THE VIETNAM WAR

The Vietnam War

Handbook of the Literature and Research

James S. Olson

Greenwood Press
WESTPORT, CONNECTICUT • LONDON

Library of Congress Cataloging-in-Publication Data

The Vietnam War : handbook of the literature and research / [edited
by] James S. Olson.
    p. cm.
    Includes bibliographical references and index.
    ISBN 0–313–27422–3 (alk. paper)
    1. Vietnamese Conflict, 1961–1975—United States. I. Olson,
James Stuart.
  DS558.V58 1993
  959.704—dc20   92–25626

British Library Cataloguing in Publication Data is available.

Library of Congress Catalog Card Number: 92–25626
ISBN: 0–313–27422–3

First published in 1993

Greenwood Press, 88 Post Road West, Westport, CT 06881
An imprint of Greenwood Publishing Group, Inc.

Printed in the United States of America

The paper used in this book complies with the
Permanent Paper Standard issued by the National
Information Standards Organization (Z39.48–1984).

10 9 8 7 6 5 4 3 2 1

Contents

Preface

The debate over the Vietnam War will continue for years, and the literature of that debate will become even more extensive than it already is. Whole volumes now exist that simply list the existing scholarly literature in bibliographic form. An April 30, 1990, issue of *Time* magazine said it all. The cover photograph showed a Vietnamese peasant walking through a rice field. The issue was devoted to "Vietnam: 15 Years Later," "In America, the Pain Endures," "In Cambodia, the Killing Continues." The lead story claimed that "guilt and recrimination still shroud America's perceptions of the only war it ever lost." Vietnam is still with us. Questions about Democratic presidential candidate Bill Clinton's war record dogged him throughout the 1992 campaign, and stories about Vietnamese gangs in southern California in 1992 frightened thousands of people. The Vietnam War has become part of the popular culture as well as the political culture in the United States. Middle-aged Americans are still trying to sort out their feelings about the war, and a new generation of young adults has grown up wondering what all the fuss is about. They, too, are now ready for answers.

It is seventeen years since the helicopters lifted off the roof of the U.S. embassy in Saigon (Ho Chi Minh City). That's still too soon for any definitive judgments, but it is also enough time to have gained at least a measure of perspective about the war, to have learned whatever lessons there are to learn. *The Vietnam War: Handbook of the Literature and Research* is an attempt to provide a perspective on the Indochina conflict. It is not, of course, an exhaustive discussion of all the literature on the war. Such a discussion would take volumes, and the literature is being produced so quickly that it would soon be out of date. Instead, I have attempted to look back on the war through the different lenses used by scholars, discussing most of the major works and providing a selected bibliography for each discussion. The decision on which literature to include was governed by several considerations. First, we looked primarily at scholarly literature published after the end of the war in 1975. Second, we avoided popular literature in favor of scholarly discussions of the war, except for those topics dealing with popular culture—films, comic books, television programs, fiction, and personal narratives. Third, we confined ourselves primarily to English-language publications, with an emphasis on items published in the United States. Our primary motivation in the book is to look at the war from an American perspective. Books and articles by French and Vietnamese scholars were used only if they have been translated into English. Because of the political and economic holocaust that swept through Indochina after 1975, that scholarship has been extremely limited.

I am grateful to the other scholars who made contributions to the book and to the librarians at the Newton Gresham Library of Sam Houston State University for their assistance. I have written all of the unsigned chapters in the book.

Introduction

On November 7, 1961, at 4:30 in the afternoon, Undersecretary of State George Ball arrived at the White House for a meeting with President John F. Kennedy. Ball was more than a little agitated. Maxwell Taylor and Walt W. Rostow, the president's advisors, had recently returned from Vietnam on a fact-finding mission and were recommending an increase in military aid, larger numbers of military advisors, and the placement of an 8,000-man logistical task force in South Vietnam to serve as soldiers and/or economic and political workers. Ball vociferously opposed the plan. He told Kennedy that the geography of Indochina "was totally unsuitable for the commitment of American forces" and that any serious American military effort there "would have the most tragic consequences." Ball then uttered the prophetic warning that has endeared him to a generation of scholars who opposed the Vietnam War: "If we go down that road we might have, within five years, 300,000 men in the rice paddies of the jungles of Viet-Nam and never be able to find them.... You [Kennedy] better be damned careful."

Kennedy and Lyndon B. Johnson were not careful enough, and from 1961 to 1966, while serving as undersecretary of state, George Ball was the lone voice in the wilderness, criticizing Vietnam policy at every turn. David L. DiLeo's *George Ball, Vietnam, and the Rethinking of Containment* is a brilliant analysis of the undersecretary's tenure in the Kennedy and Johnson administrations. Blessed with access to Ball and to his personal papers, relevant archival material from around the country, and interviews with most of the surviving individuals who made the fateful decisions to escalate the war, DiLeo has weaved together a fascinating story of Ball's futile attempt to change the American course in Vietnam. At virtually every turn, Ball stood his ground. He openly criticized the domino theory as unrealistic, narrow-minded, and ideologically tainted.

The fall of South Vietnam to the Communists, he believed, would have little impact on American national security. Ball also criticized the attempt to transplant the containment doctrine from Eastern Europe, where Communism had been imposed by an external power, to Asia, where it had become synonymous with nationalism in many countries. Because of his years with the U.S. Bombing Survey after World War II, Ball was always skeptical of the contention that strategic bombing of North Vietnam would bring Hanoi to the negotiating table. Ball went on to argue that the United States could not achieve a military victory there and that the use of extensive firepower might actually make the achievement of political objectives impossible as well. From the very beginning of the conflict, George Ball argued that it was the wrong war in the wrong place at the wrong time for the wrong reasons.

When Ball told Kennedy in 1961 that the United States might end up with more than 300,000 soldiers in Vietnam, the president was incredulous and a bit irritated. He quickly retorted: "George, you're just crazier than hell. I always thought you were one of the brightest guys in town, but you're crazy. That just isn't going to happen." But it did, and how soon we forget. The Gulf War ended in the spring of 1991, and the GIs gradually began returning home from Saudi Arabia and Iraq. The demobilization was a gradual and steady process. They were treated as conquering heroes; no ancient Roman legion marching down the Appian Way from adventures abroad ever received a more enthusiastic welcome. Small towns and large cities across the country rolled out the red carpet and staged military parades complete with tanks, armor, high school marching bands, overhead jet fighters flying in formation, artillery pieces, Boy Scout and Girl Scout troops, and soldiers, lots of soldiers. The demand for soldiers to march in parades was so high that large military bases in the United States actually had some of their day-to-day operations disrupted by the need to supply units for the weekly parades.

The most striking image in those parades was not the military hardware or spit-polished young men and women marching in unison. The victory celebrations also attracted tens of thousands of middle-aged warriors—balding, overweight men, wearing flak jackets and faded military green, walking down the streets of America or rolling down them in wheelchairs, with smiles on their faces. They had pinned their old medals on again. The Vietnam vets were finally getting their due, their parades, delayed by fifteen or twenty or twenty-five years of guilt, angst, and anger over what had taken place in Indochina and in the United States. For millions of Americans, the Gulf War provided the opportunity for an act of mass, collective repentance. After a decade of films and books like *Coming Home, Platoon, Born on the Fourth of July,* and *Full Metal Jacket,* the whole country wanted to atone for the wretched way they had treated those same Vietnam veterans a generation ago.

But more than expiation was involved in the relationship between Vietnam and Desert Storm. As President George Bush said when Iraq finally capitulated in 1991, "We finally have the Vietnam monkey off our backs." Politicians wanted to make sure that this war was handled better, that firepower was used more effectively and efficiently, and that political objectives of the war were clearly communicated to the American people. Military leaders desperately wanted to rewrite their image, to erase the memories of depressed GIs smoking marijuana and fragging their officers, and to appear competent and professional once again. The public wanted a victory, a memory more akin to the mass celebrations in Times Square in 1945 than to the television pictures of helicopters rescuing the last Americans from the roof of the U.S. embassy in Saigon in 1975. Everybody got what they wanted.

There was something unnerving, however, about the easy analogies between Desert Storm and Vietnam, proof of how vulnerable we are to political rhetoric and our own short memories. When the desert dust finally settled in Saudi Arabia and Iraq, large numbers of Americans were convinced that the Gulf War and the war in Vietnam were similar conflicts that should have had similar outcomes, that the reasons for our defeat in Vietnam were exactly the same as the explanations for our victory in Desert Storm. Victory in the Persian Gulf came because we did not "fight with one hand tied behind our back." Who can forget the exhilaration, the technological orgasm so many Americans felt when General Norman Schwartzkoff showed the films of "smart bombs" sneaking their way down the air shafts of Baghdad buildings? The obvious implication, of course, is that Vietnam, too, could have been a glorious American victory if only we had fought "the right way"—to win. Air Force General T. R. Milton best summarized this point of view when he wrote that the intensive bombing campaigns of Linebacker II in 1972 were "an object lesson in how the war might have been won, and won long ago, if only there had not been such political inhibitions." Several years later, Milton wrote, "The Christmas bombings of 1972 should have taken place in 1965."

If only life and history were that simple. They are not. Vietnam and the Persian Gulf were separated by more than a continent and a generation. They took place in completely different worlds, even different realities. For the last seventeen years, scholars and military analysts have tried to make sense of the Vietnam War, to draw some "lessons" from the conflict to guide future American policies. Most scholars have concluded that the war was a mistake, a colossal blunder in public policy. Their reasons, of course, often vary. New Left scholars like Lloyd C.

Gardner, in his book *Approaching Vietnam* (1989), saw American involvement in Indochina as part of a much broader post–World War II drive
on the part of the United States to achieve global hegemony. A similar
argument can be found in Patrick J. Heardon's *The Tragedy of Vietnam*
(1990). The primary factor in American foreign policy was the need for
world economic hegemony, and the United States committed its resources in the postwar world to the achievement of that control—to make
sure that the "liberal capitalist world system" triumphed around the
globe. Other scholars, like Frances FitzGerald (*Fire in the Lake*, 1972) and
Stanley Karnow (*Vietnam: A History*, 1983), felt the United States suffered
from historical ignorance, confusing Communism with nationalism and
embarking on a war that had no hope of political success. Even so-called
revisionists, like Guenter Lewy (*America in Vietnam*, 1978), who felt American intentions in Vietnam were noble, argue that United States policymakers confused means with ends, ignoring such questions as
economic and political development in favor of a naive commitment to
military firepower.

The idea that the United States could have achieved a military victory
in Vietnam has until recently been confined to in-house military journals
like the *Air University Review* and the arguments of people like Colonel
Harry Summers (*On Strategy: A Critical Analysis of the Vietnam War*, 1982).
For Summers, the American effort in Vietnam was hopelessly compromised at every level. The command and control structure was jerry-built
and confusing; the politicians failed to communicate a clear set of objectives to the military and to the American people; the fears of a Chinese
military intervention were grossly exaggerated; and the United States
could have won the war through conventional means by mining Haiphong harbor, invading Cambodia, North Vietnam, and Laos, and cutting off all sources of supplies to the enemy. North Vietnam did not win
the war, according to Harry Summers. The United States lost it by not
fighting intelligently.

The debate, of course, will not be over soon, not as long as those
people writing history were participants on some level in the Vietnam
era. In fact, because the Vietnam era generation is now entering middle
age and the positions of power associated with it, their role in the war
will continue to be a matter of public scrutiny. Periodically the question
of MIAs will raise its head again, and there will be new movies and
television programs about the war. Stories about the plight of "boat
people" and Vietnamese refugees in Asian camps will push their way
into newspapers and news broadcasts. The question of extending diplomatic recognition to the Socialist Republic of Vietnam will be a controversy in the 1990s, and every time Jane Fonda shows up to speak
somewhere, there will be protests. Vietnam is here to stay for our generation.

PART I

General Background and Primary Sources

1   Published Primary Sources

During the past twenty-five years, the volume of published primary source material dealing with the American involvement in Southeast Asia has expanded at an incredible rate. The American fascination with the war continues unabated. Books, movies, talk shows, radio and television programs, support groups, professors, students, and veterans associations continue to focus on the war and its effects on American culture and American foreign policy. Historians writing about Vietnam have an ever-increasing body of published government documents, autobiographies, oral histories, and memoirs to use in reconstructing the course of the war and interpreting its origins, successes, failures, and consequences.

GOVERNMENT DOCUMENTS

A wealth of government documents deals with the U.S. involvement in Southeast Asia. For an analysis of the unpublished sources, see George C. Herring's article in the *Newsletter of the Society for Historians of American Foreign Relations* and Ronald Spector's one-volume survey of the subject. The premier collection of published government documents dealing with the Vietnam War consists of what have since become known as the Pentagon Papers. In 1967, with his doubts about the Vietnam War intensifying, Secretary of Defense Robert McNamara commissioned a secret, internal study of the history of American involvement in the war. One of the senior researchers on the project was Daniel Ellsberg, a Harvard graduate and Marine Corps veteran who had worked on Vietnam policy for the Rand Corporation and for the National Security Council. After a few months of research, Ellsberg became convinced that American policy in Vietnam was a complete disaster born of the political fact that "no American President, Republican or Democrat, wanted to be the President who lost the war.... That fear was sustained by years of duplicity, lies, exaggerations, and cover-ups." Like McNamara, Ellsberg's doubts about the war were growing, and throughout 1968 he called for a bombing halt and wrote policy papers for Senator Robert Kennedy and then Senator George McGovern. When Richard Nixon was elected president in November 1968, Ellsberg sank into a deep depression, and early in 1969 he began photocopying the secret Pentagon study and carrying it page by page to his Washington apartment. Ellsberg began secretly delivering the documents to Senator J. William Fulbright, chairman of the Senate Foreign Relations Committee, hoping that the documents would strengthen the case of the antiwar movement.

Officially titled "The History of the U.S. Decision Making Process on Vietnam," the Pentagon Papers consisted of thousands of pages of essays and documents written and collected by individuals in the Department of Defense who were responding to McNamara's request for a study of the war. In its totality, it contains 2.5 million words in forty-three volumes. Documents were gathered from the Department of Defense, the White House, the Department of State, the Central Intelligence Agency, and the Office of the Joint Chiefs of Staff. Many of the individuals writing essays produced only the most self-serving analyses, while there were thousands of documents consisting of proposals by Pentagon bureaucrats that never even reached the desks of Presidents Eisenhower, Kennedy, and Johnson. What the documents blatantly revealed, however, was that American leaders had consistently misled the public about the course of the war—that American involvement had been deeper and more longterm than anyone had expected and that policymakers, from presidents to press secretaries, had frequently lied to the public about the American presence in Southeast Asia.

Daniel Ellsberg was not content to let Senator J. William Fulbright decide what to do with the documents. The Winter Soldier Investigations in February 1971, in which a number of veterans confessed to committing horrible atrocities in Vietnam, profoundly affected Ellsberg, deepening his sense of personal responsibility for the war. When he learned of the invasion of Laos later in February 1971, he decided to hand over the secret documents to the *New York Times*. On June 13, 1971, the *Times* began publishing the documents, and the press dubbed them the "Pentagon Papers." President Richard Nixon was incensed, particularly because the appendixes of the study contained highly classified documents revealing U.S. intelligence-gathering methods and intelligence sources. The Justice Department secured a court order stopping the *New York Times* from publishing the documents, but the *Boston Globe* and the *Washington Post* continued to make the documents public. On June 30, 1971, the Supreme Court, by a six to three vote, overturned the injunction against publishing the Pentagon Papers, citing the First Amendment freedoms of speech and the press. The Pentagon Papers proved conclusively the reality of the so-called credibility gap—government officials telling the public one thing and actively pursuing different military and political policies, in particular, being involved in Vietnam sooner and to a greater extent than the public had ever assumed.

Although researchers can sift through the microfilmed pages of the *New York Times*, the *Boston Globe*, and the *Washington Post* for copies of the documents, there are three other published volumes of the Pentagon Papers. The first of them is the *New York Times* edition. The *Times* assigned four of its best journalists and scholars—Neil Sheehan, Hedrick Smith, E. W. Kenworthy, and Fox Butterfield—to condense the narrative analyses in the Pentagon Papers. The result was a well-written work of 677 pages, which is excellent on American policy in the 1960s but less useful for the 1940s and 1950s. This single volume also included a number of important documents. It was published by Bantam Books as a paperback in 1971. Even more useful is the extensive collection known as the Gravel edition, named after Senator Michael Gravel of Alaska, who chaired the Senate Subcommittee on Public Buildings and Grounds. Gravel and his staff collected the documents at a time when the Nixon administration was desperately trying to stop publication of the papers. It consists of four volumes and 2,899 pages of documents. A fifth volume in the Gravel edition indexes the documents and provides scholarly commentary on the papers. The edition was published in paperback by the Beacon Press in 1971. When it became clear to President Richard Nixon that Senator Gravel was going to publish a multivolume version of the Pentagon Papers, the administration decided to release its own version of documents, the vast majority of which were unclassified material from the Department of Defense. They were released to Congressman Edward Hébert, chairman of the House Armed Services Committee. The U.S. Government Printing Office published them as twelve volumes. To provide a revealing look at the negotiations to end the Vietnam War, Professor George C. Herring selected the documents in the Pentagon Papers dealing with diplomacy and published them, along with his own commentary, in a single volume.

During the early stages of the Vietnam War, the hearings of the Senate Foreign Relations Committee, under the chairmanship of Senator J. William Fulbright of Arkansas, provided the best survey of official opinion about the conduct of the war. Those hearings were published in the usual way by congressional committees, and excerpts appeared in *The Congressional Record*. In 1966, however, Fulbright also edited a selection of the testimony of major administration officials as well as opponents of the war. The book was published by Random House and titled *The Vietnam Hearings*.

Although there is no other published collection of documents that rivals the Pentagon Papers, at least as far as scholars are concerned, there are, nevertheless, a number of other valuable collections. Over the years, the U.S. Department of State has published its monumental *Foreign Relations of the United States*, and those volumes are available through 1963, providing valuable insights into early American policy in Indochina. They consist of dispatches, policy reports, and correspondence integral to policy formulation. In 1989, University Publications of America released an extensive microfilmed collection of State Department documents dealing with the Vietnam War. The collection consists of 145 reels of microfilm and focuses on the period from 1940 to 1958. University Microfilms has also made available a large series of Vietnam war documents. Douglas Pike edited *The History of the Vietnam War* collection, which contains more than 365,000 pages of material, much of it primary sources. More recently, under the editorial direction of John T. Hickey, University Microfilms has released *The Echols Collection: Selections on the Vietnam War*, a multi-volume work available in microfiche. The material is taken from the vast John M. Echols Collection on Southeast Asia at Cornell University. The *Foreign Broadcast Information Service*, as well as the *Joint Publications Research Service*, provides ongoing current materials relevant to understanding the war. The best of the current primary source materials is edited by Douglas Pike and published quarterly as the *Indochina Chronology* by the Indochina Project at the University of California at Berkeley. For public documents, press conferences, and speeches, see the *Public Papers of the Presidents of the United States*. There are also individual collections of documents by such scholars as William Appleman Williams, Gareth Porter, Robert J. McMahon, and Andrew J. Rotter.

MEMOIRS AND AUTOBIOGRAPHIES

After World War II, American involvement in Vietnam was not apparent to the public at large. As the United States' commitment to the French and to South Vietnam grew and American leadership began to place a greater emphasis on Southeast Asia, the American press and public watched the escalation of the conflict with growing apprehension. As criticism of American goals and strategy objectives gained momentum, the men of decision—presidents, military leaders, advisors, and policy planners—formulated an intellectual defense of the positions they held and the choices they had made. When they retired from public service, many of them wrote accounts of the Vietnam tragedy. The timing of their departure affected the accounts they produced. Dwight D. Eisenhower, in *The White House Years* (1965), carefully explained the domino theory. In Arthur M. Schlesinger's biography of Kennedy, published the same year, the domino theory was called true, but moralistic. In 1971, when the belief that Vietnam was a nationalist war for freedom was at its height, Averell Harriman wrote that monolithic Communism did not apply. North Vietnam was not under any ideological stranglehold by Moscow or Beijing that would lead to the fall of Southeast Asia to Communism. The domino theory was very much out of favor. It was not difficult for George Ball quickly to scoff at the idea of the domino theory in 1982 in *The Past Has Another Pattern*. Between Eisenhower's dry definition of the domino theory in 1965 and the unprecedented volume of literature in the 1980s, American attitudes about Communist aggression and the use of military power had undergone significant change.

Presidents Eisenhower, Johnson, and Nixon all were careful to point out to readers that Vietnam was an inheritance, that they individually were not responsible for what was going on there when they came into the White House. The irony, of course, is that the war continued for more than two decades, with none of its major protagonists claiming any responsibility. Eisenhower's memoirs, published in 1963 and 1965, were not as defensive as the memoirs of those who followed him. In *The White House Years: Mandate for Change 1953–1956*, Eisenhower outlines the background of U.S. involvement in Vietnam, from aid to France to the U.S. advisory period. Believing that the French struggle was for freedom and not simply colonial domination, Eisenhower defends American financial aid to the French cause in Vietnam. In *The White House Years: Waging Peace 1956–1961*, Eisenhower uses the domino theory to support American involvement in Vietnam. Advocating firm dealings with Communists around the world, Eisenhower insists that the Soviets and the Chinese must be made to understand "the adequacy of our military power." For Dwight D. Eisenhower, from the vantage point of the early 1960s, the American commitment to South Vietnam was completely justified.

President Lyndon B. Johnson's presidency was ruined by the Vietnam War, and because of the failure he encountered there, he decided not to run for reelection in 1968. His memoirs, *The Vantage Point: Perspectives of the Presidency, 1963–1969*, were published in 1971. In his memoirs Johnson emphasizes that U.S. involvement in Vietnam did not begin with him. Citing his respect for the commitments of previous administrations, Johnson believes his actions represented a continuation of the policies of Eisenhower and Kennedy. He gives his account of the decision-making process that led to the increased troop commitment, the bombings, and the search for peace. Johnson claims he listened to a broad diversity of opinion before making the choices that became so unpopular at home. He blames much of the unpopularity of the war on the press. Not seeing detailed daily reports, he argued, kept Americans from realizing the true picture and caused the United States to defeat itself. When he left the presidency in 1969, Johnson still felt strongly that peace should be pursued but that Americans should not walk out on the commitment they had made.

Richard Nixon has been a prolific writer since resigning the presidency in 1974. Spanning the years 1978–1988, his books have all defended the administration's Indochinese policies. In *RN: The Memoirs of Richard Nixon*, Nixon writes his autobiography. Some discussion of Vietnam is inevitable, but the subject does not dominate the book. Inheriting the conflict from his predecessors, Nixon had several options, most of which he rejected. Believing that the American public wanted a "knockout blow," Nixon nevertheless refused that option, arguing that it would have required bombing dikes or a nuclear attack, clearly unacceptable. Escalation was another option Nixon dismissed because American casualties would have been too high. Abandoning South Vietnam was also rejected because, he believed, it would have damaged the international image in the United States and the trust of American allies. Nixon's goal when he came to office was to maintain American commitments while ending the conflict as quickly and as honorably as possible through a negotiated settlement. That settlement, the president believed, had to ensure the independence of South Vietnam.

In *No More Vietnams* Nixon disputes many commonly held beliefs about the Vietnam War, especially the assumptions that the Vietnam conflict was a civil war; that the domino theory has been proven false; that the antiwar movement shortened the war; that the Johnson administration was the first to send troops into combat; that the United States purposefully bombed civilian targets in North Vietnam; that the Vietcong won the hearts and minds of the Vietnamese people; and that life is better in Vietnam now that the United States is gone. A large portion of the book is spent "debunking" these "myths." His stated intention is to correct the "misimpressions" of the American public. The phrase "no more Vietnams" has been misused, according to Nixon; it poisons American foreign policy by making the United States ashamed of its own power and unwilling to use it to protect its own interests. Nixon also disagrees strongly that Ho Chi Minh was a nationalist. Ho was a committed Marxist-Leninist. Back in 1954, as vice president, Nixon favored American military intervention to help the French at Dien Bien Phu, and in 1980, when *No More Vietnams* was published, he still believed that. The Communist policies in Indochina have been murderous and the United States has been too critical of herself. The former president concludes that the United States must learn to fight unconventional, limited wars against Communist aggression. One required change to pursue that goal, he believes, is that Congress must stop limiting the president's ability to wage such an unconventional war. The control of the Third World is at stake, and the United States has been left with a psychological disadvantage. Like President Johnson, Nixon criticizes the role of the press in the Vietnam conflict, but he takes the additional step of blaming both the press and war dissenters for lengthening the conflict. In 1985, writing well after the war ended, Nixon instructs the American people in the lessons to be learned from Vietnam in *No More Vietnams*. Although his lessons for the United States may be different from those of others, it is not surprising that this type of book is written after the conflict. Others will follow.

In another 1980 book—*The Real War*—Nixon argues that the real war facing the United States is the war against Soviet expansion. Vietnam is just one battle of World War III, and it was fought by guerrilla tactics, which avoid direct confrontation. Nixon cites three major American mistakes of Vietnam. The first was taking the Central Intelligence Agency (CIA) out of control and putting the Pentagon in the driver's seat after the Taylor-Rostow report. The failure to prevent the use of Laos to establish the Ho Chi Minh Trail was the second mistake. The third error was allowing Ngo Dinh Diem to fall. Acknowledging that Diem had his faults, Nixon blames the press for giving a one-sided view of Diem to the American people, who did not understand the situation or the difference in Asian methods. Nixon is proud of the goal of Vietnamization, calling the Americanization of the conflict by Johnson a mistake. He also believes that America won the war militarily in Vietnam but lost it politically at home. Nixon is also critical of the restrictions Congress has placed on presidential powers, which kept the United States from enforcing the Paris agreements and led to greater tragedies in Cambodia and Afghanistan. The wrong lesson from Vietnam, insists Nixon, is not getting involved, not using American power. Rather, the lesson from Vietnam that Richard Nixon wants the American people to learn is that power should not be abused but definitely should be applied wisely.

In *1999 Victory Without War*, Nixon analyzes the twentieth century and outlines his concept of what America should do to have peace, freedom, and prosperity in the next century. References to Vietnam are scattered throughout the book. Nixon believes America learned the wrong lessons from Vietnam. The right lesson, Nixon holds, is that progress in foreign relations comes from a position of strength and that when America appears weak, the Soviet Union and other countries become more aggressive. Nixon criticizes the limitations placed on the presidency by Congress, which he feels have led to the belief by other countries that the United States will not interfere with Communist aggression in other parts of the world, and he cites Afghanistan, Vietnam, and Cambodia as examples.

Another perspective on the American effort in Southeast Asia comes from the military people who supervised the U.S. operations there. Military leaders prefer military solutions to political ones, and criticism of civilian leadership is expected. This position, in general, holds true. Most American military leaders had some criticism of civilian leadership, either with embassy officials in Vietnam or officials back in Washington. All of the leaders advocated military solutions; however, two individuals brought backgrounds of counterinsurgency expertise to the Vietnam arena. American CIA operative Edward Geary Lansdale and British counterinsurgency specialist Sir Robert Thompson advocated political warfare and limited military resources to achieve political goals. Other military authors, like William Westmoreland and U.S.G. Sharp, display their own faith in conventional warfare. Frustrated by the limited war they were asked to fight, they advocated a stronger use of American power. Even General Maxwell Taylor, who also served as a civilian in the post of ambassador to Vietnam, emphasized military solutions.

The defensive posture is evident in the writings of the military leaders. The publication dates range from 1972 to 1978, when criticism of the military was high and military prestige was at an all-time low. Westmoreland, Sharp, and Taylor all complain of the tactics of the press. As mentioned previously, civilian leadership was blamed, usually for a lack of clear goals, poor communication, inefficient administration of programs, a lack of understanding of the situation in Vietnam, and restrictions on all-out warfare. Westmoreland defends various military strategies and tactics, many of which he developed, such as attrition, search and destroy, and free fire zones. Westmoreland supports his choices by building a case for each. From a unique perspective, Sir Robert Thompson blames the American people as a whole for the loss of Vietnam to Communism. Citing the familiar cry of a "lost will to win," Thompson gives a European, historical flavor to his criticism by reminding Americans that they took too long to enter World Wars I and II.

Edward Lansdale's *In the Midst of Wars: An American's Mission to Southeast Asia* is a highly personal account of the years he spent in the Philippines and Vietnam as a former CIA agent. Lansdale discusses the history, culture, personalities, and problems he encountered. Bringing his Philippine experiences in counterinsurgency to Vietnam, the former air force general participated in the teaching of the South Vietnamese in counterguerrilla measures. He participated in the development of propaganda to support the regime of Ngo Dinh Diem, with whom he had a close personal relationship. Although a military man, Lansdale was at times frustrated by civilian and military officials who were sent to Vietnam but who did not understand Vietnamese culture and political needs. Lansdale includes notes on Vietnamese culture, personalities, and political and religious organizations. He is absolutely convinced that the United States should have maintained its commitment to the South Vietnamese leadership and should have continued to employ counterinsurgency techniques in fighting the Vietcong.

That emphasis on counterinsurgency was also the premier theme of Sir Robert Thompson's *Peace Is Not at Hand*. An expert in counterinsurgency who engineered the British victory in Malaya over Communist guerrillas, Thompson was head of the British advisory mission to Vietnam. He is highly critical of America's withdrawal from Vietnam. In fact, Thompson blasts the United States for its isolated, "let's not get involved" attitude. Calling this attitude the "desire to duck," he recalls the U.S. hesitation to get involved in World Wars I and II. Thompson believes that pacification and Vietnamization were successful and that America withdrew its support just when North Vietnam was weak and had been defeated militarily. He blames the American loss on a lack of will and the failure of the American press to report objectively. Thompson feels the domino theory is still true in a general way. He sees Western civilization as threatened by the damage done to American credibility because the United States did not keep her commitment to South Vietnam. Other powers will be encouraged to test the resolve of the United States, and until American resolve is once again quite clear to the entire world, the West is psychologically at risk.

The book *Strategy for Defeat* by Admiral Ulysses S. Grant Sharp takes a more traditional military approach to the war. As commander in chief–Pacific from 1964 to 1968, Sharp felt firsthand the frustration of the Vietnam War from the military's point of view. Advocating all-out conventional warfare—including land invasions of Cambodia, Laos, and North Vietnam—Sharp supports the Christmas bombings of 1972 and believes the United States should have used maximum air power on Hanoi much earlier. Frustrated with the limited objectives of the war, Sharp blames both the civilian political leadership and the press for the Vietnam debacle. He argues that American fears of a Chinese intervention were ill-founded, particularly because of the political havoc the Cultural Revolution was having on Chinese society. An all-out effort to win the war militarily was Sharp's recipe for success.

General Maxwell D. Taylor had a similar, if somewhat more sophisticated, point of view. In his 1972 book *Swords and Plowshares*, Taylor recounts his years of involvement in the Vietnam War. Back in 1960, Taylor had come to the attention of the Kennedys because of his bestselling book *An Uncertain Trumpet*. Taylor criticized the Eisenhower defense policy, which had placed too much emphasis on strategic nuclear war and not enough on conventional combat and counterinsurgency efforts. After a distinguished career in the U.S. Army, Taylor retired in

1957 but was later appointed as chairman of the Joint Chiefs of Staff during the Kennedy administration. He also served one tour as ambassador to South Vietnam.

Taylor, the inventor of the "flexible response" military posture as opposed to "massive retaliation," brings his confidence and a paternalistic style to *Swords and Plowshares*. On an investigative trip to South Vietnam in 1961, Taylor probed Ngo Dinh Diem for signs of change and tried his tactics of persuasion on the South Vietnamese leader. His report to Kennedy advocated social and economic assistance as well as a small contingent of American ground troops, ostensibly to aid in flood relief. Although Kennedy rejected the troop recommendation, he had high praise for the rest of the report.

Taylor feels the overthrow of Diem hurt the United States since there was no one to replace him. He contends the press and Kennedy, who displayed public disapproval, bear part of the blame for Diem's downfall. Taylor complains that under Lyndon B. Johnson, the Joint Chiefs of Staff (JCS) did not get political guidance concerning the goals of foreign policy. However, the JCS counseled Johnson both to intensify counterinsurgency and to begin selective air and naval attacks in North Vietnam. Military action in the North, he believes, would need to come before political and military stability in the South could be achieved. He also tends to be critical of civilian leadership. The White House liked making new plans instead of measuring the success of the old ones. Embassy officials did not know how to work with the Vietnamese, and Johnson's advisors changed their position under pressure from the press. Taylor concludes by noting that American prestige has been hurt and the ability to deter war damaged because other nations perceive that the United States has lost the will to interfere.

The best exposition of military thinking on the course of the Vietnam War is William C. Westmoreland's *A Soldier Reports*. General Westmoreland, Vietnam field commander from 1964 to 1969, saw his duties in Vietnam as primarily military. The book deals with military aspects of the Vietnam conflict, although South Vietnamese politics are mentioned. Westmoreland defends his use of strong conventional forces against guerrillas. His big units were necessary, he believes, to defend important strategic areas in South Vietnam, and they could be broken down into smaller units for mobility if the need arose. The strategy of attrition and the tactic of search and destroy are legitimate methods in war, according to the Westmoreland. Evacuations of villages and the creation of free fire zones were necessary and humanitarian due to the nature of the guerrilla tactics of the enemy. He even defends the use of defoliants because they reduced the ambushes of American soldiers. Westmoreland supports the bombing of Cambodia to destroy enemy supply bases during the Nixon administration, but he is critical of Johnson's use of "graduated response." The slowly escalating bombing gave North Vietnam the chance to absorb and adapt to the damage. Westmoreland would have preferred either an all-out effort or a limited one, as long as it was carefully conceived. He finds fault with the embassy bureaucracy, the restrictions placed on the military by Washington, the press, and antiwar demonstrators, all of whom prolonged the war. Westmoreland is dumbfounded about the great irony of the Vietnam War: the United States won the war on the battlefield but lost it at home.

A similarly harsh assessment, this time from a naval perspective, is contained in Admiral Elmo R. Zumwalt, Jr.'s, *On Watch*. Zumwalt served as commander U.S. Navy Forces, Vietnam, from 1968 to 1970. The book deals with the Vietnam War, although that is not its main focus. Zumwalt is convinced that the naval forces were poorly employed during the conflict, that Haiphong should have been mined early in the war, and that the U.S. Navy should have imposed an airtight blockade of the entire North Vietnamese coast. He also argues that the Vietnamization program of turning over huge volumes of equipment to the South Vietnamese navy should have been better planned and implemented more slowly and methodically. Zumwalt is especially critical of the Nixon administration for its handling of the peace negotiations, arguing that South Vietnam was treated high-handedly and that the U.S. agreement amounted to an all-out accession to Communist demands.

The only real exception to these memoirs is Matthew Ridgway's *Soldier: The Memoirs of Matthew B. Ridgway*. In 1954, when the embattled French army was about to fall at Dien Bien Phu, French officials were putting extreme pressure on the Eisenhower administration to intervene. Admiral Arthur Radford, chairman of the Joint Chiefs of Staff, along with Vice President Richard Nixon, strongly supported a program known as Operation Vulture, which included heavy American bombing of Vietnamese forces. Ridgway, as chief of staff of the army, opposed the intervention, arguing that it would inevitably lead to the commitment of American ground troops in Indochina, a possibility Ridgway considered extreme folly. Eisenhower listened to Ridgway, and the intervention never occurred. Ridgway was later asked to summarize his career, and he remarked: "When the day comes for me to meet my Maker...the thing I would be most humbly proud of was the fact that I fought against ... tactical schemes which would have cost the lives of thousands of men. To that list of tragic accidents that fortunately never happened I would add the Indochina intervention."

The men who served the presidents in advisory or planning capacities reflect a wide range of opinion. Pierre Salinger and Arthur Schlesinger were highly supportive of President John Kennedy. Since neither of them was actively involved in crucial decision making, they were less defensive about themselves but very defensive of Kennedy. Salinger was

John F. Kennedy's press secretary, and in his book *With Kennedy*, he observed the conflict between the government and the press develop as coverage of American involvement in Vietnam reflected a growing American presence. The problem with press relations in Vietnam during the advisory period of the Kennedy era stemmed from what Salinger calls the "non-war" situation, in which the press was not satisfied when some American activities were kept secret for security reasons. After the Maxwell Taylor report of 1961, Kennedy did not want the press to report the gradual escalation of the American commitment. Not wanting the American people to perceive a "widening" war, he tightened the rules under which correspondents could observe field personnel in action. Although Salinger places some of the blame on embassy and public information officials, he also questions some of the journalists' methods and motives. Citing examples of false reporting and the intense hatred of the press for Ngo Dinh Diem and his brother Ngo Dinh Nhu, Salinger accuses the press of a lack of objectivity and downright glory seeking. Salinger concludes with a discussion of the paradox inherent in the desire for complete openness and honesty in a free society and the need for secrecy in the interests of national security.

Arthur M. Schlesinger, Jr., the Pulitzer Prize–winning Harvard historian, served as a special assistant to the president during the Kennedy administration. In his book *A Thousand Days: John F. Kennedy in the White House*, Schlesinger had a unique vantage point from which to observe history in the making. Scattered references to Vietnam are found throughout his account of the Kennedy presidency. Although Schlesinger feels the United States is losing Third World countries to Communism, he disagrees with the moralistic quality of the domino theory that brought about American involvement in Vietnam. Seeing Ho Chi Minh as a nationalist Communist, not overly dependent on China or the Soviet Union, Schlesinger believes that previous administrations made a mistake by involving the United States in Vietnam. Kennedy felt obligated to keep the commitment to South Vietnam that had already been made. Schlesinger believes that Kennedy made a mistake by accepting most of the Taylor-Rostow report, which made Vietnam more of a military, rather than a political, problem. Consistently defending Kennedy, Schlesinger blames embassy officials and others who misled the president by their optimism. In one of his final references to Vietnam in the biography, Schlesinger denies that Kennedy or any other Americans were involved in the coup that led to the assassination of Ngo Dinh Diem. Schlesinger blamed Kennedy's growing emphasis on the military aspects of Vietnam on the Taylor-Rostow report of 1961 and optimistic advisors from 1961 to 1963.

Although Schlesinger pointed out his disapproval of Johnson's Americanization of the war, strong criticism of the conduct of the war by advisors was more evident beginning with Roger Hilsman's 1967 book *To Move a Nation*. With the exception of W. W. Rostow in 1972, the works published from 1967 to 1973 reflect the dissatisfaction of advisors with the war. This period witnessed the peak of American discontent with the war, ending in the Paris Peace Settlement of 1973. The scope of criticism by the advisors ranged from dissatisfaction with methods and strategy to outright demands that America walk out on the war.

The emphasis on the militarization of the war frustrated several civilian advisors. Two Defense Department planners advocated more civilian control over the military. As former members of Robert McNamara's staff, Alain C. Enthoven and K. Wayne Smith are highly supportive of the former secretary of defense. Enthoven headed the Office of Systems Analysis from 1965 to 1969 while Smith was his special assistant. In their book *How Much Is Enough? Shaping the Defense Program, 1961–1969*, they complain that the separate military services compete with each other, causing the Joint Chiefs of Staff to negotiate compromises between the branches, leading to poor choices. Enthoven and Smith advocate their systematic approach. When the services give inaccurate reports and seek expensive weapons systems that are not coordinated between the service branches, the Department of Defense can step in and create the best combinations. These two former defense staffers advocate the strengthening of the powers of the secretary of defense. The office they ran used an analytical approach that they believe can keep costs down, make the military more efficient, and even prevent war from escalating if the Defense Department is in control. Enthoven and Smith support such claims by citing their studies, which showed that attrition and bombing of North Vietnam were ineffective. The Pentagon should have listened.

A number of President Lyndon B. Johnson's other advisors were highly critical of the conventional aspect of the war and his increasing reliance on air power. In fact, Johnson got very little sympathy from his former advisors, especially Townsend Hoopes, Roger Hilsman, and Averell Harriman. Hilsman and Harriman did have enough respect for their old boss to laud his domestic programs. The ultimate complaint against Johnson was his "Americanization" of the war. W. Averell Harriman served as ambassador-at-large and undersecretary of state in the Kennedy administration and chief delegate to the Paris peace negotiations in 1968 under Lyndon Johnson. In his book *America and Russia in a Changing World: A Half Century of Personal Observation*, Harriman clearly rejects the theory of monolithic Communism and argues that Ho Chi Minh was primarily a nationalist whose main objective was the independence and unity of his country. Blaming John Foster Dulles, the secretary of state under Dwight D. Eisenhower, for getting America involved in Vietnam, Harriman observes that the United States should never have assisted the French.

On the presidents, Harriman proposes that Kennedy was concerned with our growing involvement and would not have become as heavily committed as Johnson did. He believes Johnson will not receive proper credit for his domestic politics due to his mistakes with Vietnam. Harriman discusses the 1968 peace talks and denies that there were any political motivations to initiate the talks. On Nixon, Harriman believes that he prolonged the war by continuing to seek a military victory. Critical of the policy of Vietnamization, Harriman called it immoral—a plan to perpetuate the fighting, not a program for peace. Harriman concludes that by getting out sooner, the United States would have prevented the loss of confidence in leadership and would actually have improved her position of worldwide influence.

Roger Hilsman served as director of the Bureau of Intelligence and Research in the State Department until 1963, when he was appointed assistant secretary of state for Far Eastern Affairs. His book *To Move a Nation* is an inside account of the working relationships of planning and policy-making. Hilsman repeatedly distinguishes the political from the military approaches to Vietnam, and he is usually quite critical of the military. The military often took an all-or-nothing approach when Vietnam required a political program that would have used limited force, tailored to send a political signal and achieve a political objective. The Vietnam conflict became a struggle among advisors over the type of strategy to be applied. Kennedy's emphasis on revolutionary warfare and counterinsurgency appealed to Hilsman, who disapproved of Johnson's emphasis on conventional warfare. Johnson's use of air power and conventional resources created hostility to the United States among the civilian population of South Vietnam, which Hilsman feels would not have happened if Kennedy's methods had been followed. Hilsman concludes that the biggest mistake that Johnson made was the Americanization of the war.

Another negative, early book on the Vietnam War was Senator Eugene McCarthy's *The Year of the People*, published in 1969. A Democratic senator from Wisconsin, McCarthy decided in 1966 that the Vietnam War was a catastrophe, and in 1967 he decided to challenge Lyndon B. Johnson's reelection in 1968. Supported by thousands of college students, McCarthy entered the New Hampshire presidential primary in February 1968 and almost defeated the president. His near-success was reported as a political victory by the press and inspired Senator Robert F. Kennedy to seek the Democratic presidential nomination as well. In the book, McCarthy gives details of his campaign for the presidency in 1968. He is highly critical of the Johnson administration and characterizes Johnson as defensive and all but violent toward his critics. Questioning the morality of the war, he cites the strategy of attrition as an example of the brutality of the conflict.

Three books published at the height of American frustration with the war in 1972 and 1973 advocated complete withdrawal of American troops. In *Papers on the War* Daniel Ellsberg admits his own guilt in the Vietnam conflict and explains his conversion to an antiwar position while reading the Pentagon Papers. As a field observer and later Vietnam War critic, Ellsberg discusses the pattern of decision making from Truman to Nixon. Blaming the presidents for America's presence in Vietnam, Ellsberg states that their fear of losing another China led them to make choices for political reasons. Denying the quagmire model, he holds that rather than being given bad information, executives made decisions over the objections of advisors and with the knowledge of other options. Ellsberg calls the war in Vietnam an immoral war of aggression by the United States. He did not always hold that position. In *Papers on the War* he explains that when he read the Pentagon Papers, he gradually came to realize he had been in the wrong. After advising Nixon to get out of Vietnam and believing that Nixon had instead chosen to prolong the war and even make it an "invisible war," Ellsberg decided to reveal the contents of the Pentagon Papers.

Townsend Hoopes was a deputy secretary of defense from 1965 to 1967 and then undersecretary of the air force until February 1969. In *The Limits of Intervention*, Hoopes gives his account of the roots of the failure of American involvement in Vietnam. He describes the conditions at the Pentagon when he arrived as lacking in explicit policy or even a central guiding principle for foreign policy. President Johnson is portrayed as uncomfortable in dealing with foreign affairs and overly dependent on W. W. Rostow for advice. Hoopes is critical of the military policy of attrition and the bombing of North Vietnam. He believes that Westmoreland and the military establishment were given too free a rein by Johnson. Johnson is described as politically crafty, deceiving the nation and attempting to hard-sell the press. Writing after Nixon took office, Hoopes is critical of Nixon's policy of the carrot-and-stick approach to achieve a settlement with North Vietnam. Hoopes advocates, instead, immediate, complete withdrawal of U.S. troops from Vietnam, a place he considered not of vital interest to the United States.

Henry Cabot Lodge, a two-time U.S. ambassador to South Vietnam, also advocates a military withdrawal from Indochina, but he wanted the pullout tied to a comprehensive, negotiated settlement. In his memoirs *The Storm Has Many Eyes*, Lodge explains his role in the fall of Ngo Dinh Diem from power in South Vietnam in 1963. Lodge hated the manipulations of Ngo Dinh Nhu, and he was convinced that Nhu must be overthrown, with or without Diem. Claiming that the Pentagon Papers

do not tell the whole story, Lodge insists that Americans did not participate in the coup d'état. The embassy was informed, however, and did
not try to interfere, just as the Kennedy administration had ordered.
Although Lodge believes the war was one against Communist aggression,
he finally decided that the cost—a loss of public confidence in government—was too high. He advocated a negotiated settlement and complete
American withdrawal with all speed.

Other books published in the 1970s took much more sympathetic
points of view about American policy. Walt W. Rostow wrote *The Diffusion
of Power, 1957–1972* in 1972. Rostow served as ad hoc consultant to
Eisenhower, personal advisor to Kennedy, chairman of the State Department's Policy Planning Council, and special assistant for national
security affairs to President Johnson. On the well-known mission with
General Maxwell Taylor to Vietnam in 1961, Rostow says that he was
given a special task by John F. Kennedy: to discover if the people of
Vietnam wanted to be independent and non-Communist or if they
wanted to join Ho Chi Minh. While Taylor was meeting with Ngo Dinh
Diem, Rostow worked on his special assignment and concluded that the
South Vietnamese did not want Communism under Ho Chi Minh. After
1961 it does not appear that Rostow ever changed his mind. Lyndon B.
Johnson was one of the best presidents in American history, according
to Rostow. Rostow believes more decisive military power earlier would
have been successful. He complains that as the United States was winning
militarily, our will to win lessened. Finally, Rostow is convinced that the
press and the antiwar movement prevented the American public from
receiving a true picture of the progress in Vietnam.

Historians have speculated in depth about the impact the death of
President John F. Kennedy in 1963 had on the course of the war in
Vietnam. Much of the speculation emerged because of the book *Johnny,
We Hardly Knew Ye* by Kenneth O'Donnell and David Powers. Both of
them were longtime aides to Kennedy, and both claimed that the president had become increasingly weary of the war by 1963 and increasingly
skeptical of the military's claims that an American–South Vietnamese
victory was possible there. They both claimed that President Kennedy
decided to abandon the American commitment to South Vietnam but
that he would implement that decision only after the election of 1964,
when he hoped to win another term in the White House. To withdraw
from South Vietnam and let it fall to the Communists before the election
would give the Republican party an election theme. Their argument,
therefore, is that had Kennedy lived, there would have been no war in
Vietnam.

A number of books from former policymakers have been published
since the end of the war, and not unexpectedly, they reflect a variety of
points of view. The best of those accounts is George Ball's *The Past Has*

Another Pattern, published in 1982. Ball had a distinguished career at the State Department, and during the Kennedy and Johnson administrations, he served as undersecretary of state. During the early 1950s, Ball had been counsel to the French embassy in Washington, and from that vantage point he observed the French debate the issue of Indochina. From the beginning of his tenure at the State Department, Ball argued that the Diem regime was corrupt, that a land war in Asia was not in the interests of the United States, and that the objective of creating a viable, democratic South Vietnam was impossible. At a 1961 meeting with President Kennedy, Ball predicted that the introduction of American troops would create its own momentum; within "five years there will be 300,000 American soldiers fighting in Vietnam." Kennedy laughed, "George, you're crazier than hell."

During the early and mid–1960s, George Ball was a voice in the wilderness, the only American policymaker of any substance who consistently took a negative view of the U.S. military presence in Vietnam. Standing virtually alone, he argued against the other advisors, who thought the United States could win and later that we could not get out. From the beginning, Ball felt that the United States should not get involved. Appalled by the Taylor–Rostow report, which called for the commitment of 8,000 ground troops, he tried to convince others of the nationalism involved in Vietnam. Ball warned that America would repeat the French experience.

Ball is highly critical of advisors in both the Kennedy and Johnson administrations who sought to present the presidents with a consensus of opinion rather than involving them in the adversarial process that would have presented a full range of options. Johnson was out of his element, according to Ball, and his advisors were particularly bad. Even after they began to accept the absurdity of the domino theory, Ball complains that they clung to the equally absurd notion that the United States could not afford the loss of the world's confidence if American forces were simply withdrawn. Ball explains the process by which other advisors came to his position, leading to Johnson's decision to seek peace and withdraw from the presidential race in 1968. In this book Ball also criticizes the performance of Nixon and Kissinger, whose obsession with air power invited the disrespect of other nations. Ball also contends that the duo made negotiating mistakes, such as withdrawing troops at the wrong times, which left the United States with no diplomatic leverage. The failure to separate the interests of the United States and those of Saigon also contributed to the delay in achieving peace.

Henry Kissinger, Nixon's national security advisor and then secretary of state, wrote his memoirs in three volumes. Two of them, *The White House Years* (1979) and *Years of Upheaval* (1982), covered the years of the Nixon presidency. As far as Vietnam was concerned, Kissinger considered it the height of folly. The United States should have never become bogged down in such a war. At best, Indochina was tangential to U.S. national security. Mindless fears and moralistic assumptions about stopping global Communism back in the 1950s and early 1960s pushed the United States into an untenable situation. Kissinger believed that a military victory in South Vietnam was out of the question unless the United States was willing to increase its combat strength to as many as 1.3 million men, something that Tet made politically impossible. For Kissinger, the United States had no choice but disengagement. How to do that was the question. Just before Nixon's inauguration, Kissinger wrote that the United States was "so powerful that Hanoi is simply unable to defeat us militarily.... It must negotiate about it. Unfortunately, our military strength has no political corollary; we have been unable so far to create a political structure that could survive military opposition from Hanoi." Kennedy and Johnson gave South Vietnam more strategic importance than it deserved, but it was too late to withdraw. "The commitment of 500,000 Americans has settled the issue of the importance of Vietnam. For what is involved now is the confidence of American promises."

Kissinger defended both his own efforts at negotiation and Nixon's decisions, many of which were made with the advice of Kissinger. Like Nixon, he blamed the portrayal by the press of the North Vietnamese as the "good guys," and the North Vietnamese themselves for the breakdowns and delays in the peace talks. Kissinger also blamed Congress for limiting the president's ability to enforce the terms of the settlement. Like the rest of America, Kissinger says he became gradually disillusioned with the U.S. role in Vietnam, but like Nixon he did not believe the United States could just walk away from her commitment. The rest of the world would never be able to trust Americans, and the United States' ability to deter war would be in jeopardy.

The domestic situation made negotiations difficult for Kissinger, he believes, due to the perception by the North Vietnamese that the American public was eager for any settlement. Kissinger portrays the North Vietnamese negotiators as tough, conceding nothing themselves, but eagerly grabbing any concession made by the United States. The deadlocks and breakdowns were portrayed in the press as the fault of the American negotiators, never the Vietnamese. Kissinger denies that he was naive about the Paris Agreement of January 27, 1973. He believed South Vietnam, with the aid of American air power, would serve as a deterrent to North Vietnamese aggression. However, Nixon's preoccupation with Watergate and the prohibitions placed by Congress on further military involvement kept the president from retaliating when the North Vietnamese began to violate the agreement. Although Kissinger notes Richard Nixon's faults, he gives him credit for being given an enormous task and achieving it.

Frederick Nolting's recently published memoirs—*From Trust to Tragedy: The Political Memoirs of Frederick Nolting, Kennedy's Ambassador to Diem's Vietnam*—provides a more positive view of American operations in South Vietnam during the years of the Kennedy administration. Although the book was published in 1988, Nolting remains completely convinced that the government of South Vietnam was a viable political unit and that President Ngo Dinh Diem was an able political leader. As far as Nolting was concerned, Diem was the only anti-Communist nationalist in all of Vietnam, and had the United States maintained its commitment to him, he would have managed to thwart the efforts of the Vietcong to seize control.

In 1989 William Colby, former CIA station chief in Saigon, wrote *Lost Victory* with James McCargar. For Colby, the real problem of U.S. policy was the result of American leadership's inability to understand the political nature of the war. The military was unable to integrate political factors into its war strategy and failed to understand that the foundations of good counterinsurgency were intelligence, an understanding of the threatened country's culture, low-intensity warfare, and interaction with the police. Because the military could not adapt to fighting a guerrilla war, it placed great faith in technology and its ability to crush the Communists into submission. The instability of the South Vietnamese government was another factor that resulted in a strategy of attrition, instead of counterinsurgency. Not until the immediate threat to the government of South Vietnam was overcome could effective counterinsurgency be pursued. Yet even with all the setbacks, by the early 1970s, Colby believed that the war was being won. The only thing that really gave the North Vietnamese a victory in 1975 was the American decision not to stay the course.

The recent memoirs of Clark Clifford, *Counsel to the President: A Memoir*, provide an outstanding look at American policy toward Vietnam during 1968 and 1969. A Kansas native and graduate of the Washington University Law School, Clifford had been special counsel to Harry Truman in 1946 and became Truman's most trusted advisor. He returned to government as head of the Foreign Intelligence Advisory Board in 1961, where he had oversight responsibilities for the CIA. Clifford directed Lyndon Johnson's reelection campaign in 1964. During the early years of the conflict, Clifford was a "hawk" who supported the escalation of the conflict. But by 1967 he was growing increasingly skeptical about the military's assessment of the conflict. In 1968 Clifford replaced Robert McNamara as secretary of state, and he immediately opposed Westmoreland's request to raise American troop levels to 750,000 men. Instead, Clifford proposed and set in motion the program of "Vietnamization," which the Nixon administration later fully implemented—returning the bulk of the fighting to South Vietnamese troops.

Clifford had decided that a military victory for the United States in Vietnam was impossible.

Finally, the recent memoirs of Dean Rusk—*As I Saw It*—constitute a defense of the policies of the Kennedy and Johnson administrations. A native of Georgia and the son of poor farmers, Rusk eventually became a Rhodes Scholar and then secretary of state under John F. Kennedy and Lyndon B. Johnson. Throughout his entire life, Rusk was a "cold warrior" who was convinced that Soviet expansionism threatened the free world and that the Russians understood only firmness. Even in his memoirs, in spite of the prevailing point of view in the United States and around the world, Rusk remained convinced that the American campaign in Vietnam was a righteous cause and that had the United States been able to stay the course politically, the South Vietnamese government could have achieved long-term stability and Indochina would not have fallen to Communism as it did in 1975.

Critically important to an understanding of the war is the view of the conflict from the North Vietnamese perspective. There are a number of important books dealing firsthand with their point of view. Although Ho Chi Minh did not write directly about his experiences with the Americans, his *Prison Diary* (1966) and *Selected Works, 1962–1964* (1965) recount his experiences at the hands of the French in the 1940s, and there are published interviews with him, most notably Jean Lacouture's *Ho Chi Minh and His Followers: A Personal Memoir* (1968). All of them reveal similar themes about Ho: that he was as driven by a Marxist–Leninist view of economics as he was by his passion for Vietnamese independence; that he was willing to stay the military course for as long as it was necessary to drive out the French and the Americans; and that he was willing to make any level of sacrifice of people and resources to achieve his objectives.

Van Tien Dung's *Our Great Spring Victory: An Account of the Liberation of South Vietnam* is among the best. Dung was commander of North Vietnamese forces during the spring 1975 offensive, which led so quickly to the collapse of the South Vietnamese government. Although Dung expected what he thought would be a "glorious victory," he had no idea that it would come so easily, that the South Vietnamese military forces would implode so completely, and that the events leading up to the unification of the country and the creation of the Socialist Republic of Vietnam would come so soon. The individual who engineered the Vietnamese victory over the French in the early 1950s and over the South Vietnamese and the United States in the 1960s and early 1970s was Vo Nguyen Giap. Giap's memoirs—*Unforgettable Days*—provide an invaluable account of the political, strategic, and tactical courses of the two wars. Giap was convinced, from the very beginning of both wars, that the Vietnamese forces would prevail over the French and the Americans simply because of staying power. The foreign enemies would tire of the conflict, decide it was not in their strategic or political interests, and ultimately withdraw. That, of course, is exactly what happened. Also see Giap's *How We Won the War*. The perspective of the southern Communists—the Vietcong—is related in Truong Nhu Tang, *A Viet Cong Memoir*. The book is especially valuable because of how clearly it reveals the depth of the Vietcong commitment, their growing resentment of the North Vietnamese, and the horrible destruction they suffered at the hands of the Americans during the Tet Offensive of 1968. For an inside look at North Vietnamese politics during the war, particularly the strategic debates over conduct of the war, see Tran Van Dinh, *This Nation and Socialism Are One: Selected Writings of Le Duan*. Nguyen Thi Dinh provides a very revealing account of the war from the perspective of the Vietcong and the National Liberation Front. A native southerner, she emerged as the official spokesperson for the National Liberation Front (NLF) in 1968 and represented the NLF as its delegate to the Paris peace negotiations. Her memoir *No Other Road to Take* reveals the tenacity of the Vietcong, the terrible impact the Tet Offensive had on them, and their commitment to wresting South Vietnam from the Americans and the older Francophile Vietnamese leadership.

A different perspective on the war—different from the American, North Vietnamese, and Vietcong perspectives—comes from former South Vietnamese officials who watched their country decline steadily until its demise was guaranteed. The best examples of their point of view consist of Cao Van Vien and Dong Van Khuyen's *Reflections of the Vietnam War* and Nguyen Cao Ky's *Twenty Years and Twenty Days*. Cao Van Vien and Dong Van Khuyen were South Vietnamese army officers, and Nguyen Cao Ky was once president and then the longtime vice president of the Republic of Vietnam. Both works argue that the United States essentially abandoned South Vietnam to the Vietcong and North Vietnamese by steadily refusing to conventionally widen the war into Cambodia, North Vietnam, and Laos; by beginning to withdraw American ground troops in 1969, just when the Tet Offensive had badly weakened the enemy and made victory a distinct possibility; and by cutting financial support of South Vietnam just before the massive North Vietnamese offensive.

BIBLIOGRAPHY

Government Documents

Cameron, Allan W., ed. *Viet-Nam Crisis: A Documentary History 1940–1956*. Ithaca, N.Y.: Cornell University Press, 1971.

Cohen, Stephen. *Vietnam: Anthology and Guide to a Television History*. New York: Knopf, 1983.

Cole, Allan B. *Conflict in Indo-China and International Repercussions: A Documentary History 1940–1956*. Ithaca, N.Y.: Cornell University Press, 1956.

Confidential State Department Documents on Southeast Asia. Frederick, Md.: U.S. Government Printing Office, 1988.

The Declassified Documents Quarterly, 1975–1988. Washington, D.C.: Carrollton Press, 1975–1981; Woodbridge, Conn.: Research, 1982–1988.

Fulbright, J. William, ed. *The Vietnam Hearings*. New York: Random House, 1966.

Gelb, Leslie. "The Pentagon Papers and the Vantage Point." *Foreign Policy* 6 (Spring 1972): 28.

Gold, Gerald, Allan M. Siegel, and Samuel Abt, eds. *The Pentagon Papers as Published by The New York Times*. New York: Quadrangle, 1971.

Griffen, William L., and John Marciano. *Lessons of the Vietnam War: A Critical Examination of School Texts & Interpretive Comparative History Utilizing the Pentagon Papers & Other Documents*. New York: Allanheld, 1980.

Herring, George C., ed. *The Secret Diplomacy of the Vietnam War: The Negotiating Volumes of the Pentagon Papers*. Austin: University of Texas Press, 1983.

Herring, George C., ed. "Sources for Understanding the Vietnam Conflict." *Society for Historians of American Foreign Relations Newsletter* 16 (March 1985): 8–30.

Hickey, John T., ed. *The Echols Collection: Selections on the Vietnam War*. Ann Arbor, Mich.: University Microfilms International, 1990.

Kahin, George McT. "The Pentagon Papers: A Critical Evaluation." *American Political Science Review* 69 (1975): 675–84.

Lacouture, Jean. *Ho Chi Minh and His Followers: A Personal Memoir*. New York: Random House, 1968.

McMahon, Robert J., ed. *Major Problems in the History of the Vietnam War*. Lexington, Mass.: D. C. Heath, 1990.

The Pentagon Papers: The Defense Department History of the United States Decision-Making Process on Vietnam: The Senator Gravel Edition. Boston: Beacon Press, 1971–1972.

Pike, Douglas. *Indochina Chronology*. Berkeley: University of California Press, ongoing quarterly publication.

Pike, Douglas, ed. *The History of the Vietnam War*. Ann Arbor, Mich.: University Microfilms International, 1987.

Porter, Gareth, ed. *Vietnam: The Definitive Documentation of Human Decisions*. 2 vols. Stanfordville, N.Y.: E. M. Coleman Enterprises, 1979.

Porter, Gareth, ed. *Vietnam: A History in Documents*. New York: New American Library, 1981.

Public Papers of the Presidents of the United States: Dwight D. Eisenhower, 1953–1961 (in separate volumes). Washington, D.C.: U.S. Government Printing Office, 1954–1962.

Public Papers of the Presidents of the United States: John F. Kennedy, 1961–1963 (in separate volumes). Washington, D.C.: U.S. Government Printing Office, 1962–1964.

Public Papers of the Presidents of the United States: Lyndon B. Johnson, 1963–1969 (in separate volumes). Washington, D.C.: U.S. Government Printing Office, 1964–1970.

Public Papers of the Presidents of the United States: Richard M. Nixon, 1969–1974 (in separate volumes). Washington, D.C.: U.S. Government Printing Office, 1970–1975.

Public Papers of the Presidents of the United States: Gerald R. Ford, 1975. Washington, D.C.: U.S. Government Printing Office, 1976.

Roche, John P. "The Pentagon Papers." In *Sentenced to Life.* New York: 1974.

Rotter, Andrew J., ed. *Light at the End of the Tunnel. A Vietnam War Anthology.* New York: St. Martin's Press, 1991.

Sheehan, Neil, Hedrick Smith, E. W. Kenworthy, and Fox Butterfield. *The Pentagon Papers as Published by the New York Times.* New York: *New York Times,* 1971.

Spector, Ronald H. *Researching the Vietnam Experience.* Washington, D.C.: U.S. Army Center of Military History, 1984.

Taylor, Maxwell D. *The Uncertain Trumpet.* New York: Harper, 1960.

Truong Nhu Tang. *A Vietcong Memoir.* New York: Harcourt Brace Jovanovich, 1985.

U.S. Department of State. *American Foreign Policy: Current Documents, 1956–1975* (in separate volumes). Washington, D.C.: U.S. Government Printing Office, 1960–1979.

U.S. Department of State. *Foreign Relations of the United States, 1961–1963. Vols. I-III. Vietnam.* Washington, D.C.: U.S. Government Printing Office, 1985–1988.

U.S. Senate Committee on Foreign Relations. *Background Information Relating to Southeast Asia and Vietnam.* Washington, D.C.: U.S. Government Printing Office, 1982.

United States–Vietnam Relations, 1945–1967: Study Prepared by the Department of Defense. Washington, D.C.: U.S. Government Printing Office, 1971.

Williams, William Appleman, ed. *America in Vietnam: A Documented History.* New York: Norton, 1985.

Westerfield, H. Bradford. "What Use Are Three Versions of the Pentagon Papers." *American Political Science Review* 69 (1975): 685–96.

Major Memoirs and Autobiographies

Ball, George W. *The Past Has Another Pattern.* New York: Norton, 1982.

Cao Van Vien. *The Final Collapse.* Washington, D.C.: U.S. Army Center of Military History, 1982.

Cao Van Vien, and Dong Dan Khuyen. *Reflections of the Vietnam War.* New York: U.S. Army Center of Military History, 1980.

Carter, Jimmy. *Keeping Faith.* New York: Bantam, 1982.

Clifford, Clark. *Counsel to the President. A Memoir.* New York: Random House, 1991.

Colby, William E., and James McCargar. *Lost Victory: An Insider's Account of Our Sixteen-Year Involvement in Vietnam.* Chicago: Contemporary Books, 1989.

Colby, William E., and Peter Forbath. *Honorable Men: My Life in the CIA.* New York: Simon & Schuster, 1978.

Collins, J. Lawton, Jr. *The Development and Training of the South Vietnamese Army, 1950–1972*. Washington, D.C.: U.S. Army Center of Military History, 1975.

Dung, Van Tien. *Our Great Spring Victory: An Account of the Liberation of South Vietnam*. New York: Monthly Review Press, 1977.

Eisenhower, Dwight D. *The White House Years: Mandate for Change 1953–1956*. Garden City, N.Y.: Doubleday, 1963.

Eisenhower, Dwight D. *The White House Years: Waging Peace 1956–1961*. Garden City, N.Y.: Doubleday, 1965.

Ellsberg, Daniel. *Papers on the War*. New York: Simon and Schuster, 1972.

Enthoven, Alain C., and K. Wayne Smith. *How Much Is Enough? Shaping the Defense Program, 1961–1969*. New York: Harper and Row, 1971.

Fall, Bernard, ed. *Ho Chi Minh on Revolution*. New York: Harper and Row, 1968.

Giap, Vo Nguyen. *Dien Bien Phu*. New York: Foreign Language Publishing House, 1962.

Giap, Vo Nguyen. *Big Victory, Big Task*. New York: Foreign Language Publishing House, 1967.

Giap, Vo Nguyen. *How We Won the War*. New York: Reconstruction, 1976.

Giap, Vo Nguyen. *Unforgettable Days*. New York: Foreign Language Publishing House, 1978.

Harriman, W. Averell. *America and Russia in a Changing World: A Half Century of Personal Observation*. Garden City, N.Y.: Doubleday, 1971.

Hilsman, Roger. *To Move a Nation*. Garden City, N.Y.: Doubleday, 1967.

Ho Chi Minh. *Selected Works, 1962–1964*. New York: Foreign Language Publishing House, 1965.

Ho Chi Minh. *Prison Diary*. New York: Foreign Language Publishing House, 1966.

Hoopes, Townsend. *The Limits of Intervention*. New York: David McKay, 1973.

Javits, Jacob. *Who Makes War? The President Versus Congress*. New York: Harper and Row, 1973.

Johnson, Lyndon Baines. *The Vantage Point: Perspectives of the Presidency, 1963–1969*. New York: Holt, Rinehart and Winston, 1971.

Kissinger, Henry. *The White House Years*. Boston: Little, Brown, 1979.

Kissinger, Henry. *Years of Upheaval*. Boston: Little, Brown, 1982.

Lansdale, Edward Geary. *In the Midst of Wars: An American's Mission to Southeast Asia*. New York: Harper and Row, 1972.

Le Duan. *The Vietnamese Revolution: Fundamental Problems and Essential Tasks*. Ann Arbor, Mich.: University Microfilms, 1972.

Lodge, Henry Cabot. *The Storm Has Many Eyes: A Personal Narrative*. New York: Norton, 1973.

McCarthy, Eugene. *The Year of the People*. Garden City, N.Y.: Doubleday, 1969.

Nguyen Cao Ky. *Twenty Years and Twenty Days*. New York: Stein and Day, 1976.

Nguyen Thi Dinh. *No Other Road to Take: Memoir of Mrs. Nguyen Thi Dinh*. Ithaca, N.Y.: Cornell University Southeast Asian Publications, 1976.

Nixon, Richard M. *RN: The Memoirs of Richard Nixon*. New York: Grosset and Dunlap, 1978.

Nixon, Richard M. *No More Vietnams*. New York: Arbor House, 1980.

Nixon, Richard. *The Real War*. New York: Warner Books, 1980.

Nixon, Richard M. *1999 Victory Without War*. New York: Simon and Schuster, 1988.

Nolting, Frederick. *From Trust to Tragedy: The Political Memoirs of Frederick Nolting, Kennedy's Ambassador to Diem's Vietnam*. New York: Praeger, 1988.

O'Donnell, Kenneth, and David Powers. *Johnny, We Hardly Knew Ye*. Boston: Little, Brown, 1978.

Ridgway, Matthew B. *Soldier: The Memoirs of Matthew B. Ridgway*. New York: Harper, 1956.

Rostow, W. W. *The Diffusion of Power, 1957–1972*. New York: Macmillan, 1972.

Rusk, Dean. *As I Saw It. The Memoirs of Dean Rusk*. New York: Norton, 1990.

Salinger, Pierre. *With Kennedy*. Garden City, N.Y.: Doubleday, 1966.

Schlesinger, Arthur M., Jr. *A Thousand Days: John F. Kennedy in the White House*. Boston: Houghton Mifflin, 1965.

Sharp, U.S.G. *Strategy for Defeat: Vietnam in Retrospect*. Novato, Calif.: Presidio Press, 1978.

Sharp, U.S.G., and William Westmoreland. *Report on the War in Vietnam*. Washington, D.C.: U.S. Government Printing Office, 1968.

Sorensen, Theodore. *Kennedy*. New York: Harper and Row, 1965.

Taylor, Maxwell D. *Swords and Plowshares*. New York: Norton, 1972.

Thompson, Robert. *No Exit from Vietnam*. New York: David McKay, 1970.

Thompson, Robert. *Peace Is Not at Hand*. New York: Chatto and Windus, 1974.

Tran Van Dinh. *This Nation and Socialism Are One: Selected Writings of Le Duan*. New York: Foreign Language Publishing House, 1977.

Tran Van Tra. *Ending the Thirty Years War*. Washington, D.C., 1977.

Vance, Cyrus. *Hard Choices*. New York: Simon and Schuster, 1983.

Westmoreland, William. *A Soldier Reports*. New York: Doubleday, 1976.

Zumwalt, Elmo R., Jr. *On Watch*. New York: Quadrangle, 1976.

2 Personal Narratives and Oral Histories

While the collections of published government documents and the memoirs and autobiographies of prominent American participants provide a firsthand look at roles played by, and opinions of, major policymakers, there is also a sizable collection of oral histories and recollections of secondary personnel—the working- and middle-class Americans and Vietnamese who found themselves fighting a war that other men and women had made. Those oral histories and books can be classified by race, sex, and ethnicity. The most comprehensive of the oral histories were collected by Al Santoli, Harry Maurer, and Mark Baker. They all tend to reiterate similar themes—how innocence gave way to skepticism, how commitment disintegrated into survivalism, how hope turned into cynicism, and how relief at coming home became bitterness. There is also a premier universal theme to all of the first-person recollections: how Vietnam had a powerful bonding effect on men and women who found themselves supporting themselves under such extraordinarily difficult conditions. Michael Norman's *These Good Men* (1991) is an excellent description of those feelings. They are best illustrated by a marine whom Norman quotes: "Men don't talk about love very well as far as men loving other men. But when it comes down to it, I've loved more men than women." For an analysis of these themes in the Vietnam literature, see Lloyd B. Lewis, *The Tainted War: Culture and Identity in Vietnam War Narratives*. The American soldiers, civilian workers, and nurses realized soon after their arrival in Southeast Asia that most Vietnamese—northern as well as southern—did not want them there. Vietnam would not be like World War II, when French, Dutch, and Belgian peasants had welcomed the conquering GIs with open arms. No battle better illustrates those feelings than what happened at Khe Sanh in 1967 and 1968, when American marines underwent a horrific siege, expecting the North Vietnamese to launch an all-out assault, only to be left sitting there when the Tet Offensive began in other parts of South Vietnam. Eric Hammel's *Khe Sanh: Siege in the Clouds: An Oral History* tells in gruesome detail the carnage of the battle and the frustration the marines felt when they later abandoned the mountain, only then to see it reoccupied by enemy troops. Gerald R. Giglio's *Days of Decision* provides dozens of recollections by conscientious objectors serving in the military during the Vietnam era.

As the war progressed, a noticeable shift in attitude became apparent in its American participants. The gung ho patriotic attitude that prevailed early in the war changed to disillusionment as soldiers realized that there would be no military victory and that most Vietnamese peasants did not even want them in the country. Few soldiers could find any cause to rally behind and give the war some meaning. Deterioration of morale and discipline occurred after 1969, when the Nixon administration began its phased withdrawal of American troops. The eventual fall of South Vietnam to the Communists came as no surprise to most of the men who served in Vietnam.

A recent oral history by J. T. Hansen, A. Susan Owen, and Michael Patrick Madden compares the experiences of American soldiers in Vietnam and Soviet soldiers in Afghanistan. *Parallels* (1992) is an extraordinary work because of the similarities of both experiences. Soviet soldiers found themselves a long way from home, trapped in an alien culture and fighting a war that none of them understood against an enemy that was fanatically committed. Like so many millions of Americans who fought in Vietnam, they found the war laced with absurdities, random violence, and political manipulation.

The individual stories of those who fought in Vietnam are available in a rapidly growing number of memoirs and autobiographies. Several of those memoirs tell of young, idealistic men who were lured to war in the 1960s by President John F. Kennedy's inaugural pledge to "pay any price, bear any burden, meet any hardship, support any friend, oppose any foe to assure the survival and the success of liberty." This gung ho patriotic attitude is revealed in *The Letters of Pfc. Richard E. Marks, USMC.* Marks spent fifteen months in Vietnam before his death there at the age of nineteen. In his letters, written at an early stage of the war, Marks expressed the conviction that the war was a noble effort and that his death would not be too high a price to pay for victory over Communism. Phillip Caputo's *A Rumor of War* and Ron Kovic's *Born on the Fourth of July* both reflect the initial impact of the idealism of the Kennedy era, but eventually, both men turned against the war. Caputo's book describes his tour with the First Battalion, Third Marine Division, in the Danang area between March and September 1965. Caputo quickly became disillusioned about the nature of the war, and by 1968 he was actively opposing American involvement in Indochina. Caputo came to feel that the war was unwinnable and American lives there were wasted. Survival was the only victory for those who endured the war. Ron Kovic also joined the Marine Corps. Kovic joined the military for reasons similar to Caputo's, but his disgust and disillusionment with the war were brought about by a severe wound that left him paralyzed from the waist down. As he was lying wounded, Kovic remembered feeling "the worthlessness of dying in that place, at that moment, for nothing." The book focuses on his life after his injury and describes vividly his hospitalization, rehabilitation, and involvement in the antiwar movement. Collective memoirs reflect the same patriotic themes and the same eventual disillusionment. Peter Goldman's *Charlie Company* and Charles Anderson's *The Grunts* describe the horrors of war and the changes in perception of those who had to fight it. *The Grunts* portrays the experiences of Bravo Company, First Battalion, Third Marine Division, on a fifty-eight day operation launched on April 29, 1969. The book captures the growing hatred the marines felt for all Vietnamese, the increasing levels of atrocities, and the deepening bitterness of the troops after their return to the United States. Goldman's book deals with sixty-five members of Charlie Company, Twenty-eighth Infantry Regiment, First Infantry Division, who fought together in Vietnam in 1968 and 1969. They were not naive about the war in 1968, but most of them believed that it was their patriotic duty to serve when they were called. But they soon became disillusioned. They felt that the practice of rotating men in and out of the country individually rather than as a unit undermined morale. Winning seemed increasingly remote and became secondary to staying alive. They questioned the tactics as well as the broad objectives of the war.

In *Chickenhawk*, Robert Mason tells of going to war because of a sense of duty of another kind. He went to Vietnam not for any idealistic reasons but because he owed the army three years for teaching him to fly helicopters. Mason did not believe in the war and questioned its military objectives. He had no respect for the South Vietnamese armed forces. In Mason's opinion, the American presence in Indochina was doomed because the United States did not have the support of the people it was supposed to be saving, and those people did not have the will to fight their own war. Most South Vietnamese he encountered believed that Ho Chi Minh would eventually prevail, and many of them hoped for that kind of victory.

While some soldiers went to war with high ideals, others were influenced by the John Wayne version of war. They sought to prove themselves and their manhood but were disillusioned when the reality of war turned out to be vastly different from their perceptions. W. D. Ehrhart, author of *Vietnam-Perkasie: A Combat Marine Memoir*, served as an intelligence assistance with the First Battalion of the First Marine Regiment from 1967 to 1968. He expected the war to be triumphant glory and conquered beachheads, but he found only shame. He was told by a South Vietnamese scout that wherever Americans took their firepower and arrogance, the Vietcong would grow like "new rice in the fields." During Ehrhart's tour of duty, he began slowly to understand what the scout meant, and, in looking back at his experience, he questioned his blind loyalty to the war. David Regan, in his book *Mourning Glory: The Making of a Marine*, also tells of losing his illusions and innocence about heroism and glory as he went through boot camp and then faced the realities of war in Vietnam.

A combination of support for the war and an inability to adjust to a society that had changed led Matthew Brennan to reenlist in 1968 for a second tour in Vietnam. He served with the First Air Cavalry Division of the U.S. Army. In his book, *Brennan's War: Vietnam 1965–1969*, Brennan describes the changes he noticed upon his return to Vietnam. The confident, disciplined soldiers of 1967 had been replaced by an army of draftees who did not have the same toughness or aggressiveness as before. He felt that the generals, being more worried about public opinion and casualties than fighting a war, had adopted defensive tactics that ultimately led to the disintegration of discipline and morale. He told of instances where soldiers literally turned on each other; in fact, some young platoon leaders were more afraid of their own men than the Vietcong. At one time he had been convinced of the justice of the U.S. presence in Vietnam but eventually came to realize that this was not a war against Communism, but rather a war against nationalism that American troops would not win.

Not all of the participants were influenced by a glorified view of war. Some had no illusions about the war and went unwillingly. In John Ketwig's *...And a Hard Rain Fell* and Tim O'Brien's *If I Die in a Combat Zone*, both men expressed their opposition to the war and their thoughts of fleeing to Canada to avoid the draft. However, each ended up serving in Vietnam, but neither ever found a reason to support the war. Ketwig was appalled by the waste of lives and was unable to trust the South Vietnamese, who acted friendly to Americans by day but at night were Vietcong. He also felt that military leaders exhibited a lack of concern for the soldiers and became so obsessed with power that they viewed soldiers as expendable. To Tim O'Brien the war was about "dinks and slopes—kill them or avoid them." He told of the hate he developed toward the villagers, the anger he felt at the death of his friends by mines, booby traps, and snipers, and his frustration at having no one to strike back against. Torching huts was the only way to get some measure of revenge, but these actions destroyed the strategy of "winning the hearts and minds" of the South Vietnamese. His main goal was survival, and it was evident that this was also the main goal of the men he served with as fraggings and self-inflicted wounds became common.

Women who served in Vietnam perceived the war with the same bitterness and disillusionment as the men. Lynda Van Devanter and Christopher Morgan, in *Home Before Morning*, expressed anger at the devastation she witnessed as a combat nurse. She explained the emotional and physical toll of working long hours in understaffed operating rooms. In Al Santoli's book, *Everything We Had*, Gayle Smith told of going to Vietnam, in spite of her objections to the war, for the purpose of bringing home the men who did not belong there. She told of the emotional impact of treating severely injured young men and how she turned this pain into hatred and anger for the Vietnamese. According to her, the rules of war allowed for the killing of women and children because they, too, were potential enemies. Three books are particularly good: Keith Walker, *A Piece of My Heart: The Stories of 26 American Women Who Served in Vietnam*; Kathryn Marshall, *In the Combat Zone: An Oral History of American Women in Vietnam*; and Dan Freedman and Jacqueline Rhoads, *Nurses in Vietnam: The Forgotten Veterans*. Most of the American women who served in Vietnam were nurses, and their experiences were just as frustrating as those of the men there, except they also had to deal with the problems of sexism from male physicians, the psychological stress of dealing every day with severely wounded and dying men, and the overwhelming sense of seeing so much pain and suffering wasted in such an ignoble cause. They also had to deal with the issue of how technology permitted human beings to bring so much death and slaughter to each other. For the perspective of a male physician, see John A. Parrish's *Twelve, Twenty and Five: A Doctor's Year in Vietnam*.

The attitudes of minority group soldiers about the war can be found in Wallace Terry's *Bloods: An Oral History of the Vietnam War by Black Veterans* and David Parks's *G.I. Diary*. Early in the war blacks reflected the same gung ho attitudes as whites, but as the war progressed and opposition to the war grew in the United States, especially among the leaders of the civil rights movement, black troops began to question more and more their participation in what many felt was the wrong war. By 1968 the war made little sense to most black soldiers, who had no idea what they were fighting for in Vietnam. Although black veterans often expressed the feeling that out in the field, when combat units were in "harm's way," a sense of mutual support was almost always evident in Vietnam, things changed back at base camps and in Saigon, where anti-black racism was common. Black soldiers also frequently wondered— because of the racial rebellions, the assassination of Martin Luther King, Jr., and the discrimination against Muhammad Ali—why they were even fighting in Vietnam. They were also aware of the higher number of black draftees in the military and, during the early years of the war, of their higher casualty rates. Many felt the real war was back in the United States. By 1971 blacks saw the struggle as senseless, and those who served in the rear areas reported incidents of racial violence and frequent clashes between blacks and whites. Hard drugs and racial incidents were more of a threat to their lives than the enemy. The will to survive became the main concern as it became clear that the United States was not willing to win the war. Larry Lee's *American Eagle: The Story of a Navajo Vietnam Veteran* tells a similar story from an American Indian's perspective, while Charley Trujillo's *Soldados: Chicanos in Vietnam* gives the points of view of Hispanic troops fighting the war. The themes are the same: doubts, disillusionment, and bitterness.

Personal accounts written by military officers revealed a different perspective on the war, even though many felt the same frustrations about the war as the enlisted men. John Trotti's *Phantom over Vietnam* and Jack Broughton's *Thud Ridge* give the reader a realistic account of the war as seen by pilots involved in the air war over North Vietnam. Trotti, a marine pilot who flew the F–4, began to question the value of strategic bombing and the destruction it caused while Broughton expressed his frustration in trying to fight a restricted and limited air war against a determined enemy. Broughton flew the F–105. As the air war was carried out, leaders of the ground forces were engaged in a war of attrition with an elusive and deadly enemy. James McDonough recounted in *Platoon Leader* that his initial idealism about the war and his eagerness to serve were eventually replaced by doubt as his platoon was slowly wiped out by booby traps. He kept his doubts to himself because he felt leadership must always be positive. On the other hand, Frederick Downs, Jr., author of *The Killing Zone*, has no qualms about his military service. He viewed it as a job to be done, and anything he had to do, even the killing of civilians, was justified. He later wondered if the people of Vietnam were worth his trouble after seeing their lack of cooperation. Even though officers were in a position where they could not openly question the war, many had their own private doubts.

A collection of letters written to family members and friends compiled by Bernard Edelman in *Dear America* reveals a wide range of attitudes about the war in Vietnam and, in many ways, mirrors the division that existed in the country as a whole. Some soldiers had no trouble justifying why they were there. These men felt they were in Vietnam to maintain a democratic society. Some express guilt for the things they did while they were there, while others reflect disillusionment toward the war and resentment toward the Vietnamese. Still others are frustrated by the limitations that were imposed on them. Most letters were written by young men who did not want to go there and wanted nothing more than to get out alive.

The changing attitudes of the men who fought the war and the resulting bitterness and cynicism that developed can best be examined in works that include the recollections of many veterans of Vietnam. The best of these works include Al Santoli's *Everything We Had*, Mark Baker's *Nam*, and Donald Kirk's *Tell It to the Dead*. In many cases their recollections are violently graphic and extremely profane and provide a clear picture of the horrors of the war as seen through the eyes of the men who fought it.

In Santoli's *Everything We Had*, soldiers tell of going to Vietnam willingly to fight for their country because it was expected of them by their fathers, who had fought in World War II. Others believed they were doing the right thing. Many of the men interviewed questioned their training and did not feel they were adequately prepared to fight a guerrilla war until their tour of duty was nearly over. The reality of guerrilla warfare and the brutal deaths of their buddies was something that most of the men were unprepared to deal with. The purpose of the war was never clear to most of the men, and, for many, survival became the main goal. As the war progressed and the number of casualties increased, many veterans began to question the military tactics being used. Others could not understand why the people who had the most to gain by winning the war were so reluctant to fight it. More than one veteran questioned the motives of their own commanding officers and wondered if they had any concern for the lives of the men they were leading. Others found it difficult to trust anyone who was Vietnamese for there was no easy way to determine the enemy. As it became apparent that the United States was not going to win the war but was going to withdraw its forces, those left in Vietnam had no desire to expose themselves to danger and earn the dubious distinction of being the last American to die there. Many veterans felt this decision to withdraw from the war without victory meant that lives lost there had been lost in vain.

Mark Baker's book, *Nam*, reflects many of the same attitudes, but these were expressed with more bitterness and anger. Soldiers remembered wanting to test their manhood and being influenced by the John Wayne mystique. The war in Vietnam turned out to be a brutal never-never land where little boys grew old before their time and war was reduced to one simple fact—survival. One veteran expressed the feeling that the ideals he had gone to Vietnam with, freedom and democracy, were shattered. He felt used by the U.S. government and felt that the war was a fraud. Veterans expressed a deep sense of frustration over the waste of lives caused by what they perceived as mismanagement of the war by the military.

Harry Maurer's *Strange Ground: Americans in Vietnam, 1945–1975. An Oral History* (1988) is a more generic oral history of the war. Maurer interviewed a wide range of individuals who were involved in the war, from those who helped Ho Chi Minh fight the Japanese during World War II to others who left on the last day, fighting for helicopter space on the roof of the U.S. embassy in Saigon. They included soldiers, from privates to generals, prisoners of war and antiwar activists, and civilians and diplomats.

Donald Kirk's *Tell It to the Dead* chronicles the change in attitude toward the war, particularly after 1969. Kirk was a journalist for the *Chicago Tribune* who spent a great deal of time in Vietnam between 1965 and 1972. The change in U.S. military strategy brought about a rapid deterioration in morale and discipline. Soldiers felt the war was a waste as areas were abandoned that had once been the site of the heaviest fighting and heaviest losses. By 1971, the struggle was viewed as senseless, and many felt that the soldiers should have been out two years earlier. Drug use increased, fraggings were more common, and racial incidents occurred more often, particularly in the rear areas. Soldiers in the field questioned continued military effort while the withdrawal of troops was taking place. By 1972, the men had become extremely bitter and cynical, and the only ones who had anything to gain in Vietnam were the career-conscious officers. By this time, many felt that all military personnel should have been moved to the rear until they were pulled out and no American soldier should have been asked to risk his life for a cause that the United States had abandoned.

A few books insist that the intention of the war was right but the war was lost because it was fought the wrong way. David Donovan, author of *Once a Warrior King*, received army training in counterinsurgency and was assigned to a five-man mobile advisory team in the Mekong Delta. He recalls being inspired by John Kennedy and initially found his work in Vietnam as a member of a mobile advisory team exciting and rewarding. Ultimately, these feelings were replaced by bitterness and frustration. This disillusionment was not with the war itself, but with the way the war was fought. Donovan expressed regret that the nation found the war "a price too high, a burden too heavy, a friend too incompetent, a foe too intractable for us to continue to hold high in the cause of liberty." He felt that the country betrayed the young men it sent to war there. Al Santoli's *To Bear Any Burden* seems to reflect the feeling that the tactics used in fighting the war were wrong, but the purpose for which the war was fought was correct. Some have not given up on the hope that someday Southeast Asia will be free of Communist tyranny.

In conclusion, the viewpoint of the grunts toward the Vietnam War cannot be dealt with in absolute terms. Some had no qualms about what they did and felt justified that the cause was right. Others felt the loss of the war could not be blamed on the inability of the soldiers themselves, but rather on military tactics and strategy. Some even felt that a strategy based on different tactics without restrictions and limitations might have resulted in the war's being won. But, by and large, most of the men who fought in Vietnam feel that the war was doomed from the beginning because of an undefined purpose, questionable military strategy, a lack of commitment on the part of the South Vietnamese to assume their share of the burden for the fight, the brutal nature of the war and the tremendous number of casualties that occurred from the tactics used by the enemy, and the gradual loss of the support of the people back home for the war. Their bitterness and anger are apparent, their disillusionment and disenchantment with the war evident, as they relate the stories many felt needed to be told, stories that, for too many, had been bottled up too long.

Another genre of memoirs and oral histories deals with the final days of the conflict and with the South Vietnamese perspective on the war. Larry Engelmann's *Tears Before the Rain: An Oral History of the Fall of South Vietnam* deals with the unbelievable chaos of the last days of the war and the overwhelming sense of betrayal so many South Vietnamese felt at the time. That bitterness is especially clear in Stephen T. Hosmer's *The Fall of South Vietnam: Statements by Vietnamese Military and Civilian Leaders.* Al Santoli's *To Bear Any Burden: The Vietnam War and Its Aftermath in the Words of Americans and Southeast Asians* deals with the frustrations of returning veterans, the economic chaos North Vietnam inflicted on South Vietnam after 1975, and the holocaust visited on Cambodia by the Khmer Rouge. The South Vietnamese view of the war is made especially clear in Don Luce and John Sommer, *Vietnam: The Unheard Voices.* For a riveting account of how the war brought hardship, destruction, torture, and rape to the life of a young South Vietnamese peasant woman, see Le Ly Hayslip, *When Heaven and Earth Changed Places: A Vietnamese Woman's Journey from War to Peace.*

There are several collections of letters between soldiers and their families during the war as well as recollections and feelings about the meaning of the war for American society. The Vietnam War Memorial in Washington, D.C., has produced an extraordinarily painful and poignant collection of letters and mementos left behind by relatives viewing the names of the dead. Laura Palmer's *Shrapnel in the Heart: Letters & Remembrances of the Vietnam Memorial* provides a powerful collection of those feelings. Also see V. L. Breckstone, John F. Stone, and Philip Wilson's *Front Lines: Soldiers' Writings from Vietnam.* Perhaps the best of the collections is Bernard Edelman, ed., *Dear America: Letters Home from Vietnam.*

In addition to the memoirs and personal recollections of pilots and foot soldiers, there is a small but powerful group of memoirs by former American prisoners of war. The best collective oral history is Stephen A. Rowan, *They Wouldn't Let Us Die: The Prisoners of War Tell Their Story.* For an individual account, see Jeremiah Denton, *When Hell Was in Session.* The themes of these prisoner-of-war books tend to be the same, since so many of the captured men shared a similar experience: periodic interrogations and occasional torture sessions, long periods of little or no contact with other colleagues, constant tension about future treatment, an almost complete lack of information about the course of the war or the negotiations, and concern about just how long their captivity would last. The memoirs also talk about the problems of returning home after a long absence and reestablishing family relationships.

There is a small but very revealing literature of memoirs and oral histories of North Vietnamese and Vietcong participants. The best of them is David Chanoff and Doan Van Toai's *Portrait of the Enemy*. It consists of interviews with North Vietnamese officials and officials of the Vietcong, as well as with Vietcong and North Vietnamese soldiers and peasants. Like all good oral histories, the book destroys monolithic assumptions by exposing the extraordinary commitment of the Vietnamese for independence, the resentments and ancient rivalry between northern and southern Vietnamese Communists, their incredulity at the firepower the Americans assembled and the stupidity with which they used it, and the deepening fatigue they were feeling toward the end of the conflict.

The experience of common people in Cambodia and Laos during and after the Vietnam War has not been the subject of much literature, but Sydney Schanberg's *The Death and Life of Dith Pran* provides a chilling account of what the Khmer Rouge did in Cambodia in the late 1970s. Schanberg was a reporter for the *New York Times* in Cambodia, and Dith Pran was his photographer. After the Khmer Rouge seized control of Phnom Penh in 1975, Pran was left behind and spent several harrowing years in concentration—"reeducation"—camps. He managed to escape into Thailand, where Schanberg eventually found him. Pran tells a grisly story of mass torture and mass death in what the Khmer Rouge called their "Year Zero."

During the 1980s, as American culture came to terms with the Vietnam War, a number of soldiers and war correspondents decided to return to the battlefield that had done so much to shape their lives. Their return to the United States had been so abrupt, so disillusioning, and so painful that they had often been unable to deal with it psychologically. For most of them, Vietnam was the watershed period of their lives, and in order to understand its impact and perhaps finally to put the war behind them, they decided to return for a visit to Indochina. Vietnam, desperate for hard currency, began to encourage their return. Mark E. Thompson described his visit in *Return to Despair: A Vietnam Story*, as did W. D. Ehrhart in *Going Back: An Ex-Marine Returns to Vietnam*. Those returning to South Vietnam for visits after the war were universally impressed with the economic malaise throughout the country as well as the friendliness with which the South Vietnamese greeted them. In *Flashbacks: On Returning to Vietnam*, CBS reporter Harry Reasoner recalls his journalistic tour of duty in Vietnam. Reasoner had come to top national attention in August 1965 when he filmed U.S. marines using Zippo lighters to burn down 150 village huts in Cam Ne. Returning to Vietnam in 1989, Reasoner describes the economic destruction the Communists have brought to the country, the friendliness of the Vietnamese toward Americans, and, in his interview with Vo Nguyen Giap, how determined the Vietnamese leadership was during the 1960s and 1970s to prevail in spite of the American firepower.

Among the best firsthand accounts of the war in Vietnam are those produced by journalists and scholars who served there. A number of French journalists spent time in Indochina during the 1950s and 1960s, and they were able to provide a comparative perspective on the two wars in Vietnam. The best of those journalists was Bernard Fall, whose major books are *The Viet Minh Regime* (1956), *Le Viet Minh, 1945–1960* (1960), *Street Without Joy* (1961), *The Two Viet Nams* (1963), *Viet Nam Witness* (1966), *Hell in a Very Small Place* (1966), and *Last Reflections on a War* (1967). Fall served with the French army until 1946, when he came to the United States. He earned a Ph.D. at Syracuse University and first went to Vietnam in 1951 on a Fulbright Scholarship. He returned there for a sixth period of study in 1966 on a Guggenheim Fellowship. Fall had a passion for Vietnam and its people, and he viewed both wars there as tragedies. Although he was deeply concerned about the threat of Communism to the free world, Fall was committed to the idea of an independent Vietnam, free of any kind of foreign domination. He was a critic of both French colonialism and American intervention. Fall was also an admirer of the Vietminh and the Vietcong, especially because of their group commitment and their tenacity. Bernard Fall was killed in Vietnam on February 21, 1967, when a Vietcong booby trap exploded near him.

A similar argument is made by Peter Sholl-Latour's *Death in the Rice Fields: An Eyewitness Account of Vietnam's Three Wars, 1945–1979* (1985). Sholl-Latour was in and out of Indochina for more than thirty years, and he argues that the French and the Americans made the same mistakes in Vietnam: confusing Communism and nationalism, being unable to focus on a coherent political objective, and assuming that victory in Indochina was a military, rather than a political, event. Both countries alienated the peasants by their arrogance and their indiscriminate use of firepower; both countries mistakenly assumed that they could successfully fight a guerrilla war with conventional techniques; and both sides eventually ignored effective counterinsurgency programs in favor of big-unit military action.

David Halberstam was a journalist for the *New York Times* in Vietnam between 1962 and 1964. He won a Pulitzer Prize for his reporting of the war. Although, at the time, Halberstam agreed with American policymakers that Vietnam was strategically significant and that the spread of Communism should be opposed there, he was highly critical of the nature of the U.S. effort there. Halberstam came to believe that the South Vietnamese government was hopelessly corrupt and that the Communists actually had the loyalty of most Vietnamese—northerners and southerners. In his 1964 book *The Making of a Quagmire*, Halberstam proved prophetic in his claim that the U.S. effort, as long as it was tied to the existing South Vietnamese government, was doomed to failure.

Neil Sheehan worked for United Press International in South Vietnam during the mid–1960s. During those years in Vietnam, Sheehan became acquainted with John Paul Vann, an American army officer who completed several tours there, three with the military and one with a civilian aid program. In 1988, Sheehan published his best-selling *A Bright and Shining Lie: John Paul Vann and America in Vietnam*. The book is a biography of Vann as well as a history of the American war in Vietnam, most of it written from Sheehan's firsthand perspective. Sheehan's major argument about the war was that American military firepower, by inadvertently inflicting millions of casualties on South Vietnamese civilians, made it impossible for the United States to win the "hearts and minds" of the people. The South Vietnamese, whether Communist or non-Communist, came to hate the United States for the sheer devastation American bombers and artillery shells brought to the country. Other reporters wrote similar surveys of the Vietnam War from their firsthand perspective. The best of them are by Stanley Karnow, a reporter for *Time*, and Peter Arnett of the Associated Press.

BIBLIOGRAPHY

Anderson, Charles R. *The Grunts.* Novato, Calif.: Presidio Press, 1976.

Anderson, Charles R. *Vietnam: The Other War.* Novato, Calif.: Presidio Press, 1982.

Arnett, Peter, and Michael Maclear. *The Ten Thousand Day War.* New York: St. Martin's Press, 1981.

Baer, Gordon, and Nancy Howell-Koehler. *Vietnam: The Battle Comes Home.* New York: Norton, 1984.

Baker, Mark. *Nam: The Vietnam War in the Words of the Men and Women Who Fought There.* New York: Morrow, 1981.

Balaban, John. *Remembering Heaven's Face: A Moral Witness in Vietnam.* New York: Poseidon Books, 1990.

Beesley, Stanley W. *Vietnam: The Heartland Remembers.* Norman: University of Oklahoma Press, 1987.

Berg, Rick, and Paul Vangelisti, eds. *The Plague in Saigon: A Vietnam Chronicle.* New York: Pennywhistle Press, 1983.

Bernard, Edward. *Going Home.* New York: Battery Press, 1973.

Bingaman, H. H. *Reckonings: Stories of the Air War over North Vietnam.* New York: Vantage, 1988.

Bleier, Rocky, and Terry O'Neil. *Fighting Back.* New York: Scarborough House, 1980.

Bowers, Curt, and Glen Van Dyne. *Forward Edge of the Battle Area: A Chaplain's Story.* Boston: Beacon Hill, 1987.

Bows, Ray. *Vietnam Military Lore, 1959–1973: Another Way to Remember.* New York: Bows and Sons, 1988.

Brant, Toby L. *Journal of a Combat Tanker Vietnam, 1969.* New York: Vantage, 1988.

Breckstone, V. L., John F. Stone, and Philip Wilson, eds. *Front Lines: Soldiers' Writings from Vietnam.* New York: Indochina Curriculum Group, 1975.

Brennan, Matthew. *Brennan's War: Vietnam 1965–1969.* Novato, Calif.: Presidio Press, 1985.

Brennan, Matthew. *Headhunters: Stories from the 1st Squadron, 9th Cavalry, in Vietnam.* Novato, Calif.: Presidio Press, 1987.

Brennan, Matthew, ed. *Hunter Killer Squadron: Aero-Weapons, Aero-Scouts, Aero-Rifles: Vietnam 1965–1972.* Novato, Calif.: Presidio Press, 1992.

Briscoe, Edward G. *Diary of a Short-Timer in Vietnam.* New York: Holt, Rinehart, and Winston, 1970.

Broughton, Jack. *Thud Ridge.* Philadelphia: Lippincott, 1969.

Brown, John M. *Rice Paddy Grunt: Unfading Memories of the Vietnam Generation.* New York: Regency-Brown, 1986.

Browne, Malcolm. *The New Face of War.* New York: Bobbs-Merrill, 1968.

Burchett, Wilfred G. *Vietnam: Inside Story of the Guerrilla War.* New York: International, 1965.

Caputo, Philip. *A Rumor of War.* New York: Holt, Rinehart, and Winston, 1977.

Caron, Philip D. *Eagles & Other Prey: A Vietnam Experience in Prose & Poetry.* New York: Volunteer, 1989.

Cassidy, John. *A Station in the Delta.* Philadelphia: Scribner's, 1982.

Chanoff, David, and Doan Van Toai. *Portrait of the Enemy.* New York: Random House, 1986.

Chinnery, Philip D. *Life on the Line: Stories of Vietnam Air Combat.* New York: St. Martin's Press, 1988.

Christian, David, and William Hoffer. *Victor 6: The Saga of One of Vietnam's Most Highly Decorated Soldiers.* New York: McGraw-Hill, 1990.

Clark, Johnnie. *Guns Up!* New York: Ballantine Books, 1984.

Cleland, Max. *Strong at the Broken Places.* Oklahoma City: Cherokee Press, 1980.

Clodfelter, Michael. *Mad Minutes & Vietnam Months: A Soldier's Memoir.* New York: McFarland, 1988.

Cook, John L. *The Advisor.* New York: Dorrance, 1973.

Crapser, William. *Remains: Stories of Vietnam.* New York: Sachem Press, 1988.

Currey, Richard. *Crossing Over: A Vietnam Journal.* Boston: Little, Brown, 1980.

Davidson, Phillip B. *Secrets of the Vietnam War.* Novato, Calif.: Presidio Press, 1990.

Deforest, Orrin M., and David Chanoff. *Slow Burn: The Rise and Bitter Fall of American Intelligence in Vietnam.* New York: Simon and Schuster, 1990.

Dengler, Dieter. *Escape from Laos.* New York: Zebra Press, 1982.

Denton, Jeremiah. *When Hell Was in Session.* New York: Reader's Digest Press, 1976.

Donovan, David. *Once a Warrior King: Memories of an Officer in Vietnam.* New York: McGraw-Hill, 1985.

Dorr, Robert. *Air War Hanoi.* London: Blandford Press, 1988.

Dougan, Clark. *A War Remembered.* Boston: Addison-Wesley, 1991.

Downs, Frederick, Jr. *The Killing Zone: My Life in the Vietnam War.* New York: Norton, 1978.

Drury, Richard S. *My Secret War.* New York: McGraw-Hill, 1979.

Dunstan, Simon. *Vietnam Choppers.* London: Osprey Books, 1988.

Edelman, Bernard, ed. *Dear America: Letters Home from Vietnam.* New York: Norton, 1985.

Ehrhart, W. D. *Vietnam-Perkasie: A Combat Marine Memoir.* Jefferson, N.C.: McFarland, 1983.

Ehrhart, W. D. *Going Back: An Ex-Marine Returns to Vietnam.* Jefferson, N.C.: McFarland, 1987a.

Ehrhart, William. *Going Back: A Poet Who Was Once a Marine Returns to Vietnam.* New York: Pendle Hill Press, 1987b.

Ehrhart, W. D. *Passing Time: Memoir of a Vietnam Veteran Against the War.* Jefferson, N.C.: McFarland, 1988.

Engelmann, Larry. *Tears Before the Rain: An Oral History of the Fall of South Vietnam.* New York: Oxford University Press, 1990.

Englebrecht, Charles V. *The Guns Fell Silent and the War Began.* New York: Englebrecht, 1987.

Esper, George. *The Eyewitness History of the Vietnam War, 1961–1975.* New York: Associated Press, 1983.

Estep, Jame. *Comanche Six: Company Commander in Vietnam.* Novato, Calif.: Presidio Press, 1991.

Fall, Bernard. *The Viet Minh Regime.* New York: Praeger, 1956.

Fall, Bernard. *Le Viet Minh, 1945–1960.* New York: Praeger, 1960.

Fall, Bernard. *Street Without Joy.* New York: Praeger, 1961.

Fall, Bernard. *The Two Viet Nams.* New York: Praeger, 1963.

Fall, Bernard. *Hell in a Very Small Place.* New York: Pall Mall Press, 1966.

Fall, Bernard. *Viet Nam Witness.* New York: Praeger, 1966.

Fall, Bernard. *Last Reflections on a War.* New York: Praeger, 1967.

Fletcher, Harvey D. *Visions of Nam.* New York: Jo-Ely Press, 1987.

Fletcher, Jerry J. *Devils with Green Faces: Navy Seals in Vietnam.* Germantown, Md.: Shann Press, 1990.

Flynn, Robert. *A Personal War in Vietnam.* College Station: Texas A & M University Press, 1989.

Freedman, Dan, and Jacqueline Rhoads, eds. *Nurses in Vietnam: The Forgotten Veterans.* Austin: Texas Monthly Press, 1987.

Gadd, Charles. *Line Doggie: Foot Soldier in Vietnam.* Novato, Calif.: Presidio Press, 1989.

Garrett, Richard. *P.O.W.: The Uncivil Face of War.* New York: Borgio Press, 1981.

Giglio, Gerald R. *Days of Decision: An Oral History of Conscientious Objectors in the Military During the Vietnam War.* New York: Broken Rifle Press, 1989.

Goff, Stanley, Robert Sanders, and Clark Smith. *Brothers. Black Soldiers in the Nam.* Novato, Calif.: Presidio Press, 1982.

Goldman, Peter. *Charlie Company: What Vietnam Did to Us*. New York: Morrow, 1983.

Grady, John, and Sarah Rogovin, eds. *Let Me Tell You Where I've Been: Photographs and Interviews with Seven Vietnam Veterans*. New York: Stonybrook Press, 1988.

Grauwin, Paul. *Doctor at Dienbienphu*. New York: J. Day, 1955.

Gritz, James B. *A Nation Betrayed*. New York: Lazarus Press, 1989.

Hackworth, David H., and Julie Sherman. *About Face: The Odyssey of an American Warrior*. New York: Simon and Schuster, 1990.

Hakes, Thomas L. *A Soldier's Diary of Thoughts, Memories and Letters*. New York: St. Martin's Press, 1987.

Halberstam, David. *The Making of a Quagmire: America and Vietnam During the Kennedy Era*. New York: Knopf, 1964.

Halstead, Fred. *Out Now! A Participant's Account of the American Movement Against the Vietnam War*. New York: Anchor, 1978.

Hammel, Eric. *Khe Sanh: Siege in the Clouds: An Oral History*. New York: Crown, 1989.

Hammel, Eric. *Ambush Valley*. Novato, Calif.: Presidio Press, 1990a.

Hammel, Eric. *The Assault on Khe Sanh: An Oral History*. New York: Warner Books, 1990b.

Hansen, J. T., A. Susan Owen, and Michael Patrick Madden. *Parallels: The Soldiers' Knowledge and the Oral History of Contemporary Warfare*. Hawthorne, N.Y.: Aldine de Gruyter, 1992.

Harrison, Marshall. *A Lonely Kind of War: Forward Air Controller, Vietnam*. Novato, Calif.: Presidio Press, 1989.

Hayslip, Le Ly. *When Heaven and Earth Changed Places. A Vietnamese Woman's Journey from War to Peace*. New York: Doubleday, 1990.

Hennen, John. *Caught Up in Time: Oral History Narratives of Appalachian Vietnam Veterans*. New York: Aegina Press, 1989.

Herbert, Anthony B. *Soldier*. New York: Holt, Rinehart, and Winston, 1973.

Herr, Michael. *Dispatches*. New York: Avon Books, 1978.

Herrington, Stuart A. *Peace with Honor? An American Reports on Vietnam, 1973–1975*. Novato, Calif.: Presidio Press, 1983.

Herrod, Randy. *Blue's Bastards: A True Story of Valor Under Fire*. New York: Regency Gateway, 1989.

Hoang Ngoc Lung. *The General Offensive of 1968–1969*. New York: Dalley Book Service, 1989.

Hosmer, Stephen T. *The Fall of South Vietnam: Statements by Vietnamese Military and Civilian Leaders*. Santa Monica, Calif.: Rand, 1978.

Howard's Hill and Other True Stories: Small Unit Marine Action in Vietnam. New York: Diane, 1987.

Hubble, John G. *POW: A Definitive History of The American Prisoner of War Experience in Vietnam, 1964–1973*. New York: Reader's Digest Press, 1976.

Hutchens, James M. *Beyond Combat*. New York: Shepherds Press, 1986.

Jaunal, Jack W. *Vietnam 68: Jack's Journal*. New York: Denson Press, 1989.

Jensen, Jay R. *Six Years in Hell: A Returned Vietnam POW Views Captivity, Country and the Future*. New York: Publications of Worth, 1989.

Jones, James. *Viet Journal*. New York: Praeger, 1973.

Joyner, William. *Vietnam Heroes: That We Have Peace*. London: Horizon Press, 1983.

Kamazi, I. S. *Nam Book*. New York: Morningland, 1981.

Kane, Ron. *Veteran's Day*. New York: Orion Books, 1990.

Karnow, Stanley. *Vietnam: A History*. New York: Viking, 1983.

Ketwig, John. . . . *And a Hard Rain Fell: A G.I.'s True Story of the War in Vietnam*. New York: Macmillan, 1985.

Kim, Samuel. *The American POWs*. New York: Branden, 1978.

Kirban, Salem. *Goodbye Mr. President*. New York: Kirban, 1974.

Kirk, Donald. *Tell It to the Dead: Memories of a War*. Chicago: Nelson-Hall, 1975.

Klein, Joe. *Payback: Five Marines After Vietnam*. New York: Knopf, 1984.

Kovic, Ron. *Born on the Fourth of July*. New York: McGraw-Hill, 1976.

Lanning, Lee. *The Only War We Had: A Platoon Leader's Journal of Vietnam*. New York: Ivy Books, 1987.

Lanning, Michael L. *Vietnam Nineteen Sixty-Nine to Nineteen Seventy: A Company Commander's Journal*. New York: Ivy Books, 1988.

Lee, Larry. *American Eagle: The Story of a Navajo Vietnam Veteran*. Tucson, Ariz.: Packrat Press, 1977.

Levinson, J. L. *Alpha Strike Vietnam*. Novato, Calif.: Presidio Press, 1989.

Lewis, Lloyd B. *The Tainted War: Culture and Identity in Vietnam War Narratives*. Westport, Conn.: Greenwood Press, 1985.

Linedecker, Clifford. *Kerry: Agent Orange and an American Family*. New York: St. Martin's, 1982.

Luce, Don, and John Sommer. *Vietnam: The Unheard Voices*. Ithaca, N.Y.: Cornell University Press, 1969.

McCauley, Anna K. *Miles from Home*. New York: AKLM, 1984.

McDonough, James R. *Platoon Leader*. Novato, Calif.: Presidio Press, 1985.

McKeown, Bonni. *Peaceful Patriot: The Story of Tom Bennett*. New York: Peaceful Patriot Press, 1987.

Manning, Robert. *The Vietnam Experience: Vietnam Remembered*. Boston: Boston, 1986.

Marks, Richard E. *The Letters of Pfc. Richard E. Marks, USMC*. Philadelphia: Lippincott, 1967.

Marshall, Kathryn, *In the Combat Zone: An Oral History of American Women in Vietnam*. Boston: Little, Brown, 1987.

Marshall, Kathryn. *Nurses in Vietnam: The Forgotten Veterans*. Boston: Little, Brown, 1987.

Marshall, Samuel L. *Ambush*. New York: Battery Press, 1982.

Marshall, Samuel L. *Bird: The Christmastide Battle*. New York: Battery Press, 1983.

Marshall, Samuel L. *Campaigning in the Central Highlands, Vietnam, Summer 1966*. New York: Battery Press, 1984.

Mason, Robert. *Chickenhawk*. New York: Viking Press, 1983.

Maurer, Harry. *Strange Ground: Americans in Vietnam, 1945–1975. An Oral History*. New York: Holt, 1988.

Mecklin, John. *Mission in Torment: An Intimate Account of the U.S. Role in Vietnam*. New York: Doubleday, 1965.

Merritt, William E. *Where the Rivers Ran Backward*. Garden City, N.Y.: Doubleday, 1990.

Miller, Franklin D., and Elwood J. C. Kureth. *Reflections of a Warrior*. Novato, Calif.: Presidio Press, 1991.

Miller, Stephen P. *An Act of God: Memories of Vietnam*. Boston: Northeast View Press, 1987.

Mulligan, James A. *The Hanoi Commitment*. New York: RIF Marketing, 1981.

Myers, Thomas. *Walking Point: American Narratives of Vietnam*. New York: Oxford, 1988.

Ngo Vinh Long. *Before the Revolution: The Vietnamese Peasants Under the French*. New York: Praeger, 1973.

Nguyen Ngoc Ngan. *The Will of Heaven*. New York: Dutton, 1981.

Noel, Chris. *Matter of Survival*. New York: Branden, 1987.

Noel, Reuben, and Nancy Noel. *Saigon for a Song: The True Story of a Vietnam Gig to Remember*. New York: USC Press, 1987.

Norman, Michael. *These Good Men. Friends Forged from War*. New York: Crown, 1991.

O'Brien, Tim. *If I Die in a Combat Zone*. New York: Delacorte, 1973.

Page, Tim. *Tim Page's Nam*. New York: Knopf, 1983.

Page, Tim. *Page After Page*. New York: Macmillan, 1990.

Palmer, David R. *Summons of the Trumpet*. New York: Ballantine Books, 1984.

Palmer, Laura. *Shrapnel in the Heart: Letters and Remembrances from the Vietnam Veterans Memorial*. New York: Random House, 1988.

Parks, David. *G. I. Diary*. New York: Harper and Row, 1968.

Parrish, John A. *Twelve, Twenty and Five: A Doctor's Year in Vietnam*. New York: Bantam Books, 1989.

Parry, Francis Fox. *Three-War Marine: The Pacific, Korea, Vietnam*. Novato, Calif.: Presidio Press, 1992.

Prashker, Ivan. *Duty, Honor, Vietnam: Twelve Men of West Point Tell Their Story*. New York: Morrow, 1988.

Pratt, John Clark. *Vietnam Voices: Perspectives on the War Years 1941–1982*. New York: Penguin, 1984.

Puller, Lewis B., Jr. *Fortunate Son: The Healing of a Vietnam Vet*. New York: Grove Weidenfeld, 1991.

Reasoner, Harry. *Flashbacks: On Returning to Vietnam*. New York: Random House, 1990.

Reed, Craig. *The Cost of War*. New York: Hurricane Ridge Press, 1989.

Regan, David J. *Mourning Glory: The Making of a Marine*. Old Greenwich, Conn.: Devlin-Adair, 1981.

Risner, Robinson. *The Passing of the Night: My Seven Years as a Prisoner of the North Vietnamese*. New York: Ballantine Books, 1989.

Roberts, Craig, and Charles W. Sasser. *The Walking Dead: A Marine's Story of Vietnam*. New York: Putnam's, 1989.

Roche, John. *Sentenced to Life: Reflections on Politics, Education, and Law*. New York: Macmillan, 1974.

Rosenberger, Mary S. *Harmless as Doves*. Philadelphia: Brethren Press, 1988.

Roskey, William. *Muffled Shots: A Year on the DMZ*. New York: Dell, 1987.

Rowan, Stephen A. *They Wouldn't Let Us Die: The Prisoners of War Tell Their Story*. New York: Reader's Digest Press, 1975.

Rowe, James N. *Five Years to Freedom*. New York: Ballantine Books, 1984.

Rubin, Jerry. *Growing Up (at 37)*. New York: M. Evans, 1976.

Sack, John. *Lieutenant Calley: His Own Story*. New York: Viking, 1971.

Santoli, Al. *Everything We Had. An Oral History of the Vietnam War by Thirty-three American Soldiers Who Fought It*. New York: Random House, 1981.

Santoli, Al. *To Bear Any Burden: The Vietnam War and Its Aftermath in the Words of Americans and Southeast Asians*. New York: Dutton, 1985.

Schanberg, Sydney. *The Death and Life of Dith Pran*. New York: Penguin Books, 1985.

Sheehan, Neil. *A Bright and Shining Lie: John Paul Vann and America in Vietnam*. New York: Random House, 1988.

Sheppard, Don. *Riverine: A Brown-Water Sailor in the Delta, 1967*. Novato, Calif.: Presidio Press, 1992.

Sholl-Latour, Peter. *Death in the Rice Fields: An Eyewitness Account of Vietnam's Three Wars, 1945–1979*. London: Fields and Smith, 1985.

Simpson, Charles M., III. *Inside the Green Berets: The First Thirty Years*. Novato, Calif.: Presidio Press, 1983.

Sisk, Robert W. *Wings for the Valiant*. New York: Flores, 1989.

Smith, Hilary. *Lighting Candles: Hospital Memories of Vietnam's Montagnards*. New York: Howard Smith, 1988.

Snepp, Frank. *Decent Interval: An Insider's Account of Saigon's Indecent End*. New York: Random House, 1977.

Spencer, Ernest. *Welcome to Vietnam, Macho Man: Reflections of a Khe Sanh Vet*. San Diego: Marine Corps Press, 1988.

Steer, John L., and Cliff Dudley. *Vietnam, Curse or Blessing*. New York: New Leaf Press, 1982.

Stockdale, Jim, and Sybil Stockdale. *In Love and War: The Story of a Family's Ordeal and Sacrifice During the Vietnam Years*. Washington, D.C.: Naval Institute Press, 1984.

Terry, Wallace. *Bloods: An Oral History of the Vietnam War by Black Veterans*. New York: Random House, 1984.

Thompson, Mark E. *Return to Despair: A Vietnam Story*. New York: Carlton Press, 1991.

Tran Tri Vu. *Lost Years: My One-Thousand Six Hundred and Thirty-Two Days in Vietnamese Re-Education Camps*. New York: International East Asian Series, 1989.

Trotti, John. *Phantom over Vietnam: Fighter Pilot, USMC*. Novato, Calif.: Presidio Press, 1981.

Trujillo, Charley, ed. *Soldados: Chicanos in Vietnam*. Albuquerque, N. Mex.: Chusma House, 1989.

Truong Van Dinh. *A Viet Cong Memoir*. New York: Harper and Row, 1985.

Tuso, Joseph F. *Singing the Vietnam Blues. Songs of the Air Force in Southeast Asia*. College Station: Texas A & M University Press, 1990.

Van Devanter, Lynda, and Christopher Morgan. *Home Before Morning: The Story of an Army Nurse in Vietnam*. New York: Beaufort, 1983.

Veninga, James, and Harry A. Wilmer. *Vietnam in Remission*. College Station: Texas A & M University Press, 1990.

Vitel, Mike. *Charlie's Paradise: Nineteen Sixty-Seven to Sixty-Eight*. New York: Vantage Press, 1987.

Walker, Keith. *A Piece of My Heart: The Stories of 26 American Women Who Served in Vietnam.* Novato, Calif.: Presidio Press, 1985.

Webb, Kate. *On the Other Side: 23 Days with the Viet Cong.* New York: Quadrangle, 1972.

Willenson, Kim. *The Bad War. An Oral History of the Vietnam Conflict.* New York: New American Library, 1987.

Williams, Reese, ed. *Unwinding the Vietnam War: From War to Peace.* New York: Comet Press, 1987.

Willson, David A. *REMF Diary.* Seattle, Wash.: Black Heron Press, 1989.

Willwerth, James. *Eye in the Last Storm.* New York: Praeger, 1972.

Yezzo, Dominick. *A G.I.'s Vietnam Diary, 1968–1969.* New York: Franklin Watts, 1974.

Zalin, Grant. *Survivors: American POWs in Vietnam.* New York: Berkley Press, 1987.

3 General Background and Surveys

ROOTS OF AMERICAN INVOLVEMENT

Ironically, given the events of the 1960s and 1970s, the United States rejected its first opportunity to intervene militarily in Southeast Asia. In 1954, with General Vo Nguyen Giap and his Vietminh troops surrounding the French outpost at Dien Bien Phu, France asked the United States to rescue them. President Dwight D. Eisenhower asked Admiral Arthur Radford, chairman of the Joint Chiefs of Staff, to consider the request and make a recommendation. Radford hatched Operation Vulture—the use of Philippine-based B–29s, accompanied by aircraft from the USS carriers *Essex* and *Boxer*—to knock out Vietminh artillery. In case the air strike did not lift the siege, Radford was prepared to use atomic weapons. Stephen Jurika, Jr., edited Radford's memoirs (*From Pearl Harbor to Vietnam: The Memoirs of Admiral Arthur W. Radford*) and quoted Radford as saying: "Whether these [air strikes] alone would have been successful in breaking the siege of Dien Bien Phu is debatable. If we had used atomic weapons, we probably would have been successful."

The issue that President Eisenhower had to decide was whether to follow Radford's advice. John Prados, in *The Sky Would Fall: Operation Vulture: The U.S. Bombing Mission in Indochina, 1954*, describes how Eisenhower decided not to intervene militarily. Secretary of State John Foster Dulles could not muster much support for the strike within the North Atlantic Treaty Organization (NATO) alliance, and Congress would not go alone. The specter of war in Vietnam, so soon after the armistice in Korea, was too much for them. What really convinced Eisenhower, however, was the opposition of General Matthew Ridgway, chief of staff of the U.S. Army. In his memoirs *Soldier: The Memoirs of Matthew B. Ridgway*, the general recalled his conviction that the air strike would not lift the siege and that American ground troops would have to be called in. Ridgway wrote to Eisenhower and asked about the depth of the water around Saigon, the quality of the harbor and dock facilities, the warehouse capacity for storing supplies, the quality of the highway system, and the nature of the climate, rainfall, and tropical diseases. Nobody knew the answers, including Radford. Eisenhower knew what infantry combat was like; Ridgway's questions provided the president with his answer. Operation Vulture was scuttled. The French outpost at Dien Bien Phu fell a few weeks later.

No issue surrounding the American role in the Indochina conflict has been more intensely debated than the question of why and how the United States originally became involved there. Toward the end of World War II, President Franklin D. Roosevelt worried about the future of colonialism. He believed World War II would destroy European co-lonialism, and one colony ripe for rebellion was French Indochina. In March 1943 Roosevelt suggested to the British foreign secretary, Anthony Eden, that when the war was over, Indochina should be placed under international trusteeship, like the older World War I mandates. In a private conversation with Secretary of State Cordell Hull in 1944, the president remarked: "France has had the country—thirty million inhabitants—for nearly one hundred years, and the people are worse off than they were at the beginning. . . . The people of Indochina are entitled to something better than that." But as historians like Christopher Thorne (*Allies of a Kind: The United States, Britain, and the War Against Japan, 1941–1945*) and William Roger Louis (*Imperialism at Bay: The United States and the Decolonization of the British Empire*) have pointed out, Great Britain and France were intensely interested in reviving their colonial empires after World War II, and eventually Presidents Franklin D. Roosevelt and Harry S. Truman went along with that revival.

During the 1950s and early 1960s, the contemporary explanations of the American involvement in Indochina emerged from a traditional cold war point of view. The anti-Communist hysteria of the late 1940s swept through the United States and shaped, as well as was shaped by, the prevailing perceptions of the Soviet Union. Senator J. William Fulbright has written that American policymakers were obsessed with the theory of "monolithic Communism"—the conviction that there was a single, international Communist conspiracy to take over the world and that the conspiracy was directed from the Kremlin in Moscow. All manifestations of Communism, anywhere in the world, could be traced directly to the Russians.

The first battleground of the cold war was Central Europe, where the United States, Great Britain, and France expected the Soviet Union to be particularly aggressive, especially after she had refused to withdraw her troops from Eastern Europe at the end of World War II. George Kennan wrote his famous article in *Foreign Affairs* in 1947 and proposed what became known as the "containment doctrine"—a foreign policy in which the United States would oppose, militarily and politically, Soviet expansion in Europe. The Truman Doctrine, the Marshall Plan, and the Berlin Airlift were all "containment" responses to Soviet political and military activity.

After the fall of China to Mao Zedong in 1949 and the outbreak of the Korean War in 1950, American policymakers began to apply the containment doctrine to Asia as well, a point of view with which George Kennan took great exception. Anthony Short's *The Origins of the Vietnam War* (1989) argues that it was a mistake for the United States to internationalize the French war in Indochina and that the U.S. decision to intervene was aimed as much at China as at North Vietnam. Regardless of Kennan's objections, American policymakers focused on the Communism in Ho Chi Minh's ideology, not on the anti-French, pro-Vietnamese nationalism. The early U.S. decision to provide financial support to the French was based on the Eisenhower administration's desire to stop the spread of Communism in Asia. For them, the major front of the cold war had shifted to Asia. During the years of the John F. Kennedy administration, as well as the first years of the Lyndon B. Johnson administration, that cold war interpretation of the struggle in Indochina prevailed. It also appeared in most of the memoirs of the individuals who made and implemented American military and foreign policy during the 1960s and early 1970s. People like Lyndon B. Johnson, Dwight D. Eisenhower, Richard Nixon, Henry Cabot Lodge, Frederick Nolting, William Westmoreland, Walt W. Rostow, Dean Rusk, W. Averell Harriman, Pierre Salinger, and Theodore Sorensen all reflected that cold war mentality in their memoirs or early histories of the war.

Even the earliest critics of the American military adventure in Vietnam accepted the cold war ideology as the operative interpretation of what was going on in Indochina. David Halberstam's book *The Making of a Quagmire: America and Vietnam During the Kennedy Era*, originally published in 1964, was highly critical of American policy in South Vietnam, but not because of any fundamental flaw in the way American leaders perceived the nature of the conflict. Halberstam served as a journalist for the *New York Times* in Vietnam between 1961 and 1963, and during his years there he concluded that the South Vietnamese government, which the United States was trying to support, was hopelessly corrupt and out of touch with the peasant masses of the country. Halberstam concluded that the war there was a quagmire simply because the narrow-minded, corrupt policies of the Ngo Dinh Diem administration were alienating most Vietnamese from the Diem government as well as from the United States. As long as American policy was expressed through the Diem family, the U.S. effort was doomed.

Historian Robert A. Divine has called this interpretation the "liberal internationalist" perspective, and the most articulate spokesman for this intellectual approach was Arthur M. Schlesinger, Jr., the Harvard historian and former advisor to the Kennedy administration. In his book *The Bitter Heritage: Vietnam and American Democracy, 1941–1966*, Schlesinger argued that well-meaning presidents—Truman, Eisenhower, Kennedy, and Johnson—had slowly, incrementally, and unintentionally escalated the American involvement in Vietnam to the point that withdrawal posed its own set of painful alternatives. The threat of Communism was very real in the world, but the United States undertook to fight it on the wrong battlefield in Vietnam. Schlesinger wrote:

We have achieved our present entanglement, not after due and deliberate consideration, but through a series of small decisions. . . . Each step in the deepening of the American commitment was reasonably regarded at the time as the last step that would be necessary. Yet, in retrospect, each step led only to the next, until we find ourselves entrapped today in that nightmare of American strategists, a land war in Asia—a war which no President, including President Johnson, desired or intended. The Vietnam story is a tragedy without villains. (Pp. 31–32)

What Schlesinger was not calling for in *The Bitter Heritage* was any fundamental reevaluation of American foreign policy. The policy was not wrong; it had just been misapplied in South Vietnam. Halberstam's later book—*The Best and the Brightest*—was highly critical of the arrogance and high-handedness of people in the Kennedy and Johnson administrations, but he did not question the basic foundations of American foreign policy that brought the country to Vietnam.

Another group of historians and policymakers puts a new twist on the incremental escalation interpretation. They argued that the cold war mentality was so strong in the United States in the 1960s that American policymakers went into Indochina knowing their efforts would probably fail to save South Vietnam from Communism. What the world needed to know, they believed, was that the United States was serious about its desire to stop the spread of Communism. Even if South Vietnam did fall to the Communists, at least American credibility would remain intact because of a sincere military, economic, and political effort to prevent it from happening. They knew that the war was essentially a stalemate, but each time a Communist victory seemed imminent, they felt compelled to make another good faith offering—more money, more firepower, more personnel. Lawrence Gelb and Richard K. Betts, in *The Irony of Vietnam: The System Worked*, argued that throughout the conflict, officials in the CIA and the State Department realized that there were severe limitations to American policy in Vietnam, but the world needed to see that the United States had at least made a serious effort to save South Vietnam.

One of the best descriptions of the impact of the containment ideology and the notion of monolithic Communism on American foreign policy in Indochina can be found be R. B. Smith's *An International History of the Vietnam War, Volume 1: Revolution Versus Containment, 1955–1961*. During the Eisenhower years, the United States threw its support behind the regime of Ngo Dinh Diem. American policymakers were not denying the potency of nationalism in Vietnam during the 1950s; they just hoped that Ngo Dinh Diem, who was a nationalist and an intense anti-Communist, would be able to rally South Vietnamese peasants around him and prevent the Vietcong and North Vietnamese from taking over the country. Eventually, Diem was undone not by his anti-Communism or by his nationalism; it was his personal paranoia, his hatred of Buddhism, and his attempt to consolidate all political power within the confines of his family that destroyed him politically.

Daniel Ellsberg, the former marine and Rand Corporation intellectual who eventually released the Pentagon Papers to the press, claimed in his book *Papers on the War* that domestic political concerns, rather than any real threat of Communism abroad, explain the escalating commitment of the United States in Vietnam. According to Ellsberg, the most significant event for post–World War II United States foreign policy was the fall of China to the Communists in 1949. Right-wing Republicans blamed President Harry S. Truman and the Democratic party for the fall of China, arguing that if the United States had shown more backbone, Mao Zedong and the Chinese Communists would not have prevailed. Their criticism led to the Democrats' defeat in the election of 1952. After that, moderate Republicans like Dwight Eisenhower and Democrats like John F. Kennedy and Lyndon B. Johnson became almost paranoid about being saddled with the "loss of Vietnam" criticism. No American president wanted to be perceived as the individual who lost Vietnam, so each of them steadily escalated the American commitment in order to save South Vietnam. Ultimately, the escalation became so great that President Johnson found himself fighting the dreaded "land war in Asia."

The Kennedy administration found itself trying to sort out these political issues, and its answer to them was an escalation of the war. When Dwight Eisenhower left the White House in 1961, there were fewer than 1,000 American military personnel in South Vietnam, but in 1963, when John F. Kennedy was assassinated, that number had increased to more than 17,000 people. Several historians have looked at the approach the Kennedy administration took to the Vietnam War. David Halberstam's *The Best and the Brightest* and Gregory Palmer's *The McNamara Strategy and the Vietnam War: Program Budgeting in the Pentagon, 1961–1968* both look at the extraordinary faith the Kennedy people had in the power of American technology and the "systems" approach to politics and military conflict. That confidence, indeed arrogance, allowed them to escalate the conflict without serious qualms. John Galloway's *The Kennedys and Vietnam* does, however, describe the significance of domestic political affairs in preventing the administration from de-escalating the American commitment. As Thomas C. Reeves points out in his recent book *A Question of Character: A Life of John F. Kennedy*, the president was growing increasingly frustrated with the domestic political instability in South Vietnam and with his own generals' requests for more troops, but he was also worried about the election of 1964 and the need to avoid right-wing criticism that he was soft on Communism. John M. Newman's recent *JFK and Vietnam: Deception, Intrigue, and the Struggle for Power* (1992) concludes that Kennedy would have withdrawn from Vietnam after the 1964 election. For a New Left critique of the Kennedy administration's role in the Vietnam War, see Bruce Miroff's *Pragmatic Illusions: The Presidential Politics of John F. Kennedy.*

For most historians, the watershed event in the early history of the Vietnam War was the Tonkin Gulf incident in 1964. President Lyndon B. Johnson complained that North Vietnamese forces had deliberately attacked American warships in international waters off the coast of North Vietnam. Johnson then used the incident to secure an overwhelming resolution of support from Congress to justify the beginning of the air war against North Vietnam. Although there were skeptics at the time who questioned whether the attack had really occurred, it was not until the publication of books like Joseph C. Goulden's *Truth Is the First Casualty: The Gulf of Tonkin Affair—Illusion and Reality* (1969) and John Galloway's *The Gulf of Tonkin Resolution* (1970) that Americans realized that the attack had not really occurred and that the president had misled the public in order to escalate the war.

The complexity of the political climate in the United States is carefully analyzed in important books by Larry Berman and Kathleen J. Turner. In *Planning a Tragedy: The Americanization of the War in Vietnam* and *Lyndon Johnson's War: The Road to Stalemate in Vietnam*, Berman argues that Lyndon Johnson was not a mindless warmonger but a moderate more preoccupied with domestic politics than with international affairs. More than anything else, Johnson wanted to make sure that the war in Vietnam did not destroy the political support he needed to implement his Great Society programs at home: civil rights, antipoverty, education, and Medicare legislation. Slowly but surely, President Johnson found himself getting deeper and deeper into the war, not out of any forthright commitment to military victory but out of compromise and moderation, taking the middle road between those Neanderthals who wanted to bomb the enemy back into the Stone Age and the weak-kneed pacifists who wanted out at any cost. Each escalation of the conflict was taken as a compromise, and each step was taken with the conviction that just a little more firepower would win the day. Throughout the war, Johnson perceived himself as acting prudently, carefully, and moderately. For a comparison of presidential decision making about Vietnam in 1954 and 1965, see John P. Burke and Fred I. Greenstein, *How Presidents Test Reality: Decisions on Vietnam, 1954 and 1965* (1991).

Kathleen J. Turner's book *Lyndon Johnson's Dual War: Vietnam and the Press* (1985) argues that the so-called credibility gap was inevitable. Like Berman, she sees the Great Society programs as critical to an understanding of Lyndon Johnson's decision-making process during the war. The dilemma the president faced was extraordinarily difficult: if South Vietnam fell to the Communists, Johnson risked taking the kind of political heat Harry Truman had taken back in the early 1950s over China, but at the same time, he had to avoid an all-out war commitment. Such a commitment would take so much money that the Great Society programs would be starved, and in the antiwar movement that would expand as the war escalated, Johnson was threatened with a loss of the support he had on the political left. For Turner, the "dual war"—which Johnson eventually lost—involved trying to convince the American public that he was doing enough to save South Vietnam without their perceiving that he was doing too much. The press soon believed that the Johnson administration was both holding back critical information about the extent of American involvement in Vietnam and actually misleading them about that commitment.

Several historians have claimed that the American effort in South Vietnam simply emerged out of a misapplication of the containment doctrine. A major explanation for that problem was the fact that the same American elite that had waged World War II and that had constructed the anti-Soviet foreign policy ideology of the 1940s and 1950s was still making policy in the 1960s. These people—including W. Averell Harriman, Dean Acheson, George Kennan, Robert Lovett, John McCloy, Charles Bohlen, and others—all remembered the Munich incident of 1938, when Neville Chamberlain and the British had caved in to Adolf Hitler's bullying over Czechoslovakia, only to see the world soon embroiled in a global war that cost tens of millions of people their lives. They believed in the "never again" approach to military and political policy, and they applied that mentality to the Soviet Union and to her clients in the world, including Ho Chi Minh and the Vietnamese Communists. These elite policymakers gave Presidents John F. Kennedy and Lyndon B. Johnson bad advice because they could see only Communism in Vietnam, not nationalism. For the best descriptions of this argument, see John C. Donovan, *The Cold Warriors: A Policy-Making Elite*, and Walter Isaacson and Evan Thomas, *The Wise Men. Six Friends and the World They Made*.

George Herring's important survey of the war—*America's Longest War: The United States and Vietnam, 1950–1975*—pursues a similar argument. The containment policy was very effective in Europe in the 1940s and early 1950s, primarily because in European history, Communism and nationalism had not become intertwined. Indeed, throughout the Eastern bloc, Communism was the antithesis of nationalism. The American effort to contain Soviet expansion was a policy that enjoyed tacit support among the people of Lithuania, Latvia, Estonia, Poland, Czechoslovakia, Hungary, Romania, and Yugoslavia. But containment was not applicable in much of Asia where Communism had often become the vehicle for expressing anti-Western, anti-imperial nationalism. For Herring, the American involvement in Vietnam "was a logical, if not inevitable outgrowth of a world view and a policy, the policy of containment, which Americans in and out of government accepted without serious question for more than two decades. The commitment in Vietnam expanded as the containment policy itself grew. In time, it outlived the conditions which had given rise to that policy" (x). Eventually, the United States abandoned nationalism in Asia because the survival of Great Britain, France, and Japan as non-Communist allies seemed more important. Historian George Herring has argued that "America's Indochina policy continued to be a hostage of its policy in Europe."

In more recent years, the interpretation of how and why the United States became so deeply involved in Indochinese affairs has turned to economic issues. Historians like Andrew J. Rotter (*The Path to Vietnam: Origins of the American Commitment to Southeast Asia*), Gabriel Kolko (*Anatomy of a War: Vietnam, the United States, and the Modern Historical Experience*), Robert M. Blum (*Drawing the Line: The Origin of the American Containment Policy in East Asia*), Richard J. Barnet (*Roots of War*), Lloyd C. Gardner (*Approaching Vietnam: From World War II Through Dienbienphu*), and Lisle Abbott Rose (*Roots of Tragedy: The United States and the Struggle for Asia, 1945–1953*) see more concrete issues than domestic politics and ideology behind the United States' willingness to invest so much in Indochina. For Rotter and Blum, there was more to the domino theory than anti-Soviet rhetoric and anti-Communist paranoia. Communist expansion was no idle threat in the region. In the 1950s, the Philippines were dealing with Communist guerrillas, and in Malaya and Burma and British government faced similar threats. Radical insurgents in Indonesia were undermining the Dutch colonial regime. Political leaders in Australia and New Zealand were genuinely concerned about the prospects of a Communist victory in Vietnam. The fall of Vietnam might topple Malaya, the Philippines, and Indonesia, and once Indonesia fell, so might Australia and New Zealand.

In strategic and economic terms, Southeast Asia was also critical to American interests. The fall of Southeast Asia would threaten the island chain stretching from Japan to the Philippines, cutting off American air routes to India and South Asia and eliminating the first line of defense in the Pacific. Australia and New Zealand would be isolated. The region was loaded with important natural and strategic resources, including tin, rubber, rice, copra, iron ore, copper, tungsten, and oil. Not only would the United States be cut off from those resources, but huge potential markets for American products would be threatened. Communist victories in Indochina, Malaya, and Indonesia would also place a geopolitical noose around the Philippines. In 1940 the United States had faced a similar threat when Japanese expansion threatened Indochina, Malaya, and Indonesia, and the outcome had been World War II. How long could the Philippines stay free of Communism if its neighbors fell?

For historians like Gabriel Kolko and Richard J. Barnet, the United States seemed bent on world hegemony in the 1950s and early 1960s— committed to the triumph of American democracy and free enterprise capitalism everywhere on earth. Many Americans found a connection between Southeast Asia, the survival of Western Europe, and their own economic prosperity. In 1949 Great Britain was still in the economic doldrums and dangerously low in dollar reserves. The recovery of the British economy required huge capital investments, and the entire British empire needed to increase its exports to the United States. Southeast Asia was critical to that process. Before World War II, a vigorous triangular trade existed among Great Britain, the United States, and British Malaya, which had valuable rubber and tin assets. That trade needed to be revived. Nor could the French economy be restored to health as long as the war in Indochina was such a financial drain. Finally, American leaders had believed ever since the end of World War II that the Japanese economy would have to revive dramatically to prevent the spread of Communism there. The key to the Japanese revival, they thought, was the presence of the huge Chinese market for Japanese goods. But when China fell to Mao Zedong in 1949, that market ceased to exist; many international economists then looked to Southeast Asia as a market for Japanese products. The fall of Vietnam to Communism would eliminate that market as well. American policymakers looked at all of these possibilities.

According to Lloyd C. Gardner, American involvement in Indochina was part of a much broader post–World War II drive by the United States to achieve global hegemony. A similar argument from the New Left school of American historiography can be found in Patrick J. Hearden's *The Tragedy of Vietnam*. The primary factor in American foreign policy was the need for world economic hegemony, and the United States committed its resources in the postwar world to the achievement of that control—to make sure, in Hearden's words, that the "liberal capitalist world system" triumphed around the globe. For these New Leftists, talk about the domino theory or the importance of domestic politics in motivating American policymakers is just subterfuge—carefully contrived rhetoric designed to mask more fundamental economic needs.

GENERAL SURVEYS

Because of the extent to which the Vietnam War has captured the
American imagination and preoccupied American culture in the past
two decades, it is not surprising that there is a wide variety of general
survey histories of the war. Although most of them fall into the broad
ideological center in their interpretations, some works take a revisionary
perspective. On the far left, historians like Martin McLaughlin, in books
like his *Vietnam and the World Revolution: A Trotskyite Analysis*, argue that
the Vietnam War proved the internal contradictions of capitalism and
imperialism by bringing the world's great capitalist power to its knees.
For McLaughlin, Ho Chi Minh and the Vietnamese Communists proved
that "people's wars," as Mao Zedong had predicted, would inevitably
prevail over American hegemony. The United States of America, the
world's premier economic and military superpower, had been unable to
defeat a small, underdeveloped country because the "hearts and minds"
of the peasant masses supported revolution. Patrick J. Hearden's *The
Tragedy of Vietnam* takes a New Left approach to the war, but his arguments are far more reasonable and well executed than the knee-jerk
mentality of McLaughlin.

Marxist conspiracies, however, are quite uncommon in the general
literature of the Vietnam War. Also uncommon, but with at least a
measure of credence, were the "revisionary" arguments of the late 1970s
and 1980s about the Vietnam War. The consensus, of course, has been
that the Vietnam War was a horrible mistake, that it was unwinnable,
and that the United States sacrificed tens of thousands of its own young
men and women, as well as millions of Vietnamese, in a poorly conceived,
if not immoral, military campaign. Revisionists, however, dispute that
point of view. In his 1978 book *Never Again: Learning from America's
Foreign Policy Failures*, Earl C. Ravenal argued that the United States
should not decide, because of the Vietnam debacle, to avoid other Third
World struggles. For Ravenal, the United States must continue to oppose
Communist expansion in the world if it is going to protect its own strategic interests. Norman Podhoretz's *Why We Were in Vietnam* argues that
throughout the Vietnam War the United States occupied the high moral
ground—that North Vietnam was a totalitarian, Communist state that
deserved to be restrained by containment policies.

Another revisionary point of view of the war argues that the United
States could have won the war. Timothy J. Lomperis's book *The War
Everybody Lost—And Won* argues that the United States had actually won
the war. After the Tet Offensive of 1968, the Vietcong were finished as
a political and military force; North Vietnam had no choice but to adopt
a conventional strategy to continue the war. By fighting a conventional
war and not defaulting because of political weaknesses at home, the

United States could have finished off North Vietnam for the long run, giving the South Vietnamese government years to build its own legitimacy. Harry G. Summers, Jr., in his book *On Strategy*, also claims that the United States could have won the war. For Summers, the American effort in Vietnam was hopelessly compromised at every level. The command and control structure was jerry-built and confusing; the politicians failed to communicate a clear set of objectives to the military and to the American people; the fears of a Chinese military intervention were grossly exaggerated; and the United States could have won the war through conventional means by mining Haiphong harbor, invading Cambodia, North Vietnam, and Laos, and cutting off all sources of supplies to the enemy. North Vietnam did not win the war, according to Harry Summers. The United States lost it by not fighting intelligently.

A more comprehensive revisionist work is Guenter Lewy's *America in Vietnam*. Lewy argues that the U.S. cause in Vietnam was a just one, but that American policymakers did not make enough of an investment in the political question. For Lewy, Vietnam was primarily a political question, not a military campaign. Had the United States spent more time and money on pacification, economic development, and counterinsurgency, the South Vietnamese peasants could have been won over politically. Lewy also argues persuasively that the entire issue of civilian casualties in Vietnam has been severely exaggerated. The United States did not engage, as far as Lewy is concerned, in genocide or wanton destruction of the Vietnamese economy, social structure, or topography.

But the left-wing interpretations of the war, as well as the revisionist perspective, constitute minority opinions about the United States and Vietnam. The prevailing consensus among American historians argues that the Vietnam War was a terrible mistake. It cost the United States the lives of nearly 60,000 of its citizens, ruined American credibility throughout the world, and led to the deaths of millions of people in Indochina. But although each of the major histories of the war comes from that intellectual perspective, there are significant differences in their points of emphasis. The first of the surveys of the war was Francis FitzGerald's *Fire in the Lake: The Vietnamese and the Americans in Vietnam*, which was published in 1972. FitzGerald's greatest contribution was to show to American audiences the depth and longevity of Vietnamese nationalism. As George C. Herring argued in *America's Longest War*, the United States' greatest error in Vietnam was applying the containment doctrine to Asia and then misgauging the relative importance of nationalism and Communism. FitzGerald was one of the first to point out how intensely the Vietnamese hated the presence of foreign occupation forces—whether they were Chinese, French, Japanese, or Americans— and how that hatred long predated the arrival of Communism on the world scene. Although critics have taken FitzGerald to task for portraying the Vietcong as romantic heroes, while they were actually vicious, committed nationalists, *Fire in the Lake* was nevertheless a major contribution to the literature of the Vietnam War. Since it was published in 1972, it was also useful to some American policymakers in deciding to withdraw American forces completely from the region.

Stanley Karnow's *Vietnam: A History* was written in conjunction with the acclaimed Public Broadcasting Corporation television series in 1983. Karnow first went to Vietnam in the early 1950s as a journalist reporting on the disintegration of the French military effort, and during the next twenty years he spent most of his professional life dealing with the Indochina issue. He was back in Vietnam in the 1960s as a reporter for *Time* magazine. Like FitzGerald, Karnow begins his book in the distant past of 2,000 years ago when Vietnamese heroes expelled Chinese invaders from their country, and he, too, argues that nationalism was the driving force in Vietnamese culture. What makes Karnow's work unique, at least in addition to its elegant writing, was the number of interviews he held over the years with major players in the conflict, including Ho Chi Minh, Le Duan, Pham Van Dong, Vo Nguyen Giap, Ngo Dinh Diem, Nguyen Cao Ky, Nguyen Van Thieu, and many others. Those interviews only confirmed the ancient histories: the North Vietnamese and Vietcong had captured the Vietnamese nationalist imagination, while the South Vietnamese were perceived only as those who did the bidding of the French, Japanese, or Americans.

The idea of the Vietnamese as committed nationalists became the consensus, and although that point of view has prevailed, some more recent histories have painted complex pictures of the interaction in Vietnamese culture between Communism and nationalism and between regional perspectives. William S. Turley's *The Second Indochina War: A Short Political and Military History, 1945–1975* relies heavily on Vietnamese documents, and because of that focus he is able to show that internal bickering among Vietnamese Communists was commonplace and often threatened to undermine their campaign. The Vietcong, who were primarily from South Vietnam, resented the assertiveness and arrogance of the North Vietnamese and often believed they were being sacrificed to the American war machine so that the northerners would not have to suffer. Many of the Vietcong, according to Turley, were not as committed ideologically to Communism as the North Vietnamese. They tended to be more interested in nationalist questions rather than issues revolving around the economic and social structure.

A number of recent general surveys of the war have emphasized the American failure to win the "hearts and minds" of the Vietnamese people. Books falling into this genre include Neil Sheehan's *The Bright and Shining Lie: John Paul Vann and America in Vietnam*, James S. Olson and Randy Roberts's *Where the Domino Fell: America and Vietnam, 1945–1990*, and Marilyn Young's *The Vietnam Wars, 1945–1990*. All of them argue that the U.S. commitment to Vietnam failed because the United States was blinded to the power of nationalism by the cold war's emphasis on Communism; that the United States tried unsuccessfully to transform the conflict from a political to a military struggle; that the American people, intoxicated by the success of the American military and economy during World War II, overestimated their own power and seriously underestimated the power and resiliency of the Vietnamese enemy; and that any American attempt to win the "hearts and minds" of Vietnamese peasants was ruined by the incredible volume and indiscriminate use of American firepower during the war. Too many South Vietnamese peasants had their lives disrupted or destroyed by the American military machine to ever develop a sense of patriotic loyalty.

REFERENCE WORKS

During the past decade a number of good reference works have dealt with the Vietnam War. The best of them are by John S. Bowman, James S. Olson, and Harry G. Summers, Jr. Bowman's *The Vietnam War: An Almanac* would have been more appropriately called a chronology of the Vietnam War. It contains an elaborate, extensive chronology of the war that covers several hundred pages. The book also has descriptive essays on the histories of the four major military branches during the war. The books by Summers and Olson are encyclopedias covering hundreds of topics of the war. Olson's *Dictionary of the Vietnam War* is the more extensive of the two books. The book covers more than 700 topics—battles, individuals, political issues, major controversies, and various military organizations and political interest groups. Summers's *Vietnam War Almanac* covers much the same ground as Olson's book, although its coverage is not as extensive. Also, Summers tends to focus primarily on military issues. There is, however, a more significant difference between the two reference works. Olson's book takes a decidedly antiwar posture, arguing that the Vietnam War was a perfect example of political and military folly and that it was unwinnable from the very beginning. Summers, on the other hand, argues that American execution of the war was politically and militarily flawed. The war was winnable if the United States would have been willing to expand its conventional military operations—that is, a long-term invasion of Cambodia, Laos, and North Vietnam, and mining of Haiphong harbor—as well as maintain its political commitment. The reference works by Olson and Summers reflect the continuing debate, in military circles at least, over the nature of the Vietnam War. For a look at the special jargon that soldiers developed during the Vietnam War, see Linda Reinberg, *In the Field: The Language of the Vietnam War* (1991).

Another genre of reference works is the "order of battle" books dealing with the histories of individual military units during the war. By far the best of these is Shelby L. Stanton's *Vietnam Order of Battle*. It is an extraordinary book, written with a sense of meticulous detail, outlining the activities of the U.S. Army's advisory level, and corps level command; divisions, task forces, and brigades; armored, artillery, aviation, cavalry, and infantry combat units; such service units as support command groups, the adjutant general, the composite service, maintenance, medical, ordnance, quartermaster, and transportation units; such special warfare units as the Army Security Agency, military intelligence, Civil Affairs and Psychological Operations, Special Forces, and MACV Special Operations; the other service units, including the air force, Marine Corps, and U.S. Navy construction units; and the military units associated with American allies—Australia, New Zealand, Philippines, Thailand, South Korea, and South Vietnam. The book also contains excellent appendixes on army aircraft, weapons, vessels, vehicles, Medal of Honor recipients, casualties, deployments and stations, military terms and slang, and maps. No historian of the Vietnam War can avoid using Stanton's book.

BIBLIOGRAPHY

General Background

Arnett, Peter, and Michael Maclear. *The Ten Thousand Day War: Vietnam 1945–1975*. New York: St. Martin's Press, 1981.

Austin, Anthony. *The President's War*. Philadelphia: Lippincott, 1971.

Baral, Jaya. *The Pentagon and the Making of U.S. Foreign Policy*. New York: Humanities Press, 1978.

Barnet, Richard J. *Roots of War*. New York: Simon and Schuster, 1972.

Berman, Larry. *Planning a Tragedy: The Americanization of the War in Vietnam*. New York: Norton, 1982.

Berman, Larry. *Lyndon Johnson's War: The Road to Stalemate in Vietnam*. New York: Norton, 1989.

Blum, Robert M. *Drawing the Line: The Origin of the American Containment Policy in East Asia*. New York: Norton, 1982.

Boettcher, Thomas D. *Vietnam: The Valor and the Sorrow*. Boston: Little, Brown, 1985.

Braestrup, Peter, ed. *Vietnam as History: Ten Years After the Paris Peace Accords*. Washington, D.C.: University Press of America, 1984.

Brodie, Bernard. *War and Politics*. New York: Macmillan, 1973.

Burke, John P., and Fred I. Greenstein. *How Presidents Test Reality: Decisions on Vietnam, 1954 and 1965*. New York: Russell Sage Foundation, 1991.

Butterfield, Fox. "The New Vietnam Scholarship." *New York Times Magazine* (February 13, 1983): 26–32, 45–60.

Campagna, Anthony S. *The Economic Consequences of the Vietnam War*. Westport, Conn.: Praeger, 1991.

Capps, Walter H. *The Unfinished War: Vietnam and the American Conscience*. Boston: Beacon Press, 1990a.

Capps, Walter H., ed. *The Vietnam Reader*. New York: Rutledge, Chapman, and Hall, 1990b.

Charlton, Michael, and Anthony Moncrief. *Many Reasons Why: The American Involvement in Vietnam*. New York: Hill and Wang, 1978.

Cohen, Warren. *Dean Rusk*. New York: Cooper Square, 1980.

Cooper, Chester. *The Last Crusade: America in Vietnam*. New York: Fawcett, 1970.

Davidson, Phillip B. *Vietnam at War: The History, 1945–1975*. Novato, Calif.: Presidio Press, 1988.

Davidson, Phillip B. *Secrets of the Vietnam War*. Novato, Calif.: Presidio Press, 1990.

Divine, Robert A. "Vietnam Reconsidered." *Diplomatic History* 12 (Winter 1988): 79–94.

Donovan, John C. *The Cold Warriors: A Policy-Making Elite*. Lexington, Mass.: D. C. Heath, 1974.

Drachman, Edward R. *United States Policy Toward Vietnam, 1940–1945*. Rutherford, N.J.: Fairleigh Dickinson University Press, 1970.

Eisenhower, Dwight D. *The White House Years: Mandate for Change 1953–1956*. Garden City, N.Y.: Doubleday, 1963.

Eisenhower, Dwight D. *The White House Years: Waging Peace 1956–1961*. Garden City, N.Y.: Doubleday, 1965.

Ellsberg, Daniel. *Papers on the War*. New York: Simon and Schuster, 1972.

Evans, Rowland, and Robert Novak. *Lyndon B. Johnson: The Exercise of Power*. New York: New American Library, 1966.

Fincher, E. B. *The Vietnam War*. Philadelphia: Franklin and Watts, 1980.

FitzGerald, Francis. *Fire in the Lake: The Vietnamese and the Americans in Vietnam*. Boston: Little, Brown, 1972.

Galloway, John. *The Gulf of Tonkin Resolution*. New York: Associated University Presses, 1970.

Galloway, John. *The Kennedys and Vietnam*. New York: Facts on File, 1971.

Gardner, Lloyd C. *Approaching Vietnam: From World War II Through Dienbienphu*. New York: Norton, 1989.

Gelb, Lawrence, and Richard K. Betts. *The Irony of Vietnam: The System Worked*. Washington, D.C.: Brookings Institution, 1979.

Geyelin, Philip. *Lyndon B. Johnson and the World*. New York: Knopf, 1969.

Gibbons, William C. *The U.S. Government and the Vietnam War, 1961–1964*. Princeton, N.J.: Princeton University Press, 1975.

Goldman, Eric. *The Tragedy of Lyndon Johnson*. New York: Knopf, 1969.

Goulden, Joseph C. *Truth Is the First Casualty: The Gulf of Tonkin Affair—Illusion and Reality*. New York: Rand McNally, 1969.

Graebner, Norman A. *Nationalism and Communism in Asia: The American Response*. Lexington, Mass.: D. C. Heath, 1977.

Grinter, Lawrence E., and Peter M. Dunne. *The American War in Vietnam: Lessons, Legacies, and Implications for Future Conflicts*. Westport, Conn.: Greenwood Press, 1987.

Halberstam, David. *The Making of a Quagmire: America and Vietnam During the Kennedy Era*. New York: Knopf, 1965.

Halberstam, David. *The Best and the Brightest.* New York: Random House, 1972.

Harriman, W. Averell. *America and Russia in a Changing World: A Half Century of Personal Observation.* Garden City, N.Y.: Doubleday, 1971.

Harrison, James P. *The Endless War: Vietnam's Struggle for Independence.* Riverside, N.J.: Free Press, 1983.

Hartmann, Robert T. *Palace Politics: An Inside Account of the Ford Years.* New York: McGraw-Hill, 1980.

Hayes, S. P., ed. *The Beginning of American Aid to Southeast Asia: The Griffin Mission of 1950.* Lexington, Mass.: Aldine, 1971.

Hearden, Patrick J. *The Tragedy of Vietnam.* New York: Harper-Collins, 1991.

Herring, George C. "The Truman Administration and the Restoration of French Sovereignty in Indochina." *Diplomatic History* 1 (1977): 97–117.

Herring, George C. *America's Longest War: The United States and Vietnam, 1950–1975.* New York: Knopf, 1986.

Hess, Gary R. *Vietnam and the United States: Origins and Legacy of War.* Boston: Twayne, 1990.

Isaacson, Walter, and Evan Thomas. *The Wise Men. Six Friends and the World They Made.* New York: Simon and Schuster, 1986.

Joes, Anthony J. *The War for South Vietnam: Nineteen Fifty-Four to Nineteen Seventy-Five.* Westport, Conn.: Praeger, 1989.

Johnson, Lyndon Baines. *The Vantage Point: Perspectives of the Presidency, 1963–1969.* New York: Holt, Rinehart, and Winston, 1971.

Josephs, Paul. *Cracks in the Empire: State Politics in the Vietnam War.* Boston: South End Press, 1981.

Jurika, Stephen, Jr., ed. *From Pearl Harbor to Vietnam: The Memoirs of Admiral Arthur W. Radford.* Stanford, Calif.: Hoover Institution Press, 1980.

Kahin, George McT. *Intervention: How America Became Involved in Vietnam.* New York: Random House, 1986.

Kahin, George McT., and John W. Lewis. *The United States in Vietnam: An Analysis in Depth of the History of American Involvement in Vietnam.* New York: Dell, 1967.

Karnow, Stanley. *Vietnam: A History.* New York: Viking, 1984.

Kattenburg, Paul. *The Vietnam Trauma in American Foreign Policy, 1945–1975.* Rutgers, N.J.: Transaction Books, 1981.

Kearns, Doris. *Lyndon Johnson and the American Dream.* New York: Harper and Row, 1976.

Kendrick, Alexander. *The Wound Within: America in the Vietnam Years, 1945–1975.* Boston, Mass.: Little, Brown, 1974.

Kennan, George. "The Sources of Soviet Power." *Foreign Affairs* 25 (July 1947): 566–82.

Kolko, Gabriel. *Anatomy of a War: Vietnam, the United States, and the Modern Historical Experience.* New York: Pantheon, 1985.

Lawson, Don. *The War in Vietnam.* Philadelphia: Franklin and Watts, 1981.

Lee, Sam. *The Perfect War.* New York: Valentine Press, 1990.

Lewy, Guenter. *America in Vietnam.* New York: Oxford University Press, 1978.

Lodge, Henry Cabot. *The Storm Has Many Eyes: A Personal Narrative.* New York: Norton, 1973.

Lomperis, Timothy J. *The War Everyone Lost—And Won: America's Intervention in*

Vietnam's Twin Struggles. Baton Rouge: Louisiana State University Press, 1984.

Louis, William Roger. *Imperialism at Bay: The United States and the Decolonization of the British Empire*. New York: St. Martin's Press, 1978.

McCloud, Bill. *What Should We Tell Our Children About Vietnam?* Norman: University of Oklahoma Press, 1990.

McLaughlin, Martin. *Vietnam and World Revolution: A Trotskyite Analysis*. New York: Labor, 1985.

McQuaid, Kim. *The Anxious Years: America in the Vietnam-Watergate Era*. New York: Basic Books, 1989.

Manhattan, Avro. *Vietnam: Why Did We Go?* New York: Chick, 1984.

Miller, Merle. *Lyndon: An Oral Biography*. New York: Ballantine Books, 1980.

Millett, Allan R., ed. *A Short History of the Vietnam War*. Bloomington: Indiana University Press, 1978.

Miroff, Bruce. *Pragmatic Illusions: The Presidential Politics of John F. Kennedy*. New York: David Mackay, 1976.

Morrison, Wilbur H. *The Elephant and the Tiger: The Full Story of the Vietnam War*. New York: Hippocrene Books, 1989.

Moss, George. *Vietnam: An American Ordeal*. Englewood Cliffs, N.J.: Prentice-Hall, 1989.

Newman, John M. *JFK and Vietnam: Deception, Intrigue, and the Struggle for Power*. New York: Warner Books, 1992.

Nickelsen, Harry. *Vietnam*. New York: Lucent Books, 1989.

Nixon, Richard M. *RN: The Memoirs of Richard Nixon*. New York: Grosset and Dunlap, 1978.

Nixon, Richard M. *No More Vietnams*. New York: Arbor House, 1980a.

Nixon, Richard. *The Real War*. New York: Warner Books, 1980b.

Nixon, Richard M. *1999 Victory Without War*. New York: Simon and Schuster, 1988.

Nolting, Frederick. *From Trust to Tragedy: The Political Memoirs of Frederick Nolting, Kennedy's Ambassador to Diem's Vietnam*. New York: Praeger, 1988.

O'Donnell, Kenneth, and David Powers. *Johnny, We Hardly Knew Ye*. Boston: Little, Brown, 1978.

Olson, James S., and Randy Roberts. *Where the Domino Fell: America and Vietnam, 1945–1990*. New York: St. Martin's Press, 1991.

Palmer, Bruce, Jr. *The Twenty-five Year War: America's Military Role in Vietnam*. Lexington: University Press of Kentucky, 1984.

Palmer, Dave. *Summons of the Trumpet: America and Vietnam in Perspective*. Novato, Calif.: Presidio Press, 1978.

Palmer, Gregory. *The McNamara Strategy and the Vietnam War: Program Budgeting in the Pentagon, 1960–1968*. Westport, Conn.: Greenwood Press, 1978.

Patti, Archimedes L. *Why Vietnam? Prelude to America's Albatross*. Berkeley: University of California Press, 1981.

Podhoretz, Norman. *Why We Were in Vietnam*. New York: Simon and Schuster, 1982.

Poole, Peter. *Eight Presidents and Indochina*. New York: Krieger, 1978.

Prados, John. *The Sky Would Fall: Operation Vulture: The U.S. Bombing Mission in Indochina, 1954*. New York: Dial, 1982.

Ravenal, Earl C. *Never Again: Learning from America's Foreign Policy Failures*. Philadelphia: Lippincott, 1978.

Reeves, Richard. *A Ford Not a Lincoln*. New York: Harcourt Brace Jovanovich, 1975.

Reeves, Thomas C. *A Question of Character: A Life of John F. Kennedy*. New York: Free Press, 1991.

Ridgway, Matthew B. *Soldier: The Memoirs of Matthew B. Ridgway*. New York: Harper and Brothers, 1956.

Roberts, Charles. *LBJ's Inner Circle*. New York: Delacorte Press, 1965.

Rose, Lisle Abbott. *Roots of Tragedy: The United States and the Struggle for Asia, 1945–1953*. Westport, Conn.: Greenwood Press, 1976.

Rostow, W. W. *The Diffusion of Power, 1957–1972*. New York: Macmillan, 1972.

Rotter, Andrew J. *The Path to Vietnam: Origins of the American Commitment to Southeast Asia*. Ithaca, N.Y.: Cornell University Press, 1989.

Rotter, Andrew J. *Light at the End of the Tunnel: A Vietnam War Reader*. New York: St. Martin's Press, 1991.

Rusk, Dean. *As I Saw It. The Memoirs of Dean Rusk*. New York: Norton, 1990.

Rust, William J. *Kennedy in Vietnam: American Foreign Policy, 1960–1963*. New York: Da Capo Press, 1987.

Salinger, Pierre. *With Kennedy*. Garden City, N.Y.: Doubleday, 1966.

Salisbury, Harrison, ed. *Vietnam Reconsidered: Lessons from a War*. New York: Harper and Row, 1984.

Schlesinger, Arthur M., Jr. *A Thousand Days: John F. Kennedy in the White House*. Boston: Houghton Mifflin, 1965.

Schlesinger, Arthur M., Jr. *The Bitter Heritage: Vietnam and American Democracy, 1941–1966*. Boston: Houghton Mifflin, 1967.

Schlesinger, Arthur M., Jr. *Robert Kennedy and His Times*. Boston: Houghton Mifflin, 1978.

Sevy, Grace, ed. *The American Experience in Vietnam: A Reader*. Norman: University of Oklahoma Press, 1989.

Shafer, Michael, ed. *Legacy: The Vietnam War and the American Imagination*. Boston: Beacon Press, 1992.

Sharp, Melvin. *The Vietnam War and Public Policy*. Fayetteville, N.Y.: Policy Studies Association, 1991.

Sharp, U.S.G. *Strategy for Defeat: Vietnam in Retrospect*. Novato, Calif.: Presidio Press, 1978.

Sharp, U.S.G., and William Westmoreland. *Report on the War in Vietnam*. Washington, D.C.: U.S. Government Printing Office, 1968.

Sheehan, Neil. *The Bright and Shining Lie: John Paul Vann and America in Vietnam*. New York: Random House, 1988.

Short, Anthony. *The Origins of the Vietnam War*. White Plains, N.Y.: Longman, 1989.

Smith, R. B. *An International History of the Vietnam War. Volume 1: Revolution Versus Containment, 1955–1961*. New York: St. Martin's Press, 1984.

Smith, R. B. *An International History of the Vietnam War: The Kennedy Strategy*. New York: St. Martin's Press, 1987.

Smith, R. B. *An International History of the Vietnam War: The Johnson Strategy*. New York: St. Martin's Press, 1990.

Sorensen, Theodore. *Kennedy*. New York: Random House, 1965.

Sullivan, Michael P. *The Vietnam War: A Study in the Making of American Foreign Policy*. Lexington: University Press of Kentucky, 1985.

Summers, Harry G., Jr. *On Strategy: A Critical Analysis of the Vietnam War*. Novato, Calif.: Presidio Press, 1982.

Taylor, Maxwell D. *Swords and Plowshares*. New York: Norton, 1972.

Thayer, Thomas. *Vietnam: War Without Fronts*. Boulder, Colo.: Westview Press, 1985.

Thomson, James. "How Could Vietnam Happen? An Autopsy." *Atlantic Monthly* 221 (April 1968): 47–53.

Thorne, Christopher. *Allies of a Kind: The United States, Britain and the War Against Japan, 1941–1945*. New York: Oxford University Press, 1978.

Trewhitt, Henry. *McNamara*. New York: Harper and Row, 1971.

Turley, William S. *The Second Indochina War: A Short Political and Military History, 1945–1975*. Boulder, Colo.: Westview Press, 1986.

Turner, Kathleen J. *Lyndon Johnson's Dual War: Vietnam and the Press*. Chicago: University of Chicago Press, 1985.

Vance, Cyrus. *Hard Choices*. New York: Random House, 1983.

Villaini, Jim, ed. *Vietnam: An Anthology*. New York: Pig Iron Press, 1987.

Westmoreland, William. *A Soldier Reports*. New York: Dell, 1976.

Windchy, Eugene G. *Tonkin Gulf*. Garden City, N.Y.: Doubleday, 1971.

Young, Marilyn. *The Vietnam Wars, 1945–1990*. New York: Harper-Collins, 1991.

Reference Works/Encyclopedias

Armstrong, R. E. *The Vietnam Veterans Trivia Book*. Oklahoma City: Vietnam Veterans of America, 1989.

Bowman, John S., ed. *The Vietnam War: An Almanac*. New York: World Almanac Publications, 1985.

Bowman, John S., ed. *The Vietnam War: Day by Day*. New York: Mall Books, 1989.

Clark, Gregory R. *Words of the Vietnam War: The Slang, Jargon, Abbreviations, Acronyms, Nomenclature, Nicknames, Pseudonyms, Slogans, Specs, Euphemisms, Double-talk, Chants, and Names and Places of the Era of United States Involvement in Vietnam*. Jefferson, N.C.: McFarland, 1990.

Clodfelter, Michael, and John Musgrave. *The Vietnam Years: 1000 Questions and Answers*. New York: Quinlan Press, 1986.

Dawson, Alan. *The Official Vietnam Trivia Book*. Bangkok, Thailand: Thai Watana Press, 1987.

Duiker, William J. *Historical Dictionary of Vietnam*. Metuchen, N.J.: Scarecrow Press, 1989.

Konerding, Erhard. *Vietnam War Facts Quiz: The Truth and Drama of American Involvement*. Middletown, Conn.: Southfarm Press, 1986.

Olson, James S. *Dictionary of the Vietnam War*. Westport, Conn.: Greenwood Press, 1988.

Reinberg, Linda. *In the Field: The Language of the Vietnam War*. New York: Facts on File, 1991.

Stanton, Shelby L. *Vietnam Order of Battle: A Complete Illustrated Reference to the*

U.S. Army Ground Forces in Vietnam, 1961–1973. New York: Galahad Books, 1981.

Stein, Jeff. *The Vietnam Fact Book*. New York: Dell, 1987.

Strait, Jerry L., and Sandra S. Strait. *Vietnam War Memorials: An Illustrated Reference to Veterans Tributes Throughout the United States*. Philadelphia: McFarland, 1988.

Summers, Harry G., Jr. *Vietnam War Almanac*. New York: Facts on File, 1985.

Thompson, Leroy. *The US Army in Vietnam*. Devon, Eng.: David and Charles, 1990.

Whitfield, Danny J. *Historical and Cultural Dictionary of Vietnam*. Metuchen, N.J.: Scarecrow Press, 1976.

Reference Works/Bibliographies

Adair, Gilbert. *Vietnam on Film*. New York: Proteus Books, 1981.

Arnoldt, Robert P. *Insights: A Guide to the American Experience in Vietnam, 1940 to the Present*. New York: Visions Unlimited, 1989.

Ashmun, Lawrence F. *Resettlement of Indochinese Refugees in the United States: A Selective and Annotated Bibliography*. DeKalb, Ill.: Center for Southeast Asian Studies, Northern Illinois University, 1984.

Baldwin, Neil. "Going After the War." *Publishers Weekly* (February 1983): 34–38.

"A Bibliography of Unusual Sources on Women and the Vietnam War." *Vietnam Generation* 1 (Summer–Fall 1989): 274–77.

Breakstone, John. *The Vietnam Era: A Guide to Teaching Resources*. New York: Indochina Curriculum Group, 1978.

Brown, F. C. *POW/MIA Indochina, 1946–1986: An Annotated Bibliography of Nonfiction Works Dealing with Prisoners of War/Missing in Action*. San Francisco: Rice Paddy Press, 1988.

Brown, F. C., and B. Laurie. *Annotated Bibliography of Vietnam Fiction 500 Titles Dealing with the Conflict in Vietnam, Cambodia, and Laos*. San Francisco: Rice Paddy Press, 1986.

Bryan, C.D.B. "Barely Suppressed Screams: Getting a Bead on Vietnam Literature." *Harper's* 268 (June 1984), 67–72.

Calloway, Catherine. "Vietnam War Literature and Film: A Bibliography of Secondary Sources." *Bulletin of Bibliography* 43 (September 1986): 149–58.

Camp, Norman M., Robert H. Stretch, and William C. Marshall. *Stress, Strain and Vietnam: An Annotated Bibliography of Two Decades of Psychiatric and Social Sciences Literature Reflecting the Effects of the War on the American Soldier*. Westport, Conn.: Greenwood Press, 1988.

Casciato, Arthur D. "Teaching the Literature of the Vietnam War." *Review* 9 (1987): 125–47.

Colonnese, Tom, and Jerry Hogan. "Vietnam War Literature, 1958–1979: A First Checklist." *Bulletin of Bibliography* 38 (January-March 1981): 26–51.

DeLano, Skip. "Selected Bibliography: GI and Veterans' Movement Against the War, 1965–1965." *Vietnam Generation* 2 (No. 2): 110–18.

Dunn, Joe P. "The P.O.W. Chronicles: A Bibliographic Review." *Armed Forces and Society* 9 (Spring 1983): 495–514.

Dunn, Joe P. "The Vietnam War POW/MIAs: An Annotated Bibliography." *Bulletin of Bibliography* 45 (June 1988): 152–57.

Dunn, Joe P. "Women and the Vietnam War: A Bibliographic Review." *Journal of American Culture* 12 (Spring 1989): 85–92.

Eckert, Edward K., and William J. Searle. "Creative Literature of the Vietnam War: A Selective Bibliography." *Choice* 24 (January 1987): 725–35.

Harnley, Caroline D. *Agent Orange and Vietnam: An Annotated Bibliography*. Metuchen, N.J.: Scarecrow Press, 1988.

King, William. *Bibliography of Sources Dealing with Minority Issues* 1 (Summer-Fall 1989): 151–59.

Kohar, Roy A., ed. *Vietnamese Holdings in the Library of Congress: Bibliography*. Washington, D.C.: Library of Congress, 1982.

McDonald, Ben. *The Vietnam Book List*. New York: Bibliography Unlimited, 1990.

Miller, E. Willard, and Ruby M. Miller. *The Third World: Vietnam, Laos, and Cambodia, A Bibliography*. New York: Vance Bibliographies, 1989.

Newman, John and Ann Hilfinger. *Vietnam War Literature: An Annotated Bibliography of Imaginative Works about Americans Fighting in Vietnam*. Metuchen, N.J.: Scarecrow Press, 1988.

Smith, Myron J., Jr. *Air War Southeast Asia, Nineteen Sixty-One to Nineteen Seventy-Three: An Annotated Bibliography and 16mm Film Guide*. Metuchen, N.J.: Scarecrow Press, 1979.

Stewart, Margaret E. "Vietnam-War Novels in the Classroom." *Teaching History: A Journal of Methods* 6 (Fall 1981): 60–66.

There: Eyewitness Accounts of the War in Southeast Asia, 1956–1975 Aftermath: Annotated Bibliography of Books, Articles and Topic-Related Magazines, Covering Writings Both Factual and Imaginative. Paradise, Calif.: Dust Books, 1984.

Wilson, James C. *Vietnam in Prose and Film*. Jefferson, N.C.: McFarland, 1981.

Wittman, Sandra M. *Writing About Vietnam: A Bibliography of the Literature of the Vietnam Conflict*. Boston: G. K. Hall, 1989.

Reference Works/Albums, Guidebooks, and Illustrated Histories

Barnes, Jeremy. *Pictoral History of the Vietnam War*. New York: Gallery Books, 1988.

Beckett, Brian. *The History of the Vietnam War*. New York: Gallery Books, 1985.

Berger, Carl. *The United States Air Force in Southeast Asia: An Illustrated Account*. Washington, D.C.: Office of Air Force History, 1984.

Berry, F. Clifton, Jr. *The Illustrated History of the Vietnam War: Air Cav*. New York: Bantam, 1988.

Bonds, Ray, ed. *The Vietnam War: The Illustrated History of the Conflict in Southeast Asia*. New York: Crown, 1979.

Carhart, Tom. *Battles and Campaigns: Vietnam, 1954–1984*. Greenwich, Conn.: Bison, 1987.

Chinnery, Phil. *Air War Vietnam*. Greeenwich, Conn.: Bison, 1987.

Clifford, Geoffrey, and John Balabad. *Vietnam: The Land We Never Knew*. New York: Chronicle Books, 1989.

Cohen, Barbara. *The Vietnam Guidebook*. New York: Harper and Row, 1990.

Dougan, Clark. *The American Experience in Vietnam*. New York: Norton, 1988.

Drendel, Louis. *Air War Over Southeast Asia*. Carrollton, Tex.: Squadron/Signal Publications, 1984.

Esper, George, and Associated Press. *The Eyewitness History of the Vietnam War*. New York: Ballantine, 1983.

Fischer, Julene, and Robert Stone. *The Vietnam Experience: Images of War*. Boston: Boston Publishing, 1986.

Generous, Kevin M. *Vietnam: The Secret War*. New York: Gallery Books, 1985.

Heubeck, Kerry. *Where Feasts Come Rarely: A Viet Nam Album*. Los Angeles: Pomegranate Press, 1989.

Jones, John R. *Guide to Vietnam*. New York: Hunter, 1989.

Jury, Mark. *The Vietnam Photo Book*. New York: Vintage, 1986.

Kamps, Charles T. *The History of the Vietnam War: An Illustrated History of the War in South East Asia*. New York: The Military Press, 1988.

Lawson, Don. *An Album of the Vietnam War*. New York: Franklin and Watts, 1986.

Manning, Robert. *The Vietnam Experience: Combat Photographer: Vietnam Through G.I. Lenses*. Boston: Boston Publishing, 1987.

McJunkin, James N., and Max D. Crace. *Visions of Vietnam*. Novato, Calif.: Presidio, 1983.

Moeller, Susan D. *Shooting War: Photography and the American Experience of Combat*. New York: Basic Books, 1990.

Myerson, Joel D. *Images of a Lengthy War: The United States Army in Vietnam*. Washington, D.C.: Center of Military History, 1986.

Newcomb, Richard F. *A Picture History of the Vietnam War*. Garden City, N.Y.: Doubleday, 1987.

Page, Tim. *Nam*. New York: Knopf, 1983.

Page, Tim. *Ten Years Later: Vietnam Today*. New York: Knopf, 1987.

Page, Tim, and John Pimlott. *NAM: The Vietnam Experience*. New York: Mallard Press, 1988.

Welsh, Douglas. *The History of the Vietnam War*. New York: Bison/Exeter Books, 1981.

Series: The Vietnam Experience

Casey, Michael. *The Vietnam Experience: Flags into Battle*. Boston: Boston Publishing, 1987.

Doleman, Edgar. *The Vietnam Experience: Tools of War*. Boston: Boston Publishing, 1984.

Dougan, Clark. *The Vietnam Experience: TET: The Crucial Year of Nineteen Sixty-eight*. Boston: Boston Publishing, 1983.

Dougan, Clark, and Samuel Lipsman. *The Vietnam Experience: A Nation Divided*. Boston: Boston Publishing, 1984.

Dougan, Clark, and Samuel Lipsman. *The Vietnam Experience: Flags into Battle II*. Boston: Boston Publishing, 1987.

Dougan, Clark, and Stephen Weiss. *The Vietnam Experience: Nineteen Sixty-eight.* Boston: Boston Publishing, 1983.

Doyle, Edward G., and Samuel Lipsman. *The Vietnam Experience: Passing the Torch.* Boston: Boston Publishing, 1981a.

Doyle, Edward G., and Samuel Lipsman. *The Vietnam Experience: Setting the Stage.* Boston: Boston Publishing, 1981b.

Doyle, Edward G., and Samuel Lipsman. *The Vietnam Experience: Fighting for Time: The War Changes Time, 1969–1970.* Boston: Boston Publishing, 1983.

Doyle, Edward G., and Samuel Lipsman. *The Vietnam Experience: America Takes Over the Big Build-Up.* Boston: Boston Publishing, 1984.

Doyle, Edward, and Stephen Weiss. *The Vietnam Experience: A Collision of Cultures.* Boston: Boston Publishing, 1984.

Doyle, Edward, and Terrence Maitland. *The Vietnam Experience: The Aftermath: The Legacy of War, 1975–1985.* Boston: Boston Publishing, 1985.

Fischer, Julene, and Robert Stone. *The Vietnam Experience: Images of War.* Boston: Boston Publishing, 1986.

Fulghum, David, and Terrence Maitland. *The Vietnam Experience: South Vietnam on Trial: The Test of Vietnamization, 1970–1973.* Boston: Boston Publishing, 1984.

Harding, Gordon. *The Vietnam Experience: Words of War: An Anthology of Vietnam War Literature.* Boston: Boston Publishing, 1988.

Lipsman, Samuel, and Stephen Weiss. *The Vietnam Experience: A False Peace: The Beginning of the End.* Boston: Boston Publishing, 1985.

Maitland, Terrence, and Peter McInerney. *The Vietnam Experience: A Contagion of War.* Boston: Boston Publishing, 1983.

Maitland, Terrence, and Stephen Weiss. *The Vietnam Experience: Raising the Stakes.* Boston: Boston Publishing, 1982.

Manning, Robert. *The Vietnam Experience: North Vietnam.* Boston: Boston Publishing, 1986a.

Manning, Robert. *The Vietnam Experience: Vietnam Remembered.* Boston: Boston Publishing, 1986b.

Manning, Robert. *The Vietnam Experience: The Army at War.* Boston: Boston Publishing, 1987a.

Manning, Robert. *The Vietnam Experience: The Fall of the South.* Boston: Boston Publishing, 1987b.

Manning, Robert. *The Vietnam Experience: Pawns of War.* Boston: Boston Publishing, 1987c.

Manning, Robert. *The Vietnam Experience: The American Experience in Vietnam.* Boston: Boston Publishing, 1988a.

Manning, Robert. *The Vietnam Experience: Secret Wars: Covert Operations in Vietnam.* Boston: Boston Publishing, 1988b.

Manning, Robert. *The Vietnam Experience: War in the Shadows.* Boston: Boston Publishing, 1988c.

Mills, Nick. *The Vietnam Experience: Combat Photographer: Vietnam Through G.I. Lenses.* Boston: Boston Publishing, 1987.

Morocco, John. *The Vietnam Experience: Rain of Fire, Air War.* Boston: Boston Publishing, 1984.

Morocco, John. *The Vietnam Experience: Thunder from Above: The War in the Air Through 1968*. Boston: Boston Publishing, 1984.

Series: The Illustrated History of the Vietnam War

Arnold, James R. *Artillery*. New York: Bantam Books, 1987a.
Arnold, James R. *Tunnel Warfare*. New York: Bantam Books, 1987b.
Berry, F. Clifton, Jr. *Sky Soldiers*. New York: Bantam Books, 1987.
Berry, F. Clifton, Jr. *Air CAV*. New York: Bantam Books, 1988a.
Berry, F. Clifton, Jr. *Chargers*. New York: Bantam Books, 1988b.
Berry, F. Clifton, Jr. *First Team*. New York: Bantam Books, 1988c.
Berry, F. Clifton, Jr. *Gadget War*. New York: Bantam Books, 1988d.
Berry, F. Clifton, Jr. *Strike Aircraft*. New York: Bantam Books, 1988e.
Cook, John L. *Dustoff*. New York: Bantam Books, 1988.
Davies, James C. *GIAP*. New York: Bantam Books, 1988.
Dorr, Robert F. *Skyraiders*. New York: Bantam Books, 1988.
Ewing, Mike. *Khe Sanh*. New York: Bantam Books, 1987.
Rufus Publications Staff. *Armor*. New York: Bantam Books, 1988a.
Rufus Publications Staff. *Carrier Operations*. New York: Bantam Books, 1988b.

Series: The Lessons of the Vietnam War

Borton, Lady. *Boat People and Vietnamese Refugees in the United States*. New York: Center for Social Studies, 1988.
Cohen, Stephen, and Millard Clements. *Was the Vietnam War Legal?* New York: Center for Social Studies, 1988.
Duiker, William J. *Introduction to Vietnam: Land, History and Culture*. New York: Center for Social Studies, 1988.
Dunn, Joe P., and Jerold M. Starr. *How the U.S. Fought the War*. New York: Center for Social Studies, 1988.
Herring, George C., and Kevin Simon. *The Vietnam War: Lessons from Yesterday for Today*. New York: Center for Social Studies, 1988.
Starr, Jerold M. *America at War in Vietnam: Decisions and Consequences*. New York: Center for Social Studies, 1988a.
Starr, Jerold M. *Who Fought for the U. S.?* New York: Center for Social Studies, 1988b.
Starr, Jerold M., and Charles Di Beneditti. *Taking Sides: The War at Home*. New York: Center for Social Studies, 1988.
Starr, Jerold M., and Christopher W. Wilkens. *When War Becomes a Crime*. New York: Center for Social Studies, 1988.
Starr, Jerold M., ed. *The Lessons of the Vietnam War: A Modular Textbook*. New York: Center for Social Studies, 1988.
Wilcox, Fred, and Jerold M. Starr. *The Wounds of War and the Process of Healing*. New York: Center for Social Studies, 1988.

4 The First Indochina War: Perceptions and Realities of French and American Policy

Joan L. Coffey

The Geneva Accords of July 1954 are generally perceived as a major defeat for the Western world but particularly for France and the United States. These two traditional allies had maintained a joint military and political presence in Indochina since World War II, each pursuing its own national interests and goals and, in the pursuit thereof, seemingly undermining those of the other. Critics of American policy in Indochina include Victor Bator in *Vietnam: A Diplomatic Tragedy*, Maurice Duverger of *Le Monde*, Ellen J. Hammer in *The Struggle for Indochina: 1940–1955*, George C. Herring in *America's Longest War: The United States and Vietnam, 1950–1975*, and Arthur M. Schlesinger, Jr., in *The Bitter Heritage: Vietnam and American Democracy, 1941–1966*. To them, American policy was passive, half-measured, Manichean, and failed, a policy that was ephemeral at best and that served only to highlight the inaction and disunity among the Western allies. The policy that oversaw French disengagement from its imperial presence in Indochina was also not above reproach. Although perceived as less elusive than its American counterpart, the policy was criticized for its lack of direction or, according to Alistair Horne in *The French Army and Politics, 1870–1940*, its misplaced direction. Yet, there are historians and political commentators, albeit a minority, whose perceptions of events from February through July 1954 stand in marked contrast to the prevailing view of failed foreign policies. Philippe Devillers and Jean Lacouture in *End of a War*, Henri Pierre of *Le Monde*, and Robert F. Randle in *Geneva 1954: The Settlement of the Indochinese War* assert that American policy was not inflexible or puritanical or vague. It was, on the contrary, astute, intricate, and purposeful. French policy of the era is lauded for being quintessential *realpolitick*. In fact, then, the Geneva Accords demonstrated that despite conducting foreign policies with ostensibly contradictory goals, those foreign policies were, in the final analysis, complementary. Franco-American diplomacy of the spring and summer of 1954 succeeded in achieving the basic aims of each nation. The perception of disharmony between the United States and France was, in large measure, due to the fact that the foreign policies of the two nations were not identical. Public opinion and domestic politics dictated otherwise.

The Eisenhower administration, elected to office in 1952 on a program of peace, faced three options in Indochina: to unleash full military might on the side of France, to intervene in some limited way, or to opt for complete disengagement. The choice was largely determined by American public opinion and congressional sentiment. In the spring of 1954, editorial opinion overwhelmingly favored a limited involvement in Southeast Asia. According to Carl Krog in his article "American Journals of Opinion and the Fall of Vietnam, 1954" (1979), only three journals, two of which were Catholic publications and the other a business periodical, favored a military intervention. A Gallup poll further confirmed the noninterventionist mood among the American public in that spring of 1954, for while over 50 percent approved financial aid to the French war effort, only one in ten would send American troops into the Indochina jungles. Not surprisingly, the mood of Congress mirrored that of the American public.

George C. Herring and Richard H. Immerman noted in "Eisenhower, Dulles, and Dienbienphu: 'The Day We Didn't Go to War' Revisited" (1984) that the Republican party enjoyed only the slimmest of majorities in Congress (48–47–1 in the Senate and 221–212–1 in the House) and had to contend with a resurgent right wing that was notoriously unreliable in its support of the administration. William Knowland, the Senate majority leader, was an ardent supporter of the Bricker Amendment, one of the principals of the China lobby, and an isolationist who contested the label. As reported in *Le Monde* on April 10, 1954, Knowland charged that "the true isolationists are not in the United States but among certain allies who are willing to concede communist victory in Indochina, not realizing that Europe will be next." The minority leader of the Senate, Lyndon Johnson, and the Democratic party in general supported administration policy throughout 1953, but by the spring of 1954, they had begun to challenge the bipartisan relationship. As the administration considered various policy alternatives in the waning days of the first Indochina War, Johnson remained steadfast, as *Le Monde* pointed out on April 28, 1954, in his belief that it was "folly to get militarily involved . . . Americans are practically unanimous in not wanting to get involved." Besides, according to Senator John Stennis, as reported in the March 12, 1954, issue of *Le Monde*, military involvement in Indochina would "lead to World War III." Furthermore, *Le Monde* stated on May 14, 1954, that most people in Congress viewed the conflict as a French civil war and were not inclined to sanction colonialism by an American military presence.

Within the administration itself, few followed Vice President Richard Nixon in advocating a "strike at the head [China]," commented *Le Monde* on May 18, 1954. Instead, Herring in *America's Longest War* demonstrates that the Republican cabinet, acting like good businessmen, wanted to balance the budget and adhere to the "New Look" defense policy, inaugurated by President Eisenhower and calling for a reduction in both defense spending and the number of American ground troops. Devillers and Lacouture in *End of a War* maintain that Secretary of Defense Charles Wilson expressed the prevailing mood toward the Indochina situation when he said, "We cannot destroy ideas with bullets" (218). It was his contention and that of most of Washington that the Indochina imbroglio was the result of the political decision in Paris not to grant complete independence to the Associated States of French Indochina.

The domestic constraints imposed upon American policymakers in 1954 by public opinion and congressional sentiment were exacerbated by the foreign policy of the past. Herring writes in "The Truman Administration and the Restoration of French Sovereignty in Indochina" (1977) that from the time of the Truman administration, the United States accepted French sovereignty in Indochina as a quid pro quo for French support of American policy in Europe. Specifically, the United States asked for French participation in the Marshall Plan, NATO, and, in 1954, the European Defense Community (EDC). In return, according to Schlesinger in *The Bitter Heritage*, the United States supported the French war effort by an ever-increasing financial outlay. By 1954, 78.5 percent of the war budget was being absorbed by the United States but without an expanded role in determining war policy. This arrangement granted considerable leverage to the French, who delayed voting on the EDC until August 1954.

Events in mainland China in 1949 and the outbreak of the Korean War in 1950 placed additional constraints on American policy in Indochina and resulted in the decision of February 1950 to recognize Bao Dai as head of the State of Vietnam and leader of the Vietnamese. Gary R. Hess in his article "The First American Commitment in Indochina: The Acceptance of the Bao Dai Solution, 1950" (1978) says that Americans of the McCarthy era were not interested in endorsing an "Asian Tito," that is, the popular Ho Chi Minh, but they were vitally interested in containing Asian Communism. From 1950, then, the French civil war became identified with a larger global struggle, and as interpreted by Eisenhower and recorded in the *Public Papers of the Presidents...1954*, "the fighting going on in Indochina, no matter how it started, has very manifestly become one of the battlegrounds of people that want to live their own lives against this encroachment of communist aggression"

(341). Frenchmen, like General de Lattre, welcomed a "joint crusade against Asian communism" (Devillers and Lacouture, vii), and soon the mission assumed concrete form. The Navarre Plan, named after Colonel Henri Navarre and partially designed by the American Joint Chiefs of Staff, was a political-military operation that called for the following:

1. The buildup of the French Union Forces to 550,000, mainly by enlisting additional Vietnamese soldiers;

2. The granting of independence to the Associated States as a means to gather popular support and, thereby, encourage enlistment in the French Union Forces;

3. The limiting of military operations south of the 18th parallel and employing "strategic defense" north of the 18th parallel with the purpose of avoiding major engagements until the French Union Forces were revitalized.

As of spring 1954, then, American policy in Indochina, while operating under considerable constraint, was also clearly delineated. Its chief tenet was the containment of Asian Communism, while its battle plan found expression in the words, recorded in *Le Monde* on March 24, 1954, of Senator Mike Mansfield: "Firstly, the French should continue the military effort [Navarre Plan] while granting full independence to the Associated States; secondly, the national leaders in Indochina [Bao Dai] should work at rallying their people against communism; and thirdly, the United States should continue to aid the war effort, but no American troops were to be sent to the jungles of Asia." The subsequent weeks were to sorely test both the chief tenet and the battle plan of this American policy and also to demonstrate that the French government was operating under its own set of political constraints.

The coalition government of Joseph Laniel, which came to power in the summer of 1953, was considered a caretaker government, but such international exigencies as the Berlin, Bermuda, and Geneva conferences kept the Mouvement Republicain Populaire (MRP) administration in place until June 1954. As monitored in the Pentagon Papers, French policy for Indochina remained consistent through 1953, but as in the United States, the deteriorating situation on the jungle battlefields in the spring of 1954, coupled with increased pressure from public opinion and the National Assembly, resulted in a change in the means, if not the ends, of the Indochina policy of France. *L'Annee Politique* for the year 1954 graphically records the political fallout.

Until the early summer of 1954, the Laniel administration maintained its delicate balance within the 625-member National Assembly, whose members were elected in 1951 and reflected a significant change in the French political spectrum from the previous national election of 1946. The 1951 Assembly represented a shift to the political right from what was the situation in 1946. Specifically, the 1951 electorate sent 83 additional Gaulists (Parti de Rassemblement du Peuple Francais) to the Assembly for a total of 118 seats and an additional 5 socialist members for a total SFIO. (Section Francaise de l'Internationale Ouvriere) head count of 104. The parties that lost ground in the National Assembly were the Communists, who unseated 74 to retain 103 members, and the MRP, which gave up 58 seats and counted 85 members as of 1951.

Further erosion of MRP political power occurred with the local elections of May 1954. Voters stayed away from the polls in large enough numbers to have political analysts comment on the apathy of the French public, the movement toward the political left, and the growing disaffection with the MRP, the party of Joseph Laniel. The disaffection appeared to be linked to the increasing distaste for the government's Indochina policy. In fact, by May 1953, 65 percent of the French public wanted an end to the war.

Since 1947, when the Communists were ousted from the French cabinet, the MRP had directed the Indochina policy. While they and the Socialists were considered by Edward Rice-Maximin in "The United States, France, & Vietnam, 1945–1950: The View from the State Department" (1982) as the most pro-American of the French parties, they were also among the staunchest defenders of the French Union, an association of France and its colonies that was incorporated within the constitution of the Fourth Republic. Modeled somewhat on the British Commonwealth, French citizenship was readily dispensed among its members, but autonomy for the individual states was given parsimoniously. Support of the French Union, not suppression of Asian Communism per se, became the cornerstone of French policy for Indochina, and it signified something more than institutional cohesiveness. In the words of François Mitterrand, "When the war in Indochina broke out, France was able to believe that the 1940 defeat was nothing more than a lost battle, and that the armistice of 1945 was going to restore its power at the same time as its glory" (Horne, *The French Army and Politics*, 74).

Yet, France, under mounting pressure from both the United States and the Associated States, relinquished some control over the Indochinese members of the French Union. The Elysée Agreement of March 1949 recognized Vietnam's independence, but foreign affairs and defense matters remained in French hands, and membership in the French Union continued to be mandatory. This arrangement resulted in a major contradiction within French policy and became the chief point of contention between the United States and France. With the granting of independence to the Associated States, France was, in essence, working to undermine its presence in Indochina and, consequently, to impugn the very raison d'être of its Indochina policy. In addition, should France achieve military victory in Indochina, it would signify triumphant colonialism, a commodity that was anathema to the United States. The United States pressed the French to continue the war and, simultaneously, disengage itself politically. For the French, the two American demands were incompatible. Foreign Secretary Georges Bidault reportedly told Secretary of State John Foster Dulles that the "French would not support the war in Indochina if the French Union could not continue to exist" (Herring and Immerman, 356).

Nevertheless, Hammer wrote in *The Struggle for Indochina: 1940–1955* that the Laniel government responded to these foreign pressures by broadening its political relationships in Indochina. Instead of dealing with only Bao Dai, it increasingly entered into discussion with the Associated States. This subtle shift in emphasis was reflected in Laniel's proposed policy for Indochina as announced in the National Assembly in October 1953. It called for (1) the armies of the Associated States to be enlarged and trained (Navarre Plan); (2) the full independence of the Associated States, but within the French Union; and (3) the maximum effort given to ending the war, including negotiation. According to Alfred Grosser, in *La IV Republique et la Politique Exterieure*, Laniel responded by saying: "Enough speaking of war. It is necessary to negotiate. . . . France is engaged in an unpopular war and wisdom calls for its ending as soon as possible" (289). The Laniel government had committed itself to peace, but its critics pointed to the absence of a definite program to achieve that peace. By supporting his minister of defense, Rene Pleven, in trying to "create the military conditions that were the most favorable for a political solution of the conflict" (297), Laniel's commitment to peace became suspect.

The Gaullists' Indochina policy was also multidimensional, thereby open to criticism that it was ill-defined and suspect as to its genuine desire for peace. Charles de Gaulle called the administration to account when he charged that under its aegis "the determination to win the war had alternated with the desire to make peace without anyone being able to decide between the two" (Horne, 74). Yet De Gaulle personally sponsored both methods as means to bring an end to the war. On one occasion, he suggested that "France ought to pursue the fight in Indochina with all the necessary means and determination" (Grosser, 140). On another occasion he wanted "to talk, when possible, with all who are truly representative of Indochina, provided they are not enemies of France" (Devillers and Lacouture, 10).

The French Communists, on the other hand, called for direct negotiations with Ho Chi Minh, who in November 1953 suggested talks between France and the Democratic Republic of Vietnam. R.E.M. Irving, writing in *The First Indochina War: French and American Policy 1945–1954*, argued that by the early 1950s most Socialists and a growing number of MRP deputies had joined the Communists in advocating direct negotiations with Ho Chi Minh as the way to end the Indochina war. The principal spokesman for this popular alternative was Pierre Mendes-France, a Radical-Socialist, who argued that France had neither the men nor the money to solve the problem by force.

Consequently, the spring of 1954 found the Laniel government fighting to retain both its delicate balance in the National Assembly and its commitment to continue the war effort amidst a crescendo of public opinion demanding a negotiated peace. Developments in Indochina itself would orchestrate the shifts and turns in French politics and diplomacy in the crucial weeks before the Geneva Conference, and nowhere was this so dramatically demonstrated as in Northwest Tonkin at a place called Dien Bien Phu.

The Navarre Plan had, for the most part, operated as intended until late 1953, when the Vietminh invasion of Laos led to Colonel Navarre's decision to position 10,000 elite French troops at Dien Bien Phu in northwest Tonkin. The French hoped to attract large numbers of Vietminh and engage them in a decisive battle, somewhat removed from the context of jungles and guerrilla warfare. The Vietminh, under the command of General Vo Nguyen Giap, responded to the challenge and, by mid-March, were on the offensive. For the French, Dien Bien Phu quickly took on the aura of past heroic resistance. But despite reference to the "Verdun dans la jungle" and Navarre, like Petain, declaring, "Ils ne passeront pas" (*Le Monde*, March 23, 1954), the French position at Dien Bien Phu rapidly deteriorated, and additional American aid was requested for the beleaguered outpost.

Secretary of State John Foster Dulles, having announced on January 12 that "all new aggression would meet with an immediate response" (*Le Monde*, March 18, 1954), rejected the French request because of the prevailing congressional temper. Senator Alexander Wiley, chairman of the Senate Foreign Relations Committee, recognized that "the West would be in a terrible fix if the French did not carry on with the war" (Devillers and Lacouture, 111), and Charles Wilson, secretary of defense, maintained that "victory in Indochina is still possible" (*Le Monde*, February 11, 1954). *Le Monde* noted on March 24, 1954, that Senator Knowland and his supporters continued to resist both American military involvement and negotiation with the enemy, while Senator Mansfield remained suspicious of French intentions fully to disengage from the Associated States. Consequently, he was opposed to any step-up in American involvement in France's colonial war.

The French, for their part, were more hopeful in March 1954 of a solution to the Indochina War than at any time in the previous seven years. Some maintained that a military solution was close at hand. For example, Foreign Secretary Bidault insisted that "Ho Chi Minh is at the point of capitulating. . . . We are going to beat him" (Grosser, 297), while

Laniel refused to negotiate with the leader of the Democratic Republic of Vietnam and persisted in the war effort because "it is the energy expended on the last battles that will determine the relative position of the negotiators" (*L'Annee Politique*, 1954, 304). Still others anticipated a negotiated solution. For them the Geneva Conference and its promise of peace became the national polestar. The Americans were simply obstructionists. As early as January 8, 1954, *Le Monde* carried the words of François Mauriac, who charged that "Americans would have French blood run." *Le Monde* commentator Jacques Fauvet, writing on March 6, 1954, argued that "the time is past when peace causes more fear than war." On March 11, 1954, his colleague, Henri Pierre, asked "Why not tell the United States, in the words of Clemenceau, 'Vous faites la guerre?'" On March 25, 1954, the paper declared that "the only language Americans know is that of war.... They don't believe another solution is possible, the one around 'le tapis vert.'"

General Paul Ely, special envoy of France who was chief negotiator of French policy in Washington, visited the American capital in late March for just that purpose. The point of departure for these discussions was Operation Vulture. It called for limited and temporary bombing of the Vietminh supply areas at Dien Bien Phu by sixty American B–29s, escorted by 150 fighters from the aircraft carriers of the U.S. Seventh Fleet. This proposed unilateral, offensive action on the part of the United States was of dubious legality. According to Herring and Immerman in "Eisenhower, Dulles, and Dienbienphu" (1984), the French argued that while Chinese troops were not engaged at Dien Bien Phu, their war matériel was and, consequently, legitimated an American reprisal. Navarre deemed it workable, but the saturation bombing would have to be "massive" and "immediate." He was supported by General Paul Ely and Admiral Arthur Radford, chairman of the American Joint Chiefs of Staff.

The Pentagon Papers disclose, however, that other members of the JCS, principally Generals Ridgway and Twining, argued that Operation Vulture was ineffective without the deployment of American ground troops, and, given the public mood, that alternative was politically inadvisable. Instead, the American administration placated the French with sixty-five additional B–26 bombers. Dulles, although declaring that "Communist victory in Indochina cannot be entertained" (*Le Monde*, March 25, 1954), saw no reason to abandon the Navarre Plan as the mode of operation. President Eisenhower, while acknowledging that the United States had a "military mission" (*Public Papers of the Presidents*, 226) in Indochina, was not interested in military escalation: "No one could be more bitterly opposed to ever getting the United States involved in a hot war in that region than I am, consequently, every move that I authorize is calculated, so far as humans can do it, to make certain that that does not happen" (*Public Papers of the Presidents*, 250).

Yet the administration's actions might call into question the veracity of those presidential words. Herring and Immerman, in "Eisenhower, Dulles, and Dienbienphu," tell of one highly significant event in those crucial weeks. On April 3, 1954, Dulles and Radford called a meeting of congressional leaders in order to discuss the military situation at Dien Bien Phu and, more significantly, to request that Congress issue the president a blank check resolution that would give him "discretionary authority to use air and sea powers" and would have a time limit of June 30, 1955. Congressional leaders, particularly Democratic senators Lyndon Johnson and Richard Russell, remained adamant in their refusal to condone unilateral action in Indochina. It has been suggested by Devillers and Lacouture in *End of a War* that the blank check proposal was nothing more than a political cover for Operation Vulture and, therefore, the administration's way to obtain congressional approval for more direct American involvement in the Indochina War. Grosser in *La IV Republique et la Politique Exterieure* concurs by saying that the blank check proposal represented a direct and positive response to the French situation at Dien Bien Phu and ran the risk of creating a "hot war" (298).

The French, acting upon a recommendation by Admiral Radford, formally requested Operation Vulture on April 4 and again on April 22, with the added enticement of an American-commanded operation, but the reply on both occasions was a negative one. The April 3 meeting, therefore, sealed the fate of Dien Bien Phu, as well as limiting the administration's policy options to one: United Action.

First announced in a speech to the Overseas Press Club on March 29, 1954, United Action, writes Allan B. Cole in *Conflict in Indo-China and International Repercussions*, was Dulles's program to move the United States from thoughts of unilateral military action to those of a multilateral nature. As Dulles himself explained, "Recent statements have been designed to impress upon potential aggressors that aggression might lead to action at places and by means of free-world choosing, so that aggression would cost more than it would gain. . . . This should be met with United Action" (172). It called for a regional defense pact to consist of the United States, Great Britain, France, the three Associated States of Indochina, Australia, New Zealand, Thailand, and the Philippines. According to the April 16, 1954, edition of *Le Monde*, Senator Knowland and the China lobby wanted to include South Korea and Taiwan, but, in the end, the only positive responses came from Thailand and the Philippines.

On April 1, 1954, *Le Monde* suggested that foreign diplomats, including Bidault, saw something Machiavellian about United Action, namely, the creation of a more general war at French expense. For this reason, *L'Annee Politique* noted that both the Communist and Socialist parties in the National Assembly refused to debate the proposal. This was the reason, according to the April 16 edition of *Le Monde*, that during the subsequent Bidault-Dulles talks of mid-April, United Action was relegated to the future. For the time being, French policy remained unchanged and reaffirmed: France would have free hand at Geneva and the United States would not block a cease-fire; the idea of an ultimatum to the People's Republic of China was abandoned; and the independence of the Associated States, within the French Union, would proceed. This independence program was ostensibly advanced when, on April 28 at the conclusion of several weeks of discussion, the governments of France and the State of Vietnam (SVN) issued a statement of intentions that allocated greater autonomy to the SVN.

United Action remained the idée fixe of American diplomacy throughout the spring and summer of 1954 and would ultimately find form, albeit in an altered state, with the creation of the Southeast Asia Treaty Organization (SEATO). But with the approach of the Geneva Conference, neither the domino theory prognosis of Eisenhower nor the threats of Senator Knowland to terminate aid to those allies who failed to endorse the military coalition succeeded in budging America's Western allies. They did not want to jeopardize Geneva by the further internationalization of the Indochina War. The only concession to United Action was the promise of future consideration should Geneva fail to produce peace.

Still, even after the fall of Dien Bien Phu on May 7, 1954, France pressed for the deployment of American ground troops; the United States talked of only air and naval support. Consequently, according to Herring and Immerman in "Eisenhower, Dulles, and Dienbienphu," modification of the Navarre Plan never occurred during the critical spring months of 1954 when the Vietminh began to threaten the Red Delta area. Shortly before the actual May 7 surrender of Dien Bien Phu, the American administration publicly recognized that a negotiated settlement might be the only way out of the military morass. In an address before the U.S. Chamber of Commerce on April 26, 1954, Eisenhower noted that "we turn our eyes to Geneva, and we see representatives of great—and some antagonistic—powers meeting there, trying to arrive at some situation that at least we could call a modus vivendi" (*Public Papers of the Presidents*, 422). The presidential shift toward conciliation ostensibly brought the United States and France into diplomatic realignment, but at least two books of the period, namely, Devillers and Lacouture's *End of a War* and Randle's *Geneva 1954*, note the disturbing effect this had on the French administration. An aggressive United States, that is, a United States that threatened military intervention, was a deterrent to Communist aggression in Indochina. A conciliatory United States, in the minds of Laniel and Bidault (and, reportedly, Dulles, too) did not serve the best interests of France in its negotiations at Geneva.

The surrender of Dien Bien Phu resulted in a further adjustment of American policy. *Le Monde* was keenly aware of the change. It reported in its May 9–10 issue that the domino theory became invalidated when Dulles commented on the defeat by saying, "A battle is lost but not the war" and, in the May 14 edition, that Indochina remained "important" but no longer "essential." The military solution to the Indochina War appeared, in May 1954, to be more elusive than ever, but Dulles continued to press France to persist in the war effort and to reconsider the mutual pact. These were difficult requests, assert Herring and Immerman in "Eisenhower, Dulles, and Dienbienphu," since Bidault personally remained unconvinced that Eisenhower was incapable of implementing some sort of executive action that could have saved Dien Bien Phu. They were also difficult because it was yet unknown whether the French would regard the loss of Dien Bien Phu as a Verdun or a Sedan. Would the French rally and renew the war resolve, queried *Le Monde* on May 12, 1954, or would they demand the resignation of the Laniel government?

As of May 6, 1954, the Laniel government still had a clear majority (311 to 262) in the National Assembly, with the MRP and other moderate parties being the mainstay of its support and the Communists and Socialists its chief opposition. But the news of the fall of Dien Bien Phu, arriving late Friday afternoon of May 7 and occurring ironically on the tenth anniversary of the victory of 1944, had a profound effect on public opinion. *Le Figaro*, the newspaper most consistent in its loyalty to the government, admonished the Laniel administration and characterized it as "a used team. . . . The government is nothing more than a bunch of administrators, without a foreign policy and without a collective will" (*L'Annee Politique*, 1954, 27–28).

L'Annee Politique further noted that when Laniel spoke before the National Assembly, he pleaded against "accepting a spirit of capitulation," while the president of the MRP, Robert Lecourt, asked for "continued support for the government which wanted to carry on the fighting while negotiating at Geneva" (29). The Laniel government was able to survive, but with only a limited mandate. The Assembly voted by 289 to 287, with 33 abstentions, to retain the Laniel administration. However, it was apparent that the "majority" was disoriented and had no real confidence in the ministerial team. Holding to its promise to continue the war effort, France, on May 28, called up its reserve units in order to free its regular troops for duty in Indochina. But according to Randle in *Geneva 1954* (261), the sole military directive from this point until the cease-fire was to "protect the French Expeditionary Forces."

The reprieve for the Laniel government was indeed a temporary one.

The political fallout from years of frustration in the jungles of Indochina, capped by the surrender of Dien Bien Phu, occurred on June 12, 1954. *L'Annee Politique* (1954, 40–50) recorded the historic events that took place in the Chamber of Deputies. By a vote of 306 to 293, the Assembly refused to give the government a vote of confidence. On June 17, with 419 for, 47 against, 143 abstentions (74 MRPs), and 12 not present, Pierre Mendes-France was elected premier of France. There was no doubt why Mendes-France was chosen, for in his own words: "Indochina is at the center of our thoughts. . . . I am firmly convinced that peaceful solution to the conflict is possible." The desire for a negotiated settlement to the war cut across party lines, thereby bearing witness to a genuine national consensus. The Communist party voted for the investiture of the president of the National Assembly (Mendes-France) for the first time since 1950 and continued in its support of the government through the month of July. Charles de Gaulle thought that "this new chapter would be decisive." The MRP, newly installed in its opposition role, awaited the outcome of the Geneva Conference in relative silence but with a critical eye, for the personal attacks of Mendes-France against Bidault had left a legacy of bitterness.

The reaction of the United States to these events in Paris was not long in coming. Randle in *Geneva 1954* writes that on June 13, Bedell Smith, undersecretary of state, followed in the wake of Dulles and withdrew from the Geneva peace talks, thereby signaling a further reduction in the "stature" of the American delegation. The United States had tied itself to the politics of the MRP, and, consequently, its removal from power disoriented the Americans. Accustomed to treating the French political scene in a trivial manner, the premiership of Mendes-France had a sobering effect on the Americans. The June 15, 1954, edition of *Le Monde* reported that the Americans initially perceived it as a "victory for the Kremlin," since, according to Senator Knowland, "Mendes-France's thirty-day deadline played into the hands of the communists." Mendes-France had become a "French Kerensky." Yet a subtle shift was detected in American opinion by *Le Monde* when the new premier was no longer called a "neutralist" by Americans but, instead, a "realist."

Le Monde further noted that the French viewed the dilution of the American delegation at Geneva as a dangerous precedent, which fed into the natural proclivity for nationalistic and isolationist tendencies vis-à-vis its Western allies. Of a more immediate French concern was that the absence of Dulles and Smith curtailed the bargaining position of Mendes-France, who responded to the new turn of events by requesting from the National Assembly additional troops for Indochina. The Franco-American diplomatic strains were ameliorated, however, when, acting upon the invitation of Mendes-France, Dulles arrived in Paris on July 14, 1954. It was an opportunity for personal appraisal and policy clarification, and Randle writes in *Geneva 1954* (323) that the meeting was characterized as successful on both counts. Mendes-France assured Dulles that the French would not accept "peace at any price," and Dulles pledged not to veto French peace terms.

As a gesture of renewed confidence in French political leadership and policy, Eisenhower endorsed the proposal that Bedell Smith return to Geneva. *Le Monde* reported in its July 11–12, 1954, issue that the under-secretary's presence, rather than that of Dulles, lessened the risk of congressional criticism of American involvement with the "Asian Munich." But as *Le Monde* pointed out on July 14, Dulles, by coming to Paris, was symbolically participating at Geneva, and this gesture was significant because he was the least free of the Western foreign ministers.

By contrast, Pierre Mendes-France, functioning in the dual role of prime minister and foreign secretary, arrived in Geneva with a mandate from the National Assembly for a negotiated peace, a peace promised within thirty days or the new government would tender its resignation. During his long political career, Mendes-France was known as an "outsider" to party politics and intrigue, preferring, instead, a "personal politics." This same style operated during the remaining weeks of the Geneva Conference, where from June 23 until the final Accords were signed, he was engaged in private talks with Chou Enlai and the Vietminh representatives, much to the consternation of the Americans. He was assisted in these discussions by his own excellent team of negotiators: General Delteil, Colonel de Brebisson, and, above all, Jean Chauvel. Grosser writes in *La IV Republique et la Politique Exterieure* (307) that the determination of the new French delegation to work toward a negotiated settlement of the Indochina conflict was reflected in a closer working relationship with the English delegation, under the leadership of Anthony Eden, who believed that Molotov sincerely wanted peace, and a movement away from the Bidault practice of cooperating closely with the Americans. In sum, Mendes-France had the courage to move in new directions at Geneva and was presented with the fortuitous circumstances to allow it to happen. Nevertheless, Mendes-France did not opt to divorce France completely from its American partner, for the threat of American military intervention continued to be a factor at the peace talks. This was particularly so, as Irving in *The First Indochina War* (124) notes, after the French were forced to evacuate the Red Delta area on July 3, 1954.

Actually, the American threat was largely illusory. With no firm battlefield plan and no real support for United Action, the United States had to be somewhat flexible at Geneva and participate, if only, as Dulles said, "in the role of a friend" (*Le Monde*, June 10, 1954). On July 17, 1954, *Le Monde* reported that acceptance of a modus vivendi in Indochina displayed a certain intrepidity on the part of Eisenhower and

Dulles, who acted in spite of congressional opposition to a policy of accommodation. Indeed, Senator Knowland earlier predicted that "the American people will not consent to a Far Eastern Munich" (*Time*, March 8, 1954), and the fall congressional elections were fast approaching. The Pentagon Papers disclose that, except for the partition of Vietnam, the Seven-Point Program of the Western allies represented the maximum Western position, given the military facts of life. Still, the Eisenhower administration, operating without a national mandate for a negotiated peace in Indochina, would only "take note" of the final agreement. Time, the factor that seemingly worked against Franco-American policy until July 21, 1954, became the new American ally after the Geneva Conference, for time seemingly promised the buildup of the Vietnamese forces and popular support for the State of Vietnam.

The cease-fire in Indochina represented a triumph of the personal diplomacy of Mendes-France and was recognized as such on both sides of the Atlantic. The French expeditiously responded to his fulfilled promise of peace when, on July 23, the National Assembly overwhelmingly voted to endorse the Accords with 501 for, 93 against, and 86 abstentions (70 MRPs).

Although much of the American press and many in government circles placed Mendes-France in the ranks of Disraeli and Churchill on July 22, 1954, *Le Monde* observed that the American Congress was less forthcoming in both praise and commentary on the actual Geneva articles. Senator Knowland did not remain silent, however, for in his opinion, Geneva represented "one of the greatest communist victories of the decade" (*Le Monde*, July 23, 1954). The American president and his secretary of state, the principal architects of American policy for Indochina, were more judicious in their commentary on the Accords. At his news conference of July 21, 1954, and in response to a question that related to cease-fire agreement to appeasement, Eisenhower said: "Well, I hesitate to use such words . . . I would say this . . . this agreement, in certain of its features, is not satisfactory to us. It is not what we would have liked to have had . . . but I don't know, when I am put up against it at this moment, to find an alternative, to say what we would or could do. Then if I have no better plan, I am not going to criticize what they have done" (*Public Papers of the Presidents*, 647). John Foster Dulles, speaking at a news conference on July 23, 1954, had this to say: "The Geneva negotiations reflected the military development in Indochina. After nearly eight years of war, the forces of the French Union had lost control of nearly one-half of Vietnam, their hold on the balance was precarious, and the French people did not want to prolong the war" (Cole, *Conflict in Indo-China*, 176).

This assessment of the Geneva settlement reflected some of the frustrations and limitations imposed upon American policy in the preceding weeks and months. It concurred with the French analysis of the Accords, for in the words of Mendes-France: "I do not have an illusion about the contents of the agreement. The texts are sometimes cruel because they consecrate facts that are cruel" (Randle, *Geneva 1954*, 355). The Geneva Conference represented, then, a convergence of Franco-American policy and the successful, albeit qualified, completion of the respective aims for Indochina held by France and the United States.

France had extricated itself from the war in Indochina with the French Union more or less preserved, and there was even the possibility that investment in North Vietnam might be salvaged. The French military could now concentrate on events in Europe and North Africa, areas of more vital national interest. Furthermore, the government of Mendes-France, riding the crest of popular approval, emerged from the Geneva Conference with renewed political strength. Geneva gave the United States time to build up native forces and popular support and to develop a mutual defense pact free from the mantle of French colonialism. Communist aggression was contained at the 17th parallel. Consequently, the Eisenhower administration could face the fall elections with a program of peace and a measure of success in its ongoing battle to contain Communism.

The Franco-American success at Geneva was not always so readily discernible. Indeed, the diplomacy of the two countries pursued ostensibly different goals until after 1950, when, with the injection of an ideological factor, the Indochina War produced a common enemy, if not a common rationale. From this point forward, the military solution pursued by France and the United States was doomed to fail without the popular support of the Vietnamese. Consequently, a negotiated settlement became the only recourse, and in light of political constraints imposed upon the French and American administrations by domestic public opinion, a complementary policy, rather than an identical one, was created.

With the deterioration of the battlefield situation, the French public demanded an end to the war by way of a negotiated settlement. The American public, by contrast, dictated a limited one. The option of a "hot war," though considered by the administration, was vetoed by both American public opinion and congressional sentiment. When the president moved toward realignment with the French conciliatory mood and spoke of adopting a modus vivendi solution in Indochina, the French administration, sensing a threat to its interests, reacted negatively. As a result, the joint policy that led to the qualified success at Geneva was a complementary one. The French gathered around the peace table while the Americans threatened military intervention. The foreign policies of the two nations became one at the moment when the French delegates signed the July Accords and their American counterparts merely noted them.

BIBLIOGRAPHY

Acheson, Dean. *Present at the Creation 1949–1959.* New York: Holt, Rinehart, and Winston, 1974.
Alexander, Charles C. *Holding the Line: The Eisenhower Era 1952–1961.* Bloomington: Indiana University Press, 1975.
Ambler, John. *The French Army in Politics 1945–1962.* Canton: Ohio State University Press, 1966.
Barnett, A. Doak. *Communist China and Asia.* New York: Random House, 1960.
Bator, Victor. *Vietnam: A Diplomatic Tragedy.* Dobbs Ferry, N.Y.: Oceana, 1965.
Beal, J. R. *John Foster Dulles 1888–1959.* New York: Harper and Row, 1960.
Bohlen, Charles. *Witness to History 1929–1969.* New York: Norton, 1973.
Brandon, Henry. *Anatomy of Error: The Inside Story of the Asian War on the Potomac, 1954–1969.* Boston: Gambit Press, 1969.
Buhite, Russell D. *Soviet-American Relations in Asia 1945–1954.* Norman: University of Oklahoma Press, 1981.
Buttinger, Joseph. *Vietnam: A Dragon Embattled.* New York: Praeger, 1967.
Caridi, Ronald J. *The Korean War and American Politics: The Republican Party as a Case Study.* Philadelphia: University of Pennsylvania Press, 1968.
Carlton, David. *Anthony Eden: A Biography.* London: Allen Lane, 1981.
Chen, King C. *Chinese Aid to the Viet-Minh 1938–1954.* Princeton, N.J.: Princeton University Press, 1959.
Cole, Allan B., ed. *Conflict in Indo-China and International Repercussions.* Ithaca, N.Y.: Cornell University Press, 1956.
Cooper, Chester. *The Lost Crusade: America in Vietnam.* New York: Dodd, Mead, 1970.
Deutscher, Isaac. *Russia, China and the West: A Contemporary Chronicle, 1953–1966.* London: Oxford University Press, 1970.
Devillers, Philippe, and Jean Lacouture. *End of a War.* New York: Praeger, 1969.
Divine, Robert. *Eisenhower and the Cold War.* New York: Oxford University Press, 1981.
Eden, Anthony. *Full Circle: Memoirs of Anthony Eden.* Boston: Cassell, 1960.
Ely, General Paul. *Memoires: L'Indochine dans la Tourmente.* Paris: Plon, 1964.
Fall, Bernard B. *Street Without Joy.* Harrisburg, Pa.: Stackpole Books, 1961.
Fall, Bernard B. *Hell in a Very Small Place.* New York: Lippincott, 1966a.
Fall, Bernard B. *Vietnam Witness 1953–1966.* New York: Praeger, 1966b.
Gaddis, John Lewis. *Strategies of Containment: A Critical Appraisal of Postwar American National Security Policy.* New York: Oxford University Press, 1982.
Geelhold, E. Bruce. *Charles E. Wilson and Controversy at the Pentagon, 1953–1957.* Detroit: Wayne State University Press, 1979.
George, Alexander L., David K. Hall, and William E. Simons. *The Limits of Coercive Diplomacy: Laos, Cuba, and Vietnam.* Boston: Little, Brown, 1971.
Gettleman, Marvin E. *Viet-Nam.* New York: Fawcett, 1965.

Gorce, Paul-Marie de la. *The French Army*. New York: George Braziller, 1963.

Grosser, Alfred. *La IV Republique et la Politique Exterieure*. Paris: Librarie Armand Colin, 1961.

Guhin, Michael. *John Foster Dulles: A Statesman and His Times*. New York: Columbia University Press, 1972.

Gurtov, Melvin. *The First Vietnam Crisis: Chinese Communist Strategy and United States Involvement 1953–1954*. New York: Columbia University Press, 1967.

Halberstam, David. *The Best and the Brightest*. New York: Random House, 1972.

Hammer, Ellen J. *The Struggle for Indochina, 1940–1955*. Stanford, Calif.: Stanford University Press, 1966.

Herring, George C. "The Truman Administration and the Restoration of French Sovereignty in Indochina." *Diplomatic History* 1 (Spring 1977): 98–117.

Herring, George C. *America's Longest War: The United States and Vietnam, 1950–1975*. New York: Wiley, 1979.

Herring, George C., and Richard Immerman. "Eisenhower, Dulles, and Dienbienphu: 'The Day We Didn't Go To War' Revisited." *Journal of American History* 60 (September 1984): 343–63.

Hess, Gary R. "The First American Commitment in Indochina: The Acceptance of the Bao Dai Solution, 1950." *Diplomatic History* 3 (Fall 1978): 331–50.

Hoopes, Townsend. *The Devil and John Foster Dulles*. Boston: Little, Brown, 1973.

Horne, Alistair. *The French Army and Politics, 1870–1940*. New York: Peter Bedrich Books, 1984.

Irving, R.E.M. *The First Indochina War: French and American Policy 1945–1954*. London: Room Helm, 1975.

Jurika, Stephen, Jr., ed. *From Pearl Harbor to Vietnam: The Memoirs of Admiral Arthur W. Radford*. Stanford, Calif.: Hoover Institution Press, 1980.

Keegan, John. *Dien Bien Phu*. New York: Ballantine, 1974.

Kelley, George A. *Lost Soldiers: The French Army and Empire in Crisis 1947–1962*. Cambridge, Mass.: MIT Press, 1965.

Krog, Carl. "American Journals of Opinion and the Fall of Vietnam, 1954." *Asian Affairs* 22 (May-June 1979): 324–32.

Lacouture, Jean. *Between Two Truces*. New York: Random House, 1966.

Lacouture, Jean. *The End of a War: Indochina 1954*. New York: Praeger, 1969.

Lancaster, Donald. *The Emancipation of French Indochina*. New York: Oxford University Press, 1961.

Langlais, Pierre. *Dien Bien Phu*. Paris: Presses Pocket, 1963.

L'Annee Politique, 1951–1954. Paris: University of Paris, 1951–1954.

Le Monde. January-December 1954.

Leuthy, Herbert. *France Against Herself*. New York: Meridian, 1955.

McAlister, John T. *Vietnam: The Origins of Revolution*. Garden City, N.Y.: Doubleday Anchor, 1971.

Navarre, Henri. *Agonie de l'Indochine 1953–1954*. Paris: Librairie Plon, 1966.

Nixon, Richard. *RN: The Memoirs of Richard Nixon*. New York: Warner Books, 1978.

O'Ballance, Edgar. *The Indochina War, 1945–1954*. London: Faber and Faber, 1964.

O'Neill, Robert J. *Indochina Tragedy 1945–1954*. Melbourne, Australia: F. W. Cheshire, 1968.

O'Neill, Robert J. *General Giap: Politician and Strategist*. New York: Praeger, 1969.

Paret, Peter. *French Revolutionary Warfare in Indochina and Algeria*. New York: Praeger, 1964.

Public Papers of the Presidents, Dwight D. Eisenhower, 1954. Washington, D.C.: U.S. Government Printing Office, 1960.

Randle, Robert F. *Geneva 1954: The Settlement of the Indochinese War*. Princeton, N.J.: Princeton University Press, 1969.

Rice-Maximin, Edward. "The United States, France & Vietnam, 1945–1950: The View from the State Department." *Contemporary French Civilization* 1 (1982): 36–53.

Rocole, Pierre. *Pourquoi Dien Bien Phu?* Paris: Flammarion, 1968.

Roy, Jules. *The Battle of Dien Bien Phu*. Paris: Julliard, 1963.

Schlesinger, Arthur M., Jr. *The Bitter Heritage: Vietnam and American Democracy, 1941–1966*. Boston: Houghton Mifflin, 1966.

United States Vietnam Relations 1945–1967. Vol. 1, Parts 1–4. Washington, D.C.: U.S. Government Printing Office, 1971.

Werth, Alexander. *France 1940–1955*. Boston: Beacon Press, 1966.

PART II

The Strategy of the War

5 Military Strategy

The consensus among contemporary military and political strategists is that the United States should have invested a good deal more effort in counterinsurgency programs during the course of the Vietnam War. By losing sight of long-term political objectives and focusing, instead, on a conventional military strategy, the United States walked the same path the French had walked earlier, and although the American effort was characterized by infinitely more firepower and had an infinitely more dramatic impact on the Vietnamese people, the end result was the same— withdrawal and defeat. With the twenty-twenty hindsight of historians, it is relatively easy to reach such conclusions. It was not so easy back in the 1960s and 1970s, when the war was being fought. The strategy of attrition that the United States eventually adopted in Vietnam had its historical antecedents, and during the conflict there was abundant criticism, from the right and from the left, about the approach the United States was taking in Vietnam. Most of the contemporary criticisms of American policy in Vietnam have their counterparts in those earlier critiques as well.

THE NEW ENEMY

The initial strategic issue confronting post–World War II America was identifying the new strategic threats to the United States. That proved easy. The Soviet Union was the new enemy. During the 1950s and early 1960s, the contemporary explanations of the American involvement in Indochina emerged from a traditional cold war point of view. The anti-Communist hysteria of the late 1940s swept through the United States and shaped, as well as was shaped by, the prevailing perceptions of the

Soviet Union. Senator J. William Fulbright has written that American policymakers were obsessed with the theory of "monolithic Communism"—the conviction that there was a single, international Communist conspiracy to take over the world and that the conspiracy was directed from the Kremlin in Moscow. All manifestations of Communism, anywhere in the world, could be traced directly to the Russians.

The first battleground of the cold war was Central Europe, where the United States, Great Britain, and France expected the Soviet Union to be particularly aggressive, especially after she had refused to withdraw her troops from Eastern Europe at the end of World War II. George Kennan wrote his famous article in *Foreign Affairs* in 1947 and proposed what became known as the "containment doctrine"—a foreign policy in which the United States would oppose, militarily and politically, Soviet expansion in Europe. The Truman Doctrine, the Marshall Plan, and the Berlin Airlift were all containment responses to Soviet political and military activity.

After the fall of China to Mao Zedong in 1949, as Robert M. Blum points out in *Drawing the Line: The Origin of the American Containment Policy in East Asia,* and the outbreak of the Korean War in 1950, American policymakers began to apply the containment doctrine to Asia as well, a point of view with which George Kennan took great exception. In testimony before the Senate Foreign Relations Committee in 1966, Kennan argued strongly that Vietnam was not strategically significant to the United States and that America should "liquidate the involvement just as soon as possible." Few people besides Senator J. William Fulbright, however, were listening. Regardless of Kennan's objections, American policymakers focused on the Communism in Ho Chi Minh's ideology, not on the anti-French, pro-Vietnamese nationalism. The early U.S. decision to provide financial support to the French was based on the Eisenhower administration's desire to stop the spread of Communism in Asia. For them, the major front of the cold war had shifted to Asia.

The specific application of the containment doctrine to Asia led inevitably to what became known as the "domino theory." As Soviet-American relations deteriorated in the 1940s and 1950s and as Mao Zedong came to power in China, the domino theory became the mainstay of U.S. foreign policy. For a time in the 1950s and early 1960s, it was central to the way Americans interpreted the world, rivaling the Monroe Doctrine and the Open Door in importance. It appeared as if the whole free world depended upon the survival of French Indochina. If Ho Chi Minh succeeded in conquering Tonkin, Annam, and Cochinchina (the three geographical regions of Vietnam), it would be only a matter of time before Laos and Cambodia fell. With Indochina in Communist hands, dominoes would fall in two directions: Thailand and Burma would go under, then Pakistan and India. Afghanistan, Iran, and the rest of the

Middle East would follow. Then Communism would infect North Africa and the entire Mediterranean.

During the years of the John F. Kennedy administration, as well as the first years of the Lyndon B. Johnson administration, that cold war interpretation of the struggle in Indochina prevailed. It also appeared in most of the memoirs of the individuals who made and implemented American military and foreign policy during the 1960s and early 1970s. People like Lyndon B. Johnson, Dwight D. Eisenhower, Richard Nixon, Henry Cabot Lodge, Frederick Nolting, William Westmoreland, Walt W. Rostow, Dean Rusk, W. Averell Harriman, Pierre Salinger, and Theodore Sorensen all reflected that cold war mentality in their memoirs or early histories of the war.

THE FAITH IN FIREPOWER

Simultaneous with the growing fear of the Soviet Union was the increasing faith in the efficacies of technology and military firepower. A post–World War II consensus intoxicated American culture. During World War II, the United States had become the premier economic and military force in the world, and the war had been characterized by euphoria, missionary zeal, national unity, prosperity, and an overpowering sense of virtue. There seemed nothing that American power could not achieve. That conviction permeated American culture in the late 1940s and 1950s, as Neil Sheehan has argued in *The Bright and Shining Lie*. It colored the way policymakers reacted to social and political change. Communists, not fascists, were the embodiment of evil. The answer was to line up the world and force people to take sides. America would provide the money, the leadership, and the technology to defeat the new threat. The best description of that prevailing sense of cultural hegemony and moral supremacy is Loren Baritz's *Backfire: A History of How American Culture Led Us into Vietnam and Made Us Fight the Way We Did*. Baritz examines the myths of American culture that led the United States into Vietnam—the conviction of moral supremacy and the faith that just as American technology and economic production had produced victory in World War II, they could do so again anywhere in the world. *Backfire* shows how the American sense of invincibility explains the failure of Washington bureaucrats to develop an effective war strategy. At the peak of the Vietnam War, the antiwar treatise by linguist Noam Chomsky (*American Power and the New Mandarins*) made the same argument.

During the 1950s, in order to develop "more bang for the buck," the faith in firepower assumed ominous dimensions in terms of military and foreign policy. Late in 1953, when President Dwight D. Eisenhower expressed some reservations about the mushrooming defense budget, Admiral Arthur Radford, chairman of the Joint Chiefs of Staff, proposed his "New Look" defense policy. Stephen Jurika, Jr., edited Radford's memoirs (*From Pearl Harbor to Vietnam: The Memoirs of Admiral Arthur W. Radford*) and describes how Radford proposed, and Eisenhower and Secretary of State John Foster Dulles accepted, the notion that instead of planning for a variety of military contingencies—strategic nuclear war, tactical nuclear war, conventional war, limited nuclear war, and guerrilla war—the United States should plan for a war in which nuclear weapons would be used wherever they were strategically advantageous. Such an approach would be less expensive than a more comprehensive response system. Dulles used the logic in his famous "massive retaliation" speech of January 12, 1954, when he threatened to use strategic nuclear weapons whenever and wherever the Soviet Union fomented rebellion.

But as President Eisenhower shifted American military strategy to rely on the use of nuclear weapons to deter any foreign aggression against the United States or its allies, he effectively put all the American eggs in one basket. Eisenhower viewed the "threat" of nuclear war to be sufficient enough to manipulate other nations to comply with American desires. No nation on earth would dare defy the United States and risk nuclear annihilation. The military strategy of massive retaliation became America's solution to the threat of modern war.

But as a number of historians and military analysts have pointed out, the New Look policy was actually a weak defense strategy. Richard A. Aliano, in *American Defense Policy from Eisenhower to Kennedy: The Politics of Changing Military Requirements, 1957–1961*, shows how the Soviet launch of Sputnik in 1957 manifested itself in the United States and resulted in the "missile gap" controversy. The Eisenhower administration began to debate a shift in U.S. defense policy from a strategy of nuclear sufficiency to one of nuclear superiority and from the doctrine of massive retaliation to one of flexible response. The reorientation in national security policy had great influence on American foreign policy and eventually provided the Kennedy administration with the means and rationale for massive intervention in Southeast Asia.

Books by Edgar M. Bottome and John M. Collins tell a similar story. Bottome's *The Balance of Terror: A Guide to the Arms Race* is a general work looking at the evolution of American strategy, particularly against Communist aggression, after World War II. Bottome begins with Eisenhower's massive retaliation and mutual destruction approaches and continues through the Kennedy policy of flexible response and second-strike counterforce. The United States is committed to the containment policy, and America must realize that containment cannot work with the threat of nuclear weapons alone. Eventually the strategic policy shifts to use conventional forces in limited engagements with massive superior firepower, and this is the strategy that was applied to the Vietnam War. John M. Collins's *U.S. Defense Planning: A Critique* argues that technology was the U.S. trump card, which was designed to employ increasing volumes of firepower until all opposition was crushed. Military victories were the major aim of strategy. Collins claims that U.S. planners failed to form sound strategy for a revolutionary war of economic, social, and psychological pressures.

A leading figure in the reorientation of American defense policy from massive retaliation to flexible response was General Maxwell Taylor. Taylor had served as chief of staff of the army during the late 1950s, and he retired in 1959. He had been a frustrated chief of staff. The New Look defense strategy was good for the air force and navy, which could deliver nuclear warheads, but bad for the army, which became a military stepchild. The New Look, for Taylor at least, was pure folly, forcing the United States to resort to nuclear terror every time a political or military crisis developed somewhere in the world. Instead, Taylor pushed his flexible response military policy. Nuclear weapons should be available for reacting to a nuclear attack, but a strong, well-equipped army and Marine Corps should be available for conventional threats. Finally, the president should have a counterinsurgency option to respond to guerrilla wars and political uprisings where conventional forces were inappropriate. Taylor's flexible response theory became a best-seller in his 1959 book *The Uncertain Trumpet*.

President John F. Kennedy and Attorney General Robert F. Kennedy were impressed with Taylor's ideas, and he became a national security advisor to the administration. In 1962 they named him chairman of the Joint Chiefs of Staff. As William J. Rust (*Kennedy in Vietnam: American Foreign Policy, 1960–1963*) and R. B. Smith (*An International History of the Vietnam War: The Kennedy Strategy*) point out in their books on the Kennedy administration and Vietnam, a dramatic shift occurred in American defense policy in the early 1960s toward limited or flexible response. Kennedy no longer wanted a policy of just nuclear sufficiency or balance with the Soviet Union; he wanted nuclear superiority. Kennedy also did not accept the concept of massive retaliation in the event of war and, instead, wanted a flexible response with conventional forces or possibly even the use of strategic nuclear weapons in a limited military theater. This reorientation in national policy provided the Kennedy administration with the means and rationale for intervention in Southeast Asia. That rationale was explained by John Galloway in his book *The Kennedys and Vietnam* (1990). Lindsay looks at the problems of organizing effective countermeasures to the tactics of guerrilla insurrection employed by Communist rebels since World War II. He contends that although the instruments employed are military, the objectives are essentially political.

The key to success in Vietnam is the establishment of a set of political goals that the average person in Vietnam can understand and accept. A systematic effort must be made by the United States to work out techniques and train experts in the political aspects of village warfare. Unless the United States accepts an unconventional strategy to unconventional warfare, the war in South Vietnam will fail.

The Kennedy administration eventually expected to use such counterinsurgency forces as the Green Berets to train the South Vietnamese army to fight its own battles, employing only limited American conventional military power when absolutely necessary. Robert McNamara, secretary of defense, designed and implemented the Kennedy defense program. It moved the United States away from a massive retaliation policy to one of a limited military strategy. It also included military assistance for the underdeveloped world to stop Communist aggression and proposed a limited war policy. It became Kennedy's policy justification for U.S. involvement in Vietnam. For a look at how this became the policy of the Kennedy administration, see William W. Kaufmann, *The McNamara Strategy* (1964).

Most strategic thinkers at the time expected the policy to be successful in Vietnam. In his *Limited War and American Defense Policy* (1964), Seymour Deitchman looks at American strategy in Vietnam and offers three tactics that could be successful against guerrilla insurgency. The United States must make a determined effort to gain the support of the people through political, cultural, and economic activities. The people and their machinery of law and order must be defended against enemy guerrilla campaigns. The government must take the offensive attack against the guerrillas in their own territory and send troops against the enemy. Peter Paret and John W. Shy, in a 1965 article entitled "Guerrilla Warfare and United States Military Policy: A Study," called for an expansion of America's unconventional warfare capabilities in the 1960s. They supported the move away from massive retaliation and dependence on more conventional troops and limited warfare, and they identified the modern guerrilla as a weapon of insurrection aimed at capturing political power and as an instrument of foreign aggression.

Still, a number of analysts argued that counterinsurgency alone would not work in Vietnam. In several articles in 1963 and 1964, Frank N. Trager offered a modification of U.S. strategy in Vietnam. He urged a full U.S. military commitment and discussed the requirements for victory. Trager noted three areas of military attention: border areas, areas of Communist concentration, and areas of Communist opportunity. Trager observed that each area requires its own war plan and forces because each sector represents a different type of warfare. Ultimate U.S. success can be achieved only by a clear-cut military victory over the Vietcong and by winning the political loyalty of the South Vietnamese people.

Trager also encouraged the American policy of containment in response to Communist aggression in Asia and Vietnam but stressed that if the war was fought on Communist terms, the United States would fail. In order to make the policy of containment work, it will be necessary to "penetrate, undermine, threaten, and if necessary attack Hanoi and North Vietnam." This will require an extension and deepening of U.S. commitment to South Vietnam and Asia as a whole. If Asia is allowed to fall, then the first line of defense for the Americas would be lost to Communism. The next to fall would be Japan, Ryukyus, and the Philippines. The United States has committed itself to South Vietnam, and we cannot withdraw and still remain a first-class dominant power.

Others urged a deeper conventional commitment to Vietnam on the part of the United States. In *Design for Survival* (1965), General Thomas S. Power, retired commander of the Strategic Air Command (SAC), advocated expanding the role of SAC. U.S. strategy must lie in manufacturing more nuclear bombs to have massive superiority over any other nation on the earth. The United States should then use its superiority as a bargaining chip to gain what it wants in negotiations. But if negotiations fail or, in the case of Vietnam, where conventional forces reach an impasse, the bomb should be used to end the conflict. Then as long as the United States held vast superiority in nuclear devices, no nation would dare attack without fear of overwhelming retaliation. Few American policymakers, of course, took the nuclear option seriously. It would simply cause too much collateral damage against our allies, produce radiation that would hurt neutral and even pro-American countries, and turn world opinion strongly against the United States.

Major John S. Pustay, in *Counterinsurgency Warfare* (1965), also doubted whether counterinsurgency tactics in South Vietnam would be sufficient to defeat the enemy. The United States could be extremely compromised if it proved unable to maintain the containment policy embarked on after World War II. Pustay supports U.S. strategy in Vietnam but tries to place the strategy in greater focus. Pustay advocates greater and more intensified control of the Vietnamese population. Then the Vietcong insurgents must be forced to expose themselves and weaken their position. Finally the insurgents could then be engaged and defeated in conventional military combat.

The critics proved to be correct. The counterinsurgency programs did not do the job, as outlined in Chapter 6, primarily because the United States was not patient enough to take the time they required and because military planners kept pushing the idea of a conventional military victory. In 1966 Sir Robert Thompson, the British expert on counterinsurgency who had engineered the successful campaign against Communist guerrillas in Malaya, wrote *Defeating Communist Insurgency*. Thompson evaluated U.S. involvement in counterinsurgency activities in Vietnam. He stressed the need for patience, determination, and an offensive spirit. He also warned the U.S. government not to be diverted by critics of its operations seeking a simpler or quicker solution. The United States must keep its nerve and be confident of its ultimate success. America must concentrate not just on military operations but on destroying the subversive political organization operating in Vietnam by establishing political and economic stability there.

They were convinced that American firepower, applied in steadily increasing doses, would quickly destroy the enemy and free South Vietnam from its fears of a Communist victory. Russell F. Rhyne, in "Victory in Vietnam" (1970), proposed a three-stage program to achieve a U.S. victory in the Vietnam War. First, the United States must "persuade" the North Vietnamese to abandon their invasion of South Vietnamese territory. Second, the U.S. military must disperse the Vietcong units operating in South Vietnam with the methods employed in Algeria by the French. Finally, the United States must implement continuous patrolling to disperse guerrillas by techniques similar to those used by the British in Malaya. Rhyne urged the development of counterinsurgency techniques and strategy. Unfortunately, as the political situation deteriorated in South Vietnam, the military situation deteriorated as well. The South Vietnamese military could not control Communist activities, and during 1963 the Kennedy administration became particularly worried that South Vietnam might fall to Communism. More and more military advisors were sent to Vietnam. When John F. Kennedy was assassinated, there were nearly 17,000 American military personnel in South Vietnam, compared with only 900 when Dwight Eisenhower left office. Douglas S. Blaufarb points out in *The Counter-Insurgency Era: U.S. Doctrine and Performance, 1950 to the Present* (1977) that counterinsurgency was dead as a real option in American policy-making circles by the onset of the Lyndon B. Johnson administration.

As the war escalated and guerrilla activities increased and as the United States abandoned counterinsurgency, the military switched to a "search and destroy" strategy. The military was unable to engage the Vietcong in open combat and was forced to attempt short-term missions of searching for the Vietcong and attempting to destroy them in ambush. Eventually, this approach developed into the strategy of attrition—to kill as many of the Vietcong and North Vietnamese as possible until their forces were so drained in manpower that they would be willing to negotiate a settlement on U.S. terms. But as Chester L. Cooper pointed out in *The Lost Crusade: America in Vietnam* (1970), that soon involved the Johnson administration in a tragedy of errors. Cooper emphasizes that the failure of American diplomatic strategy was linked to military objectives. The United States' strategy to negotiate with Hanoi was a fiasco by not working for reunification and by not taking the diplomatic discussions seriously. The United States wanted to bargain from a position of strength, not realizing that Hanoi was already in a position of strength.

There were, of course, important dissenters to the idea of escalating the war, but their voices were neither loud enough nor numerous enough. Former general James Gavin, for example, called for the "enclave strategy." During the Kennedy administration, Gavin served as ambassador to France, and he learned much about fighting in Indochina from the French. They let Gavin know that the Vietnamese were a relentlessly militaristic people and that the United States would bog down in the jungles just as the French had. When he returned to the United States in 1964 and in his 1968 book *Crisis Now*, Gavin argued that if American ground troops were going to be introduced to South Vietnam, they should be used to defend only "coastal enclaves"—major cities along the South China Sea. Securing all of South Vietnam would take more than a million troops and at least a decade. Casualties would be severe, as would political criticism. Better to use fewer soldiers to hold coastal enclaves and therefore prove to North Vietnam that the United States was willing to remain in place indefinitely. General Maxwell Taylor, as he makes clear in his memoirs, *Swords and Plowshares*, basically supported the enclave strategy. An even greater dissent came from George Ball, undersecretary of state during the Kennedy and Johnson administrations. Ball argued that the United States should withdraw from Vietnam, that it would become a bloody ground war in Asia that could not be won. He told President Johnson, "Once on the tiger's back, we cannot be sure of picking the place to dismount." Ball's memoirs—*The Past Has Another Pattern* (1982)—describe his futile attempts to prevent the escalation at every stage of the Kennedy and Johnson administrations. At a 1961 meeting with President Kennedy, Ball predicted that the introduction of American troops would create its own momentum and that within five years there would be 300,000 American soldiers fighting in Vietnam. Kennedy laughed and said, "George, you're crazier than hell."

The problem with Ball's proposal, of course, was the political ramifications of an American withdrawal from Indochina and the inevitable fall of Vietnam to the Communists. The Republican right wing would then accuse the Democrats of having "lost" another part of the world to Communism. No Democrat was willing to take that political heat. The problem with the enclave strategy was that it envisioned the United States remaining indefinitely in South Vietnam, taking casualties along the way. That, too, had its own political risks, especially when the military and the right wing were calling for a military victory there.

President Johnson found himself in an impossible position. Most of his advisors kept advocating an escalation of the conflict—invest more and more resources and more and more firepower until the enemy was broken. Those arguments appeared in the strategic writings of military analysts. Frank E. Armbruster, in his book *Can We Win in Vietnam?* (1968), tried to clarify the reasons for U.S. involvement in South Vietnam. It was essentially to stop Communist inroads in Indochina. Armbruster examined U.S. strategy and advocated escalation of U.S. involvement and an expansion of the strategic hamlets. Armbruster also urged a systematic outward advance from Saigon with the military laying waste to the entire countryside in a continually expanding security zone, forcing the Communists out of South Vietnam.

But at the same time, Johnson wanted to contain the war, to maintain it as a limited conflict. When it became apparent that limited measures were not effective, the United States began to rely more and more on its massive military firepower to stop the spread of Communism in South Vietnam. The U.S. military began massive bombings in Communist-controlled territory in South Vietnam and eventually carried the bombing into Laos and North Vietnam. The American military attempted to approach the conflict on the same terms that the nation fought under in World War I, World War II, and the Korean War. Admiral Arleigh Burke, for example, in an article in the military journal *Ordnance*, suggested increasing the ground forces in Vietnam and increasing the amount of firepower being deployed. In addition, the United States should escalate involvement in the conflict by blockading North Vietnam, mining Haiphong Harbor, and closing the enemy supply routes along the Ho Chi Minh Trail. Burke refused to give up South Vietnam to the Communist insurgents and advocated escalation.

E. J. Carroll, Jr., in his article "Limited War—Limited Peace?" for a 1966 edition of *United States Naval Institute Proceedings*, compared U.S. involvement in the Korean War with activities in the Vietnam War. Using the example of Korea as the war that was not a war but that ended in a peace that was not a peace, Carroll raised questions about U.S. involvement in South Vietnam. He observed that limited wars end in only temporary peace and only total war can conclude in a lasting peace. Only victory brings peace. Carroll went on to suggest that the United States should take a firm course of military action and advocated the escalation of the conflict by U.S. forces and firepower. Only a complete destruction of Communism or North Vietnam could bring a lasting peace to Southeast Asia. Lieutenant Colonel John R. D. Cleland made essentially the same argument in a 1966 article for *Military Review*. Cleland reiterates the military solution to South Vietnam's problems and encourages continued U.S. involvement in Southeast Asia to stop Communist aggression. Otto Heilbrunn, in a 1968 article for *Ordnance*, supported the erection of effective buffer areas to stop the Communist infiltration into South Vietnam. He challenged the United States to confront the Vietcong at every opportunity in Vietnam. The United States must expand its strategy of erecting and maintaining the Demilitarized Zone to thwart North Vietnamese aggression across the border into South Vietnam.

The logic of firepower carried to its most ludicrous extreme was the question of using nuclear weapons against the enemy. A few writers suggested it in the early 1960s, and as the war effort became more and more expensive in the late 1960s, the nuclear alternative surfaced again, although it was still not taken seriously. In a 1969 article for the *United States Naval Institute Proceedings*, Marc E. Geneste reflected on his own experience in Southeast Asia and compared the U.S. efforts with those of the French military forces. Geneste raised the question of the use of limited nuclear weapons to end the war. He questioned whether the United States could afford to waste so much manpower and resources in Vietnam, and he argued that the use of nuclear weapons would, in the end, be beneficial for concluding the war on U.S. terms. Geneste does not worry at all about the worldwide consequences of the use of nuclear weapons on U.S. relations with other nations.

Although John F. Kennedy and Lyndon B. Johnson resisted the most extreme demands for escalation, they also refused to withdraw from the conflict, and over the course of eight years they made dozens of "compromise" decisions to increase modestly the American commitment and the level of firepower. Eventually, that series of modest decisions led to an extraordinary escalation. Between 1964 and 1973, the United States detonated more than 7 million tons of explosives on North Vietnam and South Vietnam, a greater volume of firepower than was employed during all of World War II. The tactical initiative remained with the enemy forces, and the United States evolved into what became known as the "strategy of attrition." The only way to win the war was to kill so many enemy troops that they could no longer field combat-ready military units.

The strategy of attrition ultimately became a numbers game in which the United States was obsessed with body counts. In order to find the enemy, American military officials imposed relocation programs on millions of South Vietnamese peasants, removing them from ancestral villages and placing them in secured relocation camps. The removal of "friendly" civilians supposedly then left the jungles inhabited only by the "bad guys," so the United States declared those areas to be "free fire zones" and unloaded huge volumes of explosives. To expose the enemy, the United States even launched Operation Ranch Hand, an aerial defoliation campaign in which American aircraft sprayed the jungles with anti-plant chemicals. The United States essentially laid waste to much of South Vietnam. The more desperate the United States became, the more frequent and violent the bombings became.

But as John Mueller has argued in "The Search for the 'Breaking Point' in Vietnam," the arithmetic of attrition was flawed from the very beginning. By any estimates, the United States would have had to kill as many as 250,000 enemy troops a year even to begin seriously to limit North Vietnam's ability to field decent combat units. The United States, of course, did not believe North Vietnam would be willing to absorb such heavy losses. But the United States badly underestimated their sense of commitment. They were willing to sacrifice up to a quarter of a million troops a year, but in order to inflict those kinds of losses, the United States would have had to have more than 1 million combat troops in Vietnam and to be willing to accept as many as 35,000 dead troops of its own a year. While North Vietnam was prepared politically to make that kind of commitment, the United States was not, and North Vietnam knew it.

CRITICS OF STRATEGY

As the war became more and more controversial during the late 1960s and American success in achieving a military victory seemed more and more remote, a number of criticisms of U.S. strategy began to emerge. As described earlier, one group continued to advocate more firepower. They were frustrated with the idea of limited warfare and wanted the United States to fight a complete, full-scale conventional war against North Vietnam, including massive bombing of Cambodia, Laos, and North Vietnam; an invasion of Laos, Cambodia, and North Vietnam; and the mining of North Vietnam's port facilities.

Three new critical schools of thought also emerged in the late 1960s about American conduct of the war. An important argument was that the U.S. strategy was fatally flawed because political objectives were muddled at best. The second major strategic critique involved the confused command and control apparatus of the military effort in Vietnam, which prevented the development and implementation of effective political and military policies. Finally, there were a savage assault on the extent of the firepower the United States was employing and the conviction that the application of so much military firepower was actually contradicting political progress.

The first criticism—that American policymakers did not have a clear focus on their political objectives—surfaced in a variety of ways. Ralph K. White, in his book *Nobody Wanted War: Misperception in Vietnam and Other Wars* (1968), provided a psychological analysis of the factors common to World War I, World War II, and the Vietnam War. White looked at how the United States drifted into the war in Vietnam and argued that vague notions of foreign governments and ways of life greatly distorted our perception of reality and people. Marvin Kalb and Elie Able in *Roots of Involvement* (1971) said that U.S. involvement in Vietnam was based on massive American ignorance of Southeast Asia. It was compounded by failures in military and political strategy, questionable intelligence, and overblown presidential rhetoric. Kalb and Able stressed the refusal to recognize that the national interests of the United States cannot be stretched to encompass the entire globe without risking disaster at home. Presidential strategy appeared to be out of touch with the real world. Francis FitzGerald, in *Fire in the Lake* (1972), also claimed that American officials were grossly ignorant of the people they were supposedly fighting for and against.

Richard J. Barnet's *Intervention and Revolution: The United States in the Third World* (1972) offered a different twist on the problem of political objectives. Barnet stated that until the United States concedes its inability to manage social and political changes throughout the world, there will be no peace. He reviewed the history of the war and showed that even though the war was lost, America could not bring itself to end it. Barnet stressed that the United States could not solve its social problems at home, so how could it solve problems halfway around the world on foreign soil? Barnet continues to call on the United States to change its strategy for peace from a military to a social reform strategy that will improve life in America first. Only then, with the domestic front fully in support of military endeavors, can the United States hope to be successful.

The command and control problem also received heavy criticism. Hanson W. Baldwin, the prize-winning journalist for the *New York Times*, criticized in his book *Strategy for Tomorrow* (1970) the use of civilian advisors in military decision making and argued that the major failure in Vietnam War strategy was civilian usurpation of military prerogatives. The failures in Vietnam were failures in command and control at the top levels in Washington, D.C. Military officers in Vietnam had great responsibilities but little or no real authority to carry out the war. The U.S. government also failed to marshal the economic and psychological strength of the nation by trying to conduct the war while domestically continuing business as usual.

In *The Straw Giant* (1968), Arthur T. Hadley stressed the problem of overcontrol by top civilian and military officials in Washington. Flying visits and electronic communication thwarted the decisions on technique and tactics that should have been decided by commanders in the field. Civilian advisors became so bogged down in statistics and details that they were unable to face the moral and political implications squarely. The strategy of running a war through advisors halfway round the world failed. War aims and issues that should have been dealt with on the civilian end never materialized. Field commanders who should have been prosecuting the war found themselves without any authority to do so. The Vietnam War demonstrated a neglect of strategic questions and a plethora of tactical details. Brigadier General S.L.A. Marshall, in *Battles in the Monsoon: Campaigning in the Central Highlands, South Vietnam, 1966*

(1967), argued that command and control problems directly affected tactical operations. Marshall conducted a tactical study of three battles fought in the central highlands and stressed the lack of higher command coordination in making effective strategic decisions. Marshall tended to support the efforts of the enlisted men in the military and claimed that the failure in Vietnam was in the hands of their commanding officers.

Zeb B. Bradford, Jr., in his 1972 article "U.S. Tactics in Vietnam," contended that U.S. military forces should have focused more on utilizing and capitalizing on U.S. advanced organizational and technical developments. The United States should never have tried to develop a guerrilla counterinsurgency but should have relied more on crucial military tactical power, primarily by using air power or sea power. This would have enabled the army ground forces to devote their efforts to tactical missions without having to utilize their resources to secure and maintain supply routes. The armed services and Bradford tend to evaluate failure by ground troops as resting on the failure of command and control procedures in the other branches of the armed services. James A. Thomas, in "Limited War: The Theory and the Practice" (1973), argued, regarding U.S. involvement, that the Korean and Vietnam wars were limited conflicts in which expectations clashed with goals. The result, in both, was dissatisfaction within the military. He proposed that the army thoroughly study limited war and participate in appropriate field exercises to prepare for such a conflict in the future. As it now stands, the strategy employed in past limited conflicts did not work and greater emphasis must be placed on newer theories and strategies of war.

But by far the major criticism of American strategy in Vietnam during the war was the belief that too much firepower was being used—that the collateral damage on civilians, the environment, and the economy, although devastating to enemy troops, was equally devastating to American political objectives. William J. Lederer, in *Our Own Worst Enemy* (1968), wrote that Vietnam was actually several wars being fought at one time: the bomber war, body-count war, guerrilla war, major-encounter war, and the political war for the loyalty of the Vietnamese people. Lederer contended that U.S. strategy was losing all the wars but especially the political war. Without winning the contest for the people, victory can be obtained only at the cost of vast destruction, and even then victory will be only temporary. The American strategy of attrition, designed to win the war and the hearts of the Vietnamese people, had just the opposite effect in driving them into the camp of the Vietcong. Jonathan Schell wrote two books describing the effects of American firepower. In *The Village of Ben Suc* (1967), Schell examined Ben Suc, a relatively prosperous farming village on the edge of the Iron Triangle. It became a target for the pacification program. Ben Suc was believed to be a Vietcong stronghold and had been pacified several times by the U.S. Army. Schell examines the military strategy that eventually pacified Ben Suc, completely destroying it and evacuating its inhabitants. The refugees were moved to a barren, treeless, "safe" area where they were "pacified" and then sank into apathy and despair. In *The Military Half: An Account of Destruction in Quang Ngai and Quang Tin* (1968), Schell examined rural pacification gone haywire as a result of not being able to identify the Vietcong from the civilian Vietnamese population. Schell discussed the failure of pacification to win the hearts and minds of the people and the tragic consequences when American troops, unable to deal with the strain of Vietcong identification, destroyed Quang Ngai and Quang Tin in 1967.

Theodore Draper and George McT. Kahin were more analytical in their descriptions, but their conclusions were the same. In *Abuse of Power* (1967), Draper was critical of the militarization of the Vietnam struggle by U.S. armed forces. The political and economic considerations, which were much more important, were abandoned in favor of a military solution. American strategy failed from the very beginning by abandoning diplomatic and economic approaches until the United States could force the enemy to "fade way" by the application of overwhelming firepower. In *The United States in Vietnam* (1969), Kahin and George Lewis argue that U.S. military strategy had become devoted to preventing the Vietcong from winning a military victory and stopping them from overrunning Saigon and other major cities and towns. But to do this, the United States resorted to warfare that destroyed the rural Vietnamese society. The application of such horrendous military power progressively weakened the potential for social cohesion, making the achievement of any lasting political solutions remote. Unending military campaigns prevented the Vietcong from establishing its authority in the rural areas, but it also denied this to the South Vietnamese government. D. F. Fleming, in *America's Role in Asia* (1969), made essentially the same argument. He criticized American strategy in Vietnam. U.S. methods to end the war served instead greatly to exacerbate it, generating hatred among the Vietnamese people and inspiring Vietcong reprisals against Americans. The U.S. strategy using napalm, bombers, needle shrapnel, defoliants, and noxious gas only caused rebellion to gather strength among the South Vietnamese people. Raymond Barrett, in "Graduated Response and the Lessons of Vietnam" (1972), examined the application of firepower against Vietcong military targets and argued that it was not surprising that the policy of graduated response failed to achieve its goals because of massive destruction of civilian targets. The United States must seek, he said, alternative methods to deal with the problem of insurgency in South Vietnam. Massive firepower will not bring victory in South Vietnam.

Other critics of American firepower focused their attention on the problem of ecocide in the Vietnamese jungles. In *Ecology of Devastation: Indochina* (1971), John Lewallen discussed the American strategy of using chemical weapons in the Vietnam War. Lewallan concluded that the chemical weapon strategy caused ecological disaster for the countries of Vietnam and Cambodia. He covered the Vietnam War's effect on all forms of life (human, animal, and vegetation) in connection with bulldozing, bombs, and fires. He argued that the relocation of civilian populations, driven from their homes to unstable urban areas, offered the most telling example of ecological disaster. J. B. Neilands, in *Harvest of Death: Chemical Warfare in Vietnam and Cambodia* (1972), was also passionately critical of the U.S. strategy of deploying chemical weapons in the Vietnam War. He was not critical of their failure but of their success in destroying the land and disillusioning the Vietnamese people concerning American "assistance." The United States had no hope of winning the hearts and minds of the South Vietnamese people with a military strategy that destroyed the civilian population's very existence, which was so closely tied to the land.

Several contemporary critics of the American strategy in Vietnam argued that the United States had essentially abandoned counterinsurgency in favor of conventional warfare. Although the United States managed to marshal infinitely more firepower than the French had, the two policies were essentially the same. Bernard B. Fall, a journalist who observed both the fall of the French empire in Indochina in the early 1950s and the American effort in the 1960s, wrote *The Two Vietnams* in 1967, shortly before he was killed in Vietnam. Fall showed how little the United States had deviated from the pattern that had led the French to defeat. The United States repeated the same French mistakes, clinging all the time to an ill-founded optimism. Fall detailed the bombing of North Vietnam and questioned the use of massive firepower, criticizing the American tendency to approach the war militarily instead of politically. Dennis J. Duncanson, in *Government and Revolution in Vietnam* (1968), echoed Fall's concerns. The U.S. objective, he argued, was to force the guerrillas to fight a conventional war so that superior firepower could be brought to bear. Vietcong strength could be eroded by inflicting heavy casualties, and if the armed units could be rendered harmless, the subversive political wing would collapse. Any political weaknesses and corruption in the South Vietnamese government could be rectified after the military victory. Duncanson felt this strategy failed in Vietnam.

Sir Robert Thompson, the British expert on counterinsurgency, offered the same criticism in his 1969 book *No Exit from Vietnam*. Thompson argued that American strategy was misconceived and American firepower misapplied. American efforts failed because the United States misunderstood the nature of revolutionary warfare, demanded results faster than they could be obtained, relied on conventional military force in the field rather than on attacking the political substructure of the insurgents, and elected to halt the bombing and seek negotiations at the wrong time. In a war concerned with people and immune to the application of firepower, the United States cannot be impulsive or desire quick results. As a military solution to a political problem, the strategy of attrition was doomed to fail. Geoffrey Fairbairn, in *Revolutionary Warfare and Communist Strategy: The Threat to Southeast Asia* (1968), agreed with Thompson's assessment.

Other critics at the time recognized that the entire policy of limited war in Asia, which the United States had pursued ever since the outbreak of the Korean conflict in 1950, demanded reconsideration. Robert E. Osgood, in his 1969 article "The Reappraisal of Limited War," argued that limited war is defined traditionally as a matter of national policy to gain a better bargaining position for future diplomatic negotiations. Osgood reviewed the concept of limited war and its objectives and applied them to the U.S. strategy in Vietnam. He concluded that Vietnam did not fit any of the existing models of limited warfare and that limited war will not lead to predictable or universal rules of the game as the United States expected. American strategic thinkers lacked the necessary imagination to adapt new military concepts and practices from the old romantic style that glorified the offensive spirit by overwhelming the enemy with brute force. Frank Trager's 1970 article "The Future of Mainland Asia" made a similar argument. Trager's evaluation of U.S. strategy had dramatically changed since the early 1960s. By 1970 he felt the American military presence was undermining the stability of Vietnam and its neighbors. Trager argued that United States must assume a new, nonaggressive role. As a Pacific power, the United States must first recognize Asian nations as equals and become more supportive of Asian–Pacific regionalism.

POSTMORTEMS ON THE VIETNAM STRATEGY

In the years after the conclusion of the U.S. war in Vietnam, strategy critics pursued the arguments that had been outlined during the conflict. The major criticism of U.S. strategy in Vietnam involved the failure of American policymakers to grasp the political nature of the conflict there. Truong Nhu Tang, in *A Vietcong Memoir* (1985), sharply criticizes U.S. strategy in Vietnam. Tang wishes that U.S. officials had been able to view the conflict as a revolutionary war to end foreign interference and destroy the corrupt South Vietnamese government rather than a simple case of cold war Communist expansionism. If the United States had molded its strategy around those two precepts, the results of American intervention would have been very different. Robert B. Asprey, in *War in the Shadows: The Guerrilla in History* (1975), argued that the failure of

American strategy in Vietnam resulted in the government's embarking on a course of action in which nebulous ambitions replaced specific political and military goals. The administration never formulated specific objectives for victory in Vietnam. Asprey blames the ultimate failure in Vietnam on American citizen apathy. Citizens should have forced the government to correct its failing strategy because citizens are the ultimate check and balance on government action. Defeat in Vietnam was not because of the U.S. government or the military but because of the actions or nonactions of American citizens at home. Wesley K. Clark's 1979 article "Gradualism and American Military Strategy" examined the theory of graduated response and measured escalation. A powerful tension emerged from the application of military firepower to a political problem. Clark was critical of substituting a military solution for a political solution. The United States failed in South Vietnam, he claimed, because it had no clear plan of how the conflict would end. Political leaders in the United States failed in their responsibility to provide a political solution to the problems in South Vietnam. Herbert Y. Schandler made the same argument in his 1984 article "America and Vietnam: The Failure of Strategy." For Schandler, American failure was caused by the lack of realization in Washington, D.C., that military power alone could not solve a long-range political problem and that the competence and political stability of the South Vietnamese government were overlooked as an issue. American strategic strength and power were never directed toward solving the political problems. The United States failed to develop an agreed upon strategy for success because it continued to attempt to impose a military solution on a political problem.

Because of the essentially political nature of the war, the strategy of attrition was doomed from the very beginning. In the first place, the numbers were just not there. As Larry Berman has pointed out in *Lyndon Johnson's War* (1989), the strategy of attrition would have succeeded only if the United States had been able to kill more than 250,000 enemy troops a year, but in spite of all the firepower employed, enemy casualties never even came close to that figure. To inflict that many deaths on the Vietcong and North Vietnamese, the United States would have needed dramatically to escalate its troop commitments beyond the 543,000 level of mid–1968, something that by then was politically impossible at home. In his book *War Without Fronts* (1985), Thomas C. Thayer was especially critical of American strategy in Vietnam. He analyzed the information that was used by Secretary of Defense Robert McNamara's systems analysis team and then by decision makers in Washington, D.C., and Saigon. Thayer stressed that the Vietnam War was without battlefronts and was different from any previous war ever fought by the U.S. military. This difference made it difficult for U.S. civilian and military policymakers to develop effective strategy. The American attrition strategy and tactics that won the war in Korea were doomed to fail in Vietnam. In *The McNamara Strategy and the Vietnam War* (1978), Gregory Palmer is also critical of McNamara's strategy in the Vietnam War and how he tried to conduct the war from Washington, D.C. Palmer believed it was not feasible to subvert Communist countries or to attempt to push back their frontiers, but he did believe in containing Communism where it already existed. Palmer criticized McNamara as a naive rationalist who developed an impossibly generic strategy to the problems faced in Vietnam.

Other critics focused on just how the military strategy developed— essentially, how counterinsurgency strategies were abandoned in favor of conventional military tactics that emphasized firepower. Gabriel Kolko, in *Anatomy of a War: Vietnam, the United States, and the Modern Historical Experience* (1985), had a left-wing perspective on the American experience in Vietnam. He examined the causes of the Vietnam War and tried to explain the politics that motivated different factions to make the crucial decisions that led to the U.S. defeat. Kolko evaluated the dilemma of the U.S. strategy to fight a limited war in an age of dependence on advance technology and weapons. Guenter Lewy's *America in Vietnam* (1978) is diametrically opposed, in many ways, to Kolko's analysis. Lewy provides a revisionary look at the American experience in Vietnam, arguing that the apocalyptic descriptions of American war crimes and destruction of South Vietnamese civilians have been grossly exaggerated, but he, too, is extremely critical of the strategy of attrition, arguing that the United States should have been more interested in counterinsurgency programs, rebuilding the South Vietnamese government, and focusing on political as well as military objectives.

In spite of Lewy's argument that the United States did not wreak wholesale devastation on South Vietnam, most critics of American strategy argue to the contrary. Douglas S. Blaufarb's *The Counter-Insurgency Era: U.S. Doctrine and Performance, 1950 to the Present* examined the U.S. strategy of counterinsurgency in the Vietnam War from 1963 to 1972. Too much emphasis was placed on doctrine and management and far too little on the importance of a real understanding of Vietnamese culture. The biggest failure in Vietnam was not the U.S. government but the extraordinary politicization of the Vietnamese army and the fact that the government of South Vietnam had so little support among its own people. The U.S. strategy in Vietnam failed because it relied on massive firepower instead of trying to perceive the realities of the situation. Also see Lawrence E. Grinter, "South Vietnam: Pacification Denied" (1975).

The most recent evaluations of American strategic policy in Vietnam, written by such scholars and journalists as Marilyn Young, James S. Olson, Randy Roberts, Gary Moss, Larry Berman, and Neil Sheehan, argue that whatever hopes the United States had of winning the support of the South Vietnamese people were destroyed by the extraordinary havoc American policies created there. By the end of the war, more than 1 million Vietnamese had been killed in combat, and another 500,000 South Vietnamese civilians had been killed accidentally. As many as 1 million South Vietnamese civilians had received a wound as a result of American firepower during the war, and several million had had their homes destroyed by air and artillery bombardment. The hope of building political loyalties amidst such unprecedented destruction was ludicrous. American firepower ran amok in South Vietnam and lost the war politically in the "hearts and minds" of the peasant masses.

Another source of real criticism was the command and control problems that emerged out of interservice rivalries and the tendency of civilian officials in Washington, D.C., to make tactical as well as strategic decisions about the conduct of the war. Lieutenant General Phillip B. Davidson, *Vietnam at War: The History 1946–1975* (1988), cited the problem of command and the lack of ability for military officers to act without guidance from Washington, D.C. The United States failed because its leaders did not develop a strategy superior to that of the Vietcong. The United States never determined clearly what its national objectives were in Vietnam. In his article "The American Army" (1983), Peter M. Dunn was highly critical of U.S. strategy in the Vietnam War, and he was especially sharp in his denunciations of the extent to which Washington bureaucrats fought the war from Washington, D.C. The policy of having national security advisors like William Bundy and McGeorge Bundy or Walt W. Rostow actually selecting bombing targets was patently absurd. A breakdown in military command, falsification of reports, overemphasis on firepower, and an endemic inability to understand the real social and political aspects of the war characterized U.S. strategy.

The overall strategy in Vietnam was also handicapped by theoretical, bureaucratic rigidity among military and civilian planners. Andrew F. Krepinovich, Jr., in *The Army and Vietnam* (1986) claimed that the war was lost before the army even had a chance to fight it. The army's failure was in its assumption that it could transplant to Indochina the operational methods that had been successful in the European battle theaters of World War II. The American mind-set of more bombs and troops proved ill-suited to the war in Vietnam. Vietnam was a war of insurgency and the resolution of political and social problems, but American military commanders refused to place emphasis on this. In *Without Honor: Defeat in Vietnam and Cambodia* (1983), Arnold R. Isaacs investigated the personal implications of political decisions made a world away from Vietnam. He criticized the intelligence failure that misled American officials as to the conduct of the war. Isaacs also examined the consequences of the American military and political policies that sustained the war effort. What America lacked in Vietnam was not persistence but the flexibility to change policies and strategies that had proven ineffective. Paul Joseph makes similar arguments in *Cracks in the Empire: State Politics in the Vietnam War* (1987).

Edward N. Luttwak, in his article "On the Need to Reform American Strategy" (1981), claimed that U.S. military organizations were structured, equipped, and trained for warfare on a large scale against regular forces. But this strategy has never really adapted to entirely different circumstances by evolving appropriate small unit structure. The military developed neither operational methods related to the context of the Vietnam War nor tactics responsive to those of the enemy, which were radically different from traditional methods and tactics. U.S. strategy in Vietnam failed because the military could not adapt to the new kind of warfare employed by the Communist insurgency. Stanley J. Michael, Jr.'s, "Vietnam: Failure to Follow the Principles of War" in 1977 claimed that the enemy followed the correct strategy while the United States neglected to adhere to the principles of war in Vietnam. Correct strategy requires the military to change in the event that the strategy is not working. The Vietcong quickly recognized that the rules of conventional warfare would not work in the struggle against the U.S. military. The Vietcong changed their strategy to one of guerrilla activities while the United States continued to follow its outdated conventional warfare strategy. The United States failed to win the war because it refused to follow the basic rules that require change.

Richard A. Gabriel and Paul L. Savage argued in *Crisis in Command: Mismanagement in the Army* (1987) that the army leadership was at fault for the strategic defeat in Vietnam. The U.S. officer corps was more concerned with furthering individual careers than with developing cohesion. As the war progressed, U.S. forces moved into a state of advanced disintegration. Honor, integrity, and personal responsibility were abandoned to selfish ends. The strategic problems that surfaced in the Vietnam War were not caused by the war but were already inherent in the U.S. military. Vietnam only exacerbated the problems. Gabriel and Savage maintain that the same military exists today and that no matter what strategy is used, the mismanagement in command will continue to thwart success. A similar argument was made in Cincinnatus's *Self-Destruction: The Disintegration and Decay of the United States Army During the Vietnam Era* (1981). Published under a pseudonym by a career senior field-grade officer who served in the Vietnam War, the book discusses the failures of the military command staff, which was more concerned with a rotating opportunity to command in battle and acquire medals useful to officer promotion than with achieving real military progress. Reports of tactical failures were ignored, and facts contrary to command opinion were suppressed. American strategy and military efforts showed a lack of understanding of the very nature of the war. Without commanders willing to see beyond their own personal advancement and understand

Vietnam in its totality, defeat was inevitable. American strategy in Vietnam was a total failure. Also see Robert L. Gallucci's *Neither Peace nor Honor: The Politics of American Military Policy in Vietnam* (1975).

Postwar strategy critics also focused on other elements of the command and control structure. Harry G. Summers, Jr., in his 1982 book *On Strategy*, blasted American policymakers for creating a command and control structure that was almost guaranteed to fail. Military Assistance Command Vietnam (MACV) was in charge of the war. But MACV was a "subordinate unified command." Although General William Westmoreland eventually commanded 543,000 American troops fighting a land war in Asia, real authority over the war was in Honolulu with CINCPAC (Commander-in-Chief, Pacific Command). During Westmoreland's four years in South Vietnam, CINCPAC was Admiral Ulysses S. Grant Sharp. To get more requests to, and decisions from, the president and the Joint Chiefs of Staff, Westmoreland had to go through CINCPAC. Command of air operations was even more complicated. Westmoreland controlled the air force sorties inside South Vietnam and on the southern parts of the Ho Chi Minh Trail in Laos, but CINCPAC controlled naval air strikes over North Vietnam and northern Laos. To say the least, the command and control structure often prevented a unified battle plan. In *Rolling Thunder: Understanding Policy and Program Failure* (1980), James Clay Thompson focuses on the bureaucratic inertia that prevented effective use of air power during the war.

Most critics of the Vietnam War are convinced that the war could not have been won from the very beginning, but during the late 1970s and 1980s two other schools of thought criticized American strategy from another direction, arguing that the war could have been won had the United States employed a different strategic approach. One of those perspectives—counterinsurgency, economic development, and political education—is covered in Chapter 6, but the second perspective argues vociferously that the United States could have won the war in Vietnam. Books like Harry G. Summers, Jr.'s, *On Strategy* (1981), William Westmoreland's *A Soldier Reports* (1976), Guenter Lewy's *America in Vietnam* (1980), Robert L. Gallucci's *Neither Peace Nor Honor* (1975), Bruce Palmer, Jr.'s, *The 25-Year War: America's Military Role in Vietnam* (1984), and U.S. Grant Sharp's *Strategy for Defeat* (1978) argue not only that the United States should have fought in Vietnam but that the war was winnable. The U.S. military expended huge amounts of firepower but still fought the war under crippling restrictions. Because of an unwarranted fear of Chinese or Russian military intervention, the United States did not use its resources fully, preferring a "limited war," which unloaded millions of tons of explosives but refused to do what was necessary to isolate North Vietnam from its troops and supporters in South Vietnam and its suppliers in the People's Republic of China and the Soviet Union. These critics argue that the United States should have mined Haiphong harbor at the beginning of the war, steadily bombed all rail lines linking North Vietnam with China, consistently pursued enemy troops into their Cambodian sanctuaries, invaded and occupied portions of eastern Laos in order to interdict the inflow of supplies down the Ho Chi Minh Trail, and even invaded the southern portion of North Vietnam. By doing that and remaining in Indochina indefinitely, the United States could have achieved a military victory.

Shelby L. Stanton, in *The Rise and Fall of an American Army* (1985), argued that the Vietnam War all but destroyed the U.S. Army. Because of the conventional restraints on expanding the theater of operations, military officials were not able to conduct the war in an effective manner. Because of the nature of the terrain and guerrilla warfare, the tactical initiative was almost always with the enemy. Because of political considerations at home, Presidents Johnson and Nixon refused to call up the reserves, and as a result, American military readiness around the world was compromised as more and more troops were drained off into Vietnam. Finally, troop morale took a savage beating once the gradual withdrawals began. Everyone realized there would be no military victory, and survival, rather than service, became the premier goal of every soldier.

Lewis W. Walt, in *Strange War, Strange Strategy* (1976), offered his perspective on the war. Walt had been commander of the Third Marine Division and then the III Marine Amphibious Force in Vietnam in 1965 and 1966. During those years he opposed General William Westmoreland's "search and destroy" strategy of attrition in Vietnam. During the early years of the war, the Marine Corps argued for a strategy based more on counterinsurgency. They found themselves in I Corps—the northern provinces of South Vietnam. In I Corps, more than 90 percent of the Vietnamese population lived within ten miles of the South China Sea, while the other 10 percent were scattered throughout the mountainous highlands. Most of the Vietcong and North Vietnamese troops, however, operated in the mountains. The marines wanted to remain in the lowlands, working politically and economically with the vast majority of the peasants in counterinsurgency programs. If the enemy troops wanted to attack out of the mountains, then Walt and the marines were ready for them. The battles would have been fought in areas where American firepower could have been used effectively. But implicit in Walt's strategy was the reality that the United States would have to be in South Vietnam for years, perhaps even decades, to prepare the country for political self-sufficiency. American policymakers did not have that much time. General William Westmoreland's "search and destroy strat-

egy" forced the marines to patrol into the mountains, where they inflicted, but also sustained, heavy casualties. The Marine Corps
counterinsurgency programs were essentially abandoned.

The widening of the war, of course, finally occurred during the Nixon
administration, but it was the result of the Vietnamization strategy, not
of any comprehensive strategic thinking. Although most scholars have
seen Vietnamization—turning the war over to the South Vietnamese—
as a policy of the Nixon administration, it actually originated in the
Johnson administration, as Clark Clifford has pointed out in his recent
memoirs *Counsel to the President* (1991). Actually, Vietnamization had
been French and American policy for twenty years. The only difference
in 1969 was that the United States had little choice. As long as the war
enjoyed political support or at least neutrality at home, Presidents Eisenhower, Kennedy, and Johnson had been able to escalate the American
commitment, always with the intention of turning the war over to the
South Vietnamese. Those days were over by 1969. Richard Nixon had
little choice but to turn the war over to South Vietnam and begin withdrawing American troops. Vietnamization was his only political option.
The antiwar movement was gaining momentum, in Congress as well as
on the streets.

But as Nixon began the phased withdrawal of American troops in the
spring of 1969, he faced a new dilemma. South Vietnam was not ready
to assume the burden of the fighting, and as United States troops left,
a power vacuum materialized. Unless the president made some tactical
and strategic innovations, the North Vietnamese would take over as soon
as the last Americans left. The only substitute for American troops was
increases in American firepower and a widening of the war. The secret
bombing campaigns over Cambodia and Laos, the invasion of Cambodia
in 1970, the invasion of Laos in 1971, and the mining of Haiphong
harbor in 1972 all represented such tactical innovations, but they proved
to be too little, too late.

BIBLIOGRAPHY

Aliano, Richard A. *American Defense Policy from Eisenhower to Kennedy: The Politics
of Changing Military Requirements, 1957–1961*. New York: Random House,
1976.
Armbruster, Frank E. *Can We Win in Vietnam?* New York: Harper and Row,
1968.
Arnett, Peter, and Michael Maclear. *The Ten-Thousand Day War*. New York: St.
Martin's Press, 1981.
Asprey, Robert B. *War in the Shadows: The Guerrilla in History*. 2 vols. New York:
Doubleday, 1975.
Baldwin, Hanson W. *Strategy for Tomorrow*. New York: Harper and Row, 1970.
Ball, George. *The Past Has Another Pattern*. New York: Norton, 1982.

Bank, Aaron. *From OSS to Green Berets: The Birth of Special Forces*. Novato, Calif.: Presidio Press, 1990.

Baritz, Loren. *Backfire: A History of How American Culture Led Us into Vietnam and Made Us Fight the Way We Did*. New York: Morrow, 1984.

Barnet, Richard J. *The Economy of Death*. New York: Atheneum, 1969.

Barnet, Richard J. *Intervention and Revolution: The United States and the Third World*. New York: Atheneum, 1972a.

Barnet, Richard J. *Roots of War*. New York: Simon and Schuster, 1972b.

Barrett, Raymond. "Graduated Response and the Lessons of Vietnam." *Military Review* 52 (May 1972): 80–91.

Bender, David L., ed. *The Vietnam War: Opposing Viewpoints*. New York: Greenhaven, 1984.

Berman, Larry. *Planning a Tragedy: The Americanization of the War in Vietnam*. New York: Norton, 1982.

Berman, Larry. *Lyndon Johnson's War: The Road to Stalemate in Vietnam*. New York: Norton, 1989.

Blaufarb, Douglas S. *The Counter-Insurgency Era: U.S. Doctrine and Performance, 1950 to the Present*. New York: Free Press, 1977.

Blum, Robert M. *Drawing the Line: The Origin of the American Containment Policy in East Asia*. New York: Norton, 1982.

Bottome, Edgar M. *The Balance of Terror: A Guide to the Arms Race*. Boston: Beacon Press, 1971.

Bradford, Zeb B., Jr. "U.S. Tactics in Vietnam." *Military Review* (February 1972): 63–76.

Braestrup, Peter, ed. *Vietnam as History: Ten Years After the Paris Peace Accords*. Washington, D.C.: University Press of America, 1984.

Broughton, Jack. *Going Downtown: The War Against Hanoi and Washington*. New York: PB, 1990.

Brown, Harold. *Thinking About National Security: Defense and Foreign Policy in a Dangerous World*. Boulder, Colo.: Westview Press, 1983.

Burchett, Wilfred G. *Vietnam North: A First-Hand Report*. New York: International, 1967.

Burke, Arleigh. "Alternatives in Vietnam." *Ordnance* 50 (May-June 1966): 611–13.

Butterfield, Fox. "The New Vietnam Scholarship." *New York Times Magazine* (February 13, 1983): 26–32, 45–60.

Carroll, Captain E. J., Jr. "Limited War—Limited Peace?" *United States Naval Institute Proceedings* 92 (December 1966): 30–37.

Cash, John A., ed. *Seven Firefights in Vietnam*. Washington, D.C.: U.S. Government Printing Office, 1984.

Chomsky, Noam. *American Power and the New Mandarins*. New York: Knopf, 1968.

Chomsky, Noam. *At War with Asia*. New York: Pantheon Books, 1970.

Cincinnatus. *Self-Destruction: The Disintegration and Decay of the United States Army During the Vietnam Era*. New York: Norton, 1981.

Clark, Wesley K. "Gradualism and American Military Strategy." *Military Review* 55 (1979): 3–13.

Clarke, Jeffrey J. *Advice & Support, The Final Years, 1965–1973*. Washington, D.C.: U.S. Government Printing Office, 1988.

Cleland, Lieutenant Colonel John R. D. "Principle and Objective and Vietnam." *Military Review* 46 (July 1966): 82–86.

Clifford, Clark. *Counsel to the President. A Memoir.* New York: Random House, 1991.

Collins, John M. *U.S. Defense Planning: A Critique.* Boulder, Colo.: Westview Press, 1982.

Cooper, Chester L. *The Lost Crusade: America in Vietnam.* New York: Fawcett, 1970.

Corson, William R. *The Consequences of Failure.* New York: Norton, 1990.

Davidson, Lt. General Phillip B. *Vietnam at War: The History 1946–1975.* Novato, Calif.: Presidio Press, 1988.

Davis, Charles H. "Evolution of Policy and Strategy in the Vietnam Conflict." *Society for Historians of American Foreign Relations Newsletter* 21 (1990): 10–31.

Deitchman, Seymour. *Limited War and American Defense Policy.* Cambridge: MIT Press, 1964.

Divine, Robert A. "Vietnam Reconsidered." *Diplomatic History* 12 (Winter 1988): 79–94.

Donovan, John C. *The Cold Warriors: A Policy-Making Elite.* Lexington, Mass.: D. C. Heath, 1974.

Draper, Theodore. *Abuse of Power.* New York: Viking Press, 1967.

Duncanson, Dennis J. *Government and Revolution in Vietnam.* New York: Oxford University Press, 1968.

Dunn, Peter M. "The American Army: The Vietnam War, 1965–1973." In *Armed Forces and Modern Counter-Insurgency,* ed. Ian F. W. Beckett and John Pimoltt. London: Smyth and Weems, 1983.

Eisenhower, Dwight D. *The White House Years: Mandate for Change 1953–1956.* Garden City, N.Y.: Doubleday, 1963.

Eisenhower, Dwight D. *The White House Years: Waging Peace 1956–1961.* Garden City, N.Y.: Doubleday, 1965.

Ellsberg, Daniel. *Papers on the War.* New York: Simon and Schuster, 1972.

Fairbairn, Geoffrey. *Revolutionary Warfare and Communist Strategy: The Threat to Southeast Asia.* London: Faber and Faber, 1968.

Fall, Bernard B. *The Two Vietnams: A Political and Military Analysis.* New York: Pall Mall Press, 1967.

Fincher, E. B. *The Vietnam War.* Philadelphia: Franklin and Watts, 1980.

FitzGerald, Francis. *Fire in the Lake: The Vietnamese and the Americans in Vietnam.* Boston: Little, Brown, 1972.

Fleming, D. F. *America's Role in Asia.* New York: Dell, 1969.

Francillon, Rene J. *Tonkin Gulf Yacht Club: U.S. Carrier Operations.* Washington, D.C.: Naval Institute Press, 1988.

Frey-Wouters, Ellen, and Robert Laufer. *Legacy of a War: The American Soldier in Vietnam.* New York: M. E. Sharpe, 1986.

Fromkin, David, and James Chace. "What Are the Lessons of Vietnam?" *Foreign Affairs* 63 (Spring 1985): 722–46.

Gabriel, Richard A., and Paul L. Savage. *Crisis in Command: Mismanagement in the Army.* New York: Hill and Wang, 1987.

Galloway, John. *The Kennedys and Vietnam.* Ann Arbor, Mich.: University Microfilms, 1990.

Gallucci, Robert L. *Neither Peace nor Honor: The Politics of American Military Policy
in Vietnam.* Washington, D.C.: Washington Center of Foreign Policy Research Studies in International Affairs, 1975.

Gardner, Lloyd C. *Approaching Vietnam: From World War II Through Dienbienphu.*
New York: Norton, 1989.

Gavin, James. *Crisis Now.* New York: Pantheon, 1968.

Gelb, Lawrence, and Richard K. Betts. *The Irony of Vietnam: The System Worked.*
Washington, D.C.: Brookings Institution, 1979.

Geneste, Marc E. "Vietnam ... A New Type of War?" *United States Naval Institute
Proceedings* 94 (May 1969): 66–77.

Gibson, James W. *The Perfect War: Technowar in Vietnam.* Boston: Atlantic
Monthly, 1986.

Gregory, Barry. *Vietnam Coastal & Riverine Forces.* New York: Borgo Press, 1989.

Grinter, Lawrence E. "South Vietnam: Pacification Denied." *Southeast Asia Spectrum* 3 (July 1975): 49–78.

Grinter, Lawrence E., and Peter M. Dunne. *The American War in Vietnam: Lessons,
Legacies, and Implications for Future Conflicts.* Westport, Conn.: Greenwood
Press, 1987.

Hadley, Arthur T. *The Straw Giant.* New York: Random House, 1968.

Halberstam, David. *The Making of a Quagmire: America and Vietnam During the
Kennedy Era.* New York: Knopf, 1964.

Halberstam, David. *The Best and the Brightest.* New York: Random House, 1972.

Hammel, Eric. *Ambush Valley. I Corps, Vietnam, 1967: The Story of a Marine Infantry
Battalion's Battle for Survival.* Novato, Calif.: Presidio Press, 1990.

Harriman, W. Averell. *America and Russia in a Changing World: A Half Century of
Personal Observation.* Garden City, N.Y.: Doubleday, 1971.

Hayes, S. P., ed. *The Beginning of American Aid to Southeast Asia: The Griffin Mission
of 1950.* Lexington, Mass.: D. C. Heath, 1971.

Hearden, Patrick H. *The Tragedy of Vietnam.* New York: Harper-Collins, 1991.

Heilbrunn, Dr. Otto. "U.S. Strategy in Vietnam." *Ordnance* 52 (January-February
1968): 356–59.

Herring, George C. "The Truman Administration and the Restoration of French
Sovereignty in Indochina." *Diplomatic History* 1 (1977): 97–117.

Herring, George C. "The 'Vietnam Syndrome' and American Foreign Policy."
Virginia Quarterly Review 57 (Winter 1981): 594–612.

Herring, George. "American Strategy in Vietnam: The Postwar Debate." *Military
Affairs* 46 (April 1982): 57–63.

Herring, George C. *America's Longest War: The United States and Vietnam, 1950–
1975.* New York: Knopf, 1986.

Hess, Gary R. "The Military Perspective on Strategy in Vietnam: Harry Summers's *On Strategy* and Bruce Palmer's *The 25-Year War.*" *Diplomatic History*
10 (Winter 1986): 91–106.

Hoang Ngoc Lung, Colonel. *Strategy and Tactics.* Washington, D.C.: U.S. Army
Center of Military History, 1980.

Isaacs, Arnold R. *Without Honor: Defeat in Vietnam and Cambodia.* Baltimore: Johns
Hopkins University Press, 1983.

Isaacson, Walter, and Evan Thomas. *The Wise Men. Six Friends and the World They Made.* New York: Simon and Schuster, 1986.

Joes, Anthony J. *The War for South Vietnam: Nineteen Fifty-four to Nineteen Seventy-five.* Westport, Conn.: Praeger, 1989.

Johnson, Lyndon Baines. *The Vantage Point: Perspectives of the Presidency, 1963–1969.* New York: Holt, Rinehart, and Winston, 1971.

Joseph, Paul. *Cracks in the Empire: State Politics in the Vietnam War.* New York: Columbia University Press, 1987.

Jurika, Stephen, Jr. *From Pearl Harbor to Vietnam: The Memoirs of Admiral Arthur W. Radford.* Stanford, Calif.: Hoover Institution Press, 1980.

Kahin, George McT., and John W. Lewis. *The United States in Vietnam.* New York: Dial Press, 1969.

Kalb, Marvin, and Elie Able. *Roots of Involvement.* New York: Norton, 1971.

Karnow, Stanley. *Vietnam: A History.* New York: Viking, 1984.

Kattenburg, Paul M. *The Vietnam Trauma in American Foreign Policy, 1945–1975.* Rutgers, N.J.: Transaction Books, 1980.

Kattenburg, Paul M. "Reflections on Vietnam: Of Revisionism and Lessons Yet to Be Learned." *Parameters, Journal of the US Army War College* 14 (1984): 42–50.

Kaufmann, William W. *The McNamara Strategy.* New York: Harper and Row, 1964.

Kennan, George. "The Sources of Soviet Power." *Foreign Affairs* 25 (July 1947): 566–82.

Kolko, Gabriel. *Anatomy of a War: Vietnam, the United States, and the Modern Historical Experience.* New York: Pantheon, 1985.

Krepinovich, Andrew F., Jr. *The Army and Vietnam.* Baltimore: Johns Hopkins University Press, 1986.

Lawson, Don. *The War in Vietnam.* Philadelphia: Franklin and Watts, 1978.

Lederer, William J. *Our Own Worst Enemy.* New York: Norton, 1968.

Lee, Sam. *The Perfect War.* New York: Valentine Press, 1990.

Lewallen, John. *Ecology of Devastation: Indochina.* New York: Penguin Books, 1971.

Lewy, Guenter. *America in Vietnam.* New York: Oxford University Press, 1978.

Liska, George. *War and Order: Reflections on Vietnam and History.* Washington, D.C.: Washington Center of Foreign Policy Research Studies in International Affairs, 1989.

Lodge, Henry Cabot. *The Storm Has Many Eyes: A Personal Narrative.* New York: Norton, 1973.

Lomperis, Timothy J. *The War Everyone Lost—And Won: America's Intervention in Vietnam's Twin Struggles.* Baton Rouge: Louisiana State University Press, 1984.

Louis, William Roger. *Imperialism at Bay: The United States and the Decolonization of the British Empire.* New York: Columbia University Press, 1978.

Luttwak, Edward N. "On the Need to Reform American Strategy." In *Planning United States Security: Defense Policy in the Eighties,* ed. Philip S. Kronenberg. New York: Pergamon Press, 1981.

McLaughlin, Martin. *Vietnam and World Revolution: A Trotskyite Analysis.* New York: Labor, 1985.

McQuaid, Kim. *The Anxious Years: America in the Vietnam-Watergate Era.* New York: Basic Books, 1989.

Manhattan, Avro. *Vietnam: Why Did We Go?* New York: Chick, 1984.

Marolda, Edward J., and Oscar P. Fitzgerald. *The United States Navy and the Vietnam Conflict.* 3 vols. Washington, D.C.: U.S. Government Printing Office, 1980–1988.

Marshall, S.L.A. *Battles in the Monsoon: Campaigning in the Central Highlands, South Vietnam, 1966.* Nashville, Tenn.: Battery Press, 1967.

Meuller, John. "Trends in Popular Support for the Wars in Korea and Vietnam." *American Political Science Review* 65 (1971): 358–75.

Meuller, John. "The Search for the 'Breaking Point' in Vietnam." *Strategic Studies* 24 (December 1980): 497–519.

Michael, Stanley J., Jr. "Vietnam: Failure to Follow the Principles of War." *Marine Corps Gazette* 61 (1977): 56–62.

Millett, Allan R., ed. *A Short History of the Vietnam War.* Bloomington: Indiana University Press, 1978.

Milstein, Jeffery S. *Dynamics of the Vietnam War: A Quantitative Analysis and Predictive Computer Simulation.* Columbus: Ohio State University Press, 1974.

Miroff, Bruce. *Pragmatic Illusions: The Presidential Politics of John F. Kennedy.* New York: David Mackay, 1976.

Morrison, Wilbur H. *The Elephant and the Tiger: The Full Story of the Vietnam War.* New York: Hippocrene Books, 1990.

Morrison, Wilbur H. *Vietnam: The Winnable War.* New York: Hippocrene Books, 1990.

Moss, George. *Vietnam. An American Ordeal.* Englewood Cliffs, N.J.: Prentice-Hall, 1989.

Neilands, J. B., ed. *Harvest of Death: Chemical Warfare in Vietnam and Cambodia.* New York: Free Press, 1972.

Nickelsen, Harry. *Vietnam.* New York: Lucent Books, 1989.

Nixon, Richard M. *RN: The Memoirs of Richard Nixon.* New York: Grosset and Dunlap, 1978.

Nixon, Richard M. *No More Vietnams.* New York: Arbor House, 1980a.

Nixon, Richard. *The Real War.* New York: Warner Books, 1980b.

Nixon, Richard M. *1999 Victory Without War.* New York: Simon and Schuster, 1988.

Nolan, Keith William. *Operation Buffalo: USMC Fight for the DMZ.* Novato, Calif.: Presidio Press, 1990.

Nolting, Frederick. *From Trust to Tragedy: The Political Memoirs of Frederick Nolting, Kennedy's Ambassador to Diem's Vietnam.* New York: Praeger, 1988.

O'Donnell, Kenneth, and David Powers. *Johnny, We Hardly Knew Ye.* Boston: Little, Brown, 1978.

Olson, James S., and Randy Roberts. *Where the Domino Fell: America and Vietnam, 1945–1990.* New York: St. Martin's Press, 1991.

Osgood, Robert E. "The Reappraisal of Limited War." *Problems of Modern Strategy* 54 (1969): 41–54.

Palmer, Bruce, Jr. *The 25-Year War: America's Military Role in Vietnam.* Lexington: University Press of Kentucky, 1984.

Palmer, Dave. *Summons of the Trumpet: A History of the Vietnam War from a Military Man's Viewpoint.* Novato, Calif.: Presidio Press, 1978.

Palmer, Gregory. *The McNamara Strategy and the Vietnam War: Program Budgeting in the Pentagon, 1960–1968.* Westport, Conn.: Greenwood Press, 1978.

Parker, William D. *U.S. Marine Corps Civil Affairs in I Corps, Republic of South Vietnam.* Washington, D.C.: U.S. Government Printing Office, 1970.

Paret, Peter, and John W. Shy. "Guerrilla Warfare and United States Military Policy: A Study." In *Components of Defense Policy,* ed. Davis B. Bobrow. Chicago: Rand McNally, 1965.

Parmet, Herbert. *JFK: The Presidency of John F. Kennedy.* New York: Penguin, 1983.

Patti, Archimedes L. *Why Vietnam? Prelude to America's Albatross.* Berkeley: University of California Press, 1981.

Pelz, Stephen. "Alibi Alley: Vietnam as History." *Reviews in American History* 8 (1980): 139–43.

Pelz, Stephen. "John F. Kennedy's 1961 Vietnam War Decisions." *Journal of Strategic Studies* 4 (December 1981): 356–85.

Pike, Douglas. *PAVN: People's Army of Vietnam.* Novato, Calif.: Presidio Press, 1988.

Podhoretz, Norman. *Why We Were in Vietnam.* New York: Simon and Schuster, 1982.

Poole, Peter. *Eight Presidents and Indochina.* New York: Krieger, 1978.

Power, Thomas S. *Design for Survival.* New York: Coward-McCann, 1965.

Prado, John. *The Sky Would Fall: Operation Vulture: The U.S. Bombing Mission in Indochina, 1954.* New York: Dial Press, 1982.

Pustay, John S. *Counterinsurgency Warfare.* New York: Free Press, 1965.

Ravenal, Earl C. *Never Again: Learning from America's Foreign Policy Failures.* Philadelphia: Lippincott, 1978.

Reeves, Thomas C. *A Question of Character: A Life of John F. Kennedy.* New York: Free Press, 1991.

Rhyne, Russell F. "Victory in Vietnam." *Military Review* 50 (February 1970): 37–47.

Ridgway, Matthew B. *Soldier: The Memoirs of Matthew B. Ridgway.* New York: Harper, 1956.

Rostow, W. W. *The Diffusion of Power, 1957–1972.* New York: Macmillan, 1972.

Rotter, Andrew J. *The Path to Vietnam: Origins of the American Commitment to Southeast Asia.* Ithaca, N.Y.: Cornell University Press, 1989.

Rusk, Dean. *As I Saw It. The Memoirs of Dean Rusk.* New York: Norton, 1990.

Rust, William J. *Kennedy in Vietnam: American Foreign Policy, 1960–1963.* New York: Da Capo Press, 1987.

Salinger, Pierre. *With Kennedy.* Garden City, N.Y.: Doubleday, 1966.

Salisbury, Harrison, ed. *Vietnam Reconsidered: Lessons from a War.* New York: Harper and Row, 1984.

Schandler, Herbert Y. "America and Vietnam: The Failure of Strategy." In *Vietnam as History,* ed. Peter Braestrup. Washington, D.C.: Woodrow Wilson International Center for Scholars, 1984.

Schell, Jonathan. *The Village of Ben Suc.* New York: Knopf, 1967.

Schell, Jonathan. *The Military Half: An Account of Destruction in Quang Ngai and Quang Tin.* New York: Knopf, 1968.

Schlesinger, Arthur M., Jr. *A Thousand Days: John F. Kennedy in the White House.* Boston: Houghton Mifflin, 1965.

Schlesinger, Arthur M., Jr. *The Bitter Heritage: Vietnam and American Democracy, 1941–1966.* Boston: Houghton Mifflin, 1967.

Schlight, John. *War in South Vietnam: The Years of the Offensive, 1965–1973.* Washington, D.C.: U.S. Government Printing Office, 1988.

Sevy, Grace, ed. *The American Experience in Vietnam: A Reader.* Norman: University of Oklahoma Press, 1989.

Sharp, Melvin. *The Vietnam War and Public Policy.* Fayetteville, N.Y.: Policy Studies Association, 1991.

Sharp, U.S.G. *Strategy for Defeat: Vietnam in Retrospect.* Novato, Calif.: Presidio Press, 1978.

Sharp, U.S.G., and William Westmoreland. *Report on the War in Vietnam.* Washington, D.C.: U.S. Government Printing Office, 1968.

Sheehan, Neil. *The Bright and Shining Lie: John Paul Vann and America in Vietnam.* New York: Random House, 1988.

Simmons, E. H., ed. *Marines in Vietnam.* Washington, D.C.: U.S. Government Printing Office, 1985.

Simmons, Edwin. *Marines.* New York: Bantam, 1987.

Simpson, Charles M., III. *Inside the Green Berets. The First Thirty Years.* Novato, Calif.: Presidio Press, 1991.

Smith, R. B. *An International History of the Vietnam War. Vol. 1: Revolution Versus Containment, 1955–1961.* New York: St. Martin's Press, 1984.

Smith, R. B. *An International History of the Vietnam War: The Kennedy Strategy.* New York: St. Martin's Press, 1987.

Smith, R. B. *An International History of the Vietnam War: The Johnson Strategy.* New York: St. Martin's Press, 1990.

Sorensen, Theodore. *Kennedy.* New York: Harper and Row, 1965.

Stanton, Shelby L. *The Rise and Fall of an American Army: U.S. Ground Forces in Vietnam, 1965–1973.* Novato, Calif.: Presidio Press, 1985.

Stanton, Shelby L. *Green Berets at War: U.S. Army Special Forces in Asia, 1956–1975.* Novato, Calif.: Presidio Press, 1990.

Stanton, Shelby L. *Anatomy of a Division: 1st Cav in Vietnam.* Novato, Calif.: Presidio Press, 1991.

Sullivan, Michael P. *The Vietnam War: A Study in the Making of American Foreign Policy.* Lexington: University Press of Kentucky, 1985.

Summers, Harry G., Jr. *On Strategy: A Critical Analysis of the Vietnam War.* New York: Dell, 1982.

Summers, Harry G., Jr. "A Strategic Perception of the Vietnam War." *Parameters* 13 (June 1983): 41–46.

Tang, Truong Nhu. *A Vietcong Memoir.* New York: Harcourt Brace Jovanovich, 1985.

Taylor, Maxwell D. *The Uncertain Trumpet.* New York: Norton, 1959.

Taylor, Maxwell D. *Swords and Plowshares.* New York: Norton, 1972.

Taylor, Sandra C. "Reporting History: Journalists and the Vietnam War." *Reviews in American History* 13 (1985): 451–61.

Thayer, Thomas C. *War Without Fronts: The American Experience in Vietnam*. Boulder, Colo.: Westview Press, 1985.

Theis, Wallace J. *When Governments Collide: Coercion and Diplomacy in the Vietnam Conflict, 1964–1968*. Berkeley: University of California Press, 1980.

Thomas, James A. "Limited War: The Theory and the Practice." *Military Review* 53 (1973): 75–82.

Thompson, James Clay. *Rolling Thunder: Understanding Policy and Program Failure*. Chapel Hill: University of North Carolina Press, 1980.

Thompson, Sir Robert. *Defeating Communist Insurgency*. New York: Praeger, 1966.

Thompson, Sir Robert. *No Exit from Vietnam*. New York: David McKay, 1969.

Thompson, W. Scott, and Donaldson D. Frizzell. *The Lessons of Vietnam*. New York: Crane, Russak, 1977.

Thomson, James. "How Could Vietnam Happen? An Autopsy." *Atlantic Monthly* 221 (April 1968): 47–53.

Thorne, Christopher. *Allies of a Kind: The United States, Britain and the War Against Japan, 1941–1945*. New York: Oxford University Press, 1978.

Trager, Frank N. "The Far East." In *National Security: Political, Military, and Economic Strategies in the Decade Ahead*, ed. David M. Abshire. New York: Praeger, 1963.

Trager, Frank N. "Vietnam: The Military Requirements for Victory." *Orbis* 8 (Fall 1964): 563–83.

Trager, Frank N. "The Future of Mainland Asia." *Military Review* 50 (January 1970): 3–16.

Tran Van Don. *Our Endless War. Inside Vietnam*. Novato, Calif.: Presidio Press, 1986.

Turley, William S. *The Second Indochina War: A Short Political and Military History, 1945–1975*. Boulder, Colo.: Westview Press, 1986.

Turner, Kathleen J. *Lyndon Johnson's Dual War: Vietnam and the Press*. Chicago: University of Chicago Press, 1985.

Vance, Cyrus. *Hard Choices*. New York: Random House, 1983.

Villaini, Jim, ed. *Vietnam: An Anthology*. New York: Pig Iron Press, 1982.

Walt, Lewis W. *Strange War, Strange Strategy*. New York: Funk and Wagnalls, 1976.

Westmoreland, William. *A Soldier Reports*. New York: Dell, 1976.

White, Ralph K. *Nobody Wanted War: Misperception in Vietnam and Other Wars*. New York: Doubleday, 1968.

Young, Marilyn B. "Revisionists Revisited: The Case of Vietnam." *Society for Historians of American Foreign Relations Newsletter* 10 (1979): 1–10.

Young, Marilyn B. *The Vietnam Wars, 1945–1990*. New York: Harper-Collins, 1991.

Zaffiri, Samuel. *Hamburger Hill. May 11–20, 1969*. Novato, Calif.: Presidio Press, 1988.

6 The Other War: Counterinsurgency in Vietnam

Steven Head

During White House discussions in the first half of 1965, Lyndon Johnson surveyed top advisors on the options available to the United States regarding Vietnam. The options presented to the president ranged from full-scale military intervention to a limited commitment approach (Berman, 91). Another option offered to Johnson came from Undersecretary of State George Ball, who argued that unless U.S. goals could be achieved within acceptable costs, America should cut its losses and either withdraw from Vietnam or significantly reduce its defense perimeters (Berman, 86). Ball warned that if American troops were committed, they would bog down in the rice paddies of Vietnam, while at the same time slowly blow the country to pieces (Berman, 73). When asked by Lyndon Johnson if withdrawal would result in a loss of credibility for the United States, Ball replied, "It would be worse for the United States to be defeated by a handful of guerrillas" (Berman, 110). The undersecretary's advice was never seriously considered by the president (Berman, 109). Instead, Johnson sided with those individuals who supported escalation of the war.

The United States increased its commitment in Vietnam and fought a conventional war against an unconventional enemy. As George Ball warned, American troops bogged down in Vietnam and blew the country to pieces. The greatest military power in the world was defeated by an enemy who fought a guerrilla war, with the clearly defined objectives of uniting North and South Vietnam and driving out the imperialist Westerners. The tragedy of Vietnam was the failure of American leadership to acknowledge that the strategy of attrition was not working against such an intense and disciplined enemy. While billions of dollars and tens of thousands of lives were wasted trying "to smash a fly with a sledge hammer" (Dunn, 85), the United States should have concentrated its efforts on what was known as the "other war," or counterinsurgency.

Why American political and military leaders failed to develop an effective counterinsurgency policy has been the subject of much debate. Prior to the United States' entry into Vietnam, its leaders witnessed insurgency movements in Central America, the Philippines, Malaya, and French Indochina. While differences in ethnic composition, geography, economic development, and cultural heritage limited the learning value of these prior experiences, a number of general lessons about counterinsurgency were transferable to Vietnam.

Effective counterinsurgency was a time-consuming process that emphasized patience and determination. The objective was not to kill guerrillas but to destroy their underground infrastructure. In guerrilla warfare the infrastructure was the most important weapon of guerrillas since it was the source of most of their supplies and intelligence. In order to destroy the infrastructure, counterinsurgents had to integrate themselves into the local community. Winning the "hearts and minds" of the people placed a premium on unity of command, intelligence, and knowledge of the politics and culture of the threatened population. Unity of command reduced confusion among the various internal and external organizations involved in the counterinsurgency effort. Good tactical intelligence provided the counterinsurgents with information on where the guerrillas were and what they were up to. Knowledge of the politics and culture of the threatened population enabled the counterinsurgents to gain the trust of the people, so their grievances and needs could be determined without offending them.

The counterinsurgents lived and worked with the threatened people, provided them with security, and constantly tried to eliminate the guerrillas' infrastructure. Engagements with the enemy were to be avoided if possible. When fighting occurred, counterinsurgents were to use simple weapons, such as a knife or gun. The worst approach toward insurgency was for counterinsurgents to march into an area and try to blow guerrillas away with massive firepower. Not only would this fail to destroy the guerrillas, but it would kill civilians and destroy their property, further increasing the guerrillas' appeal to the population. These general lessons were new to American officials. Yet, while they acknowledged the importance of winning the hearts and minds of the people, they followed a strategy that did just the opposite and never seriously attacked the guerrilla infrastructure in South Vietnam.

Robert Komer, who headed the Civil Operations and Revolutionary Development Support in Vietnam (CORDS), attributed this failure to develop an effective counterinsurgency strategy to institutional or bureaucratic constraints.[1] The military was a massive bureaucracy, designed to fight a conventional war against the Soviets in Central Europe. Like other bureaucracies, it was resistant to change. When confronted with a new situation, the military tried to make the situation fit its existing structures rather than change its structure to fit the situation (Komer, 17). Vietnam was viewed by most military leaders as a temporary war. They were not about to restructure or reequip their forces for a war that they saw as a diversion from their normal mission of fighting the Soviets (Komer, 73). Since counterinsurgency was not part of the military's institutional repertoire (Komer, 149), winning the hearts and minds of the people was delegated to civilian organizations (Komer, 118). The military was going to fight the Vietcong with conventional warfare. Once this course of action was decided upon, the Vietnam War was guaranteed to undergo Americanization (Komer, 41).

Through "mirror-imaging," the military turned the South Vietnamese army into a conventional fighting machine, which it later made responsible for counterinsurgency (Komer, 41, 145). Instead of keeping civilian casualties to a minimum, the military played out its repertoire or did what it was most capable and experienced at doing by fighting a war of attrition with massive firepower (Komer, 48). It reasoned that since the firepower was available, it might as well be used (Komer, 57, 55). The danger with this type of reasoning was that it increased America's investment in Vietnam and made it more difficult to change the strategy of attrition even when that strategy failed to defeat the enemy. The bulk of resources and manpower continued to go to the big-unit war, while all pacification received was lip service. Even with the establishment of CORDS, which was a civil-military structure, the military continued to view counterinsurgency as a corollary to its big-unit war (Komer, 44).

Andrew Krepinevich theorized that the failure to embrace counterinsurgency was the result of rigid military doctrine or what he called "the concept" (Krepinevich, 4–5). Like the Ten Commandments, the concept was carved in stone. It stated that in war, the government should sacrifice material goods in order to save American lives (Krepinevich, 5)—in other words, "bucks for blood." The concept was based on the premise of a conventional war against the Soviets (Krepinevich, 6). Insurgency was viewed as an abnormal or special situation (Krepinevich, 45). The army intended to keep its main force units out of counterinsurgency so their orientation would remain on the "big war" in Europe (Krepinevich, 43). Vietnam was not vital enough in the eyes of most military leaders to justify a major overhaul of the concept. Everyone expected the war to be short, and no one expected counterinsurgency to be the key to victory. The pacification literature the war did create was made to fit the concept (Krepinevich, 39–40). When the army entered Vietnam in 1965, it was not prepared for the war it was about to fight, and it had no intention of changing its doctrine on warfare.

The army decided to gamble that through attrition it could destroy the Vietcong faster than they could replace their losses (Krepinevich, 177). Great faith was placed on the ability of massive firepower to defeat the enemy (Krepinevich, 118). As the war progressed, the army's answer to any situation became "firepower." If things were not going right, do not question the validity of the concept or change strategy, just increase the intensity of the fighting (Krepinevich, 178). The army believed that if it made a big enough bang, it might bring something down (Krepinevich, 199). True pacification, which emphasized patience instead of weapons and quick results, had no place in the concept. When the marines attempted some legitimate counterinsurgency with their Combined Action Platoons (CAPs), the army accused them of not being offensive-minded (Krepinevich, 198). With this frame of mind, the army never stood a chance against the Vietcong.

Larry Cable also theorized that America's failure at counterinsurgency was the result of doctrine. U.S. counterinsurgency programs were influenced by a belief in high-tech, conventional warfare and from prior experiences with insurgency in Greece (1946–1949), Korea (1950–1953), the Philippines (1946–1954), Malaya (1948–1960), and Central America during the 1920s and 1930s. Each of these past experiences offered valuable lessons on counterinsurgency. The problem with America was that its leaders learned the wrong lessons. Instead of learning from the Philippines and Malaya the political nature of insurgency and the benefits of tactical intelligence, unity of command, and low-intensity fighting, American leadership learned only those lessons that fit into the doctrine of conventional warfare. From the insurgent movements in Greece and Korea, U.S. officials concluded that guerrillas were auxiliaries to a regular military force, sponsored and supported by an outside nation, and the first sign of a conventional attack (Cable, 28, 41). Greece and Korea also taught American leaders that guerrillas could be defeated by a combination of heavy firepower, close air support, and good mobility (Cable 28, 41). Only the marines offered a different approach to counterinsurgency.

From their experience in Central America, the marines concluded that guerrillas did exist without external support and that large search and clear operations were ineffective in fighting insurgency (Cable, 108). Instead, they advocated small, mobile, combined patrols that maximized the firepower and discipline of the marines, and the local knowledge of terrain and culture enjoyed by native personnel (Cable, 107). They recognized the need for civil development in fighting insurgency and supported various public health and education programs (Cable, 108). But the marine approach to guerrilla warfare was at variance with what the army believed (Cable, 108). Because of this difference, their ideas were poorly integrated into the nation's counterinsurgency doctrine (Cable, 5). The United States entered Vietnam believing it was prepared to fight a guerrilla war, when in reality it was a child at counterinsurgency (Cable, 4). With its perception of the Vietcong and the war distorted by faulty doctrine, American leadership was unable to adapt to what confronted them in Vietnam. The best book dealing with the Combined Action Platoon program of the Marine Corps is Michael E. Peterson's *The Combined Action Platoons: The U.S. Marines' Other War in Vietnam* (1989).

To Lyndon Johnson and his aides, Vietnam was a distraction to be resolved as quickly as possible, so they could move on to more important political areas (Cable, 284). The marines, with their slow, low-intensity approach to insurgency, were not appealing to either the president or his advisors (Cable, 284). Instead, doctrine told them that the Vietcong were the advance guard of the North Vietnamese, who were going to launch a massive attack at any moment. Likewise, doctrine said that guerrillas could be defeated by a combination of firepower, air power, and mobility. This combination was very appealing because not only would it defeat the guerrillas but it would also keep the North Vietnamese in line. The president and his advisors opted to use the instruments that could best deliver this combination; the air force and the army. When the war did not end quickly, doctrine told them to apply even more firepower. It never seemed to dawn on most of the Johnson administration that the doctrine might be wrong. They believed in the doctrine, and what they received for their belief was a slow escalation to the war and finally defeat.

Douglas Blaufarb, who worked for the CIA in Vietnam, argued that the failure of counterinsurgency was due to the overpoliticalization and corruption of the Vietnamese.[2] Blaufarb acknowledged that during the early stages of the war there was a lack of counterinsurgency programs, but as the war continued, this problem was corrected. Many of the programs developed would have been successful if politics and corruption had not doomed them.

The Strategic Hamlets program[3] failed because the Ngo family used it as a means for gaining control of village life and to build up the cult of personalism (Blaufarb, 110).[4] Nhu saw the Strategic Hamlets program as a way of forcing the peasants to achieve self-sufficiency (Blaufarb, 111). He also used the program as a means of bypassing the normal ministries in order to gain personal control of the rural apparatus (Blaufarb, 112). The Citizens Irregular Defense Groups (CIDGs) were corrupted and turned into nothing more than groups of mercenaries (Blaufarb, 107).[5] The same thing happened to the Counter Terror Teams (CTTs). They ended up as bodyguards for province chiefs, engaged in petty gangsterism, or served as "enforcers" for local political chiefs (Blaufarb, 211).[6] The Chieu Hoi (open arms) program, the Phoenix program, and the New Rural Life program all failed because of politics and corruption.[7] According to Blaufarb, the examples of pacification programs that failed due to politics and corruption were almost endless.

The most recent look at "the other war" in Vietnam is Zalin Grant's *Facing the Phoenix: The Political Defeat of the United States in Vietnam* (1991). The focus of the book is Tran Ngoc Chau, who headed up pacification programs for several years in South Vietnam and who served as secretary-general of the National Assembly. Chau's work with Edward Lansdale and later with William Colby in counterinsurgency enjoyed many local successes but was eventually destroyed by corrupt local political officials. Chau was betrayed by a brother who was a Vietcong, abandoned by the Central Intelligence Agency, capriciously jailed by President Nguyen Van Thieu, and captured by the North Vietnamese in 1975.

The Vietnamese police were deeply involved in politics throughout the country. They engaged in gangsterism and were viewed as arbitrary and hard-faced when dealing with the public (Blaufarb, 216). In the South Vietnamese army, promotions were made on the basis of friendship, relatives, or bribery, not on merit (Blaufarb, 237). Because of corruption, the rural population saw the South Vietnamese government as arbitrary, capricious, inscrutable, and exploitive (Blaufarb, 219). The solution to South Vietnam's problems was reform. But as Blaufarb noted, reform for Diem or any other subsequent regime was almost impossible while there was a war going on. The only course of action was for America to take control of the war effort and try to stabilize the South Vietnamese government. Only then could reform take place and counterinsurgency proceed, unhindered by corruption or politics.[8]

The British counterinsurgency expert Sir Robert Thompson provided two views on why he believed counterinsurgency failed in Vietnam. When he wrote in the mid–1960s, Thompson faulted the Diem regime for the failure of the Strategic Hamlets program. Nhu had imposed political control from the top instead of winning support from the bottom; he created conflict in the community between youths and elders and failed to eliminate the Vietcong infrastructure in the newly created hamlets (Thompson, *Defeating Communist Insurgency*, 126). The Strategic Hamlets program had gone too far too fast (138). This resulted in provincial forces being overextended and hamlets being created haphazardly over the countryside (138, 141). Thompson also stated that the South Vietnamese government and the United States had broken all the principles of counterinsurgency by creating a large standing army in the country (58). He urged the two governments to avoid the quick-fix approach to counterinsurgency and just face the fact that they were in for a "long, arduous, and protracted struggle" (169).

Writing later in the conflict, Thompson still supported America's involvement in Vietnam (*No Exit from Vietnam*, 11), but now he blamed the United States for the failure of pacification. Thompson attributed this failure to three causes: America's continued failure to understand the nature of the war; certain inherited disadvantages; and weaknesses in the American character (122). The inherited disadvantages were the previous errors committed by the United States, including the creation of a large South Vietnamese army and the failure to develop a competent intelligence organization (122–24). These problems should have been corrected by now, but with escalation, Americans could care less because now they could fight the war their way (125).

Sir Robert Thompson was not the only observer who offered an early criticism of America's flawed political approach in Vietnam. William J. Lederer's *Our Own Worst Enemy* devoted the entire book to examples of American incompetence and arrogance in Vietnam. He wrote: "The United States is so dominated by its technologies and its wealth that it has lost touch with people. The United States believes it can spread democracy and maneuver politics by technology and money only. This may well be a fatal error in the life of our nation" (27). This could be a perfect summation of the American experience in Vietnam.

The most extreme version of American counterinsurgency was the Phoenix program, which Douglas Valentine has described in his book by the same name (1990). The Phoenix program was launched in 1968 and continued until 1972. Its objective was to identify the Vietcong, build support among the local Vietnamese in combatting Vietcong insurgency, and eventually reduce and eliminate the Vietcong as a military and political force. The Phoenix program was administered by the Central Intelligence Agency, the Civil Operations and Revolutionary Development Support office, and the government of South Vietnam. By the end of the program, Phoenix had completed the assassination of more than 20,000 people, but inconsistent record keeping, political abuse of the program in resolving South Vietnamese political disputes, and implementation of a quota system in eliminating the Vietcong resulted in the assassination of thousands of innocent South Vietnamese.

The American character weaknesses that Thompson identified included impatience, impulsiveness, and aggressiveness. They resulted in a desire for quick results, a try-anything-once approach, and a tendency to confuse fast reaction with initiative (125–26). Americans also became emotionally involved in the fighting and believed that anything that saved an American life was acceptable, even if it wasted more lives in the long run (127). In Vietnam, resources were substituted for efficiency and organization (127). When something failed, no one questioned whether it was right or wrong; it was just assumed that resources were inadequate (127).

But the factor that really inhibited counterinsurgency was the United States' continued failure to judge the war correctly. Americans continued to view Vietnam in conventional terms, with a "find 'em and fight 'em" approach that ignored the political aspects of the war. Instead of learning from the Malayan and French experiences, Americans wrote these off as irrelevant and continued to believe the strategy of attrition would bring the North Vietnamese running to the conference table (131–35). But attrition was failing to destroy the Vietcong and North Vietnamese army's main units (144). The only ones who were really suffering from the war of attrition were the South Vietnamese peasants. The result was that attrition benefited the North Vietnamese and Vietcong far more psychologically and politically than it hurt them physically and economically (139). By following a war of attrition, Thompson believed the best the United States could hope for was a stalemate. But a stalemate was no good; for in a political war, if you were not winning, then you were losing (144).

Loren Baritz interpreted the failure of counterinsurgency from a cultural point of view. He believed that there was an American way to war, which was based on the American way of life and culture (Baritz, 8). Americans developed a national myth about themselves, which reflected the belief that they were the saviors of the world (Baritz, 36). Americans were chosen to lead the world in public morality and to teach political virtue (Baritz, 27). It was their job to fight evil in the world. After World War II, that evil was the Soviets (Baritz, 63). The past had taught the Americans that they had to stand up to aggression. In order to avoid another major war, Americans had to win the cold war (Baritz, 75).

Americans also believed that whatever saved American lives and destroyed the enemy was good (Baritz, 49) They began to believe in technology and value technological killing over face-to-face killing (Baritz, 50). This faith in technology soon led to standardized procedures, which left a large bureaucracy to manage it all (Baritz, 47–48). America's war culture was now complete. The national myth told Americans they were good, technology made them strong, and bureaucracy gave them standard operating procedures (Baritz, 54). They were now ready to save Vietnam with the dangerous combination of self-righteousness and high-power technology.

Throughout the war, Americans viewed Vietnam as the victim of external Communist aggression. Because they could not perceive the war as an internal conflict, they fought the way their culture trained them to fight aggressive Communism—with massive doses of firepower. Vietnam was another battle in the cold war, a war Americans believed they had to win if the world was going to be safe. It did not matter that the Vietcong were fighting a political war; Americans assumed the big war could be fought alongside the political war (Baritz, 243). They believed their country was so strong there was no need for them to know about the culture of others (Baritz, 326). Their faith in technology led them to believe that if enough rounds were fired and enough bombs exploded, the enemy would quit. They were to find out the hard way that the North Vietnamese and Vietcong were willing to accept more death than any American thought was rational (Baritz, 325).

Another explanation of why counterinsurgency failed was offered by retired major general Edward Lansdale. He believed counterinsurgency failed because Americans had an attitude problem. If they were going to win the hearts and minds of the people they must change their attitudes toward others. Americans must understand that all people were endowed with certain inalienable rights (Lansdale, 375–76). If they were going to assist other nations, then they needed to build a brotherhood of love, trust, and help with those nations (Lansdale, 369). Americans must realize that it was the manner in which help was given rather than what was given that counted (Lansdale, 366–67). They must learn to follow their political tenets when dealing with Asian countries (Lansdale, 369). Americans preach "In God We Trust" and place their emphasis on material goods and money (Lansdale, 369). If they were going to defeat Communism, Americans should not only be against Communism but stand for something (Lansdale, 369). Victory against insurgency would not come quickly, and Lansdale warned that "people's wars were not for fighters with short attention spans" (Lansdale, 374).

Peter Dunn attributed the failure of counterinsurgency to what he called a "combination of high-level amateurishness and an accompanying massive breakdown of professional and personal integrity" (Dunn, 100). The soldiers who fought in Vietnam had degenerated to the point where they could no longer carry out effective counterinsurgency. Vietnam had turned into a class war with tensions between all layers of commands. Conscripts hated the regulars. Those in the field had no use for headquarters. Staff disliked answering to Washington (Dunn, 102). Cover-ups and lying were widespread, and it was impossible to get the truth from generals (Dunn, 102). The moral decay of the troops manifested itself in increased desertions, mutinous outbreaks in combat units, and the murder of officers (Dunn, 101). Careerism and ticket punching did nothing for officers' leadership ability, just their careers (Dunn, 101). Counterinsurgency, with its emphasis on small, highly disciplined, and intense units, could not function in an atmosphere of such professional decay. Since soldiers were the ones responsible for all pacification in the long run, if they were incompetent or bad, counterinsurgency would fail. Individuals who were on drugs or contemplating desertion or mutiny should not even consider fighting a guerrilla. Likewise, counterinsurgency, which was low-intensity and out of the mainstream of warfare, was no place for officers who were interested only in putting in their time and advancing their careers.

George Herring believed that counterinsurgency failed in Vietnam because American leadership was still influenced by the containment theory (Herring, vii). Containment was based on the premise of halting future advances of Soviet- (later expanded to include Chinese-) inspired Communism. The turmoil in Indochina was viewed as another example of Soviet aggression (Herring, 15). American leadership worried that if Indochina was allowed to fall, the rest of Southeast Asia would follow, with disastrous political, economic, and strategic consequences to the United States (Herring, 25). They decided to draw a line in Indochina, where Communism would not be allowed to cross (Herring, 39). After the Geneva Accords of 1954, that line was drawn in Vietnam. By incorrectly attributing the conflict in Vietnam to external forces, U.S. officials made the war a test case of America's determination to uphold the world order (Herring, 279). In the process of doing this, they placed the nation's credibility on the line (Herring, 279). Because America had to win or suffer an international loss of credibility, its options on how to pursue the war were severely limited (Herring, 279). In essence, the containment theory forced the United States to abandon counterinsurgency and, instead, fight a conventional war.

Timothy Lomperis saw Vietnam as a war for national legitimacy between the South Vietnamese government and the Communists (Lomperis, 159). A government that lacked national legitimacy would be too weak and unstable to meet the challenges of insurgency or manage the assistance from benefactor nations (Lomperis, 10). The side that established legitimacy with the people was the side that would win the war. In Vietnam the Communists were able to do this.

The South Vietnamese government was too inherently weak and dependent on aid from the American "dominators" effectively to claim national legitimacy with the people (Lomperis, 103). Its leaders were viewed as cosmopolitan slobs because of their dress, demeanor, and social background (Lomperis, 162). The Communists—with their humble origins, appearances, and social proximity—were more appealing to the peasants (Lomperis, 162). They exploited the South Vietnamese government's association with the United States to portray themselves as the fighters of foreign intruders and the protectors of the homeland (Lomperis, 163).

Without the support of the people, counterinsurgency, along with attrition, was bound to fail. How can the people's hearts and minds be won when they have no desire for this to take place? America's failure in Vietnam was its inability to recognize the importance of national legitimacy in fighting a war. Instead of trying to measure the numerical strength of the enemy or the body count, officials should have developed charts and numbers that measured how the two opposing sides were meeting the challenges of national legitimacy (Lomperis, 73).

Guenter Lewy argued that the military failed to appreciate the political aspects of the Vietnam War. It did not realize that revolutionary war was different from a conventional war (Lewy, 116). Because of this, the military never developed counterinsurgency capabilities on a large scale (Lewy, 85). Instead, it clung to the illusion that Vietnam was a war that American troops could win if enough power was brought to bear (Lewy, 116).

From the Robert McNamara school of quantitative analysis was Thomas Thayer's explanation of counterinsurgency. Vietnam was a war without fronts (Thayer, 4). In the early stages of the conflict, the United States was not prepared to fight such a war. Because its prior experiences were mostly conventional, it decided to fight that type of war (Thayer, 4). In fighting conventionally, the United States gave top priority to the air and ground wars, while pacification came in a distant third (Thayer, 26). But as the war progressed, some officials began to doubt the validity of attrition. Realizing that attrition was not going to defeat the enemy, they turned their attention toward pacification. With the establishment of CORDS in 1967, pacification began to make great strides in securing the population (Thayer, 137). How does Thayer know great strides were made? Why, the numbers told him so.[9] Then why did South Vietnam fall in 1975? According to Thayer, the South Vietnamese failed to develop the ability to win (Thayer, 257). They never faced up to their peril or made the efforts to pull themselves together and keep the Communists from winning (Thayer, 257). Thayer probably has the numbers to back this up, too.

William Colby blamed the failure of early attempts at counterinsurgency on institutional and political constraints (Colby, 365). The institutional constraints were the same as Robert Komer's and were taken from his book, *Bureaucracy Does Its Thing*. The political constraints were the result of American leadership's inability to understand the political nature of the war. The military was unable to integrate political factors into its war strategy (Colby, 372). It failed to understand that the foundations of good counterinsurgency were intelligence, an understanding of the threatened country's culture, low-intensity warfare, and interaction with the police (Colby, 367, 372). Because the military could not adapt to fighting a guerrilla war, it placed great faith in technology and its ability to crush the Communists into submission (Colby, 371). The instability of the South Vietnamese government was another factor that resulted in a strategy of attrition instead of counterinsurgency (Colby, 366). Not until the immediate threat to the government of South Vietnam was overcome could effective counterinsurgency be pursued. Yet even with all the setbacks, by the early 1970s, according to Colby, the war was being won.

The establishment of CORDS had placed pacification on the correct path, and every year more of the countryside was judged secure.[10] In the spring of 1972, the South Vietnamese army was put to the test when

North Vietnam launched a massive offensive into South Vietnam. According to Colby, the South Vietnamese army passed the test because it repulsed the attack without the aid of American ground troops (Colby, 321). Colby did not consider American support in the form of ammunition, fuel, helicopters, and the massive U.S. air strikes against the North Vietnamese as playing a significant part in South Vietnam's victory (Colby, 320–21). He did not make the connection that without American support South Vietnam could not stand on its own two feet, let alone win the war. That was the reason, when South Vietnam finally fell in 1975, Colby blamed the antiwar movement for its collapse. It was the antiwar proponents who caused the United States to break its promise to help South Vietnam fight off external aggression (Colby, 325–55). He truly believed that if America would have hung in just a little longer, South Vietnam could have been saved.

Colonel Harry Summers took a completely different approach to the topic of counterinsurgency. He argued that counterinsurgency was overrated and oversold. Too much time was spent on winning the hearts and the minds of the people. Instead, that time should have been devoted to destroying the war-making ability of the North Vietnamese army and the Vietcong. When the United States became involved in Vietnam, most of its attention was focused on containing Soviet and Chinese Communism (Summers, 98). Since America's attention was diverted, clearly defined political objectives of what the United States was going to accomplish in Vietnam were never developed (Summers, 98). This lack of purpose made the United States vulnerable to the tactical smoke screen of insurgency (Summers, 90). American military leadership believed that the guerrilla movement in Vietnam was a strategy in itself (Summers, 86). They failed to remember that guerrillas were adjuncts to a conventional army with the purpose of harassing, delaying, and diverting the attention of the larger forces (Summers, 74). Because of their misperception of the Vietcong, American leaders made the military responsible for counterinsurgency instead of using it to destroy the North Vietnamese army (Summers, 79). In effect, the army concentrated its efforts on the symptom—guerrilla warfare—and not on the illness—North Vietnam. It was only after the fall of South Vietnam that American leaders realized the true nature of the war and realized that the Vietcong were only a means to an end (Summers, 96).

Counterinsurgency was not the job of the army. It should have been left either to civilian management or to the South Vietnamese. The job of the U.S. military was to protect allied nations from external threats. Internal security was the responsibility of the threatened nations (Summers, 75). By fighting a war of counterinsurgency, America followed a defensive strategy with a negative aim (Summers, 88). The United States lost in Vietnam because it did not fight to win, only to contain.

While each writer advanced a particular theory as to why counterinsurgency failed, several common themes emerged. Americans believed the war was going to be quick, misjudged the enemy and the nature of the war, and had an undying faith in the superiority of technology. Also, in the process of trying to quantify the war effort, Americans turned the Vietnamese into statistics and ended up losing touch with the very people they were trying to save.

The United States entered Vietnam with the support and blessings of its citizens. President Johnson's handling of the Gulf of Tonkin incident was approved by 85 percent of the public (Barnet, 338). As America's commitment continued to increase, support for the war still remained stable through mid–1966 (Barnett, 339–40). There was no real reason for a majority of Americans to oppose the war. The United States was fighting against the expansion of Communism, and officials told the public that the war was not going to last long. The United States was the greatest military power in the world. It had defeated the Germans and Japanese in World War II and stopped the expansion of Communism in Korea. There was no way a bunch of lightly armed guerrillas could last for an extended period of time against the military might of the United States. If the war was going to be over quickly, why engage in counterinsurgency?

The Filipino and Malayan experiences confirmed that counterinsurgency could take years to defeat a guerrilla movement. It took considerable time to establish an intelligence network and lines of communication and to integrate the civil and military aspects of the pacification effort. In a war that was going to last, at the most, only eighteen months, effective counterinsurgency would have been a waste of time and money. Why Americans accepted the idea of a quick war was the result of underestimating the enemy and having too much faith in technology's ability to win a war.

Americans believed that once they used the firepower of their war machine, the Vietcong and North Vietnamese would recognize the futility of fighting. If the enemy did persist in fighting, all the United States had to do was increase the intensity of the conflict. Sooner or later the Communists would realize that they could not win and were risking total annihilation. Humans were not equal to machines, and Americans reasoned that if they were faced with the same situation, they would stop fighting and try to negotiate a settlement. What Americans failed to realize was that the enemy had more at stake in this war than they did.

The Vietcong and the North Vietnamese were fighting to unite their country and free it from foreign domination and influence. If the United States lost, it would pack up and go home. The worst thing that could happen was that Americans might lose some prestige. The Vietcong and North Vietnamese believed if they lost, they would lose everything. They were willing to do whatever it took to win. This included accepting more death and destruction than Americans believed possible. While the U.S. war machine did its job and killed thousands, it was never able to kill enough to overcome the enemy's determination to win at all costs. As Robert Komer noted, once America had invested billions in resources and thousands in lives, it would become more difficult to change strategy (Komer, 71). Abandoning the war of attrition for counterinsurgency would have been an admission that technology was not all-powerful, that resources had been wasted, and that Americans had died in vain.

America's misperception about the significance of the war also inhibited the development of counterinsurgency. U.S. officials would not accept the idea that Vietnam was only an internal conflict. Instead, they persisted in viewing the war as another example of Soviet or Chinese Communist expansion. By doing this, they blew the significance of Vietnam out of proportion. The Vietcong were not just guerrillas but agents of the North Vietnamese. Their presence in South Vietnam could mean only one thing: a massive military attack from the North was imminent. There was also the possibility that the Soviets or the Chinese might be part of this invasion. If the United States was possibly going to fight another superpower, then it would need a conventional army in South Vietnam. By turning Vietnam into another Korea, American leaders basically wrote off any real attempts at counterinsurgency.

The "big unit" war was going to receive the bulk of the resources and manpower, and officials would be able to justify this. They could argue, What if America pursued counterinsurgency? This would require a deescalation of the war effort. Then what if the big attack came? The Communists would sweep through Vietnam, all because the American military was trying to win the hearts and minds of the people instead of trying to crush the enemy. When General Westmoreland stated that he did not have the resources to engage in counterinsurgency, he was not lying. It required more resources and manpower than Americans were willing to provide at the time. Preparing for the big conventional invasion and conducting a meaningful pacification program at the same time were impossible because of resource limitations. When faced with the choice between conventional war or counterinsurgency, officials opted for the strategy they knew had worked in the past—conventional warfare.

Loren Baritz stated that technology led to bureaucracy, which then produced standard operation procedures for the technology (Baritz, 54). Once a society had its standard operation procedures, it needed systems analysts to measure their effectiveness. During Vietnam the systems analyst finally reached maturity. Just about every aspect of the war was quantified. Success was measured by the body count, number of rounds fired, and the tonnage of bombs dropped. Computer programs stated that if *x* amount of firepower was applied, then *x* amount of destruction would take place. Officials were so engrossed in the numbers that they forgot the war involved people. They tried quantitatively to measure determination, apathy, and suffering. In the process, they turned pacification into an equation. The Vietnamese ceased to be humans and, instead, became numbers.

Noam Chomsky, the MIT intellectual and opponent of the war, wrote, "Opposition to the war in Vietnam is based very largely on its cost, and on the failure of American power to crush Vietnamese resistance" (Chomsky, 17). He was correct. Even the critics of American policy spent their time debating whether America received an acceptable return on its investment. Most agreed that the strategy of attrition was wrong, not because it caused human suffering, but rather because it did not win the war. If the fear of Soviet or Chinese intervention had not been present, most Americans would have supported any strategy, regardless of the hardship it caused the Vietnamese, that guaranteed victory. It was only when American boys began to die in large numbers and no victory was in sight that opposition to war grew. How can a nation seriously consider winning the hearts and minds of the people when it could care less whether those people lived or died? America's insensitivity to the Vietnamese may have been its most significant hindrance to effective counterinsurgency.

NOTES

1. According to Robert Komer, CORDS was a successful pacification effort and an example of how to overcome institutional constraints (118–21, 151). But CORDS was established by Komer, and he headed the organization during 1967 and 1968. His bias in favor of CORDS was apparent by his downplaying of the effects Tet–1968 had on pacification efforts from 1967 to 1972. The massive Vietcong losses suffered during Tet made pacification after Tet seem more successful than it really was.

2. Douglas Blaufarb's biases for the CIA and its programs were clearly apparent. While his theory on corruption and overpoliticalization had many good points, there were other writers who argued that many CIA pacification programs failed because they were weak from the start.

3. The Strategic Hamlets program was a national program to organize local hamlets for self-defense and to provide a new social and political base to Vietnam (Colby, 384–85).

4. Personalism was a combination of Western individualism and the collectivism of Marxism. It developed the cult of personality and emphasized personal morality, strong family life, and the merging of individual goals into a common communal purpose (Blaufarb, 110).

5. Citizens Irregular Defense Groups were an ad hoc program that mobilized local population throughout the country for self-defense and development (Colby, 384).

6. Counter Terror Teams were established by the CIA to combat Vietcong terrorism (Blaufarb, 211).

7. Chieu Hoi was a South Vietnamese amnesty program for Communist defectors (Colby, 393). The Phoenix program was an intelligence coordination to identify and combat the secret Vietcong infrastructure (Colby, 408–9). It was also accused of promoting terrorism and assassination. The New Rural Life program was another version of the Strategic Hamlets program.

8. In order to stabilize South Vietnam, the United States would have to use massive firepower, which would thwart pacification efforts and destabilize the South Vietnamese government. It was a massive catch–22. In order to save Vietnam, the United States would have to destroy it.

9. Thayer actually devoted eighty pages (pp. 137–217) to quantifying the success of pacification from 1967 to 1972. While his effort was inspiring, it was also boring. Thayer needed to be reminded that based on the numbers, the United States had won the war by 1964 (Barnet, 337).

10. For a detailed explanation of the success of pacification, read Colby, pp. 205–23 and 259–313. Colby, like his friend Komer, was very biased in favor of CORDS.

BIBLIOGRAPHY

Anderson, Charles R. *Vietnam: The Other War*. New York: Warner Books, 1990.

Andrews, William R. *The Village War: Vietnamese Communist Revolutionary Activities in Dinh Tuong Province, 1960–1964*. Columbia: University of Missouri Press, 1973.

Armbruster, Frank E., and Herman Kahn, eds. *Can We Win in Vietnam?* New York: Praeger, 1968.

Asprey, Robert B. *War in the Shadows: The Guerrilla in History*. 2 vols. New York: Doubleday, 1975.

Bank, Aaron. *From OSS to Green Berets: The Birth of Special Forces*. Novato, Calif.: Presidio Press, 1990.

Baritz, Loren. *Backfire*. New York: Morrow, 1985.

Barnet, Richard J. *The Rockets' Red Glare*. New York: Simon and Schuster, 1990.

BDM Corporation. *A Study of Strategic Lessons Learned in Vietnam*. New York: MacLean, 1979–1980.

Berman, Larry. *Planning a Tragedy*. New York: Norton, 1982.

Blaufarb, Douglas S. *The Counterinsurgency Era*. New York: Free Press, 1977.

Brandon, Henry. *The Anatomy of Error*. New York: Gambit Books, 1969.

Browne, Malcolm W. *The New Face of War*. New York: Bobbs-Merrill, 1968.

Burchett, Wilfred G. *Vietnam: Inside Story of the Guerrilla War*. New York: International, 1965.

Cable, Larry E. *Conflict of Myths: The Development of American Counterinsurgency Doctrine and the Vietnam War*. New York: New York University Press, 1986.

Central Intelligence Agency. *The Highlanders of South Vietnam, 1954–1965*. June 15, 1966 (Secret; declassified August 1974). Washington, D.C.: U.S. Government Printing Office, 1974.

Chomsky, Noam. *American Power and the New Mandarins*. New York: Pantheon Books, 1969.

Clutterbuck, Brigadier Richard L. *The Long War: Counterinsurgency in Malaya and Vietnam*. New York: Praeger, 1966.

Colby, William, and James McCargar. *Lost Victory: A Firsthand Account of America's Sixteen-Year Involvement in Vietnam*. Chicago: Contemporary Books, 1989.

Conley, Michael James. *The Communist Insurgent Structure in Vietnam: A Study of Organization and Strategy*. Washington, D.C.: Center for Research in Social Systems, American University, July 1967.

Cooper, Chester L., ed. *The American Experience with Pacification*. 3 vols. Arlington, Va.: Institute for Defense Analysis, 1972.

Currey, Cecil B. *Edward Lansdale: The Unquiet American*. Boston: Houghton Mifflin, 1988.

Delaney, Captain Robert F., USNR. "Reflections on Political Communication and Insurgency." *Naval War College Review* 22 (December 1969): 3–9.

Dunn, Peter W. *Armed Forces and Modern Counterinsurgency*. New York: St. Martin's Press, 1985.

Elliot, David W. P., and W. A. Stewart. *Pacification and the VC System in Dinh Tuong*. Santa Monica, Calif.: Rand Corporation Collection, RM–5708 ISA/ARPA, January 1969.

Fitzsimons, Louise. *The Kennedy Doctrine*. New York: Random House, 1972.

Galula, David. *Counterinsurgency Warfare: Theory and Practice*. New York: Praeger, 1962.

Gelb, Leslie H., and Richard K. Betts. *The Irony of Vietnam: The System Worked*. Washington, D.C.: Brookings Institution, 1979.

George Washington University Staff. *Bureaucracy at War: U.S. Performance in the Vietnam Conflict*. Boulder, Colo.: Westview Press, 1985.

Greene, T. N. *The Guerrilla and How to Fight Him*. New York: Praeger, 1962.

Grant, Zalin. *Facing the Phoenix: The Political Defeat of the United States in Vietnam*. New York: Norton, 1991.

Grinter, Lawrence E. "How They Lost: Doctrines, Strategies, and Outcomes of the Vietnam War." *Asian Survey* 15 (December 1975): 114–32.

Grinter, Lawrence, and Peter Dunn, eds. *The American War in Vietnam: Lessons, Legacies and Implications for Future Conflicts*. Westport, Conn.: Greenwood, 1987.

Hammel, Eric. *Ambush Valley. I Corps, Vietnam 1967: The Story of a Marine Infantry Battalion's Battle for Survival*. Novato, Calif.: Presidio Press, 1990.

Havron, M. Doan, ed. *Constabulary Capabilities for Low-Level Conflict*. MacLean: Human Sciences Research, HSR-RR–69/1-Ser., April 1969.

Heilbrunn, Otto. *Partisan Warfare*. New York: Praeger, 1962.

Heilbrunn, Otto. *Warfare in the Enemy's Rear*. New York: Praeger, 1963.

Herring, George C. *America's Longest War: U.S. Performance in the Vietnam Conflict*. New York: Knopf, 1986.

Herrington, Stuart A. *Silence Was a Weapon: The Vietnam War in the Villages*. New York: Ivy Books, 1987.

Herz, Martin F. *The Vietnam War in Retrospect*. Washington, D.C.: Georgetown University School of Foreign Service, 1985.

Hetmann, Hans, Jr., and William W. Whitson. *Can and Should the U.S. Preserve a Military Capability for Revolutionary Conflict?* Santa Monica, Calif.: Rand Corporation Collection. R–940-ARPA, January 1972.

Hilsman, Roger. *To Move a Nation.* Garden City, N.Y.: Doubleday, 1967.

Hunt, Richard A., and Richard H. Schultz, Jr., eds. *Lessons from an Unconventional War: Reasoning U.S. Strategies for Future Conflicts.* New York: Pergamon, 1982.

Isaacs, Arnold R. *Without Honor: Defeat in Cambodia and Vietnam.* Baltimore: Johns Hopkins University Press, 1983.

Jenkins, Brian M. *The Unchangeable War.* Santa Monica, Calif.: Rand Corporation Collection, RM–6278–1-ARPA, September 1972.

Johnson, Chalmers A. "Civilian Loyalties and Guerrilla Warfare." *Asian Survey* 7 (June 1968): 435–47.

Johnson, John J., ed. *The Role of the Military in Underdeveloped Countries.* Princeton, N.J.: Princeton University Press, 1962.

Karnow, Stanley. *Vietnam.* New York: Viking Press, 1983.

Kelly, F. S. *U.S. Army Special Forces, 1961–1971.* Washington, D.C.: U.S. Government Printing Office, 1973.

Koch, Jeannette A. *The Chieu Hoi Program in South Vietnam.* Santa Monica, Calif.: Rand Corporation Collection, R–1172/1-ARPA, May 1975.

Komer, Robert W. *Bureaucracy Does Its Thing: Institutional Constraints on U.S.-GVN Performance in Vietnam.* Santa Monica, Calif.: Rand Corporation Collection, R–967-ARPA, August 1972.

Krepinevich, Andrew F. *The Army and Vietnam.* Baltimore: Johns Hopkins University Press, 1986.

Lansdale, Edward G. *In the Midst of Wars: An American's Mission to Southeast Asia.* New York: Harper and Row, 1972.

Lederer, William J. *Our Own Worst Enemy.* New York: Norton, 1968.

Lewy, Guenter. *America in Vietnam.* New York: Oxford University Press, 1978.

Lomperis, Timothy J. *The War Everyone Lost—And Won.* Baton Rouge: Louisiana State University Press, 1984.

McChristian, J. *The Role of Military Intelligence, 1965–1967.* Washington, D.C.: U.S. Government Printing Office, 1974.

McCuen, John J. *The Art of Counter-Revolutionary War.* Harrisburg, Pa.: Stackpole, 1966.

The Marines in Vietnam, 1954–1973: An Anthology and Annotated Bibliography. Washington, D.C.: History and Museums Division Headquarters, U.S. Marine Corps, 1974.

Millstein, Jeffrey. *Dynamics of the Vietnam War.* Columbus: Ohio State University Press, 1974.

Nighswonger, William A. *Rural Pacification in Vietnam.* New York: Praeger, 1966.

Osborne, Milton E. *Strategic Hamlets in South Vietnam: A Survey and Comparison.* Ithaca, N.Y.: Cornell University Press, 1965.

Osgood, Robert E. *Limited War Revisited.* Boulder, Colo.: Westview Press, 1979.

Palmer, David Richard. *Summons of the Trumpet: U.S.—Vietnam in Perspective.* Novato, Calif.: Presidio Press, 1978.

Parker, F. Charles, IV. *Vietnam: Strategy for a Stalemate.* Washington, D.C.: Washington Institute Press, 1988.

The Pentagon Papers. Gravel Edition. Boston: Beacon, 1971.

Petersen, Michael E. *The Combined Action Platoons: The U.S. Marines' Other War in Vietnam.* Westport, Conn.: Praeger, 1989.

Pike, Douglas. *War, Peace, and the Viet Cong.* Cambridge: Harvard University Press, 1969.

Prados, John. *The Sky Would Fall: Operation Vulture—The U.S. Bombing Mission in Indochina, 1954.* New York: Dial Press, 1983.

Race, Jeffrey. "How They Won." *Asian Survey* 10 (August 1970): 628–51.

Race, Jeffrey. *War Comes to Long An: Revolutionary Conflict in a Vietnamese Province.* Berkeley: University of California Press, 1972.

Sanson, Robert L. *The Economics of Insurgency in the Mekong Delta of Vietnam.* Cambridge: MIT Press, 1970.

Scoville, Thomas W. "United States Organization for Pacification Advice and Support in Vietnam, 1954–1968." Ph.D. diss., Massachusetts Institute of Technology, 1976.

Sharp, Ulysses S. Grant. *Strategy for Defeat: Vietnam in Retrospect.* San Rafael, Calif.: Presidio Press, 1978.

Simpson, Charles M., III. *Inside the Green Berets. The First Thirty Years: A History of the U.S. Army Special Forces.* Novato, Calif.: Presidio Press, 1990.

Summers, Harry G. *On Strategy.* Novato, Calif.: Presidio Press, 1982.

Tanham, George K. "Some Insurgency Lessons from Southeast Asia." *Orbis* 16 (Fall 1972): 646–59.

Tanham, George K., ed. *War Without Guns: American Civilians in Rural Vietnam.* New York: Praeger, 1966.

Thayer, Thomas C. *War Without Fronts: The American Experience in Vietnam.* Boulder, Colo.: Westview Press, 1985.

Thompson, Sir Robert. *Defeating Communist Insurgency: The Lessons of Malaya and Vietnam.* New York: Praeger, 1966.

Thompson, Sir Robert. *No Exit from Vietnam.* New York: David McKay, 1969.

Thompson, Sir Robert. *Peace Is Not at Hand.* London: Chatto and Windus, 1974.

Thompson, W. Scott, and Donaldson D. Frizzell, eds. *The Lessons of Vietnam.* New York: Crane Russak, 1977.

Tolson, J. J. *Airmobility, 1961–1971.* Washington, D.C.: U.S. Government Printing Office, 1973.

U.S. Congress, Hearings Before the Senate Committee on Foreign Relations, 91st Congress, Second Session, February 17–20, 1970. *Civil Operations and Revolutionary Development Support.* Washington, D.C.: U.S. Government Printing Office, 1970.

Valentine, Douglas. *The Phoenix Program.* New York: Morrow, 1990.

Valeriano, Colonel Napoleon D., and Lt. Colonel Charles T. R. Bohannan. *Counterguerrilla Operations: The Philippine Experience.* New York: Praeger, 1962.

Walt, Lewis. *Strange War, Strange Strategy.* New York: Funk and Wagnalls, 1970.

Walton, Richard J. *Cold War and Counter-Revolution: The Foreign Policy of John F. Kennedy.* New York: Viking, 1972.

Wise, David, and Thomas B. Ross. *The Invisible Government.* New York: Random House, 1964.

Wolf, Charles, Jr. "The Logic of Failure: A Vietnam Lesson." *Journal of Conflict Resolution* 16 (September 1972): 397–403.

PART III
The Conduct of the War

7   Vietnam and International Relations

Gary M. Bell

During the course of his academic and scholarly career, Henry Kissinger came to a number of important conclusions about international relations. In his 1957 book *Nuclear War and Foreign Policy*, he advocated the use of tactical nuclear weapons in a total defense strategy. The filmmaker Stanley Kubrick, who met Kissinger at a Cambridge cocktail party, used him as the role model for the Nazi-saluting, German-accented megalomanic in his 1964 dark comedy *Dr. Strangelove*, a satire on the nuclear arms race. In his doctoral dissertation, a study of the Congress of Vienna of 1815, Kissinger had argued that diplomacy was a complicated, inter-related balancing act among the major powers. Any significant event in the life of one power automatically affected every other major power. The achievement of absolute superiority by one power imposed absolute insecurity on every other power and destabilized international politics. Every nation on earth had the right to legitimacy and security; they were prerequisites to peace.

Kissinger had a strong disdain for moralistic assumptions that prevented long-term solutions to international rivalries. Woodrow Wilson's moral diplomacy undermined the Treaty of Versailles and indirectly contributed to World War II. The irrational fears of McCarthyism in the 1950s were another case. Moralistic images replaced rational calculations and prevented the United States, the Soviet Union, and China from dealing successfully with one another. Regardless of institutional differences, the major powers had to respect their rights to govern themselves internally without external, ideological interference.

Kissinger also believed that the entrenched bureaucracies of the foreign policy establishments were tradition-bound and inflexible. Creative diplomacy, he believed, could not come out of the State Department or the Kremlin. It required a charismatic leader at home who could shape public opinion, develop new policies, and force the bureaucracies to implement them. The first requirement of a successful diplomat was "legitimizing a policy within the government apparatus." As national security advisor under Richard Nixon, Kissinger wanted to seize the foreign policy initiative from the State Department. What Kissinger claimed was happening in the United States was also occurring in all of the other major capitals of the world.

More so than any other "minor" conflict in world history, the Vietnam War revealed the complex interrelationships between the world powers and the global economy. R. B. Smith's series of volumes entitled *An International History of the Vietnam War* (1983–1990) deal with those complex interrelationships. The Geneva Conference of 1954 first revealed how all of the major powers became involved in the early stages of the conflict in Indochina. R. H. Fifield's *The Diplomacy of Southeast Asia, 1945– 1958* and Robert F. Randle's *Geneva 1954: The Settlement of the Indochinese War* deal with the peace conference that ended the first Indochinese war. All of the parties involved had their own agendas. The United States was basically opposed to any arrangement that yielded, in Secretary of State John Foster Dulles's words, "one inch of territory to the Communists." Ho Chi Minh and the Vietminh wanted a complete political settlement leading to the withdrawal of French forces and establishment of a new, independent Vietnamese nation. The French wanted only a cease-fire and time to work to retain their foothold in Indochina. The Chinese wanted to partition Vietnam. They did not want a united Vietnam—French or Vietnamese—to the south. Only the Soviet Union and Great Britain approached the talks at Geneva open-mindedly. Both of them wanted to make sure that the conflict did not get out of hand and become a confrontation between the superpowers.

Eventually, Sir Anthony Eden of Great Britain and Vyacheslav Molotov of the Soviet Union played peacemakers. Along with Chou Enlai of China, they convinced Pham Van Dong and the Vietminh to accept a temporary partitioning of Vietnam, to be followed by reunification elections. The French and Vietminh hotly debated the question of where to divide Vietnam and when to hold the elections. France wanted the dividing line as far north and the elections as far into the future as possible. Ho Chi Minh wanted the dividing line as far south and the elections as soon as possible. The Geneva Accords eventually divided Vietnam at the 17th parallel into North Vietnam and South Vietnam. With that division in place, the Accords imposed a cease-fire and provided for the withdrawal of French forces from North Vietnam and Vietminh forces from South Vietnam within the next 300 days. New foreign troop placements were prohibited throughout Vietnam, and both the French and Vietminh were to withdraw their troops from Laos and Cambodia. Finally, the Accords provided for free elections in 1956, with the goal of reunifying the two Vietnams. An International Control Commission, composed of representatives from India, Canada, and Poland, was established to monitor compliance with the Accords.

Although the French hoped to rebuild their Indochina empire using South Vietnam as a base, their hopes were never realized. Within two years of the Geneva settlement, Ngo Dinh Diem, the new leader of South Vietnam, had insisted on their withdrawal, and the United States had supported his demand. France left Vietnam for good. From that point on, the French observed the growing American involvement with a unique vantage point. Marianna P. Sullivan, in *France's Vietnam Policy: A Study in French-American Relations*, provides an excellent interpretation of the French role. Throughout the late 1950s and much of the 1960s, France was highly critical of the American escalation of the war. France knew of Vietnamese tenacity and how expensive the war would be, and she doubted whether the United States could achieve its political objectives. Archimedes Patti's *Why Vietnam? Prelude to America's Albatross* shows how well the French knew of the Vietnamese willingness to stay the course. Charles De Gaulle openly criticized American policy and also worried about the expansion of American hegemony in southern and southeastern Asia. His demand in 1966 for an American withdrawal reflected his hopes that French influence, if not French imperialism, in the region could be revived.

After the resignation of Charles De Gaulle in 1969, French policy became less anti-American and more neutral. France still believed that an American withdrawal was inevitable, but they were more diplomatic in their suggestions. North Vietnam had a great deal of trust in the French efforts, and between 1969 and 1973 France played a key role in helping to negotiate the final settlement among the United States, South Vietnam, and North Vietnam. French motives, of course, were not altogether altruistic. They, too, realized that if the United States did withdraw from the area, a power vacuum would result, and the French wanted to be one of the European powers to help fill it.

When South Vietnam eventually fell to North Vietnam in 1975, however, it was not the French who filled the vacuum. Instead, it was the Soviet Union. The origins of the Vietnam War reach back to the cold war assumption on the part of the United States that the Soviet Union was expansionist and inspiring many of the anticolonial rebellions occurring throughout the world. The containment policy was designed to deal with Soviet aggression, and it resulted in the Truman Doctrine, Marshall Plan, Berlin airlift, NATO, and the Korean War. The irony is that the Soviet Union was preoccupied with Europe after World War II, and Josef Stalin viewed Ho Chi Minh's campaign in Vietnam as more nationalistic than Communistic. The Soviet Union did not extend diplomatic recognition to the Democratic Republic of Vietnam (DRV) until 1950; Vietnam was very much outside the Soviet area of interest. Therefore, Moscow provided rhetorical support but little else for the Vietminh.

In 1954 the Soviet Union cochaired, along with Great Britain, the Geneva Conference to settle the Vietnamese question. Actually, the Soviets pursued a pro-Western course at Geneva. At the time they were currying French opinion since French Communists had done well in recent elections. Also, they wanted to dissuade France from joining the American-led European Defense Community with its plans for rearming West Germany. Finally, the Russians were interested in reaching an accommodation, if possible, with the United States. For these reasons the Soviet Union worked for an armistice acceptable to the French and agreed to a partitioning of Vietnam between a Communist North and a non-Communist South. Later, when South Vietnam and the United States balked on holding the prescribed elections, the Soviet Union carefully sidestepped Ho Chi Minh's pleas for assistance.

In his book *Vietnam and the Soviet Union: Anatomy of an Alliance*, Douglas Pike deals with the role the Soviet Union played in the international politics of the Vietnam War. Soviet interest in Indochina intensified as the independence of the People's Republic of China increased in the 1950s. Vietnam became an important counterweight to expanding Chinese influence, and, because of the historic Sino-Vietnamese rivalry, the counterweight was relatively easy to lift. Gradually the Soviet Union began to increase its shipment of military equipment, training personnel, and economic assistance to North Vietnam, and by the late 1960s Moscow was far and away the largest supplier of North Vietnam and the Vietcong. The assistance exceeded $1 billion a year by 1970. At the same time, the Soviet Union hoped that the American preoccupation with Vietnam would distract her from European concerns.

North Vietnam was unusually astute in maintaining a diplomatic balance between the Soviet Union and China, neatly playing them off against each other in a diplomatic minuet. For the Soviets, North Vietnam was maddeningly independent, especially in 1968 when Ho Chi Minh condemned the invasion of Czechoslovakia. Still, the Democratic Republic of Vietnam (North Vietnam) leaned more to Moscow than to Peking, not only because Moscow was a more reliable supplier of military equipment but because of ancient fears of Chinese expansion into Indochina. Also, the Cultural Revolution in the People's Republic of China left China too weak and internally preoccupied to be very reliable.

The United States never appreciated the independence of Vietnamese Communism. Presidents Lyndon B. Johnson and Richard Nixon both sought to have the Soviet Union restrain North Vietnam, assuming that Moscow had direct influence in Hanoi. What few understood was that Hanoi would pursue policies sanctioned neither by Moscow nor by Peking and, in fact, notoriously irritated the Russians throughout the war by taking their aid, expressing gratitude for it, but keeping them in the dark about their own war plans. The cold war was not really a monolithic event, as so many Americans believed. As Robin Edmonds points out in *Soviet Foreign Policy 1962–1973: The Paradox of a Superpower*, the Russians actually had relatively little influence over North Vietnam, and even that influence was tempered by North Vietnam's willingness to play the Russians off against the Chinese. Leif Rosenberger's book *Vietnam and the Soviet Union: An Uneasy Alliance* clearly points out how tenuous that alliance really was.

Toward the end of the war, the Soviet Union became increasingly interested in a negotiated settlement. The war threatened, along with the Watergate crisis, American political stability, and the Russians did not want the United States to become destabilized. Unstable superpowers are dangerous entities. Daniel S. Papp makes that point of view clear in his book *Vietnam: The View from Moscow, Peking, Washington*.

As the war concluded in 1975, the Soviets were considered the diplomatic victors internationally. The border skirmishes between the Vietnamese and the Chinese increased Soviet influence, and they secured important military bases at DaNang and Cam Ranh Bay. They could now challenge American military superiority in the Indian Ocean and the Western Pacific. Moreover, the Soviet line about the inevitable decline of American power received a major boost in the Vietnam defeat. Finally, the Soviets have appreciated the new "realism" in American foreign policy growing out of Vietnam, a development that they believe has given them a freer hand in Angola, Afghanistan, and Ethiopia. A war that began in order to staunch the tide of Soviet Communism has had a different result.

Historians now argue, of course, that the Soviets actually learned very little from the American experience in Vietnam. The rise of Muslim fundamentalism in the Middle East late in the 1970s threatened to spread into the Soviet Union, where Muslims constitute the majority of the population in the southern republics. To maintain a pro-Soviet government in Afghanistan, the Soviet Union invaded in 1980, and during much of the rest of the decade the Russians found themselves bogged down in a bloody war with Afghan guerrillas. It took ten years and 10,000 dead Soviet soldiers before Mikhail Gorbachev completed the withdrawal, ending "Russia's Vietnam." Both superpowers learned, the hard way, that concerted opposition by indigenous people living in rugged geography could foil even the United States and the Soviet Union.

The other major power directly involved in the Vietnam conflict was the People's Republic of China. On October 1, 1949, Mao Zedong's victorious Communist forces proclaimed the People's Republic of China in Beijing, the traditional capital. The next twenty-five years would be as tumultuous as the preceding twenty-five years of civil war. After the Chinese intervention in the Korean War, the United States attempted to freeze the People's Republic out of the international community, erecting a series of regional security pacts and mutual defense treaties among surrounding nations. In return, the Chinese predicted the demise of capitalism and American global hegemony, declaring "wars of national liberation" throughout the world. Their own People's Liberation Army was a model. Although the People's Liberation Army eventually became huge and questionable in quality, it was unsurpassed in its ability, through tightly controlled discipline and mass appeal, to politicize large numbers of people. Mao Zedong predicted that mass uprisings and guerrilla wars in capitalist countries would bring about the revolution Karl Marx had predicted.

Ho Chi Minh's People's Army of Vietnam was modeled on the People's Liberation Army, but after that the resemblance stopped. Although the United States feared the intervention of the Chinese in the Vietnam conflict, just as had happened in Korea, the People's Republic of China was not inclined to do so. As historians like Henry McAleavy (*Black Flags in Vietnam: The Story of the Chinese Intervention*), Eugene Lawson (*The Sino-Vietnamese Conflict*), and Pao-Min Chang (*Sino-Vietnamese Territorial Disputes*) have pointed out, the animosity between the Chinese and the Vietnamese runs deep. For centuries an intense and often bloody rivalry had raged between the Vietnamese and the Chinese, and the North Vietnamese would have viewed any Chinese military intervention into Indochina as simply a pretext for renewing the domination of the peninsula they had once enjoyed. At the Geneva Accords of 1954, as Melvin Gurtov demonstrates in *The First Vietnam Crisis: Chinese Communist Strategy and United States Involvement 1953–1954*, the Chinese worked diligently for the division of Vietnam into two countries, and Vietnamese nationalists like Ho Chi Minh viewed their meddling as just another example of China's ancient anti-Vietnamese expansionism.

During the Vietnam War, the Chinese found themselves in a real diplomatic dilemma. Two historians have written careful accounts outlining that dilemma—H. R. Chakrabartty (*China, Vietnam, and the United States*) and King C. Chen (*Vietnam and China, 1938–1954*). On one hand, they praised Ho Chi Minh's "war of national liberation" against "American imperialism," but at the same time they worried about the growing military strength of North Vietnam. They also worried about the increasing influence of the Soviet Union in Vietnamese affairs. Actually, China was not in much of a position to do a great deal about that dilemma. In 1962 Mao Zedong plunged the Chinese people into the Great Proletarian Cultural Revolution. Mao gained control of the army and let loose a rampaging horde of young Red Guards to terrorize government officials, scientists, and teachers. Robert G. Sutter writes in

Chinese Foreign Policy After the Cultural Revolution: 1966–1977 that the Cultural Revolution so destabilized Chinese society that concerted military effort in Indochina was not really possible. Finally, by 1971 the Chinese began to fear Soviet and even Vietnamese power more than American power, which seemed to be ebbing. With increasingly powerful Vietnamese forces to her south and Soviet forces aligned all along her long northern borders, Chinese leaders decided to seek a rapprochement with the United States. Richard Nixon and Henry Kissinger exploited that decision and normalized diplomatic relations in 1972. Although the Chinese provided some weapons and economic assistance to the North Vietnamese during the course of the war, they never posed the threat to the United States that they had twenty years earlier in Korea.

As soon as the United States was completely out of the picture in 1975, the Sino-Vietnamese dispute, so long in the making, resumed. China did not want to see the Socialist Republic of Vietnam extend its influence in Southeast Asia and East Asia. C. L. Sulzberger, in *Postscript with a Chinese Accent*, describes the February 17, 1979, invasion, in which Deng Xiaoping sent the People's Liberation Army across the border and invaded Vietnam. The bloody war lasted only a month, but 35,000 people died before it was over. On their way out of northern Vietnam, the Chinese destroyed several towns, blew up vital railway links, and obliterated important power plants and a phosphate mine responsible for most of Vietnam's fertilizer.

Throughout the 1960s, the fear of China had played a key role in the development of American policy in Vietnam. The U.S. memory for the large-scale Chinese invasion of South Korea in 1950 was still clear, and American policymakers were always concerned about the possibility of a Chinese invasion of South Vietnam and subsequent escalation of the war. Actually, as Daniel S. Papp has pointed out in *Vietnam: The View from Moscow, Peking, Washington*, the ancient Sino-Vietnamese rivalry militated against such a development, and China was in so much turmoil because of the Cultural Revolution that she could not have staged an invasion anyway. Nevertheless, one reason the United States did not pursue more aggressive conventional military policies was the fear of a hostile Chinese reaction.

Another reason was the inability of Presidents Eisenhower, Kennedy, Johnson, and Nixon to secure any real support for the war from the major allies of the North Atlantic Treaty Organization. France, of course, had vociferously opposed American escalation, but the United States could not get any real support from Canada, Great Britain, or West Germany. Two excellent books expose Canada's approach to the Vietnam War— Douglas A. Ross's *In the Interests of Peace: Canada and Vietnam, 1954–1973* and Charles Taylor's *Snow Job: Canada: the United States and Vietnam (1954–1973)*. Canada played several important roles in the Vietnam War.

Despite some disagreement over figures, it is clear that large numbers of young Americans exercised the option of becoming expatriates in Canada, either temporarily or permanently, in order to avoid the Vietnam War. Canadian immigration officials suggest that approximately 30,000 Americans settled legally there between 1965 and 1972. The Americans in Exile organization (AMEX) argued the number was closer to 80,000— 50,000 illegally and 30,000 legally. Canada was clearly an alternative for men who chose not to aid the war effort, who could not secure deferments, or who found the possibility of jail intolerable.

Canada also served, after the 1954 Geneva Accords, as a longtime member of the International Commission for Supervision and Control in Vietnam (the ICSC), created to monitor compliance with the agreement. Soon the Canadian role in the ICSC changed, especially after it became readily apparent that the 1954 Geneva Accords would not be upheld. With access to North Vietnam, Canadian members also became conveyors of messages from the United States to Hanoi, especially threats of escalation unless North Vietnam compromised its position. Critics of the war charged Canada with compliance, but Prime Minister Lester Pearson defended Canadian actions as attempts to bring the war to an end and keep lines of communication open.

Pearson also pointed out that cooperation with American requests helped Canada maintain access to the corridors of power in Washington and thus enabled Canada to influence American policy. Although Canada steadfastly would not provide material aid to the war effort, she also would not condemn American actions. Harsh criticism would have alienated the Americans, while expressions of cautious support lent credibility to urgings of moderation. The Canadian voice, along with those of other NATO allies, may have prompted more restraint in American policies and hastened the eventual disengagement.

As the United States withdrew from Vietnam, the ICSC was reconstituted in 1972 as the International Commission of Control and Supervision (ICCS), and again Canada served as a member. It had the same weakness as its predecessor. Communist forces were uncooperative to the point of taking military action against ICCS helicopters and refusing to allow teams to make required inspections. When Poland and Hungary, also ICCS members, hindered objective reporting on the military situation in South Vietnam, Canada resigned from the commission in 1973.

Policymakers in Great Britain also opposed the escalation of the war in Vietnam. Their own experiences with colonial rebellions in the post– World War II era gave the British a real appreciation for the tenacity of nationalistic movements, and they clearly saw the issue in Vietnam as one of nationalism, not Communism. As George Rosie makes clear in *The British in Vietnam: How the Twenty-Five Years War Began*, British interest in Indochina has a long history. Ever since 1945, the British have adopted a policy of relative noninvolvement with Indochina. They were preoccupied with a contraction of their own responsibilities east of the Suez Canal; were bogged down in a counterinsurgency effort in Malaysia; were undergoing substantial reductions in defense expenditures because of economic problems; were entertaining hopes of expanding trade with Communist-bloc nations; and were dealing with a powerful left-wing movement at home that resented military adventures abroad. All these problems precluded active British intervention in the problems of Vietnam.

In 1945, in order to free American troops for the anticipated invasion of Japan, the British took the Japanese surrender in Indochina, disarmed the enemy, and reestablished the prewar supremacy of the French. The British commander, Major General Douglas Gracey, actually used, however, a combined force of British and Japanese troops to fight the Vietminh, who were preparing to resist any reimposition of Western control over Vietnam. Still, on March 5, 1946, the British disengaged from the area. Eight years later, when President Dwight Eisenhower sought British support for an American air strike at Dien Bien Phu, Prime Minister Winston Churchill refused, pragmatically arguing that air strikes would accomplish little since most of Indochina was already under Vietminh control. He preferred a diplomatic solution.

In 1954, Great Britain cochaired the Geneva Conference on Vietnam, where they supported the American proposal for a division of Vietnam at the 17th parallel, with reunification elections to be held in two years. Privately, the British hoped, like the Americans, that the 17th parallel would become a recognized and permanent international boundary, with the South remaining non-Communist, out of the control of the Vietminh. When it appeared obvious that such elections would endorse the demands of Ho Chi Minh and the Vietminh, Britain supported the U.S. decision to stall and delay those elections.

As the American involvement escalated during the Lyndon B. Johnson administration, Prime Minister Harold Wilson refused all American requests for military support. In his memoirs (*Personal Record: The Labour Government, 1964–1970*), Wilson clearly expresses the British sense that the United States would not prevail against the Vietcong. Sensitive to the "special relationship" that Britain had with the United States in the postwar era, but also harassed by strongly leftist elements in his own Labour party who vocally condemned the war, Wilson maintained a delicate balance between 1964 and 1970. His government gave verbal support to American policy in Southeast Asia generally, while privately calling for an end to the bombing of North Vietnam and a negotiated settlement. Wilson's conservative successor, Edward Heath, continued the policy of limited support but no formal participation.

Britain did serve, however, as an important conduit for contact between the United States and the Soviet Union. Harold Wilson consulted frequently with Soviet leaders. The United States frequently used the British government as a sounding board, to convey negotiating positions to, or to try to bring pressure on, North Vietnam through the Soviet Union. Such contacts availed little because the United States greatly exaggerated the amount of influence the Soviet Union had with the North Vietnamese.

The approach of West Germany to the American involvement in Vietnam was just as ambiguous, as Viola Herma Drath (*Germany in World Politics*) and Wolfam Hanreider (*The Stable Crisis: Two Decades of German Foreign Policy*) have pointed out. West Germany, long conceded to be America's strongest ally in Europe next only to Great Britain, had little to do with Vietnam. Officially, West Germany supported the anti-Communist policy in South Vietnam, but privately German leaders had serious reservations about the American commitment there. More important is the question of the impact of Vietnam on West Germany. American preoccupation with Vietnam drew attention away from Europe, and, by default, West Germany assumed a much more significant role in NATO. There is some evidence that Soviet restraint in Vietnam was tacitly bought by U.S. assurances of keeping West Germany from joint nuclear control over weapons stationed on her soil. The denouement of the war contributed to a decline in American prestige in Europe and to a more independent stance by West European nations. West Germany's increasing trade and political contacts with Eastern bloc countries attest to her new independence.

Although U.S. allies in NATO were ambivalent about, or opposed to, the nature of the American involvement in Indochina, the whole issue was much more complicated in Asia, where the war had a far greater immediacy. In East Asia, the Japanese found themselves in a delicate political position. As Thomas R. Havens has pointed out in *Fire Across the Sea: The Vietnam War and Japan*, the conflict in Indochina posed a peculiar challenge to the Japanese. Japan played several important roles in the Vietnam conflict. Historically, the original drive for Vietnamese independence received substantial impetus from Japanese occupation during World War II. When Japan conquered Indochina in 1941, it chose to leave French bureaucrats in nominal control, belying Japanese wartime propaganda of "Asia for the Asians" and greatly reinforcing Vietnamese anticolonialism. Supported with U.S. supplies and advice, the Vietminh had fought against Japanese occupation forces, becoming popular heroes in the process and the de facto government in the countryside. When the French returned to power in 1946, the Vietminh simply turned their nationalist energies against them. Japan's rhetoric and occupation policies had accelerated the movement for Vietnamese independence.

Japan also served as a primary rationale for American intervention in Vietnam after the French debacle at Dien Bien Phu in 1954. China had become a Communist state in 1949; the Korean War had seemingly demonstrated the expansionist nature of Communism between 1950 and 1953; and a containment-oriented American foreign policy was worried about Communist aggression in Southeast Asia. If Vietnam fell to Communism, the United States argued, a sequence of disastrous events would follow: both Japan and the United States would lose access to Indochina's natural resources; Japanese economic expansion would be curtailed since Indochinese markets would be closed; and Japan would be forced into an accommodation with both the Soviet Union and the People's Republic of China. Japan was the United States' closest ally in Asia and had to be protected through American intervention in Vietnam. Finally, the United States had to prove to the Soviet Union, the Chinese, and the other nations of the world its commitment to stopping Communism.

During the war itself, Japan played only a peripheral role. Despite the United States–Japanese security treaty of 1960, Japan resisted American blandishments to become more involved in the conflict. They viewed the American commitment in Vietnam as excessive and ultimately as a dangerous mistake. Japan's role in the conflict was confined to playing host to the Seventh Fleet and various U.S. air wings and permitting American personnel to find necessary hospitalization and rest and recreation. Potent leftist elements periodically provoked domestic turmoil over such issues as hospitalized American soldiers in Japan conveying virulent tropical diseases to Japanese civilians or the dangers of expanding airports, especially at Narita, which could then be used for American air operations against Vietnam. The leftists were never successful, however, in convincing the Japanese public that the United States was engaged in a racist war in Vietnam. Japan also adopted a conservative posture for fear of inciting her Communist neighbors in North Korea and China. Finally, Japan wanted to maintain commerce with North Vietnam. It was the presence of Japanese ships in Haiphong that restrained initial American plans to bomb and mine the harbor.

The irony, of course, is that the Vietnam War may actually have hastened the Japanese accommodation with the Soviet Union and the People's Republic of China. With Vietnam monopolizing U.S. diplomatic interests, with the articulation of the Nixon doctrine in 1969, and with the shock of not being consulted about Henry Kissinger's secret initiatives to the People's Republic of China, Japan felt free, even compelled, to adopt a more independent diplomatic course in Asia. Although Japan remains solidly pro-Western, she is more wary about her relations with the United States and more independent in her dealings with the major powers.

At the other periphery of Asia, the Indians also found themselves in a delicate political position. In her book *Studies on India and Vietnam*, Helen B. Lamb describes the complicated geopolitical forces at work on the governments of Jawaharlal Nehru and, later, Indira Gandhi. Because of their own colonial history, the Indians understood the sincerity of Ho Chi Minh's desire to rid Vietnam of foreign control, whether it was Japanese, Chinese, French, or American. They viewed Ho Chi Minh as one of the great anticolonial leaders of the twentieth century. But at the same time, the Indians were afraid of the People's Republic of China. They worried, though not obsessively, about the nature of Chinese Communism, but they were far more concerned about historical Chinese expansionism. A. S. Whiting's *The Chinese Calculus of Deterrence: India and Indochina* deals with the relationship between China and India and how that relationship related to Indochina. Over the years India found itself in a number of border disputes with China, and the massive Chinese invasion of South Korea in 1950 had confirmed, in their own mind, the reality of Chinese expansionism. In that sense, they were somewhat sympathetic with the U.S. desire to contain Chinese aggression. But eventually, the Indians leaned more toward anticolonialism than to anti-Communism, and they, too, urged a negotiated settlement and American withdrawal from the region.

The only real assistance the United States received during the Vietnam War came from South Korea, Thailand, Australia, New Zealand, and the Philippines. As Stanley R. Larsen and J. Lawton Collins, Jr., point out in their book *Vietnam Studies: Allied Participation in Vietnam*, South Korea had a strong vested interest in extending real support to the United States. That support, of course, had little to do with any strong conviction that Ho Chi Minh was an evil individual or even that a victory for the Communists in Vietnam would seriously threaten the viability of their own government. South Korea's real worry in the late 1960s and early 1970s was North Korea. They had already experienced, between 1950 and 1953, a bloody struggle for survival against North Korean aggression, and only massive American intervention had saved them. They knew that North Korea could attack again at any time and that the presence of more than 40,000 American troops in South Korea prevented that. The South Koreans were desperate to maintain a close relationship with the United States.

The threat of North Korea was clearly illustrated in 1968, when the North Korean navy seized the USS *Pueblo*, a highly sophisticated American intelligence ship. The seizure reportedly occurred fifteen miles off the North Korean coast, although the North Koreans claimed it had violated their territorial waters. One American was killed in the attack, and four were wounded. The survivors were held in prison for more than eleven months. F. Carl Schumacher and George C. Wilson, in their book *Bridge of No Return*, describe the American response. Although the

United States immediately ordered 350 aircraft to air bases in South Korea as a show of force, it was impossible to make a more vigorous response, and military action against North Korea was out of the question. The quagmire in Vietnam had limited the American capacity to deal with the dispute.

To preserve its close relationship with the United States, South Korea eventually had as many as 49,000 troops fighting in South Vietnam. Those troops were among the country's best—the Capital Division, the Ninth Division, and the Second Marine Brigade. During the course of the war, South Korea suffered 4,407 combat deaths in Vietnam. South Korea's loyalty to the American war effort in South Vietnam, even though most Korean officials did not think the war was winnable, was a direct function of the close relationship existing between the two countries since the Korean War.

Thailand also had an important stake in the war. Unlike the other countries of Southeast Asia, the Thais managed over the centuries to avoid colonization by a European power. Their independence had often been tenuous, since they were surrounded by the French in Indochina and the British in Malaya, Burma, and India. By the 1950s and 1960s, however, the Thais felt more threatened by Communist insurgency and by the possibility of aggression from Vietnamese Communists. In all of Southeast Asia, the Vietnamese had the strongest reputation for territorial expansion, and Thai leaders saw the American presence in Vietnam as one way of protecting them from attack. D. E. Nuechterlein's *Thailand and the Struggle for Southeast Asia* looks at their tenuous political history. During the war, Thailand was a close American ally. By 1969 the Thais had a total of 12,000 combat troops in Vietnam, including the elite Queen's Cobras and the Black Panther Division of the Royal Thai Army. The U.S. 46th Special Forces Company assisted Thai forces in resisting Communist guerrilla activity along the Laotian border and in the south on the Malay Peninsula. The United States also had a strong presence in Thailand, including the 8th, 355th, 366th, and 388th Tactical Fighter Wings and the 307th Strategic Wing. Strategic bombing operations over North and South Vietnam often originated in Thailand.

No other country provided anywhere near the support level of the South Koreans and the Thais. Australia and New Zealand made token commitments to sustain the U.S. effort in Vietnam, and Peter King's *Australia's Vietnam* points out the contribution they made. Because of its charter membership in the Southeast Asia Treaty Organization, Australia found herself drawn into the American sphere of influence in the Pacific. It was a role she did not resent. After the French defeat at Dien Bien Phu in 1954, the Australians steadily warned the United States that the fall of South Vietnam would threaten democracies throughout Asia. Australian officials believed the domino theory. As early as 1962, Australia had sent thirty military advisors to work with the Army of the Republic of Vietnam (ARVN) on jungle and guerrilla tactics. After the Gulf of Tonkin Resolution in 1964, Australia increased its troop contingent in South Vietnam to 1,300 people, with a large combat battalion at Bien Hoa. Under pressure from Washington in 1965 and 1966, Australia increased that commitment, eventually to more than 8,000 troops at its peak in October 1967. Australian prime minister Harold Holt consistently offered his support to Lyndon Johnson, politically as well as militarily, even to the point of using a conscription system to supply its troop commitment. Next to the South Koreans, Australia provided the most military support to the United States in the conflict.

A charter member of the Southeast Asia Treaty Organization, New Zealand was reluctant to become too deeply involved in the Vietnam War, simply on the grounds of limited resources and limited political support at home and because the war was more than 2,000 miles away. Nevertheless, New Zealand did make a troop commitment to the conflict. Eventually, New Zealand sent about 1,000 soldiers and artillery support troops to South Vietnam because they wanted to prove their allegiance to American collective security arrangements in the Pacific and because they genuinely did not want to see a Communist takeover of Vietnam, Cambodia, and Laos.

The only other country to provide any support for the United States was the Philippines, but Filipino assistance came with strings attached. The location of the giant military complexes of Subic Bay Naval Base and Clark Air Base within the Philippines virtually assured that the country would serve as the primary staging area for the war. Most naval aircraft and ordnance passed through Subic. It served as the main repair station for the Seventh Fleet, playing host to 1,600 military personnel and 9,000 sailors at any one time. Clark Air Base became the hub for all U.S. military air traffic in the western Pacific and the operational base of the 13th Air Force.

The second role for the Philippines was support for the war effort. Manila had always been a strong champion of South Vietnam, which the Philippines considered the key to the future political direction of Southeast Asia. Three books deal with Filipino-South Vietnamese-American relations: William J. Pomeroy, *An American Made Tragedy: Neo-Colonialism and Dictatorship in the Philippines*; James Gregor, *Crisis in the Philippines: A Threat to U.S. Interests*; and Man Mohini Kaul, *The Philippines and South East Asia*. In 1965 President Lyndon B. Johnson asked for Filipino support. The new president of the Philippines, Ferdinand Marcos, initially refused, but after visits from Vice President Hubert Humphrey, Secretary of State Dean Rusk, and Senator Mike Mansfield of Montana, he relented. Marcos sent a 2,000-man combat engineering unit to South Vietnam from 1966 to 1969. His support, however, was not motivated simply by feelings of national security. Marcos negotiated aggressively for $39 million in additional American aid as well as sizable contributions of equipment to the Philippine military. He also made sure that Filipino troops had full access to U.S. military post exchanges (PXs) which they exploited, and that the United States employ Filipino civilians in South Vietnam.

A number of excellent works deal with the impact of the Vietnam War on American foreign policy as well as on the image of the United States in the international community. Paul Kattenburg deals with that problem in *The Vietnam Trauma in American Foreign Policy*, as does D. Michael Shafer in *The Legacy: The Vietnam War in the American Imagination*, but the best of the books is Ole R. Holsti and James N. Rosenau, *American Leadership in World Affairs: Vietnam and the Breakdown of Consensus*. In two important ways, the Vietnam War introduced severe indentity crises into the formulation of American foreign policy. First, the war proved that American power in the world was not unlimited, indeed, that even a small country, given the right circumstances, could bring the American military and political apparatus to its knees. Second, the Vietnam War shattered the postwar Western alliance, in which the United States had assumed the moral and military lead. Not a single major U.S. ally in the North Atlantic Treaty Organization offered any assistance, and most of them expressed open opposition to the course of the war. As a result of the Vietnam War, the United States lost its position as the unrivaled moral and political leader of the West. Wallace Thies's *When Governments Collide: Coercion and Diplomacy in the Vietnam Conflict, 1964–1968* shows how severely the Vietnam War strained the relationship between the United States and its major NATO allies.

BIBLIOGRAPHY

Abel, E. S. *The Missiles of October: Twelve Days to World War III*. London: Macmillan, 1966.

Albinski, Henry. *Politics and Foreign Policy in Australia*. Durham, N.C.: Duke University Press, 1970.

Allison, G. T. *Essence of Decision: Explaining the Cuban Missile Crisis*. Boston: Little, Brown, 1971.

Ambekar, G. V. *Documents on China's Relations with South and South-East Asia 1949–1962*. Bombay, India: C. K. Riang, 1964.

Aron, Raymond. *France Steadfast and Changing: The Fourth to the Fifth Republic*. Cambridge: Harvard University Press, 1960.

Ashmore, Harry S., and William C. Baggs. *Mission to Hanoi*. New York: Putnam, 1968.

Austin, Allen. *The Great Debate: Theories of Nuclear Strategy*. New York: Anchor Books, 1965.

Austin, Allen. *Peace and War: A Theory of International Relations*. New York: Praeger, 1967.

Austin, Allen. *The President's War*. Philadelphia: Lippincott, 1971.

Beloff, Max. *The Future of British Foreign Policy*. New York: Taplinger, 1969.

Berman, Larry. *Planning a Tragedy: The Administration of the War in Vietnam*. New York: Norton, 1982.

Berman, Larry. *Lyndon Johnson's War: The Road to Stalemate in Vietnam*. New York: Norton, 1989.

Bidault, George. *Resistance*. New York: Praeger, 1967.

Blaufarb, D. S. *The Counterinsurgency Era: US Doctrine and Performance, 1950 to the Present*. New York: Free Press, 1977.

Bohlen, Charles E. *Witness to History, 1929–1969*. New York: Norton, 1973.

Borisov, O. B., and B. T. Koloskov. *Soviet-Choice Relations 1945–1970*. Bloomington: University of Indiana Press, 1975.

Browne, M. W. *The New Face of War*. London: Macmillan, 1965.

Buckingham, W. A. *Operation Ranch Hand: The Air Force and Herbicides in Southeast Asia 1961–1971*. Washington, D.C.: U.S. Government Printing Office, 1972.

Buszynski, Leszet. *Soviet Foreign Policy and Southeast Asia*. New York: St. Martin's Press, 1986.

Cady, John. *The United States and Burma*. Cambridge: Harvard University Press, 1976.

Cairnes, James Ford. *The Eagle and the Lotus: Western Intervention in Vietnam, 1847–1968*. New York: Lansdowne Press, 1969.

Calleo, David. *The Atlantic Fantasy: The United States, NATO and Europe*. Baltimore: Johns Hopkins University Press, 1970.

Camps, Miriam. *Britain and the European Community, 1955–1963*. Princeton, N.J.: Princeton University Press, 1964.

Chakrabartty, H. R. *China, Vietnam and the United States*. Washington, D.C.: Public Affairs Press, 1966.

Charlton, M., and A. Moncrieff. *Many Reasons Why: The American Involvement in Vietnam*. New York: Hill and Wang, 1982.

Chen, King C. *Vietnam and China, 1938–1954*. Princeton, N.J.: Princeton University Press, 1969.

Colbert, E. S. *Southeast Asia in International Politics 1941–1956*. Ithaca, N.Y.: Cornell University Press, 1977.

Collins, J. Lawton. *The Development and Training of the South Vietnamese Army, 1950–1972*. Washington, D.C.: U.S. Government Printing Office, 1975.

Cooper, Chester L. *Lost Crusade: America in Vietnam*. New York: Dodd, Mead, 1970.

Crouch, H. A. *The Army and Politics in Indonesia*. Ithaca, N.Y.: Cornell University Press, 1978.

Dake, A.C.A. *In the Spirit of the Red Banteng: Indonesian Communists Between Moscow and Peking 1959–1965*. The Hague: Mouton, 1973.

DeGaulle, Charles. *The Army of the Future*. Philadelphia: Lippincott, 1941.

DeGaulle, Charles. *The War Memoirs of Charles de Gaulle*. 3 vols. New York: Simon and Schuster, 1955–1960.

Devilers, Philippe. *The Struggle for the Unification of Vietnam*. London: Ilford House, 1962.

Devilers, Philippe, and Jean Lacouture. *End of a War: Indochina, 1954*. New York: Praeger, 1969.

Dommen, Arthur J. *Conflict in Laos, the Politics of Neutralization*. New York: Praeger, 1964.

Drath, Viola Herma, ed. *Germany in World Politics*. New York: Random House, 1979.

Duiker, William J. *The Communist Road to Power in Vietnam*. Boulder, Colo.: Westview Press, 1981.

Duncanson, D. J. *Government and Revolution in Vietnam*. London: Morrow, 1968.

Eden, Anthony. *Towards Peace in Indochina*. London: Oxford University Press, 1966.

Edmonds, Robin. *Soviet Foreign Policy, 1962–1973: The Paradox of a Superpower*. New York: Oxford University Press, 1975.

Emmerson, John K. *Arms, Yen and Power: The Japanese Dilemma*. New York: Dunellen, 1971.

Fall, Bernard. *Anatomy of a Crisis: The Laotian Crisis of 1960–1961*. Garden City, N.Y.: Doubleday, 1969.

Fall, Bernard. *Street Without Joy*, 3d ed., rev. Harrisburg, Pa.: Telegraphic Press, 1961.

Fall, Bernard. *Viet-Nam Witness 1953–1966*. London: Pall Mall Press, 1966.

Fall, Bernard. *Hell in a Very Small Place*. Philadelphia: Lippincott, 1967a.

Fall, Bernard. *Last Reflections on a War*. Garden City, N.Y.: Doubleday, 1967b.

Fedder, Edwin H. *NATO: The Dynamics of Alliance in the Post-War World*. New York: Dodd, Mead, 1973.

Fifield, R. H. *The Diplomacy of Southeast Asia, 1945–1958*. New York: Columbia University Press, 1958.

Fishel, Wesley R., ed. *Vietnam: Anatomy of a Conflict*. Itasca, Ill.: Peacock, 1968.

Garner, John W. "Sino-Vietnamese Conflict and the Sino-American Rapprochement." *Political Science Quarterly* 96 (Fall 1981): 445–64.

Gavin, James M. *Crisis Now*. New York: Random House, 1968.

Gelb, L. H., and R. K. Betts. *The Irony of Vietnam: The System Worked*. Washington, D.C.: Brookings Institution, 1979.

Gettleman, Marvin E., ed. *Vietnam: History, Documents and Opinions on a Major World Crisis*. New York: New American Library, 1970.

Gibney, Frank. *Japan: The Fragile Superpower*. New York: Norton, 1975.

Gilpin, Robert. *United States Power and the Multinational Corporation*. New York: Basic Books, 1975.

Gittings, J. C. *The Role of the Chinese Army*. London: Walpole, 1967.

Gordon, David C. *The Passing of French Algeria*. London: Oxford University Press, 1966.

Goulden, J. C. *Truth Is the First Casualty: The Gulf of Tonkin Affair, Illusion and Reality*. Chicago: Quadrangle, 1969.

Gregor, James. *Crisis in the Philippines: A Threat to U.S. Interests*. New York: Knopf, 1984.

Griffith, W. E. *The Sino-Soviet Rift*. Cambridge: Harvard University Press, 1964.

Griffith, W. E. *Sino-Soviet Relations 1964–1965*. Cambridge: Harvard University Press, 1969.

Gurtov, Melvin. *The First Vietnam Crisis: Chinese Communist Strategy and United States Involvement 1953–1954*. New York: Columbia University Press, 1967.

Gurtov, Melvin. *China and Southeast Asia: The Politics of Survival*. Lexington, Mass.: D. C. Heath, 1971.

Halberstam, David. *The Making of a Quagmire*. New York: Knopf, 1965.

Halberstam, David. *The Best and the Brightest*. New York: Random House, 1972.

Halpern, A. M., ed. *Policies Toward China: Views from Six Continents*. New York: McGraw-Hill, 1965.

Hammer, Ellen J. *The Struggle for Indochina*. Stanford, Calif.: Stanford University Press, 1954.

Hanreider, Wolfam. *The Stable Crisis: Two Decades of German Foreign Policy*. New York: Harper and Row, 1970.

Harr, John. *The Professional Diplomat*. Princeton, N.J.: Princeton University Press, 1969.

Havens, Thomas R. *Fire Across the Sea: The Vietnam War and Japan*. Princeton, N.J.: Princeton University Press, 1987.

Henderson, William. *Southeast Asia: Problems of United States Policy*. Cambridge: Harvard University Press, 1963.

Herring, George C. *America's Longest War: The United States and Vietnam 1950–1975*. New York: Knopf, 1979.

Hess, John L. *The Case for de Gaulle*. New York: Morrow, 1968.

Hilsman, Roger. *To Move a Nation: The Politics of Foreign Policy in the Administration of John F. Kennedy*. Garden City, N.Y.: Doubleday, 1967.

Hinton, Harold. *Communist China in World Politics*. Boston: Houghton-Mifflin, 1966.

Hinton, Harold. *China's Turbulent Quest*. New York: Macmillan, 1970.

Hoffman, Stanley. *Gulliver's Troubles*. New York: McGraw-Hill, 1968.

Hoffman, Stanley. *Decline or Renewal? France Since the 1930s*. New York: Viking Press, 1974.

Hoffman, Stanley, ed. *In Search of France*. Cambridge: Harvard University Press, 1963.

Holsti, Ole R., and James N. Rosenau. *American Leadership in World Affairs: Vietnam and the Breakdown of Consensus*. New York: Unwyn Hyman, 1984.

Hoopes, Townsend. *The Limits of Intervention*. New York: David McKay, 1970.

Hsiao, Gene T., ed. *The Role of External Powers in Indochina*. Edwardsville: Southern Illinois University Press, 1973.

Hull, Cordell. *Memoirs*. New York: Macmillan, 1948.

Humbaraci, Arslan. *Algeria: A Revolution That Failed: A Political History Since 1954*. New York: Praeger, 1966.

Irving, R.E.M. *The First Indochina War*. London: Crown Helm, 1975.

Jain, R. K. *China and Japan 1949–76*. London: Kellogg, 1977.

James, H. T., and D. D. Scheil-Small. *The Undeclared War: The Story of Indonesian Confrontation 1962–1966*. London: Macmillan, 1971.

Johnson, Lyndon B. *The Vantage Point: Perspectives of the Presidency 1963–1969*. New York: Holt, Rinehart, and Winston, 1971.

Jones, H. P. *Indonesia, the Possible Dream*. Stanford, Calif.: Stanford University Press, 1971.

Jordan, A. A. *Foreign Aid and the Defense of Southeast Asia*. New York: Columbia University Press, 1962.

Kahin, George McT. *Intervention. How America Became Involved in Vietnam*. New York: Dial, 1986.

Karnow, Stanley. *Vietnam: A History*. New York: Viking, 1983.

Kattenburg, Paul M. *The Vietnam Trauma in American Foreign Policy, 1945–1975*. New York: Transaction Books, 1980.

Kaul, Man Mohini. *The Philippines and South East Asia*. New York: Harper and Row, 1978.

Kelly, George Armstrong. *Lost Soldiers, the French Army and Empire in Crisis*. Cambridge: MIT Press, 1965.

Khrushchev, Nikita S. *Khrushchev Remembers*. Translated by S. Talbott. Boston: Little, Brown, 1971.

King, Peter, ed. *Australia's Vietnam*. Sydney, Australia: Allen and Unwin, 1983.

Kissinger, Henry A. *Nuclear Weapons and Foreign Policy*. New York: Harper, 1957.

Kissinger, Henry A. *The Troubled Partnership: A Re-appraisal of the Atlantic Alliance*. New York: McGraw-Hill, 1965.

Kissinger, Henry A. *White House Years: The Memoirs of Henry A. Kissinger*. Boston: Little, Brown, 1979.

Kissinger, Henry A. *Years of Upheaval: The Memoirs of Henry A. Kissinger*. Boston: Little, Brown, 1982.

Klare, M. T. *War Without End: American Planning for the Next Vietnams*. New York: Praeger, 1972.

Kohl, Wilfrid L. *French Nuclear Diplomacy*. Princeton, N.J.: Princeton University Press, 1971.

Kolodiej, Edward A. *French International Policy Under de Gaulle and Pompidou: The Politics of Grandeur*. Ithaca, N.Y.: Cornell University Press, 1974.

Kraslow, David, and Stuart H. Loory. *The Secret Search for Peace in Vietnam*. New York: Vintage Books, 1968.

Kulski, Wladyslaw W. *De Gaulle and the World: The Foreign Policy of the Fifth French Republic*. Syracuse, N.Y.: Syracuse University Press, 1966.

Lacouture, Jean. *Vietnam: Between Two Truces*. New York: Vintage Books, 1966.

Lacouture, Jean. *De Gaulle*. New York: Avon Books, 1968.

Lacouture, Jean. *Ho Chi Minh*. New York: Vintage Books, 1970.

Lamb, Helen B. *Studies on India and Vietnam*. New York: Monthly Review Press, 1976.

Lancaster, Donald. *The Emancipation of French Indochina*. London: Oxford University Press, 1961.

Larsen, Stanley Robert, and James Lawton Collins, Jr. *Vietnam Studies: Allied Participation in Vietnam*. Washington, D.C.: U.S. Government Printing Office, 1975.

Lawson, Eugene K. *The Sino-Vietnamese Conflict*. Westport, Conn.: Greenwood Press, 1984.

Leifer, M. R. *Indonesia's Foreign Policy*. London: Jameson, 1983.

Linden, C. A. *Khrushchev and the Soviet Leadership 1957–1964*. Baltimore: Johns Hopkins University Press, 1966.

Liska, George. *Nations in Alliance.* Baltimore: Johns Hopkins University Press, 1962.

Liska, George. *Imperial America.* Baltimore: Johns Hopkins University Press, 1967.

Lusignan, Guy de. *French-Speaking Africa Since Independence.* New York: Praeger, 1969.

McAleavy, Henry. *Black Flags in Vietnam: The Story of the Chinese Intervention.* New York: Allen and Unwin, 1968.

McCoy, A. W. *The Politics of Heroin in Southeast Asia.* New York: Harper and Row, 1973.

MacFarquhar, R. D. *Sino-American Relations 1949–1971.* London: Newton Abbot, 1973.

Mackie, J.A.C. *Konfrontasi: The Indonesia-Malaysia Dispute 1963–1966.* Kuala Lumpur, Malaysia: Stenham, 1974.

Macridis, Roy C., ed. *De Gaulle, Implacable Ally.* New York: Harper and Row, 1966.

Maneli, Mieczyslaw. *War of the Vanquished.* New York: Harper and Row, 1971.

Mayall, J. B. "Malaysia, Indonesia and the Philippines: Prelude to Confrontation." In D. C. Watt, ed. *Survey of International Affairs 1963.* London: Beckworth, 1977.

Mecklin, J. T. *Mission in Torment: An Intimate Account of the US Role in Vietnam.* Garden City, N.Y.: Doubleday, 1965.

Modelski, George. *International Conference on the Settlement of the Laotian Question, 1961–62.* Canberra, Australia: Australian National University, Department of International Relations, 1962.

Momyer, Walter W. *Air Power in Three Wars.* Washington, D.C.: U.S. Government Printing Office, 1978.

Montgomery, J. D. *The Politics of Foreign Aid: American Experience in Southeast Asia.* New York: Harper, 1962.

Morse, Edward L. *Foreign Policy and Interdependence in Gaullist France.* Princeton, N.J.: Princeton University Press, 1973.

Newhouse, Edward. *De Gaulle and the Anglo-Saxons.* New York: Viking Press, 1969.

Nishihara, Masahi. *The Japanese and Sukarno's Indonesia: Tokyo-Jakarta Relations 1951–1966.* Kyoto: University of Kyoto Press, 1967.

Norodom Sihanouk, and William Burchett. *My War with the CIA: Cambodia's Fight for Survival.* New York: International, 1973.

Nuechterlein, D. E. *Thailand and the Struggle for Southeast Asia.* Ithaca, N.Y.: Cornell University Press, 1965.

Pachter, H. M. *Collision Course: The Cuba Missile Crisis and Coexistence.* New York: Praeger, 1963.

Palmer, David R. *Summons of the Trumpet: US–Vietnam in Perspective.* New York: Ballantine, 1978.

Pao-Min Chang. *Beijing, Hanoi, and the Overseas Chinese.* Berkeley: Institute of East Asian Studies, University of California, 1983.

Pao-Min Chang. *Sino-Vietnamese Territorial Disputes.* Westport, Conn.: Greenwood Press, 1985.

Papp, Daniel S. *Vietnam: The View from Moscow, Peking, Washington.* New York: Columbia University Press, 1981.

Patti, Archimedes. *Why Vietnam? Prelude to America's Albatross.* Berkeley: University of California Press, 1981.

Pickles, Dorothy. *Algeria and France: From Colonialism to Cooperation.* New York: Praeger, 1963.

Pickles, Dorothy. *The Uneasy Détente: French Foreign Policy and Franco-British Misunderstandings.* London: Oxford University Press, 1966.

Pike, Douglas. *Viet Cong: The Organization and Techniques of the National Liberation Front of South Vietnam.* Cambridge: Harvard University Press, 1966.

Pike, Douglas. *Vietnam and the Soviet Union: Anatomy of an Alliance.* Boulder, Colo.: Westview Press, 1987.

Pinder, Jean. *Europe Against de Gaulle.* New York: Praeger, 1963.

Pomeroy, William J. *An American Made Tragedy: Neo-Colonialism and Dictatorship in the Philippines.* New York: International Publishers, 1974.

Poole, Peter A. *The United States and Indochina from FDR to Nixon.* Hinsu. le, Ill.: Dryden Press, 1973.

Porte, A. W. de. *De Gaulle's Foreign Policy, 1944–1946.* Cambridge: Harvard University Press, 1968.

Porter, D. Gareth. *A Peace Denied: The United States, Vietnam, and the Paris Agreement.* Bloomington: Indiana University Press, 1976.

Prittie, Terence. *Willy Brandt: Portrait of a Statesman.* New York: Simon and Schuster, 1974.

Prouty, L. F. *The Secret Team.* Englewood Cliffs, N.J.: Prentice-Hall, 1973.

Randle, Robert. *Geneva 1954: The Settlement of the Indochinese War.* Princeton, N.J.: Princeton University Press, 1969.

Raskin, Marcus G., and Bernard B. Fall, eds. *The Viet-Nam Reader: Articles and Documents on American Foreign Policy and the Vietnam Crisis.* New York: Vintage Books, 1967.

Reischauer, Edwin O. *Japan: Story of a Nation.* New York: Knopf, 1974.

Robinson, Frank M., and Earl Kemp. *Report of the U.S. Senate Hearings: The Truth About Vietnam.* San Diego, Calif.: Greenleaf Classics, 1966.

Rosenberger, Leif. *Vietnam and the Soviet Union: An Uneasy Alliance.* New York: Random House, 1986.

Rosie, George. *The British in Vietnam: How the Twenty-Five Years War Began.* London: Macmillan, 1970.

Ross, Douglas A. *In the Interests of Peace: Canada and Vietnam, 1954–1973.* Ithaca, N.Y.: Cornell University Press, 1984.

Ross, Robert. *The Indochina Tangle: China's Vietnam Policy, 1975–1979.* New York: Columbia University Press, 1988.

Rostow, Walt W. *The Diffusion of Power: An Essay in Recent History.* New York: Macmillan, 1972.

Roy, Jules. *The Battle of Dienbienphu.* New York: Harper and Row, 1963.

Sainteny, Jean. *Ho Chi Minh and His Vietnam; A Personal Memoir.* Chicago: Cowles, 1972.

Scheer, Robert. *How the United States Got Involved in Vietnam.* Santa Barbara, Calif.: Center for the Study of Democratic Institutions, 1965.

Scheinman, Lawrence. *Atomic Energy Policy in France Under the Fourth Republic.* Princeton, N.J.: Princeton University Press, 1965.

Schlesinger, Arthur M., Jr. *A Thousand Days: John F. Kennedy in the White House.* Boston, Mass.: Houghton Mifflin, 1965.

Schlesinger, Arthur M., Jr. *Robert Kennedy and His Times.* Boston: Houghton Mifflin, 1978.

Schoenbrun, David. *The Three Lives of Charles de Gaulle.* New York: Atheneum, 1966.

Schumacher, F. Carl, and George C. Wilson. *Bridge of No Return.* New York: Praeger, 1973.

Schurmann, Franz, Peter Dale Scott, and Reginald Zelnik. *The Politics of Escalation in Vietnam.* Greenwich, Conn.: Fawcett, 1966.

Serfaty, Simon. *France, De Gaulle and Europe.* Baltimore, Md.: Johns Hopkins University Press, 1968.

Shafer, D. Michael, ed. *The Legacy: The Vietnam War in the American Imagination.* Boston: Beacon Press, 1990.

Shaplen, Robert. *The Lost Revolution in Vietnam 1945–1965.* New York: Harper and Row, 1965.

Smith, R. B. *An International History of the Vietnam War: The Johnson Strategy.* New York: St. Martin's Press, 1990.

Smith, R. B. *An International History of the Vietnam War. Volume 1: Revolution Versus Containment, 1955–1961.* New York: St. Martin's Press, 1984.

Smith, R. B. *An International History of the Vietnam War: The Kennedy Strategy.* New York: St. Martin's Press, 1987.

Steele, Jonathan. *Soviet Power.* New York: Simon and Schuster, 1983.

Sullivan, Marianna P. *France's Vietnam Policy: A Study in French–American Relations.* Westport, Conn.: Greenwood Press, 1978.

Sulzberger, C. L. *The Last of the Giants.* New York: Macmillan, 1970.

Sulzberger, C. L. *Postscript with a Chinese Accent.* New York: Macmillan, 1974.

Sutter, Robert G. *Chinese Foreign Policy After the Cultural Revolution: 1966–1977.* Boulder, Colo.: Westview Press, 1978.

Taylor, Charles. *Snow Job: Canada, the United States and Vietnam (1954–1973).* New York: Columbia University Press, 1974.

Thich Nhat Hanh. *Vietnam: Lotus in a Sea of Fire.* New York: Hill and Wang, 1967.

Thies, Wallace. *When Governments Collide: Coercion and Diplomacy in the Vietnam Conflict, 1964–1968.* Berkeley: University of California Press, 1980.

Truong, Buu Lam. *Patterns of Vietnamese Response to Foreign Intervention, 1858–1900.* New Haven, Conn.: Yale University Press, 1967.

Vandenbosch, Amry, and Mary Belle Vandenbosch. *Australia Faces Southeast Asia.* Lexington: University Press of Kentucky, 1967.

Vasilev, D. S., and K. R. Lvov. *Soviet Trade and Southeast Asia.* Moscow: Lenin Institute, 1959.

Weiner, J. H., and J. H. Plumb. *Great Britain: Foreign Policy and the Span of Europe, 1689–1971. A Documentary History.* London: Macmillan, 1972.

Weinstein, Franklin B. *Vietnam's Unheld Elections: The Failure to Carry Out the 1956 Reunification Elections and the Effect on Hanoi's Present Outlook.* Ithaca, N.Y.: Cornell University Southeast Asia Program, Data Paper #60, 1966.

Werth, Alexander. *De Gaulle: A Political Biography.* New York: Simon and Schuster, 1966.

Whiting, A. S. *The Chinese Calculus of Deterrence: India and Indochina.* Ann Arbor: University of Michigan Press, 1975.

Wickberg, Edgar. *Historical Interaction of China and Vietnam.* New York: Paragon Book Gallery, 1969.

Williams, Philip M. *Crisis and Compromise: Politics in the Fourth Republic.* Garden City, N.Y.: Doubleday, 1966.

Williams, Philip M. *The French Parliament.* New York: Praeger, 1968.

Willis, F. Roy. *France, Germany and the New Europe.* Stanford, Calif.: Stanford University Press, 1965.

Willis, F. Roy, ed. *De Gaulle: Anachronism, Realist or Prophet?* New York: Holt, Rinehart, and Winston, 1967.

Wilson, Harold. *Personal Record: The Labour Government 1964–1970.* Boston: Little, Brown, 1971.

Yahuda, M. B. *China's Role in World Affairs.* London: Macmillan, 1978.

Zagoria, Donald S. *Vietnam Triangle: Moscow, Peking, Hanoi.* New York: Pegasus Books, 1967.

Zagoria, Donald S., ed. *Soviet Policy in East Asia.* New Haven, Conn.: Yale University Press, 1983.

8 Air Power

Iris Love

Americans are often a culturally egotistical people. They have a "can do" attitude about almost all of their challenges. Not only did they survive the cold war, but their collective character breathes a sigh of relief and says "well done" now that the collapse of the Soviet Union has finally occurred. It may be because Americans often arrogantly view their democratic institutions as superior. The Gulf War against Iraq, 1990–1991, only served to reemphasize that sense of moral and military superiority. In no small measure, the U.S. victory in the Gulf War was a matter of air power. American pilots delivered high-tech explosives at will to carefully targeted areas of Iraq and brought a precision-based firepower unknown in human history. The success of the air war over Iran led inevitably to second-guessing about the failure of the air war in Indochina between 1964 and 1972.

HISTORICAL BACKGROUND

Before listing the arguments and logic refuting the stance of the military, it would be helpful to some to outline briefly the major bombing campaigns of the Vietnam War. Ironically, given the events of the 1960s and 1970s, the United States rejected its first opportunity to intervene militarily in Southeast Asia. American air power was not employed when the first opportunity presented itself. In 1954, with General Vo Nguyen Giap and his Vietminh troops surrounding the French outpost at Dien Bien Phu, France asked the United States to rescue them. President Dwight D. Eisenhower asked Admiral Arthur Radford, chairman of the Joint Chiefs of Staff, to consider the request and make a recommendation. Radford hatched Operation Vulture—the use of Philippines-based B–29s, accompanied by aircraft from the USS carriers *Essex* and

Boxer—to knock out Vietminh artillery. In case the air strike did not lift the siege, Radford was prepared to use atomic weapons. Stephen Jurika edited Radford's memoirs (*From Pearl Harbor to Vietnam: The Memoirs of Admiral Arthur W. Radford*) and quoted Radford as saying: "Whether these [air strikes] alone would have been successful in breaking the siege of Dien Bien Phu is debatable. If we had used atomic weapons, we probably would have been successful."

The issue that President Eisenhower had to decide was whether to follow Radford's advice. John Prados, in *The Sky Would Fall: Operation Vulture: The U.S. Bombing Mission in Indochina, 1954*, describes how Eisenhower decided not to intervene militarily. Secretary of State John Foster Dulles could not muster much support for the strike within the NATO alliance, and Congress would not go it alone. The specter of war in Vietnam, so soon after the armistice in Korea, was too much for them. What really convinced Eisenhower, however, was the opposition of General Matthew Ridgway, chief of staff of the U.S. Army. In his memoirs *Soldier: The Memoirs of Matthew Ridgway*, the general recalled his conviction that the air strike would not lift the siege and that American ground troops would have to be called in. Ridgway wrote to Eisenhower and asked about the depth of the war around Saigon, the quality of the harbor and dock facilities, the warehouse capacity for storing supplies, the quality of the highway system, and the nature of the climate, rainfall, and tropical diseases. Nobody knew the answers, including Radford. Eisenhower knew what infantry combat was like; Ridgway's questions provided the president with his answer. Operation Vulture was scuttled. The French outpost at Dien Bien Phu fell a few weeks later.

HELICOPTERS

The helicopter became the primary symbol of the American military presence in Vietnam. No other weapon system attained the high degree of visibility or identification with the war that the helicopter did. The French first used helicopters in Vietnam, primarily to evacuate wounded soldiers, and at the time of the battle of Dien Bien Phu, French military leaders were debating the use of the helicopter as a means of offsetting Vietminh mobility. The United States resolved that debate and committed itself to the helicopter very early in the war. The best book outlining the use of the helicopter in Vietnam is John J. Tolson's *Airmobility, 1961–1971* (1973). In December 1961 the 8th and 57th Transportation Companies deployed to South Vietnam. They flew the Piasecki H–21 in combat missions supporting the ARVN troops. These units were followed by a U.S. Marine helicopter squadron flying CH–34s and by a U.S. Army medical detachment using UH–1s for medical evacuation. Specially equipped UH–1 helicopter gunships arrived in the fall of 1962.

The first major offensive operation using American helicopters occurred on January 2, 1963, when ten CH–21s and five Huey gunships fought at the battle of Ap Bac. Without fixed-wing air support, they took heavy losses. The first airmobile assault of the Vietnam War was a failure, and the major lesson learned was the need to coordinate airmobile assaults with bombing and strafing runs by fixed-wing aircraft. With that lesson learned, the American military made the helicopter the key item in tactical policy. By the late 1960s the U.S. Army had 3,600 helicopters functioning in South Vietnam. Without the helicopter, the American military commitment in Vietnam would have been impossible.

STRATEGIC AND TACTICAL AIR POWER

The real American air war in South Vietnam began during the Kennedy administration, as Robert F. Futrell describes in *The United States Air Force in Southeast Asia: The Advisory Years to 1965* (1983). In April 1961 the U.S. Air Force created the 4,400th Combat Crew Training Squadron, also called Jungle Jim, and stationed it at Elgin Air Force Base in Florida. In October 1961, half of the 4,400th Combat Squadron received a new code name—Farmgate—and were deployed to an old French air base at Bien Hoa, just fifteen miles northeast of Saigon. Farmgate trained Vietnamese pilots to fly A–1H Skyraiders, dropped propaganda leaflets over Vietcong territory, and supplied Vietnamese Ranger camps and Civilian Irregular Defense Group camps along the Laotian and Cambodian borders. At first Farmgate pilots provided only covert support to Vietnamese operations. They had to fly with Vietnamese copilots in Vietnamese aircraft. As time passed, however, American pilots increasingly took over the flight duties.

OPERATION ROLLING THUNDER

Sustained American air operations over Indochina did not begin until 1964, as pointed out by James N. Eastman, Jr., Walter Hanak, and Lawrence J. Paszek (*Aces and Aerial Victories: The United States Air Force in Southeast Asia, 1965–1973*) and Carl Berger (*The United States Air Force in Southeast Asia, 1961–1973*). At the end of World War II, Vietnam was one of several nations that were artificially divided into sectors by the victorious allies. The United States was instrumental in the creation of the capitalistic Republic of South Vietnam, while the Soviet Union supported the leftist nation in North Vietnam. Each portion of Vietnam held differing political beliefs and sought to unify the nation under its rule. The United States developed a close relationship with South Vietnam during the 1950s, and as difficulties with leftist North Vietnam grew during the early 1960s, so did American commitments. Eventually, by the late 1960s, the United States had assumed the primary responsibilities of conducting the defense of South Vietnam. The first clash between North Vietnamese and American forces occurred on August 2, 1964, when a North Vietnamese force attacked an American naval vessel patrolling the Gulf of Tonkin. Two nights later, American destroyers were attacked along the Vietnamese coast. With these attacks, President Lyndon Baines Johnson ordered a retaliatory bombing strike against a North Vietnamese supply depot on August 5. The president then requested and Congress approved the Gulf of Tonkin Resolution on August 7, 1964, granting President Johnson the authority to use all measures necessary to assist South Vietnam in defending its territory. These actions set the stage for extended bombing operations against enemy targets in North Vietnam.

In an effort to preserve a non-Communist South Vietnam, civilian advisors agreed on air power tactics, and Rolling Thunder was initiated as the policy of President Johnson in 1965. Johnson's predicament was complicated, and thus, his leadership goals were mixed. His positive objective of establishing South Vietnamese independence was shaped by his negative objective of equal importance—to prevent the Chinese or Soviets from intervening in the conflict. Johnson further complicated the situation with his intention to maintain the domestic social programs that were part of his Great Society, and therefore he could not actively solicit support for the war from the American public. "The President and his advisors never really considered whether bombing was a viable political instrument, given the conflicting nature of America's war aims." Rolling Thunder thus "epitomized the discord among the President's civilian counselors over how best to employ air power to achieve the nation's war aims" (Clodfelter, 44, 101).

From the very beginning of bombing operations against enemy targets, the U.S. Air Force (USAF) experienced difficulties. Bombardment campaigns in Vietnam were substantially different from those of World War I and II and even materially different from those of Korea. First, the president was intensely concerned with the complexities and necessities of fighting a war limited both in size and scope, and he maintained firm control over all phases of planning and execution. Coordination of all bombing operations involved not only military planners but also senior State Department, Defense Department, cabinet, and numerous other government officials. Second, air force bombing doctrine underwent a striking alteration during the war as the practical differences between air interdiction and strategic bombing against North Vietnam were muted. In this conflict, all types of bombers and fighters worked together to bomb transportation, supply, and industrial targets, not just in North Vietnam but in South Vietnam as well. Third, because of the limited nature of the war in Southeast Asia, any bombing activity could never be decisive.

The initial air strikes, code-named Operation Rolling Thunder, were limited primarily to enemy radar and bridges below the 20th parallel. As the effort expanded, however, President Johnson ordered the bombing of most metropolitan areas in North Vietnam. The first of these expanded attacks took place on May 22, 1965, when USAF–105s bombed the North Vietnamese barracks at Quang Soui. While the first strikes were made by tactical aircraft, the most spectacular and destructive aircraft used in the air war were B–52 strategic bombers. These aircraft operated essentially from six large airfields in Thailand. The USAF bomber and support presence in Thailand grew from about 1,000 personnel and 83 aircraft in early 1965 to a peak of about 55,000 personnel and 600 aircraft by the time of the Tet Offensive in January and February 1968. James Clay Thompson's *Rolling Thunder: Understanding Policy and Program Failure* (1980) is an excellent evaluation of the bombing campaign over North Vietnam.

From the first handful of strikes into enemy territory in 1965 until the USAF and navy sorties were halted by presidential decree on October 31,1968, the aircraft struck at bridges, vehicles, rolling stock, military posts, assembly plants, supply depots, vessels, antiaircraft and radar sites, railroads, and highways. During nearly four years of bombing, USAF, navy, marine, and South Vietnamese aircraft had flown about 304,000 tactical and 2,380 B–52 sorties and dropped 643,000 tons of bombs on enemy targets. R. Bruce Harley (*A Short History of Strategic Bombardment*) and Walter Boyne (*Boeing B–52: A Documentary History*) consider the B–52 the most successful military aircraft ever produced. It began entering service in the mid–1950s and by 1959 had replaced the awesome but obsolete B–36 as the backbone of Strategic Air Command's (SAC) heavy bomber force. Its primary mission was nuclear deterrence through retaliation. The B–52 has been amazingly adaptable. It was initially designed to achieve very high-altitude penetration of enemy airspace. But when that concept was rendered obsolete by the development of accurate surface-to-air missiles (SAMs), the B–52 was redesigned and reconstructed for low-altitude penetration. It has undergone eight major design changes since first flown in 1952, from B–52A to B–52H. Literally, although much the same in appearance, the most recent version is a radically different aircraft, superior in every way to the first models.

When the Vietnam situation began to deteriorate in 1964, key SAC commanders began pressing for SAC to get involved in any U.S. action in Vietnam. But the first problem was mission. How could a heavy strategic bomber designed to carry nuclear bombs be used in Vietnam? The answer was to modify the B–52 again. Two B–52 units, the 320th Bomb Wing and the 2nd Bomb Wing, had their aircraft modified to carry "iron bombs," that is, conventional high-explosive bombs. After a second modification, each B–52 used in Vietnam could carry eighty-four 500-pound bombs and twenty-four 750-pound bombs on underwing racks, for a 3,000-mile, nonstop range. The two bomb wings were deployed to operate from Guam as the 133rd Provisional Wing. Later, additional units were deployed to Thailand and Okinawa to reduce in-flight time and thus warning time.

The first B–52 raids against a target in South Vietnam (and the first war action for the B–52) took place on June 18, 1965. The target was a Vietcong jungle sanctuary. The results were not encouraging. Two B–52s collided in flight to the target and were lost in the Pacific Ocean. The results of the bombing could not be evaluated because the area was controlled by the Vietcong. Although the press criticized the use of B–52s, ground commanders were much impressed with the potential of the B–52. Previous attempts to use tactical bombers and fighter-bombers to disrupt enemy troop concentrations and supply depots had not been successful. But the B–52 was a veritable flying boxcar, and the effect of a squadron-size attack was to create a virtual Armageddon on the ground.

Ironically, the most effective use of the B–52 in Vietnam was for tactical support of ground troops. B–52s were called in to disrupt enemy troop concentrations and supply areas with devastating effect. B–52 raids were also flown against targets in North Vietnam, Cambodia, and Laos. General William Westmoreland considered the B–52s essential to American efforts in Vietnam. From June 1965 until August 1973, when operations ceased, B–52s flew 124,532 sorties, which successfully dropped their bomb loads on target. Thirty-one B–52s were lost, eighteen shot down by the enemy (all over North Vietnam), and thirteen lost to operational problems. Rolling Thunder's military objective was to destroy North Vietnamese capability and will to fight. The air commanders advocated unrestricted bombing, but Rolling Thunder was in reality a graduated response without a singular objective reflecting the aims of the president. The bombing did not weaken the Communist armed forces and had a minimal impact on the North Vietnamese war-making capacity. By March 1968 Johnson was unsure that the goal of non-Communist South Vietnam was obtainable.

OPERATION MENU

Although the bombing was stopped for several months during the winter of 1968–1969, the bombing eventually resumed after President Richard M. Nixon assumed office. President Nixon was responsible for the most controversial bombing operation of the war, taking place in Cambodia after spring 1969. It was known as Operation Menu. American military leaders had long complained that leftist forces were using Cambodian jungles near the Vietnamese borders as safe havens from which to stage hit-and-run attacks against American and South Vietnamese forces. President Nixon was convinced by military leaders that he could cripple North Vietnam by destroying its Cambodian sanctuaries.

On March 18, 1969, the U.S. Air Force began Operation Menu, a series of secret, illegal B–52 bombings of National Liberation Front and North Vietnamese army sanctuaries in eastern Cambodia. The sorties, all of which were flown at night, were directed by ground control units, ensuring that not even the aircrews were told to follow explicitly all directions for the bomb release from the ground control personnel. In all, between March 18, 1969, and May 26, 1970, the B–52s flew 4,308 sorties and dropped 120,578 tons of bombs on enemy base camps in Cambodia. It continued for fifteen months until the Cambodian invasion (May 1970), when it was renamed Operation Freedom Deal and expanded to include "targets" throughout Cambodia. Freedom Deal continued until Congress prohibited funds for bombing Cambodia effective August 15, 1973. By their end 16,527 sorties had been flown and 383,851 tons of bombs dropped.

General Creighton Abrams had wanted to attack sanctuaries for some time; however, President Lyndon Johnson repeatedly refused permission. When Richard Nixon became president in January 1969, these requests were resubmitted with the justification that striking sanctuaries would reduce the National Liberation Front–North Vietnamese Army (NLF-NVA) offensive capabilities and the Central Office for South Vietnam (COSVN) (the NLF-NVA command structure) had been located and could be destroyed by either ground or air attack. After initial hesitation, Nixon approved, for reasons of his own. The bombing was to "signal" Hanoi that Nixon was "tougher" than Johnson and to lend credence to the "mad man" image he wanted to create among North Vietnamese leaders.

Officially, the American military claimed the base areas were not inhabited by Cambodian civilians, but private military reports indicated awareness of civilian presence and expectations of civilian casualties. These reports contended that although casualties should be light because the Base Areas were sparsely populated and Cambodians lived apart from the NLF-NVA, "some Cambodian casualties would be sustained ...[and] the surprise effect of attacks would tend to increase casualties ...[due to] probable lack of protective shelter around Cambodian homes." The number of Cambodians killed is unknown.

Nixon, very concerned that Operation Menu not become public knowledge, ordered elaborate security measures, which included falsification of military records, an offense punishable by court-martial under Article 107 of the Uniform Code of Military Justice, so there was absolutely no record of the bombings having occurred. Nixon and Henry Kissinger's justification was that secrecy was necessary to protect Cambodia's Prince

Norodom Sihanouk, who gave his "tacit consent." They do not provide evidence to support this proposition, and Prince Sihanouk vehemently denies he consented, tacitly or otherwise.

These bombings, according to William Shawcross in *Sideshow: Kissinger, Nixon, and the Destruction of Cambodia* (1979), temporarily hampered North Vietnamese efforts in Cambodia, but they also expanded the war into Cambodia as the North Vietnamese retaliated. By April 26, 1970, for instance, North Vietnam had taken control of large areas of the country and appeared on the verge of toppling the Cambodian government. This action prompted an American and South Vietnamese invasion of Cambodia to preserve the friendly government. During a three-month period, April 29 to June 30, 1970, these forces temporarily threw back the North Vietnamese, but with their withdrawal North Vietnam attacked Cambodia again. Throughout these operations, the USAF provided bombing support to the Cambodian army in its defensive activity, but it was insufficient. Not long after the withdrawal of the United States from Southeast Asia, the Cambodian government fell, and the puppet state of Kampuchea was created by North Vietnam.

OPERATION LINEBACKER I

On Good Friday, March 30, 1972, three North Vietnamese Army divisions crossed the Demilitarized Zone (DMZ) and invaded the Republic of Vietnam. Before the Easter weekend was over, 120,000 NVA regulars with 200 armored vehicles were in South Vietnam. Launched to strengthen Hanoi's negotiating position at Paris, the invasion prompted the second major bombing campaign over North Vietnam by the United States. Named Linebacker I, the operation continued nearly nine months and involved nearly all U.S. Air Force assets in the theater. B–52 Arc Light bombing missions against infiltration routes and staging areas increased, and B–52 forces already in the theater were strengthened by additional aircraft deployments to Guam. At the same time tactical air power forces were also reinforced. Over the next few weeks U.S. marine air squadrons deployed to several staging bases; navy carrier support doubled; and air force tactical air units rejoined the war from Korea and the United States. The major priority of returning tactical air units was to support South Vietnamese forces directly so that the ground battle in South Vietnam could be established.

On April 2, 1972, President Richard Nixon authorized air strikes against military targets and logistic supply points north of the DMZ to the parallel at 17° 25'; this was increased to 18° N on April 4 and to 19° N on April 6. On April 9, fifteen B–52s stuck railroad and supply depots at Vinh, the first use of B–52s in North Vietnam since October 28, 1968. Three days later, eighteen B–52s struck Bai Thuong airfield. On the weekend of April 15–16, navy and air force aircraft bombed military storage areas surrounding Hanoi and Haiphong.

As with most military operations, these attacks had several purposes. They disrupted the flow of war supplies supporting the invasion of South Vietnam; warned Hanoi that if it persisted in the invasion, it would face mounting raids in the north; and demonstrated continuing American support for the government of South Vietnam. Furthermore, these attacks were intended to persuade the North Vietnamese to seek a political rather, than a purely military, resolution of the conflict.

When the initial Linebacker I bombing operations brought further North Vietnamese intransigence, President Nixon announced that the North Vietnamese ports of Haiphong, Cam Pha, Hon Gai, and Thanh Hoa, as well as smaller inlets harboring North Vietnamese patrol boats, would be mined. The mines were laid on May 8 and activated two days later. Simultaneously, Nixon announced that Linebacker I air operations throughout North Vietnam would continue until a formal cessation of hostilities could be secured. Throughout the spring and summer of 1972, Linebacker I operations continued. In the fall North Vietnam indicated a willingness to negotiate, and on October 22, 1972, Nixon ended Linebacker I. Richard Nixon redefined America's objective in Vietnam. In order to achieve "peace with honor," he placed a greater emphasis on air power to accomplish this task. Although Linebacker I differed little from Rolling Thunder, Nixon had fewer negative objectives limiting the application of bombing. North Vietnam's defenses, pilot inexperience, and weather conditions were about the only operational controls on Linebacker I and II. The changing international climate and détente with China and the Soviets allowed Nixon to apply a free hand with bombing in the hopes of a negotiated peace. He used air power tactics in an endeavor to end the war quickly while providing an advantageous climate for an "honorable" peace accord (Clodfelter, 154). The nature of the war had changed somewhat after the Tet Offensive of 1968. The conventional nature of the Easter Offensive presented material need that heretofore had not been required by the Communist forces. This factor alone accounted for the successes enjoyed by Linebacker I. The North Vietnamese employed tanks and heavy cannon, requiring ammunition and oil supplies that were vulnerable to air strikes by B–52s with their enormous thirty-ton bomb loads.

OPERATION LINEBACKER II

On October 22, 1972, when it seemed the Paris peace talks were leading to an agreement, the United States halted air operations above the 20th parallel. The end of Operation Linebacker I provided a breathing spell for the North Vietnamese, who quickly strengthened air defenses in Hanoi and Haiphong. By mid-December, Hanoi had repaired rail lines to China and adjusted its supply routing to compensate for the naval mine blockade. The restored rail lines were capable of handling 16,000 tons of supplies per day, or 2.5 times Hanoi's needs. Simultaneous with the cessation of bombing, negotiations between North Vietnam and the United States stalled amid indications that Hanoi might renew its offensive in South Vietnam. By early December, an agreement that had appeared so near five weeks earlier was in a shambles. President Richard Nixon then launched Operation Linebacker II, a final, eleven-day bombing campaign, which was one of the heaviest aerial assaults of the war. The U.S. Air Force used F–105, F–4, F–111, and, for the first time, B–52 aircraft to attack Hanoi and Haiphong. Tactical aircraft flew more than 1,000 sorties, and the B–52s about 740, most of them against rail yards, power plants, communication facilities, air defense radar sites, docks and shipping facilities, petroleum stores, ammunition supply depots, air bases, and transportation facilities.

The North Vietnamese retaliated with most of their inventory of about 1,000 surface-to-air missiles and a heavy barrage of antiaircraft fire. The countermeasures were ineffective. Only twenty-seven aircraft were lost; however, eighteen B–52s were destroyed or badly damaged by missiles. In spite of this, the air attacks continued, and by December 28, North Vietnamese defenses had been all but obliterated. During the last two days of the campaign, American aircraft flew over Hanoi and Haiphong without suffering any losses. The North Vietnamese lost eight aircraft in aerial fighting during the Linebacker II campaign, as well as suffering substantial collateral damage in the raids.

Linebacker II, or the December bombings, was directed at the will of the North Vietnamese to resist. Nixon removed almost all negative controls, and the magnitude of Linebacker II surprised Northern Vietnamese leaders. William C. Westmoreland said, "When President Nixon decided to use our available military power in manner that truly hurt North Vietnam, negotiations began to move in a substantive way" (Clodfelter, 176). The conviction that air power played the decisive role in gaining an agreement with the North permeated the air force. Partially as a result of Linebacker II's success, negotiations resumed while Henry Kissinger and Le Duc Tho were in Paris on January 8, 1973. While the diplomats talked, American air attacks were restricted and confined south of the 20th parallel. U.S. air force, navy, and marine fighters flew about twenty sorties per day with B–52s, adding thirty-six to the daily total. On January 23, 1973, the Paris negotiators signed a nine-point cease-fire agreement effective January 28, 1973. The air power displayed in Linebacker II had played a significant role in extracting this agreement to end the war. Between June 1965 and August 1973, the Strategic Air Command's B–52s flew 126,615 bombing sorties, and the tactical forces flew more than 400,000 bombing sorties, in the process dropping 6,162,000 tons of munitions on enemy positions. By contrast, the total tonnage of explosives dropped in World War II had been 2,150,000 tons.

THE DEBATE

Since the end of the Vietnam War, there has been a persistent perception, nurtured by the military and some political leaders, that the proper use of air power could have achieved American political objectives in Southeast Asia and ended the conflict. In fact, the conviction of most air force officers and strategic thinkers today is that massive bombing could have "won" the war. Other politicians and military historians condemn this view as a false interpretation of Vietnam military history and a misplaced faith in weaponry. The argument focuses around the question of how to use air power, which means strategic bombing, as a political tool. Mark Clodfelter, author of *The Limits of Air Power*, states, "The supreme test of bombing's efficacy is its contribution to a nation's war aims" (xi).

In the argument concerning the use of air power during the Vietnam War, there has never been a consensus of agreement in the literature for or against its effectiveness. Instead, the questions have persisted. Did the United States win the war or end the war because of successful air strikes? Could the United States have won the war with a different tactical approach—using more or less air power? A more basic question revolves around whether air power was efficacious at all in Vietnam. The military contributes a resounding "yes" to these questions. For the most part, during the Vietnam conflict they had the support of "the best and the brightest" in the Kennedy, Johnson, and Nixon administrations. National Security Advisor McGeorge Bundy argued that bombing would bolster South Vietnamese morale. Ambassador Maxwell Taylor said that it would break Hanoi's will to fight. Secretary of State Dean Rusk assured President Lyndon B. Johnson that bombing would secure a bargaining advantage. Secretary of Defense Robert S. McNamara was convinced that air power would convey America's political resolve to Hanoi. According to Raphael Littauer and Norman Uphoff (*The Air War in Indochina*, 1972), "The whole of U.S. policy in Indochina became a function of the capabilities and limitations of air power." The only powerful critic of air power was George Ball, undersecretary of state in the Kennedy and Johnson administrations. But as David DiLeo points out in *George Ball, Vietnam, and the Rethinking of Containment* (1991), nobody listened to Ball.

Air force doctrine and tradition state that air power must strike a nation's vital centers in order to destroy war-fighting capabilities. This will then wreck the social fabric of an enemy nation and ultimately destroy their will to resist. Air force chief of staff during the Korean War, Hoyt Vandenberg, told the Air War College's class of senior officers in 1953 that "air power must not be applied except against the industrial power of the nation. And it must not be applied unless you're going to win the war with it.... Let us keep our eye on the goal of air power, which is to knock out the ability of a nation to fight" (Clodfelter, 35). This viewpoint reflects the history of the air force in World War II and Korea, with its perception of the Communists as the perpetual enemy who can be subdued only with massive air strikes. The tactics are geared toward a conventional war. A limited war, with provisional or even undefined aims, never entered the realm of thinking for air war planners. Lieutenant General George E. Stratemeyer stated in 1951 the credo accepted by the air force for the next twenty-five years. Objecting to the limited nature of the United States' war aims in Korea, he said: "It [the American military objective] is contrary to everything that every military commander that I have been associated with or from all of our history— he has never been in position where he could not win the war he started to win. That is not American. That is not American" (Clodfelter, 25). Since the military leaders of the Vietnam era matured during World War II and Korea, the traditions and experiences of those wars carried over to the military strategies used in Vietnam. As recently as 1986, General Curtis Lemay said, "Once you're in a war, or you've made the decision to use military force to solve your problems, then you ought to use it" (Clodfelter, 208). The *Air Force Manual* also states, "The employment of land, sea, and air forces in time of war should be directed toward one single aim: VICTORY." Therefore, understandably, it is the conviction of today's air force that we could have truly won the war in Vietnam with massive bombing early in the conflict and fewer, or at least clearer, political restraints throughout. For the best summary of traditional air force thinking, see Robert F. Futrell's *Ideas, Concepts, Doctrine: A History of Basic Thinking in the United States Air Force, 1907–1964* (1971). In defense of their stance concerning Vietnam and even future wars, the military logicians and historians cite precedents and the rationale for the use of air power. They argue that during World War II, air power effectively destroyed Japan's and Germany's capacity to fight through strategic attacks against war production facilities. In addition to its capacity for destroying an enemy's capacity to fight, air power can also be extremely useful in achieving major objectives of foreign policy. During the Berlin Airlift of 1948–1949, air power prevented Soviet expansion into West Berlin while at the same time preventing a violent confrontation between the two superpowers. Advocates of air power also argue that the Soviets stepped back from the Cuban missile crisis in 1962 because of the threat of air power.

The advocates of air power remain convinced today, especially after the Gulf War air attacks on Iraq in 1991, that air power can win wars and that the air war did not win the war in Vietnam because it was not applied intensely enough. Writers like Raphael Littauer and Norman Uphoff (*The Air War in Indochina*), William Momyer (*Air Power in Three Wars*), and T. R. Milton ("USAF and the Vietnam Experience") complain that civilian political leaders in Washington, D.C., tied the hands of air force planners and imposed political constraints on the military effort, implying that without those constraints they could have won the war. Jack Broughton's *Going Downtown: The War Against Hanoi and Washington* continues that argument, raising the "tying our hands behind our backs" argument to a new level. The advocates of air power all then make a similar set of arguments about the efficacy of their art: air war is "capital intensive," but it is cheap in terms of American lives; air power demonstrates the reliability of American commitments; intensive bombing achieves a bargaining counter at the diplomatic table; air power raises the cost of enemy aggression; the technology of air power can compensate for the limitations imposed by economic, geographical, and political considerations; destruction of vital military targets will destroy the enemies' will to fight; air superiority gives tactical flexibility to surface forces, and in Vietnam we were able to use their air space, but they could not use ours; and air power can inhibit the enemy's capabilities to escalate and thus provide time for the United States to achieve political goals.

The proponents of air power look to the Linebacker II bombing campaigns as proof of the efficacy of air power. The attacks were conducted against an experienced air defense network in North Vietnam, and because of their accuracy and ferocity, they brought Hanoi to the bargaining table. The military claims these bombings would have been even more effective if conducted earlier in the war against the "embryonic defense" of the North Vietnamese army. Such a bombing campaign beginning in 1965 in the North would have been deadly to be sure—to civilians as well as military personnel. But military historians like John Nichols and Barrett Tillman argue that it would not have been as deadly as the final totals of the protracted war. Linebacker II halted Communist supplies and jump-started the negotiations. According to A.J.C. Lavelle's *Air Power and the 1972 Spring Invasion*, "By interdicting the lines of communication to impede the movement of men and materials into Laos and South Vietnam, by systematically striking bridges, key choke points, port facilities, truck parks, staging areas, POL [petroleum, oil, lubricants] facilities, supply caches, and trucks moving from Hanoi south, the enemy's supply was reduced to an estimated 20 percent of his initial capabilities" (151).

John B. Nichols and Barrett Tillman, authors of *On Yankee Station*, thus conclude: "They [the veterans] know the fallacy of the belief that airpower 'failed' in Vietnam. They know instinctively . . . that airpower was misunderstood and misapplied throughout Southeast Asia for seven years or more and that when aviation was applied correctly, it achieved results" (x). They strongly recommend that our government should "not fight unless it means to win." Vice Admiral C. Turner Joy, the naval theater commander in Korea from 1950 to 1951 and chief of the United Nations truce delegation team, contributes to this traditional dogma with these words: "The speed with which agreement is reached with the Communists varies directly to the military pressure applied, and the worth of any agreement is in proportion to the military strength with which you are able and willing to enforce it" (Nichols and Tillman, 138).

There are a number of excellent works that are quite critical of the advocates of air power. The most important of those books include Mark Clodfelter's *The Limits of Air Power: The American Bombing of North Vietnam* (1989), Raphael Littauer's and Norman Uphoff's *The Air War in Indochina* (1972), James Clay Thompson's *Rolling Thunder: Undertaking Policy and Program Failure* (1980), and Earl H. Tilford, Jr.'s, *Setup: What the Air Force Did in Vietnam and Why* (1991). They argue, first of all, that the United States unloaded unprecedented volumes of explosives on North and South Vietnam. In spite of 6,300,000 tons of bombs dropped between 1965 and 1971 (nearly three times as many bombs as were detonated during all of World War II), Hanoi did not capitulate. The United States was still in the war. Bombing did not crush the Vietnamese spirit; it only made them more determined and more resentful of the United States.

Critics also claimed that the political situation in Vietnam militated against the effectiveness of air power. Air war planners never considered the case of a limited war. To air force senior officers, the Soviets were the enemy—the only enemy. According to Clodfelter, their experience was using a "preponderance of effort," a "bludgeon rather than a rapier" (10). They saw bombing as the cure-all for any contingency. But that created the problem of linking strategic targeting with national goals. Critics used Henry Kissinger to support their arguments against the use of air power. He said that "military success [achieved through air power] could not be translated into permanent political advantages" (Littauer, 3). Political reality limited the effectiveness of air power. "The determination to win," wrote Clodfelter, "was significantly modified by our fear of widening the war" (47). The United States was reluctant to strike Hanoi or Haiphong, since it would effectively amount to killing the hostage. Nor was air power able to interdict the source of North Vietnamese supplies—the Soviet Union and China—without the grave consequences of widening the war.

Another argument the critics made was that the destructiveness of the bombing was so great and its impact so enormous on the civilian population of South Vietnam that it became counterproductive. The military claimed that air power could support troops in a firefight, interdict supply lines and the lines of communication, and harass the enemy at his base. But none of these supposed advantages of air power work in a guerrilla setting. How do bombers separate insurgents from the population? If they do not attempt such a separation, there are going to be horrendous civilian casualties, and such casualties did occur. Most estimates conclude that American bombers accidentally killed between 150,000 and 400,000 South Vietnamese civilians during the war. As early as 1966, Arthur M. Schlesinger, Jr., in *The Bitter Heritage* wrote:

If we continue the pursuit of a total military victory, we will leave the tragic country gutted and devastated by bombs, burned by napalm, turned into a wasteland by chemical defoliation, a land of ruin and wreck. This is the melancholy course to which the escalation policy commits us. The effect will be to pulverize the political and institutional fabric which alone can give a South Vietnamese state that hope of independent survival which is our presumed aim. Our method in other words, defeats our goal. (Pp. 47–48)

Whatever chance the United States might have had of building an anti-Communist democracy in South Vietnam was destroyed by the destructiveness of American firepower. Undersecretary of State George W. Ball, a member of the World War II Strategic Bombing Survey and chief critic of the air campaign over Indochina, commented that the air war cast the United States as a great power raining destruction on a small power because we accused that small power of instigating what much of the world regarded as an indigenous rebellion.

The critics of the use of air power also argue that fighting a "capital intensive war" in an agricultural country is a contradiction in terms. Air power is especially useful in highly industrialized countries with complex, centralized infrastructures. Bombing those countries can play havoc with the production and distribution of goods. But North Vietnam was not that type of nation. It was overwhelmingly agricultural, with a primitive infrastructure. Dirt roads, small factories, and peasant agriculture were the norm. According to Thompson and Clodfelter, if a peasant economy is resistant to air attack, no level of bombing efficiency can make a difference. Both the American military and civilian policy-making apparatus failed to take this into consideration.

Other critics, like Neil Sheehan in *Bright and Shining Lie* (1988), convincingly argue that the arithmetic of the air war simply did not add up. The bombing campaigns over the Ho Chi Minh Trail did not succeed in cutting off the Vietcong and the North Vietnamese troops in South Vietnam from their supply bases above the 17th parallel. They just intensified Communist efforts to keep the supplies flowing by constantly improving the transportation system into South Vietnam. In 1963 the Ho Chi Minh Trail was primitive, requiring a physically demanding, month-long march of eighteen-hour days to reach the south. But by the spring of 1964, the North Vietnamese began dramatic improvements in the trail. They put nearly 500,000 peasants to work full- and part-time, building and repairing roads. In one year the peasants built hundreds of miles of all-weather roads, complete with underground fuel storage tanks, hospitals, and supply warehouses. They built ten separate roads for every main transportation route. By the time the war ended, the Ho Chi Minh Trail had 12,500 miles of high-quality roads, complete with pontoon bridges that could be removed by day and reinstalled at night and miles of bamboo trellises covering the roads and hiding the trucks.

Despite the most intense aerial pounding in history, the Ho Chi Minh Trail served continuously as the Communist lifeline. As early as mid–1965 the North Vietnamese could move 5,000 men and 400 tons of supplies into South Vietnam every month. Robert McNamara estimated that by mid–1967 more than 12,000 trucks were winding their way up and down the trail. By 1974 the North Vietnamese had even managed to build 3,125 miles of fuel pipelines down the trail to keep their army functioning in South Vietnam. Three of the pipelines came all the way out of Laos and deep into South Vietnam without being detected.

When Lyndon Johnson saw the photographs of the June 29, 1966, raid on the petroleum storage facilities in Hanoi and Haiphong, he was ecstatic, gleefully remarking to Walt Rostow that "them sons-of-bitches are finished now." But North Vietnam was not finished. The country had an agricultural economy, with few industries vital to the war effort. Anticipating an escalation of the bombing, the North Vietnamese built enough underground tanks and dispersed them widely enough to have a survival level of gasoline, diesel fuel, and oil lubricants. In 1965 and 1966 North Vietnam began evacuating nonessential people from cities and relocating industries—machine shops, textile mills, and other businesses—to the mountains, jungles, and caves. Home manufacturing filled the modest need for consumer goods. By late 1967 Hanoi's population had dropped from 1 million to 250,000 people. A little planning had robbed the American pilots of their effectiveness.

The air war was doomed. The only targets that mattered were bridges, roads, and transportation centers, and almost as soon as they were bombed, the North Vietnamese repaired them. They replaced steel bridges with ferries and easily repairable pontoon bridges. A long history of fighting the drought and flooding in the Red River Valley created a cooperative spirit among the North Vietnamese that served them well. Political teams organized people to repair roads, help troops and supplies get across rivers, and build air-raid shelters, bunkers, tunnels, and trenches. American pilots found themselves returning to the same places again and again to bomb the same targets.

The bombing was, to be sure, devastating. During the war the United States dropped 1 million tons of explosives on North Vietnam and 1.5 million tons on the Ho Chi Minh Trail. In 1967 the bombing raids killed or wounded 2,800 people in North Vietnam each month. The bombers destroyed every industrial, transportation, and communications facility built in North Vietnam since 1954, badly damaged three major cities and twelve provincial capitals, reduced agricultural output, and set the economy back a decade. Malnutrition was widespread in North Vietnam in 1967. But because North Vietnam was overwhelmingly agricultural—and subsistence agriculture, at that—the bombing did not have the devastating economic effect it would have had on centralized, industrial economy. Moreover, the Soviet Union and China gave North Vietnam a blank check, willingly replacing whatever the U.S. bombers destroyed.

Weather and problems of distance also limited the air war. In 1967 the United States could keep about 300 aircraft over North Vietnam or Laos for about thirty minutes each day. It was mathematically impossible to stop the infiltration over the thousands of miles of roads of the Ho Chi Minh Trail, especially with hundreds of thousands of Vietnamese repairing the damage on a moment's notice. Torrential rains, thick cloud cover, and heavy fogs also hampered the bombing. Trucks from North Vietnam could move when the aircraft from the carriers in the South China Sea could not.

Throughout the war North Vietnam steadily improved its air defense system. In fact, the gradualist approach Lyndon Johnson took to escalating the air war gave the North Vietnamese time to build the most elaborate air defenses in the history of the world. They built 200 Soviet SA–2 surface-to-air missile sites, trained pilots to fly MiG–17s and MiG–21s, deployed 7,000 antiaircraft batteries, and distributed automatic and semiautomatic weapons to millions of people, with instructions to shoot at American aircraft. The North Vietnamese air defense system, which was placed around Hanoi and Haiphong as well as critical points along the Ho Chi Minh Trail, hampered the air war in three ways. First, American pilots had to fly at higher altitudes, and that reduced their accuracy. Second, they were busy dodging missiles, and that consumed "time over target" and reduced the effectiveness of each individual sortie. Finally, they spent much of their time firing at missile installations and antiaircraft guns instead of supply lines. The air war did not bludgeon North Vietnam into submission; it did not even keep food out of Vietcong mouths, bullets out of NVA rifles, or North Vietnamese troops out of South Vietnam. In 1967 alone North Vietnam moved more than 90,000 troops into South Vietnam in spite of the heaviest air bombardment in history. According to Earl H. Tilford, Jr. (*Armed Forces & Society*, 1991):

The ambiguities of the Vietnam War remain. What is more certain is that warfare is more than sortie generation and firepower on targets. It incorporates many factors, including some that are traditionally considered beyond the purview of the soldier, such as politics and economics. But geography, the weather, and the many aspects of culture—one's own as well as the enemy's—are factors that determine the way nations fight their wars. Above all, warfare, especially limited warfare, is an art. As such, it requires intellectual sophistication, mental dexterity, and the ability to think abstractly. (P. 342)

The American air war over Vietnam, unfortunately, had none of those qualities.

BIBLIOGRAPHY

Anderson, William C. *BAT–21*. New York: Bantam, 1983.

Ballard, Jack S. *The United States Air Force in Southeast Asia: Development and Employment of Fixed Wing Gunships, 1962–1972*. Washington, D.C.: Office of Air Force History, 1982.

Basel, G. I. *Pak Six*. La Mesa, Cal.: Associated Creative Writers, 1982.

Berger, Carl, ed. *The United States Air Force in Southeast Asia, 1961–1973, an Illustrated Account*. Washington, D.C.: Office of Air Force History, 1977.

Bowers, Ray L. *The U.S. Air Force in Southeast Asia: Tactical Airlift*. Washington, D.C.: Office of Air Force History, 1984.

Boyne, Walter. *Boeing B–52: A Documentary History*. London: Jane's, 1981.

Branfman, Fred. *Voices from the Plain of Jars: Life Under an Air War*. New York: Harper and Row, 1972.

Broughton, Jack. *Thud Ridge*. Philadelphia: Lippincott, 1969.

Broughton, Jack. *Going Downtown: The War Against Hanoi and Washington*. New York: Orion, 1988.

Buckingham, William A., Jr. *Operation Ranch Hand: The United States Air Force and Herbicides in Southeast Asia, 1961–1971*. Washington, D.C.: U.S. Government Printing Office, 1982.

Burbage, Paul, ed. *The Battle for the Skies Over North Vietnam, 1964–1972*. Washington, D.C.: Office of Air Force History, 1976.

Chinnery, Phil. *Air War in Vietnam*. New York: Exeter Books, 1987.

Clodfelter, Mark. *The Limits of Air Power: The American Bombing of North Vietnam*. New York: Free Press, 1989.

Corum, Delbert, ed. *The Tale of Two Bridges*. Washington, D.C.: Office of Air Force History, 1976.

Davis, Larry. *Gunships*. Washington, D.C.: Squadron/Signal, 1983.

Dickson, Paul. *The Electronic Battlefield*. Bloomington: Indiana University Press, 1976.

DiLeo, David. *George Ball, Vietnam, and the Rethinking of Containment*. Chapel Hill: University of North Carolina Press, 1991.

Doglione, John A., ed. *Airpower and the 1972 Spring Invasion*. Washington, D.C.: Office of Air Force History, 1976.

Drendel, Lou. *Huey*. Carrollton, Tex.: Squadron/Signal Publications, 1983.

Drendel, Lou. *Air War over Southeast Asia: A Pictorial Record*. Washington, D.C.: Squadron/Signal, 1983–1984.

Drendel, Lou. *B–52 Stratofortress in Action*. Carrollton, Tex.: Squadron/Signal, 1984.

Drury, Richard. *My Secret War*. New York: St. Martin's Press.

Eastman, James N., Jr., Walter Hanak, and Lawrence J. Paszek, eds. *Aces and Aerial Victories: The United States Air Force in Southeast Asia, 1965–1973*. Washington, D.C.: U.S. Government Printing Office, 1976.

Eckhardt, George S. *Command and Control, 1950–1969*. Washington, D.C.: U.S. Government Printing Office, 1974.

Emerson, Gloria. *Winners and Losers: Battles, Retreats, Gains, Losses, and Ruins from a Long War*. New York: Random House, 1976.

Fox, Roger P. *Air Base Defense in the Republic of Vietnam, 1961–1973*. Washington, D.C.: Office of Air Force History, 1979.

Franklin, H. Bruce. "How American Management Won the War in Vietnam." *American Quarterly* 40 (Summer 1988): 409–26.

Frisbee, John L. "The Phoenix That Never Was." *Air Force Magazine* (February 1973), 1–10.

Frisbee, John L. "Not With a Whimper but a Bang." *Air Force Magazine* (March 1973), 1–6.

Futrell, Robert F. *Aces and Aerial Victories: The United States Air Force in Southeast Asia, 1965–1973*. Washington, D.C.: Office of Air Force History, 1976.

Futrell, Robert F. *Ideas, Concepts, Doctrine: A History of Basic Thinking in the United States Air Force, 1907–1964*. Maxwell AFB, Ala.: University Press, 1971.

Futrell, Robert F. *The United States Air Force in Southeast Asia: The Advisory Years to 1965*. Washington, D.C.: Office of Air Force History, 1983.

Gabriel, Charles A. "The Air Force: Where We Are and Where We Are Going." *Air University Review* 35 (January-February 1984): 2–10.

Gehri, Suzanne Budd. *Study War Once More: Teaching Vietnam at Air University*. Maxwell AFB, Ala.: Air University Press, 1985.

Gibson, James William. *The Perfect War: Technowar in Vietnam*. Boston: Atlantic Monthly Press, 1986.

Gropman, Alan L. *Airpower and the Airlift Evacuation of Kham Duc*. Washington, D.C.: U.S. Government Printing Office, 1979.

Hai Thu. *North Vietnam Against U.S. Air Force*. New York: Foreign Language Publishing House, 1967.

Harley, R. Bruce. *A Short History of Strategic Bombardment*. Washington, D.C.: Air University Press, 1971.

Harvey, Frank. *Air War—Vietnam*. New York: Bantam, 1967.

Hetz, Martin F. *The Prestige Press and the Christmas Bombing, 1972*. Washington, D.C.: Ethics and Public Policy Center, 1980.

Hoopes, Townsend. *The Limits of Intervention*. New York: David McKay, 1969.

Hopkins, Charles K. *SAC Tanker Operations in the Southeast Asia War*. Omaha, Nebr.: Strategic Air Command, 1979.

Johnson, Lyndon B. *The Vantage Point*. New York: Popular Library, 1971.

Jurika, Stephen, ed. *From Pearl Harbor to Vietnam: The Memoirs of Admiral Arthur W. Radford*. Stanford, Calif.: Hoover Institution Press, 1982.

Kirk, Donald. *Wider War: The Struggle for Cambodia, Laos, and Thailand*. New York: Praeger, 1971.

Lavelle, A.J.C., ed. *Airpower and the 1972 Spring Invasion*. Washington, D.C.: U.S. Government Printing Office, 1976a.

Lavelle, A.J.C., ed. *The Battle for the Skies Over North Vietnam*. Washington, D.C.: U.S. Government Printing Office, 1976b.

Lavelle, A.J.C., ed. *The Tale of Two Bridges*. Washington, D.C.: U.S. Government Printing Office, 1976c.

Lavelle, A.J.C., ed. *Last Flight from Saigon*. Washington, D.C.: U.S. Government Printing Office, 1978.

Littauer, Raphael, and Norman Uphoff, eds. *The Air War in Indochina*. Boston: Beacon Press, 1972.

McCarthy, James P. "SAC Looks to the Future." *Air University Review* 38 (January–March 1987): 13–23.

McCarthy, James R., and Allison McCarthy. *Linebacker II: A View from the Rock*. London: Unger, 1986.

McDonald, Charles, and A.J.C. Lavelle, eds. *The Vietnamese Air Force 1951–1975: An Analysis of Its Role in Combat*. Washington, D.C.: U.S. Government Printing Office, 1976.

Mason, Robert C. *Chickenhawk*. New York: Viking Press, 1983.

Mersky, Peter, and Norma Polmar. *The Naval Air War in Vietnam: 1965–1976*. Washington, D.C.: Nautical and Aviation, 1981.

Mesko, Jim. *Airmobile: The Helicopter War in Vietnam*. Washington, D.C.: U.S. Government Printing Office, 1985.

Mickish, Robert C. *B–57 Seven Canberra at War: 1964–1972*. Philadelphia: Scribner's, 1980.

Mickish, Robert C. *Flying Dragon: The South Vietnamese Air Force*. London: Osprey, 1988.

Milton, T. R. "USAF and the Vietnam Experience." *Air Force Magazine* 58 (June 1975): 51–64.

Milton, T. R. "The Lessons of Vietnam." *Air Force Magazine* 66 (March 1983): 104–22.

Momyer, William. *The Vietnamese Air Force, 1951–1975, An Analysis of Its Role in Combat*. Washington, D.C.: Office of Air Force History, 1977.

Momyer, William. *Air Power in Three Wars*. Washington, D.C.: Office of Air Force History, 1980.

Morrocco, John. *The Vietnam Experience. Rain of Fire: Air War, 1969–1973*. Boston: Boston, 1984.

Morrocco, John. *The Vietnam Experience. Thunder from Above: Air War, 1941–1968*. Boston: Boston, 1984.

Nalty, Bernard C. *Power and the Fight for Khe Sanh*. New York: Arco, 1973.

Nalty, Bernard C., George M. Watson, and Jacob Neufeld. *An Illustrated Guide to the Air War Over Vietnam*. New York: Arco, 1981.

Nichols, John B., and Barrett Tillman. *On Yankee Station: The Naval Air War Over Vietnam*. Washington, D.C.: U.S. Government Printing Office, 1987.

Parks, W. Hays. "Rolling Thunder and the Law of War." *Air University Review* 33 (January-February 1982): 2–23.

Parks, W. Hays. "Linebacker and the Law of War." *Air University Review* 34 (January-February 1983): 2–30.

Porter, Melvin F. *Linebacker: Overview of the First 120 Days*. Maxwell AFB, Ala.: Air Force Historical Research Center, 1973.

Prados, John. *The Sky Would Fall: Operation Vulture: The U.S. Bombing Mission in Indochina, 1954*. New York: Dial, 1983.

Rausa, Rosario. *Skyraider: The Douglas A–1 "Flying Dump Truck."* New York: Nautical and Aviation Publishing, 1982.

Ridgway, Matthew. *Soldier: The Memoirs of Matthew B. Ridgway*. New York: Harper, 1956.

Robbins, Christopher. *Air America*. New York: Putnam's, 1979.

Rogers, Bernard W. *Cedar Falls-Junction City: A Turning Point*. Washington, D.C.: Government Printing Office, 1974.

Salisbury, Harrison E. *Behind the Lines: Hanoi*. New York: Harper and Row, 1967.

Schemmer, Benjamin F. *The Raid*. New York: Harper and Row, 1976.

Schlesinger, Arthur M., Jr. *The Bitter Heritage: Vietnam and American Democracy, 1941–1966*. Boston: Houghton Mifflin, 1967.

Schlight, John. *The United States Air Force in Southeast Asia, The War in South Vietnam: The Years of the Offensive, 1965–1968*. Washington, D.C.: Office of Air Force History, 1989.

Shawcross, William. *Sideshow: Kissinger, Nixon, and the Destruction of Cambodia*. New York: Simon and Schuster, 1979.

Sheehan, Neil. *Bright and Shining Lie: John Paul Vann and America in Vietnam*. New York: Random House, 1988.

Smith, Melden E., Jr. "The Strategic Bombing Debate: World War II and Vietnam." *Journal of Contemporary History* 12 (January 1977): 175–91.

Snepp, Frank. *Decent Interval*. New York: Random Houe, 1977.

Szulc, Tad. "Behind the Vietnam Cease-Fire Agreement." *Foreign Policy* 15 (Summer 1974): 21–68.

Thayer, Thomas C. *War Without Fronts: The American War in Vietnam*. Boulder, Colo.: Westview Press, 1985.

Thompson, James Clay. *Rolling Thunder: Undertaking Policy and Program Failure*. Chapel Hill: University of North Carolina Press, 1980.

Tilford, Earl H., Jr. *A History of U.S. Search and Rescue in Southeast Asia, 1961–1975*. Washington, D.C.: Office of Air Force History, 1980.

Tilford, Earl H., Jr. *Setup: What the Air Force Did in Vietnam and Why*. Maxwell Air Force Base, Ala.: Air University Press, 1991.

Tilford, Earl H., Jr. "Why and How the U.S. Air Force Lost in Vietnam." *Armed Forces & Society* 17 (1991): 327–42.

Tobin, Thomas G., ed. *Last Flight from Saigon*. Washington, D.C.: Office of Air Force History, 1978.

Tolson, John J. *Airmobility, 1961–1971*. Washington, D.C.: U.S. Government Printing Office, 1973.

Westmoreland, William C. *A Soldier Reports*. Garden City, N.Y.: Doubleday, 1976.

Windchy, Eugene C. *Tonkin Gulf.* Garden City, N.Y.: Doubleday, 1971.

Van Dyke, Jon M. *North Vietnam's Strategy for Survival.* San Francisco: Pacific Books, 1972.

Vo Nguyen Giap. *People's War Against the United States: Aero-Naval War.* New York: Foreign Language Publishing House, 1975.

9   Atrocities and War Crimes

Karen Sleezer

One of the most pronounced issues of the Vietnam War was the emotionally charged debate on the conduct of the fighting forces in Vietnam. Statesmen, philosophers, artists, legal experts, military experts, and ordinary people have all, at one time or another, joined in the discourse. Of course, the central component of any discussion on what is acceptable conduct in warfare requires at least a minimal understanding of established international laws. However, there are those who would also contend that a discussion about permissible military behavior ought to include what is morally acceptable on the battlefield. In 1863 Francis Lieber, who formulated the first modern code of law for military operations, stated, "Men who take up arms against one another in public war do not cease on this account to be moral beings, responsible to one another and to God" (S. Cohen, 6). The fact that there is treatment of atrocity and war crimes in international law proves that all is not fair in war.

In the literature that deals with atrocities and war crimes in Vietnam, much of the emphasis is given to interpretations of the international laws on warfare. However, quite a few arguments contend that the laws are lacking and should incorporate a greater concern for moral and humanitarian limitations on the conduct of war. The specific issues that arise in the discussions on illegal acts of war include the conduct and policies of American forces in Vietnam; the actions of the enemy forces; the circumstances confronting the civilian population of Vietnam; the treatment of prisoners of war on both sides; the political context of American involvement in Vietnam; military strategies such as counterinsurgency, pacification, enemy attrition, and saturation bombing; the use of defoliants and technologically advanced weaponry; and finally, responsibility or guilt for illegal or immoral behavior.

In general, the evaluations of American conduct in the Vietnamese War tend to break down to those that oppose everything about American involvement in the region, those that see justifications for the American presence there, those that see justification for the presence in Vietnam but no justification for certain aspects of American policy, and those that perceive very little for which to fault the American military as a whole. The character of the works surveyed ranges from the most vocal antiwar activists, such as Bertrand Russell and Robert J. Lifton, to such official military and political participants in Vietnam as General William Westmoreland and Robert W. Komer.

In 1967 Bertrand Russell published a collection of essays and speeches dealing with the tragic and, as he alleges, criminal aspects of American involvement in the Vietnamese war. *War Crimes in Vietnam* is a direct condemnation of American policy in Vietnam on both moral and legal grounds. In Russell's opinion, America's role in the civil war of Vietnam was an act of aggression. The author also attempts to disprove Washington's claim that American forces are in the region solely as advisors to the South Vietnamese government, which Russell insists is an illegitimate government. He cites that during 1962, American planes with American pilots or copilots carried out 50,000 covert combing and strafing missions on Vietnamese villages located outside the strategic hamlets. This report, according to Russell, was broadcast on the Voice of America radio and was confirmed by the United States' Department of Defense. Russell concludes that the fighting is done by American troops and that Washington is responsible for the high civilian casualty rate—30,000 noncombatants killed in 1962, according to General Paul D. Harkins (49). Russell also charges that America's role as a belligerent violates the 1954 Geneva Accords, which is obligatory upon all nations under international law regardless of whether they were signators or not. In addition, Russell claims that the weapons being used in the conflict—napalm, "lazy dog" bombs, and chemical defoliants—are a violation of international law because of their unnecessarily cruel effects on the civilian population. The author points out that these chemical weapons, which Washington defended as "weed-killers," were actually reported to President Kennedy by his chief science advisor, Dr. Jerome Weisner, as potentially "more dangerous than radioactive fallout," and that these same "weed-killers" have been banned from use in the United States.

Russell goes on to expose the myths about American involvement in the Vietnamese conflict. He maintains that the National Liberation Front (NLF) is not a purely Communist faction in South Vietnam and that the government in North Vietnam under Ho Chi Minh would have a majority of the electoral votes throughout North and South Vietnam if the free elections, mandatory under the Geneva Accords, were allowed to take place. Furthermore, Russell contends that the United States and the South Vietnamese dictatorship under Diem have interred 8 million Vietnamese in forced relocation camps. According to Russell, the United States is not protecting the freedom of the South Vietnamese from Communist aggression. Russell attempts to show that the NLF is not controlled from outside Vietnam. "In the vernacular of the State Department, whenever Hanoi is urged to call off its 'support of the South Vietnamese insurgency,' what is really meant is that Hanoi should apply pressure and sanctions to force the rebels to submit to the United States" (69). Russell also reasons that North Vietnam and South Vietnam were separated only at the insistence of the "Great Powers" at Geneva. Therefore, in the author's view, Vietnam is one country, and North Vietnam is not an outside aggressor. The myth that the United States has been drawn into, or provoked to, attack North Vietnam in order to defend American troops is refuted by Russell on the basis that Washington has admitted that attacks from American forces on the North Vietnamese islands of Hon Me and Hon Nhu occurred before the Gulf of Tonkin incident. In short, American troops were trying to provoke the incident.

In analyzing the international scope of the Vietnamese conflict, Russell warns that the American government is seeking to extend the war into North Vietnam, inevitably drawing a response from China or Moscow. A confrontation between the Great Powers would lead to the involvement of nuclear weapons and the destruction of civilization. He pleads for worldwide resistance to American imperialistic aggression and compares Johnson's offers for a settlement with those made by Hitler. The author implores the nations of the world not to follow a policy of appeasement and to insist upon unconditional withdrawal of American forces from the region in order to save mankind from nuclear annihilation. As an appeal to the American conscience, Russell states, "With the exception of the extermination of the Jews, . . . everything that the Germans did in Eastern Europe has been repeated by the United States in Vietnam on a scale which is larger and with an efficiency which is more terrible and more complete" (121). He also claims that the government of Lyndon Johnson has committed war crimes, crimes against humanity, and crimes against peace in its violations of established international laws signed and ratified by the United States.

Bertrand Russell's *War Crimes in Vietnam* concludes with a journalistic report from Ralph Schoenman, an observer in North Vietnam in 1966. Schoenman points out that American policy and conduct in Vietnam violate not only international law but the Constitution of the United States of America as well. Particularly interesting is his argument that the drafting of American young men to serve on the illegal endeavors of the Johnson government is unconstitutional. Schoenman also reminds his readers that in the Nuremberg Tribunal after World War II, German soldiers and German citizens were held individually responsible for carrying out, or complying with, illegal orders.

Clearly, Russell's 1967 publication was the work of antiwar propagandists, designed to expose the worst horrors of the Vietnam War in order to move people to protest American involvement. The principal message of the book was the need to curtail the proliferation of the dominating influences of the Great Powers in regional conflicts, as well as international issues, and the necessity for all to realize the apocalyptic nature of ideological confrontations in an era characterized by the buildup of nuclear weapons.

In 1966 Bertrand Russell's International War Crimes Tribunal met for the first time. The tribunal was a gathering of internationally renowned philosophers, authors, historians, statesmen, and activists who met in London under no official government charter of sanction. The purpose of the meeting was to determine and publicize whether or not American policies and conduct in Southeast Asia warranted criminal charges under international law and, if so, which specific charges. The tribunal also endeavored to show guilt or innocence of the charges, in an attempt to force, by popular protests, the United States, Britain, or any nation's government to act upon the tribunal's verdicts. Jean-Paul Sartre was the executive president of the tribunal, and immediately following the proceedings in 1968 he published *On Genocide*. The introduction to this work, entitled, "A Summary of the Evidence and Judgments of the International War Crimes Tribunal," by Arlette El Kaim-Sartre, clearly defines the grounds upon which those who sought to expose American atrocities in Vietnam based their conclusions.

The United States and its supporters were found guilty on five general violations of international law. The first conviction was the waging of a war of aggression as defined by the 1928 Kellogg-Briand Pact, the U.S. Charter, and the 1954 Geneva Accords. The second conviction was the intentional bombing of civilian targets with no justifying military objective, which violated the 1923 Convention of The Hague, the 1949 Geneva Convention, and the findings of the Nuremberg Trials. The use of illegal weapons that cause undue suffering was the third conviction, based upon the statutes of the 1907 Convention of The Hague, the 1925 Geneva Protocols, the U.S. Army Handbook, *The Law of Land Warfare*, and the 1966 U.S. General Assembly Resolution outlawing "weapons of massive destruction." The United States was also convicted of crimes in dealing with prisoners of war protected under the 1949 Geneva Convention. In its actions against the Vietnamese population, the United States and its supporters and agents were convicted of crimes against the people and crimes against humanity as defined by the Nuremberg Trials and the Geneva Convention, which outlaw reprisal and deportation.

Most extreme of all of the convictions against the United States was the tribunal's finding that America's illegal actions in Southeast Asia tended toward the extermination of the population, which can legally be shown to substantiate charges of genocide. The 1949 International Convention on Genocide established that the condemnation of genocide was enforceable not only by virtue of the convention's resolutions but by international customary law, which, like common law, is obligatory to all members of society. Therefore, the United States' claim of never having ratified the statute on genocide was of no legal consequence.

Sartre's essay, *On Genocide*, attempts to substantiate the tribunal's genocide conviction by proving that Americans were killing Vietnamese because they were Vietnamese and for no other reason and that they knew they were doing it, hence, intent to commit genocide. Sartre begins by revealing the concept of total war that has evolved through modern times. According to the author, no longer do nations confront each other in war with solely military resources. Instead, present-day wars are waged with and against the entire resources of nations, including the population. Sartre sees this as acceptable when the belligerents are of an equal stature. However, the United States is waging total war on a tiny, undeveloped country that is in the midst of a civil war, not an international conflict. Sartre examines some of the possible reasons behind this situation. He maintains that when the French were opposing the Vietnamese insurrection as a colonial power, they were limited from waging total war on the hostile population because they had an economic interest in not destroying the total resources of the country. However, the United States is not as much interested in the economic gains of controlling Vietnam as it is interested in the ideological gains of forever defeating the spread of Communism in underdeveloped countries. The author points out that the United States publicly announced that its intentions in the region were to demonstrate that Communist insurgency throughout the world will not be tolerated. Sartre holds that this aspect of American policy gives the Vietnamese conflict an "admonitory" characteristic and proves that the United States intends to eradicate the forces behind the uprising. Since statistics show that a majority of the Vietnamese population supported Ho Chi Minh, Sartre concludes that the forces behind the movement to install Ho Chi Minh as leader are the Vietnamese people. The United States' vow to defeat the forces behind insurgency and the lack of restraint inherent in the "neocolonial" nature of American interests are the necessary proof of America's intentional policy of genocide in Vietnam.

Sartre concedes that the United States has offered terms of settlement to its enemies, which normally those intent on genocide do not do. However, Sartre maintains this is "genocidal blackmail"—capitulate or be exterminated. Sartre also attempts to show that if the Vietnamese people are to save themselves by capitulating to the intrusion of Amer-

ican control and the establishment of a dominating Western culture,
they will have saved Vietnamese lives but Vietnamese culture will have
been exterminated:

Look at this more closely and examine the nature of the two terms of the
alternative. In the South, the choice is the following: villages burned, the pop-
ulace subjected to massive bombing, livestock shot, vegetation destroyed by defoliants, crops ruined by toxic aerosols, and everywhere indiscriminate shooting,
murder, rape and looting. This is genocide in the strictest sense: massive extermination.... What are the Vietnamese people supposed to do to escape this
horrible death? Join the armed forces of Saigon or be enclosed in strategic
hamlets or today's "New Life" hamlets, two names for the same concentration
camps?... Even the most elementary needs are denied: there is malnutrition
and a total lack of hygiene. The prisoners are heaped together in small tents or
sheds. The social structure is destroyed. Husbands are separated from their
wives, mothers from their children; family life, so important to the Vietnamese,
no longer exists.... the birth rate falls; any possibility of religious or cultural life
is suppressed; even work—the work which might permit people to maintain
themselves and their families—is refused them. These unfortunate people are
not even slaves.... they are reduced to a living heap of vegetable existence.
When, sometimes, a fragmented family group is freed—it goes to swell the ranks
of the subproletariat in the big cities; the elder sister or the mother, with no job
and mouths to feed reaches the last stage of her degradation in prostituting
herself to the GIs.... Submission, in those circumstances, is submission to genocide. (P. 74)

Sartre also maintains that the Americans have learned that the only
way to win the war is "to free Vietnam of all the Vietnamese." Knowing
this, the policymakers consciously choose to continue their "admonitory
war in order to use genocide as a challenge and a threat to all the people
of the world." This is not only the crime against humanity that Sartre
calls "genocidal blackmail" but "atomic blackmail, that is, absolute, total
war" between the United States and its ideological foes (84).

The earliest discussions of atrocity and war crimes in Vietnam were
obviously impassioned pleas from the leaders of the burgeoning antiwar
movement. Their charges were based on the numerous and ever-present
media exposures of the circumstances in Vietnam. The war was broadcast into everyone's living rooms on the evening news and written about
in our morning papers, and increasingly more and more Americans felt
that they were becoming reluctant participants in, as well as appalled
witnesses of, the gruesome and tragic events of this American venture.
One reporter who devoted his pen to exposing the problems that American troops had in Vietnam was the *New Yorker*'s Jonathan Schell. His
firsthand account of the trials of the Vietnamese peasants who found
themselves caught up in the giant American war machine were published
in 1967 in *The Village of Ben Suc*. Schell's report makes no overt plea to

join in a fight against American policy. Yet, his interviews and observations certainly bring to mind a sense of wrongdoing in the treatment
of the Vietnamese people and their beloved country. The author is
present throughout every phase of the execution of Operation Cedar
Falls, an all-out attempt to encircle, evacuate, relocate, pacify, and destroy the Vietcong stronghold area known as the Iron Triangle, some
thirty miles north of Saigon. Approaching the operation from the perspective of a seemingly objective, third-party observer, Schell interviews
U.S. and South Vietnamese military commanders and soldiers, Vietnamese and American civilian participants, and even enemy personnel in
order to portray the ironic results of America's policies of counterinsurgency and pacification or the "other war," as our soldiers liked to call
it.

First, as if to compare and contrast, Schell concentrates on the methods
used by the NLF to win the hearts and minds of the people. After gaining
control of a village, the NLF would have victims of the war testify to the
villagers how the Army of the Republic of Vietnam (ARVN) or the
American forces had ruined their lives. The NLF would then install a
local administrative branch to organize public support through propaganda campaigns and an efficient yet fair system of taxation and conscription. There was even a welfare allotment for the very poor.
Associations of every kind were initiated among the villagers to foster a
proud feeling of participation in a worthy cause. Of course, the NLF
also did away with those who were unwilling to join their ranks, but
Schell reports that "the Front attempted to create an atmosphere com-
bining impassioned seriousness with an optimistic, energetic, improvised
gaiety that drew the villagers into participation" (7). The author notes
that by 1967 "to the villagers of Ben Suc the National Liberation Front
was not a band of roving guerrillas but the full government of their
village" (10). The intervening ARVN and American troops in the area
tried the same approach with Hamlet Festivals, handing out free food
and medical care as well as carrying off those they believed to be Vietcong. The villagers, along with the enemy ranks, gladly accepted this
infusion of aid.

When bombing and artillery increased in the area, around 1965, the
U.S. Army Psychological Warfare Office dropped leaflets in the area saying, "From now on, chase the Vietcong away from your village, so the government won't have to shell your area again" (13). Villagers were also told
to display the government flag on their storage sheds and houses to avoid
being bombed, which the Front was obliged to do. The Psychological Warfare Office dropped leaflets of every kind. "Some leaflets depict American
weapons with the teeth and claws of a beast, killing or torturing people in
the manner of fantastic devils in medieval paintings of Hell" (16). In January 1967 the Americans estimated the number of pacified villages within

the Iron Triangle to be zero. American high command decided on Operation Cedar Falls, to be executed only by Americans, without advance notice to a single Vietnamese in the area. Previous operations of this nature that sought to establish the ill-fated Strategic Hamlet programs were always a failure because of security leaks.

The new war strategy devised in Washington was that American forces would remove the villagers, engage the enemy, and lay waste to the resources of the area, while ARVN was feeding and housing those freed from NLF control. Jonathan Schell describes the events of January 8, 1967. Massive air strikes arrived first. Then a loudspeaker told the villagers to leave their bomb shelters and gather in the center of the village. If anyone was seen going in the wrong direction, he or she would be shot on sight. Leaflets were dropped and anyone wishing safe conduct could use them as a pass to enter the *chieu hoi*, or open arms camps for "defectors," who, upon arriving, would be subject to interrogation as enemy cadres. Foot soldiers proceeded to search dwellings and shelters and move the villagers to the gathering area. Schell observed a Vietnamese man traveling in the wrong direction on a bicycle. He was wearing the black "pajamas" of the rural peasantry, which American soldiers associated with the dress of Vietcong. Meanwhile, the army was busy leveling and poisoning the surrounding forest and rice paddies. Next, ARVN soldiers arrived to finish the sweep of the village and begin the task of moving the villagers.

When the first phase of the operation is Ben Suc seemed nearly completed, the count of Vietcong killed stood at twenty-four. One army officer told Schell, when asked about the enemy corpses, "We leave the bodies where they are and let the people themselves take care of them." Schell wonders who is left to do the job (61). The author reports another conversation with one American officer who was willing to kill any Vietnamese wearing black pajamas because he was certain they were Vietcong. The officer felt that no civilian working a rice field would wear black because it absorbed too much heat (64).

During the night the villagers were allowed to return to their homes to retrieve their possessions in order to take what they could carry to their new home, the camp at Phu Loi. Schell notes the amazement of the American troops with the efforts of the ARVN soldiers to load the trucks the next morning and reports that one officer said, "You pat the little Arvin on the ass and he just might do a good job" (67). Upon arriving at the site of the new camp, the huge convoy found an open, treeless field of at least ten acres. The psychological warfare trucks arrived with their loudspeakers and propaganda. Schell ventured to other areas within the Iron Triangle and reports the full-scale destruction of evacuated villages, crops, livestock, and forests. The whole Triangle was to be designated as a free fire zone where anything that moved would be considered the enemy. One army captain told Schell that the people within the Iron Triangle were either Vietcong or "hostile citizens," and this is why they were being relocated. However, one reporter notes, once they reach the camp at Phu Loi, they become "refugees," suggesting that these were people fleeing the enemy. Back at Phu Loi more than 1,000 Vietnamese were brought to the open field on the first day; they were sullen and bitter about the destruction of their village.

Two days into the operation, barbed-wire fences were installed, and the civilian accommodations consisted of open-air canopies under which each family was assigned about ten square feet in which to live with their supplies and livestock. Bathroom facilities were a long ditch dug behind a corrugated tin barrier that was about waist-high. Water and rice were trucked in each day, and when the trucks were empty, they left and did not return. The villagers were sprayed with insecticides from a machine, resembling a lawnmower, that made its way through the canopies. Schell asked if these people were going to be working at some occupation. Colonel White replied that they were given thirty-eight dollars for each family and would be farming soon. The reporter asked about the difficulties of starting rice paddies in a dry, open field. White said, "Maybe they'll grow vegetables" (95).

Schell's moving story of Ben Suc and the physical, economic, environmental, social, and cultural dislocation of Vietnamese life at the hands of the U.S. Armed Forces certainly might make one, such as Jean-Paul Sartre, conclude that American actions in Vietnam are not only a tragic circumstance of war, but an intentional and criminal neglect and even targeting of a whole population and its culture.

In 1970 Richard Hammer exposed a different sort of atrocity, one that was indisputably criminal. Hammer's book, *One Morning in the War: The Tragedy at Son My*, tells the story of the horrible massacre at My Lai. In his narrative the author makes a few charges of his own regarding the chosen policies and conduct, which, in his view, could only have resulted in one My Lai after another throughout Vietnam. While many were espousing that the massacre was an aberration of the war and that Captain Medina, Lieutenant Calley, and the men of Company C were soldiers gone mad, Hammer and others like him were beginning to examine the orders and procedures that were issued and executed from the soldier in the field all the way up to Washington.

Hammer begins by examining the complicated tactical issues that stem from the involvement of any army in a conflict fought in a strange environment between peoples with a completely different language and social structure. The author maintains American maps were wrong. Vietnamese intelligence was useless. Tactical coordination was impossible. Hammer also points out that the American forces actually attacked the wrong hamlet in what seemed to be a shot-in-the-dark attempt to act on

Vietnamese intelligence reports that Vietcong were active in a hamlet named My Lai. What the Americans were faced with was an American map that showed six different My Lai subhamlets. None of the subhamlets named on the American maps shared the same names on the Vietnamese maps. My Lai on the Vietnamese maps was a hamlet with four subhamlets, one of which was the Vietcong stronghold of subhamlet My Khe, or "pinkville." This subhamlet was named My Lai 1 on American maps. Therefore, the Vietcong were in My Lai 1 on American maps, and My Khe on Vietnamese maps. My Lai 4, where the massacre took place, was actually named Xom Lang subhamlet on Vietnamese maps and nowhere near the designated "pinkville" subhamlet or, for that matter, nowhere near the hamlet of My Lai, which was the Vietcong area reported by Vietnamese intelligence. Hammer offers no explanation of why the Americans chose to attack My Lai 4 and not My Lai 1. However, he does illustrate that the Americans' contempt, mistrust, and even hatred of the Vietnamese, including their Vietnamese allies, more than once caused other tactical errors.

Hammer also theorizes that young, inexperienced draftees, in a foreign land, confused by a foreign culture and frustrated by an invisible enemy, are driven by fear and hatred just to survive their tours of duty in order to leave this ungrateful country and return safely home. With these influences, little concern or respect for the Vietnamese can be afforded. The dehumanization of the Vietnamese people fosters the psychotic killing behavior of the soldier who is angry at not only his enemy but those who do not seem to sympathize with his situation. The men in Company C tell of common experiences in the course of their regular search and destroy missions: rape, theft, and murder of unarmed civilians. Most of the men shared the attitude that the only good Vietnamese is a dead Vietnamese, and "if it's dead, it's Vietcong."

The author exposes the army's, Washington's, and Saigon's attempt to cover up the incident. However, the circulation of the Ridenhour letter one year after the tragedy substantiated the long-existing rumors of evildoings in Vietnam. Charges of murder, rape, maiming, assault, intent to commit murder, and violations of the "laws and customs of war" were brought against the men of Company C and B. Hammer presents some of the legal questions arising from the My Lai massacre and the subsequent courts-martial. Who in the chain of command is ultimately responsible? Can there be collective responsibility? Hammer, like Bertrand Russell four years earlier, advocates the establishment of an international tribunal, much like the Nuremberg Trials after World War II. The author also argues that it is not necessarily the initial orders to attack My Lai, but the monitoring, or the lack of monitoring, of the situation that resulted in the crime of massacre. The command was ultimately responsible, in Hammer's opinion, for not ending the hour-long attack when it was learned from the outset that there was no return fire from the villagers. In addition, the command is responsible for the incorrect maps. "There are, then, many answers to the question of who gave the orders for this particular incident and who let it go to its end and the reason for those orders. No one in authority, from General Koster to Colonel Henderson to Colonel Barker to Captain Medina to Lieutenant Calley to the lowest private can escape a share of the responsibility for what happened at Xom Lang. And none of them can point to the other and say he was the one most responsible" (96).

Richard Hammer concludes with the assertion that the events that occurred in the village of Son My were not unique in Vietnam. They happened every day on a smaller scale. Lack of coordination between the forces "defending" South Vietnam, contempt, even disdain, for the Vietnamese, military strategies such as the use of napalm and chemical defoliants, saturation bombings against guerrilla enemies, declaration of free fire zones, search and destroy missions, relocation camps, and the unwillingness of the Americans, from the highest command down to the soldier in the field, to cooperate with and understand the Vietnamese people—all contributed to the participants' loss of distinction between ally and enemy. The author maintains that Washington's policies of fighting total war based upon complete annihilation of an enemy who mixes with the population can only result in mass, indiscriminate destruction and death. The cost of such a policy is, to the Vietnamese, the loss of population, the country in ruins, traditions destroyed, and culture obliterated. The cost to the Americans was phenomenal civil unrest and moral disillusionment. Hammer poignantly uses President Johnson's analogy of Americans and policemen guarding a home from housebreakers when he writes, "And what is the responsibility of the housebreaking policeman now that in his zeal to protect the house he has destroyed it?" (206).

Soon after the My Lai incident, another charge of immoral, criminal conduct on the part of the United States in Vietnam emerged from the literary community; environmental scientists made the rather complex charge of "ecocide" being perpetrated against the physical and human environments of Indochina. These charges were based on the principles of genocide as they apply to the ecology and not just the human and cultural aspects of a region. John Lewallen, a graduate of Whitman College in Washington and an alumnus of Stanford Law School, was a volunteer for International Volunteer Services in Vietnam from 1967 to 1969 and in 1971 became editor of *Clear Creek* magazine. In his 1971 publication, *Ecology of Devastation: Indochina*, Lewallen defines ecology as the integration of three levels of the natural world—the individual, the population, and the ecosystem. According to the author, the ecosystem consists of living systems, which involve the interaction of many plants, animals, and physical elements. He states, "Endless lines of biological relationships and energy flow attach to the [ecosystem] and enmesh the individual . . . in the fate of the universe" (15). Men are not only involved in natural surroundings but also in "cultural oceans." Lewallen explains that political, social, and economic milieus exist in the ecology of humankind, and people operate in the environment of rational thought and conscious invention, as well as in the natural environment.

In addition, Lewallen warns that the divisions of science are artificial and even dangerous because they limit one's ability to see the whole. Counterinsurgency is one such science, or, as Lewallen calls it, a pseudoscience. The counterinsurgent tries to destroy his enemy in three ways: capture him as if with a net, alter the ecology that supports his activities, and finally deprive him of the cover of humanity and leave him exposed. The author asserts that American activities in Vietnam have employed all three of these methods.

Lewallen's thesis defines ecocide as "the international destruction of large portions of the natural and/or man-made environments that serve to sustain human health and life" (128). Destruction of the environment in Indochina by American men and machines is massive and blatantly intentional, maintains Lewallen. It is the expressed policy of the U.S. government to deprive the Communist insurgents "of the people, land, food, shelter, medical facilities and other environmental elements that are necessary for life" (129). The author also contends that the implications of this ecocidal policy bear upon the world as a whole. Scientists are not sure of the extent of the physical damage that the world environment may experience from massive devastation to whole regions of the earth. Certainly, the most dangerous aspects of this endeavor, Lewallen claims, are the disturbances of human relationships throughout the world. He theorizes that the war in the region has, in a way, taken on a life of its own and is enmeshed in, and an active participant in, the ecosystem of the world. The only way the world can remove this addition to the ecosystem is by understanding the "technocracy" upon which it thrives.

"Technocracy may best be described as a uniting of the bureaucratic organization with modern technology"—the military-industrial complex as supported by the U.S. government and vice versa (134). The author then attempts to explain how a bureaucracy becomes a creature in its own right, striving to survive and grow by virtue of the policies it adopts through procedural adaptations. Success of a program in Vietnam was quantified on the basis of rounds fired, bodies counted, hearts and minds won, money distributed, bombs dropped, latrines built, herbicides sprayed, pigs stied, and so on. According to Lewallen, a technocratic war can do nothing but expand. Technocracy, like bureaucracy, does not know how to diminish in size and is destined to drain not only the United States but the world of economic resources because of the costly technology that it uses to sustain its survival. However, Lewallen gives the world some hope by explaining that the other essential resource necessary to the survival of the war technocracy is manpower, and it is drying up. Americans do not want to invest human lives in Indochina anymore. Therefore, after a period of excessive spending on weapons that require fewer men, possibly mercenaries, to operate, the technocracy will no longer be able to quantify its accomplishments in a cost-effective light.

With the charges of American war crimes and atrocities in Vietnam having been made throughout the late 1960s and early 1970s, the literature of the 1970s began to address concerns for legal and moral justice. Washington had finally decided to cut its losses and work toward decreasing America's involvement on Indochina. Consequently, intellectuals writing on the Vietnam issue in the 1970s focused on assessments of guilt and responsibility for the failed policies and strategies in Vietnam, lessons we were to learn from our failures, and arguments defending the American presence and conduct in Vietnam.

A superb analysis of the war crimes debate comes from a collection of essays published in 1971 by Richard A. Falk, Gabriel Kolko, and Robert J. Lifton, entitled *Crimes of War*. Contributions to this work include arguments by Jean-Paul Sartre, Seymour Hersh, Jonathan Schell, Townsend Hoopes, Kurt Vonnegut, Arthur Miller, Karl Jaspers, Erik H. Erikson, and others. In agreement with Richard Hammer, the three editors of *Crimes of War* hold that the guilt or responsibility for tragedies such as My Lai and the situations that foster criminal behavior in warfare extends beyond the soldier, and that America's overall military and political involvement in Vietnam should be a source of insight about the character of modern warfare and international law. The conclusions drawn in this collection attempt to illustrate several debates: the failure of the laws governing warfare to be an effective limitation on criminal activity, the need to revise and enforce criminal boundaries regarding international relations, and the need to compel world powers to conform to international law in the exercise of political power.

Richard Falk writes about a "circle of responsibility," beginning with the soldier in the field, extending to his commanders, and including the military planners who implement the desired goals set forth by foreign policymakers. Falk theorizes that the Nuremberg experience established a principle of every man's obligation to oppose illegal acts of war. This aspect of international law can be used to indict the government of the United States and even those living under and supporting that government. "The circle of responsibility is drawn around all who have or should have knowledge of the illegal and immoral character of the war. The Son My massacre puts every American on notice as to the character of the war" (230). Falk extends this indictment to foreign governments and ultimately to every member of the world population by pointing out that international law makes corrective action against aggression and atrocity obligatory under the Charter of the United Nations. The author suggests that the first step in a solution would be a clarification of what constitutes criminal activity in international affairs. Second, a legal method of recognizing, halting, and punishing criminal activity must be defined. Falk suggests this should be done by the establishment of an international commission of citizens who are more concerned with the maintenance of international law than with political issues.

Robert J. Lifton examines the psychological aspects of atrocity in Vietnam. According to Lifton, the soldier in Vietnam, the political leader in Washington, the American voter, and even the observer in the world community are involved in an "atrocity-producing situation" brought about by the worldwide illusion of the dreaded apocalyptic confrontation of good and evil in the age of modern nuclear warfare. Lifton illustrates this "deadly illusion" of unlimited evil and atrocity by pointing out that even Bertrand Russell exhibited the "apocalyptic imagination when he advocated that we threaten to drop the atomic bomb on Russia in order to compel her to agree to a system of international control of nuclear weapons" (22). Lifton argues that atrocity "is a perverse quest for meaning, the end result of a spurious sense of mission, the product of false witness" (23). The author explains that three psychological patterns become evident in the behavior exhibited in Vietnam. First, because of the need to deny the atrocity, atrocity built upon atrocity. As My Lai was the result of smaller crimes, so also is the extension of the war throughout Indochina a result of the shame of Vietnam. Second is a system of nonresponsibility, or the feeling that no one is to blame because everyone is to blame. Third, what Lifton calls the most terrible pattern of behavior, is the feeling of being "stuck in atrocity." The Nixon administration inherits the war. The military command in Vietnam changes personnel. The public protests are led by the next generation. Yet, nothing is done to stop atrocity. Lifton writes, "Nothing is more conducive to collective rage and totalism than a sense of being bound to a situation perceived to be both suffocating and evil" (24). Lifton suggests that only by confronting the evil of our atrocities in Vietnam can the United States throw off its illusion that it is averting, by any means available, an apocalyptic confrontation of good and evil. This illusion, according to Lifton, produces evil, and the evil is denied to preserve the illusion.

Lifton's reality is also confronted by Gabriel Kolko, who writes about America's failure to comprehend the contemporary world. According to Kolko, contemporary Third World society is characterized by upheaval and revolution, which to the majority of Americans are undesirable. However, as a nation, Americans have been taught to see Washington's role in the world community as the "open" voice of "liberalism" and "rationality." With the realities of war crimes in Vietnam, such as My Lai, Americans catch a glimpse of the truth behind what they believe about their system, contrasted to the way they truly function in the world as it really is. Kolko argues that the reasons America became involved in Vietnam and its expressed objectives, there and worldwide, seem to illustrate a repudiation of the "literal" and "rational" principles proclaimed as the American way. Once their illusions are swept aside and their eyes are opened "to the meaning and causes of our malaise at home and the terror and misery America inflicts abroad, then we close the door on the seemingly easy, but in reality futile, widely accepted means of solving problems—which is to say, we fundamentally doubt the official theory of the American political process and the requisites for changing it" (13). Kolko implies here that the defense of democratic principles, namely the electoral process, is not a reality of American involvement in Vietnam. Subsequently, if Americans see their commitment to Vietnam for what it truly is, then they threaten America itself. Therefore, Americans have chosen a safer assessment of reality, one that either treats the perpetrators of such incidents as My Lai as aberrant criminals or welcomes them home with accolades, a reality that uses body counts to quantify progress against an insurgent population, a reality that does not accurately define what America and capitalism are. Kolko seems to be trying to expose America's own disbelief in its values by pointing out that, in reality, these very values are repudiated in America's policies in Vietnam and that, when confronted with this knowledge, the American people still choose to disbelieve in order to believe.

As the presence of American military personnel in Indochina dwindled during the early 1970s, so also did the passion of the arguments urging the world to recognize the criminal tendencies of U.S. policies and conduct in the region. Instead of focusing on the urgent need for action to end the "atrocity-producing situation," discussions centered on which conclusions should be drawn from the experience in Vietnam, the verdicts that might be reached as all of the official evidence and legal discussion surface, how Americans are to live with those verdicts, and whether Americans might adapt international laws to deal better with circumstances like those in Vietnam. Certainly, not all scholars would agree with Sartre's and Russell's charges of genocide, Schell's emotional description of pacification programs, or even Lifton's and Kolko's evaluation of the American psyche. One such opposing view was presented in 1974 by Hugo Adam Bedau, noted philosopher and chairman of the Society for Philosophy and Public Affairs. Bedau's essay "Genocide in Vietnam?", published in a collection of essays entitled *Philosophy, Morality, and International Affairs*, attempts to look beyond the language of condemnation and justification in order to analyze the philosophical, legal, and social aspects of international arrangements and customs. Bedau addresses the specific legal validity of Sartre's charge of genocide.

According to Bedau, the term *genocide* as a punishable crime must be defined before one can conclude if it has been committed. Bedau points out that etymology alone fails to define genocide as a crime: "If genocide is to be thought of as criminal without exception . . . then this requires building into the concept of genocide a *mens rea* [criminal state of mind], which etymology alone fails to do" (9). Bedau also disputes whether genocide can be categorized with the notion of "crimes against humanity," as he points out that the Nuremberg texts are the basis of this notion and the concept of genocide is not addressed in the Nuremberg texts. Bedau claims that the best definition of genocide originates from the 1948 Convention on the Prevention and Punishment of the Crime of Genocide, which states what genocidal intent is, thereby legally defining genocide in terms necessary to designate it as a crime. The controversy over genocide in Vietnam revolves around intention, specific intent, and motive. The convention addresses these issues but does not provide for the responsibility, guilt, or punishment of nonindividuals. Bedau attempts to show how the considerations of definition and application have impaired our ability to form a conclusion regarding the genocide debate. Bedau discounts the arguments for guilt made by Richard Du Boff and Townsend Hoopes because their verdicts are based on the results of American policy in Vietnam and not whether or not a conscious decision to commit or allow genocide was made. In Bedau's appraisal of our legal traditions, tendencies do not equate with intention. However, Sartre's argument survives this initial test regarding intent by charging that America has made a choice to follow a policy that we know tends toward genocide in Vietnam. The key to any argument proposing America's guilt of genocide, according to Bedau, must conclude that motive to commit the crime has been acted upon. Bedau concedes that Sartre makes this allegation by pointing out that the American military policies and strategies intentionally targeted Vietnamese people and their way of life. However, the author goes one step further in asking whether the intentional killing of thousands and laying waste to the country imply specific genocidal intentions. Sartre maintains that genocidal intentions are implicit in the facts. Bedau counters by explaining that this is not how criminal law works, and arguments must be based on the actual practice of Anglo-American laws regarding malicious intent in criminal activities.

The author explains that this approach can be applied to the charges of genocide in Vietnam in two ways. First, the idea of implied malice, meaning the "reckless disregard of foreseeable consequences of military policy, tactics, and weaponry," is problematic because of the difficulty in proving that those who directed the actions had foresight of the results to come (27). Sartre argues that genocidal intent is proven by the fact that Washington proclaimed its actions to be admonitory against guerrilla warfare of any sort, and antiguerrilla warfare—counterinsurgency—is targeted at a rebellious population and entails the removal of fighting resources from it, including natural resources, shelter, and any means of survival. Bedau writes that even if anti-guerrilla warfare is equated with genocide, critics must prove that Washington's defense of not having foresight is invalid. But they must still have to prove with evidence that the goals of Washington were an admonitory action against guerrillas, such as preventing dominoes from falling elsewhere. Given official privileges regarding information from Washington's decision makers, determining their goals is very difficult. Second, the notion of express malice in criminal law may be applied to the discussion of America's actions in the war. This brings to light another fallacy in Sartre's argument—proving that antiguerrilla warfare equates with genocide. Bedau maintains that if Washington's goals were an antiguerrilla war to stop the spread of Communist insurgency worldwide, critics must still connect counterinsurgency with genocidal means and genocidal results. Here again the evidence for proving foresight will fall short. Without the ability to prove that Washington's goal was the execution of an admonitory action toward a rebellious population and without the evidence to prove that such admonitory actions result in genocide, the prosecution in this case cannot validate its argument and the verdict must be, as in British courts, not proven.

Bedau's essay in *Philosophy, Morality, and International Affairs* is accompanied in the same book by another question posed by Richard Wasserstrom's "The Responsibility of the Individual for War Crimes," in which the focus is placed not on motive but on responsibility and liability. Must it be proven that individuals knew what the outcome of their actions would be? Or is it simply enough to say such persons who make such decisions should or ought to know what will result from their actions? Wasserstrom maintains that the proof of individuals' foreknowledge regarding their decisions was not required to convict war criminals after World War II. "On the other hand, strict liability [actual knowledge] is hardly a more attractive notion for war crimes than it is in our own legal system. The appropriate test in this regard appears, therefore, to be what the leaders ought to have known or foreseen about the policies and programs under their authorship, direction, or control. It is upon this question, and not the question of their motives, that our attention ought to focus" (70).

As is apparent, these discussions of alleged war crimes committed by the United States in Vietnam did not center solely around incidents such as My Lai. Commentators also attempted to relate individual tragedies to the broader circumstances that allowed such inhumane treatment of the Vietnamese to occur. The policies and strategies of counterinsurgency, which underscored the political and military intervention in Indochina, were brought under scrutiny as the reason behind such cruelty to the Vietnamese civilian population. In 1975 Richard Falk discusses this position in *Law and Responsibility in Warfare: The Vietnam Experience*. This work is especially important because it presents opposing points of view regarding the indictments against, and defenses of, the United States in Vietnam. Falk argues that American policy and strategy in Vietnam were based on the military and political theories of counterinsurgency and pacification. He starts with the assumption that counterinsurgency is aimed at combatants who live among the civilian population, and, therefore, counterinsurgency is aimed at all civilians, noncombatants included. In general, the whole idea of counterinsurgency as employed by the United States in Vietnam is a violation of international law on the basis of its use of air power in populated areas, anitpersonnel weaponry on enemy populations, "body counts" to calculate attrition rates, crop destruction, water contamination, psychological warfare, free fire zones, search and destroy and capture and eliminate strategies. Falk maintains that the fundamental premise upon which counterinsurgency in Vietnam is based, the extent to which high-technology weaponry can be used against a civilian population in order to maintain a government in power, brings into dispute the very laws that govern warfare. International law, according to Falk, is lacking in this area because it does not deal realistically with the nature of insurgency and counterinsurgency. For example, one of the defenses claimed by the United States in justifying counterinsurgency policies is the fact that Vietnamese guerrillas had violated international law by waging war without distinguishing themselves from the civilian population. Falk argues that this principle of international law gives unfair advantage to the larger military and political powers. In addition, international law does not deal adequately with the role and responsibility of a supporter—the United States—when those receiving the support—the South Vietnamese government—are violating the laws of warfare. The Vietnamization policy of the 1970s is a prime example of this. Falk concludes that international law needs revision to incorporate a less biased view of insurgency and stronger concepts of individual responsibility.

In response to the charges against the policy of counterinsurgency and specifically the pacification programs in Vietnam, Robert W. Komer, chief pacification advisor in Vietnam, attempts to dispute each accusation made by Falk and the others. Komer employs a ten-point argument to illustrate the lack of evidence behind the allegations of war crimes and the insufficient arguments regarding criminal intent on the part of the United States. The author disputes Falk's assumption that the civilian population was the target of counterinsurgency policies by pointing out that the only evidence used to support that accusation was the ratio of civilian to military casualties, which Falk maintains was ten to one. Komer writes that this ratio was improbable. If one accepts the reported casualty figures in the *New York Times* in 1973 of nearly 1 million enemy casualties since 1961 and the figure of civilian casualties used by opponents of the war of a million or more, no evidence exists of a ten-to-one ratio of civilian to military casualties. Komer does not explain how "enemy" casualties were distinguished.

In answer to the question of whether or not the United States was responsible for most civilian casualties, Komer points out that more civilian casualties were attributed to mines and mortar than to shelling and bombing. Vietcong and North Vietnamese used mines and mortar more than the United States and South Vietnamese did. In addition, the civilian casualty figures date back to 1960, before the United States was involved on a large scale. Komer disagrees with Falk's thesis that civilians were the target of counterinsurgency policies and indiscriminate attack strategies. Furthermore, the author maintains that the Vietnamese war was more than just an insurgency and that the United States was fighting organized regular forces in relatively unpopulated areas. Most civilian casualties took place in five rural provinces, and Komer judges that 75 to 95 percent of U.S. offensive combat operations took place in sparsely populated jungle areas.

Arguing against the accusation that genocidal patterns of thought existed in the strategies employed by the United States in Vietnam, Komer excuses the functional calculations of "body counts" and "kill ratios" as standard procedure in a war of attrition, which he contends was the only strategy the United States and the South Vietnamese could think of in this conflict. The accusation that indiscriminate air power was used against the civilian population is unfounded, according to Komer, who maintains that in 1969 only 5 percent of the population lived near heavily bombed targets and by 1971 that figure had been reduced to less than 1 percent. This, Komer points out, illustrates a deliberate effort to drive the enemy out of populated areas. To dispute further the charges of genocide and ecocide, Komer uses statistics that show a 3 percent per annum increase in the South Vietnamese population during the 1960s and the largest rice crop in South Vietnamese history during 1970 and 1971. Regarding the issue of forced resettlement or "forced-draft urbanization," the author writes that the predominant policy was to drive the enemy away from the population and bring in U.S. or South Vietnamese protection instead of relocating the people to protected areas. Furthermore, urbanization was already a trend in Vietnamese society, and universally this trend is accelerated by war. According to Komer, only 2 to 3 percent of all refugees were due to forced relocations. While Komer admits that a staggering 5 million refugees were reported in Indochina for the years 1964 to 1970, he asserts that not all were homeless or dislocated during the entire time. The number of "refugees" included those making property or casualty damage claims. Furthermore, many of these refugees can be attributed to enemy attacks, and in recent years the number of refugees has been reduced considerably.

Another issue that is important to Falk's argument was the nature and origins of the enemy forces. Komer points out that U.S. policy maintained that allied forces were more an obstacle to invasion than military reinforcement to one side of a civil war. The fact that most of our efforts, air strikes and artillery fire, were targeted toward attacks on main forces and not insurgents proves this. In addition, by 1968, North Vietnamese outnumbered Vietcong in enemy forces, and this tended to reinforce the idea that the United States was helping South Vietnam expel an aggressor. Falk's theory that the internal crisis in Vietnam was directed from Washington and the South Vietnamese were puppets is hardly believable to Komer, who notes the numerous reports that quite often the South Vietnamese functioned, militarily and politically, beyond our wishes.

Finally, the author defends pacification programs as "basically constructive in both intent and execution." Implying that the programs were mainly the duty of the South Vietnamese, Komer states the emphasis was on "arming the people to protect themselves, restoring village autonomy, rural development through self-help, economic revival, refugee care, land reform." Komer contends that critics tend to focus only on the Phoenix program, which he maintains had been the complete responsibility of the South Vietnamese government and military. The United States was involved only in "collation and intelligence procedures." The author's definition of the Phoenix program states: "It was a wartime attempt to put out of action the politico-administrative-military cadres who ran the enemy side of the war," not a program of "capture and assassination or civilian suspects. . . . Excesses were committed, but the record will show that the chief critics of the Phoenix Program were the United States advisors themselves" (100).

In conclusion, Komer argues that there is no more evidence supporting the accusations of war crimes than there is evidence to the contrary. The author admits that the counterinsurgency effort of the United States in Vietnam was highly counterproductive and ineffective in terms of its costs, but this cannot equate with an indictment against counterinsurgency strategies in general or against the participants in the effort.

One year after Richard Falk and Robert Komer presented their opposing views, General William C. Westmoreland published *A Soldier Reports*. In his account of the years he spent commanding the military actions of the U.S. forces in Vietnam, Westmoreland briefly responds to the literature of the previous decade, including the accusations of war crimes and illegal policies and strategies. The author expresses his opinion on questions such as who should be held accountable for individual incidents of criminal behavior and misguided policy-making as well as the controversial and tragic nature and outcome of the Vietnam War. On the subject of specific incidents such as My Lai, Westmoreland holds the opinion that these situations were the result of aberrant behavior on the part of individual soldiers who were poorly commanded. The author believes that, at most, the blame can extend only to the immediate commanders of that particular incident and the cover-up that followed. While warning that the methods of recruitment of candidates into the officer corps, namely the deferment of college students, had reduced the standards for officers during the Vietnam War, Westmoreland points to men like Lieutenant Calley as the prime example of army incompetence. For officers like Calley, the policymakers of the U.S. Army and the House Armed Services Committee must bear the blame for its draft policies. Public sympathy for Calley as a fall guy for the brass and questions relating to the Nuremberg and Yamashita trials after World War II brought about accusations that Westmoreland and civilian officials in Washington may have criminal liability for My Lai. However, Westmoreland employs the principle that an officer's intent and efforts to prevent war crimes must be applied to any discussions of responsibility, as was the practice after World War II. Under these standards Westmoreland is quite sure his record stands for itself. The general also maintains that the disparity between enemy killed and weapons recovered, shown in the original report of 11th Infantry Brigade's action in Son My, did not alert him to what had occurred because, as Westmoreland points out, "As opposed to warfare against the enemy's big units, high body counts and low numbers of weapons collected in the war against guerrillas in hamlet and village were not uncommon (the dead were presumed to be armed combatants, not civilians)" (379). An indication of Westmoreland's detachment from the troops in the field is evident from his next statement. "Having passed up the chain of command, the reports gained added credibility from at least implicit endorsement of the intermediate headquarters: company, battalion, brigade, division, field force, and U.S. Army Vietnam. We had to rely on the presumed and generally established veracity of the reports and the chain of command" (379). Westmoreland goes on to admit that a number of "battlefield irregularities" occurred, but his emphasis rests on the premise that "an army is the sum of the caliber of its officer crops.... aspects of leadership that I consider to be imperative.... Absolute integrity of an officer's word, deed and signature" (380).

Westmoreland also addresses the issues of pacification raised by accounts such as Jonathon Schell's. The general comments that relocation of the civilian population into camps was the most humane alternative to exposing them to the destruction of free fire zones. "That it was infinitely better in some cases to move the people from areas long sympathetic to the Viet Cong was amply demonstrated later by events that occurred when the discipline of an American company broke down at a place called My Lai" (151). Noting that human error was also a factor in civilian casualties—mistargeting of bombs and artillery, maps showing wrong coordinates, weapons malfunctioning—Westmoreland pleads that relocation of civilians into camps became one solution to the dilemma of balancing the safety of the civilians with the safety of the troops while achieving the military objective. In addition, Westmoreland explains that a war of attrition was our only alternative in fighting the Vietcong, who were reinforced by North Vietnamese regulars, because invasion of North Vietnam to decrease the number of enemy troops was politically impossible. With this method of attrition, one strategy was to remove the civilians as a source of conscription and support for the enemy ranks. Relocation camps were the means to this end as well as an attempt to minimize the civilian casualties that were "bound to occur in villages that the enemy turned into fortified camps" (152–53).

In response to allegations of blatant racism among American troops toward the Vietnamese, the general believes that this did not result in indiscriminate killings of noncombatants. Westmoreland writes that soldiers display racist behavior as "merely a defense mechanism for men engaged in perilous and distasteful duties." Reports of criminal behavior by American troops were exaggerated, according to Westmoreland, who explains the crime rate was no more than in urbanized areas of the United States. At peak strength the Americans in Vietnam numbered about the same as a city the size of Buffalo or Cincinnati, where crimes of violence are daily occurrences. Unlike the population of a city, the Americans and Vietnamese were armed and operating in a hostile environment. "Thus the remarkable fact may well be that crimes occurred but they were as few as they were." Westmoreland notes, in addition, that of the fifty-nine soldiers tried for war crimes, thirty-six were convicted. The General claims that this rate is better than civilian justice (254–57).

Rebuttals like Westmoreland's were plentiful during the late 1970s. It seemed that the more distance and time we gained away from the experience of Vietnam, the more acceptable a point of view sympathetic to the official or military position became. *America in Vietnam*, written by Guenter Lewy and published in 1978, addresses the issues of criminal actions of Americans during our involvement in Vietnam. Dealing with accusations of genocide, irresponsible bombings of populated areas, illegal weaponry and herbicides, and individual atrocities, Lewy theorizes that the Vietnam War was more popularly opposed primarily because of our false strategic approach, counterinsurgency.

Lewy begins by addressing antiwar literature like Bertrand Russell's and the numerous allegations of atrocity and war crimes that followed. According to Lewy, Vietnam was an "international civil war," and each side claimed a different status under the international laws. This is the reason sanctions and corrective actions were not applied consistently to the conduct of the belligerents, the command staff, or the policy planners. At the same time, many protections afforded to noncombatants and provided for under intentional law, while deemed applicable in one respect, were seen as impractical by other considerations. The author attempts to illustrate this paradox as it applies to the general policies and strategies of each side in the conflict. Lewy also tries to analyze how the contradictions and ambiguities in international law apply to the rights and actions of individuals.

Beginning with the roots of American involvement in Vietnam, Lewy discusses the allegations that America was an aggressor in a country that was in the midst of a civil conflict. The author brings to light evidence that shows the NLF was formed at the instigation of the Communist party in Hanoi. The argument over the 1954 Geneva Accords and the status of Vietnam as one country or two is much more complicated. However, Lewy maintains that the only aspect of the Accords that may be considered binding was the cease-fire agreements, which were signed by all parties. The final declaration was not signed by all participants. Lewy doubts, therefore, that the failure of Diem to hold free elections legally justifies a resumption of the military struggle. The cease-fire was signed and obligatory, and the free elections stipulation was not. But can North Vietnam's instigation of hostilities be seen as aggression upon a sovereign state? Did the Geneva Accords constitute South Vietnam as a nation separate from North Vietnam? For that matter, could South Vietnam be a party to the Geneva Conference without standing as a sovereign state? Or is South Vietnam still bound by the obligations assumed by France on its behalf? Lewy concludes that South Vietnam was not bound by international laws formulated before it came into existence. Lewy also stipulates that, according to French foreign minister Georges Bidault, Vietnam had been recognized as a sovereign state by thirty-five nations.

The issue of the sovereign status of South Vietnam bears directly on the arguments for and against the legitimacy of American intervention in the Vietnamese war. However, Lewy maintains that it was never the intention of either side to leave the country divided. According to the author's presentation of the evidence, the North was actively pursuing a strategy of recruiting and training the supposedly indigenous NLF in South Vietnam. In response to this subversion the United States initiated the Southeast Asia Treaty Organization for collective security of all "free" states in the region. In 1960 both Hanoi and the NLF announced publicly their intentions of unifying Vietnam under the Communist leadership of Ho Chi Minh. Given substantial cause to believe that subversion from the North existed, the question became, To what extent should the United States aid the South Vietnamese? Before the Geneva Accords, a contingent of military and political advisors had been sent to the area, and Lewy maintains this degree of involvement was legal under the Accords and international law. The dispute over the legitimacy of the infusion of American personnel arises after December 1961, when the State Department concluded that under international law a breach of an agreement by one party releases the other parties from compliance with that provision. "The United States now felt entitled to disregard the Geneva ceilings on both U.S. personnel and the shipping of military equipment to South Vietnam" (23).

Next, the author answers critics whose objection to American involvement centers around the Gulf of Tonkin Resolution and the supposed ruse the Johnson administration used to coerce Congress into escalating American involvement in the war and sanctioning overt attacks on North Vietnam. Lewy points out that, after American ships had been attacked once by North Vietnamese torpedo boats and had ignored the incident, the ships were moved away from areas where the South Vietnamese were attacking North Vietnamese islands. Well outside of North Vietnamese waters, the ships were attacked by North Vietnam again two days later. The author points out that records from staff meetings and task assignments show no evidence that the American ships were preparing a retaliatory attack on the North Vietnamese coast prior to the North Vietnamese attack. Had there been a plan to provoke the attack on American forces, preparations for follow-up would have been evident in the records. Lewy also points out that in 1964 three North Vietnamese regular infantry units had joined the fighting in the South. Communists, not Americans, first escalated the conflict.

In his answer to the critics of an attrition strategy, which places the emphasis on "body counts" when no one really knows who is civilian and who is Vietcong, Lewy agrees that command pressure for quantified progress in the form of "body counts" often led soldiers in the field to count all killed in action as enemy dead. Lewy also concedes that this also might have led to the same nondiscrimination during the battle. Neglect of the security of the population, corruption and unpopularity of the South Vietnamese forces and government officials, damage to civilian property, forced relocation, free fire zones, refugees—all led to the failure of the pacification component necessary to a successful strategy of counterinsurgency. Another reason that Lewy gives for the failure of American efforts in Vietnam was the breakdown of discipline and morale among the troops and officers. Again, Lewy's thesis centers on the strategy of counterinsurgency and its inevitable failure as the cause behind the world's outrage over American involvement in Vietnam (223).

Beyond this observation, Lewy offers his conclusions on the application of international laws to specific American policies and actions in Vietnam, namely population relocation in declared free fire zones. While maintaining that, in general, many of the laws governing warfare "do not really fit the special conditions of modern insurgency warfare," the author explains that, regardless of how the nature of the conflict is viewed—international or internal in character—all of the demands of international laws point toward a duty to remove civilians from a combat zone (225). In addition, there is no prohibition in international law concerning the deprivation of resources to the enemy. Lewy contends that, in the case of counterinsurgency warfare, this strategy of deprivation of resources means the removal of the population that is the enemy's source of cover, recruitment, and supply. The author maintains that in some instances free fire zones can be equated with the scorched earth tactic. However, the American forces employed the strategy in accordance with international law by providing for those civilians dislocated from the free fire zones. American motives were not the disruption of Vietnamese society and the destruction of the natural environment in order to force a political objective on the civilian population, as critics allege, but a conscious effort to forewarn civilians of impending military action in the area, to help them evacuate to a safer place, and to stop the Vietcong from feeding off the noncombatant civilians.

Lewy also points out that, according to international law, once a populated area is occupied and fortified by combatant forces, it may become a legitimate military objective to which any attacking force must apply the rule of proportionality—that is, the loss of life and property must be in proportion to the military advantage achieved by the attack. Compliance with this rule on the use of firepower is, according to Lewy, left up to the judgment of the commanding officer, who, unless grossly negligent, cannot be held criminally responsible for incorrect estimates of the military objective. Furthermore, Lewy contends that international law supports the defense that once civilians become supporters of a combatant force, they cease to be noncombatants and are subject to attack themselves. In general, the blame for the necessity of relocation, the laying to waste of whole villages and hamlets, and the high civilian casualty rates can be blamed on the insurgents, who took to the cover and fortification of populated areas in the first place.

On the question of command responsibility, Lewy compares the case of General Yamashita, Japanese commander during World War II, with that of General Westmoreland. Yamashita was convicted of war crimes because he knew atrocities were occurring and failed to do anything to prevent them or punish the perpetrators. In addition, according to the interpretation given to the law of war by the U.S. Supreme Court, it was a commander's responsibility to control his troops when he should have known that his troops were violating the laws of war. Lewy, therefore, concludes that Westmoreland could be held responsible for incidents such as My Lai because he should have known that the rules of engagement (ROE) were not suited to the Vietnam situation and could have led to violations of the laws of war. The author states the high civilian casualties and the incidents of fighting around populated areas should have alerted the command staff that rules aimed at protecting civilian life were not being applied or were not sufficient rules in those circumstances. After My Lai, the rules were revised to protect civilian life better. However, Lewy agrees with Richard Wasserstrom when he contends that the blame for military conduct before My Lai could be placed with Westmoreland because of a clear dereliction of duty or perhaps criminal negligence for not correcting a problem that he knew existed.

Next, the author discusses the legitimacy of some of the weaponry used by the American and South Vietnamese forces in Vietnam. Incendiary weapons, various types of tear gases, and chemical defoliants are, in Lewy's opinion, legitimate weapons if they are used properly. However, Lewy agrees that tracer bullets, napalm, white phosphorous, and other weapons that cause severe suffering were sometimes employed without consideration to the rule of proportionality, thereby causing more civilian suffering than was justified by the military achievement. Nevertheless, the author supplies evidence that the occurrences of injuries to civilians from these weapons were very low and grossly exaggerated by the antiwar propagandists.

With regard to defoliants and crop destruction, Lewy supplies arguments from legal authorities that support the legitimacy of a strategy of destroying food supplies used by the enemy. In addition, in certain circumstances it is legal to deprive civilians of food supplies, if those supplies are thought to benefit the enemy. However, Lewy concedes that in most cases crop destruction hurt the civilian population in a manner disproportionate to the military achievements of such actions. The author also reviews the evidence regarding the poisonous effects of herbicides on the population and concludes that, as of the time of his book, there was no conclusive evidence of any long-term danger to human health from the presence of herbicides in Vietnam. According to Lewy, charges of "ecocide," although never defined by international law, are also unsupported by the recent studies of Vietnamese soil and timber stocks. Lewy reminds the critics of crop destruction that the international law dealing with this issue addresses only the effects of food deprivation on civilians.

In rebuttal to the charges that the American and South Vietnamese air war in Vietnam was illegal because it targeted a great deal of non-military objectives, Lewy points out that, while the laws governing air warfare permit the bombing only of targets that have a military significance, civilians living near these targets are afforded very little protection. In short, if there is a military presence, a war industry, or defensive weapons located in an area, it may be considered a legitimate target for air attack. International law does prohibit the bombing of an area for psychological effect of bombing disproportionately to the military advantage sought by the attack. Lewy does, however, concede that U.S. motives for bombing North Vietnam included an effort to pressure the North Vietnamese government to negotiate a withdrawal of their support for the insurgency in the south and that bombings were accelerated by an interservice rivalry. However, the author points out that objective observers in North Vietnam, Cambodia, and Laos confirmed that the majority of the cities that had suffered air attack were located in or around military targets. Furthermore, the actual civilian casualty rate was lower than that of the air war in Europe during the Second World War. Lewy adds that as North Vietnam employed more antiaircraft weapons, the civilian casualty rate was also affected by North Vietnamese ammunition. Military records, according to Lewy, also show that many sorties were ineffective and several pilots were lost because of the precaution taken to safeguard civilian life and property. Charges that hospitals, residential areas, and dikes were intentional targets of the U.S. air war in Vietnam are shown by Lewy to be erroneous by numerous accounts from nonofficial investigations of bombed areas. In each case the observer can see the intended military target and justify the incidental damage to civilian life as a problem inherent in the inaccurate nature of air warfare. Finally, Lewy argues that secret bombings that took place after Johnson had officially repudiated the use of air power against North Vietnam were possibly a violation of U.S. rules of command, but, since the secret bombings were directed at military targets, they were not a violation of international law.

Lewy dedicates two chapters in his book to the issue of atrocities and individual war crimes. The author tends to agree with the assessment of Lifton when he states, "Aggressive behavior is often the result of frustration and anxiety, and American servicemen in Vietnam experienced both of these states of mind in abundance" (309). The racism of the soldiers is also explained by the fact that the soldiers felt trapped in a situation where no Vietnamese could be trusted. However, Lewy argues that the antiwar press even helped to develop the attitude in the soldier that the South Vietnamese were no more worth protecting than the enemy. The author criticizes the "war crimes industry" as completely one-sided and irrational in its assessments of what was really happening in Vietnam. According to Lewy, self-styled war crimes tribunals employed questionable standards of evidence, decorum, and impartiality. The author cites several testimonies from the tribunals to illustrate the lack of merit in the prosecution's case. Witnesses were forced to speculate. Hearsay was admissible evidence. Charges of illegal actions were made against whole groups of people, and no names were requested in the testimonies. In general, the war crimes tribunals sought to carry the responsibility for atrocities on the battlefield all the way to the top policymakers, while the court-martial cases, like that of Lieutenant Calley, rejected a defense plea based on the defendant's obedience of a superior's orders. Although Lewy is of the opinion that the command is not without blame for neglecting its responsibility to take all possible actions to prevent war crimes, the author also states, "While collective guilt... may have a place in theology, it is not part of Anglo-American jurisprudence. Here guilt is always personal, and if all are guilty then in effect nobody is guilty" (315).

Lewy also questions the actions of certain groups that claimed to be helping the returning veterans of the war with their postwar problems. Veterans were encouraged to discuss their guilty feelings about things they had done in the war and to join the antiwar protestations. The author implies that some mental health professionals, Lifton included, were relying on the testimonies of the veterans, obviously disturbed by the experience of war, as evidence behind the charges of war crimes occurring on a large scale in Vietnam. After the massacre at My Lai became public and in light of the prolonged cover-up effort, the charges that massacres happened on a daily basis seemed to gain acceptance. Yet Lewy maintains that "in view of the openness of the fighting in South Vietnam to journalists and the encouragement which the My Lai affair gave to other servicemen to come forward with reports of atrocities, it is highly unlikely that anything like the My Lai massacre did escape detection" (326). Even those witnesses to the My Lai massacre regarded it as out of the ordinary. In conclusion, Lewy argues that atrocities were bound to happen in an atmosphere such as that in Vietnam. However, atrocities were not daily occurrences or standard procedure. The individual soldier is responsible for his own acts of frustration, and the commanders are responsible for seeing that rules of engagement fit the situation and are enforced to the best of their abilities. The author also agrees with General Westmoreland and the contention that the manpower demands of the Vietnam conflict led to lower standards not only for officers but also for enlisted men and that a resulting breakdown in discipline and morale was a major cause of aberrant criminal behavior.

To disprove the charges of genocide made by the "war crimes industry," Lewy's views correspond with those of Hugh Adam Bedau. There exists no evidence that proves the United States intended to destroy the Vietnamese people and their way of life. Lewy points to statistics that show an increase in Vietnamese population during the years of American involvement. The author also asserts that American military policy called for steps to protect the population. Programs were initiated to improve health care and further technological and economic development. The rules of engagement were adapted to the Vietnamese theater of war in order to protect civilian life better. Violators of the laws of war were prosecuted and punished. Lewy also disputes Falk's contention that, because international law was biased and put them at a distinct disadvantage, the insurgents were justified in operating amidst the civilian population. Lewy maintains that Vietcong tactics were an illegal and intentional strategy that cost far more civilian lives than the strategies employed by the United States and South Vietnam. The thesis of Lewy's book is that a policy that is debatable on humanitarian grounds, regardless of its legality, is largely counterproductive and self-defeating, and this is why policies and strategies used by America in Vietnam were protested so widely.

After assessments such as Guenter Lewy's were published in the late 1970s, it seemed that charges of excessive violations of international laws on the part of the United States in Vietnam were overstated in the antiwar press. Most Americans accepted the belief that, while what we did in Vietnam was nothing to be proud of, Johnson was not another Hitler and our soldiers were not mass murderers. America's attention was turning to the lessons to be learned from the mistakes and how best to confront the problems in the American system that the Vietnam War had exposed. The same year that Guenter Lewy's book put a lot of American minds to rest, another student of international law and the military, Peter Karsten, published a telling appraisal of how American attitudes and international rules concerning warfare were lacking in humanitarian considerations. *Law, Soldiers, and Combat* addresses the assumptions and moral principles upon which the existing international and customary laws governing war are based. The author suggests that revisions be made beyond those of the 1970s in order to adapt the laws to existing world relationships and establish a stronger foundation for humanitarian concerns. When placing the emphasis of his discussion on the experiences in Vietnam, Karsten agrees with Bedau and Lewy in arguing that the *mens rea* aspect of criminal law, or the culpable state of mind, must be applied to any appraisal of the questionable policies and behavior exhibited by the military and government personnel involved in the Vietnamese war. However, Karsten rejects the defense that where there is war, unfortunately and unavoidably there is also great damage to civilian life. Karsten relates that in addition to strict and narrow applications of the laws of war, there are also the practical aspects, or the spirit of the laws. International laws are based in part on moral, ethical, and religious grounds in providing for protection to defenseless, innocent noncombatants. Even when policies and actions can be shown to be within the legal limits, violations of the ethical and moral spirit of the laws, according to Karsten, "degrade a belligerent's purposes and principles, weaken discipline in one's own forces, leave the soldier with guilty, or worse, a sense of social sanction, injure one's own relations with other nations, and many provoke reprisals." The moral considerations behind the laws also govern the decision to go to war, and Karsten believes these decisions contribute greatly to the formation of what Falk refers to as the "atrocity-producing situation." In addition, moral transgressions committed by "freedom fighters" are no less wrong than those committed by an "imperialist." Karsten reviews the agreements and treaties that compose the twentieth-century laws of warfare—the Hague Convention of 1907, Geneva 1925, the war crimes tribunals after World War II, and Geneva 1949—and concludes that in each accord the emphasis was on protection for noncombatants and their property in undefended areas. The use of gases was outlawed. Deportation, slave labor, and the imprisonment of noncombatants were prohibited. Wholesale destruction of civilian property was restricted. Of course, these laws dealt with the destructive effects of the weapons technology at that time. However, Karsten attempts to relate that some modern advances in weaponry and strategies, though not specifically forbidden by the older laws, may violate the spirit of those laws. The author also explains that military trials and courts-martial have used *The Law of Land Warfare* as the legal basis for criminal charges and convictions. This volume incorporates international agreements and treaties, including the more recent accords reached in 1956 at Geneva, in 1965 at Vienna, in 1969 at Istanbul, and during the 1970s at Geneva, and deals more effectively with the modern technology of warfare.

Karsten theorizes that a number of factors play a role in causing war crimes: an individual soldier's values and attitudes, the conditions of an individual's military service, the theater, the command, the weaponry, the ethnocentricity of the fighting forces, a soldier's personal insecurity, military peer pressure, frustration turned to aggression, fear, revenge, misperception, ideology, conscience, and finally, illegal orders. The author advances numerous suggestions to mitigate these problems: better screening of officers and recruits, extensive training in the laws of war and the guiding moral principles of these laws, and better weapons control, including a legal review process such as an international or national board to review the effects of new weapons. In addition, Karsten advocates the formulation of better command procedures to facilitate the ability of high commanders to know or predict what will happen as a result of accepted practices. A system for reviewing unlawful orders and rewarding soldiers who uphold the legal and moral restrictions on warfare would also preclude the occurrence of war crimes. Finally, the international community should continually strive to modernize and update the codification of international limits on warfare. In conclusion,

Karsten warns that a nation that is free of guilt in committing unscru-
pulous acts is not released from its duty to uphold the spirit of international laws. The author reminds his audience that two wrongs do not
make a right. Perhaps as a direct statement regarding American involvement in the Vietnamese war, Karsten writes, "that some may violate the
laws is no reason for others to violate them in reprisal against the criminals" (201).

In the 1980s attitudes about the Vietnam experience paid closer attention to the veterans of the war. America was finally starting to acknowledge the Vietnam veterans, their problems, their sacrifices, and
their judgments about the war. One book that uses this approach in
assessing America's guilt is Ellen Frey-Wouters and Robert S. Laufer's
Legacy of a War (1986). In this study—a comparison of veteran and
nonveteran perspectives—the authors attempt to evaluate and form conclusions regarding the conduct of the American military in Vietnam by
concentrating on the "Vietnam generation's views of the conduct of the
war.... [embracing] four specific areas: the war against the civilians and
the environment, the use of unnecessarily cruel weapons, the treatment
of prisoners, and perspectives on individual responsibility in war" (xxxi).
For the purposes of this chapter, the treatment that this work gives to
the effects of American actions on the noncombatant population will be
presented.

Frey-Wouters and Laufer advance the general idea that the "humanitarian law of armed conflict suffers from the same 'weakness' of all
international law: there is no effective supernatural organization to enforce it." The authors point out that in the case of the Vietnamese
conflict, loopholes for each side of the conflict existed in the laws and
minimized its effectiveness in protecting the civilian population. However, the authors argue, "It must be remembered that the main international legal instruments of this century have a clear provision that in
cases not covered by conventional or customary international law, civilian
populations and combatants remain under the protection of the principles of humanity and the dictates of the public conscience" (175–76).

"The dictates of the public conscience" or the perceptions of those
involved in or observing the war, the Vietnam generation, are the foundations of this book's conclusions about America's responsibility for the
war against the civilian population and the environment. Veterans and
prowar and antiwar nonveterans by and large agreed that violent acts
against individual civilians and, likewise, bombardment of cities to force
the enemy's capitulation were both unlawful. However, not all were in
agreement that environmental warfare was illegal. According to the
study, the Vietnam generation also feels that the enemy was more to
blame for abuse of civilians than the American forces. Regarding the
American involvement in abusive acts of violence against the population,

three conclusions surfaced. First, some veterans felt that violent acts upon the population were

> inherent not in the men but in the circumstances under which they had to live and fight.... With no visible enemy on whom one could avenge [their] losses. ... Apparent civilians were actually combatants; women and children engaged in hostile acts. Gradually the whole Vietnamese population became cause for fear ... men who do not expect to receive mercy eventually lose their inclination to grant it.... In such a scenario.... the need to prosecute the war against the enemy which hid among the people legitimized the use of a broad range of actions against civilians. (P. 205)

Second, another group of veterans argued that "though some of the abuse was unavoidable, most of it could have been prevented or stopped. They often blamed military and political leaders for their unwillingness to forgo certain military strategies directed against civilians and for their indifference to the human costs involved" (205). The third perspective comes from nonveterans. "For them, this pattern of violence against civilians became the basis for arguing that a war fought under such conditions cannot be justified" (205–6).

Frey-Wouters and Laufer's study of how the Vietnam generation viewed the use of unnecessarily cruel weapons indicates two separate viewpoints of public conscience: the perspective of those who experienced the theater of the Vietnam War and the ideology of those who experienced the war at a distance. "Most Vietnam veterans are reluctant to renounce the use of these weapons. Their dilemma ... arises from the fact that 'cruel' weapons were often perceived as protecting [soldiers] from harm, the enemy's use of equally brutal weapons required retaliation, or the success of the mission depended on the use of these devices. ... The majority of Vietnam veterans would limit the use of these weapons to the battlefield" (231). Among nonveterans, especially antiwar activists, stronger emphasis is placed on humanitarian considerations. The study found "stronger support here for the banning of 'cruel' devices. The use of these weapons even against military personnel is rejected outright, in part because of the suffering they cause and also because the battlefield in Vietnam often blurred the distinctions between civilians and combatants" (231). Frey-Wouters and Laufer comment that much of the argument justifying the use of "cruel" weapons is based on military necessity. However, the authors note that there is consensus that these weapons often resulted in the hostile civilian attitude toward the allied objectives of war, canceling out any military advantage to be gained by using these weapons near civilian areas. Thus, according to the authors, the conclusion of the study is that, even among those directly involved in the war, "there is serious concern for the issues raised by the cruelty of weaponry" (231–32).

In their conclusions drawn from the evaluation of the Vietnam generation's perspectives on individual responsibility in war, Frey-Wouters and Laufer state that American soldiers generally made a distinction between regular soldiers and their commanders—officers and politicians—and believed that they did have a responsibility to enforce the laws of war and the rules of engagement. The soldiers also believed, however, that misconduct was sometimes going to happen because of the stress of battlefield conditions (284).

In general, Frey-Wouters and Laufer's assessments rest on the principle most predominant in their study: individual outrages and heavy civilian suffering can be morally justifiable if there exists a clear-cut ethical justification, such as a war between good and evil. However, according to the authors, the absence of this component clouds the Vietnam generation's perceptions of the conduct of those participating and undercuts the ability to understand the full implications of America's involvement in the Vietnamese war. The authors remind the reader that the recent revisions in, and additions to, international laws illustrate that much of the world viewed the Vietnam conflict in the light of war crimes. Nevertheless, they maintain that the Vietnam generation feels that where the charge of war crimes can be substantiated against individuals, more effort should be made to allow for redress against those "who actively stripped individual soldiers of control over their behavior" (287).

This popular view is noticeable still in the 1990s. Concern for the moral and ethical environments of soldiers sent into battle can be observed in the media discussions about the United States' recent deployment of troops to the Middle East. President George Bush's statement that a confrontation with Iraq would not be another Vietnam illustrates that the political, military, legal, and moral lessons learned from Vietnam are not forgotten.

A survey of the literature presented in this chapter illustrates that attitudes about atrocities and war crimes in Vietnam evolved significantly with the passing of time. From 1965 to 1975, discussions centered on condemnation of American actions and motives. The early 1970s also brought forth several analyses of international law. Most of the literature in defense of the United States' involvement and conduct in Vietnam came from the military community and Washington. Until the American presence in Vietnam began to diminish, "the war crimes industry," as Guenter Lewy calls it, presented forceful enough views on the subject of war crimes in Vietnam to influence a whole generation of Americans. The antiwar movement, from which the accusations of criminal actions and motives on the part of the United States flowed, eventually influenced, in one way or another, not only the policies of Washington, but the makeup of international law as well.

Since 1975, debates on the character of American intervention in

Vietnam have concentrated, not on war crimes and punishment for war crimes, but on the failed policies and strategies of Washington and the military. While espousing several reasons for America's failures in Vietnam, most of these discussions also attempt to relate the lesson that a lack of humanitarian considerations in the waging of war is self-defeating. The literature since the war shows that attitudes about atrocities and war crimes in Vietnam have mellowed, but the lessons learned have become part of the national conscience of America.

BIBLIOGRAPHY

Bain, David Howard. *Aftershocks: A Tale of Two Victims*. New York: Methuen, 1980.

Barry, John Stevens. *Those Gallant Men: On Trial in Vietnam, 1968–69*. Novato, Calif.: Presidio Press, 1984.

Bedau, Hugo A., Virginia Held, Sidney Morgenbesser, and Thomas Nagel. *Philosophy, Morality, and International Affairs*. New York: Oxford University Press, 1974.

Bromley, Dorothy Dunbar. *Washington and Vietnam: An Examination of the Moral and Political Issues*. Dobbs Ferry, N.Y.: Oceana, 1966.

Browning, Frank, and Dorothy Forman, eds. *The Wasted Nations*. New York: Harper and Row, 1972.

Buckingham, William A., Jr. *Operation Ranch Hand: The Air Force and Herbicides in Southeast Asia, 1961–1971*. Washington, D.C.: U.S. Government Printing Office, 1982.

Chan, Steve. "Temporal Delineation of International Conflicts: Poison Results from the Vietnam War, 1963–1965." *International Studies Quarterly* 22 (June 1978): 237–65.

Chomsky, Noam. *At War with Asia*. New York: Pantheon Books, 1970.

Chomsky, Noam. "Vietnam: How Government Became Wolves." *New York Review of Books* (June 1972): 23–31.

Citizens Commission of Inquiry. *Dellums Committee Hearings on War Crimes in Vietnam*. New York: Vintage Press, 1972.

Cohen, Marshall, Thomas Nagel, and Thomas Scanlon. *War and Moral Responsibility*. Princeton, N.J.: Princeton University Press, 1974.

Cohen, Sheldon M. *Arms and Judgment: Law, Morality, and the Conduct of War in the Twentieth Century*. Boulder, Colo.: Westview Press, 1989.

Committee of Concerned Asian Scholars. *The Indochina Story*. New York: Bantam, 1970.

Corson, William R. *The Betrayal*. New York: Norton, 1968.

Dinstein, Y. T. *The Defense of Obedience to Superior Orders in International Law*. Leyden: A. W. Sijthoff, 1965.

Drinan, Robert F. *Vietnam and Armageddon: Peace, War and the Christian Conscience*. New York: Sheed and Ward, 1970.

Duffet, John, ed. *Against the Crime of Silence: Proceedings of the International War Crimes Tribunal*. New York: Clarion, 1970.

Dunn, Colonel Jerry F. "A New Look at Pacification." *Military Review* 50 (January 1970): 84–87.

Falk, Richard A. *Law and Responsibility in Warfare: The Vietnam Experience.* New York: Praeger, 1975.

Falk, Richard A. "Son My: War Crimes and Individual Responsibility, A Legal Memorandum." *Trans-Action* 7 (1970): 33–40.

Falk, Richard A., ed. *The Vietnam War and International Law.* 4 vols. Princeton, N.J.: Princeton University Press, 1968–1976.

Falk, Richard A., Gabriel Kolko, and Robert Lifton, eds. *Crimes of War.* New York: Random House, 1971.

Farer, T. J. *The Laws of War 25 Years After Nuremberg.* New York: Carnegie Endowment for International Peace, 1971.

Frey-Wouters, Ellen, and Robert S. Laufer. *Legacy of a War.* Armonk, N.Y.: M. E. Sharpe, 1986.

Fried, John H. *Vietnam and International Law.* New York: Consultative Council, Lawyer's Committee and American Policy Toward Vietnam, 1968.

Friedman, Leon, and Burt Newborne. *Unquestioning Obedience to the President: The ACLU Case Against the Illegal War in Vietnam.* New York: Norton, 1972.

Gelb, Leslie, and Richard Betts. *The Irony of Vietnam: The System Worked.* Washington, D.C.: Brookings Institution, 1979.

Gershin, Martin. *Destroy or Die: The Story of Mylai.* New Rochelle, N.Y.: Arlington House, 1971.

Goldstein, Joseph, Burk Marshall, and Jack Schwartz. *The My Lai Massacre and Its Cover-up: Beyond the Reach of Law?* New York: Free Press, 1976.

Greenhaw, Wayne. *The Making of a Hero: The Story of Lieut. William Calley, Jr.* Louisville, Ky.: Touchstone, 1971.

Halperin, Morton H. *The Lawless State: The Crimes of the U.S. Intelligence Agencies.* New York: Penguin Books, 1976.

Hammer, Richard. *One Morning in the War: The Tragedy at Son My.* New York: Coward-McCann, 1970.

Hammer, Richard. *The Court-Martial of Lt. Calley.* New York: Coward-McCann, 1971.

Hart, Lieutenant Colonel Franklin A. "Yamashita, Nuremberg, and Vietnam: Command Responsibility Reappraised." *Naval War College Review* 25 (September-October 1972): 19–36.

Held, Virginia, Sidney Morgenbesser, and Thomas Negel, eds. *Philosophy, Morality, and International Affairs.* New York: Oxford University Press, 1974.

Herman, Edward S., and Richard B. Du Boff. *America's Vietnam Policy.* Washington, D.C.: Public Affairs Press, 1966.

Hersh, Seymour M. *Chemical and Biological Warfare: America's Hidden Arsenal.* Indianapolis, Ind.: Bobbs-Merrill, 1968.

Hersh, Seymour M. *My Lai 4: A Report on the Massacre and Its Aftermath.* New York: Random House, 1970.

Hersh, Seymour M. *Cover-up: The Army's Secret Investigation of the Massacre at My Lai 4.* New York: Random House, 1972.

Hoopes, Townsend. *The Limits of Intervention.* New York: David McKay, 1969.

Hull, Roger H., and John C. Novogrod. *Law and Vietnam.* Dobbs Ferry, N.Y.: Oceana, 1968.

Karsten, Peter. *Law, Soldiers, and Combat*. Westport, Conn.: Greenwood Press, 1978.

Knoll, Erwin, and Judith Nie McFadden, eds. *War Crimes and the American Conscience*. New York: Holt, Rinehart, and Winston, 1970.

Kolko, Gabriel. *Anatomy of a War: Vietnam, the United States, and the Modern Historical Experience*. New York: Pantheon, 1986.

Komer, Robert W. *Bureaucracy Does Its Thing: Institutional Constraints on the U.S.– G.V.N. Performance in Vietnam*. Santa Monica, Calif.: Rand Corporation, 1972.

Kunen, James Simon. *Standard Operating Procedure*. New York: Avon Books, 1971.

Kuper, Leo. *Genocide: Its Political Use in the Twentieth Century*. New Haven, Conn.: Yale University Press, 1981.

Lane, Mark. *Conversations with Americans*. New York: Simon and Schuster, 1970.

Lang, Daniel. *Casualties of War*. New York: McGraw-Hill, 1969.

The Law of Land Warfare. Field Manual 27–10. Washington, D.C.: Department of the Army, 1956.

LeFever, Ernest W., ed. *Ethics and World Politics: Four Perspectives*. Baltimore: Johns Hopkins University Press, 1972.

Leventman, S., and P. Camacho. "The 'Gook' Syndrome: The Vietnam War as a Racial Encounter." In *Strangers at Home*, ed. C. R. Figley and S. Leventman. New York: Praeger, 1980.

Lewallen, John. *Ecology of Devastation: Indochina*. Baltimore: Penguin Books, 1971.

Lewy, Guenter. *America in Vietnam*. New York: Oxford University Press, 1978.

Lifton, Robert J. *Home from the War: Vietnam Veterans Neither Victims Nor Executioners*. New York: Simon and Schuster, 1973.

Littauer, Raphael, and Norman Uphoff, eds. *The Air War in Indochina*. Boston: Beacon Press, 1972.

Luce, Don, and John Sommer. *Viet Nam—The Unheard Voices*. Ithaca, N.Y.: Cornell University Press, 1969.

McCarthy, Mary. *Medina*. New York: Harcourt Brace Jovanovich, 1972.

McCarthy, Mary. *The Seventeenth Degree*. New York: Harcourt Brace Jovanovich, 1974.

Mallin, Jay. *Terror in Viet Nam*. Princeton, N.J.: Van Nostrand, 1966.

Melman, Seymour. *In the Name of America: The Conduct of the War in Vietnam by the Armed Forces of the United States as Shown by Published Reports, Compared with the Laws of War Binding on the United States Government and Its Citizens*. New York: Clergy and Laymen Concerned About Vietnam, 1968.

Menzel, Paul T., ed. *Moral Argument and the War in Vietnam: A Collection of Essays*. Nashville, Tenn.: Aurora, 1971.

Mezerik, Avrahm G., ed. *Viet Nam and the U.N.—1967: National and International Policy*. Vol. 13, No. 95. New York: International Review Service, 1967.

Millet, Stephen M. "The Air Force, the Courts, and the Controversial Bombing of Cambodia." *Air University Review* 27 (July-August 1976): 80–88.

Millis, Walter. *War and Revolution Today*. Santa Barbara, Calif.: Center for the Study of Democratic Institutions, 1965.

Moore, John Norton. *Law and the Indo-China War*. Princeton, N.J.: Princeton University Press, 1972.

National Research Council. *The Effects of Herbicides in South Vietnam*. Washington, D.C.: National Academy of Sciences, 1974.

Neilands, J. B. *Harvest of Death: Chemical Warfare in Vietnam and Cambodia*. New York: Free Press, 1972.

The *New York Times*, *The Pentagon Papers*. New York: Quadrangle Books, 1971.

Palmer, Bruce. *The 25-Year War: America's Military Role in Vietnam*. New York: Simon and Schuster, 1984.

Parks, W. Hays. "Linebacker and the Law of War." *Air University Review* 34 (January-February 1983): 2–30.

Parks, W. Hays. "Rolling Thunder and the Law of War." *Air University Review* 33 (January-February 1982): 2–23.

Peers, William R. *The My Lai Inquiry*. New York: Norton, 1979.

Powers, Thomas. *The War at Home, Vietnam and the American People, 1964–1968*. New York: Grossman, 1973.

Russell, Bertrand. *War Crimes in Vietnam*. London: George Allen and Unwin, 1967.

Sack, John. *Lieutenant Calley/His Own Story*. New York: Viking Press, 1970.

Sartre, Jean-Paul. *On Genocide*. Boston: Beacon Press, 1968.

Scheehan, Neil. *Bright and Shining Lie*. New York: Random House, 1988.

Schell, Jonathan. *The Village of Ben Suc*. New York: Knopf, 1967.

Schell, Jonathan. *The Military Half: An Account of the Destruction in Quang Ngai and Quang Tin*. New York: Knopf, 1968.

Schevitz, Jeffrey M. *The Weaponsmakers: Personal and Professional Crisis During the Vietnam War*. Cambridge, Mass.: Schenkman, 1979.

Spector, Ronald H. *Advice and Support: The Early Years of the U.S. Army Involvement in Vietnam—1941–1960*. New York: Free Press, 1985.

Standard, William L. *Aggression: Our Asian Disaster*. New York: Random House, 1971.

Stanton, Shelby L. *The Rise and Fall of an American Army: U.S. Ground Forces in Vietnam, 1965–1973*. Novato, Calif.: Presidio Press, 1985.

Stockholm International Peace Research Institute. *Incendiary Weapons*. Cambridge: MIT Press, 1975.

Stockholm International Peace Research Institute. *Ecological Consequences of the Second Indochina War, Weapons of Mass Destruction and the Environment*. Stockholm: SIPRI, 1974.

Taylor, Telford. *Nuremberg and Vietnam: An American Tragedy*. Chicago: Quadrangle Books, 1970.

Trooboff, Peter D., ed. *Law and Responsibility in Warfare: The Vietnam Experience*. Chapel Hill: University of North Carolina Press, 1975.

U.S. Congress. Senate. Subcommittee to Investigate Problems Connected with Refugees and Escapees, Committee on the Judiciary. *Aftermath of War: Humanitarian Problems of Southeast Asia*. Staff Report, 94th Congress. Washington, D.C.: U.S. Government Printing Office, 1976.

U.S. Congress. Senate. Committee on Foreign Relations. *Moral and Military Aspects of the War in Southeast Asia*. Hearings...May 7 and 12, 1970. 91st

Congress. 2d Session. Washington, D.C.: U.S. Government Printing Office, 1970.

U.S. Department of Defense. "Pacification in Vietnam." In *Vietnam Review II* (December 1969). Washington, D.C.: Armed Forces Information Service, U.S. Government Printing Office, 1970.

U.S. Department of State, Office of the Legal Adviser. "The Legality of United States Participation in the Defense of Viet Nam." *Department of State Bulletin* 54 (March 1966).

Vennama, Alje. *The Viet Cong Massacre at Hue.* New York: Vantage Press, 1976.

Vietnam Veterans Against the War. *The Winter Soldier Investigation: An Inquiry into American War Crimes.* Boston: Beacon Press, 1972.

Wakin, Malham, ed. *War, Morality, and the Military Profession.* Boulder, Colo.: Westview Press, 1986.

Walzer, M. *Just and Unjust Wars.* New York: Basic Books, 1977.

Wasserstrom, Richard, ed. *War and Morality.* Los Angeles: Wadsworth, 1970.

Weller, Jack. "Good and Bad Weapons for Vietnam." *Military Review* 48 (October 1968): 56–64.

Wermuth, Colonel Anthony L. "Deputies of Zeus: Morality and the Vietnam War." *United States Naval Institute Proceedings* 100 (August 1974): 26–34.

West, Francis J., Jr. *The Village.* New York: Harper and Row, 1972.

Westmoreland, William C. *A Soldier Reports.* Garden City, N.Y.: Doubleday, 1976.

10   The Peace Negotiations

Mark Lambert

Of all the topics concerning the Vietnam War, the actual peace negotiations are probably the most neglected. There are several reasons for
the neglect. The fact that the final peace agreement was so anticlimactic—
completed long after the most severe fighting was over—is certainly one
reason. Another reason, no doubt, is the fact that the long-term outcome
of the negotiations was so negative in terms of South Vietnamese, Cambodian, Laotian, and American interests. Finally, the lack of access to
Vietnamese government documents concerning the negotiations has
clouded the issue and made new research less likely to occur. After more
than fifteen years, no significant reinterpretations of the negotiations
themselves have emerged, and almost all the principal Americans involved in the war and the peace negotiations have stood fast to the ideas
that motivated them at the time. Most texts concerning the peace process
were either released during the war or immediately afterward and are
highly critical of American involvement. Most memoirs by the persons
involved were also released within ten years of the end of the war, so
no new perspectives have appeared from firsthand observers.

George C. Herring, who has written one of the most respected histories
of our total involvement in Vietnam (*America's Longest War*) is also editor
of *The Secret Diplomacy of the Vietnam War: The Negotiating Volumes of the
Pentagon Papers* (1983). This text is a collection of documents and materials from the Pentagon Papers, and reviews the whole process in its
873 pages. *Secret Diplomacy* is a good starting point for anyone interested
in the peace process and all its intricate convolutions.

Almost all the books written on peace talks focus on the early negotiations in Paris during the Johnson years. They are uniformly critical
in their evaluation of the American position. *Mission to Hanoi: A Chronicle
of Double-Dealing in High Places* (1968) was written by Harry S. Ashmore

and William C. Baggs, who acted as go-betweens in 1967 for early peace seekers from both sides. Both men were private citizens and members of the Center for the Study of Democratic Institutions, a private organization formed in 1964 to "clarify the basic issues of our time and widen the circles of discussion about them." Ashmore was the organization's executive vice president, and Baggs was a member of its board of directors as well as editor for the *Miami News*.

The center originally concerned itself with relations between the superpowers in Europe, but in 1965, as the difficulties multiplied, problems in Southeast Asia were added to the agenda. Through a neutral third party, Ashmore and Baggs obtained a meeting with Ho Chi Minh. Since the men had to notify the U.S. government of their travel to the country, the State Department began using the two men as go-betweens for unofficial peace initiatives. At the same time, Lyndon Johnson was sending strongly worded notes by regular channels, and was escalating the war at the same time. When Ashmore and Baggs had had enough of the two-sided dealings, they opted out. In *Mission to Hanoi*, they reserve their strongest criticism for U.S. foreign policy-making apparatus, which they found to be hopelessly bureaucratic, inflexible, and conservative. Senator William Fulbright, chairman of the Senate Foreign Relations Committee, agreed with them. The book also contains a short history of U.S.-Vietnamese involvement since 1945.

Also concerned with early peace efforts is David Kraslow and Stuart H. Loory's *The Secret Search for Peace in Vietnam* (1968). They discuss early peace attempts by the Johnson administration, using formal and informal methods, which were sometimes aided by such intermediaries as Poland, Canada, and the United Nations. Kraslow and Loory conducted interviews with current and former members of the Johnson administration, as well as research in the public records. The authors reveal that peace attempts usually ended in failure because of American bombing escalation at times when breakthroughs seemed imminent. Therefore, they conclude that President Johnson probably missed early opportunities at peace, or at least lost the propaganda advantages that would have developed at home had the North Vietnamese started and then terminated the negotiations.

Janos Radvanyi's *Delusion and Reality: Gambits, Hoaxes and Diplomatic One-Upmanship in Vietnam* (1978) tells of the author's personal involvement in the early peace process as the former chargé d'affaires in the Hungarian embassy in Washington, D.C. He acted as a go-between for the U.S. government. The book also reveals the roles of the Soviets, the Chinese, and the East Europeans in this sideshow of the cold war. Radvanyi starts by explaining Stalin's own Vietnam policy as early as 1945, describes the negotiations involving Hungary in 1965 and 1966, and concludes with his own involvement in the process from 1965 to 1967.

Although the book is biased from a Communist point of view, Vietnam is nevertheless viewed as just one playing field of the cold war. He points out that both the Chinese and the Soviets in the long run did not end up with the influence they thought they would gain in Vietnam when the war was over.

Another analysis of the Johnson years is Wallace J. Thies's *When Governments Collide: Coercion and Diplomacy in the Vietnam Conflict, 1964–1968* (1980). It is the most thorough work on the early negotiating process and discusses the various international relations theories, bombing strategies, and peace feelers from the perspective of both sides. Blame for early failures is placed on both sides, Hanoi for not understanding the political realities pushing on Washington and Johnson for never really knowing what he was fighting for or sufficiently articulating it to the American people. Johnson's attempts at coercion by bombing halts/escalations are also faulted for their naïveté in the face of a well-disciplined and long-tenured leadership in the North.

Morton Kaplan, Abraham Chayes, Warren Nutter, Paul Warnke, John Roche, and Clayton Fritchey have put together a text entitled *Vietnam Settlement: Why 1973, Not 1969?* (1973), which is derived from their televised February 1973 debates concerning the Vietnam peace treaty. They examine whether the negotiations of the last four years had gained anything substantial since the opening of the talks in May 1969. Most of the men are academics, one is a journalist, and some are former government officials during the war. The text is broken into three lecture/rebuttal formats, with a discussion following each. This book does a good job at framing the issues Nixon and Kissinger had to deal with at the time. The participants do not come to any conclusions, but the book, which is short and easy reading, is an excellent introduction for someone not aware of the issues at stake.

The only text that is thorough and exhaustive in its coverage of the final peace negotiations that led to the Paris treaty is *A Peace Denied: The United States, Vietnam and the Paris Agreement* (1975) by Gareth Porter. Porter used extensive interviews with unnamed U.S. government officials as well as officials of the Central Committee of the Lao Dong party of North Vietnam. He points out that the United States and South Vietnam worked hard in the 1950s to eliminate all opposition to their policies, which they blamed on the Communists, even though cadre infiltration from the North did not start until 1959. Porter is also quick to point out the U.S. delaying tactics during peace negotiations, but he fails to mention these tactics when used by Hanoi. The main thesis of the text is that the war ended in a Communist victory in 1975 because the United States would not accept even partial representation of the Communists in the South Vietnamese government after the final cessation of hostilities in the political negotiations leading to the settlement of 1973.

In *The Lost Peace: America's Search for a Negotiated Settlement of the Vietnam War* (1978), Allen E. Goodman suggests that a Communist victory was always the only objective, and all peace negotiations by the North were just delaying tactics. There is nothing the United States could have done that would have brought North Vietnam to the peace table without a guarantee of independence and reunification of the country. Goodman looks at the negotiations from 1962 to 1973, and he sees the failure in diplomacy as just an inevitable result of dramatically conflicting points of view. For the United States, the negotiations were a bargaining process seen in the larger context of the global American geopolitical arena, attempting to maintain a balance between détente with the Soviet Union, rapprochement with the Chinese, and actual warfare in the Middle East. The North used the negotiations as a tactic of warfare, and the ultimate goal was still the liberation of the South from outside influences.

Tad Szulc, in his *The Illusion of Peace: Foreign Policy in the Nixon Years* (1978), sets aside a great deal of the book to the negotiations and set-tlement in Vietnam. He is harsh on Nixon, who is seen as a statesman of peace, but whose real story has not been revealed. Szulc blames Nixon for killing and maiming hundreds of thousands for an unenforceable settlement. He acknowledges that both sides to the final agreement vi-olated the cease-fire 1973–1975, but he argues that American involve-ment was unnecessarily prolonged by four years. He sums up his treatment of Nixon by saying that the president extracted a large price from Americans and the world, producing in the process only an "illusion of peace."

Also important to the peace negotiations on Vietnam were the major characters involved. While literally hundreds of people are responsible on both sides for bringing the two sides to the negotiating table, the people who made the policies or are directly responsible for their en-forcement had the major hand in what was achieved at the negotiations. Lyndon Johnson, the president who made the commitment of American combat troops in Vietnam, wrote about his thoughts on the war in *The Vantage Point: Perspectives of the Presidency, 1963–1969* (1971). Johnson is quick to point out that although he escalated the war, he was in touch regularly with Hanoi either through normal State Department channels or through such intermediaries as Poland, Hungary, the Soviet Union, or Canada for any possible peace overtures. He even lists the numerous peace initiatives the United States made from 1965 to 1968 in a chart at the back of his book, and he states repeatedly that even a small chance for peace was always worth a bombing halt. He places all the failure at peace attempts during his administration on the North Vietnamese, say-ing that their insistence on the Four Point Plan was simply Hanoi de-manding a settlement on its own terms. Johnson supposes that his constant attempts at peace might have convinced the North that he desired peace at any price. More likely, Johnson argues, the North Vietnamese had little incentive to negotiate since from early on in the conflict, they thought they were winning on the political battlefield.

Secretary of State Dean Rusk issued his memoirs, *As I Saw It*, in 1990. Rusk is unapologetic about his stance during the war years, and he believes the United States could have won had different tactics been utilized. He also thinks the United States made genuine efforts in good faith for peace negotiations, and he agrees with Johnson that those constant attempts at peace may have given the North the misleading impression that he wanted peace at any price. Rusk does concede that the United States underestimated North Vietnam's will in prosecuting the war, but he also states they never made one single genuine peace initiative in his eight years in office. Rusk was surprised at the Nixon administration's handling of the war. He felt the election of 1968 was a mandate by the American people to end the war soon, and yet it continued for four more years.

In his memoirs, *The Education of a Public Man: My Life and Politics* (1976), Vice President Hubert H. Humphrey is quick to point out that he was an early critic of the war, agreeing to bombing missions only to protect the American troops already involved and then pushing for a gradual disengagement. He reveals that even though he was a statute-authorized member of the National Security Council, his views were not in demand, and in fact President Johnson began discussing the war more heavily in informal meetings with his own selected advisors, excluding Humphrey's input almost totally. Johnson may have been removing the all-important linkage to public opinion on the war by later relying only on those who were in agreement with his views. Humphrey states he also realized that North Vietnam probably took the constant U.S. attempts at negotiations as a sign of weakness and conceded that our efforts probably did not look too sincere since American troop levels were constantly on the increase.

George W. Ball, deputy secretary of state for Presidents Kennedy and Johnson, was the only member of their advisory staffs consistently to oppose the war. In his book *The Past Has Another Pattern* (1982), he explains that as early as November 1961, he was advising Kennedy against any American involvement in Vietnam, because unlike Korea, the conflict was a purely internal civil matter. Bell was also surprised in 1965 to find Clark Clifford in agreement with his views against an Americanization of the war, but neither Clifford nor Ball could make that impression on Johnson. Ball did get the authorization for several low-key peace initiatives between 1964 and 1966, but when he gained no ground with either North Vietnam or President Johnson, he resigned in 1966.

In 1967, however, Johnson asked Ball and several other retired government officials—W. Averell Harriman, George Kennan, Dean Acheson, Robert Lovett, Charles Bohlen, and John McCloy—to advise him about Vietnam on an informal basis. They became known as the Senior Advisory Group, or the "Wise Men," as Walter Isaacson and Evan Thomas point out in *The Wise Men: Six Friends and the World They Made* (1986). When the Senior Advisory Group came out against any further escalation of the war in March 1968 after the Tet Offensive, Johnson decided to limit future actions in the combat area and strongly pursue peace options. He also decided that peace could best be accomplished if he decided not to run for reelection.

Clark Clifford, one of President Johnson's personal advisors and later defense secretary following Robert McNamara's resignation, has written the most recently published memoirs—*Council to the President: A Memoir* (1991). In 1965 Clifford was one of only a few advisors telling President Johnson not to expand the war, but he credits the hawks with being more persuasive, thus leading to a greatly enlarged war. In 1966 and 1967 Clifford supported troop increases so as not to lose ground in South Vietnam, but by early 1968 he was again viewing American chances at success dimly. When the Senior Advisory Group, including former secretary of state Dean Acheson, also reported that the war looked hopeless, Johnson swung around to Clifford's view and pushed harder for peace. Clifford also states in hindsight that Vietnam was an unwinnable war and that the United States erred badly in risking its prestige in a needless war.

President Nixon has explained his views on the war and the peace negotiations in *RN: The Memoirs of Richard Nixon* (1978) and *No More Vietnams* (1985). He still comes across as an unrepentant hardliner, explaining his prosecution of the war and pursuit of negotiations as trying to salvage a "peace with honor." Much of the blame for Vietnam is placed on President John Kennedy (not surprising, considering Nixon lost the presidency to him), and, in fact, President Johnson's work elicits much praise from Nixon. In December 1968 Nixon indicated to Hanoi his interest in a fair settlement. Efforts at sincere peace negotiations failed, and since political considerations at home kept large troop operations out of the question, Nixon decided to rely on bombing as a way to bring the North Vietnamese to the negotiating table. For three years all attempts by Kissinger at negotiations were for naught, but when it began to look as if Nixon would be reelected in 1972, North Vietnam proposed new talks, probably thinking they could get better terms before his election than after. In October 1972, Hanoi made a proposal in which they agreed on most major issues. By that time, of course, the United States had already agreed to most of Hanoi's earlier demands, including the withdrawal of American troops, a coalition government in South Vietnam, and permission for North Vietnamese to remain in South Vietnam.

The peace was signed in January 1973. Richard Nixon was happy with the peace accords, arguing that the United States won the war only to see Congress lose the peace in not living up to Nixon's financial commitment to South Vietnam in the postwar years.

Henry A. Kissinger, Nixon's national security advisor and later secretary of state, has explained his ideas on the war and peace in two huge volumes: *White House Years* (1979) and *Years of Upheaval* (1982). He describes Nixon's peace ideas as "face-saving," and he writes that he believed in ending the war in a way compatible with maintaining American self-respect. He believes that the breakthrough in negotiations came when North Vietnam finally accepted what it had long denied: the continued existence of the Saigon government. He rejects the idea that he was just working on a "decent interval" of peace before South Vietnam collapsed and says he actually demanded a decent settlement for them. Kissinger is much more contemplative in his analysis of the negotiations than Nixon, and he states that even at the time he knew that North Vietnam would probably not abide by the agreement.

The Vietnam War peace negotiations have been reasonably well documented concerning the early years, and Wallace J. Thies's *When Governments Collide: Coercion and Diplomacy in the Vietnam Conflict, 1964–1968* is the most thorough approach. The later negotiations, conducted by Kissinger and directed by Nixon, which led to the actual peace, may have to await the opening of the archives for a thorough treatment, because of the very high premium that both men placed on secrecy and because of their almost total exclusion of the State Department from the process. Whether the tough dealing as espoused by Nixon and Kissinger won the peace or whether North Vietnam's desire just to sign something to hasten the Americans' exit will remain a question until then.

BIBLIOGRAPHY

Ashmore, Harry S., and William C. Baggs. *Mission to Hanoi: A Chronicle of Double-Dealing in High Places*. New York: Berkeley, 1968.

Ball, George W. *The Past Has Another Pattern*. New York: Norton, 1982.

Clifford, Clark. *Counsel to the President: A Memoir*. New York: Random House, 1991.

Dillard, Walter Scott. *Sixty Days to Peace: Implementing the Paris Peace Accords, Vietnam 1973*. Washington, D.C.: National Defense University Press, 1975.

Goodman, Allen E. *The Lost Peace: America's Search for a Negotiated Settlement of the Vietnam War*. Stanford, Calif.: Hoover Institution Press, 1978.

Herring, George C. *America's Longest War: The United States in Vietnam, 1950–1975*. New York: Wiley, 1979.

Herring, George C. *The Secret Diplomacy of the Vietnam War: The Negotiating Volumes of the Pentagon Papers*. Austin: University of Texas Press, 1983.

Herrington, Stuart A. *Peace with Honor? An American Reports on Vietnam, 1973–1975*. Novato, Calif.: Presidio Press, 1983.

Humphrey, Hubert H. *The Education of a Public Man: My Life and Politics*. Garden City, N.Y.: Doubleday, 1976.

Isaacson, Walter, and Evan Thomas. *The Wise Men: Six Friends and the World They Made*. New York: Simon and Schuster, 1986.

Johnson, Lyndon B. *The Vantage Point: Perspectives of the Presidency, 1963–1969*. New York: Holt, Rinehart, and Winston, 1971.

Kaplan, Morton A., Abraham Chayes, Warren Nutter, Paul Warnke, John Roche, and Clayton Fritchey. *Vietnam Settlement: Why 1973, Not 1969?* Washington, D.C.: American Enterprise Institute for Public Policy Research, 1973.

Kissinger, Henry A. *White House Years*. Boston: Little, Brown, 1979.

Kissinger, Henry A. *Years of Upheaval*. Boston: Little, Brown, 1982.

Kraslow, David, and Stuart H. Loory. *The Secret Search for Peace in Vietnam*. New York: Random House, 1968.

Nixon, Richard M. *RN: The Memoirs of Richard Nixon*. New York: Grosset and Dunlap, 1978.

Nixon, Richard M. *No More Vietnams*. New York: Arbor House, 1985.

Porter, Gareth. *A Peace Denied: The United States, Vietnam and the Paris Agreement*. Bloomington: Indiana University Press, 1975.

Radvanyi, Janos. *Delusion and Reality: Gambits, Hoaxes and Diplomatic One-Upmanship in Vietnam*. South Bend, Ind.: Gateway Editions, 1978.

Rusk, Dean. *As I Saw It*. New York: Norton, 1990.

Szulc, Tad. *The Illusion of Peace: Foreign Policy in the Nixon Years*. New York: Viking Press, 1978.

Thies, Wallace J. *When Governments Collide: Coercion and Diplomacy in the Vietnam Conflict, 1964–1968*. Berkeley: University of California Press, 1980.

PART IV

Indochinese History

11   Vietnamese History

Almost as soon as the United States escalated the war in Vietnam, historians began issuing warnings that American policymakers did not really understand the nature of Vietnamese history. The Vietnamese were not a simple people ready to cave in to a militarily superior foreign power. On the contrary, their entire history was based on resistance to such foreign powers, and the United States would only be the latest in a series of Chinese, French, and Japanese conquerors to learn a hard lesson in the jungles of Indochina. The premier scholar among those historians was Joseph Buttinger, whose *The Smaller Dragon* (1958) and two-volume *Vietnam: A Dragon Embattled* (1967) are the classics in the field. For a historical description from a Vietnamese perspective, see Nguyen Van Thai's *A Short History of Vietnam* (1958) and Thich Nhat Hanh's *Vietnam: Lotus in a Sea of Fire* (1967), both of which focus on the intensity of Vietnamese identity.

Years ago, a Chinese historian remarked that the "people of Vietnam do not like the past." As Edgar Wickberg makes clear in his book *Historical Interaction of China and Vietnam* (1969), Vietnam developed in the shadow of Chinese imperialism. In 208 B.C. the Han dynasty expanded into southern China and Vietnam, and over the centuries the Chinese brought their "mandarin" administrative system, technology, language, and Confucian social philosophy to Vietnam. Alexander Woodside's *Vietnam and the Chinese Model* (1971) clearly describes Vietnamese values and institutions, as well as their roots in Chinese history. But the Vietnamese managed to resist assimilation. Intensely ethnocentric, the Vietnamese, while welcoming many Chinese institutions, refused to accept a Chinese identity.

The result, of course, was a history of resistance and rebellion against Chinese authority. An old Vietnamese proverb stated that "Vietnam is too close to China, too far from heaven." Periodically, the Vietnamese rose up in rebellion, and in the process they produced their national heroes: the Trung sisters, who led an anti-Chinese insurrection in A.D. 40; Trieu Au, the Vietnamese Joan of Arc, who led a rebellion in A.D. 248; Ngo Quyen, the military leader of the revolution of 938; Tran Hung Dao, who led the anti-Chinese military effort of the 1280s; and Le Loi, who invented guerrilla warfare in Vietnam in the early 1420s. Truong B. Lam's *Resistance—Rebellion—Revolution: Popular Movements in Vietnamese History* (1984) clearly demonstrates how the centuries-long struggle against China left its mark on Vietnamese culture, creating a warrior-hero cult and elevating martial strengths as moral virtues. Anti-Chinese resistance became the cutting edge of Vietnamese identity, as King Chen makes clear in *Vietnam and China, 1938–1954* (1969).

As Joseph Buttinger has pointed out, the Vietnamese first developed as a self-conscious group thousands of years ago in Tonkin, the northern-most region of Vietnam. They were an aggressive, expansionist people from the very beginning. Michael Cotter's 1968 article "Toward a Social History of the Vietnamese Southward Movement" shows how the Vietnamese moved steadily down the coast of the South China Sea, eventually dislodging the Champa and Khmer people, who had dominated central and southern Vietnam during the Middle Ages. Over the years, two Vietnams actually emerged, one northern and the other southern. The northerners viewed the southerners as a lazy, backward people who enjoyed little sense of community, while southerners felt the northern Vietnamese were pushy and aggressive.

According to Georges Coedes (*The Making of South East Asia,* 1964) and Daniel Hall (*A History of Southeast Asia,* 1955), life in southern Vietnam was easy, at least compared with Tonkin. The Mekong River Delta was rich and productive, with water movements predictable and agriculture simple. Land was abundant and available, and after the defeat of the Khmers, a frontier spirit developed in southern Vietnam, with farmers acquiring larger landholdings and possessing self-serving lifestyles. Population density in southern Vietnam was less than in the north. A more rural culture developed. In Tonkin, on the other hand, the Red River Delta was rich but unpredictable. The river flooded frequently, and over the centuries the northern Vietnamese had to work together to build and supervise thousands of miles of dikes. Population density was heavy and demanded more political and economic organization. Peasant landholdings were much smaller, but the sense of community was much stronger.

Vietnamese religion magnified those differences, as historians Sukumar Dutt (*Buddhism in East Asia,* 1966), Pierro Gheddo (*The Cross and the Bo Tree: Catholics and Buddhists in Vietnam,* 1970), and Thich Thien An (*Buddhism and Zen in Vietnam,* 1975) make clear. Buddhism came to Vietnam from two directions. The Chinese brought Mahayana Buddhism to Vietnam, but the Indians brought Theravada Buddhism to Champa and the Khmer. Theravada Buddhism was archaic and conservative. It viewed salvation as a future state distinct from the present; individuals find nirvana by transcending the present and detaching themselves from worldly cares. The Theravada tradition was strong in southern Vietnam. But in northern Vietnam, there was only Mahayana Buddhism. It was progressive and rested on the belief that anybody could become Buddha and enjoy salvation. It identified morally redeemed people as those committed to acts of love and charity, who focused on the present and postponed their salvation until they helped others achieve theirs. Mahayana Buddhism bequeathed a communal spirit to northerners that was not as well developed in the South. When the time came to resist the Chinese, Japanese, and French intruders, the communal nature of northern culture provided an ideal atmosphere for political organization.

THE FRENCH EMPIRE

France first became involved in Vietnam because of the European missionary movement in Asia. As John F. Cady points out in *The Roots of French Imperialism in Eastern Asia* (1954), the French formed the Society of Foreign Missions and an East India Company in the seventeenth century to move into Indochina, and by the mid-nineteenth century a combination of religious and business pressures led France to a formal, imperial intervention. At first, the French were primarily interested in seeing if the Mekong River could give them a conduit to the China trade, as described in Milton E. Osborne, *River Road to China, The Mekong River Expedition, 1866–1873* (1975). By the 1880s France was in complete control of Vietnam, renaming it in terms of its three major geographical sections: Tonkin, Annam, and Cochinchina.

A number of historians have described the functioning of the French empire in Indochina, including Chester Bain (*A History of Vietnam from the French Intervention to 1939*, 1957), James Ford Cairns (*The Eagle and the Lotus: Western Intervention in Vietnam, 1847–1968*, 1969), Thomas E. Ennis (*French Policy and Developments in Indochina*, 1936), Milton E. Osborne (*The French Presence in Cochinchina and Cambodia: Rule and Response (1859–1905)*, 1969), and Virginia Thompson (*French Indochina*, 1937). French colonial administration was "direct" in that it usually employed Frenchmen rather than ruling through indigenous culture and institutions. A few Vietnamese collaborators enjoyed a false status, but most occupied low-level positions in the imperial bureaucracy. France ruthlessly seized land, imposed onerous taxes on peasants, and exploited Vietnamese labor in mines and rubber plantations. But as Alexander

Werth makes clear in *France 1940–1955* (1956), all that came to an end in 1940. France's surrender to Germany undermined, throughout Indochina, the myth of French invincibility. Both Vichy and Free France officials talked about the importance of the empire, but they could not defend it. Japan took over French Indochina 1940–1941, and the Japanese occupation forces even encouraged Vietnamese nationalism.

Vietnamese nationalism had been long in the making. For Truong B. Lam (*Vietnam's Will to Live: Resistance to Foreign Aggression from Early Times Through the Nineteenth Century*, 1973), resentment of, and resistance to, foreign intruders had been a central feature of Vietnamese history for thousands of years. But it was not until the nineteenth century, in the face of French exploitation, that Vietnamese nationalism began to assume a systematic political and military profile. A number of prominent Vietnamese nationalists emerged in the nineteenth century—such as Phan Chu Trinh and Phan Dinh Phung—but none of them was as important a figure, according to Vinh Sinh's *Phan Boi Chau and the Dong-Vu Movement* (1988), as Phan Boi Chau. He was a leader of the Scholar's Revolt of 1885, the Nghe Tinh Uprising of 1893, and the Poison Plot of 1907. But as William J. Duiker makes clear in his brilliant *The Rise of Nationalism in Vietnam 1900–1941* (1975), Phan Boi Chau was not destined to lead the struggle against the French. That task would fall to Ho Chi Minh.

Ho Chi Minh was born to a revolutionary family in Nghe An province. At his father's knee he learned to hate the French empire and the Vietnamese who did their bidding. The best of Ho Chi Minh's biographers—David Halberstam, *Ho*, 1971; Jean Lacouture, *Ho Chi Minh: A Political Biography*, 1968; and Charles Fenn, *Ho Chi Minh: A Biographical Introduction*, 1973—describe Ho's unassuming personality and unquenchable passion for Vietnamese independence. He traveled the world as a young man, ended up in Paris during World War I, and from there emerged as the leading Vietnamese nationalist. He also became a dedicated Communist after reading Vladimir Lenin's essay "Thesis on the National and Colonial Question." Lenin argued that imperialism was the natural consequence of capitalism. Industrial monopolies and their financial backers, to secure new sources of raw materials and new markets, expand into the underdeveloped world and exploit colonial peoples. He argued that there were two enemies to be confronted: Western imperialists and Asian feudalists. A tiny minority of Asian natives, protected by European technology, control enormous economic assets, intensifying the suffering of peasants and workers. Revolution was the answer. Throw off the imperial yoke and redistribute property to the peasant masses.

In later years Americans would debate which was Ho's true love, nationalism or Communism. Anti-Communists would see only his Communism, arguing that nationalism was just a subterfuge for his role in advancing the international Communist conspiracy. Antiwar critics, on the other hand, claimed that deep down Ho Chi Minh was a nationalist, that Communism was simply the most effective tool for bringing about independence. But as the best of recent research is taken into account— such as the works of Robert F. Turner (*Vietnamese Communism: Its Origins and Development*, 1975), Douglas Pike (*History of Vietnamese Communism, 1925–1976*, 1978), and William J. Duiker (*The Communist Road to Power in Vietnam*, 1981)—both points of view were self-serving and naive. Ho hated the French empire for what it had done to his country, but he also hated the elitism of the mandarin class and French-speaking Vietnamese Catholics who enriched themselves at the expense of poor peasants. Ho Chi Minh was a devout Communist because in Communism he saw the resolution of both evils.

Between 1920 and 1945, Ho Chi Minh lived in France, the Soviet Union, China, Thailand, and Vietnam, honing his political skills, building a coterie of handpicked associates, and building what eventually became the Lao Dong, or Indochinese Communist party. He fought against French imperialism and then resisted the Japanese conquest of Indochina during World War II. As David G. Marr makes clear in *Vietnamese Tradition on Trial, 1920–1945* (1981), those were precarious years for Ho Chi Minh. With assistance from the United States, however, as well as his own political and military skills, he built a dedicated following among Vietnamese peasants, and at the end of World War II, he proclaimed Vietnamese independence.

But it was not to be. No issue surrounding the American role in the Indochina conflict has been more intensely debated than the question of why and how the United States originally became involved there. Toward the end of World War II, President Franklin D. Roosevelt worried about the future of colonialism. He believed World War II would destroy European colonialism, and one colony ripe for rebellion was French Indochina. In March 1943 Roosevelt suggested to the British foreign secretary, Anthony Eden, that when the war was over, Indochina should be placed under international trusteeship, like the older World War I mandates. In a private conversation with Secretary of State Cordell Hull in 1944, the president remarked: "France has had the country— thirty million inhabitants—for nearly one hundred years, and the people are worse off than they were at the beginning.... The people of Indochina are entitled to something better than that." But as historians like Christopher Thorne (*Allies of a Kind: The United States, Britain, and the War Against Japan, 1941–1945*) and William Roger Louis (*Imperialism at Bay: The United States and the Decolonialization of the British Empire*) have pointed out, Great Britain and France were intensely interested in reviving their colonial empires after World War II, and eventually Presidents Franklin D. Roosevelt and Harry S. Truman went along with that revival. In 1946 France returned to Vietnam, and Ho Chi Minh and his followers went into hiding in the mountains near the Chinese border.

But France's tenure in Vietnam was destined to be short-lived as well. Although French military officials in Vietnam urged the French government in Paris to provide more and more assistance, officials paid little heed in the early stages of the conflict. The Vietminh forces of Ho Chi Minh operated as guerrillas, and with Mao Zedong's victory in China in 1949, new forms of assistance to the Communists became readily available. Several historians have written about the fall of French Indochina— Ellen Jay Hammer, *The Struggle for Indochina, 1940–1955* (1966); Donald Lancaster, *The Emancipation of French Indochina* (1974); Lucien Bodard, *The Quicksand War: Prelude to Vietnam* (1967); Bernard Fall, *Street Without Joy* (1964); and Edgar O'Ballance, *The Indo-China War 1945–1954: A Study in Guerrilla Warfare* (1964). Ho Chi Minh's forces were able to inflict increasingly devastating casualties on French forces through hit-and-run tactics, and at the same time they managed to garner more and more political support from the Vietnamese masses who resented French colonialism. As French casualties and costs mounted with no victory in sight, so did discontent at home. Replacement of commanders, even the appointment of renowned General Jean de Lattre de Tassigny, was of no avail.

The decisive and final battle of the conflict took place at Dien Bien Phu in the spring of 1954. The battle has been more than adequately described by such historians as Bernard Fall (*Hell in a Very Small Place: The Siege of Dien Bien Phu*, 1966) and Jules Roy (*The Battle of Dien Bien Phu*, 1965), as well as by General Vo Nguyen Giap (*Dien Bien Phu*, 1962), who commanded the Vietminh forces there. The French had been hoping for just such a confrontation of conventional military forces, but the valley of Dien Bien Phu proved to be a trap. Giap laid siege to the French fortress, cut off its supplies, and bombarded them with artillery. Of the 12,000 French defenders, 2,293 were killed and 5,134 were wounded. The French surrendered on May 7, 1954. By that time, the "quicksand war" in Vietnam had cost France 90,000 casualties. Enough was enough. The diplomatic talks at Geneva settled the issue, at least as far as France was concerned.

During and after the defeat of French forces at Dien Bien Phu in 1954, an international convention met in Geneva, Switzerland, to determine the political future of Indochina. Delegates from the United States, the Soviet Union, the People's Republic of China, Great Britain, France, India, the State of Vietnam, the Democratic Republic of Vietnam, Laos, and Cambodia attended the meetings. For a time the conference tried to work out some method of reuniting North and South

Korea, but all efforts failed. The conference did manage to draft a number of complicated political arrangements for Vietnam.

As Robert F. Randle (*Geneva 1954*, 1969) and Philippe Devillers and Jean Lacouture (*End of a War: Indochina, 1954*, 1969) make clear, the accords divided Vietnam at the 17th parallel into two countries: South Vietnam (Republic of Vietnam) and North Vietnam (Democratic Republic of Vietnam). With the division in place, the Geneva Accords imposed a cease-fire throughout Vietnam as well as cease-fire provisions for the peaceful withdrawal of French forces from North Vietnam and Vietminh forces from South Vietnam. New foreign troop placements were prohibited throughout Vietnam, and all troops were to be withdrawn from Laos and Cambodia. Finally, provisions were made for free elections in both North and South Vietnam in 1956, with the goal of reunification and elimination of the artificial barrier at the 17th parallel. An International Supervisory Commission, composed of representatives from India, Canada, and Poland, was established to monitor compliance with the Accords. Although the United States did not sign the Accords, it did agree with them and promised to avoid the use of military force in the area and to support the principle of self-determination throughout Indochina. South Vietnamese representatives also neglected to sign the Accords but nevertheless expressed public support for its major provisions. By not signing the agreement, the United States had the advantage of appearing supportive without being bound by its provisions. Two years after the Geneva Conference, when it appeared that the followers of Ho Chi Minh had majority support in North as well as South Vietnam, the United States scuttled the free elections and threw all of its economic and military support behind the South Vietnamese regime.

SOUTH VIETNAM

The government of South Vietnam was personified by Ngo Dinh Diem and his family, who dominated the political and economic system. Denis Warner (*The Last Confucian*, 1963) and Anthony T. Bouscaren (*The Last of the Mandarins: Diem of Vietnam*, 1965) have described Diem as a hopelessly out-of-touch tyrant who was incapable of stopping the Communist takeover of his country. Son of a counselor to Emperor Thanh Thai, Ngo Dihn Diem was born in 1901 and claimed to descend from mandarins. The third of six sons, Diem graduated first in his class from a Catholic school in Hue and studied for the civil service at a French college in Hanoi. Rising rapidly through administrative ranks, he became minister of the interior in 1933 but resigned two months later because of French unwillingness to grant Vietnam greater autonomy. An ardent nationalist and early opponent of Communism, Diem retired from public life for twenty years, having nothing further to do with the French and refusing offers from the Japanese during World War II. His anti-communism strengthened when Vietminh forces killed one of his brothers and a nephew. Diem refused Ho Chi Minh's offer to join his government, denouncing him as a "criminal." In 1950 Diem went to the United States, where he met Cardinal Spellman and Senators John Kennedy and Mike Mansfield. These contacts served Diem well when he accepted Emperor Bao Dai's 1954 offer to become prime minister of what would become the Republic of Vietnam. One of Diem's first acts was to request American assistance.

Diem proved unable to build a new nation. He was a devout Catholic who hated Buddhists; the irony, of course, was that South Vietnam was a Buddhist nation. Reclusive and paranoid, he depended almost exclusively on his family, refused to delegate authority, and did little to build a broadly based, popular government. Diem was surprisingly adept in meeting challenges to his government. In 1955, he rejected the reunification elections specified in the Geneva Accords, disposed of Emperor Bao Dai in a fraudulent election (winning 98.2 percent of the vote), neutralized the powerful Cao Dai and Hoa Hao religious sects, and defeated the Binh Xuyen, Vietnam's organized crime group, in open combat. He survived a 1960 coup attempt, which rendered him even more dependent on his immediate family, especially his brother Ngo Dinh Nhu.

But his repressiveness only helped the Vietminh Communists, now known as the Vietcong, in gaining more and more control in South Vietnam. The best historian of the Vietcong is Douglas Pike, whose books provide a brilliant portrait of the Vietnamese Communists in South Vietnam during the 1950s, 1960s, and 1970s. Pike's most important works include *History of Vietnamese Communism, 1925–1976* (1978); *Viet Cong: The Organization and Techniques of the National Liberation Front of South Vietnam* (1966); *The Viet-Cong Strategy of Terror* (1971); and *War, Peace and the Viet Cong* (1969). In 1954, after the Geneva Conference on Indochina, Ho Chi Minh, just as he had promised, ordered his forces to withdraw into North Vietnam, where he would wait for the results of the promised elections to reunite the country in 1956. Included in the withdrawing troops were those Vietminh originally from southern Vietnam. Some of them undoubtedly stayed in the South, but they were few in number and restrained by Hanoi. But five years later, with the government of Ngo Dinh Diem firmly in control of the Republic of Vietnam and the elections canceled, Ho Chi Minh decided to rejoin the battle in the South. He permitted southern Communists to return home, recruit new supporters, and prepare for the "revolutionary struggle." Southern Communists engaged in a frenzy of assassination and terrorism to destabilize the Saigon regime. On December 20, 1960, Ho Chi Minh organized the National Liberation Front (NLF) of South Vietnam, with Nguyen Hu Tho serving as chairman. The purpose of the NLF, as Michael Conley's *The Communist Infrastructure in South Vietnam: A Study of Organization and Strategy* (1967) clearly shows, was to foment a general uprising in the Republic of Vietnam to bring about a Communist revolution that would unite the South with the North. It remains arguable how firmly southern Communists controlled the NLF and how firmly Hanoi controlled the southern Communists.

During the Kennedy administration, the southern insurgents became stronger. South Vietnamese President Ngo Dinh Diem, seeking to deride the insurgency, called the guerrillas the Vietcong (short for Vietnamese Communists). American troops later called them VC, or "Charlie." But the VC soon appeared more than a match for Diem's government forces. At the Battle of Ap Bac, for example, in January 1963, the Vietcong were outnumbered ten to one but managed to inflict a humiliating defeat on the South Vietnamese. By late 1963, American intelligence analyses found that the Vietcong controlled more villages in the South than did the Saigon government. At that point, the United States decided to abandon Diem and try to build a new government in South Vietnam, and one more capable of dealing successfully with the Vietcong.

Ellen J. Hammer's *Death in November: America in Vietnam 1963* (1987) is a brilliant analysis of the demise of the Diem regime. Administratively, Diem could not set priorities, choosing to spend a long afternoon with a journalist while members of his government and the military waited for audiences. Governing through repression and intrigue, he tried to kill or imprison the Vietcong infrastructure along with most other potential opponents. His oppressiveness and refusal to implement reforms tried the patience of the United States and drove the peasants into Communist hands. By 1963, he was finished. The final blow was Ngo Dinh Nhu's vicious attacks on Buddhist dissidents and the ensuing national paralysis. Although not involved in the coup, the United States signaled that it would accept a change in government. On November 1, the generals moved; Diem and his brother were murdered the next day.

The Vietcong high-water mark came in 1963–1964. In 1965 President Lyndon B. Johnson began committing the first of what became more than a half million troops and a vast array of weaponry. Hanoi responded with its own buildup of North Vietnamese regular troops. The Vietcong were battered by American forces and taken over gradually by North Vietnamese Army cadres. The Tet Offensive, as Dan Oberdorfer points out in *Tet!* (1971), was a political disaster for the United States, but it was also the death stroke for the independence of the Vietcong. By the end of 1968, as William J. Duiker describes in his *The Communist Road to Power in Vietnam* (1981), the Vietcong had suffered deep and disastrous losses, and North Vietnamese troops were largely responsible for the war effort in South Vietnam. In 1969 the Provisional Revolutionary Government of South Vietnam superseded the Vietcong-NLF.

But although the corrupt Diem administration was gone and the Vietcong had been all but destroyed, the U.S. military effort in Vietnam did not achieve the political objectives Presidents Kennedy, Johnson, and Nixon hoped to achieve. Part of the problem, of course, was that those political objectives were muddled and poorly conceived, but beyond that the political and economic conditions in South Vietnam were not conducive to an American political victory. Douglas C. Dacy's outstanding book *Foreign Aid, War, and Economic Development: South Vietnam, 1955–1975* (1986) describes how the presence of billions of dollars of American money changed the Vietnamese economy and triggered monumental demographic changes. The entire economy became geared to serving the American war machine, and in the process millions of South Vietnamese poured into such cities as Saigon, Hue, Cam Ranh Bay, and Nha Trang. The problem, of course, was that the flow of American dollars was creating an artificial prosperity and introducing a host of social problems that would be devastating for the local government once any American withdrawal began. The U.S. objective of building a viable, anti-Communist government of South Vietnam was doomed. As soon as the United States withdrew and reduced the volume of money flowing to South Vietnam, the resulting unemployment and economic dislocation would undermine any political support the government had earned.

All along, that political support was problematic. As Allan E. Goodman (*Politics in War: The Bases of Political Community in South Vietnam*, 1973) and John C. Donnell and Charles Joiner (*Electoral Politics in South Vietnam*, 1974) have written, there was no grass-roots support in the villages for the government of South Vietnam. In fact, the government of South Vietnam had not even been in existence until 1954; it hardly existed in the minds of most peasants. When they did think of the government, most perceived it as a corrupt, anti-Buddhist entity that deprived them of their traditional rights. Nor was there any real sense of democracy in South Vietnam, except at the village level. Any hope the United States had of building a nation in South Vietnam with a foundation of political democracy was naive at best. Most South Vietnamese looked to Ho Chi Minh, not Ngo Dinh Diem or his successors, as the rightful leader of the Vietnamese people. Also see Samuel L. Popkin, *The Rational Peasant: The Political Economy of Rural Society in Vietnam* (1979).

Whatever political support the United States was trying to build in South Vietnam was also undermined by the extent of the military effort there. By far the major criticism of American strategy in Vietnam during the war was the belief that too much firepower was being used—that the collateral damage on civilians, the environment, and the economy, although devastating to enemy troops, was equally devastating to American political objectives. William J. Lederer, in *Our Own Worst Enemy* (1968), wrote that Vietnam was actually several wars being fought at one time: the bomber war, body-count war, guerrilla war, major-encounter war, and the political war for the loyalty of the Vietnamese people. Lederer contended that U.S. strategy was losing all the wars but especially the political war. Without winning the contest for the people, victory can be obtained only at the cost of vast destruction, and even then victory will be only temporary. The American strategy of attrition, designed to win the war and the hearts of the Vietnamese people, had just the opposite effect in driving them into the camp of the Vietcong. Jonathan Schell wrote two books describing the effects of American firepower. In *The Village of Ben Suc* (1967), Schell examined Ben Suc, a relatively prosperous farming village on the edge of the Iron Triangle. It became a target for the pacification program. Ben Suc was believed to be a Vietcong stronghold and had been pacified several times by the U.S. Army. Schell examines the military strategy that eventually pacifies Ben Suc, completely destroying it and evacuating its inhabitants. The refugees were moved to a barren, treeless "safe" area where they were "pacified" and then sank into apathy and despair. In *The Military Half: An Account of Destruction in Quang Ngai and Quang Tin* (1968), Schell examined rural pacification gone haywire as a result of not being able to identify the Vietcong from the civilian Vietnamese population. Schell discussed the failure of pacification to win the hearts and minds of the people and the tragic consequences when American troops, unable to deal with the strain of Vietcong identification, destroyed Quang Ngai and Quang Tin Provinces in 1967. A host of other books have also dealt with the problem of how massive American firepower affected South Vietnamese peasants, including James Walker Trullinger, Jr., *Village at War: An Account of Revolution in Vietnam* (1980); William A. Nighswonger, *Rural Pacification in Vietnam* (1966); Richard Hammer, *One Morning in the War: The Tragedy at Son My* (1970); Gloria Emerson, *Winners and Losers* (1978); Fred Gloechner, *A Civilian Doctor in Vietnam* (1972); Ken Post, *Revolution, Socialism, and Nationalism* (1989); Jeffrey Race, *War Comes to Long An Province* (1972); and Jonathan Schell, *The Time of Illusion* (1975).

By the early 1970s, the political, economic, and military problems associated with the American effort in Vietnam destroyed the government of South Vietnam and led to the Communist victory of 1975. Because of the antiwar movement at home, political support for the war declined dramatically after 1968, and in the process appropriations for the war dropped as well. President Richard Nixon implemented his "Vietnamization" policy and turned the war over to the South Vietnamese government, and the flow of American money to South Vietnam began to erode. The economic consequences were immediate: unemployment and political discontent skyrocketed, especially in urban areas. The government of South Vietnam had little support among the masses of South Vietnamese, and the resentment of the United States, primarily because of the years of destruction, was intense. When the peace treaty was signed in 1973, policymakers in Saigon, Hanoi, and Washington, D.C., knew that it was only a matter of time before South Vietnam fell. When North Vietnamese troops launched their final assault on South Vietnam at the end of March 1975, it was all over in a month. The South Vietnamese government and military imploded.

AFTERMATH

The fall of South Vietnam in the spring of 1975 led to a euphoric celebration through North Vietnam and much of South Vietnam. Saigon was renamed Ho Chi Minh City, and the names Democratic Republic of Vietnam (North Vietnam) and Republic of Vietnam (South Vietnam) were abandoned in favor of the Socialist Republic of Vietnam. The first order of business, as Ginetta Sagan and Stephen Downey (*Violations of Human Rights in the Socialist Republic of Vietnam*, 1983) and Nguyen Van Canh (*Vietnam Under Communism, 1975–1982*, 1983) make clear, was the political reeducation of the people of South Vietnam. Vietnamese Communists wanted to wipe out every vestige of democracy, capitalism, vice, and American popular culture throughout the country, and that involved establishing "re-education" campaigns for the South Vietnamese who had been closely associated with the Americans. In the process, the Socialist Republic of Vietnam became one of the most repressive regimes in the world.

The Vietnamese also soon found themselves involved in a third Indochina war. The expulsion of France in 1954 had brought the first Indochinese conflict to an end, and the withdrawal of the Americans in 1975 had put a conclusion to the second war. But as David W. P. Elliott (*The Third Indochina Conflict*, 1981) and Edgar O'Ballance (*The Wars in Vietnam, 1954–1980*, 1981) argue, Indochina was still not destined for peace. In 1979 Vietnam found itself once again at war with China, this time over a long-held border dispute between the two countries. Vietnam also invaded Cambodia in order to eliminate the Khmer Rouge, who were subjecting the country to a genocidal rage. Both wars were very expensive for Vietnam, especially after the years of conflict with France and the United States, and they exaggerated Vietnam's already serious economic problems.

Most of those economic problems were of their own making. Leaders in Hanoi were also quick to impose a socialist economy on South Vietnam. William Duiker's two books (*Vietnam: Nation in Revolution*, 1983, and *Vietnam Since the Fall of Saigon*, 1989), as well as Joel Charney and John

Spragens, Jr., *Obstacles to Recovery in Vietnam and Kampuchea* (1984) describe the process by which the government in Hanoi eliminated private entrepreneurship and small business, collectivized agriculture, and tried to accelerate industrialization through the establishment of state industries. The results amounted to an economic catastrophe. Per capita income, worker productivity, industrial and agricultural production, and the gross national product declined precipitously. As Robert E. Long points out in *Vietnam Ten Years After* (1985), such an economic decline was ironic, since the Vietnamese have traditionally been one of the most hardworking and enterprising people in the world. By the late 1980s, Communism had transformed the Socialist Republic of Vietnam into an economic basket case. In fact, conditions were so bad that Vietnamese leaders began to think the unthinkable: seeking a rapprochement with the United States in order to secure economic assistance.

BIBLIOGRAPHY

General Histories

Archer, Robert. *Vietnam: The Habit of War*. New York: Catholic Institute of International Relations, 1983.

Beresford, Melanie. *Vietnam: Politics, Economics and Society*. London: Pinter, 1988.

Boettcher, Thomas D. *Vietnam: The Valor and the Sorrow*. Boston: Little, Brown, 1985.

Burchett, Wilfred. *Grasshoppers and Elephants*. New York: Urizen Books, 1977.

Burchett, Wilfred. *Catapult to Freedom: The Survival of the Vietnamese People*. New York: Quartet Books, 1982.

Buttinger, Joseph. *The Smaller Dragon*. New York: Praeger, 1958.

Buttinger, Joseph. *Vietnam: A Dragon Embattled*. New York: Praeger, 1967.

Cairns, James Ford. *The Eagle and the Lotus: Western Intervention in Vietnam, 1847–1968*. New York: Lansdowne Press, 1969.

Chesneaux, Jean. *The Vietnamese Nation: Contribution to a History*. New York: Current Book Distribution, 1966.

Coedes, Georges. *The Making of South East Asia*. Berkeley: University of California Press, 1964.

Fishel, Wesley, ed. *Vietnam: Anatomy of a Conflict*. New York: Peacock, 1968.

FitzGerald, Francis. *Fire in the Lake: The Vietnamese and the Americans in Vietnam*. Boston: Little, Brown, 1972.

Gettleman, Marvin E., ed. *Vietnam*. New York: Fawcett, 1965.

Hall, Daniel. *A History of Southeast Asia*. New York: St. Martin's Press, 1955.

Hammer, Ellen Jay. *Vietnam: Yesterday and Today*. New York: Holt, Rinehart, and Winston, 1966.

Harrison, James P. *The Endless War: Fifty Years of Struggle in Vietnam*. New York: Free Press, 1982.

Harrison, James P. *The Endless War: Vietnam's Struggle for Independence*. New York: Columbia University Press, 1989.

Karnow, Stanley. *Vietnam: A History*. New York: Viking, 1983.

Lederer, William. *Our Own Worst Enemy*. New York: Norton, 1968.

Nguyen Van Thai. *A Short History of Vietnam*. New York: Times, 1958.

Thich Nhat Hanh. *Vietnam: Lotus in a Sea of Fire*. New York: Hill and Wang, 1967.

Welty, Paul. *The Asians: Their Heritage and Their Destiny*. Philadelphia: Lippincott, 1963.

Pre–1945 Vietnam

Bain, Chester. *Vietnam: The Roots of Conflict*. Englewood Cliffs, N.J.: Prentice-Hall, 1967.

Chen, King. *Vietnam and China, 1938–1954*. Princeton, N.J.: Princeton University Press, 1969.

Chesneaux, Jean. "Stages in the Development of the Vietnamese National Movement, 1862–1940." *Past and Present* 37 (1955): 63–75.

Cotter, Michael. "Toward a Social History of the Vietnamese Southward Movement." *Journal of Southeast Asian History* 9 (1968): 12–24.

Drachman, Edward R. *United States Policy Toward Vietnam, 1940–1945*. Rutherford, N.J.: Fairleigh Dickinson University Press, 1970.

Duiker, William J. *The Rise of Nationalism in Vietnam 1900–1941*. Ithaca, N.Y.: Cornell University Press, 1975.

Gran, Guy. "Vietnam and the Capitalist Route to Modernity: Village Cochinchina 1880–1940." Ph.D. Diss. University of Wisconsin, 1973.

Lam, Truong B. *Resistance—Rebellion—Revolution: Popular Movements in Vietnamese History*. New York: Gower, 1984.

Lamb, Helen B. *Vietnam's Will to Live: Resistance to Foreign Aggression from Early Times Through the Nineteenth Century*. New York: Monthly Review Press, 1973.

Louis, William Roger. *Imperialism at Bay: The United States and the Decolonization of the British Empire, 1941–1945*. New York: Oxford University Press, 1978.

McAleavy, Henry. *Black Flags in Vietnam: The Story of the Chinese Intervention*. Boston: Allen and Unwin, 1968.

MacAlister, John T., Jr. *Vietnam: The Origins of Revolution*. New York: Knopf, 1969.

Marr, David G. *Vietnamese Tradition on Trial, 1920–1945*. Berkeley: University of California Press, 1981.

Sinh, Vinh, ed. *Phan Boi Chau and the Dong-Vu Movement*. New Haven, Conn.: Yale University Southeast Asia Program, 1988.

Thorne, Christopher G. *Allies of a Kind: The United States, Britain, and the War Against Japan, 1941–1945*. London: Hamilton, 1978.

Truong B. Lam. *Vietnam's Will to Live: Resistance to Foreign Aggression from Early Times Through the Nineteenth Century*. New York: International Publishers, 1973.

Whitmore, John K. *Vietnam, Ho Quy, and the Ming*. New Haven, Conn.: Yale University Southeast Asian Studies Program, 1985.

Wickberg, Edgar. *Historical Interaction of China and Vietnam*. New York: Paragon Book Gallery, 1969.

Woodside, Alexander. "The Development of Social Organization in Vietnamese Cities in the Late Colonial Period." *Pacific Affairs* 64 (1921): 39–63.

Woodside, Alexander. *Vietnam and the Chinese Model.* Cambridge: Harvard University Press, 1971.

Vietnamese Culture

Crawford, Ann. *Customs and Culture of Vietnam.* New York: Tuttle, 1966.

Dutt, Sukumar. *Buddhism in East Asia.* New York: Indian Council for Cultural Relations, 1966.

Fall, Bernard B. "The Political Religious Sects of Vietnam." *Pacific Affairs* 28 (1955): 235–53.

Gheddo, Pierro. *The Cross and the Bo Tree: Catholics and Buddhists in Vietnam.* New York: Sheed and Ward, 1970.

Groslier, Bernard. *The Art of Indochina.* New York: Crown, 1962.

Hejzlar, J. T. *The Art of Vietnam.* New York: Hamlyn, 1973.

Hickey, Gerald C. *Free in the Forest: Ethnohistory of the Vietnamese Central Highlands, 1954–1976.* New Haven, Conn.: Yale University Press, 1982a.

Hickey, Gerald C. *Sons of the Mountains: Ethnohistory of the Vietnamese Central Highlands to 1954.* New Haven, Conn.: Yale University Press, 1982b.

Hickey, Gerald C. *Kingdom in the Morning Mist: Mayrena in the Highlands of Vietnam.* Philadelphia: University of Pennsylvania Press, 1988.

Mole, Robert L. *The Montagnards of South Vietnam: A Study of Nine Tribes.* New York: Tuttle, 1970.

Nguyen Din Hoa. *The Vietnamese Language.* Saigon: Department of National Education, 1960.

Nguyen Ngoc Bich. *A Thousand Years of Vietnamese Poetry.* New York: Knopf, 1975.

Oliver, Victor L. *Cao Dai Spiritualism: A Study of Religion in Vietnamese Society.* New York: Brill, 1976.

Schultz, George F. *Vietnamese Legends.* New York: Tuttle, 1965.

Sharma, Ritu. *Vietnam.* New Delhi, India: Sterling, 1988.

Smith, Ralph B. "An Introduction to Cao Daism: I. Origins and Early History." *London University Bulletin of the School of Oriental and African Studies* 33 (1970a): 335–49.

Smith, Ralph B. "An Introduction to Cao Daism: II. Beliefs and Organization." *London University Bulletin of the School of Oriental and African Studies* 33 (1970b): 573–89.

Smithsonian Institution. *Art and Archaeology of Vietnam.* Washington, D.C.: Smithsonian Institution, 1961.

Thich Thien An. *Buddhism and Zen in Vietnam.* New York: Tuttle, 1975.

The French Intervention

Bain, Chester. *A History of Vietnam from the French Intervention to 1939.* Ann Arbor, Mich.: University Microfilms, 1957.

Bodard, Lucien. *The Quicksand War: Prelude to Vietnam.* Boston: Little, Brown, 1967.

Cady, John F. *The Roots of French Imperialism in Eastern Asia.* Ithaca, N.Y.: Cornell University Press, 1954.

Cady, John F. "The French Colonial Regime in Vietnam." *Current History* 50 (1966): 72–78, 115.

Cairns, James Ford. *The Eagle and the Lotus: Western Intervention in Vietnam, 1847–1968.* New York: Lansdowne Press, 1969.

Chen, King. *Vietnam and China, 1938–1954.* Princeton, N.J.: Princeton University Press, 1969.

Devillers, Philippe, and Jean Lacouture. *End of a War: Indochina, 1954.* New York: Praeger, 1969.

Duong, Pham C. *Vietnamese Peasants Under French Domination, 1861–1945.* Lanham, Md.: University Press of America, 1985.

Ennis, Thomas E. *French Policy and Developments in Indochina.* Chicago: University of Chicago Press, 1936.

Fall, Bernard. *The Two Vietnams: A Political and Military Analysis.* New York: Praeger, 1963.

Fall, Bernard. *Street Without Joy.* New York: Macmillan, 1964.

Fall, Bernard. *Hell in a Very Small Place: The Siege of Dien Bien Phu.* London: Pall Mall Press, 1966.

Garner, Reuben. "Watchdogs of the Empire: The French Colonial Inspection Service in Action: 1815–1913." Ph.D. diss., University of Rochester, 1970.

Ghosh, Manomohan. "French Colonization of Vietnam: The First Phase (1861–1885)." *Calcutta Review* 172 (1964a): 119–29.

Ghosh, Manomohan. "French Conquest of Vietnam." *Calcutta Review* 170 (1964b): 273–310.

Giap, Vo Nguyen. *Dien Bien Phu.* New York: Foreign Language Publishing House, 1962.

Gurtov, Melvin. *The First Vietnam Crisis: Chinese Communist Strategy and United States Involvement, 1953–54.* New York: Columbia University Press, 1967.

Hammer, Ellen Jay. *The Struggle for Indochina, 1940–1955.* Palo Alto, Calif.: Stanford University Press, 1966.

Lacoutre, Jean. *Vietnam: Between Two Truces.* New York: Random House, 1966.

Lancaster, Donald. *The Emancipation of French Indochina.* New York: Octagon Books, 1974.

Langlais, Pierre. *Dien Bien Phu.* Paris: Editions France-Empire, 1963.

Marr, David G. *Vietnamese Anticolonialism, 1885–1925.* Berkeley: University of California Press, 1971.

O'Ballance, Edgar. *The Indo-China War 1945–1954: A Study in Guerrilla Warfare.* New York: Faber and Faber, 1964.

Osborne, Milton E. *The French Presence in Cochinchina and Cambodia: Rule and Response (1859–1905).* Ithaca, N.Y.: Cornell University Press, 1969.

Osborne, Milton E. *River Road to China, The Mekong River Expedition, 1866–1873.* London: Liveright, 1975.

Randle, Robert F. *Geneva 1954: The Settlement of the Indochinese War.* Princeton, N.J.: Princeton University Press, 1969.

Smith, Ralph B. "The Development of Opposition to French Rule in Southern Vietnam 1880–1940." *Past and Present* 54 (1972): 94–129.

Sullivan, Marianna P. *France's Vietnam Policy: A Study in French-American Relations.* Westport, Conn.: Greenwood Press, 1978.

Thompson, R. Stanley. "The Diplomacy of Imperialism: France and Spain in Cochinchina, 1858–1863." *Journal of Modern History* 12 (1940): 334–56.

Thompson, Virginia. *French Indochina.* New York: Allen and Unwin, 1937.

Truong Buu Lam. *Patterns of Vietnamese Response to Foreign Intervention, 1858–1900.* New Haven, Conn.: Yale University Press, 1967.

Werth, Alexander. *France 1940–1955.* Boston: Beacon Press, 1956.

Vietnamese Communism

Andrews, William R. *The Village War. Vietnamese Communist Revolutionary Activities in Dinh Tuong Province, 1960–1964.* Columbia: University of Missouri Press, 1973.

Aptheker, Herbert. *Mission to Hanoi.* New York: International, 1966.

Archer, Jules. *Ho Chi Minh: Legend of Hanoi.* New York: Crowell-Collier Press, 1971.

Ashmore, Harry S., and William C. Baggs. *Mission to Hanoi.* New York: Putnam, 1968.

Asprey, Robert B. *War in the Shadows: The Guerrilla in History.* Garden City, N.Y.: Doubleday, 1975.

Burchett, Wilfred G. *Vietnam: Inside Story of the Guerrilla War.* New York: International, 1965.

Burchett, Wilfred G. *Vietnam North.* Ann Arbor, Mich.: University Microfilms, 1986.

Cameron, James. *Here Is Your Enemy.* New York: Holt, Rinehart, and Winston, 1966.

Carver, George. "The Faceless Viet Cong." *Foreign Affairs* 44 (April 1966): 347–72.

Chaliand, Gerard. *The Peasants of North Vietnam.* New York: Penguin, 1969.

Chen, King C. "Hanoi's Three Decisions and the Escalation of the Vietnam War." *Political Science Quarterly* 90 (Summer 1975): 239–60.

Cole, Allen, ed. *Conflict in Indochina and Its International Repercussions.* Ithaca, N.Y.: Cornell University Press, 1956.

Conley, Michael. *The Communist Infrastructure in South Vietnam: A Study of Organization and Strategy.* Washington, D.C.: American University Press, 1967.

Davidson, W. P., and J. J. Zasloff. *A Profile of Viet Cong Cadres.* Santa Monica, Calif.: Rand Corporation, 1966.

DuBerrier, Hilaire. *Background to Betrayal: The Tragedy of Vietnam.* Boulder, Colo.: Westview Press, 1965.

Duiker, William J. "The Red Soviets of Nghe-Tinh: An Early Communist Rebellion in Vietnam." *Journal of Southeast Asian Studies* 4 (1973): 185–98.

Duiker, William J. *The Communist Road to Power in Vietnam.* Boulder, Colo.: Westview Press, 1981.

Duiker, William J. *Vietnam: Nation in Revolution.* Boulder, Colo.: Westview, 1983.

Duncanson, Dennis J. *Government and Revolution in Vietnam.* New York: Oxford University Press, 1968.

Durr, John C., ed. *The North Vietnamese Regime: Institutions and Problems.* Washington, D.C.: American University Press, 1969.

Fall, Bernard. *The Viet-Minh Regime: Government and Administration in the DRVN.* San Francisco, Calif.: Institute of Pacific Relations, 1956.

Fall, Bernard. *Viet-Nam Witness, 1953–1966.* New York: Praeger, 1966.

Fall, Bernard. *The Two Vietnams.* New York: Praeger, 1967.

Fenn, Charles. *Ho Chi Minh: A Biographical Introduction.* New York: Scribner's, 1973.

Gerassi, John. *North Vietnam: A Documentary.* Chicago: Bobbs-Merrill, 1968.

Giap, Vo Nguyen. *Dien Bien Phu.* Hanoi: Foreign Language Publishing, 1962.

Giap, Vo Nguyen. *People's Army: The Viet Cong Insurrection Manual for Underdeveloped Countries.* New York: Praeger, 1962.

Gourou, Pierre. *The Peasants of the Tonkin Delta.* Washington, D.C.: Human Relations Area File, 1955.

Gurtov, Melvin. *Vietcong Cadres and the Cadre System: A Study of the Main and Local Forces.* Santa Monica, Calif.: Rand Corporation, 1967.

Halberstam, David. *Ho.* New York: Knopf, 1971.

Hoang Van Chi. *From Colonialism to Communism—A Case History of North Vietnam.* New York: Praeger, 1964.

Hoang Van Thi. *Some Aspects of Guerrilla Warfare in Vietnam.* New York: Praeger, 1964.

Honey, P. J. *Communism in North Vietnam.* Cambridge: MIT Press, 1963.

Honey, P. J., ed. *North Vietnam Today.* New York: Praeger, 1962.

Kellen, K. T. *A Profile of the PAVN Soldier in South Vietnam.* Santa Monica, Calif.: Rand Corporation, 1966.

Knobel, Kuno. *Victor Charlie: The Face of War in Viet-Nam.* New York: Praeger, 1967.

Lacouture, Jean. *Ho Chi Minh: A Political Biography.* New York: Random House, 1968.

Le Duan. *On the Socialist Revolution in Vietnam.* New York: Foreign Language Publishing House, 1965.

Le Duan. *The Vietnamese Revolution.* New York: International, 1971.

Le Duan. *Selected Writings.* New York: Foreign Language Publishing House, 1972.

McCarthy, Mary. *The Seventeenth Degree.* New York: Harcourt Brace Jovanovich, 1974.

McCoy, Alfred W. *The Politics of Heroin in Southeast Asia.* New York: Harper and Row, 1972.

McGarvey, Patrick J. *Visions of Victory: Selected Vietnamese Communist Military Writings 1965–1968.* Palo Alto, Calif.: Hoover Institute Press, 1969.

Maneli, Mieczyslaw. *War of the Vanquished.* New York: Harper and Row, 1971.

Molnar, Andrew R., ed. *Undergrounds in Insurgent, Revolutionary, and Resistance Warfare.* Washington, D.C.: American University Press, 1963.

Nguyen Ngoc Ngan. *The Will of Heaven.* New York: Dutton, 1982.

Nguyen Tien Dung. *Economic Development of Socialist Vietnam, 1955–1980.* New York: Praeger, 1977.

Oberdorfer, Dan. *Tet!* Garden City, N.Y.: Doubleday, 1971.

Ojwa, Ishwer. "China and North Vietnam: The Limits of the Alliance." *Current History* 54 (January 1968): 42–47.

O'Neill, Robert. *General Giap*. New York: Praeger, 1969.

Papp, Daniel S. *Vietnam: The View from Moscow, Peking, Washington*. New York: McFarland, 1981.

Pike, Douglas. *Viet Cong: The Organization and Techniques of the National Liberation Front of South Vietnam*. Cambridge: MIT Press, 1966.

Pike, Douglas. *War, Peace and the Viet Cong*. Cambridge: MIT Press, 1969.

Pike, Douglas. *The Viet-Cong Strategy of Terror*. Saigon: U.S. Mission, 1971.

Pike, Douglas. *History of Vietnamese Communism, 1925–1976*. Palo Alto, Calif.: Hoover Institution Press, 1978.

Pike, Douglas. *PAVN: People's Army of Vietnam*. New York: Pergamon Press, 1986.

Pimlott, John, ed. *Vietnam: The History and the Tactics*. New York: Crescent Books, 1982.

Prados, John. *President's Secret Wars: CIA and Pentagon Covert Operations Since World War II*. New York: Morrow, 1986.

Race, Jeffrey. *War Comes to Long An: Revolutionary Conflict in a Vietnamese Province*. Berkeley: University of California Press, 1972.

Sainteny, Jean. *Ho Chi Minh and His Followers: A Personal Memoir*. New York: Cowley, 1968.

Salisbury, Harrison E. *Behind the Lines: Hanoi*. New York: Harper and Row, 1967.

Sheehan, Susan. *Ten Vietnamese*. New York: Knopf, 1967.

Stern, Kurt, and Jeanne Stern. *Ricefields, Battlefield: A Visit to North Vietnam*. New York: Seven Seas, 1969.

Tanham, George Kilpatrick. *Communist Revolutionary Warfare: From the Vietminh to the Viet Cong*. New York: Praeger, 1967.

Trullinger, James Walker, Jr. *Village at War: An Account of Revolution in Vietnam*. New York: Longman, 1980.

Truong Chinh. *Primer for Revolt: The Communist Takeover in Vietnam*. New York: Praeger, 1963.

Truong Chinh. *Forward Along the Path Charted by Karl Marx*. New York: Foreign Language Publishing House, 1969.

Truong Nhu Tang. *A Vietcong Memoir*. New York: Harcourt Brace Jovanovich, 1985.

Turner, Robert F. *Vietnamese Communism: Its Origins and Development*. Stanford, Calif.: Hoover Institution Press, 1975.

Van Dyke, Jon M. *North Vietnam's Strategy for Survival*. San Francisco: Pacific Books, 1972.

Van Tien Dung. *Our Great Spring Victory*. New York: Monthly Review Press, 1977.

Vo Nguyen Giap. *Big Victory, Great Task*. New York: Praeger, 1968.

Vo Nguyen Giap. *Selected Writings*. New York: Foreign Language Publishing House, 1977.

Zagoria, Donald. *Vietnam Triangle*. New York: Pegasus, 1967.

Zasloff, Joseph J., and MacAlister Brown, eds. *Communism in Indochina*. New York: Lexington Books, 1975.

Zasloff, Joseph J., and Allan E. Goodman, eds. *Indochina in Conflict: A Political Assessment*. New York: Lexington Books, 1972.

South Vietnam

Adair, Dick. *Dick Adair's Saigon*. New York: Weather Hill, 1971.

Amter, Joseph A. *The Vietnam Verdict*. New York: Continuum, 1982.

Bamford, James. *The Puzzle Palace*. New York: Penguin, 1983.

Bonds, Ray, ed. *The Vietnam War*. New York: Crown, 1979.

Bouscaren, Anthony T. *The Last of the Mandarins: Diem of Vietnam*. Pittsburgh, Pa.: University of Pittsburgh Press, 1965.

Boyle, Richard. *The Flower of the Dragon*. New York: Ramparts Press, 1972.

Butler, David. *The Fall of Saigon: Scenes from the Sudden End of a Long War*. New York: Simon and Schuster, 1985.

Dacy, Douglas C. *Foreign Aid, War, and Economic Development: South Vietnam, 1955–1975*. Cambridge: Cambridge University Press, 1986.

Dawson, Alan. *55 Days: The Fall of South Vietnam*. Englewood Cliffs, N.J.: Prentice-Hall, 1977.

Donnell, John C., and Charles Joiner, eds. *Electoral Politics in South Vietnam*. New York: Lexington Books, 1974.

Emerson, Gloria. *Winners and Losers*. New York: Harcourt Brace Jovanovich, 1978.

Falabala, Robert. *Vietnam Memoirs*. New York: Pageant Press International, 1971.

Garms, Robert. *With the Dragon's Children*. New York: Exposition Press, 1973.

Gloechner, Fred. *A Civilian Doctor in Vietnam*. New York: Winchell, 1972.

Goodman, Allan E. *Politics in War: The Bases of Political Community in South Vietnam*. Cambridge: Harvard University Press, 1973.

Goodman, Allan E. *The Lost Peace: America's Search for a Negotiated Settlement of the Vietnam War*. Palo Alto, Calif.: Hoover Institution Press, 1978.

Haas, Harry, and Nguyen Bao Cong. *Vietnam: The Other Conflict*. New York: Sheed and Ward, 1971.

Haley, Robert T. *Congress and the Fall of South Vietnam and Cambodia*. New York: Associated University Presses, 1982.

Hammer, Ellen J. *Death in November: America in Vietnam 1963*. New York: Dutton, 1987.

Hammer, Richard. *One Morning in the War: The Tragedy at Son My*. New York: Coward-McCann, 1970.

Haviland, H. Field, Jr. *Vietnam After the War: Peacekeeping and Rehabilitation*. Ann Arbor, Mich.: University Microfilms, 1982.

Hefley, James C. *By Life or Death*. Grand Rapids, Mich.: Zondervan, 1969.

Hendry, James B. *The Small World of Khanh Hau*. New York: Aldine, 1964.

Herrington, Stuart A. *Silence Was a Weapon: The Vietnam War in the Villages. A Personal Perspective*. Novato, Calif.: Presidio Press, 1982.

Hickey, Gerald. *Village in Vietnam*. New Haven, Conn.: Yale University Press, 1964.

Hosmer, Stephen. *Viet Cong Repression and Its Implications for the Future*. Lexington, Mass.: D. C. Heath, 1970.

Hosmer, Stephen T., et al. *The Fall of South Vietnam: Statements by Vietnamese Military and Civilian Leaders*. New York: Crane Russak, 1980.

Hughes, Larry. *You Can See a Lot Standing Under a Flare in the Republic of Vietnam*. New York: Morrow, 1969.

Isaacs, Arnold. *Without Honor: Defeat in Vietnam and Cambodia*. Baltimore, Md.: Johns Hopkins University Press, 1983.

Kissinger, Henry. *The Memoirs of Henry Kissinger: The White House Years*. Boston: Little, Brown, 1979.

Kissinger, Henry. *The Memoirs of Henry Kissinger: Years of Upheaval*. Boston: Little, Brown, 1982.

Knappman, Edward W. *South Vietnam. U.S.-Communist Confrontation in Southeast Asia*. Vol. 7, 1972–1973. New York: Facts on File, 1973.

Lansdale, Edward Geary. *In the Midst of Wars: An American's Mission to Southeast Asia*. New York: Harper and Row, 1972.

Lavalle, A.J.C., ed. *Last Flight from Saigon*. Washington, D.C.: U.S. Air Force, 1979.

Lindholm, Richard W. *Viet-Nam: The First Five Years*. Lansing: Michigan State University Press, 1959.

Loory, Stuart. *Defeated*. New York: Random House, 1973.

Ly Qui Chunh. *Between Two Fires*. New York: Praeger, 1970.

May, Julian. *In the Jaws of History: Bui Diem with David Chanoff*. New York: Ticknor and Fields, 1987.

Mecklin, John. *Mission in Torment*. Garden City, N.Y.: Doubleday, 1965.

Nguyen Cao Ky. *Twenty Years and Twenty Days*. New York: Stein and Day, 1976.

Nighswonger, William A. *Rural Pacification in Vietnam*. New York: Praeger, 1966.

Nixon, Richard M. *RN: The Memoirs of Richard Nixon*. New York: Warner Books, 1978.

Oberdorfer, Dan. *Tet!* Garden City, N.Y.: Doubleday, 1971.

O'Neill, Robert J. *The Strategy of General Giap Since 1964*. Melbourne: Australian National University, 1969.

Pham Van Dong. *Forward! Final Victory Will Be Ours!* New York: Foreign Language Publishing House, 1968.

Pickerell, James H. *Vietnam in the Mud*. New York: Bobbs-Merrill, 1966.

Popkin, Samuel L. *The Rational Peasant: The Political Economy of Rural Society in Vietnam*. Berkeley: University of California Press, 1979.

Post, Ken. *Revolution, Socialism, and Nationalism*. New York: Wadsworth, 1989.

Race, Jeffrey. *War Comes to Long An Province*. Berkeley: University of California Press, 1972.

Schell, Jonathan. *The Village of Ben Suc*. New York: Knopf, 1967.

Schell, Jonathan. *The Military Half: An Account of Destruction in Quang Ngai and Quang Tin*. New York: Knopf, 1968.

Schell, Jonathan. *The Time of Illusion*. New York: Vintage Books, 1975.

Scigliano, Robert. *South Vietnam: Nation Under Stress*. Westport, Conn.: Greenwood Press, 1964.

Shaplen, Robert. *The Road from War: Vietnam 1965–1970*. New York: Harper and Row, 1970.

Shaplen, Robert. *Time Out of Hand: Revolution and Reaction in Southeast Asia*. New York: Harper and Row, 1970.

Shultz, Richard H., Jr., and Richard A. Hunt. *Lessons from an Unconventional War*. New York: Pergamon Press, 1982.

Snepp, Frank. *Decent Interval*. New York: Vintage Books, 1977.

Sobel, L. A., ed. *South Vietnam: U.S.-Communist Confrontation in Southeast Asia, Vol. 1, 1961–1965*. New York: Facts on File, 1966.

Sobel, L. A., ed. *South Vietnam: U.S.-Communist Confrontation in Southeast Asia, Vol. 2, 1966–1967*. New York: Facts on File, 1969.

Sobel, L.A., ed. *South Vietnam: U.S.-Communist Confrontation in Southeast Asia, Vol. 3, 1968*. New York: Facts on File, 1970.

Sobel, L. A., ed. *South Vietnam: U.S.-Communist Confrontation in Southeast Asia, Vol. 4, 1969*. New York: Facts on File, 1973.

Sobel, L. A., ed. *South Vietnam: U.S.-Communist Confrontation in Southeast Asia, Vol. 5, 1970*. New York: Facts on File, 1973.

Sobel, L. A., ed. *South Vietnam: U.S.-Communist Confrontation in Southeast Asia, Vol. 6, 1971*. New York: Facts on File, 1973.

Statford, Ann. *Saigon Journey*. New York: Taplinger, 1960.

Trullinger, James Walker. *Village at War: An Account of Revolution in Vietnam*. New York: Longman, 1980.

Turpin, James. *Vietnam Doctor*. New York: McGraw-Hill, 1966.

Warner, Denis. *The Last Confucian*. New York: Macmillan, 1963.

West, Richard. *Sketches from Vietnam*. New York: Jonathan Cape, 1968.

Woodruff, Lloyd W. *The Study of a Vietnamese Rural Community*. Lansing: Michigan State University Press, 1960.

Woodside, Alexander. *Community and Revolution in Modern Vietnam*. Boston: Houghton-Mifflin, 1976.

After the Fall

Barron, John, and Anthony Paul. *Murder of a Gentle Land*. Pleasantville, N.Y.: Reader's Digest Press, 1977.

Charney, Joel, and John Spragens, Jr. *Obstacles to Recovery in Vietnam and Kampuchea*. New York: Oxfam America, 1984.

Duiker, William. *Vietnam: Nation in Revolution*. Boulder, Colo.: Westview Press, 1983.

Duiker, William. *Vietnam Since the Fall of Saigon*. Columbus: Ohio University Press, 1989.

Elliott, David W. P., ed. *The Third Indochina Conflict*. Boulder, Colo.: Westview Press, 1981.

Garner, John W. "Sino-Vietnamese Conflict and the Sino-American Rapprochement." *Political Science Quarterly* (Fall 1981).

Hien, Minh, and Luthfi Pirabeau. *Vietnam, Vietnam*. New York: Vantage, 1976.

Keylin, Arleen, and Duri Boiangiu. *Front Page Vietnam*. New York: Ayer, 1989.

Long, Robert E., ed. *Vietnam Ten Years After*. New York: Wilson, 1985.

Nguyen Long. *After Saigon Fell*. Cambridge, Mass.: Institute for East Asian Studies, 1981.

Nguyen Van Canh. *Vietnam Under Communism, 1975–1982*. Stanford, Calif.: Hoover Institution Press, 1983.

O'Ballance, Edgar. *The Wars in Vietnam, 1954–1980.* New York: Hippocrene Books, 1981.

Pike, Douglas. "The USSR and Vietnam." *Asian Survey* 19 (December 1979): 16–31.

Pike, Douglas. "Southeast and the Superpowers: The Dust Settles." *Current History* 82 (April 1983): 146–57.

Sagan, Ginetta, and Stephen Downey. *Violations of Human Rights in the Socialist Republic of Vietnam.* New York: Aurora Foundation, 1983.

Salzburg, Joseph S. *Vietnam: Beyond the War.* New York: Sovereign Books, 1975.

Tran Van Don. *Our Endless War: Inside Vietnam.* Novato, Calif.: Presidio Press, 1978.

Truong Nhu Tang. *A Vietcong Memoir.* New York: Harcourt Brace Jovanovich, 1985.

12   Laos and the Vietnam War

Covering 92,429 square miles in mountainous Southeast Asia, Laos is one of the most underdeveloped nations in the Third World. Its population of more than 4 million people in 1990 were primarily engaged in rice cultivation, and more than 80 percent of them are illiterate. Joel M. Halpern's *Government, Politics, and Social Structure of Laos: A Study of Tradition and Innovation* and Frank M. Lebar's and Adrienne Suddard's *Laos: Its People, Its Society, Its Culture* describe Laotian social history. The largest Laotian city is Vientiane, with a population of approximately 155,000 people, but the capital city is Luang Prabang, with a population of 55,000. Approximately 75 percent of the population are ethnic Lao or Kha, and 25 percent consist of tribes of Thais who have spilled over from the Khorant Plateau of eastern Thailand. The country is completely landlocked, surrounded by China, Cambodia, Vietnam, Burma, and Thailand. During the years of the Indochina War, Laos found itself a pawn caught between the geopolitical objectives of the superpowers and the ancient drives of the Vietnamese people.

In his book *Laos: Keystone of Indochina*, Arthur J. Dommen looks at how Laotian geography and ethnography influenced Laotian history. The long eastern border between Laos and Vietnam follows the crest of the Annamite Mountains. The terrain of Laos is steeply mountainous, and jungle covers most of the country. There are no railroads and relatively few roads. With such a limited infrastructure, the movement of goods and products is difficult at best, especially during the rainy season. The Lao language is a Thai dialect, and most Lao speakers actually live in northeastern Thailand. In Laos, they dwell in the Mekong River Valley. In the highlands there are hill tribes such as the Ho, Yao, and Meo, who are closely related to tribes in Chinese Yunnan. These highland tribes are animist in their religion, while the lowland Laos are

Buddhist. Laos is hardly a nation state in the modern sense. Ethnic diversity and a severe geography have hindered national unity and retarded political development. The vast majority of Laotians have profoundly local, rather than national, perspectives about life.

Laotian origins are in China. During the twelfth and thirteenth centuries the Laos moved from southwest China into territory that had been controlled by the great Khmer empire, which at the time was in a state of decline. The Laos fell into a pattern of internal squabbling, and the kingdom was divided in three, with capitals at Luang Prabang in the north, Vientiane in the center, and Champassak in the south. Disunity invited Siamese intervention. The Thais asserted suzerainty over all of Laos in 1828. The Thais remained in political control of the region until the arrival of the French imperial apparatus.

The classic work describing the early expansion of the French into Indochina is Virginia Thompson's *French Indochina*. Also see John F. Cady's *The Roots of French Imperialism in Indochina*. Both of them tell the story of French Laos. There was little European contact with Laos until the French began to carve out their Indochinese empire. After establishing a foothold in Cochinchina and then, in the 1880s, reducing Annam, Tonkin, and Cambodia to protectorate status, France sought to buffer her new holdings against Siam and the rival British, who had already moved into Burma. French motives for incorporating Laos into Indochina also included a desire to keep the British, as Milton Osborne points out in *River Road to China*, from what they vainly hoped would be a navigable route into China up the Mekong or Red River valleys. The Himalaya Mountains made that plan stillborn.

French conquest of Laos was accomplished nearly single-handedly by the extraordinary Auguste Pavie, who promised to protect Laos from Siam and claimed that a dubious Annamese right of suzerainty over Laos had passed to France. Siam protested, but a French naval blockade of Bangkok settled the issue. In 1893 Siam renounced all rights to land east of the Mekong. France reunited Laos and added some more territory to it by another treaty with Siam in 1907. The role of the Thais in Laotian history is clearly explained in John F. Cady's *Thailand, Burma, Laos, and Cambodia* and Bardwell L. Smith's *Religion and Legitimation of Power in Thailand, Laos, and Burma*. French imperialism was hardly oppressive. The Laotian king remained on his throne in Luang Prabang, while the rest of the country was divided into eight provinces, each governed by a French *resident*. A *resident superieur* exercised supreme power from Vientiane, but the French seemed to think of Laos as a quaint colonial backwater whose innocent people needed protection from modern ways. Few Laotians even knew they lived under French jurisdiction. Life went on as always in the self-sufficient villages. The French set up only a few schools and no industry. A few towns emerged to export rice, opium, tea, coffee, and sugarcane, but none of them was large enough to be called a city.

The colonial idyll came to an end after World War II. In 1945 the Lao Issara (Free Lao), a protonationalist movement, declared Laos independent of France. In his autobiography, *Lao Issara: The Memoirs of Oun Sananikone*, Gudone Sananikone looks at the anti-French rebellion in Laos during and just after World War II. Eventually, what began as jockeying for political influence between rival branches of the Laotian royal family gradually became transformed into a cold war struggle between left-wing nationalists and a right-wing military.

Prince Boun Khong fathered twenty children, including Prince Souvanna Phouma and his half brother Prince Souphanouvong. They were both raised, after their father's death, by Prince Phetsart, the eldest brother. David K. Wyatt's *Iron Man of Laos: Prince Phetsarath Ratanavongsa* looks back at the dynastic struggles that eventually fractured the royal family of Laos. All three sons received French educations, and all three were committed nationalists. Prince Souphanouvong, however, was the most radical of the brothers, and Prince Souvanna Phouma the most conservative. Phetsart charted a middle course. In August 1945, Souphanouvong expelled the French from Laos and established an independent government, with Phetsart and Souvanna Phouma serving as ministers. But the French soon reasserted themselves and defeated royal Laotian forces. Souphanouvong retreated into the jungles and began forming anti-French resistance forces, while Souvanna Phouma and Phetsart went into exile in Thailand. Eventually, the French talked Souvanna Phouma into returning and establishing a provisional government, but Phetsart stayed in Bangkok, refusing to have anything to do with the French. Souphanouvong stayed in the countryside, forming a guerrilla army, which he called the Pathet Lao, and he began to cooperate closely, militarily, and ideologically with Ho Chi Minh's Vietminh forces. For an excellent history of the Pathet Lao, see Joseph Zasloff's *The Pathet Lao*.

The emergence of a Communist guerrilla movement in Laos was not unlike Ho Chi Minh's development of the Vietminh in Vietnam. During the late nineteenth and early twentieth centuries, there were a variety of anti-French, nationalist movements in Indochina. Because of his own charisma, Ho Chi Minh emerged as one of the leading figures. While his intense nationalism addressed the problem of French imperialism, his Communist ideology seemed to address the poverty of the region. Ho Chi Minh's Lao Dong party became the political vehicle of Communism, and the Pathet Lao emerged from it. As Macalister Brown and Joseph J. Zasloff make clear in *Apprentice Revolutionaries: The Communist Movement in Laos, 1930–1985*, Communism and nationalism fused in Laos as they had in Vietnam. That nationalism had an anti-French flavor to it until 1954 and then an anti-American flavor throughout the 1950s, 1960s, and 1970s.

The internal struggle for power in Laos, as Perala Ratnam has pointed out in *Laos and the Super Powers*, became a much broader conflict when the United States, France, the Soviet Union, and the People's Republic of China became intimately involved in it. After the fall of China to Mao Zedong in 1949 and the outbreak of the Korean War in 1950, American policymakers began to apply the containment doctrine to Asia as well. In Laos, American policymakers focused on the Communism in Souphanouvong's ideology, not on his anti-French, pro-Laotian nationalism. The United States began to see both Souphanouvong and Souvanna Phouma as "bad guys"—Souphanouvong because of his ties to the Vietminh and Souvanna Phouma because of his increasing neutrality. France set up a puppet regime in Laos under a right-wing collaborator—Phoumi Nosovan. France, of course, was intent on maintaining her imperial outpost in Laos and similarly saw Souphanouvong as a real threat and Souvanna Phouma as a potential threat.

The early U.S. decision to provide financial support to the French in Laos was based on the Eisenhower administration's desire to stop the spread of Communism in Asia. For them, the major front of the cold war had shifted to Asia. During the years of the John F. Kennedy administration, as well as the first years of the Lyndon B. Johnson administration, that cold war interpretation of the struggle in Indochina prevailed. It also appeared in most of the memoirs of the individuals who made and implemented American military and foreign policy during the 1960s and early 1970s. People like Lyndon B. Johnson, Dwight D. Eisenhower, Richard Nixon, Henry Cabot Lodge, Frederick Nolting, William Westmoreland, Walt W. Rostow, Dean Rusk, W. Averell Harriman, Pierre Salinger, and Theodore Sorenson all reflected that cold war mentality in their memoirs or early histories of the war. The People's Republic of China and the Soviet Union both began to compete in the 1950s for the mantle of leadership in the Communist world as well as in the smaller world of Indochina.

Vietnamese nationalists also became acutely interested in Laotian politics. During the 1940s and 1950s, that interest was primarily economic. Ho Chi Minh and the Vietminh financed their military campaign against France with money from heroin sales. The rugged mountains of Laos supplied the heroin, which the Vietminh bought and then sold to Asian drug kingpins. With the money from the sales, the Vietminh purchased the weapons they needed. When the French established their outpost at Dien Bien Phu in northwestern Vietnam in 1953, Ho Chi Minh was at least somewhat worried that the base would cut off the Vietminh's heroin source in Laos. Alfred W. McCoy's *The Politics of Heroin in Southeast Asia* and Anna L. Strong's *Cash and Violence in Laos* both deal with the history and politics of that heroin traffic in Laos.

The interest became even more compelling after the Geneva Accords of 1954. At the battle of Dien Bien Phu in 1954, Souphanouvong's Pathet Lao had assisted the Vietminh in the defeat of French forces, and at the Geneva Conference on Indochina the United States made sure that the Pathet Lao did not have representation. Martin E. Goldstein makes it clear in his book *American Policy Toward Laos* that the United States had no intention of allowing either Souvanna Phouma or Souphanouvong to take control of an independent Laos. Eventually, the Geneva Accords called for negotiations among all three factions in Laos—the right-wingers under Phoumi Nosovan, the neutralists under Souvanna Phouma, and the leftists under Souphanouvong.

For North Vietnam, which had become independent in 1954, Laos suddenly had an even greater significance. When it became increasingly clear in the 1950s that there would be no free elections to reunite North Vietnam and South Vietnam, Ho Chi Minh realized that Laos would be strategically critical in order to ship troops and supplies into South Vietnam. What became known as the Ho Chi Minh Trail traversed hundreds of miles through Laos and from there into the northern regions of South Vietnam. Paul F. Langer and Joseph J. Zasloff, in *North Vietnam and the Pathet Lao: Partners in the Struggle for Laos,* describe how the North Vietnamese began providing resources and training to the Pathet Lao in the late 1950s and how that relationship became closer and firmer during the years of the Vietnam War.

Throughout the 1950s and into the 1960s, Souvanna Phouma and Souphanouvong tried to establish and maintain a united coalition government, but superpower involvement in Laos prevented that. The United States was dead-set opposed to any Pathet Lao participation in the national government. In his book *The End of Nowhere: American Policy Toward Laos Since 1954,* Charles A. Stevenson shows how the United States repeatedly sabotaged all attempts to establish a coalition government in Laos. John Prados, in *President's Secret Wars,* also described how the United States, between 1954 and 1960, conducted a secret war, led by the Central Intelligence Agency, to destabilize the efforts of both Souvanna Phouma and Souphanouvong. The United States was frustrated with Souvanna Phouma's unwillingness to use the Royal Laotian Army to attack the Pathet Lao troops of Souphanouvong. The Eisenhower administration had the CIA fund a right-wing mercenary army under the corrupt Phoumi Nosovan in an attempt to take over the country. Souvanna Phouma and Souphanouvong then joined hands and defeated Nosovan's troops. The defeat of Nosovan's mercenaries precipitated the "Laotian crisis" of 1962 and the Geneva agreements that year, as Sisouk Na Champassak describes in *Storm over Laos.*

The Geneva Conference of 1962 has been of some controversy among historians. Contemporary works by people like Arthur M. Schlesinger, Jr. (*A Thousand Days*) or Theodore Sorensen (*Kennedy*) treated the conference as a major achievement of the Kennedy administration, as if the United States orchestrated a great triumph by establishing a neutral government under Souvanna Phouma. The agreements did give the Pathet Lao a minor voice in the new government, called for neutrality, provided for an end of CIA-based military activities, insisted on the expulsion of all foreign military personnel (meaning any North Vietnamese troops), prohibited Laos from entering into any military alliances, and arranged for the election of a national legislature.

Contemporary historians have reached far more critical conclusions. The works of people like Thomas C. Reeves (*A Question of Character: A Life of John F. Kennedy*), Michael R. Beschloss (*The Crisis Years: Kennedy and Khrushchev 1960–1963*), Bruce Miroff (*Pragmatic Illusions: The Presidential Politics of John F. Kennedy*), Charles A. Stevenson (*The End of Nowhere: American Policy Toward Laos Since 1954*), and William J. Rust (*Kennedy in Vietnam: American Foreign Policy, 1960–1963*) all see the United States playing a more devious role at Geneva, still conspiring to prevent any truly neutralist, coalition government from gaining power and still working to elevate right-wing groups. Although all parties to the agreement eventually violated its provisions, the United States never intended anything more than a pretense of compliance.

In fact, the ink on the Geneva documents was hardly dry before the CIA was back in business subverting the Laotian government. The Pathet Lao were essentially driven into the two northern provinces and the eastern border of the country, where they became even more closely connected with the North Vietnamese army in protecting the Ho Chi Minh Trail. As Christopher Robbins writes in *Air America: The Story of the CIA's Secret Airlines* and *The Ravens: The Men Who Flew in America's Secret War in Laos*, as well as John Prados in *President's Secret Wars*, the CIA began a campaign of assassinations against left-wing and even neutralist political officials in Laos, while U.S. Special Forces teams began recruiting and training an army of 12,000 Meo tribesmen to go to war against the Pathet Lao. On a more formal level, as Gudone Sananikone describes in *The Royal Lao Government and U.S. Army Advice and Support*, U.S. military personnel provided training to Royal Lao forces. Late in 1964, under the pretext of bombing the supplies moving south down the Ho Chi Minh Trail, the United States began a concerted bombing campaign against the Pathet Lao that lasted for the next decade. Eventually, the United States unloaded more than 2 million tons of explosives on Laos during the Vietnam War.

During the course of the Vietnam War, Laos was an important element in the political and military conflict. The Ho Chi Minh Trail, over which North Vietnam sent troops and supplies into South Vietnam, stretched through northeastern Laos. In 1964 the trail was primitive, and the journey down it was arduous and exhausting. But after the U.S. buildup beginning in 1964, North Vietnam, according to Jon M. Van Dyke (*North Vietnam's Strategy for Survival*), began extending the trail and expanding its capacity. That effort continued until 1975. Over the years the Ho Chi Minh Trail became a series of 12,000 miles of paved and unpaved roads complete with petroleum pipelines and storage facilities, hospitals, and vast supply caches. The United States operated Special Forces camps near the trail, CIA-trained Meo tribesmen fought to cut the trail, and American bombers secretly bombed it. By 1975 enough supplies were moving down the Ho Chi Minh Trail to support twelve full divisions of North Vietnamese troops.

Laos also played an important role in the strategic and tactical debates going on in the Lyndon B. Johnson and Richard M. Nixon administrations. To people like General William Westmoreland, commander of U.S. troops in Vietnam, and Admiral Ulysses S. Grant Sharp, head of American naval forces, it was important to cut the Ho Chi Minh Trail in half and interrupt the flow of enemy supplies to South Vietnam. Although the United States was secretly conducting an intensive aerial bombing campaign against the Ho Chi Minh Trail, President Johnson was reluctant to send ground troops into Laos. Not only would it have violated Laos's official neutrality, but it would have constituted a widening of the war, something Johnson wanted to avoid. A military invasion of Laos may have been militarily prudent, but it involved too many political risks. Johnson did not permit it.

President Richard Nixon eventually did permit it. Beginning in 1969, Nixon launched what he called the Vietnamization program, in which Vietnamese troops assumed more and more responsibility for the ground war. American troops were gradually withdrawn from combat and from the theater of the war. But it became apparent by early 1970 that the South Vietnamese troops were going to have a difficult time resisting the North Vietnamese divisions. By withdrawing American combat troops before the South Vietnamese were prepared to assume all of the fighting, President Nixon left himself no alternative but to increase the bombing and broaden the war. The 1970 invasion of Cambodia was part of that effort, as was the ill-fated 1971 invasion of Laos.

For Americans, the invasion of Laos was known as Operation Dewey Canyon II, but for the South Vietnamese it was known as Operation Lam Son 719. Nguyen Duy Hinh has written *Lam Son 719*, and Keith William Nolan has written *Into Laos: The Story of Dewey Canyon II/Lam Son 719, Vietnam 1971*. President Richard Nixon and Henry Kissinger anticipated heavy infiltration of North Vietnamese troops and supplies down the Ho Chi Minh Trail during the dry season of 1971, in preparation for a major North Vietnamese invasion during the 1972 American elections. Nixon wanted to test the Vietnamization by seeing if ARVN could handle a major invasion, and he hoped to cut the Ho Chi Minh Trail in half.

But the invasion was an unmitigated disaster. In order to maintain as much secrecy as possible, planning for the invasion was confined to relatively few people in Washington and Saigon. The ARVN division commanders actually had very little time to prepare or plan for the invasion. Another problem was posed by congressional restrictions on the use of American ground troops in Laos, which kept American advisors from accompanying the ARVN units into battle and coordinating artillery, helicopter, and tactical air support. Although General Creighton Abrams wanted four ARVN divisions to be committed to the battle, South Vietnam agreed to send only two. On the road to Tchepone, which was their objective, they encountered four battle-seasoned North Vietnamese divisions. The terrain was rugged, and the weather damp and rainy, limiting American tactical air support. During the battle, the North Vietnamese subtly drew the ARVN troops deeper into Laos and farther away from U.S. air support, lengthening ARVN supply lines in the process. The North Vietnamese counterattack was a huge success, inflicting a 50 percent casualty on the ARVN units. Without massive American aerial bombardment of North Vietnamese forces, the destruction would have been complete. For South Vietnam, Lam Son 719 was a rout.

The American withdrawal from South Vietnam continued in 1971 and 1972, and in Congress President Nixon was unable to maintain control of Southeast Asia policy. Late in June 1973 Congress attached a rider to a supplemental appropriations bill cutting off funds for American bombing in Cambodia. Nixon vetoed the bill on June 27, but when it became clear that an override was a distinct possibility, he compromised, guaranteeing to Congress that all American military activity in Cambodia and Laos would be over by August 15, 1973. Congress passed the legislation ending all American combat activities in Indochina by August 15. Nixon signed the bill on July 1, 1973.

With no more American bombing of Laos, North Vietnam initiated massive increases in the infiltration of troops and supplies into South Vietnam and provided huge amounts of matériel to the Pathet Lao. The Pathet Lao controlled most of northern Laos by 1974. Prince Souvanna Phouma had signed the comprehensive cease-fire for Indochina in 1973, which the United States, Cambodia, South Vietnam, and North Vietnam had also signed, but North Vietnam had no intention of agreeing with the cease-fire and withdrawing its troops from Laos. Souvanna Phouma pleaded with Kissinger and Nixon to keep pressure on North Vietnam, but it was to no avail. The United States was getting out of Indochina, and North Vietnam was going to be able to have its way there.

Late in March 1975, as North Vietnamese troops were preparing for their final assault on South Vietnam, the Pathet Lao launched an offensive against the Souvanna Phouma government, attacking Vang Pao and Sala Phou Khoun and then driving south along Route 13 toward the capital city of Vientiane. Antigovernment riots and demonstrations erupted in Vientiane during the offensive, and Souvanna Phouma was unable to suppress them. Similar antigovernment activities took place in towns and cities throughout Laos. The Pathet Lao infiltrated guerrilla troops into Vientiane and such cities as Pakse, Savannakhet, and Thakhek along the border with Thailand. They could smell victory. At the end of April 1975, North Vietnam completed its conquest of South Vietnam, and the North Vietnamese 325th, 471st, and 968th divisions then headed for Laos. The Pathet Lao conquered Vientiane in August 1975 and proclaimed the People's Democracy of Laos. For historians like Charles A. Stevenson (*The End of Nowhere: American Policy Toward Laos Since 1954*), the United States had spent twenty years opposing the left-wing and the moderate center in Laotian politics, and because of those policies all but guaranteed the triumph of the Pathet Lao.

BIBLIOGRAPHY

Adams, N. T., and A. R. McCoy, eds. *Laos: War and Revolution*. New York: Harper and Row, 1970.

Andelman, David A. "Laos After the Takeover." *New York Times Magazine*, October 24, 1976.

Beschloss, Michael R. *The Crisis Years: Kennedy and Khrushchev 1960–1963*. New York: HarperCollins, 1991.

Brown, MacAlister, "Laos." *Current History* 82 (April 1983): 158–61.

Brown, Macalister, and Joseph J. Zasloff. "New Stages of Revolution in Laos." *Current History* 71 (December 1976): 218–21.

Brown, MacAlister, and Joseph J. Zasloff. *Apprentice Revolutionaries: The Communist Movement in Laos, 1930–1985*. Stanford, Calif.: Hoover Institution Press, 1986.

Burchett, Wilfred G. *The Furtive War: The United States in Vietnam and Laos*. New York: International, 1963.

Burchett, Wilfred. *The Second Indochina War: Cambodia and Laos Today*. New York: Lorrimer, 1970.

Butwell, Richard. "From Feudalism to Communism in Laos." *Current History* 69 (December 1975): 223–26.

Cady, John F. *The Roots of French Imperialism in Eastern Asia*. Ithaca, N.Y.: Cornell University Press, 1954.

Cady, John F. *Southeast Asia*. New York: McGraw-Hill, 1964.

Cady, John F. *Thailand, Burma, Laos, and Cambodia*. Englewood Cliffs, N.J.: Prentice-Hall, 1966.

Chavez, Arlene. *Mission Laos: Top Secret*. New York: Sandia, 1991.

Coedes, Georges. *The Making of South East Asia*. Berkeley: University of California Press, 1967.

Coedes, Georges. *The Indianized States of Southeast Asia*. New York: East-West Center Press, 1968.

Dengler, Dieter. *Escape from Laos*. New York: Zebra Press, 1982.

Dommen, Arthur J. "Laos in the Second Indochina War." *Current History* 59 (December 1970): 326–32.

Dommen, Arthur J. *Conflict in Laos*. New York: Praeger, 1971.

Dommen, Arthur J. *Laos: Keystone of Indochina*. Boulder, Colo.: Westview Press, 1985.

Ennis, Thomas. *French Policy and Developments in Indochina*. Chicago: University of Chicago Press, 1936.

Fifield, Russell H. *The Diplomacy of Southeast Asia, 1945–1958*. New York: Harper and Row, 1958.

Fox, Martin Stuart. *Laos*. Palo Alto, Calif.: Hoover Institution Press, 1986.

Goldstein, Martin E. *American Policy Toward Laos*. Rutherford, N.J.: Fairleigh Dickinson University Press, 1973.

Hall, D.G.E. *A History of South-East Asia*. New York: St. Martin's Press, 1968.

Halpern, Joel M. *Government, Politics, and Social Structure of Laos: A Study of Tradition and Innovation*. New York: Dalley Book Service, 1990.

Halpern, Joel M., and W. S. Turley, eds. *The Training of Communist Cadres in Laos*. Paris: Centre d'étude du Sud-est Asiatique et de l'Estreme Orient, 1977.

Hammer, Ellen J. *The Struggle for Indochina, 1940–1955*. Palo Alto, Calif.: Stanford University Press, 1955.

Hannah, Norman B. *The Key to Failure: Laos and the Vietnam War*. New York: Madison Books, 1990.

Keomanichanh, Virachith. *India and Laos: A Study in Early Cultural Contacts*. New York: Scholarly, 1980.

Kirk, Donald. *Wider War: The Struggle for Cambodia, Thailand, and Laos*. New York: Praeger, 1971.

Lacouture, Jean. "From the Vietnam War to an Indochina War." *Foreign Affairs* 48 (July 1970): 617–28.

Langer, Paul F., and Joseph J. Zasloff. *North Vietnam and the Pathet Lao: Partners in the Struggle for Laos*. Cambridge: Harvard University Press, 1970.

Leary, William M. *Perilous Missions: Civil Air Transport and CIA Covert Operations in Asia*. Tuscaloosa: University of Alabama Press, 1984.

Lebar, Frank M., and Adrienne Suddard, eds. *Laos: Its People, Its Society, Its Culture*. New Haven, Conn.: Human Relations Area Files, 1960.

McCoy, Alfred W. *The Politics of Heroin in Southeast Asia*. New York: Harper and Row, 1972.

Meeke, Odeen. *The Little World of Laos*. New York: Scribner's, 1959.

Miroff, Bruce. *Pragmatic Illusions: The Presidential Politics of John F. Kennedy*. New York: David McKay, 1976.

Nguyen Duy, Hinh. *Lam Son 719*. Washington, D.C.: U.S. Army Center of Military History, 1979.

Nolan, Keith W. *Into Laos: The Story of Dewey Canyon II/Lam Son 719, Vietnam 1971*. Novato, Calif.: Presidio Press, 1986.

Osborne, Milton. *River Road to China*. New York: Liveright, 1975.

Prados, John. *President's Secret Wars: CIA and Pentagon Covert Operations Since World War II*. New York: Morrow, 1986.

Randle, Robert F. *Geneva 1954*. Princeton, N.J.: Princeton University Press, 1969.

Ratnam, Perala. *Laos and the Super Powers*. New York: Praeger, 1980.

Reeves, Thomas C. *A Question of Character: A Life of John F. Kennedy*. New York: Free Press, 1991.

Robbins, Christopher. *Air America: The Story of the CIA's Secret Airlines*. New York: Putnam's, 1979.

Robbins, Christopher. *The Ravens: The Men Who Flew in America's Secret War in Laos*. New York: Crown, 1987.

Rust, William J. *Kennedy in Vietnam: American Foreign Policy, 1960–1963*. New York: De Capo Press, 1987.

Salinger, Pierre. *With Kennedy*. Garden City, N.Y.: Doubleday, 1966.

Sananikone, Gudone. *The Royal Lao Government and U.S. Army Advice and Support*. New York: Dalley Book Service, 1981.

Sananikone, Gudone. *Lao Issara: The Memoirs of Oun Sananikone*. New York: Dalley Book Service, 1983.

Schlesinger, Arthur M., Jr. *A Thousand Days: John F. Kennedy in the White House*. Boston: Houghton Mifflin, 1965.

Sisouk Na Champassak. *Storm over Laos: A Contemporary History*. New York: Praeger, 1961.

Smith, Bardwell L., ed. *Religion and Legitimation of Power in Thailand, Laos, and Burma*. New York: Anima, 1978.

Smith, R. B. *An International History of the Vietnam War. Volume I: Revolution Versus Containment, 1955–1961*. New York: St. Martin's Press, 1984.

Smith, R. B. *An International History of the Vietnam War: The Kennedy Strategy*. New York: St. Martin's Press, 1987.

Sorensen, Theodore. *Kennedy*. New York: Harper and Row, 1965.

Stevenson, Charles A. *The End of Nowhere: American Policy Toward Laos Since 1954*. Boston: Beacon Press, 1972.

Strong, Anna L. *Cash and Violence in Laos*. Peking: New World Press, 1961.

Stuart-Fox, Martin. *Laos: Politics, Economics, and Society*. Boulder, Colo.: Lynne Rienner, 1986.

Stuart-Fox, Martin, ed. *Contemporary Laos: Studies in the Politics and Society of the Lao People's Republic*. New York: St. Martin's Press, 1982.

Tate, D.J.M. *The Making of Modern South-East Asia*. New York: Oxford University Press, 1971.

Thompson, Virginia. *French Indochina*. New York: Octagon Books, 1968.

Toye, Hugh. *Laos: Buffer State or Battleground*. New York: Oxford University Press, 1968.

Van Dyke, Jon M. *North Vietnam: Strategy for Survival*. San Francisco: Pacific Books, 1972.

Vongsavanh, Soutchay. *RLA Military Operations and Activities in the Laotian Panhandle*. New York: Dalley Book Service, 1981.

Wyatt, David K., ed. *Iron Man of Laos: Prince Phetsarath Ratanavongsa*. Ithaca, N.Y.: Cornell University Southeast Asia Program, 1978.

Zasloff, Joseph. *The Pathet Lao*. Lexington, Mass.: D. C. Heath, 1973.
Zasloff, Joseph, and MacAlister Brown, eds. *Communism in Indochina*. New York: Lexington Books, 1975.
Zasloff, Joseph, and Leonard Unger. *Laos: Beyond the Revolution*. New York: St. Martin's Press, 1991.

13 Cambodia and the Vietnam War

William J. Topich

The majority of significant works on early Cambodia are general histories of Southeast Asia that include sections on Cambodia. Georges Coedes's *The Indianized States of Southeast Asia* does an excellent job depicting the history of Southeast Asia prior to 1500. Coedes's survey of the formation of Cambodian civilization is fascinating and easy to comprehend. Furthermore, Coedes pays great attention to the early civilizations in Southeast Asia, an area often overlooked. A classic work on Southeast Asian history that devotes ample coverage to Cambodia is Daniel Hall's *A History of South-East Asia*. This work was an extensively researched, detailed outline of Southeast Asian political and dynastic life from prehistoric times to the modern period. Hall's work is impressive and capable of overwhelming even a knowledgeable reader in its detail. Indeed, this detailed and accurate chronology has made Professor Hall's *History* a basic reference work on Southeast Asian studies; no other single-volume text contains so much information.

The only modern work in English that deals exclusively with early Cambodia is David P. Chandler's *A History of Cambodia*. The author surveys Cambodian history from earliest times to the achievement of independence in 1953. Chandler gives outstanding testimony to his mastery of the literature dealing with Cambodian history. He draws on an impressive range of materials in English, French, Cambodian, and Thai, using his own linguistic talents. He has also been able to make use of relevant Vietnamese materials. For the first time, the often jumbled history of Cambodia before and during the colonial period is presented in a coherent form. This work, written for the student and general reader rather than the specialist, is likely to remain the standard text for many years to come. One of the book's strengths is the extent to which Chandler's work is informed by his wide-ranging reading of materials not strictly historical in character. His grasp of political sociology and his understanding of anthropology create a broader view of the development of Cambodian society than Chandler's predecessors have achieved in their reviews of discrete periods of Cambodian history.

The only detailed study of the first half of French rule in Cochinchina and Cambodia is Milton Osborne's *The French Presence in Cochinchina and Cambodia: Rule and Response (1859–1905)*. The author is the first historian to have made extensive use of archives and newspapers pertaining to this period. His research led him from Paris to Saigon, to Phnom Penh, and even London, where he found a manuscript on Cambodian relations with Singapore in the mid-nineteenth century. The Cambodian story is treated in a series of excellent historical chapters featuring the role of King Norodom and his relations with a succession of resident French officials. Over a forty-year period, the tradition-oriented king maintained a surprisingly effective resistance to French interference in behalf of "reform." The decaying monarchy clung desperately to its traditional moorings, a situation that both invited and impeded French efforts to take over control. Whereas the French became definitely interested both economically and culturally in Cochinchina and its people, they regarded Cambodia as a kind of museum piece, serving as a buffer against assumed British influence in Siam and Malaya. For thirty years, the French kept a spare, princely puppet available against the eventuality of Norodom's death or displacement. He took a long time dying, and even during his eclipse in the late 1890s, he continued to exert a measure of influence amid palace intrigue and regional disaffection.

Osborne's account can be criticized on the grounds that his historical context is too limited. Some attention must be paid to the political developments within France that affected policy developments in Indochina. However, with the publication of Osborne's book, a major gap has been filled; scholars and students of the history of French Indochina will be grateful to him for this most worthy contribution.

THE EVOLUTION OF CAMBODIAN COMMUNISM

From 1954 to 1975 the Cambodian Communists waged a struggle against two forces. From 1954 to 1970 the Communists fought Norodom Sihanouk, who controlled the legislature (Sangkum) and had near total support from the masses. Following Sihanouk's overthrow and his subsequent alliance with his former adversary (the Khmer Rouge), the enemy of the left became the Khmer Republic under Lon Nol.

Several works on the emergence of the Khmer Communist movement have been published. Ben Kiernan's 1985 seminal work, *How Pol Pot Came to Power*, traces the history of Cambodian Communism from its early period of solidarity with Vietnam in the 1930s through the seizure of power by the Khmer Rouge in 1975. Kiernan brilliantly details the long, complex struggle for control of the Communist Party of Kampuchea (CPK), discussing the ideological and political struggle that brought Pol Pot to the leadership position. The conflict between factions loyal to Vietnamese Communism and those loyal to a strongly nationalist group whose outlook was marked by chauvinism and racism is a principal theme of this book. The roles of the United States, China, and Vietnam in the Cambodian experience through 1975 are thoroughly addressed.

The first two chapters of *How Pol Pot Came to Power* discuss Cambodia from the 1920s through 1949. Kiernan addresses the role of the Indochina Communist party, the rise of the modern Khmer elite, and the contending colonial interests in Cambodia. The material in these chapters is ground-breaking research and thoroughly documented. Chapters 3 and 4 detail the period from 1949 through 1954. The conflicting nationalist movements and the early attempts at organizing revolutionary cells are addressed. The urban and rural strategies of the resistance are also documented, along with the reasons for the limited success of the antigovernment efforts.

The international efforts of the Geneva Conference and the effective policies of Sihanouk in the early years are the theme of Chapter 5, "International Supervision." The political struggle from 1955 through 1966 is the focus of Chapter 6. A segment detailing the events from 1962 to 1966 that led Cambodia to the brink of civil war is fascinating. Kiernan's extensive use of interviews and declassified government documents makes for solid, insightful research.

The seventh chapter, "The First Civil War 1967–1970," details the beginning of armed insurrection against the leadership of Prince Sihanouk. The polarization of Cambodian society is a main theme in Kiernan's work. Other issues discussed include the rebellion in Samlaut and what that would mean for the revolution; the role of the Communist party during the start of full-scale armed insurrection; and the development of the Khmer Rouge army and political infrastructure.

The final chapter, "Contending Communisms: The Second Civil War, 1970–1975" is probably the best chapter of the book. Kiernan shows how Cambodia was drawn into the Vietnam War by the Nixon administration and its total disregard for the neutrality of Cambodia. Furthermore, Kiernan discusses the possibility of U.S. involvement in the 1970 overthrow of Prince Sihanouk. A thorough review of the CPK's strategy and policy decisions is a major theme in this chapter. Kiernan shows the animosity between the Communist movements in Cambodia and Vietnam, along with regionalism in the ranks of the Khmer Rouge.

How Pol Pot Came to Power will be required reading for anyone wishing to study the evolution of the most notorious revolutionary movement in modern history. Kiernan's study of the rise to power of the radical

Communists led by Pol Pot is the most comprehensive account of the Khmer Rouge written to date.

Craig Etcheson's *The Rise and Demise of Democratic Kampuchea*, published in 1984, is a study of Cambodian Communism from 1930 to 1979. The major difficulty with this work was that the author attempted to cover far too much ground for one study. Many themes addressed by the author were not fully developed. The fact that the author has no first-hand experience in Cambodia is also a negative. However, Etcheson's work is useful for the nonspecialist who desires an overview of the development of Khmer Communism. Especially impressive is the author's analysis of the 1970–1975 civil war period. Etcheson's strong political science background is very apparent in his discussion of foreign policy dealings. The international interplay between the different parties interested in geopolitical dominance of Cambodia is well done. Etcheson also makes good use of graphical presentations in discussions dealing with demographic trends, Communist party leadership, and military circumstances. Impressive use of maps is another benefit of Etcheson's work. Most of the analysis of the Khmer Rouge comes from the research of scholars such as Stephen Heder, Michael Vickery, and Ben Kiernan. It would have been appropriate if Etcheson could have implemented more primary sources in dealing with the Khmer Communist movement.

AMERICAN INVOLVEMENT IN CAMBODIA

One of the earliest accounts of American involvement in Cambodia was Malcolm Caldwell and Lek Tan's *Cambodia in the Southeast Asian War*. Published in 1973, this work gives a leftist perspective on the events in Cambodia from the time of the French Protectorate through the early 1970s. The heavy emphasis of this work is on the Sihanouk years and Cambodia's fight to maintain its neutrality. The early sections of the book compare French policies during the Protectorate period, 1864–1954, with those of American control over Cambodia following the establishment of Lon Nol's Khmer Republic in 1970. According to the authors, remarkable parallels can be detected in the patterns of resistance to foreign control that emerged in the French period compared with the resistance to American involvement in the early 1970s. The authors believe that by the late 1950s Cambodia was the victim of direct aggression from Thailand and the Saigon regime and subsequently of continued harassment by CIA-directed mercenaries operating out of South Vietnam. Direct U.S.-ARVN air, land, and sea attacks began in the mid-1960s. Peasant discontent over these actions led to open rebellion by 1967.

Caldwell and Tan also discuss the American involvement in Sihanouk's overthrow and the subsequent invasion by U.S. and ARVN troops in

1970. The destruction of the Cambodian life-style and the obvious appeal of the resistance groups on the peasants at this time are also brought out by the authors, misery and destruction that can never be forgotten, according to Caldwell and Tan. Anyone reading *Cambodia in the Southeast Asian War* should remember that the book was being written during the worst bombing campaigns of the war. The fact that American policy-makers share the blame for the destruction of Cambodia is undeniable. The authors make a strong case in condemning the way Cambodia was drawn into the Vietnam conflict. As with many antiwar activists, Caldwell and Tan did not see the destructive nature of the regime that was eventually to replace Lon Nol's Khmer Republic. Caldwell himself would be murdered while visiting Pol Pot's Democratic Kampuchea in December 1978.

My War with the CIA: The Memoirs of Prince Norodom Sihanouk (1973) details the relations between Cambodia and the United States from the mid–1950s until the overthrow of Sihanouk's regime in March 1970. Sihanouk's account is told to Australian journalist Wilfred Burchett. This work, written in the early 1970s, was composed during the time of Si-hanouk's alliance with the Khmer Rouge in the "Royal Government of National Union." Sihanouk's neutrality-for-peace policies were looked down upon by U.S. policymakers, especially the Central Intelligence Agency. From the time of the Geneva Accords until the successful coup against Sihanouk, it was the goal of U.S. foreign policy to see Cambodia thrown into the camp of the South Vietnamese government. Early attempts through the Dulles brothers were made to convince Sihanouk to abandon his neutralist ideas. It quickly became evident that diplomatic, political, and economic pressure would not cause Sihanouk to change his stance. Thus, a period of plots and assassination attempts followed.

Sihanouk claims that numerous plots to overthrow him failed between 1955 and 1970. Only total devotion to the U.S. line would be tolerated, according to the prince. This work was written so close to the actual overthrow that Sihanouk's anger and bitterness are clearly evident. *My War with the CIA* gives a unique insight into the international interplay that went on between the Geneva agreement and the 1970 coup. This work was obviously written too early to incorporate the animosity that was developing between the Cambodian and Vietnamese revolutionary movements. However, this book is worthwhile for gaining an understanding of the Cambodian government and its international dealing during the Sihanouk era.

Another work dealing exclusively with the Sihanouk years in power is Milton Osborne's *Before Kampuchea: Prelude to Tragedy* (1979). This work is very critical of the prince, who Osborne believes was not a capable or competent leader. The author suggests that Sihanouk was ready to make sweeping decisions at a moment's notice but he seldom thought through the long-term implications. In 1966, Osborne reports, the French advisors around him were uniformly contemptuous of him. Sihanouk's private scribe said: "Sihanouk's policies seemed to change from day to day. Was America an enemy or not? Nobody seemed to know." Sihanouk had an almost absolute incapacity to listen to contrary advice, let alone criticism of his policies, according to Osborne. Furthermore, as far as Sihanouk was concerned, the elections were "part of a national ritual, not part of a process that would greatly affect his determination of policy." When he stopped handpicking the candidates, they were simply bought by the "most conservative forces in Cambodian politics."

Before Kampuchea is highly critical of the Sihanouk years. In many instances Osborne has valid criticisms of the prince. However, Cambodia was heavily pressured by all of the major superpowers, and Sihanouk's neutrality stance has to be admired. Osborne was probably too harsh on the prince. After seeing the types of governments set up in Cambodia from 1970 to 1990, many Khmer may wish that the prince was still running the government of Cambodia. The author should be commended for dealing with an area where very little research has been done.

A classic work on the American involvement in Cambodia is *Sideshow: Kissinger, Nixon, and the Destruction of Cambodia* by William Shawcross (1979). This work is one of the most significant investigations of American foreign policy ever written. The author brilliantly depicts the horrifying American bombing campaign waged against Cambodia by American policymakers, most notably Henry Kissinger and Richard Nixon. *Sideshow* gives a comprehensive look at the Nixon administration's dealings with Cambodia.

The conduct of U.S. policy in Cambodia is Shawcross's main story. The author used personal interviews and U.S. government documents released under the Freedom of Information Act to recount the U.S. policies. Shawcross believes that Cambodia was "the foreign-policy side of Watergate." Shawcross's research asserts the two were, indeed, related. The Nixon administration came to corrupt the ordinary institutions and practices of the government. At first, this involved keeping the Cambodian operations off the books, then to maintain the secrecy in the face of press leaks, wiretapping was begun. In turn, this fed into the various extrainstitutional and illegal practices that became part of the larger Watergate crisis. The basic thesis in *Sideshow* is that if Nixon and Kissinger had not done what they did, Pol Pot and his associates would not have been able to do what they did. Shawcross does not, however, try to excuse the Khmer Rouge. The author has always been one of the most vocal critics of Pol Pot and his regime. As Ben Kiernan (1985) stated: "The Pol Pot leadership of the Khmer Rouge can in no way be exonerated from responsibility for committing genocide against their own people.

But neither can Nixon or Kissinger escape judgment for their role in the slaughter that was a prelude to the genocide. Worse, but for that extreme example of United States militarism, the Pol Pot group may have been denied their opportunity."

THE KHMER ROUGE IN POWER

The first work to analyze postwar Cambodia was François Ponchaud's *Cambodia: Year Zero*. Ponchaud's book is based on his personal experiences as a priest in Cambodia from 1965 until the capture of Phnom Penh, plus extensive interviews with refugees and reports from the Cambodian radio. Published in France in 1977, it was the earliest account of what was happening in Cambodia during the first year of Communist rule. Ponchaud's book is serious and worthwhile reading. He gives a grisly account of what refugees reported to him about the barbarity of their treatment at the hands of the Khmer Rouge. He also reminds us of the terrible conditions prior to 1975. Peasants were massacred, their lands stolen and villages destroyed by the police and army in 1966. Many peasants joined in the movement out of a hatred for a government responsible for such misery. He reports the enormous destruction and murder resulting directly from the American attack on Cambodia, the starvation and epidemics as the population was driven from the countryside by American military terror and the U.S.-incited civil war, leaving Cambodia economically devastated. He also gives a rather positive account of Khmer Rouge programs of social and economic development, while deploring much brutal practice in working for egalitarian goals and national independence.

As noted, Ponchaud relies overwhelmingly on refugee reports. Further, his account is secondhand, with many of the refugees reporting what they claimed to have heard from others. Another problem with Ponchaud is his loose use of numbers. Ponchaud cites a Cambodian report that 200,000 people were killed in American bombings from March 7 to August 15, 1973. No source is offered, but suspicions are aroused by the fact that the Phnom Penh radio announced on May 9, 1975, that there were 200,000 casualties of the American bombing in 1973, including killed, wounded, and crippled for life. Ponchaud cites "Cambodian authorities," who give the figures 800,000 killed and 240,000 wounded before liberation. The figures are implausible. By the usual rule of thumb, wounded amount to about three times killed; quite possibly he has the figures reversed.

Also problematic is Ponchaud's account of the evacuation of Phnom Penh in April 1975. He reports the explanation given by the revolutionary government that the evacuation was motivated by impending famine. But this he rejects on the grounds that rice stocks in Phnom

Penh would have sufficed for two months, with rationing. He gives no source for this estimate and fails to observe a *New York Times* report that "according to Long Boret, the old Government's last Premier, Phnom Penh, had only eight days worth of rice on hand on the eve of the surrender." Nor does he cite the testimony of U.S. Agency for International Development (AID) officials that Phnom Penh had only a six-day supply of rice.

Another early work dealing with the Khmer Rouge in power is George C. Hildebrand and Gareth Porter's *Cambodia: Starvation and Revolution* (1976). Hildebrand and Porter present a carefully documented study of the destructive American impact on Cambodia. However, time has shown Hildebrand and Porter's calculations on the Khmer Rouge to be seriously flawed. In the chapter on Cambodia's agricultural revolution, the claim that the Khmer Rouge had alleviated famine during 1975 was inaccurate. Massive starvation did take place throughout the reign of Pol Pot. Furthermore, the author's claim that "Cambodia had for the first time both a coherent national development plan and the organizational ability to put it into effect" has been proven inaccurate. Another area where the book fails is in its evaluation of the industrial sector of postrevolutionary Cambodia. For example, claims of textile mills being reopened and industries running at normal pre–1970 rates were not substantiated. Hildebrand and Porter do a good job of pointing out the destruction and misery that had been wrought as a result of civil war. The fact that America and its client regime bear some responsibility for the tragedy in Cambodia is undeniable. However, the book's attempt to defend the Khmer Rouge regime by quoting unsubstantiated facts and figures lessens the impact of *Cambodia: Starvation and Revolution*.

Another early account of the Khmer Rouge was written by Timothy Michael Carney. *Communist Party Power in Kampuchea: Documents and Discussion*, published in January 1977, describes the growth of the Communist party of Kampuchea, with particular attention to the period 1970–1975. Carney discusses the policies and programs of the movement, using captured documents and reports prepared by Khmer Rouge defector Ith Sarin. Carney's experience as a member of the U.S. embassy in Phnom Penh from 1972 to 1975 provides interesting insights into the Communist movement from the American perspective. This work was published prior to the September 1977 announcement of the existence of the Communist Party of Kampuchea. The September announcement by the party contradicted Carney's assertion that the CPK was formed in 1951, rather than the 1960 date that was stated by CPK officials.

One of the main themes of Carney's work is to contradict the assumption that the Cambodian peasants suffered at the hands of landlords and usurers. The basis of Carney's skepticism is derived from the conclusions drawn by French scholars Jean Delvert and Remy Prud'-

homme. It is important to note, however, that questions can be raised concerning the extent to which the Delvert and Prud'homme findings provide a truly complete picture of what life was like in rural Cambodia in the 1950s and 1960s. For example, the problem of landlordism was severe in many areas of Cambodia, even though it did not exist in all areas. Notwithstanding this point, Carney's work on party power in Cambodia is valuable to anyone wishing to gain a greater understanding of the Cambodian left.

One of the most significant contributions in the field of Cambodian studies is *Peasants and Politics in Kampuchea, 1942–1981* (1982). Edited by Ben Kiernan and Chanthou Boua, the book brings together works by Cambodian writers translated for the first time from the French and Khmer. Also included are several essays by Ben Kiernan, along with an essay by Michael Vickery. Following Kiernan's provocative overview of history and socioeconomic structure from the colonial period, the book is divided into three parts. An analysis by two leading Cambodian intellectuals is the basis of the first part. Hou Yuon's "The Peasantry of Kampuchea: Colonialism and Modernization" is probably the most detailed and penetrating analysis of the Cambodian rural socioeconomic structure available. Translated from the French original, Hou Yuon (1955) addresses the factors affecting the living standards of the Khmer peasantry. Hu Nim's "Land Tenure and Social Structure in Kampuchea" (1965) stresses the exploitation of peasants in prerevolutionary Cambodia and the need for social and economic reform. Both Hou Yuon and Hu Nim studied in France during the 1950s and were exposed to Marxist ideology. During Pol Pot's reign both were killed in purges.

Part II of *Peasants and Politics in Kampuchea* begins with Cambodian historian Michael Vickery's discussion on political developments from 1942 to 1976. The establishment of independence and policies of Prince Sihanouk, both domestic and foreign, are discussed. Finally the destruction of Cambodia during the period of Lon Nol's leadership is investigated. Buchan Mul's "The Umbrella War of 1942" discusses the Cambodian resistance to Japanese occupation during World War II. The author, a former official under Lon Nol, describes the anticolonial activities of early Khmer nationalists in the 1930s and 1940s. An additional three pieces in Part II, written by Ben Kiernan, deal with pivotal events during the period of Cambodian independence (1954–1970). The Khmer Issarak, the Samlaut Rebellion of 1967–68, and the anti-Lon Nol protests of 1970 are investigated. Also included is a second piece from Hou Yuon entitled "The Cooperative Question," written in 1964. The purpose of this work was to outline a blueprint for socialist transformation in Cambodia.

The third part of this book is dominated by Ben Kiernan's outstanding essay entitled "Pol Pot and the Kampuchean Communist Movement."

This article provides a detailed analysis of the Cambodian revolution and the fascinating factionalism within the Communist movement. According to Kiernan, the three factions comprising the CPK were Pol Pot's faction, which was committed to political and economic autarky; a pro-Chinese faction, including Hu Nim; and a pro-Vietnamese faction comprising those leaders who spent years in Hanoi. Kiernan also addresses issues of the origins of Khmer Communism, ideologies, and social policies. Also included are a section entitled "Testimonies: Life Under the Khmer Rouge" and a final piece, "Kampuchea Stumbles to Its Feet." *Peasants and Politics in Kampuchea 1942–1981* is a book of great importance to anyone interested in gaining greater insight into the politics, economics, and contemporary history of Cambodia. Ben Kiernan and Chanthou Boua do a superb job in detailing significant events that dominated Cambodia's recent past. Kiernan exhibits thought-provoking insights, a high level of intelligence, and evidence of thoroughly investigated research in putting this book together.

Revolution and Its Aftermath in Kampuchea: Eight Essays (1983), edited by David P. Chandler and Ben Kiernan, discusses Cambodia's recent past. The papers published in the book came out of a conference sponsored by the Social Science Research Council held in August 1981 in Chiangmai, Thailand. The central focus is the Pol Pot regime and the revolution that brought it to power. Several Western academics specializing in Cambodia are prominent in this book. Essays by Chandler and Serge Thion discuss the historical and ideological perceptions of the Khmer Rouge. Thion's belief that the leadership was not in control of some policies carried out in certain regions is somewhat flawed. Time has shown that the central leadership of the Communist Party of Kampuchea was, in effect, responsible for most of the brutalities carried out in Democratic Kampuchea. The party employed regional strongmen such as Ta Mok and Ke Pauk to carry many of the draconian policies. However Thion's article does a splendid job in analyzing many of the ideological influences on Khmer Communism. Chandler's work on how the Khmer Rouge reinterpreted Cambodian history is also very informative and well written.

Lacking in this compilation is the foreign policy of Democratic Kampuchea. A notable exception to this is Gareth Porter's article entitled "Vietnamese Communist Policy Towards Kampuchea 1930–1970." Porter addresses two major issues in Vietnamese Communist policy: the geopolitical role of Cambodia in the Indochina conflict and the potential for Marxist-Leninist revolution in Cambodia. Porter's regional expertise on both Cambodia and Vietnam is apparent in the analysis. The only problem was that the theme was not expanded into the post–1970 period.

The next two essays deal with regional variations within Democratic Kampuchea. Michael Vickery's "Democratic Kampuchea: Themes and

Variations" discusses regionalism within Cambodia under Pol Pot's rule. Ben Kiernan's "Wild Chickens, Farm Chickens, and Cormorants: Kampuchea's Eastern Zone Under Pol Pot" also addresses the theme of variations within the different zones of Democratic Kampuchea. Kiernan's thorough research on the Eastern Zone of Cambodia is to be condemned. His in-depth interviews of peasants who survived Pol Pot's massacre of eastern Cambodia showed the lack of regional coordination from the party center. Furthermore, the brutality of the regime against dissent is brought out. Anthony Barnett's essay examines the high level of centralization within the government of Democratic Kampuchea. The decisions to evacuate the cities, attack religion, and eliminate property and commerce were, in Barnett's opinion, directed by Pol Pot and his closest associates. According to this conclusion, the regime's leadership bears responsibility for the tragedy.

William Shawcross's "Cambodia: Some Perceptions of a Disaster" addresses the way the Western media handled the Cambodian tragedy. The author attempts to show how the media were reluctant to believe Western governments' charges that a massacre of enormous proportion was occurring in Cambodia. There are problems with the Shawcross assertion that the media downplayed what was occurring in Cambodia. Noam Chomsky and Edward Herman's *After the Cataclysm: Postwar Indochina and the Reconstruction of Imperial Ideology* is attacked by Shawcross for being somewhat skeptical of refugee reports coming out of Cambodia during the early years of Khmer Rouge control. The media showed caution because of a sense of paranoia over the possibility of Western intelligence's "cooking up a bloodbath to say, we told you so," according to Shawcross. The fact that early reports denouncing the Khmer Rouge turned out to be correct does not change the fact that works such as John Barron's *Murder of a Gentle Land* were inaccurate propaganda. The Shawcross piece is interesting, especially for anyone interested in the debate over the media's role in reporting international politics. The final piece by Chanthou Boua, entitled "Observations of the Heng Samrin Government 1980–1982," discusses the recovery of the Cambodian people in the years following the ouster of Pol Pot. This time period in Cambodia has thus far been neglected by scholars and the media alike. A highly detailed chronology of Khmer Communism by Serge Thion closes out the book.

Probably the most comprehensive political history of the Democratic Kampuchean regime is Michael Vickery's *Cambodia 1975–1982*. Published in 1984, Vickery gives a balanced and comprehensive overview of the 1975–1982 period. The author's expertise in the Khmer language and in Cambodian history and society is evident throughout the book. In a clear and convincing manner Vickery attacks much of the previous work done on Cambodia, including *Murder of a Gentle Land* and François

Ponchaud's *Cambodia: Year Zero*. Vickery asserts that "class" rather than the "Khmer personality" accounts for the direction the Cambodian revolution took. Another major theme addressed by Vickery is regionalism within Democratic Kampuchea. The seven zones within Pol Pot's Cambodia retained considerable autonomy after April 1975. A number of vengeful acts committed in Democratic Kampuchea were, in Vickery's estimation, sporadic and confined to certain areas. The treatment of peasants varied depending on the attitudes of local cadre.

The third chapter of *Cambodia 1975–1982*, entitled "The Zero Years," does ground-breaking research into several untouched areas of Pol Pot's Cambodia. Sections on political and economic issues, postwar returnees, medicine and education in Democratic Kampuchea, the family, religion, and a controversial section on the human cost make this chapter both fascinating and informative. Vickery also discusses the occupation and evacuation of Phnom Penh, along with a region-by-region breakdown of Democratic Kampuchea. The fourth chapter, entitled "Kampuchea: From Democratic to People's Republic," addresses such topics as the war with Vietnam, the Salvation Front, and a description of the People's Republic of Kampuchea (PRK) regime. This chapter draws on extensive interviews with refugees who survived the Pol Pot period. The final section of the chapter covers the 1981–1982 period.

"The Nature of the Cambodian Revolution" is the title of the fifth and final chapter of this book. Vickery looks at Marxism in Cambodia and some of the ideological views of the Democratic Kampuchean leadership. Comparisons between the Cambodian revolution and revolutions in China, Russia, and Yugoslavia are made. Vickery believes that the vital element driving the Cambodian revolutionaries was concern for the peasants. The ideological concern and the reality of the revolution were, of course, quite different. Vickery further speculates that the Cambodian Communists were utopians whose "violent excesses lay in the very nature of a peasant revolution, which was the only kind of revolution possible in Cambodia." The final area addressed by Vickery is the lessons of the Cambodian revolution. The book closes with a look at the events of 1983. *Cambodia 1975–1982* was the first comprehensive look at the Cambodian revolution. Michael Vickery's thorough knowledge of the history and politics of the region is apparent to anyone who reads this book. Extensive research and interviewing of survivors of Pol Pot's terror are evident in Vickery's work. A major plus is that this book is readable, and it addresses a wide variety of areas on the Pol Pot regime. Without a doubt *Cambodia 1975–1982* is the definitive work on the Democratic Kampuchean period and the early years of the People's Republic of Kampuchea.

Journalist Elizabeth Becker's *When the War Is Over: The Voices of Cambodia's Revolution and Its People* is an attempt to write a full-scale history of the Cambodian revolution. The author was a reporter for the *Wash-*

ington Post during the final month of Pol Pot's rule in December 1978. The author also visited the People's Republic of Kampuchea in 1983. Becker's insight from being in Cambodia during the different eras of recent Cambodian history is apparent. The most significant part of this book is the section where Cambodians tell personal stories of revolutionary Cambodia. The tragic histories of individuals who were tortured and killed in Pol Pot's incarceration center are compelling. The reader learns how the lives of Cambodian citizens were devastated during the Democratic Kampuchean era. Becker's firsthand account of how Cambodian society was changed by Khmer Rouge rule is striking. The description of the characteristics of the Khmer Rouge rule is impressive. The collectivization, evacuation, and wide-scale uprooting of Cambodia from 1975 to 1978 are thoroughly accounted.

However, this book is not without its shortcomings. Becker tries to cover too much material. For example, her discussion of the conflict between the Cambodian and Vietnamese Communists has been covered more thoroughly by scholars such as Stephen Heder and Nayan Chanda. Also, the question of why so many peasants followed the Khmer Rouge is never fully addressed by Becker. Furthermore, the fact that Becker does not know the Khmer language is a hindrance in many key areas of the book. Overall, Elizabeth Becker is to be commended for putting together one of the most important books yet to appear on Cambodia during the 1970s. Her firsthand insights into the events of the Lon Nol regime and of the final days of Pol Pot's dictatorship make this book a valuable contribution to the study of revolutionary Cambodia.

Norodom Sihanouk's second book about Cambodia was entitled *War and Hope: The Case for Cambodia* (1980). The book marked Sihanouk's reemergence on the international scene. The author makes a compassionate plea for a multinational conference on Cambodia that would restore its neutrality. As the dominant figure in Cambodian politics for over five decades, Sihanouk is able to share with the reader his insights into the intricate relationships between Cambodia and its stronger neighbors. After reading the pleas of Sihanouk that the Khmer people must be saved from further devastation, it was even more disheartening to see him once again join a coalition with the Khmer Rouge less than two years after the publication of *War and Hope*. Several chapters of the book detail the brutality of the Khmer Rouge regime. Many of the author's family members were killed in the carnage that engulfed Cambodia during the late 1970s. Another major theme of *War and Hope* is the condemnation of the Vietnamese occupation of Cambodia. Sihanouk fears that the longer the occupation of Cambodia continues, the more difficult it will be to come to a diplomatic solution to the crisis.

Sihanouk believes that he is the only hope for the future of Cambodia. The United Nations (UN) seat should not be held by the Khmer Rouge, according to the prince. It was both surprising and unfortunate that Sihanouk caved in to Chinese pressure and joined in the "coalition government of Kampuchea" with the Khmer Rouge in 1982. Many of the statements made by the prince in *War and Hope* seem directly to contradict the attitude and action taken by Sihanouk since 1982. Overall, *War and Hope* is useful in letting the reader see how the most influential person in Cambodian politics of the last half decade viewed the Cambodian situation following the Vietnamese conquest of 1979. Much of the book is rhetoric, blasting both the Khmer Rouge and the Vietnamese occupation forces. Sihanouk's plan for a settlement parallels the current UN attempts to mediate the Cambodian conflict. The prince, however has lost the respect of many people because of the alliance he formed with the hated Khmer Rouge in 1982. If Sihanouk would have continued on the path of nonalignment he proposed in *War and Hope*, maybe the Khmer Rouge would have not been the force they are today.

Cambodia 1975–1978: Rendezvous with Death (1989) is a collection of nine essays dealing with numerous aspects of the Democratic Kampuchean reign of terror. Edited by Karl Jackson, this series deals with such topics as the ideology of revolutionary Cambodia, the social and economic policies of the regime, and the structure of authority and power in Pol Pot's government. The majority of the chapters were completed in the early 1980s, but the book was not published until 1989. No explanation is given for the lengthy delay in publication. Areas such as population control, military policy, and foreign support for the revolution are not covered. Jackson attempts to bring together a group of people with unique experiences and expertise to explain the Cambodian revolution. The majority of contributors to *Cambodia 1975–1978* are U.S. government employees. It would have been appropriate to see a more diverse group of scholars if the goal was to "design a book that would illuminate the most salient dimensions of revolutionary Cambodia." Several seminal works on the Cambodian revolution were not mentioned, either as references in the bibliography or as citations by any of the authors.

Two chapters by Timothy Carney, "The Unexpected Victory" and "The Organization of Power," are enlightening. Carney's first essay discusses the period leading up to the Khmer Rouge victory. The author's experience and firsthand knowledge of Cambodia during the pre–1975 period is evident. Segments on the beginning of armed struggle and the war years were provocative and insightful. The best overall essay in the book is Carney's discussion of "power" within Democratic Kampuchea. Carney's analysis of class organization, party building, and party instruction is ground-breaking.

Charles Twining's "The Economy" was another worthwhile selection from this work. The author must be commended for investigating an area that has been neglected, for the most part, by scholars who study Cambodia. Sections on the goals, rationale, and organization of the economy were informative. Twining's analysis of regime performance was also well researched. Areas such as irrigation, rice development, export-import trade, and nutrition were investigated. The regime's economic development was based on the idea of complete self-reliance, according to Twining. The author used captured government documents and press releases from the regime in drawing conclusions on economic decision making. Overall, Twining gave a detailed picture of the economic strategies and policies of the Democratic Kampuchean regime.

The intellectual and ideological origins of the Khmer Rouge were the focus of two essays by Karl Jackson. In "The Ideology of Total Revolution," Jackson rejects the propositions that explain Cambodian events as "mere by-products of either American foreign policy or the madness of a few Khmer leaders." He believes that it is critically important to understand Democratic Kampuchea on its own terms by analyzing the goals of its leadership. The author suggests that the revolution's ideology was dominated by four interrelated themes: (1) total independence and self-reliance, (2) preservation of the dictatorship of the proletariat, (3) total and immediate economic revolution, and (4) complete transformation of Khmer social values. Downplaying American responsibility for the turn of events in Cambodia, as Jackson does, is flawed analysis. There are also problems with the author's treatment of the Cambodian revolutionaries as a whole, rather than addressing the different factions involved. For the most part, Jackson's analysis of the ideology is accurate, although the article was still somewhat disappointing. It would have been helpful to see more detailed comparisons with other Communist ideological movements such as China's Great Leap Forward.

The second piece by Jackson, entitled "Intellectual Origins of the Khmer Rouge," is speculative, but the author must be praised for dealing with an area that has been enormously frustrating for Cambodian scholars. The basic theme of the chapter was, Where did the Khmer Rouge get their ideas? Jackson believes the sources included "Maoism, European Marxism, Fanonism, perhaps Stalinism, and certainly Khmer nationalism." There is no evidence as to what the leadership of the Khmer Rouge read. The ideological origins of the movement remain a mystery. Jackson's speculations might be correct, but no evidence is there to support his hypothesis.

François Ponchaud's "Social Change in the Vortex of Revolution" attempts to discover associations between the revolution and Khmer culture. The author traces how certain elements of Khmer culture were eradicated by the Khmer Rouge. For example, the elimination of Buddhism and the Cham Muslims is investigated. Another section of Ponchaud's work looks at the revolt of the youth against the elders. The

author's use of refugee reports and Democratic Kampuchean government documents is skillful. The section on the Cham persecution has
been more thoroughly done by Kiernan (see *Bulletin of Concerned Asian
Scholars*). Overall, Father Ponchaud's work is an important contribution
in the understanding of revolutionary Cambodia.

Kenneth Quinn also had two contributions in *Cambodia 1975–1978:
Rendezvous with Death*. "The Pattern and Scope of Violence" discussed
the goals of Pol Pot's regime. Quinn believes that Pol Pot had four specific
goals: "1. Breaking the System; 2. Socioeconomic Transformation; 3.
Political Prophylaxis; and 4. Defending against External Threat." This
chapter does an excellent job describing each of these four goals and
how Pol Pot attempted to achieve each. The author's analysis of the use
of terror and violence in Cambodia is well-written and thoroughly documented. The second piece by Quinn, entitled "Explaining the Terror,"
seeks to answer the question of what Pol Pot sought to accomplish with
the extensive use of force and terror in Democratic Kampuchea. This
question is not sufficiently answered by the author. By use of comparative
analysis, Quinn attempts to blame the Khmer Rouge policies on "a Maoist
plan to create a pure socialist order in the shortest possible time." The
author also cites Stalinist mentors teaching young cadres to destroy the
cultural underpinnings of Khmer civilization. On both accounts the comparisons are not adequately developed. Early theories that leveled at
least a part of the blame on the American air war against Cambodia
from 1970 to 1973 are totally written off by Quinn. The idea of a strict,
centralized decision-making apparatus is put forth. Most of the assertions
made by Quinn need further development. Also, the author's tendency
to see Cambodian radicalism as a social science problem to be solved,
rather than as something that was lived and fought for by Cambodians
for over a decade, lessens the significance of this article.

David P. Chandler, Ben Kiernan, and Chanthou Boua's *Pol Pot Plans
the Future: Confidential Leadership Documents from Democratic Kampuchea,
1976–1977*, is a translation and annotation of eight documents from the
Pol Pot regime. This work is a major contribution in the study of the
government decision making of Communist Cambodia. Very few internal documents from the regime exist, so the importance of this work
cannot be overestimated. These documents are fascinating for what they
can tell us about such things as strategy, ideology, and the Khmer Rouge
view of the future. Seven of the eight documents discuss the Khmer
Rouge thinking and planning during the 1976–1977 period. The government's plan for the economy, agriculture, and industry are included
in the chapter. The party's history and state organization are also discussed. The final chapter is the forced confession of Hu Nim, the DK
minister of information, one of the most prominent figures with the
pre–1975 revolutionary movement. The utopian goals of the Khmer

Rouge are apparent from the documents dealing with the economic outlook of the regime. Unbelievably high outputs were expected from the regions within Cambodia. Historic outputs for regions were ignored, and failure of an area to live up to the leadership's expectations meant treason.

Pol Pot Plans the Future also shows evidence of the paranoia and xenophobia of the Democratic Kampuchean leadership. The relationship between the Khmer Rouge and other Communist regimes such as China and Vietnam is rejected. The movement claimed to be indigenous, inspired only by the ancient Khmer empire. The final document, the forced confession of Hu Nim, is basically a fabricated story to serve the interests of Pol Pot and his henchmen. He confesses to being a double agent of the Soviet State Security Committee (KGB) and CIA during the 1960s through the mid–1970s. Hu Nim's confession is an example of what happened to Khmer Rouge leaders who became critical of the direction that Pol Pot was leading the revolution. Part of the value of Hu Nim's confession is that it gives us a glimpse as to what went on at the incarceration centers set up by Pol Pot's security apparatus. Nearly 20,000 individuals (mostly party members or government officials) were executed at the torture center at Tuol Sleng. Many other top party officials who made forced confessions were treated in a similar fashion as Hu Nim.

The reader of *Pol Pot Plans the Future* comes away with the belief that there was, indeed, genocide perpetrated in Cambodia that was a direct result of decisions made by the Communist party leadership. This book is obviously a key link in understanding the Cambodian revolution. A greater understanding of the plan of the government, along with making major strides for future scholarship on Cambodia, will come from this book.

REFUGEE ACCOUNTS

There is an abundance of material from refugees who survived the horrors of Pol Pot's Cambodia. At least six major works from survivors have received widespread circulation. I will briefly discuss the major contributions of these works. Laurence Picq's *Beyond the Horizon: Five Years with the Khmer Rouge* tells a Western woman's firsthand account of brutality and cruelty of the Cambodian Communists. This book is the only Western account of Pol Pot's regime. Picq was the wife of a Khmer Rouge official who lived in Cambodia during the entire reign of the Khmer Rouge. Her idealism of how the Khmer Rouge would set up a utopian society was quickly crushed. The story of how her family was put through the hell-like reality of Cambodia from 1975 to 1978 is vividly described. This thought-provoking, insider's look at revolutionary Cambodia is must reading in understanding the reality of the Khmer Rouge holocaust.

Haing Ngor: A Cambodian Odyssey by Haing Ngor and Roger Warner, the story of Haing Ngor's ordeal living through the Khmer Rouge years, is another fine work. Ngor is the medical doctor who won an Oscar for playing the role of Dith Pran in *The Killing Fields*. The full horror of life under Pol Pot's rule is graphically depicted by Haing Ngor. Ngor believes that the Khmer Rouge wanted to destroy everything that was not Cambodian. They were hypocrites, however, because everything from their uniforms to their ideology was borrowed from China. Ngor levels much of the blame for the disaster on the Khmer themselves. This point is widely debated by scholars of revolutionary Cambodia even today.

To Destroy You Is No Loss: The Odyssey of a Cambodian Family, by Joan D. Criddle and Teeda Butt Mam, is another compassionate look at the horrors of Pol Pot's Cambodia. This book traces one courageous young woman and her remarkable family during those years of servitude and genocide when Pol Pot and his Khmer Rouge held Cambodia in a death grip. This work is an example of the affirmation of the human spirit, of the will to prevail. A deeply disturbing real-life story, *To Destroy You Is No Loss* gives the reader a tiny glimpse into the carnage that engulfed Cambodia during the 1975–1978 period.

The Murderous Revolution: Death in Pol Pot's Kampuchea, by Martin Stuart-Fox, is the story of holocaust survivor Bun Heang Ung. The recollections and drawings of Bun Heang Ung form the backbone of this work. Stuart-Fox's text is a straightforward account of the Pol Pot years for the general reader. The depiction of the Eastern Zone massacres and the evacuation of Phmom Penh was especially well done. The drawings of Bun Heang Ung, a political cartoonist, vividly convey the crowding, turmoil, and repression that were Democratic Kampuchea. *The Murderous Revolution* is the best of the refugee accounts. Several other refugee accounts are worth mentioning. Molyda Szymusiak's *The Stones Cry Out: A Cambodian Childhood, 1975–1980* and James Fenton's *Cambodian Witness: The Autobiography of Someth May* are both worthy contributions to the growing literature from Cambodian survivors of the Pol Pot years.

BIBLIOGRAPHY

Ablin, David, and Marlowe Hood. *The Cambodian Agony*. Armonk, N.Y.: Sharpe, 1987.

Abrams, Floyd, and Diane Orentlicher. *Kampuchea, After the Worst: A Report on Current Violations of Human Rights*. New York: Lawyers Committee for Human Rights, 1985.

Amin, Samir. *Accumulation on a World Scale: A Critique of the Theory of Underdevelopment.* New York: Monthly Review Press, 1970.

Anderson, Benedict. *Imagined Communities.* London: Verso, 1970.

Barron, John. *Murder of a Gentle Land: The Untold Story of Communist Genocide in Cambodia.* New York: Reader's Digest Press, 1977.

Becker, Elizabeth. *When the War Is Over: The Voices of Cambodia's Revolution and Its People.* New York: Simon and Schuster, 1986.

Berger, Carl, ed. *The United States Air Force in Southeast Asia.* Washington, D.C.: Office of Air Force History, 1977.

Briggs, Lawrence. "Siamese Attacks on Angkor Before 1430." *Far Eastern Quarterly* 8 (1948): 3–33.

Briggs, Lawrence. *The Ancient Khmer Empire.* Philadelphia: American Philosophical Society, 1951.

Burchett, Wilfred. *The Second Indochina War: Cambodia and Laos Today.* New York: Lorrimer, 1970.

Burstein, Dan. *Kampuchea Today: An Eyewitness Report from Cambodia.* Chicago: Call, 1978.

Buttinger, Joseph. *Vietnam: A Political History.* New York: Praeger, 1968.

Cady, John F. *Southeast Asia: Its Historical Development.* New York: McGraw-Hill, 1964.

Cady, John F. *The Roots of French Imperialism in Eastern Asia.* Ithaca, N.Y.: Cornell University Press, 1967.

Caldwell, Malcolm, and Lek Tan. *Cambodia in the Southeast Asian War.* New York: Monthly Review Press, 1973.

Carney, Timothy Michael. *Communist Party Power in Kampuchea: Documents and Discussion.* Ithaca, N.Y.: Cornell University Press, 1977.

Chanda, Nayan. "When the Killing Had to Stop." *Far Eastern Economic Review* 94 (1976): 20–23.

Chanda, Nayan. *Brother Enemy: The War After the War.* New York: Harcourt Brace Jovanovich, 1986.

Chandler, David P. "The Constitution of Democratic Kampuchea: The Semantics of Revolutionary Change." *Pacific Affairs* 49 (Fall 1976): 506–15.

Chandler, David P. *A History of Cambodia.* Boulder, Colo.: Westview Press, 1983a.

Chandler, David P. "Revising the Past in Democratic Kampuchea: When Was the Birthday of the Party?" *Pacific Affairs* 56 (Summer 1983b): 288–300.

Chandler, David P. "A Revolution in Full Spate: Communist Party Policy in Democratic Kampuchea, December 1976." *International Journal of Politics* 16 (Fall 1986): 131–49.

Chandler, David P., and Ben Kiernan, eds. *Revolution and Its Aftermath in Kampuchea: Eight Essays.* New Haven, Conn.: Yale University Press, 1983.

Chandler, David P., Ben Kiernan, and Chanthou Boua. *Pol Pot Plans the Future: Confidential Leadership Documents from Democratic Kampuchea, 1976–1977.* Ithaca, N.Y.: Cornell University Press, 1989.

Chatterjee, Bijan R. *Indian Cultural Influences in Cambodia.* New York: AMS Press, 1928.

Chomsky, Noam, and Edward Herman. *After the Cataclysm: Postwar Indochina and the Reconstruction of Imperial Ideology.* Boston: South End Press, 1979.

Coedes, Georges. *The Making of Southeast Asia*. Berkeley: University of California Press, 1967.

Criddle, Joan D., and Teeda Butt Mam. *To Destroy You Is No Loss: The Odyssey of a Cambodian Family*. New York: Atlantic Monthly Press, 1989.

Elliott, David W. P., ed. *The Third Indochina Conflict*. Boulder, Colo.: Westview Press, 1981.

Ennis, Thomas E. *French Policy and Developments in Indochina*. Chicago: University of Chicago Press, 1936.

Etcheson, Craig. *The Rise and Demise of Democratic Kampuchea*. Boulder, Colo.: Westview Press, 1984.

Fenton, James. *Cambodian Witness: The Autobiography of Someth May*. New York: Random House, 1987.

Girling, J.L.S. "Crisis and Conflict in Indochina." *Orbis* 14 (Summer 1970): 349–65.

Grant, Jonathan, ed. *Cambodia: The Widening War in Indochina*. New York: Washington Square Press, 1971.

Groslier, Bernard P. *Indochina*. London: Muller, 1966.

Haley, Edward P. *Congress and the Fall of South Vietnam and Cambodia*. New York: Associated University Press, 1982.

Hall, Daniel. *A History of South-East Asia*. New York: St. Martin's Press, 1955.

Hammer, Ellen Jay. *The Struggle for Indochina, 1940–1955*. Palo Alto, Calif.: Stanford University Press, 1966.

Hawk, David. "International Human Rights Law and Democratic Kampuchea." *International Journal of Politics* 16 (Fall 1986): 3–38.

Heder, Stephen. "Origins of the Conflict." *Southeast Asia Chronicle* 64 (1978): 3–18.

Heder, Stephen. "Kampuchea's Armed Struggle: The Origins of an Independent Revolution." *Bulletin of Concerned Asian Scholars* 2 (1979): 2–24.

Heder, Stephen. "Kampuchea 1980: Anatomy of a Crisis." *Southeast Asia Chronicle* 77 (1981): 3–11.

Hersh, Seymour. *The Price of Power*. New York: Simon and Schuster, 1983.

Herz, Martin F. *A Short History of Cambodia from the Days of Angkor to the Present*. New York: Praeger, 1958.

Hildebrand, George C., and Gareth Porter. *Cambodia: Starvation and Revolution*. New York: Monthly Review Press, 1976.

Honda, Katuiti. *Journey to Cambodia*. Tokyo: Committee of Journey to Cambodia, 1981.

Isaacs, Arnold R. *Without Honor: Defeat in Vietnam and Cambodia*. Baltimore, Md.: Johns Hopkins University Press, 1983.

Jackson, Karl. "Cambodia 1977: Gone to Pot." *Asian Survey* 18 (1979): 76–90.

Jackson, Karl. "Cambodia 1978: War, Pillage, and Purge in Democratic Kampuchea." *Asian Survey* 19 (1979): 72–84.

Jackson, Karl, ed. *Cambodia 1975–1978: Rendezvous with Death*. Princeton, N.J.: Princeton University Press, 1989.

Khieu, Samphan. *Cambodia's Economy and Industrial Development*. Ithaca, N.Y.: Cornell University Press, 1979.

Kiernan, Ben. "Conflict in the Kampuchean Communist Movement." *Journal of Contemporary Asia* 10 (1980): 7–74.

Kiernan, Ben. "Origins of Khmer Communism." *Southeast Asian Affairs* 6 (1981): 161–80.

Kiernan, Ben. *How Pol Pot Came to Power*. London: Verso, 1985.

Kiernan, Ben. *Cambodia: The Eastern Zone Massacres*. New York: Columbia University, Center for the Study of Human Rights, 1986a.

Kiernan, Ben. "Kampuchea's Ethnic Chinese Under Pol Pot: A Case of Systematic Social Discrimination." *Journal of Contemporary Asia* 16 (1986b): 18–29.

Kiernan, Ben. "Orphans of Genocide: The Cham Muslims of Kampuchea Under Pol Pot." *Bulletin of Concerned Asian Scholars* 20 (1988): 2–33.

Kiernan, Ben. "The American Bombardment of Kampuchea." *Vietnam Generation* 1 (1989): 4–41.

Kiernan, Ben, and Chanthou Boua, eds. *Peasants and Politics in Kampuchea, 1942–1981*. London: Zed Press, 1982.

Kiljunen, Kimmo, ed. *Kampuchea—Decade of the Genocide*. London: Zed Press, 1984.

Kirk, Donald. *Wider War*. New York: Praeger, 1971.

Kissinger, Henry. *White House Years*. Boston: Little, Brown, 1979.

Kosut, Hal, ed. *Cambodia and the Vietnam War*. New York: Facts on File, 1971.

Lancaster, Donald. *The Emancipation of French Indochina*. New York: Oxford University Press, 1961.

Leifer, Michael. *Cambodia: The Search for Security*. New York: Praeger, 1967.

Leifer, Michael. "Kampuchea 1979: From Dry Season to Dry Season." *Asian Survey* 20 (January 1980): 33–41.

Leighton, Marian Kirsch. "Perspectives on the Vietnam-Cambodia Border Conflict." *Asian Survey* 18 (May 1978): 448–57.

Littauer, Raphael, and Norman Uphoff, eds. *The Air War in Indo China*. Boston: Beacon Press, 1972.

McCoy, Alfred. *The Politics of Heroin in Southeast Asia*. New York: Harper and Row, 1972.

Marshall, S.L.A. *West to Cambodia*. New York: Cowles, 1968.

Munson, Fred P. *Area Handbook for Cambodia*. Washington, D.C.: U.S. Government Printing Office, 1968.

Myrdal, Jan. "When the Peasant War Triumphed." *Southeast Asia Chronicle* 77 (1981): 12–15.

Ngor, Haing, and Roger Warner. *Haing Ngor: A Cambodian Odyssey*. New York: Macmillan, 1987.

Osborne, Milton. *The French Presence in Cochinchina and Cambodia: Rule and Response (1859–1905)*. Ithaca, N.Y.: Cornell University Press, 1969.

Osborne, Milton. "King-making in Cambodia: From Sisowath to Sihanouk." *Journal of Southeast Asian Studies* 4 (1973a): 169–85.

Osborne, Milton. *Politics and Power in Cambodia*. New York: Longman, 1973b.

Osborne, Milton. *River Road to China, The Mekong River Expedition, 1866–1873*. London: Liveright, 1975.

Osborne, Milton. *Before Kampuchea: Preludes to Tragedy*. London: Allen and Unwin, 1979.

Penfold, Helen. *Remember Cambodia*. New York: OMF Books, 1979.

Picq, Laurence. *Beyond the Horizon: Five Years with the Khmer Rouge.* New York: Random House, 1989.

Ponchaud, François. *Cambodia: Year Zero.* New York: Holt, Rinehart, and Winston, 1977.

Poole, Peter. *Expansion of the Vietnam War into Cambodia.* Miami: Ohio University Press, 1970.

Quinn, Kenneth M. "Cambodia 1976: Internal Consolidation and External Expansion." *Asian Survey* 17 (January 1977): 43–54.

Reddi, V. M. *A History of the Cambodian Independence Movement.* Tirupati, India: Sri Venkateswara University, 1970.

St. Cartmail, Keith. *Exodus Indochina.* New York: Heinemann, 1983.

Samphan, Khieu. *Cambodia's Economy & Industrial Development.* Ithaca, N.Y.: Cornell University Press, 1979.

Schanberg, Sydney H. *The Death and Life of Dith Pran.* New York: Penguin, 1980.

Shaplen, Robert. *Time Out of Hand: Revolution and Reaction in Southeast Asia.* New York: Harper and Row, 1969.

Shaplen, Robert. *The Road from War, 1965–1970.* New York: Harper and Row, 1970.

Shaplen, Robert. *Bitter Victory.* New York: Harper and Row, 1986.

Shawcross, William. *Sideshow: Kissinger, Nixon, and the Destruction of Cambodia.* New York: Simon and Schuster, 1979.

Shawcross, William. *The Quality of Mercy: Cambodia, Holocaust, and Modern Conscience.* New York: Simon and Schuster, 1984.

Sihanouk, Norodom. *My War with the CIA: The Memoirs of Prince Norodom Sihanouk.* New York: Pantheon, 1973.

Sihanouk, Norodom. *War and Hope: The Case for Cambodia.* New York: Pantheon, 1980.

Simon, Sheldon W. *War and Politics in Cambodia: A Communications Analysis.* Durham, N.C.: Duke University Press, 1974.

Smith, Roger M. *Conflict in Indochina: A Reader on the Widening of War in Laos and Cambodia.* New York: Vintage Books, 1970.

Snepp, Frank. *Decent Interval.* New York: Random House, 1978.

Stuart-Fox, Martin. *The Murderous Revolution: Death in Pol Pot's Kampuchea.* Chippendale, N.S.W., Australia: Alternative, 1986.

Summers, Laura. "Cambodia: Model of the Nixon Doctrine." *Current History* 63 (December 1972): 259–62.

Sutsakhan, Sak. *The Khmer Republic at War and the Final Collapse.* Washington, D.C.: U.S. Government Printing Office, 1980.

Szulc, Ted. *The Illusion of Peace: Foreign Policy in the Nixon Years.* New York: Viking, 1978.

Szymusiak, Molyda. *The Stones Cry Out: A Cambodian Childhood, 1975–1980.* New York: Hill and Wang, 1986.

Tamby, Zaleha, ed. *Cambodia: A Bibliography.* New York: Gower, 1982.

Thion, Serge. "The Ingratitude of the Crocodiles: The 1978 Cambodian Black Paper." *Bulletin of Concerned Asian Scholars* 4 (1980): 38–54.

Thion, Serge. "The Pattern of Cambodian Politics." *International Journal of Politics* 16 (Fall 1986): 110–30.

Thompson, Virginia. *French Indochina.* New York: Allen and Unwin, 1937.

Thomson, R. Stanley. "The Establishment of the French Protectorate Over Cambodia." *Far Eastern Quarterly* 4 (1945): 314–30.

Van Der Kruef, Justus. "Cambodia: From Democratic Kampuchea to People's Republic." *Asian Survey* 19 (1979): 731–50.

Vats, Bhagat. *The Kampuchea Holocaust and Its Aftermath*. Helsinki, Finland: World Peace Council, 1981.

Vella, Walter. *The Indianized States of Southeast Asia*. Kuala Lumpur, Malaysia: University of Malaya Press, 1967.

Vickery, Michael. "Democratic Kampuchea—CIA to the Rescue." *Bulletin of Concerned Asian Scholars* 14 (1982).

Vickery, Michael. *Cambodia 1975–1982*. Boston: South End Press, 1984.

Vickery, Michael. *Kampuchea: Politics, Economics, and Society*. London: Frances Pinter, 1986.

Wilmott, W. E. "Analytical Errors of the Kampuchean Communist Party." *Pacific Affairs* 54 (1981): 209–27.

Zasloff, Joseph, and MacAlister Browne, eds. *Conflict in Indochina: A Political Assessment*. Lexington, Mass.: D. C. Heath, 1972.

Zasloff, Joseph, and MacAlister Browne, eds. *Communism in Indochina: New Perspectives*. Lexington, Mass.: D. C. Heath, 1975.

PART V

Minorities and the War

14 Women in a Man's World: American Women in the Vietnam War

Lenna Allred

Almost twenty years after the last combat troops pulled out of Vietnam, Americans are still trying to come to terms with the war. Thousands of works—histories, memoirs, combat narratives, collections of oral interviews, fiction, drama, poetry, movies, television series, and documentaries—have attempted to reveal the truth that was the war in Vietnam. The truth revealed in most of these works is decidedly one-sided—the war from the perspective of the American male. The majority ignore the effect of the war on the Vietnamese, the Australian and Korean troops, and the American women who also served. Many Americans are still unaware that the Australians and Koreans participated in the war. Only within the last few years, through the popular TV series "China Beach," have people begun to recognize the contributions of American women.

An estimated 7,500 to 11,000 American military women were posted to Vietnam during the war. Because the Department of Defense failed to categorize recruits by sex, there is no official count of the number of women who served. Most of the female military in Vietnam were nurses. Only about 1,300 nonmedical servicewomen drew billets in Southeast Asia. They included WACs (Women's Army Corps), WAFs (Women in the Air Force), WAVEs (Women Accepted for Voluntary Service in the Navy), and Women Marines. They worked in a wide variety of specialties, such as intelligence, air traffic control, photography, cartography, secretarial, and supplies. An estimated 50,000 civilian women worked for private and government agencies in Vietnam. They served as nurses, teachers, journalists, missionaries, Red Cross doughnut dollies, entertainers, flight attendants, or Special Services personnel. Very few of these women wrote about their experiences.[1]

War is considered a man's work—an initiation experience—a way for boys to become men. Most of the literature about the American experience in Vietnam ignores women or treats them as background figures. Many of the women who served there could not overcome the gender stereotyping that affected everyone's concept of war and the part they played. One female veteran wrote: "Vietnam was not a woman's place. My up-bringing dictated that war was a man's job" (Van Devanter, 302). Women's contributions were considered marginal. They did not fire guns. They were not in combat. They did not consider themselves heroes. Courage and heroism were something men were supposed to exhibit. Women were supposed to nurture and support life, not destroy it. Women in Vietnam lived in a man's world. Most of them worked side by side with men. Female nurses worked daily with male nurses and doctors. Servicewomen in nonmedical specialties worked closely with their male counterparts. They experienced the same danger as the men with whom they served. But because they were women, they were treated differently. Because their outlook was colored by female culture, they experienced the war in a different way than men did.

The small body of literature that has thus far been produced by or about the American women who served in Vietnam demonstrates both the similarities and the differences of their experiences and expands our knowledge of the Vietnam War. It includes memoirs, collections of oral histories, a few articles, a history of American nurses in Vietnam, and works of fiction. There are also several books of a broader nature that include sections about the women who served in Vietnam.

The earliest literature, written in the 1960s and 1970s, consisted of war memoirs—personal narratives of individual experiences. They evidence little insight into the politics of the war. *Lucky-Lucky: A Nurse's Story of Life at a Hospital in Vietnam* by Marva Hasselblad with Dorothy Brandon (1966) was the first of that genre. Hasselblad, who served as a missionary nurse in a civilian hospital in Nhatrang (usually spelled "Nha Trang") between 1962 and 1965, provides a sympathetic portrait of the Vietnamese people. She describes the food, native customs, and the hospital staff and patients. Working in a civilian hospital prior to the commitment of ground troops to Vietnam, Hasselblad experienced no more than the rumors of war. The patients she cared for were civilians suffering from diseases common to Third World countries, rather than war injuries.

While Hasselblad provides a sympathetic view of the Vietnamese people with whom she worked, Diane L. Trembly, in *Petticoat Medic in Vietnam: Adventures of a Woman Doctor* (1976), callously judges the South Vietnamese as low-class "peasants." In this breezy account of her work as a volunteer physician in Vietnam between 1970 and 1972 under the American Medical Association's Volunteer Physicians for Vietnam and later as a participant in Project Concern, she criticizes the South Vietnamese people for their lack of industry, ambition, and organization. She presents the United States as the "good guys" who are doing their best to help an ungrateful people. During her tour in Vietnam, she rotated through various hospitals and clinics every few months. She served in a number of civilian hospitals and at a clinic in Lien Hiep and participated as a member of a Military Public Health Assistance Program team working with Montagnards at Boa Loc. Her account provides a glimpse of the variety of medical programs created to fight "the other war in Vietnam"—the battle to win the hearts and minds of the people (259).

A number of female journalists worked in Vietnam during the war and wrote about their experiences. In 1965 Marguerite Higgins related her observations of the last days of the Diem regime during the summer and fall of 1963 in *Our Vietnam Nightmare* (1965). Mary McCarthy visited South Vietnam in 1967 and wrote a polemical treatise about the war in the book *Vietnam* (1967). A second book, *Hanoi* (1968), recounts her experiences in that city as part of an unofficial peace delegation. Journalist Gloria Emerson covered the war for the *New York Times* from 1970 to 1972. The book *Winners and Losers* (1977) emerged out of her experiences in Vietnam and numerous interviews she conducted across the country after she returned. War correspondent Helen "Patches" Musgrove recounts her experiences in excruciating detail in a massive two-volume book, *Vietnam, Front Row Center* (1986).

Home Before Morning (1983), the most substantive memoir and the first book-length narrative of a combat nurse in Vietnam, relates Lynda Van Devanter's experience as a surgical nurse at the 71st Evacuation Hospital in Pleiku and the Evac Hospital at Qui Nhon between 1969 and 1970. Van Devanter was unprepared for the reality of Vietnam—the steady flow of mangled young bodies, the gruesome effects of napalm, the terror of mortar attacks, the smells and the filth, the long hours of work that led to almost constant fatigue, and the seeming senselessness of the war. She volunteered as an idealistic, patriotic young woman ready to answer Kennedy's call to serve her country. By the time she returned home 365 days later, her idealism had turned to disillusionment and her patriotism to distrust.

Coming home offered no relief. No one wanted to hear her war stories. Vietnam was not a socially acceptable topic. She tried to repress her memories of the war, to put the war behind her. But the war was not so easily repressed. She experienced many of the same symptoms male veterans exhibited on coming back to "the world"—flashbacks, nightmares, depression, inability to stay in one place or with one job for any length of time or to form long-lasting relationships. After years of living a nightmare, she finally obtained help from a Veterans Administration counselor who recognized her symptoms as PTSD, post traumatic stress disorder. This disorder had been associated with combat veterans, not with female noncombatants. Veteran officials were slow to recognize the needs of servicewomen. VA hospitals were not equipped to handle women, and most veteran support groups were hostile to them. They did not feel comfortable with women in their groups. Van Devanter became a strong advocate for the needs of women veterans and was eventually appointed the National Women's Director of the Vietnam Veterans of America.

Van Devanter's courage in speaking out about the problems of female veterans gave others courage to speak out. Some agreed to interviews to tell their story to the world. Most women found that dredging up old memories of their Vietnam experience was both painful and therapeutic. One woman wrote to Keith Walker after he interviewed her: "I have a mental picture of you traveling across the country leaving a wake of devastated women. After you left, I spent a week recovering" (Walker, 120). Another women wrote: "It brought back memories, a lot of things that I've suppressed and a lot of things I hadn't thought about.... So I'm glad I did it" (Walker, 34). Many of the interviews were compiled and published as collections of oral histories.

Two early collections, Al Santoli's *Everything We Had* (1981) and Mark Baker's *Nam: The Vietnam War in the Words of the Men and Women Who Fought There* (1981), combine the recollections of both men and women. Santoli's book records the words of thirty-three Vietnam veterans, including two women who served as army nurses between 1969 and 1971. Baker's account, a compilation of the experiences of an unidentified number of Vietnam veterans, including at least one female in the Army Nurses Corps, pounds home the brutality and senselessness of the conflict with the effectiveness of a sledgehammer. This is a book filled with anger, obviously edited to present the harshest and ugliest experiences of those who served. "We sanitize war with romantic adventure and paranoid propaganda to make it tasteful enough for us to live with it," wrote Baker. "Because Vietnam veterans lived through it, the account they give is as raw and shocking as an open wound."[2]

The "women" (or woman) of the title served as a nurse in an unidentified army hospital in Vietnam. She related her introduction to Vietnam—landing at Bien Hoa air base during a mortar attack. She described the sweaty, stale smell that hit her as she ran from the plane and the bugs on the toilet and in the shower. She described the maimed bodies of young men scarcely out of their teens, the green pus that oozed out of many of their dressed wounds, the rage and helplessness she felt in the face of death, and the nervous breakdown of one of the doctors. She told of the shock of coming home, feeling alienated and out of touch, missing Vietnam in spite of the horrors experienced there. Then she described her own nervous breakdown eight years after she came home. "Survivor syndrome," the psychiatrist labeled it. Finally she spoke of her guilt. As a nurse she was supposed to do all she could to save life. In Vietnam she had denied medicine to her Vietnamese patients in order to save it for the GIs. She had also silently acquiesced to the murder of Vietnamese patients to provide beds for American soldiers. At the time of the interview she was still under psychiatric care (Walker, 345).

Between 1985 and 1987, three oral histories emerged focusing exclusively on the experiences of American women in the war: Keith Walker, *A Piece of My Heart: The Stories of 26 American Women Who Served in Vietnam* (1985), Kathryn Marshall, *In the Combat Zone: An Oral History of American Women in Vietnam, 1965–1975* (1987), and Dan Freedman and Jacqueline Rhoads, *Nurses in Vietnam: The Forgotten Veterans* (1987). These oral history collections are all written in the same format. They begin with a short introduction followed by individual interviews of women who served or worked in some capacity in Vietnam during the war. While each account is very personal, there are many similarities in the women's collective experiences.

Women played a variety of roles in Vietnam, but the majority served as nurses. Most of them volunteered for duty in Southeast Asia. However, a few who signed up for the army student nurse program under the impression that they would not be sent to the war zone were unpleasantly surprised when they received their orders for Vietnam. Most served for many of the same reasons as the male volunteers—to answer the call of patriotism, to find adventure, to escape oppressive family situations. Other reasons were essentially feminine—to provide nurture to the fighting men, boost their morale, and heal their broken bodies and spirits.

In spite of their classification as noncombatants, most of the women reported experiencing many of the dangers of war—rocket and mortar attacks and sniper fire. A few reported another danger—rape. There was little threat of rape by the enemy; it was their own troops that they feared. Many men accepted the old stereotype of military women as either whores or lesbians. There was a saying in Vietnam: "Nurses do it for free, but the Red Cross girls charge" (Marshall, 68–69). This attitude could create serious problems. One woman, a Red Cross Volunteer, accepted a ride with a couple of enlisted men. They assumed she had been "putting out" for the brass and became violent and angry when she refused their advances.

Constant exposure to the savage toll war inflicts on the bodies and minds of young men was even more devastating to the women than the physical danger they experienced. Red Cross workers told of boys who came back from the boonies too haunted to talk. Others proudly showed them their souvenirs—strings of ears, scalps, and fingers and jars of carefully preserved body parts. Nurses told of having to make life-and-death decisions in triage. During mass casualty calls there were often not enough doctors and nurses to take care of the injured. Triage was a system designed to care for the patients who had the best chance of survival. Those who were not expected to live were set aside. Hospital personnel developed their own jargon, which tended to dehumanize patients and combat the grim reality. Patients not expected to live were termed "expectants." "Crispy critters" were napalm victims; "gorks," brain-damaged; and "train wrecks," massive multiple injuries. There were also "sucking chest wounds" and "turtles," those who lost both arms and legs (Walker, 79).

Dredging up war memories demanded that these women face both the best and the worst of themselves and others. They remembered the intensity of friendships that developed in Vietnam and the love affairs that helped them retain a sense of their humanness in a world of pain and death. They told of fear and boredom and the numbness they cultivated in order to survive. They told how alcohol and drugs helped to block their nightmares and get them through the night. They spoke of "gooks" and "slant-eyes" and used other racial epithets that tended to dehumanize the enemy. They spoke of pride in the skills they developed. They also told of disillusionment and alienation.

These stories are valuable as raw material—the first step in beginning to understand the female experience in Vietnam. However, none of the interviewers probed beyond the surface to examine the political and cultural implications of the experiences. Very rarely did the women question the system that sent them to war. They did not connect official policies or cultural values with the devastating consequences of what happened to them and others in Vietnam.

While memoirs and oral histories are valuable in recognizing individual experiences, quirks of memory and self-serving unconscious or conscious mechanisms often interfere and keep the author from digging deep enough to discover the whole truth. After her interview with Keith Walker, Jill Ann Mishkill wrote: "I want to tell everyone, make them understand. But even after [reading] eighteen pages of my story, I feel I haven't said it, that there must be another story I have forgotten that could explain it" (Walker, 120). John Clark Pratt observed that "to understand and apprehend the truth (which after all is the only real fact) of war, I suggest . . . that one can best learn about the Vietnam War through the works of art: the poetry, drama, and fiction."[3]

Hundreds of works of fiction have been written about the war. In John Newman's 1988 edition of *Vietnam War Literature*, over 700 works—poetry, drama, short stories, and novels—are listed. Of those 700 works, only about twenty deal with American women who served in Vietnam. Only one of the twenty treats the contributions of American women seriously. Most works of fiction about American servicewomen in Vietnam are either adolescent nurse novels, romance novels, or adult fiction bordering on or blatantly pornographic. Characterization of the women in these novels tends to be thinly drawn stereotypes. Newman's annotated bibliography lists five stories entitled either *Vietnam Nurse* or *Nurse in Vietnam*. The plot of these romance novels revolves around the relationship between a beautiful nurse and a handsome, very masculine officer. They fall in love and manage to have one or more dangerous adventures. In most of these stories the officer rescues the nurse, and they live happily ever after. Other works are blatantly pornographic. These include Parma Malik's *Viet Cong Defilers* (1976), in which a WAC corporal is captured and sexually tortured by the Vietcong, *Vietcong Rape Raiders* (1983), a story about the brutal violation of an American nurse by her Vietcong captors, and several other anonymous works published by the War Horrors Press—*Nurse Prisoners of the Cong, Captive Nurses of the Viet Cong*, and *Victims of the Cong*. These works provide little insight into the real experiences of women who served in Vietnam.

One romance novel, *Bend with the Wind* (1980) by Elizabeth Simms Moore, is unique in its attempt to provide cultural background on Vietnam. The love story of nurse Marty Fountain and Dr. Peter Cain, set in a small civilian hospital to Quang Ngai province in 1962, is interspersed with thinly disguised lectures about the people, culture, and government of Vietnam. Moore brings some firsthand experience to the work. Her biographical information indicates that she worked as an X-ray technician in Vietnam but does not tell when she was there or in what part of the country. While this work presents information on such things as Vietnamese wedding customs, the Buddhist and Cao Dai religions, the Montagnards, and efforts to help the Vietnamese people through international relief organizations, the stereotypical portrayals of the female characters provide little insight into the reality of their experiences in Vietnam.

Forever Sad the Hearts (1982) by Patricia L. Walsh is undoubtedly the best novel about women in the Vietnam War. In contrast to the other novels, the characterization, language, and experiences presented in this work are completely consistent with Van Devanter's memoir and the oral histories. The story is told by Kate Shea, a nurse anesthetist, who volunteers for an eighteen-month tour of duty in Vietnam with the government-funded Better World Organization (BWO). Arriving in Saigon in early 1967, she is assigned to a civilian hospital in Danang. Walsh vividly describes the deplorable conditions in the hospital—the stench of rotted flesh and blood, garbage cans overflowing with putrid dressings, swarms of flies crawling over the operating tables, inadequate equipment and lack of supplies. Kate quickly learns that most of the supplies BWO sends the hospital are siphoned off to the black market.

Because agency officials refuse to face the problem, nurses "crumshawed" most of their supplies from the navy and air force to keep the hospital going.

Like most Vietnam novels, *Forever Sad the Hearts* is a novel of initiation, of lost innocence. In this version, however, innocence is lost through treating the victims of combat rather than through participation in combat. Kate came to Vietnam believing the American myth. Americans were the good guys in the white hats who were in Vietnam to help fight Communism and preserve democracy. She was soon disillusioned. When the marines brought truckloads of wounded civilians to the hospital, Kate asked, "Why are American military called to pick up civilians?" "They don't have to be called," she was told. "They're the other half of the fire fight" (Walsh, 26). A young lieutenant put it more bluntly when he exclaimed, "You mean we shoot 'em and you fix them up?" (109). Here, the paradox of this war is brought clearly in focus. The patients whom the American government was paying her to heal were wounded by the soldiers the government was paying to fight.

Unlike most of the other works presented, *Forever Sad the Hearts* seriously examines the politics of war and its consequences. Kate becomes increasingly concerned as she observes numerous discrepancies between what is being reported and what she can see firsthand. After an attack that leaves a large number of Americans dead, Kate wonders how the government would report this back home. She notes the difference between what the papers report and the actual numbers of dead and maimed soldiers (119). There is another concern. What would happen to the young men Uncle Sam so casually offers up for slaughter who come home mutilated but still alive, whose lives are destined never to be normal again? (114).

While many novels of Vietnam deny or trivialize the danger faced by noncombatants in the "rear," Walsh presents the danger as very real and reminds the reader that there were no safe areas in Vietnam. All of Vietnam was a combat zone. The nurses, doctors, and everyone else in town and on the base were subject to frequent rocket attacks. Both the hospital and Kate's living quarters were in unsecured areas. Rockets sometimes exploded close enough to shatter the glass in the windows of her house. During heavy attacks the nurses had to drive to a bunker in town. One time they went to the base to seek shelter, only to find that the base was the center of the firefight. In Vietnam, Kate stated, there was "no safe place in which to hide" (116).

At one point the hospital became the target. While Kate and her fellow coworkers calmly watched the firefight through the broken windows of the hospital, a newly arrived doctor went into hysterics and demanded immediate evacuation. In this interesting scene, the author debunks the stereotypical gender roles. The image of the strong male who faces danger with courage and offers the defenseless women his protection is shattered. When the doctor screams: "We're Americans! I demand that we be evacuated immediately," Kate calmly takes him to a window and points toward a raging fire. "See that?" she said. "That's the air base" (72). The ways in which both men and women coped with the stresses of the war were individual—defined more by their personal reserves of strength and resilience than by their gender.

They found different ways of dealing with the danger that surrounded them. Finding humor in even the blackest situations was one way. When passing a Vietnamese house of prostitution, one of the nurses, Jean, explains to newly arrived Kate that several soldiers "have been killed by V.C. grenades while they were in there screwing." "Talk about the earth moving," said Jean (160). At a Green Beret party a soldier offered Kate some "grass." She declined, saying, "I'd be afraid I wouldn't be able to get myself to a bunker fast enough if I had to." "We don't really give a damn where our bodies are," the soldier replied, "just so our minds are out of Viet Nam" (110).

Besides danger, the nurses and doctors had to cope with the bloody human wreckage that streamed through the hospital. Hardest to deal with were the children. They came to the hospital horribly burned by napalm, with their arms and legs blown off, and sometimes clinging to parents who were already dead. Most of the nurses and doctors fought off nightmares by drinking themselves to sleep. They also reached out to one another to reaffirm their humanity. Many of Kate's fellow nurses entered into affairs with married men. Kate did not. She rejected the advances of a married officer, then met, fell in love, and became engaged to a young marine officer, Dan Cowan. Unlike most of the romance novels, the love plot of *Forever Sad the Hearts* is realistic and evolves naturally. There is no happy ending, however. Dan is killed, betrayed by the ARVN troops he had been training.

Kate is sent home when her back is injured during the Tet Offensive. "The preparations for leaving were simpler than I'd expected," she comments. "I was given a bottle of pills to flush the parasites from my intestines. I thought it unfortunate they couldn't give me something to flush my mind as well." Kate returned home completely disillusioned. Flying out, she notes that "the landscape was no longer the lush green it had been the day I'd first flown into Da Nang. It had all been cruelly defoliated; stripped as naked as I had" (384).

Forever Sad the Hearts meets Tim O'Brian's definition of a true war story. "It comes down to gut instinct," he wrote in *The Things They Carried* (1990). "A true war story, if truly told, makes the stomach believe" (84). This book has the feel of truth. Patricia Walsh, like the heroine of her novel, spent fourteen months in a civilian hospital in Danang run by the U.S. Agency for International Development (AID). Many of the events of the novel actually occurred during her tour of duty. Walsh has taken her own experiences and embellished and reshaped them to present her truth of the Vietnam War.

In most novels of the war, women are either absent or secondary. Works by male doctors set in hospitals in Vietnam present nurses as shadow figures, faceless beings—an extra pair of hands to help the doctor. Ronald J. Glasser's novel, *Another War, Another Peace*, can serve as an example. The hero in this war novel is a doctor named David. The only other character that rates much attention is Tom, the driver who takes David out on Med Caps to strategic hamlets near the hospital. When Tom is killed, David becomes disillusioned. With the Tet Offensive, he begins to realize that the officers in charge have no real strategy. Like *Forever Sad the Hearts*, this is a novel of loss of innocence and disillusionment. However, unlike Walsh's work, Glasser does not provide full characterization for both the male and female characters. He merely acknowledges the presence of a few nurses without giving them names or faces. Nurses are automatons with a job to do. That is all. Women in this novel are not only secondary; they are mere fixtures.

Glasser is not the only doctor to write about hospitals in Vietnam without giving nurses a face. In an article by John A. Parrish, "Journal of a Plague Year: The Recollections of a Doctor at War," Parrish begins by noting that "Dong Ha had about twelve doctors, half general medical officers, the rest some kind of surgeons." No nurses are mentioned until the last page of the article, when "a nurse with giant tits and an awful face" becomes part of a surreal dream (62, 70).

Where were all the nurses in these works? In both the fictional and nonfictional accounts of women in Vietnam, nurses worked side by side with male doctors, often performing minor surgery that would be done by physicians in the States. Nurses saw themselves as major contributors. They stabilized and prepared the wounded, they had the responsibility of triage, and they were the ones who held the hands of the dying. That doctors neglected to credit nurses for their contributions tells something about American culture. That most other war stories exclude women is also telling.

Few serious works recognize the contributions of women in the war zone as a legitimate part of the war's history. From the American Revolution to Desert Storm, women have provided vital services during wartime. Their experiences, if acknowledged at all, are segregated as separate "female" experiences. In Myra MacPherson's overly long, rambling account of the effect of Vietnam on the sixties generation, *Long Time Passing: Vietnam and the Haunted Generation* (1984), one chapter is dedicated to the experiences of women. In that chapter, MacPherson tells the stories of mothers who lost their sons in war, the women who supported the war, and the women who demonstrated against the war.

The account of women who served in the war occupies two pages and mainly focuses on the problems they faced on returning home.

Post-Traumatic Stress Disorders, a compilation of articles about PTSD edited by Tom Williams (1987), is another book that segregates the female veterans' experience to a single chapter. That chapter, "Women Vietnam Veterans," written by Rose Sandecki, details the similarities and differences found between male and female vets suffering from PTSD.

Two general histories of servicewomen—*Women in the Military: An Unfinished Revolution* by Jeanne Holm (1982) and Shelley Saywell's *Women in War* (1985)—contain one chapter each on women and the Vietnam War. Saywell's chapter, entitled "Twilight Zone, Vietnam, 1965–1972," presents the oral histories of six women who served as nurses in the war. They report experiences very similar to those of the nurses in the works by Walker, Marshall, and Freedman and Rhoads. The chapter on Vietnam in Holm's work tells the little-known story of the struggle nonmedical servicewomen experienced in order to be assigned a billet in Southeast Asia. During the war, thousands of servicewomen applied for assignment to Vietnam, but only an estimated 1,300 nonmedical servicewomen were sent. Holm conducted an investigation to determine why so many women volunteers were denied duty there while the Department of Defense was having difficulty drafting enough men to serve. She discovered that the decision to assign women to Vietnam rested primarily with the personnel officer in the Department of Defense and with individual commanding officers. Their reluctance to send women to Vietnam tells much about masculine attitudes toward women in the military.

Recently, several articles have appeared that deal with the literature of women in the Vietnam War—Kathleen M. Puhr's "Women in Vietnam War Novels" (1988) and "Women and the Vietnam War" (1989) by Joe P. Dunn. Puhr analyzes three war novels, *Vietnam Nurse* by Evelyn Hawkins, "a poorly crafted romance set in Vietnam"; Leonard Scott's *Charlie Mike*, a novel about Army Rangers in An Khe that presents American nurses and Red Cross volunteers as "mere accessories to the men"; and *Forever Sad the Hearts* by Patricia Walsh, the only "credible" portrayal of American women in Vietnam among the three works cited (Puhr, 176, 178, 182). Dunn presents a bibliographic review of works produced by and about women who either served in Vietnam or were touched in some way by the war. He reviews memoirs, oral histories, works of fiction, and films about military and civilian nurses, journalists, missionaries, wives, mothers, and girlfriends of servicemen, and women involved in the antiwar movement. The women in the works he presents include American, French, German, and Vietnamese.

Of the works on women in the war, only one attempts a historical synthesis of their experiences. *Women at War: The Story of Fifty Military*

Nurses Who Served in Vietnam by Elizabeth Norman (1990) documents the experiences of fifty nurses who served in the army, navy, or air force Nurses Corps in Vietnam between 1965 and 1973. Norman describes how these experiences differed according to when and where they served. The first group of nurses sent to South Vietnam in 1965 went as advisors to train South Vietnamese nurses. They wore civilian clothes and worked with the local people in a trusting, reciprocal relationship. They reported a positive, rewarding experience. Nurses who served between 1965 and 1967 recalled a sense of purpose and "esprit de corps." They felt that what they did made a difference. After 1967, however, morale sagged. A sense of futility began to permeate all branches of the armed forces after the Tet Offensive of January 31, 1968. Antiwar demonstrations at home became more intense, the South Vietnamese appeared indifferent to the sacrifices Americans were making in their behalf, and the number of casualties grew. Esprit de corps diminished, and nurses began to see large numbers of senseless injuries—self-inflicted wounds, injuries from barroom brawls, and drug overdoses. These women reported their experiences in much less positive terms. However, virtually all the nurses in this study recognized their year in Vietnam as one of exceptional professional growth. Vietnam gave them a sense of confidence—much had been demanded, and they had performed. They had survived Vietnam.

As the first published work that attempts a historical synthesis of the women who served in the Vietnam War, *Women at War* makes an important contribution to the literature. It adds a missing link in the picture of the American experience in Vietnam. However, much more is needed. Most of the oral histories, memoirs, and the one historical synthesis on women in the war deal with the nurses who served. We know much less about the experiences of the nonmedical servicewomen or the estimated 50,000 civilian women who worked in Vietnam during the war. Carol Lynn Mithers addresses the reasons behind this lacuna in "Missing in Action: Women Warriors in Vietnam" (1991). "There has always been a place for women to serve in war," Mithers states, "but there is no place for them in its mythology" (81).

Our culture assumes that men will go to war to protect their women and children. Women stay behind to keep the home fires burning for the returning warriors. Our mythology of war serves to reinforce deeply held cultural assumptions of gender roles. Women's war stories challenge these assumptions and, therefore, are not accepted as valid. An incident reported in Van Devanter's book can serve as an example. While men fled a flaming helicopter on a hospital landing pad, one nurse refused to leave a wounded man. Yelling for help, she tried to lift him by herself while the chief screamed at her, "He's gonna die anyway. . . . Forget about him" (195). The man was rescued just before the chopper blew. He lived.

The head nurse ordered a Bronze Star with "V" for valor to be given to the heroic nurse. When the medal came, the "V" was missing. Women were not awarded things like that, the head nurse was told.

In our society, war has been, and will continue to be, defined in masculine terms. We make heroes of men who kill. The greater the slaughter, the more the honor. We call it courage. We consider the contributions of the healers, the doctors and nurses who patch up the broken bodies of casualties, as secondary. As noncombatants they are not considered heroic material. The insights gained by this contribution of women to the Vietnam War contradict the stereotypical images of women at war. Women, though classified as noncombatants, faced the same danger as the men with whom they served. They demonstrated courage under difficult and hazardous conditions. While they were only a very small minority in a vast sea of men who served in Vietnam, they made a difference, and their contributions must be recognized.

NOTES

1. Marshall, 4, cites Department of Defense estimates of 7,500 servicewomen in Vietnam between 1962 and 1973. She also states that 1,300 nonmedical military women served in Vietnam, although she does not name her source. Holm, 241, states that neither the Veterans Administration (VA) nor the Department of Defense (DOD) has reliable statistics on how women served in Vietnam or how many were decorated. Norman, 4, cites a 1985 newsletter published by the Vietnam Veterans of America that puts the number of female Vietnam veterans at 11,000. Walker, 335–45, includes an appendix at the end of his book that identifies the organization of female military personnel in Vietnam by service.

2. Baker, xiv. Each section of Baker's book deals with one aspect of Vietnam— enlistment or getting drafted, arrival in country, operations, war stories, and coming home. It is possible, in this book, to follow one voice of the nurse (usually one in each section), but it sounds so much the same throughout the book that it appears that all the female voices are coming from one woman.

3. John Clark Pratt, "Bibliographic Commentary: 'From the Fiction, Some Truths,' " in Lomperis, 98.

BIBLIOGRAPHY

Anisfield, Nancy. "Sexist Subscript in Vietnam Narratives." *Vietnam Generation* 1 (Summer-Fall 1989): 109–14.

Baker, Mark. *Nam: The Vietnam War in the Words of the Men and Women Who Fought There*. New York: Morrow, 1981.

Beidler, Philip D. "The Good Women of Saigon: The Work of Cultural Revision in Gloria Emerson's *Winners and Losers* and Frances FitzGerald's *Fire in the Lake*." *Genre* 21 (Winter 1988): 523–34.

"A Bibliography of Unusual Sources on Women and the Vietnam War." *Vietnam Generation* 1 (Summer-Fall 1989): 274–77.

Carter, Susanne. "Visions of Vietnam in Women's Short Fiction." *Vietnam Generation*, 1 (Summer-Fall 1989), 74–89.

Christie, N. Bradley. "What Happened on the Inside: Women Write About Vietnam." Educational Resources Information Center (ERIC). No. ED 296 340 (March 1988): 1–19.

Christopher, Renny. " 'I Never Really Became a Woman Veteran Until...I Saw the Wall': A Review of Oral Histories and Personal Narratives by Women Veterans of the Vietnam War." *Vietnam Generation* 1 (Summer-Fall 1989): 33–45.

Dunn, Joe P. "Women and the Vietnam War: A Bibliographic Review." *Journal of American Culture* 12 (Spring 1989): 79–86.

Emerson, Gloria. *Winners and Losers: Battles, Retreats, Gains, Losses, and Ruins from a Long War*. New York: Random House, 1977.

Freedman, Dan, and Jacqueline Rhoads. *Nurses in Vietnam: The Forgotten Veterans*. Austin: Texas Monthly Press, 1987.

Glasser, Ronald J. *Another War, Another Peace*. New York: Summit Books, 1985.

Hasselblad, Marva, with Dorothy Brandon. *Lucky-Lucky*. Greenwich, Conn.: Fawcett, 1966.

Higgins, Marguerite. *Our Vietnam Nightmare*. New York: Harper and Row, 1965.

Holm, Jeanne. *Women in the Military: An Unfinished Revolution*. Novato, Calif.: Presidio, 1982.

Jason, Philip K. "Sexism and Racism in Vietnam War Fiction." *Mosaic* 23 (Summer 1990): 125–37.

Lawson, Jacqueline. " 'She's a pretty woman...for a gook': The Misogyny of the Vietnam War." *Journal of American Culture* 12 (Fall 1989): 55–65.

Lomperis, Timothy J. *"Reading the Wind": The Literature of the Vietnam War*. Durham: Duke University Press, 1987.

MacPherson, Myra. *Long Time Passing: Vietnam and the Haunted Generation*. Garden City, N.Y.: Doubleday, 1984.

Marshall, Kathryn. *In the Combat Zone: An Oral History of American Women in Vietnam, 1965–1975*. Boston: Little, Brown, 1987.

McCarthy, Mary. *Hanoi*. New York: Harcourt, Brace & World, 1968.

Meyers, Kate Beaird. "Fragmenting Mosaics: Vietnam War 'Histories' and Postmodern Epistemology." *Genre* 21 (Winter 1988): 535–52.

Mithers, Carol Lynn. "Missing in Action: Women Warriors in Vietnam." In John Carlos and Rick Berg, eds. *The Vietnam War and American Culture*. New York: Columbia University Press, 1991.

Moore, Elizabeth Simms. *Bend with the Wind*. Port Washington, N.Y.: Ashley Books, 1980.

Musgrove, Helen. *Vietnam, Front Row Center*. New York: Knopf, 1986.

Newman, John. *Vietnam War Literature: An Annotated Bibliography of Imaginative Works About Americans Fighting in Vietnam*. Metuchen, N.J.: Scarecrow Press, 1988.

Norman, Elizabeth. *Women at War: The Story of Fifty Military Nurses Who Served in Vietnam*. Philadelphia: University of Pennsylvania Press, 1990.

O'Brien, Tim. *The Things They Carried*. Boston: Houghton Mifflin, 1990.

Parrish, John A. "Journal of a Plague Year: The Recollections of a Doctor at War." *Harpers* (February 1972): 62–70.

Puhr, Kathleen M. "Women in Vietnam War Novels." In William J. Searle, ed. *Search and Clear: Critical Responses to Selected Literature and Films of the Vietnam War*. Bowling Green, Ohio: Bowling Green State University Popular Press, 1988.

Sandecki, Rose. "Women Veterans." In Tom Williams, ed. *Post-Traumatic Stress Disorders: A Handbook for Clinicians*. Cincinnati, Ohio: Disabled American Veterans, 1987.

Santoli, Al. *Everything We Had: An Oral History of the Vietnam War by Thirty-three American Soldiers Who Fought It*. New York: Random House, 1981.

Saywell, Shelley. *Women in War*. New York: Viking Penguin, 1985.

Shell, Cheryl A. "Making Sense of Vietnam and Telling the Real Story: Military Women *In the Combat Zone*." *Vietnam Generation* 1 (Summer-Fall 1989): 59–67.

Smith, Lori. "Back Against the Wall: Anti-Feminist Backlash in Vietnam War Literature." *Vietnam Generation* 1 (Summer-Fall 1989): 115–26.

Tal, Kali. "Feminist Criticism and the Literature of the Vietnam Combat Veteran." *Vietnam Generation* 1 (Summer-Fall 1989): 190–201.

Tal, Kali. "The Mind at War: Images of Women in Vietnam Novels by Combat Veterans." *Contemporary Literature* 31 (Spring 1990): 76–96.

Trembly, Diane L. *Petticoat Medic in Vietnam: Adventures of a Woman Doctor*. New York: Vantage, 1976.

Van Devanter, Lynda. *Home Before Morning: The Story of an Army Nurse in Vietnam*. New York: Beaufort Books, 1983.

Walker, Keith. *A Piece of My Heart: The Stories of 26 American Women Who Served in Vietnam*. Novato, Calif.: Presidio, 1985.

Walsh, Patricia L. *Forever Sad the Hearts*. New York: Avon Books, 1982.

Williams, Thomas. *Post-Traumatic Stress Disorders*. New York: American Psychological Association, 1987.

15 Blacks and the Vietnam War

Ernest M. B. Obadele-Starks and
Amilcar Shabazz

From the range of basic questions of historical inquiry we ask this one question: What was the meaning of the Vietnam War to African Americans? The question is quite old; indeed, it was asked as far back as the early 1960s, following the first major escalation of the U.S. military presence in Southeast Asia. What remains ever new about this question is merely that it must be asked again and again. The history of blacks and the Vietnam War has barely begun to unfold, and many aspects have yet to be explored. Overall, this field of professional study is still at an embryonic stage of development, and much more needs to be done before we can adequately evaluate its nature. Such a note of caution notwithstanding, an overview of its status might still be useful in determining historiographical gaps and problem areas and in pointing out research directions. What follows is a discussion of the status of this new literature and an exploration of some of its major arguments and themes.

The written material currently available for the professional study of blacks and the Vietnam War divides into two general areas: that produced by academic writers for scholarly audiences and that produced by nonacademic writers for a general readership. Sociologists, psychologists, political scientists, and scholars in other disciplines rank favorably in their contribution to the documentation of the Afro-Vietnam experience. In the nonacademic realm, political interests and concerns, as might be expected, tend to pervade the literature in both overt and subtle ways. To be sure, subjectivity, particularly the issue of patriotism, has more often than not winnowed its way into the literature of both the academic and the popular realms; but, in the case of the latter domain, patriotism, whether for or against, tends to be the central question.

The scholarly historical literature on African Americans' relationship

to the Vietnam War, like its popular counterpart, characteristically contemplates the same axiological questions: What was the war's worth to
the black soldier? What was its value for the black man or woman in
uniform? What were the effects of the wartime experience on African
Americans as a whole, both those who served there and their families
and friends who did not? Such questions are an appropriate area of
inquiry, given the fact that blacks were essentially marginalized from the
political, military, and diplomatic centers of power and decision making.
Nevertheless, an Afrocentric perspective challenges historians to probe
deeper and to ask exactly what role the blacks played in shaping the
history of America's involvement in Southeast Asia. Other than an occasional reference to a few celebrated instances of black protest to the
war, blacks are largely invisible in the political and diplomatic histories
of the Vietnam War. Even some of the best general accounts of the war,
such as the works of George Herring, James Olson, and Randy Roberts,
and the controversial analysis of Gabriel Kolko fail to give much attention
to blacks.

As for the traditional military histories, the black experience in Vietnam is also largely ignored. The actual reality of the war is typically
treated as a monolithic phenomenon. What the white soldier experienced, all soldiers experienced. Recently, more balanced and sophisticated studies have gone beyond such a reductive depiction of the war
and have emphasized the fact that the wartime experience of blacks,
Puerto Ricans, and other nonwhite soldiers included not only the battles
with the Vietcong, but internal battles with racism, ethnic and linguistic
chauvinism, and prejudice and other forms of discrimination as well.
This dual or separate experience for African Americans is addressed
most often in one of two ways. The most common argument is that the
pressures of the daily fight for survival against the Vietcong brought
black and white soldiers together across the color line. The alternative
argument focuses on the rise of a defensive ideology of black nationalism
that manifested itself in such superficial and symbolic forms as "Afro"
hair styles, black power salutes, spirited handshakes, amulets, and other
fashion statements. There is ample evidence to support both lines of
interpretation of the black soldier's story in Vietnam.

For the student of history, the indispensable starting point for an
understanding of the Vietnam War and African Americans is as yet in
the basic documents or primary sources. Morris J. MacGregor and Bernard C. Nalty have compiled some of the more important of the wartime
press releases, government memoranda, letters, and reports. *Blacks in
the United States Armed Forces: Basic Documents* (Vol. 13, Equal Treatment
and Opportunity: The McNamara Doctrine) contains sixty-four documents reproduced in the form they originally appeared between 1962
and 1973. Most of the documents are from government or military

sources and address issues involving the armed forces in general, but there are a few nonofficial pieces included, as well as documents that specifically focus on black soldiers in Southeast Asia. MacGregor and Nalty have also edited a more compact volume, *Blacks in the Military: Essential Documents*, in which the last two chapters contain many of the same documents included in the aforementioned volume. In the *Essential Documents* volume, however, each piece is briefly introduced, annotated, and typeset, which makes for easier reading.

Nalty's *Strength for the Fight* is one of the more recently published general summaries of blacks in U.S. military history. The portion of his book that considers the Southeast Asian conflict is somewhat tedious and needlessly argumentative. A better introduction can be found in Jack D. Foner's *Blacks and the Military in American History*. Neither book is designed with the advanced reader or specialist in mind, but their contrasting interpretations may be read together with profit. Another good, although also limited, overview is in Mary Frances Berry and John W. Blassingame's *Long Memory: The Black Experience in America*. These works represent virtually the sum total of professional historians' contribution to our understanding of blacks and the Vietnam War. An important general work written by a professor of speech communication is Robert W. Mullen's *Blacks in America's Wars*. In the portion of his book that covers the conflict in Vietnam, basically a restatement of his 1971 doc-fjtoral dissertation, "An Analysis of the Issues Developed by Select Black Americans on the War in Vietnam," Mullen contrasts the rhetorical strategies or positions that developed among "revolutionary," "separatist," and "assimilationist" black leaders regarding blacks and the Vietnam War.

Social scientists, particularly military sociologists and psychologists, have done the most to document and analyze the black fight in Vietnam. Charles C. Moskos, Jr., stands out as one of the most prolific and perceptive of sociologists who have written about racism in the armed forces. His *The American Enlisted Man* is still the best work available on the attitude of blacks and their role in the war in Vietnam during its early phase. Martin Binkin's *Blacks and the Military* devotes a portion of its first chapter to a consideration of "Vietnam and the New Era of Racial Representation."

In May 1972, Major Jonathan F. Borus of the U.S. Army, along with his colleagues in the Psychiatry Department at Walter Reed Hospital, launched a study of "racial polarization" in the armed services. This study was the most significant wartime attempt within the armed forces scientifically to assess the reality of racial tension in the military. Borus's article, "Racial Perceptions in the Army: An Approach," offers historians useful material on which they can begin to build more sophisticated interpretations of the black wartime experience. After conducting an "inventory" of racial division within the army, on the basis of his study, he concludes that blacks and whites perceive the Army experience differently and that blacks are more likely than whites to see racial discrimination.

In an effort to capture the psychological tension that Borus and other social scientists observed in black soldiers, fiction writers have produced three fine novels on the black-Vietnam war theme: George Davis's *Coming Home*, John A. Williams's, *Captain Blackman*, and Wesley Brown's *Tragic Magic*. Norman Harris, a professor of English, in "Blacks in Vietnam: A Holistic Perspective Through Fiction and Journalism," has written a fine commentary on these novels and on the major newspaper and magazine treatments of the black soldier's experience during the Vietnam War. He concludes his literary analysis by suggesting that in these novels black soldiers discovered that Vietnam was simply another "act in the contradictory drama of Afro-America: the concurrent manifestation of opportunity and exploitation . . . another bridge into an Afro-American past that illuminates the present while throwing light on the future" (126). Likewise, as black soldiers in Vietnam became more historically conscious, they began to demand "magazines and books that had black life as their content," which served to relieve the "psychological tension" of serving in the war machine of a country that denied them their full democratic rights. Harris argues that mainstream journalism during the war spread a "propaganda of integration" based upon what he calls the "historical amnesia" that swept American newsrooms.

Harris's findings lead us into a consideration of the second general area of literature on blacks and the Vietnam War: written material intended for a general readership. Larger and more subjective than its scholarly cousin, the popular literature on the Afro-Vietnam experience is presently more diverse and revealing, once one gets beyond the political bias of the author. The popular branch of the literature splits into a patriotic limb that either ignores the morality of the war or wholeheartedly endorses the fight against Communist subversion of a "democratic" government. Or it splits into an antiwar limb that criticizes the war as unjustifiable and sometimes decries the U.S. government as unworthy of black loyalty and support on any level. While both discourses were present during the war and can still be heard today, antiwar writers seemed to have overshadowed the promilitary writers by the middle of the 1960s. An understanding of the development of each literary group is essential for the student of Afro-Vietnam history.

The majority of the articles and books in the patriotic group spring almost entirely from black military officers and enlisted men and women or from authors writing about blacks in the officer corps during the war. Obligation and opportunity are the watchwords of those writing in this mode. High-ranking black soldiers are profiled from the vantage point of their commitment and their ability to do the job. A recent piece from this group is Marvin Fletcher's *America's First Black General: Benjamin O. Davis, Sr., 1880–1970*. Although Davis was not directly involved in combat activity in Vietnam, his support of the war and government policy made and continues to make him a symbol for the United States to present to other blacks who join the military. Davis comes through as a man who never questions his superiors. His sense of military obligation is revealed in his assertion: "I did my duty. That's what I set out to do— to show that I could make my own way if I knew my job." Another soldier who did see combat in Vietnam and later became the first black to chair the Joint Chiefs of Staff, among other top military posts, is Colin L. Powell. Like Davis, he, too, is held up as a symbol of the upward mobility available to blacks in the armed forces. In a 1990 interview Powell explained his perspective on the military service: "My approach has been that racism is there. . . . The only thing I can do is outperform it." The title of this interview itself speaks to the symbol-making process that occurs now as it did during the Vietnam War: "Colin L. Powell: The Most Important Soldier in the World." Other examples during the war include *Sepia* articles on the navy's first black to achieve the rank of admiral, Samuel Gravely, and another on the black four-star general Daniel "Chappie" James. The article on James, which appeared in 1968 and was subtitled "Big Man, Big Message," praised him for his unswerving dedication to the military in Vietnam and provides him with a platform from which he proclaimed his 100 percent American patriotism.

Among the black soldiers in Vietnam of lower rank, two figures attest to the fact that at the rank-and-file level there were blacks who, like their high-ranking counterparts, completely identified themselves as American soldiers, proud to be in the service of "their country." Sergeant Samuel Vance, author of *The Courageous and the Proud* in 1970, produced a full-length narrative about his service in Vietnam in 1965. His bravery in combat won him a Silver Star for "gallantry in action." Vance's work is deliberately conceived as an answer to those who opposed the Vietnam War, especially the participation of blacks as fighting units there. To the "figures that show that more Negroes have died in Vietnam than any other group," Vance explains that they are not proof of racial discrimination in battle area assignments (where white officers may have put black soldiers in the most dangerous areas because they were viewed as more expendable than whites), but evidence of the fact that "all commanders use their best people, and often these men are Negroes." Vance tells us he "went to Vietnam to prove something. . . . I'm glad I had a chance to go and play my part as a black American. I'm glad to say that I know for a fact that the Negro soldiers are outstanding, and that we are truly helping the South Vietnamese" (158–59).

Woody Wanamaker, the sole black person among the dozens of persons whose recollections of the Vietnam War appear in Harry Maurer's *Strange Ground: Americans in Vietnam, 1945–1975; An Oral History*, is the second example of a nonofficer black who apparently supported America's political posture in Vietnam. His story, however, is quite different from Vance's. Between 1966 and 1973 Wanamaker did five tours of duty in Vietnam—a total of fifty-four months. After he completed his first tour, he was already a sergeant at nineteen and a half years old, and at the time (1967), he recalled: "I thought my shit didn't stink. I thought I had the world by the balls, and I was unstoppable" (240). Nevertheless, he found it "strange being back in the States," and thus he reenlisted. He simply states he "wasn't peace." Peace, however, was not what he would find in Vietnam. In the summer of 1968 he witnessed a "full-scale race riot" at the camp he was stationed at in Cu Chi. In the aftermath of this affray, pitting "blacks against whites, whites against Puerto Ricans, blacks against Puerto Ricans," Wanamaker and a white "buddy" named Al, also a sergeant, set up a "race relations group" within their company. He and Al, so close they were referred to by some as "Salt and Pepper," led classes that were designed to educate other soldiers and make them more sensitive to feelings of others of a different race or social background. From discussions on black history, greater friction was stirred up between black and white soldiers than less. Wanamaker claims other black soldiers soon tagged him an Uncle Tom, and he believes at least one of his black enemies was responsible for a tragic incident that changed the course of his life. On August 21, 1968, while he and Al were sitting in Al's room "bullshitting," someone tossed a grenade into the room. Al was killed, and Wanamaker took some shrapnel. Army officials falsely designated his death as the result of incoming enemy fire, but Wanamaker had to live with the truth. He began to drink heavily, picked up a habit of shooting morphine, and went on an unsuccessful "crusade" to find the man he suspected was responsible for the "fragging" of his friend. "It destroyed me, in a way," he says. In 1985 he entered a posttraumatic stress program at the VA Hospital in Menlo Park, California. Ironically, he kicked his morphine habit after participating in an antiwar march in 1968. He states, however, he was turned off to the peace movement after some protestors shouted, "Killers! Killers! Killers!"

Much has been written on the anti–Vietnam War movement, but the literature that addresses the antiwar sentiment of African Americans remains relatively underdeveloped. The literature, largely targeted to a popular audience, rather than an academic one, may be demarcated into three distinct phases. The earliest writings examined the paradox of America's deployment of African-American soldiers in the face of the dire social, economic, and political conditions of African-American citizens on the home front. In this phase, the literature makes a clear link between the origins of antiwar sentiment within African-American communities and among African-American soldiers with the maturation of the civil rights movement in the 1960s. In the next phase writers frequently viewed the Vietnam conflict as an exercise in racial genocide aimed at people of color throughout the world. The trend of the literature then moved in the third phase in the direction of acknowledging racism within the armed services of the United States, but without the harsh rhetoric of "racial genocide." Additionally, African-American statements and African-American soldiers were primarily responsible for generating a large percentage of the antiwar literature in each of these phases between 1963 and 1974.

The coming of age of the civil rights movement in the 1960s intensified concerns about drafting blacks into the Vietnam War. Concerns, moreover, quickly emerged into loud and critical social protest. Many African Americans began to feel that the sending of black soldiers to Southeast Asia in defense of America's foreign policy could no longer be justified. President John F. Kennedy was soon compelled to recognize the need for the federal government to speak to the concerns of African Americans on the home front, if for no other reason than to assuage the criticisms of blacks that they were being taken to fight for the rights of people in Vietnam that they did not themselves enjoy in the United States. Kennedy asserted, in an address on civil rights a little more than four months before his assassination, that "when Americans are sent to Vietnam or West Berlin we do not ask for whites only." This admission unequivocally indicates an awareness that the demands of blacks could no longer be ignored on the home front, if the United States wished to fulfill its military objectives in Vietnam.

Kennedy's concern, at least in part, can be attributed to the outspoken criticism of leaders in the black community who forcefully attacked his Vietnam policy and the use of African-American soldiers in Southeast Asia. Much of the early protest came from Malcolm X, the charismatic and relentlessly critical black Muslim leader. "Kennedy has time to take a stand against Khrushchev, against Castro, against lay-offs, against U.S. Steel, against South Vietnam; but when it comes to correcting the injustices that are being inflicted upon negroes in this country, Kennedy fiddles while Birmingham is burning" (quoted in the film *Malcolm X*, 1972). Malcolm's attack on the president and the government created the ideological springboard for later writers and orators who would look critically at the African-American involvement in Vietnam.

Malcolm's criticism of the U.S. Vietnam War policy relative to African Americans continued until his death. Speaking before the militant Labor Forum in 1965, Malcolm vigorously attacked U.S. activities in Vietnam. In his "Two Minutes on Vietnam," Malcolm X charged that the war "is a shame" for the country and for blacks. Malcolm suggested that blacks who criticized the war risked being perceived as anti-American and un-intelligent. In 1970, the Malcolm X Association published an article reflecting the antiwar sentiment of its soldiers in Vietnam and their radical challenge to the military hierarchy.

Another noteworthy discussion of the misuse of black soldiers in Vietnam appeared in a 1967 *Freedomways* article. "Muhammad Ali—The Measure of a Man" argued that the undoing of heavyweight boxing champion Muhammad Ali revealed the ability of the U.S. government to deny or circumvent individuals' exercise of their constitutional right of protest. In a philosophy similar to that of Malcolm X, the author suggested that it is inexplicable for any black American, including Ali, to cloak himself in U.S. military gear and jet thousands of miles away from home to defend the policy of a country that denies its black citizens basic human and civil rights. *Freedomways* also published Martin Luther King, Jr.'s "A Time to Break the Silence." Taken from his address to fellow clergy and lay leaders at Riverside Baptist Church in New York City, Dr. King declared that to remain silent on the Vietnam War was to betray morality, justice, black Americans, and humanity. King's attack on Vietnam differed slightly from Malcolm X's and the editorial on Muhammad Ali. Dr. King chose to extend the criticism of the Vietnam War to include the exploitation and destruction of poor whites and Vietnamese. Other important contributions to the black antiwar literature can be found in Dr. King's "Beyond Vietnam," James Baldwin's "The War Crimes Tribunal," and Julian Bond's "The Roots of Racism and War," which are reprinted in Clyde Taylor's *Vietnam and Black America: An Anthology of Protest and Resistance.*

Some of the writings on the war focused attention on racism in the military itself. "Black Soldiers Fight Two Enemies in Vietnam," while acknowledging political attempts to end segregation and discrimination in the military, charged that the political reforms failed to solve the real problem of racial prejudice directed at black soldiers. Double standards relative to conduct and military promotions were two distinct points of concern for the black soldier. The black soldier "is convinced that he is a victim of two sets of standards" and is a part of a "racist military." "The War in Vietnam," a 1965 *Freedomways* article, went beyond the normal charge of racial prejudice in the military and asserted that racism in the armed services was a reflection on the U.S. government, which throughout history had allowed racism to flourish within military and civilian life. Past wars against Indians, Mexicans, Filipinos, Cubans, Haitians, and Asians were "but one chapter in a sordid record of crimes that would disgrace a race of savages." In "Whites Against Blacks in Vietnam," the *New Republic* exposed the tension existing between African-American and white soldiers. The "crime of '68," as the King assassination was known, and the continuous battle against discrimination led to race riots, triggered random beatings, and ultimately resulted in the death of soldiers of both races.

The shift to a more strident version of antiwar rhetoric perhaps has no clearly definable moment. The assassination of Martin Luther King in April 1968 undoubtedly unleashed pent-up frustrations and rage in many African Americans. Nathan Hare's "It's Time to Turn the Guns the Other Way" (in Clyde Taylor's *Vietnam and Black America*), as much as any black antiwar expression, reflected the new tenor that began to emerge in the late sixties in the black community. Hare attacked President Nixon's Vietnam policy and the deployment of black American soldiers to a war in which the objective was "annihilation" of black people. Hare, like many antiwar writers, argued that the real enemy was not the Vietcong, but rather "white America."

An added change in the antiwar literature that occurred during the latter part of the 1960s was the shift from articles to books. A significant work that reveals this transition is Eldridge Cleaver's *Soul On Ice*. In his book, Cleaver implies that the exploitation and destruction of blacks transcended the Vietnam War. Cleaver argues that racial genocide was a problem not unique to blacks in the United States, but rather was a critical concern for people of color throughout the world. One of the more compelling works of the genocide thesis to appear was Samuel Yette's *The Choice: The Issue of Black Survival in America*. Yette's award-winning book extended upon Cleaver's argument and suggested that the Vietnam War was but one strategy that one oppressive government was employing to "destroy an obsolete people." Like Cleaver, Yette claimed that the problem of racial genocide was a global phenomenon. The writings of Cleaver, Yette, and several others, most notably psychiatrist Frances Cress Welsing, pivot on a conceptualization of white paranoia and immortality that reached into the very pinnacle of corporate and governmental power.

By the early 1970s the antiwar literature being written in the paranoid style began to fade from popular view as quickly as it had risen. The search for the underlying motives of racism in the government's Vietnam policy and the treatment of nonwhite soldiers were replaced by a simple acknowledgment of military racism. Jack White, in "The Angry Black Soldier," searched for an explanation of racial tension. White discovered that concessions to "the black power boys," interracial dating, and a southern white male–dominated military that still preserved racial discrimination combined to increase racial hostilities.

Another article that reflected the growing concern over military racism was Mark Allen's "The Case of Billy Dean Smith." This 1972 *Black Scholar* article offers a compelling scenario of a black man who resists the Vietnam draft but was still inducted into the service, where he quickly develops a militant and rebellious attitude toward the army, the United

States, and its racist policy in Vietnam. As a consequence of his stance, Smith was charged with the murder of two white officers. He was later acquitted. The trial of Billy Dean symbolizes the dissonance many black soldiers in Vietnam encountered among their moral sensibility, their military obligations, and their confrontation with racial prejudice.

Reflecting on the years of racial strife in the military, William Stuart Gould presented an interesting reevaluation of U.S. Army policies toward African-American soldiers. In "Racial Conflict in the U.S. Army," Gould examined the roots of racial tension and federal government attempts to eliminate racial hostility and "ensure equal treatment" for the African-American soldier. Gould concluded that the army needed to recognize that there was a different "behavioral pattern" among African-American soldiers in regard to the "traditional structure" of the military and that this made it necessary for the military to modify some of its policies.

A final area of popular material on the black experience of the Vietnam War lies in the handful of firsthand accounts and oral histories that have been published in the last two decades. Terry Whitmore's *Memphis-Nam-Sweeden: The Autobiography of a Black American Exile* was one of the initial major works on the Vietnam War as seen by the black soldier. The author, a marine during the war, traced a personal journey from his hometown of Memphis to Southeast Asia and ultimately to Sweden, where he lived in exile following a tour of duty in Vietnam. During the war, like many black soldiers, Whitmore developed antiwar sentiments and found it increasingly difficult to justify his part in helping "Sam do his dirty work" in Vietnam. Also reaching negative conclusions about the war, although less negative than Whitmore's, were David Parks's *GI Diary* and Fenton A. Williams's *Just Before the Dawn: A Doctor's Experiences in Vietnam*. Parks, son of the famed black photojournalist and author Gordon Parks, published his diary in 1968, less than a year after his father's *A Choice of Weapons* was published. Like his father's narrative account of his experiences in the Second World War, the younger Parks's story is driven more by a sense of race and racial discrimination, than of any sense of obligation or opportunity. Williams, a black medical doctor and captain during his tour in Vietnam, wrote in 1971 a moving account of the war from a different standpoint from that of the combat regular. He details the suffering and anguish of war from one who saw brutalities inflicted by both sides on each other. In his conclusion he writes: "If America learns nothing else from the loss of 44,000 lives in Vietnam, she should learn that in this day and age she cannot police the world and force her values on other people. America cannot think she has all to teach and nothing to learn" (127).

Stanley Goff and Robert Sanders's *Brothers: Black Soldiers in the Nam*, published in 1982, is a more recent firsthand account of war. In this book the authors, two black men who met and became close friends in Vietnam, discuss their day-to-day tribulations, many of which relate to their interactions with white soldiers. Goff and Sanders, however, do not present themselves as radicals or as consumed by any anger with whites and their racism. They stress that in the heat of combat the racial animosity harbored in the minds and hearts of black and white soldiers had to become subordinate to the primary objective of survival. "Blacks realize, I'm stuck out here in the boonies and the white guy from the South is stuck out here, and it's life and death" (62). *Brothers* is one of the most balanced of the black soldier accounts.

One of the more powerful works of the African American soldier's experience in Vietnam is Wallace Terry's *Bloods: An Oral History of the Vietnam War by Black Veterans*. Terry's collection of oral interviews of African-American soldiers contains some unique and poignant glimpses into the black reality during the Vietnam War. Story after story attests to the idea that the black soldier's perception of the war underwent a profound transformation. Initially, many black soldiers "supported the war effort." However, the intensification of the civil rights struggle in the States, along with increased racism and discrimination on the war front, served to awaken a dormant antiwar instinct among African-American soldiers. Like Goff and Sanders, Terry's interviews show that beyond the racial crisis on the home front and at base camp, black and white soldiers pulled together in the life-or-death times of combat. Terry's work is particularly useful for at least two reasons. First, the author relates social phenomena on the home front to the plight of the soldier on the war front. Second, he is able to present the war from the minds and hearts of the soldier on the front lines. Terry's ability to unite these dynamics offers the reader an excellent source on the African-American experience in Vietnam.

As this review indicates, the professional study of the history of African Americans and Vietnam is still in its infancy. Presently it faces at least three major problems. First, there is a critical need to provide solid empirical data illustrating the specific character and content of the black soldier's experience in Vietnam, as well as of the impact the war had on black communities in the United States. Second, there is a need for additional studies focusing on the experience of black servicemen and servicewomen away from Vietnam during the 1960s and 1970s. These experiences should then be merged with the Vietnam story in order that an integrated picture of black military life can be produced. Finally, and perhaps most important, a synthesis and interpretation are desperately needed to create a visible order in this field and thereby encourage additional research.

This new field might also profit from exploration of new areas. The new military history, which has risen to prominence with the ascendancy of the "new" social history, could, for example, identify new methodological avenues and topical concerns for history literature in this area. Large social questions need answering. What were the socioeconomic backgrounds of black soldiers in the struggle in Vietnam? What were their religious affiliations and average level of educational attainment? What locations did they come from? Moreover, how did these various factors of economic, regional, educational, religious, and other differences affect their experience of, and adjustment to, the war?

Another specific area of inquiry is the spread of drug addiction among black soldiers both in Vietnam and elsewhere. Did military service increase the likelihood of an African American's becoming addicted to illegal narcotics? Also, what role did military officials play in discouraging or encouraging the abuse of drugs? Furthermore, new studies comparing and contrasting the military experiences of African Americans in Vietnam with other minorities, as well as with the white majority, would be useful. It is yet unclear how similar or dissimilar the wartime experiences of individuals of African descent were to those of other historically dispossessed groups such as Puerto Ricans, Mexican Americans, and Native Americans. One question that emerges is whether black prisoners of war fared better, the same, or worse than whites or other nonwhites of similar rank. Comparative studies of both behavioral and attitudinal variations would provide a greater understanding of the differential experiences of all these groups and would add a new dimension to our understanding of the Vietnam War and its enduring legacy.

The search for the African-American experience in Vietnam must not, moreover, be abandoned for the sake of a convenient, homogenized, and oversimplified picture of the American soldier. The unique way in which African Americans encountered and were a part of the Vietnam War era, once its dark, complex, and sometimes misleading veneer is penetrated, may well open a new door to the very marrow of social conflict and consensus, dissent and loyalty, and anarchic and cohesive impulses in America. The potential is there; let the battle begin.

BIBLIOGRAPHY

Adler, Bill. *The Black Soldier: From the American Revolution to Vietnam*. New York: Morrow, 1971.

Allen, Mark. "The Case of Billy Dean Smith." *Black Scholar* (October 1972): 15–17.

Allen, Robert L. *Black Awakening in Capitalist America: An Analytic History*. Garden City, N.Y.: Anchor Books, 1969.

Badillo, Gilbert, and G. David Curry. "The Social Incidence of Vietnam Casualties: Social Class or Race?" *Armed Forces and Society* 2 (Spring 1976): 397–406.

Berry, Mary Frances. *Military Necessity and Civil Rights Policy: Black Citizenship and the Constitution, 1861–1868.* Port Washington, N.Y.: Kennikat Press, 1977.

Berry, Mary Frances, and John W. Blassingame. *Long Memory: The Black Experience in America.* New York: Oxford University Press, 1982.

Binkin, Martin, and Mark J. Eitelberg, with Alvin J. Schexnider and Marvin M. Smith. *Blacks and the Military.* Washington, D.C.: Brookings Institution, 1982.

"Black Soldiers Fight Two Enemies in Vietnam." *Sepia* 18 (February 1969): 61–62.

Booker, Simon. "Negroes in Vietnam: We, Too, Are Americans." *Ebony* 21 (November 1965): 89–90.

Borus, Jonathan F., Albert F. Dowd, Byron G. Fiman, M. Duncan Stanton. "Racial Perceptions in the Army: An Approach." *American Journal of Psychiatry* 27 (1972): 1369–74.

Boyd, George M. "A Look at Racial Polarity in the Armed Forces." *Air University Review* 21 (September-October 1970): 42–50.

Brown, Wesley. *Tragic Magic: A Novel.* New York: Random House, 1978.

Browne, Robert S. "The Freedom Movement and the War in Vietnam." *Freedomways* 5 (Winter 1965): 467–80.

Butler, John S., and Charles C. Moskos. *Blacks in the Military Since World War II.* Washington, D.C.: National Research Council, 1987.

Butler, John S., and Kenneth L. Wilson. "The American Soldier Revisited: Race Relations and the Military." *Social Science Quarterly* 59 (December 1978): 442–52.

Card, Josefina J. *Lives After Vietnam: The Personal Impact of Military Service.* Lexington, Mass.: Lexington Books, 1983.

Chiricos, Theodore, Michael A. Pearson, and James M. Fendrich. "Status Inconsistency, Militancy and Black Identification Among Black Veterans." *Social Science Quarterly* 51 (December 1970): 572–86.

Clarke, John. *Black Soldier.* Garden City, N.Y.: Doubleday, 1968.

Cleaver, Eldridge. *Soul on Ice.* New York: McGraw-Hill, 1968.

Coates, Charles H. *Military Sociology: A Study of American Military Institutions and Military Life.* University Park, Md.: Social Science Press, 1965.

"Colin L. Powell: The Most Important Soldier in the World." *Black Issues in Higher Education* 7 (April 2, 1990): 2–6.

"Daniel Chappie James: Big Man, Big Message." *Sepia* 17 (April 1968): 64–66.

Darby, Henry E., and Margaret N. Rowley. "King on Vietnam and Beyond." *Phylon* 47 (March 1986): 43–50.

David, Jay, and Elaine Crane. *The Black Soldier from the American Revolution to Vietnam.* New York: Morrow, 1971.

Davis, George. *Coming Home.* New York: Random House, 1972.

Davis, Lenwood G., and George Hill. *Blacks in the American Armed Forces, 1776–1983: A Bibliography.* Westport, Conn.: Greenwood Press, 1985.

Duvall, Henry. "Former Vietnam Official Questions Use of Secret Diplomacy." *About Time* 15 (March 1987): 8–9.

Fairclough, Adam. "Martin Luther King, Jr., and the War in Vietnam." *Phylon* 45 (Spring 1984): 19–39.

Fletcher, Marvin. *America's First Black General: Benjamin O. Davis, Sr. 1880–1970*. Lawrence: University of Kansas Press, 1989.

Foner, Jack D. *Blacks and the Military in American History*. New York: Praeger, 1974.

Goff, Stanley, and Robert Sanders. *Brothers: Black Soldiers in the Nam*. New York: Berkeley Books, 1982.

Gould, William S. "Racial Conflict in the U.S. Army." *Race* 15 (July 1973): 1–27.

Grant, Zalin B. "Whites Against Blacks in Vietnam." *New Republic* 160 (January 18, 1969): 15–16.

Greene, Robert E. *Black Defenders of America, 1775–1973*. Chicago: Johnson, 1974.

Grimes, Kyle. "The Entropics of Discourse: Michael Harper's Debridement and the Myth of the Hero." *Black American Literature Forum* 24 (Fall 1990): 417–40.

Halstead, Fred. *GI's Speak Out Against the War: The Case of the Fort Jackson Eight*. New York: Pathfinder Press, 1970.

Harris, Norman. "Blacks in Vietnam: A Holistic Perspective Through Fiction and Journalism." *Western Journal of Black Studies* 10 (Fall 1986): 121–31.

Herring, George C. *America's Longest War: The United States and Vietnam, 1950–1975*. New York: Random House, 1990.

Hope, Richard O. *Racial Strike in the U.S. Military*. New York: Praeger, 1979.

Johnson, Haynes, and George C. Wilson. *Army in Anguish*. New York: Pocket Books, 1972.

Johnson, Jesse J. *Black Armed Forces Officers, 1736–1971*. Hampton, Va.: Hampton Institute, 1971.

Johnson, Jesse J. *Black Women in the Armed Forces, 1942–1974*. Hampton, Va.: Hampton Institute, 1974.

Johnson, Thomas T. "Negroes in the Nam." *Ebony* (August 1968): 31–40.

Jones, Nathaniel R. *The Search for Military Justice: Report of an NAACP Inquiry into the Problems of Negro Servicemen in West Germany*. New York: NAACP Special Contribution Fund, 1971.

King, Coretta Scott, ed. *The Words of Martin Luther King, Jr.* New York: Newmarket, 1983.

King, Edward L. *The Death of the Army*. New York: Saturday Review Press, 1972.

King, Martin Luther. "A Time to Break the Silence." *Freedomways* 7 (Spring 1967): 103–17.

Knight, Cranston Sedrich, ed. *Tour of Duty: Vietnam in the Words of Those Who Were There*. Richford, Vt.: Samisdat, 1986.

Kolko, Gabriel. *Anatomy of a War*. New York: Pantheon Books, 1985.

Lee, Ulysses. "Draft and the Negro." *Current History* (July 1968): 28–33.

Lewis, Lloyd B. *The Tainted War: Culture and Identity in Vietnam War Narratives*. Westport, Conn.: Greenwood Press, 1985.

MacGregor, Morris J. *Blacks in the Military: Essential Documents*. Wilmington, Del.: Scholarly Resources, 1981a.

MacGregor, Morris J. *Defense Studies: Integration of the Armed Forces*. Washington, D.C.: Center of Military History, 1981b.

MacGregor, Morris J., and Bernard C. Nalty, eds. *Blacks in the United States Armed*

Forces: Basic Documents (Vol. 13). Wilmington, Del.: Scholarly Resources, 1977.

MacPherson, Myra. *Long Time Passing: Vietnam and the Haunted Generation.* Garden City, N.Y.: Doubleday, 1984.

McGovern, James R. *Black Eagle: General Daniel "Chappie" James, Jr.* Tuscaloosa: University of Alabama Press, 1985.

McKissick, Floyd B., and Whitney M. Young, Jr. "The Negro and the Army: Two Views." *New Generation* 48 (Fall 1968): 10–15.

Maurer, Harry. *Strange Ground: Americans in Vietnam, 1945–1975; An Oral History.* New York: Henry Holt, 1989.

Moskos, Charles C., Jr. "The American Dilemma in Form: Racism in the Armed Forces." *American Journal of Sociology* 72 (September 1966): 132–48.

Moskos, Charles C., Jr. "Racial Integration in the Armed Forces." *American Journal of Sociology* 72 (September 1966): 132–48.

Moskos, Charles C., Jr. *The American Enlisted Man.* New York: Russell Sage Foundation, 1970.

Moskos, Charles C., Jr. "Racial Integration in the Armed Forces." *Annals* 406 (March 1973): 94–106.

"Muhammad Ali—The Measure of a Man." *Freedomways* 7 (Spring 1967): 101–2.

Mullen, Robert W. *Blacks in America's Wars.* New York: Pathfinder Press, 1973.

Mullen, Robert W. *Blacks and Vietnam.* Washington, D.C.: University Press of America, 1981.

Nalty, Bernard C. *Strength for the Fight: A History of Blacks in the Military.* New York: Free Press, 1986.

Newlry, John Henry, Jr. "An Assessment of the Relationship Between Racial Perceptions and Patterns of Leadership Behavior Among Black and White Army Company Commanders." Ph.D. diss., Catholic University of America, 1973.

Olson, James S., and Randy Roberts. *Where the Domino Fell: America and Vietnam, 1945 to 1990.* New York: St. Martin's Press, 1991.

Parks, David. *GI Diary.* New York: Harper and Row, 1968.

Parks, Gordon. *A Choice of Weapons.* New York: Harper and Row, 1965.

Rowe, John C., and Richard Berg. *The Vietnam War and American Culture.* New York: Columbia University Press, 1991.

Schexnider, Alvin James. "The Development of Nationalism: Political Socialization Among Blacks in the U.S. Armed Forces." Ph.D. diss., Northwestern University, 1973.

Schexnider, Alvin James. "Blacks in the Military: The Victory and the Challenge." In *The State of Black America 1988*, ed. Janet Dewart. New York: National Urban League, 1988.

Schubert, Fank N. "Black Soldiers on the White Frontier: Some Factors Influencing Race Relations." *Phylon* 32 (Winter 1971): 410–15.

Scruggs, Jan C., and Joel L. Swerdlow. *To Heal a Nation: The Vietnam Veterans Memorial.* New York: Harper and Row, 1985.

Southall, Rita. *The Black Letters: Love Letters from a Black Soldier in Vietnam.* Washington, D.C.: Nuclassics and Science, 1972.

Stewart, Ted. "The Marines Vs. Prejudice." *Sepia* 20 (August 1971): 32–39.

Stillman, Richard J. *The Integration of the Negro in the U.S. Armed Forces.* New York: Praeger, 1968.

Stillman, Richard J. "Negroes in the U.S. Armed Forces." *Phylon* 30 (Summer 1969): 139–59.

Taylor, Clyde, ed. *Vietnam and Black America: An Anthology of Protest and Resistance.* Garden City, N.Y.: Anchor Books, 1973.

Terry, Wallace. *Bloods: An Oral History of the Vietnam War by Black Veterans.* New York: Random House, 1984.

Terry, Wallace. "Bloods: An Oral History of the Vietnam War by Black Veterans." *Afro-Americans in New York Life and History* 10 (January 1986): 76–86.

"Two Black Generals." *Negro History Bulletin* 34 (April 1971): 93.

U.S. Commission on Civil Rights. South Dakota Advisory Committee. *Negro Airmen in a Northern Community, Discrimination in Rapid City, South Dakota.* Washington, D.C.: U.S. Government Printing Office, 1963.

U.S. President's Committee on Equal Opportunity in the Armed Forces. *Equality of Treatment and Opportunity for Negro Military Personnel Stationed Within the U.S.* Washington, D.C.: U.S. Government Printing Office, 1963.

Vance, Samuel. *The Courageous and the Proud.* New York: Norton, 1970.

"Vietnam." In *The Negro Almanac: The Afro-American.* New York: Wiley Press, 1980.

"The War in Vietnam." *Freedomways* (Spring 1965): 229–30.

Watson, D. L. "Search for Justice Continues." *Crisis* 43 (October 1971): 258–59.

Watts, Daniel H. "Reverend King and Vietnam." *Liberator Magazine* (May 1967): 3.

Webb, Percy R. *Memoranda of a Soldier.* New York: Vantage Press, 1961.

Weigert, Kathleeen Maas. "Stratification and Minority Group Ideology: Black Soldiers' Beliefs About Military and Civilian Opportunity." Ph.D. diss., University of Notre Dame, 1972.

White, Jack. "The Angry Black Soldier." *Progressive* 34 (March 1970): 22–26.

White, James S. "Race Relations in the Army." *Military Review* 50 (July 1970): 3–12.

White, Milton. "Malcolm X in the Military." *Black Scholar* 1 (May 1970): 3–12.

Whitmore, Terry. *Memphis-Nam-Sweden: The Autobiography of a Black American Exile.* Garden City, N.Y.: Doubleday, 1972.

Williams, Fenton A. *Just Before the Dawn: A Doctor's Experiences in Vietnam.* New York: Exposition Press, 1971.

Williams, John A. *Captain Blackman.* Garden City, N.Y.: Doubleday, 1972.

Williams, Juan. *Eyes on the Prize.* New York: Viking, 1987.

Willis, Williams S. "Divide and Rule: Red, White and Black in the Southeast." *Journal of Negro History* 48 (July 1963): 157–76.

Yarmolinsky, Adam. *The Military Establishment: Its Impact on American Society.* New York: Harper Colophon, 1971.

Yette, Samuel. *The Choice: The Issue of Black Survival in America.* Silver Spring, Md.: Cottage Books, 1971.

Zaroulis, Nancy, and Gerald Sullivan. *Who Spoke Up: American Protest Against the War in Vietnam.* Garden City, N.Y.: Doubleday, 1986.

Zelik, Melvin. "The Census and Selective Service." *Eugenics Quarterly* 15 (September 1968): 173–76.

PART VI

The Home Front and American Culture

16   The Antiwar Movement

Marilyn Clark

The Vietnam War, the longest military conflict in U.S. history, deeply divided the nation in the 1960s and early 1970s. Public opinion polls reflected the disunity of the American people on the issue of the Vietnam War, discord that increased as American involvement in the war escalated. The war was a principal cause of the turmoil that was a characteristic of this era of recent American history. Much has been written about the various aspects of the Vietnam War, including the movement that developed in opposition to it. The literature of the antiwar movement fits into two broad categories: books that describe the entire movement and those that focus on some particular element of the opposition to the war. The first group of books provides the big picture of the movement, offering an overall view of the different groups that comprised the opposition to the Johnson and Nixon administrations. The second group of books turns its attention to the individual segments of the nation that objected to the war—intellectuals, blacks, veterans, pacifists, religious leaders, and others.

Thomas Powers offers his account of the antiwar movement in *Vietnam: The War at Home, Vietnam and the American People, 1964–1968*. Published in 1984, Powers confines his examination of the movement to the years of the Johnson administration, 1964–1968. Powers, an opponent of the war, is concerned that the antiwar movement is in danger of being written out of history, and he seeks to emphasize the movement's achievements. *Vietnam: The War at Home* presents the picture of a movement that was able to create the conditions that necessitated Johnson's shift from further escalation of the war to disengagement in Southeast Asia. By 1968 the opponents of the war had successfully pursued two strategies that forced the president to abandon his policy of escalation. They had

operated within the nation's political system, and they had taken their
opposition to the war into the streets.

   Ordinary citizens, firm in their belief that the war was wrong, employed a wide variety of tactics to express their opposition. Using demonstrations, teach-ins, petitions, draft resistance, involvement in electoral
politics, public fasting, and other methods, a broad-based opposition
brought the United States to a very serious crisis in late 1967 and early
1968. The major public figures who became critics of the war were led
by the antiwar movement, rather than leading the opposition to the war.
Those who opposed the war, often disagreeing among themselves about
tactics, refused to allow the issue to die, escalating their efforts even as
the Johnson administration expanded American military efforts in Vietnam.

   Powers argues that North Vietnam and the National Liberation Front
were encouraged to continue fighting not because they believed that the
antiwar movement possessed any potential political power, but because
of the way the United States elected to pursue its military objectives.
Hanoi seemed to assume that an opposition would arise in the United
States when America failed in Vietnam. Powers contends that the antiwar
movement was not responsible for the failure of American policy. However, the movement functioned to compel the government to acknowledge its unsuccessful policy.

   Published in 1984, *Who Spoke Up? American Protest Against the War in
Vietnam, 1963–1975* surveys the protest movement from 1963 through
1975. In this sympathetic portrayal of the opponents of the war, Nancy
Zaroulis and Gerald Sullivan argue that the movement represented a
unique protest—it was the first time that so many citizens had freely told
their government that it was pursuing the wrong policy in wartime.
Expressing their outrage at their government's policy, the war's opponents used many methods to attempt to persuade their officials to alter
what they believed to be a disastrous policy—lobbying, civil disobedience,
destruction of draft board records, letters, refusal to pay taxes, and many
more. The authors characterize the antiwar movement as originating in
a sense of patriotism, refuting suggestions that it was in any way anti-
American. They believe that the movement survived the government's
attempts to destroy it because it actually spoke for America's best interests. The movement restored the nation's honor by telling the truth about
American policy to people who were not eager to hear it. Zaroulis and
Sullivan compare the antiwar movement with the abolitionists of the
nineteenth century, maintaining that both groups acted according to
their consciences.

   Who Spoke Up? is concerned with establishing the correct image of the
war's opponents because the authors believe that the antiwar movement
has been incorrectly characterized by some people, especially those who

disagreed with it. Several inaccurate perceptions of the movement are refuted, including the notion that foreign powers inspired or led it. Zaroulis and Sullivan assert that opposition to the Vietnam War was "a homegrown movement of the Left which eventually encompassed the entire political spectrum; it was American born and bred" (xii). The movement, begun and led by pacifists, was not a violent one. In addition, it was not simply a movement of young people. It is presented as a movement that was "conceived, nurtured, and largely directed by adults" (xii). Young people played an important role in the efforts to end the war, but a large segment of the movement's membership was composed of people over thirty.

The authors set out to correct other false perceptions of the war's critics, declaring that the movement was not made up of people too cowardly to fight for their country. Those who opposed the war often did so at great personal cost. The leaders of the movement were primarily people who lived a conventional life-style, and opponents of the war did not represent "a movement of licentious counterculturals living a sexually promiscuous lifestyle" (xii). The movement was an "often uneasy coalition of groups and individuals who often disagreed on every issue except their hatred of the war" (xii). There was no party line followed by everyone who opposed the Vietnam War, and throughout its existence the movement was split by internal disputes over tactics, basic philosophy, policy, and programs it should advocate. Arguing that the war and the movement to end it "consumed the passions of a generation" (xiv), Zaroulis and Sullivan state their belief that the Vietnam generation was only detoured by the war. As *Who Spoke Up?* appeared in 1984, they felt that the Vietnam generation's political power was beginning to have an impact in American life.

Charles DeBenedetti and Charles Chatfield provide a more thorough evaluation of the antiwar movement than Zaroulis and Sullivan in *An American Ordeal: The Antiwar Movement of the Vietnam Era* (1989). They set the antiwar movement in its social context—peace reform—arguing that the movement started liberal, then became radical, finally returning to being liberal. The movement, which tended to be more antiwar than it was peace-seeking, "was a loose alignment of elements which changed in style, tactics, and thrust during the era" (1). During the 1960s the movement grew from a few dozen organizations to more than 1,200. The majority of the groups were local and transient in nature, the movement failing to develop "a single directing agency, common leadership, or ideology" (2).

The antiwar movement, which was in the long tradition of citizen peace activism that had addressed such issues as international disarmament and had been antagonistic to an interventionist foreign policy, made use of a wide range of methods to call attention to the government's incorrect policy in Southeast Asia. These tactics varied from letter writing, lobbying, prayer vigils, electoral politics, and teach-ins, to bombings, destruction of draft records, and self-immolation. The authors suggest that the "very diversity of dissent increased its outreach, for its leadership permeated the society from the most elite and conventional to the most antisocial elements" (2). The movement should be measured by the influence it exercised, not the number of people who comprised its constituency. The actions undertaken by the war's critics thrust the Vietnam War into the public arena, spawned an organized opposition to intervention in Indochina, and drove the government to make increasingly larger claims for the war.

The antiwar movement was linked to the other cultural and social protests of the 1960s, a relationship not emphasized by Zaroulis and Sullivan in their analysis of the movement. DeBenedetti and Chatfield also cite another characteristic of the movement: it was vulnerable to fragmentation, a trait they attribute to its leaders' differing over the most appropriate tactics and whether to devote the movement's energies only to ending the war or to creating an extensive coalition to work for social change in the United States. The opponents of the Vietnam War basically argued that the military involvement in Asia was having a detrimental effect on the United States. *An American Ordeal* asserts that even though the war was fought in Vietnam, "the ordeal for the antiwar movement and the citizens it sought to mobilize was in and over America" (5).

A 1991 addition to the literature of the antiwar movement is *The Debate Over Vietnam*, a new study written by Professor David W. Levy of the University of Oklahoma. According to Levy, the movement acquired its form in the twenty months after the beginning of 1964. With the increasing American involvement in the war and the growing frustration with the progress of the war, the movement gathered strength and knitted together large portions of the American public in opposition to the war.

Levy emphasizes that the debate over the war was carried out in traditional terms; it was debated in the context of whether or not Vietnam was a just war. He places the Vietnam War in the broad framework of America's military involvements throughout its history, noting that the lack of unity with regard to Vietnam was much more typical of responses to other war efforts than it was unique. The central argument of the war's opponents involved an attack upon the morality of the conflict, the accusation of immorality remaining the central core of resistance to government policy.

Americans who opposed all wars were among the first to voice their disapproval of the Vietnam War, but the most forceful dissent came from people who "were revolted by the Vietnam War in particular" (48). There were three issues in the debate over the morality of the war: its legality, the question of whether the war in Vietnam was an invasion or a civil war, and the nature of the fighting. Opponents of the war maintained that there was no legal basis for the war, that the struggle in Vietnam was a civil war in which the United States did not need to be involved, and that the war was "a war of destruction upon a primitive, peasant, agricultural society" (55). Critics of the war were especially vehement in their attacks upon the extensive bombing program, noting that two-thirds of the tonnage was dropped on South Vietnam.

Levy points out that the antiwar movement, in spite of its successes, weakened by the end of the decade. The movement was afflicted by two major problems: internal quarreling over goals and methods and the fact that as the war wound down through the process of Vietnamization, fewer people were eager to protest the continuing war. The movement was also weakened in 1972 as the presidential election siphoned off its energies. The weak and ineffective protest that was voiced at the December 1972 bombing of North Vietnam was a measure of the movement's declining strength.

William F. Gausman's *Red Stains on Vietnam Doves* is a polemic against the antiwar movement. Gausman, a minister who believes that anti-Americanism was rampant in the United States in the 1960s, proclaims that the baby-boomer generation was an easy target for pro-Communist ideas and that the argument that the United States was intervening in a civil war in Vietnam was the primary justification for the position taken by critics of the war. The antiwar movement became a real power in the United States, its radicals defeating each presidential action designed to win the war. Gausman criticizes the liberal clergy who aligned themselves with the antiwar movement, labeling Clergy and Laymen Concerned About Vietnam (CALCAV) "an extreme leftist organization" (5).

Red Stains on Vietnam Doves argues that the antiwar movement perpetuated misconceptions about the war, that pacifism was a great obstacle blocking the path to an enduring peace, and that Ho Chi Minh took advantage of the antiwar sentiment in the United States. Gausman indicts the war's critics for being responsible for causing Johnson and Nixon to withhold the force needed to achieve a victory in Vietnam and for providing a "great boost to Communist morale" through their dissent (170).

The words used to express opposition to the government's war policy are analyzed in *Rhetoric and American Democracy: Black Protest Through Vietnam Dissent* (1985). Randall M. Fisher examines the arguments of those who protested, arguments that ranged from calls for a quick and total military victory to demands for the immediate withdrawal of American forces. The message of the peace movement implied that the war should be ended without the achievement of a definite victory, a suggestion that "created so much dissonance for so many Americans that it stimulated every defense mechanism available" (258). Fisher finds no evidence that the antiwar rhetoric was responsible for Americans' coming to the conclusion that the war was a mistake. He argues that the length of the conflict, the high casualty rate, and the failure to win a decisive victory probably caused people to turn against the war. The antiwar movement, which was strongly identified with the hippies and flower children of the era, was more unpopular than the war itself. Fisher maintains that the principal reason the antiwar movement failed to convince the public of its views was that some of its participants had damaged the reputation of the entire movement. The movement was generally peaceful, but the entire movement suffered when violence did occur, even though the violence was usually not initiated by protesters. Although no study provided proof that the rhetoric of the peace movement was controlled by Communist participants, Johnson and Nixon explained dissent as being inspired by Communists.

Comparing the rhetoric of the civil rights and antiwar movements, Fisher concludes that the antiwar movement was less effective in accomplishing its objectives. The antiwar movement, unlike the civil rights movement, suffered from several handicaps: no competent central leadership and organization, no protection for the credibility of its communicators, the failure to make its position clear enough so that the public would accurately perceive it, and the inability to advance a realistic, definite course of action. The civil rights movement, avoiding all these pitfalls, was much more successful in reaching its goals.

Rhetoric and American Democracy also points out that the hawks, who spent more time attacking the war's critics than providing their own specific proposals, also "failed in their argumentative goals" (234). Dismissing the notion that protest shortened the war, Fisher believes that a better argument can be made that the rhetoric of the antiwar movement was responsible for altering the way the war was prosecuted or that it had no effect on war policy or that it lengthened the war.

Irving Louis Horowitz, a professor of sociology, examines the antiwar movement in a book published during the war, *The Struggle Is the Message: The Organization and Ideology of the Anti-War Movement* (1970). The author arrives at several key conclusions about the movement, which he notes had a definite pacifist bias and "grew out of the stimulus provided by the civil rights movement" (13, 26). The antiwar movement, which was controlled by white liberals and radicals, was basically a nonviolent protest. The violence associated with the antiwar movement was mostly directed against property, particularly targeting government and state property. Most of the violence that accompanied the protests was "externally generated by pressures upon law enforcement agencies to keep greater law and order" (115). The violence connected with the movement often involved "confrontations over symbols rather than over the exact issues involved in any specific struggle" (115). Although the antiwar movement frequently emulated many of the tactics of the civil rights movement, it was concerned with different issues. Where the civil rights movement focused on "problems of integration and increased participation in the benefits of American society," the critics of the Vietnam War were "clearly concerned with the issues of legitimation and alienation" (115). Writing as the war continued, Horowitz indicates that the movement was characterized by factionalism, the movement splitting into small cells, each of which was linked to a different element of opposition to the war.

Horowitz states that the destruction of the antiwar movement would have been a loss to the "integrity of American democracy" (119). The movement had several effects—causing the disruption of government operations, increasing the costs of domestic military preparedness, stimulating disaffiliation from the major political parties, and being a general nuisance for the nation's police forces. The use of pragmatic violence, emphasizing attacks on convenient symbols of the enemy instead of endeavoring to change the conventional political pattern, resulted from the "inability of either major party to mount and sustain a meaningful peace offensive" (144). At the time of his examining the antiwar movement, Horowitz concludes that "the politics of protest has been transformed into the politics of polarization" (145). The antiwar movement, having lost a great deal of its independence by the end of the decade, found its ideology and organization being included in more directly political struggles, which consisted of "party conflicts within the liberal faction and revolutionary violence within the radical faction" (145). Horowitz closes his study of the antiwar movement by predicting that the protesters had introduced issues that would not be settled in an easy, quick manner.

Melvin Small's *Johnson, Nixon, and the Doves* (1988) focuses on a different aspect of the antiwar movement—its impact on Lyndon Johnson and Richard Nixon. Making use of government documents, presidential papers, interviews, and secondary sources, Small concludes that the antiwar movement did influence the policy decisions of both administrations, the greater impact being made on the Johnson administration. The first major example cited by Small involves the initial bombing of North Vietnam, an escalation of the war that resulted in protests, including teach-ins, at several universities around the country. Johnson administration officials reacted to the fledgling peace movement in several ways, including dispatching administration spokesmen to present the government's case on college campuses, assisting organizers of parades designed to support the troops, and calling in the Federal Bureau of Investigation (FBI) and the CIA to harass and investigate the activities of the movement. The doves played a role in Johnson's decision to halt temporarily the bombing of North Vietnam in May 1965. The antiwar

activists' attacks upon administration officials contributed to the resig-
nations of McGeorge Bundy and Robert McNamara.

Through its unenthusiastic and even hostile attitude toward Hubert
Humphrey in the 1968 election, the movement unintentionally helped
Nixon win the presidency. Endeavoring to counter his radical and liberal
adversaries in the antiwar movement, Nixon made his famous "silent
majority" speech in 1969 and turned Vice President Agnew loose to
assail the protesters and the press. Nixon, who was more convinced than
Johnson that antiwar leaders were working with Communists, undertook
a secret intelligence war against the movement, a tactic that contributed
to the weakening of dissenters. Small credits the antiwar movement with
persuading Nixon to refrain from initiating a massive bombing attack
in 1969 and imposing Vietnamization on him as the only strategy the
nation would accept.

Small notes that *Johnson, Nixon, and the Doves* reaffirms the fact that
presidents do react to criticism and challenges to their policies, even
when it comes from a minority. The lesson Small draws from his study
is that "those who exercise their rights as citizens to gather, protest, and
petition in comparatively small numbers have much more of an impact
on their leaders than one would expect. Such a conclusion might help
to sustain others who question present and future foreign policies" (234).

One source of criticism of the Vietnam War was the intellectual community. Much of the challenge to the war policies of Johnson and Nixon
originated on university campuses. An example of this component of
the antiwar movement is a book by historian Arthur M. Schlesinger, Jr.,
The Bitter Heritage: Vietnam and American Democracy, 1941–1966. Pointing
out that the United States had become entrapped in an Asian land war
one step at a time, Schlesinger calls for a scaled-down military commitment in Vietnam. Advocating a middle course of action characterized
by no further escalation and no immediate withdrawal, *The Bitter Heritage*
suggests a policy consisting of several elements: halting bombing raids,
ceasing search and destroy efforts, confining military operations to re-
taining areas already under American control, and working out a negotiated settlement of the war. A precipitous departure would be unwise
because it would create adverse reverberations throughout Southeast
Asia, but the process of ending U.S. involvement must be begun because
the manner in which the war is being conducted is exacting a great cost
both at home and overseas. Schlesinger cautions Americans that they
confront a test of their democracy and that they must not allow the
Vietnam War to debase their national life.

Sandy Vogelgesang's *The Long Dark Night of the Soul: The American
Intellectual Left and the Vietnam War* (1974) is an analysis of the intelligentsia's critique of the longest war in American history. The intellectual
left, which had been inactive in the Eisenhower era, was unable to func-

tion as an early critic of war policy because of its connection with the liberal bipartisanship of diplomacy in the period after the Second World War. The author, a career foreign service officer in the State Department, defines the intellectual left as the group of people who centered around four publications: *The New Republic, Partisan Review, Studies on the Left,* and *New York Review of Books.*

In the early 1960s few intellectuals spoke out about the war, even though the seed of all the principal arguments that were used later in the Johnson administration existed while Kennedy was president. A symbiotic relationship existed between the Kennedy administration and the intelligentsia, and Johnson began his presidency with noticeable attempts to court the intellectual community. The first criticism of Johnson's policy was generally polite in tone, but later in the decade the intellectual left's opposition to the war was bitter, including a vendetta against Johnson because they believed the president had betrayed them after the 1964 election.

Vogelgesang traces the development of the intellectual left's criticism of the Vietnam War through three distinct stages. The first stage, beginning in the early 1960s and lasting until early 1965, was the period in which they saw the war as only a lapse in judgment, a deplorable departure from America's national interest. The first turning point in U.S. involvement, the Gulf of Tonkin incident, stunned the intellectual community, which condemned the retaliatory air strikes ordered by Johnson. The intellectual left perceived the war to be an exercise in immorality from early 1965 through the end of 1966. Finally, in 1967 and 1968, intellectuals viewed the war as a reflection of the government's political illegitimacy.

By the end of the Johnson administration, intellectuals occupied a position on the border of American politics. Divided, bitter, and powerless, they had not ended the war or caused most Americans to change their thinking about the government's policies. Vogelgesang argues that there were several causes of their failure: their inability to speak persuasively to the public, their hatred of "midcult" and fear of the "tyranny of the majority," the intermittent struggle between the left and liberals, and the internal discord that plagued their community. The intellectuals depended too much on students and blacks, two marginal segments of the population that shared their concern about the war.

Although the intellectuals failed to persuade the public or the government to adopt their moral case against the Vietnam War, they did "set in motion some important new considerations for American foreign policy" (176). First, their participation in the opposition to the war contributed to the undermining of Johnson's consensus. Second, their criticism of the Vietnam War restored the "beneficial exercise of debate of American foreign policy" (177).

One of the important constituent groups of the antiwar movement was comprised of veterans who opposed the war in which they had fought. The most significant organization in this category was the Vietnam Veterans Against the War (VVAW). The VVAW, concerned about the type of war being fought in Southeast Asia, conducted an investigation in Detroit in 1971. Veterans were invited to participate in the Winter Soldier Investigation, an event the organization described as an inquiry into American war crimes committed in Vietnam. The My Lai incident had received a great deal of public attention, but the VVAW wanted to demonstrate that My Lai was not an aberration. *The Winter Soldier Investigation: An Inquiry into American War Crimes* (1972) provides a presentation of the testimony offered by many of the veterans who attended the convention, evidence that dealt with many aspects of the soldiers' experiences in Vietnam—combat experiences, the medical care received during the war, racism, the weapons employed in the war, prisoners of war, the ravaging of Vietnam, and the psychological impact of the war on veterans. The purpose of the convention was to prevent the continuance of the inhumanity the veterans had been part of during the war. The organizers of the convention hoped that the publicizing of the experiences dramatically described in Detroit would have a positive effect on the nation as the veterans provided their realistic accounts of the war.

David S. Surrey, who counseled men during the Vietnam era on the draft and military decisions, has studied draft evaders and deserters who became exiles in Canada. The results of his study are presented in *Choice of Conscience: Vietnam Era Military and Draft Registers in Canada*, a book published in 1982. Surrey argues that class has been the most significant factor in determining liability to conscription and combat service, as well as patterns of desertion and draft resistance. Class predicted who would get out and stay out of military service. His study confirms that draft resisters tended to come from relatively privileged socioeconomic backgrounds and that men from such backgrounds were more successful than the less privileged in assimilating into Canadian society.

During the Vietnam War, members of all classes pushed the limits of resistance and avoidance to a greater degree than in any other period of American history. The attack on the military procurement system was a major contributor to ending the war. Concluding that America and the war in Vietnam were not worth fighting for in the 1960s, the draft and military resisters chose exile in Canada, with class paving different paths for each group. The higher-class draft evader, who did not have to leave America until forced to do so by imminent induction or status reclassification, had time to plan his transition into a new life in Canada. On the other hand, military deserters were usually politicized after they entered military service, a situation that left them less time and fewer choices. Both groups experienced a conversion of their attitudes, where they had once been either indifferent or patriotic, they became convinced that America's involvement in Vietnam was wrong and that military service was reprehensible. The only possible alternative for them was exile, "an act of resistance against a nation involved in an indefensible war" (Surrey, 103). Both moral commitment and personal self-interest helped shape their views.

Surrey found that the draft dodgers were more likely to be warmly welcomed into Canadian society than military deserters, the draft evaders' middle- and upper-class backgrounds blending in with "Canada's selective immigration policy" (121). Many Canadians were pleased that most of the exiles intended to become permanent residents and had compiled a positive record, facts that helped to diminish their skepticism and resentment toward the draft dodgers and deserters. Surrey notes that most of the exiles gave up on the United States, an attitude that he feels is "the saddest commentary on what the Vietnam War did to the United States" (103).

Two lawyers who served on President Ford's Clemency Board have written *Chance and Circumstance: The Draft, the War, and the Vietnam Generation*, a book that refutes the mistaken impression that affluent, well-educated radicals refused to serve in the military during the Vietnam era, their motivation being either conscience or cowardice. Lawrence M. Baskir and William A. Strauss characterize the draft as inequitable and unfair, a system in which men with money and education escaped military service while the poor and uneducated fought and died in the war. By 1971 implementation of the draft laws was in shambles, local draft boards having adopted widely varying standards for granting deferments and conscientious objector status and for prosecuting violators of the laws.

Baskir and Strauss conclude that resisters and deserters were from the same group of poor and uneducated men who did most of the fighting and dying in Vietnam, basing their conclusion on a sample of draft offenders whose cases came before the Clemency Board, which recommended pardons in 80 percent of the cases. The authors note that politically motivated deserters greatly exceeded those whose absences from their posts were not directly related to their attitude toward the war. These men, many of them blacks and Hispanics, had been unwilling or unable to take advantage of methods by which they could have escaped the draft. Young men from more privileged backgrounds had the greatest number of escape routes from military service—status deferments, physical exemptions, and safe enlistments. College graduates, who comprised a mere 2 percent of all draftees, had much greater access to draft counselors who could apprise them of their rights and options, a situation that shifted the burden of fighting the war to an even greater degree to those who were socially and economically disadvantaged. Baskir and Strauss are critical of Project 100,000, Johnson's plan to use military training and discipline to rehabilitate America's disadvantaged youth. Labeling it a cynical political act, they argue it permitted the administration to carry on the war without calling up the reserves or ending deferments for sons of the middle class, a politically sensitive constituency Johnson did not wish to offend.

Chance and Circumstance points out that many cases of draft violators were dismissed, generally for one of two reasons: procedural errors in the cases or the legal system's inability to deal with the large number of cases with which the opponents of the draft overwhelmed it. The penalties that were imposed were harsher than those handed out in World War II and the Korean War, but they were imposed more sparingly than the public was led to believe. Only 3,250 men were ever jailed for violation of the draft laws. Baskir and Strauss, arguing that Ford's clemency program and Carter's blanket pardon program were ineffective in dealing with the problem of the large-scale resistance to military service, note that just 6 percent of the eligible resisters applied for clemency, and only 99 of 265,000 resisters sought pardons through the Carter program. Writing in 1978, the authors express their fear that the nation's experience with conscription during the Vietnam War had shaken the "nation's confidence that it can order young people to fight in anything short of an unquestioned national emergency" (236).

The Resistance, an organization whose aim was to cripple the conscription system, is explained as a collective political protest in Michael Useem's *Conscription, Protest, and Social Conflict: The Life and Death of a Draft Resistance Movement* (1973). Useem, a sociologist, labels the movement radical in terms of its ideological orientation. Like the civil rights and free speech movements, it was a norm- and value-oriented movement that originally endeavored simply to avoid the draft. Later, the Resistance, which never grew to more than a few thousand members, tried to change the way the United States conducted its political business with other countries. The political and economic climate of the United States during the Vietnam War caused the organization's leaders to perceive the larger issue to be changing the political and economic philosophy of the nation, including its general concept of property, an idea that embraced youth as a form of property. Useem argues that when the movement arrived at this stage of political awareness, it assumed its radical position.

The organization, whose membership consisted mostly of white, middle-class students or former students, built its assault on the draft on the idea that its constituency was an "oppressed class," a group that could be "mobilized through traditional means of class conflict protest" (39). Their program was directed at the government, their objective being to urge "a wholesale exodus of eligible youth from the draft pool" (6). Hoping to end the war by depriving the military of its manpower needs, the protests themselves were trying to change the political arrangements of the nation, not asking the government to make changes. The Resistance, begun in the fall of 1967 and beginning to falter by the spring of 1968, was unable to build a long-term commitment to its cause, a situation resulting in its membership ranks' remaining too small to have the effect on the government it desired. Its program of noncooperation with the conscription system had little appeal for working-class youths, students holding deferments, and the radical left. Its emphasis on directly attacking government authority "left the Resistance without prospects for local campaigns that could yield small but tangible victories" (285). Useem maintains that it had originally been united by political action, not by political beliefs.

Black Americans opposed the war in Vietnam, one of the most eloquent critics of the war coming from their ranks. Stephen B. Oates's *Let the Trumpet Sound: The Life of Martin Luther King, Jr.* describes the process by which the civil rights leader came to be increasingly fearful of the Johnson administration policies in Vietnam. King openly broke with the administration over its war policy in 1967, a split that had begun in 1965 when he began to see a definite link between the government's foreign and domestic policies. King believed that the war in Asia was detrimental to efforts to create a more just society at home, but many of his advisors urged King to refrain from openly criticizing the government because such criticism could jeopardize congressional and presidential support for the domestic reform programs favored by the civil rights movement. Recognizing the generally strong support the administration enjoyed, many people in the Southern Christian Leadership Conference feared the loss of support that could result from King's criticizing the war. King, troubled by the question of how to deal with his growing opposition to the war, restricted his criticism of the war, urging an end to the bombing raids and the initiation of negotiations to end the conflict. Even this relatively mild denunciation of the war brought King a swift, hostile reaction from people who questioned his right to criticize the nation's foreign policy.

In 1967 King could no longer mute his protest, and in that year he began to speak out very forcefully on the immorality of the war, first in Los Angeles in February and especially in New York in April, when he spelled out the reasons for his condemnation of the Vietnam War. He emphasized the ways in which the war was destroying the moral fabric of the nation and the immense damage being inflicted upon the Vietnamese. His eloquent criticism of the war made him the most prominent American in the antiwar movement and its most popular voice. The Johnson administration closely monitored King's activities, hoping to discover a link to Communists, an association that could be used to discredit King and the antiwar movement. King continued his pleas to end the war until his assassination in April 1968.

Vietnam and Black America: An Anthology of Protest and Resistance, edited by Clyde Taylor, offers a wide range of writing illustrating the opposition many blacks felt toward the war. Taylor includes several forms of written denunciation of the Vietnam War—poems, essays, speeches, short stories, excerpts from novels, editorials, manifestos, interviews, and press releases. According to Taylor, there were significant differences between black and majority opposition to the war. He emphasizes the different motivations of the two groups, contending that the majority turned against the war out of a sense of "fatigue and frustration with the war's particular lack of success" (xviii). On the other hand, blacks became critics of the war because they viewed it in the context of their personal concern for human rights and racial justice. Blacks, being excluded from the discussions of national policy, needed to send a clear, well-defined message of opposition that did not merely echo the national movement. That message had to address the war in terms of the question of the health or illness of civilizations. In the early 1970s most blacks still regarded the war and racial conflicts at home as the most significant issues that needed to be addressed by Americans, while white Americans tended to state that the economy and busing were their preeminent concerns. There was a linkage between the "obscene bloodletting in Vietnam" and "the unprincipled repression aimed at their liberation struggle" at home, the origins of both events being found "deep in the fibers of American life and history" (xx).

Black opposition to the Vietnam War was characterized by several qualities: a decentralized structure, infrequent demonstrations, occasional coalitions with the national antiwar movement, and "courageous stands taken by hundreds of solitary blacks symbolized by the individual acts of resistance of King, Muhammad Ali, Julian Bond, and Malcolm X" (xx). Taylor points out that polls indicate that in the earlier phases of the war a majority of blacks agreed with national war policy, but as the war continued, black opposition to it was consistently ahead of national opposition. Taylor, noting that there was not much reasoned black opinion published supporting the war, includes no authors whose works upheld the government's policy. *Vietnam and Black America* highlights the words of a wide range of black spokesmen against America's longest and most controversial war, from "statesmen" such as Martin Luther King, Julian Bond, and Malcolm X to "radicals" such as Eldridge Cleaver, Stokely Carmichael, and Huey Newton.

E. Raymond Wilson's *Uphill for Peace: Quaker Impact on Congress* contains two chapters devoted to a description of the Friends' efforts to protest the Vietnam War. The author, a lobbyist and the first executive secretary of the Friends Committee on National Legislation (FCNL), points out that, very early, the Quakers denounced the intervention of the United States in what they regarded as fundamentally a revolution within South Vietnam against a despotic regime. In their traditionally evenhanded criticism, the FCNL also expressed its condemnation of the violence of the Vietcong and the North Vietnamese action that forced hundreds of thousands of people to flee to South Vietnam.

As early as 1954 the FCNL newsletter cautioned against U.S. involvement in a war in Vietnam, advocating instead a general settlement in Asia that "would shift the emphasis of the conflict from a military basis to a political and economic basis" (Wilson, 281). Throughout the years of American intervention in Southeast Asia, the FCNL was busy with conventional lobbying activities designed to bring an end to a conflict it described as a "war of indescribable barbarity" (276). Encouraging people to contact their congressional representatives, the Quakers set up committees to disseminate information about the war, published documents on the Tonkin Gulf Resolution and other subjects, conferred with leaders of Congress, brought speakers and experts on Vietnam to address the decision makers on Capitol Hill, and dispatched delegations to visit administration officials.

The FCNL also cooperated with other groups, such as the American Friends Service Committee, always emphasizing the cost of the war in human terms. In electoral political activity, FCNL published, without official endorsement, lists of peace candidates and urged the two major parties to adopt planks calling for an end to the war in their 1968 platforms. The organization's efforts included working on problems closely linked to the war—the draft, prisoners of war, and men missing in action.

Mitchell K. Hall analyzes one of the most important religious organizations opposing the war in *Because of Their Faith: CALCAV and Religious Opposition to the Vietnam War*. CALCAV played a key role in mobilizing the religious community to take ecumenical social action against the war. Appealing primarily to theological and social liberals in mainstream Protestant denominations, it attracted some conservatives and radicals as well as functioning as "one of the first important channels for Jewish and Catholic peace activism" (171).

Originating in New York in 1965, the group served as a protest vehicle for clergy and laity from churches that were silent on the war issue. Established to help defend the right to dissent, CALCAV, which was clearly in the mainstream of American life, argued that nothing was accomplished by escalating the war and advocated a negotiated settlement to end it. Adopting a moderate tone and asserting its patriotic motivation in opposing the Vietnam War, CALCAV combined moral and pragmatic arguments in voicing its condemnation of the war. Always careful to avoid extreme arguments and tactics, CALCAV expressed its opposition in ways that kept it on good terms with its basically white, middle-class, religiously motivated constituency, which proved to be the source of a great deal of its success. As it chose to remain formally independent of the broader antiwar coalition, its "association with the American religious mainstream earned it greater respect in the Johnson administration than most other antiwar groups" (37).

During the war its membership became larger and more varied, a development that produced tension within CALCAV, a strain growing between those who advocated focusing exclusively on ending the war and those who favored action to deal with a wider range of social justice issues. Before turning to other issues in 1975, the organization had played an important part in influencing public opinion to oppose the war, limiting the government's option in conducting the war, and helping defend the right to disagree. CALCAV, as described by Hall in *Because of Their Faith,* is certainly not the extremist organization referred to in Gausman's *Red Stains on Vietnam Doves.* Hall declares that its "religious, ecumenical, and nonpacifist nature made it more resistant than most antiwar groups to the public's negative attitudes and allowed it to communicate with a moderate, middle-class constituency that would not listen to the radical left" (175–76).

Law, Morality and Vietnam: The Peace Militants and the Courts describes the attempts of the peace movement to involve the legal system in the campaign to end the Vietnam War. John and Rosemary Bannan use the cases of the Catonsville Nine, the Fort Hood Three, the Boston Five, and other peace militants to demonstrate how they intentionally violated the law, hoping to use their trials "as forums to challenge the morality and legality of military policy"(3). These cases created a dilemma for the courts: by accepting the challenge, they risked a conflict with the other two branches of the government; on the other hand, by rejecting the challenge, the courts could be in danger of abdicating their responsibility to be the place where citizens can find justice.

Prior to the era of the Vietnam War, the peace movement had not endeavored to use the law as a way of fostering its cause. The character of the radical pacifists' approach had been passive, nonviolent witness, a tactic intended to sensitize the public to the causes it espoused. The protests expected "only a distant and indirect impact on government policy and institutions" through the use of civil disobedience (6). However, during the Vietnam War, the peace movement decided to attempt to alter national institutions directly through asking the courts to rule on the constitutionality of government policy. This new approach, which attracted nonpacifists to the peace movement, had been used successfully in the civil rights movement.

Believing that it was futile to appeal to the president and Congress to end the war, the peace movement turned to the judicial system in its challenge of the Vietnam War. Their cases were built upon a variety of legal grounds: the United Nations Charter, the Nuremberg principles, the failure of Congress formally to declare war, restrictions of First Amendment rights, the Hague and Geneva conventions, and others. The protesters believed that even if the judges failed to agree with their arguments, the peace movement would at least bring the issue before the public, thereby achieving a "raising of the level of consciousness and conscience" (15).

The courts failed to declare the war illegal, finding the issue to be a political question that was not within the province of the judicial branch to resolve. The peace militants' effort to urge the judiciary to rule against the war was costly in terms of their own lives, most of them being convicted at their trials. The authors note that in most of the trials the defendants were denied an opportunity to air their grievances against the war during the course of the court proceeding. Although the judiciary did not "satisfy the best hope of the peace movement by declaring the war illegal, not the best hope of the public for clear decisions effectively reasoned, it did provide a forum for the peace movement" (212). *Law, Morality and Vietnam* asserts that the trials were able to stir the nation's conscience in a way that "eventually made antiwar sentiment an important political current" (212). The trials played a role in Johnson's decision to leave office in 1969, and they helped build a widespread dissatisfaction with the practice of the Selective Service System.

Much of the opposition to the Vietnam War was expressed at the local level, a topic dealt with by Bradford Lyttle in *The Chicago Anti-Vietnam War Movement*. The author, a native of Chicago who was active in the campaign to end the war, including spending nine months in prison for noncooperation with the Selective Service System, notes that Chicago had several organizations that were part of the pre-Vietnam era peace movement. The Chicago Peace Council, incorporating more than thirty groups, was the second largest antiwar coalition that operated at the municipal level during the Vietnam War. In many respects the Chicago antiwar movement resembled efforts to end the war in other major cities. Its activities included organizing local demonstrations, assembling people to participate in national protests, offering draft counseling and resistance programs, and taking action on college campuses in the area. Lyttle believes that the programs to advise young men about the draft may have been better organized in Chicago than in some other cities. The antiwar movement involved a war tax resistance campaign, as well as groups of veterans and businessmen opposed to the war. Chicago was unique in being the site of an unusually large number of antiwar conventions and conferences, including the 1968 Democratic Party Convention. Lyttle attributes the violence in 1968 to three factors: the police, important elements of the antiwar movement that sought a confrontation with the authorities, and the disunity of the Chicago antiwar movement. Lyttle indicates that it was difficult for nonviolent protesters to influence the movement at the convention, the disunity of the local movement manifesting itself dramatically at the Democratic Convention.

America's involvement in the Vietnam War was a divisive, traumatic event that continues to influence the United States in the 1990s. Thus, it is to be expected that a great deal has been written about the war, including the Americans who rejected their government's war policy and worked in a variety of ways to extricate the nation from the quagmire of Vietnam. Charles DeBenedetti and Charles Chatfield accurately characterize the story of the antiwar movement as "a story of the Vietnam War on the home front" (1). The books surveyed in this chapter are only a small number of the volumes that have already appeared on this important topic. The antiwar movement continues to attract the attention of scholars and journalists, a group from whom we can anticipate further additions to the literature of the Vietnam War.

THE ROLE OF THE MEDIA

Another critical element in the literature of the antiwar movement involves the role played by the media in shaping public opinion. From the very beginning of the conflict in the early 1960s, officials of the Kennedy, Johnson, and Nixon administrations criticized the press for impeding the war effort. They wanted reporters to deliver positive news to the public, or at least news that reflected official opinion. The journalists, of course, were more interested in reporting reality. Actually, the real problem was the enormous gap between Pentagon reports on the progress of the war and the stories coming out of the Saigon press corps. The Saigon press corps kept reporting a steady decline in support for Diem and steady increases in Vietcong strength. David Halberstam of the *New York Times*, Neil Sheehan of UPI, Nick Turner of Reuters, Peter Arnett of the Associated Press, Bernard Kalb and Peter Kalisher of CBS, James Robinson of NBC, Charles Mohr of *Time*, François Sully of *Newsweek*, Pepper Martin of *U.S. News & World Report*, and Stanley Karnow of *Time* consistently argued that the regime of Ngo Dinh Diem was isolated and paranoid, that a stable democracy would never develop as long as the Ngo family held power. In short, the United States and South Vietnam were losing. After their tours of duty in Vietnam, a number of those journalists wrote influential books that continued to shape scholarly and popular opinions about the war. Halberstam's best works were *The Making of a Quagmire* (1965), *Ho* (1971), and *The Best and Brightest* (1972). Neil Sheehan's *Bright and Shining Lie* won a Pulitzer Prize in 1989.

Peter Arnett and Michael Maclear wrote *The Ten Thousand Day War* (1981), and Stanley Karnow's *Vietnam: A History* (1983) was a best-seller.

The inconsistencies between administration positions and news stories eventually became the so-called credibility gap during the Johnson administration, a public policy problem brilliantly described in Daniel C. Hallin's *The Uncensored War: The Media & Vietnam* (1986). In February 1968 White House staffer Fred Panzer wrote a position paper explaining the psychology of the credibility gap. He blamed the phrase on "antiwar and anti-Johnson forces" who focused on the charge that Johnson lied to the American people in the election of 1964 by promising to stay out of Asian wars. The term was first used by reporter David Wise in a May 23, 1965, article for the *New York Herald Tribune* and was popularized by a December 5, 1965, article by Murray Marder for the *Washington Post*. Talk about the credibility escalated when doubts developed about what actually happened in the Gulf of Tonkin in 1964, intensified during the Tet Offensive of 1968, reached a fever pitch with the publication of the Pentagon Papers in 1971, and climaxed with the Watergate revelations between 1972 and 1974.

Kathleen J. Turner's book *Lyndon Johnson's Dual War: Vietnam and the Press* (1985) argues that the so-called credibility gap was inevitable. Like Berman, she sees the Great Society programs as critical to an understanding of Lyndon Johnson's decision-making process during the war. The dilemma the president faced was extraordinarily difficult: if South Vietnam fell to the Communists, Johnson risked taking the kind of political heat Harry Truman had taken back in the early 1950s over China, but at the same time, he had to avoid an all-out war commitment. Such a commitment would take so much money that the Great Society programs would be starved, and in the antiwar movement that would expand as the war escalated, Johnson was threatened with a loss of the support he had on the political left. For Turner, the "dual war"—which Johnson eventually lost—involved trying to convince the American public that he was doing enough to save South Vietnam without their perceiving that he was doing too much. The press soon believed that the Johnson administration was both holding back critical information about the extent of American involvement in Vietnam and actually misleading them about that commitment.

The Tet Offensive in February 1968 spawned an intense scholarly debate over the nature of news reporting. Peter Braestrup's *Big Story: How the American Press and Television Reported and Interpreted the Crisis of Tet 1968 in Vietnam and Washington* (1978) argued that the press actually misled the American public about what actually happened during those critical weeks of the war. Militarily, the Tet Offensive was an unmitigated disaster for the Vietcong and North Vietnamese. They had confidently predicted a spontaneous uprising against the government of South Vietnam, but that rebellion did not occur, and American military forces decimated the Vietcong, virtually eliminating them as a fighting force. But because the press reported Tet as a triumph for the Communists, it actually became a political victory for them, demoralizing the American public and all but destroying the Johnson administration.

But that opinion remains a minority one, and even in military circles more recent research has elevated the role of the press during the Vietnam War. Army historian William Hammond's *The Military and the Media* (1991) rejects the view held by earlier analysts that negative media coverage eroded public support for the war and eventually forced an American withdrawal from Vietnam. Hammond agrees that some press reports were badly flawed, but he is also convinced that most press reports were far more accurate than public statements from administration officials. It was casualties, not negative press reports, that undermined public opinion. Even if news reports had been more positive, the American war effort would have failed because North Vietnam held the political and tactical initiative. The casualties would have continued to rise. The war was not winnable.

BIBLIOGRAPHY

Andrew, Bruce. *Public Constraint and American Policy in Vietnam.* Beverly Hills, Calif.: Sage, 1976.

Arnett, Peter, and Michael Maclear. *The Ten Thousand Day War.* New York: St. Martin's Press, 1981.

Bacciocco, Edward J. *The New Left in America: Reform to Revolution, 1956–1970.* Stanford, Calif.: Hoover Institution Press, 1974.

Baez, Joan. *And a Voice to Sing With: A Memoir.* New York: Summit, 1987.

Bailey, George. "Television War: Trends in Network Coverage of Vietnam, 1965–1970." *Journal of Broadcasting* 20 (Spring 1976): 147–58.

Bannan, John, and Rosemary Bannan. *Law, Morality and Vietnam: The Peace Militants and the Courts.* Bloomington: Indiana University Press, 1975.

Baskir, Lawrence M., and William A. Strauss. *Chance and Circumstance: The Draft, the War and the Vietnam Generation.* New York: Knopf, 1978.

Belfrage, Cedric, and James Aronson. *Something to Guard: The Stormy Life of the National Guardian, 1947–1967.* New York: Columbia University Press, 1978.

Berkowitz, William R. "The Impact of Anti-Vietnam Demonstrations upon National Public Opinion and Military Indicators." *Social Sciences Research* 2 (March 1973): 1–4.

Berman, Ronald. *America in the Sixties: An Intellectual History.* New York: Harper and Row, 1970.

Berman, William C. *William Fulbright and the Vietnam War: The Dissent of a Political Realist.* Kent, Ohio: Kent State University Press, 1988.

Berrigan, Daniel. *The Trial of the Catonsville Nine.* Boston: Beacon, 1970.

Bloom, Lynn Z. *Doctor Spock: Biography of a Conservative Radical.* Indianapolis, Ind.: Bobbs-Merrill, 1972.

Bolton, Charles D. "Alienation and Action: A Study of Peace Group Members." *American Journal of Sociology* 78 (November 1972): 537–61.

Booth, Paul. *Peace Politics: A Study of the American Peace Movement and the Politics of the 1962 Congressional Elections.* Ann Arbor, Mich.: Peace Research and Education Project, 1964.

Boyer, Paul. "From Activism to Apathy: The American People and Nuclear Weapons, 1963–1980." *Journal of American History* 70 (March 1984): 837–44.

Boyer, Paul. *By the Bomb's Early Light: American Thought and Culture at the Dawn of the Atomic Age.* New York: Pantheon, 1985.

Braestrup, Peter. *Big Story: How the American Press and Television Reported and Interpreted the Crisis of Tet 1968 in Vietnam and Washington.* New Haven, Conn.: Yale University Press, 1978.

Breins, Wini. *The Great Refusal: Community and Organization in the New Left: 1962–1969.* New York: Praeger, 1982.

Brodie, Bernard. *Vietnam: Why We Failed in War and Politics.* New York: Macmillan, 1973.

Brooks, Robin. "Domestic Violence and America's Wars: A Historical Perspective." In *The History of Violence in America: Historical and Comparative Perspectives,* ed. Hugh Davis Graham and Ted Robert Gurr. New York: Praeger, 1969.

Brown, Robert McAfee. *Vietnam: Crisis of Conscience.* New York: Association Press, 1967.

Cantor, Milton. *The Divided Left: American Radicalism, 1900–1975.* New York: Hill and Wang, 1978.

Cantrill, Albert H., and Charles W. Roll, Jr. *Hopes and Fears of the American People.* New York: University Books, 1971.

Capps, Walter H. *The Unfinished War: Vietnam and the American Conscience.* Boston: Beacon, 1982.

Carroll, Peter N. *It Seemed Like Nothing Happened: The Tragedy and Promise of America in the 1970s.* New York: Holt, Rinehart, and Winston, 1982.

Carson, Clayborne. *In Struggle: SNCC and the Black Awakening of the 1960s.* Cambridge: Harvard University Press, 1981.

Chomsky, Noam. *American Power and the New Mandarins.* New York: Pantheon, 1967.

Clecak, Peter. *Radical Paradoxes: Dilemmas of the American Left, 1945–1970.* New York: Harper, 1974.

Coffin, William Sloane. *Once to Every Man: A Memoir.* New York: Atheneum, 1977.

Cooney, Robert, and Helen Michalowski, eds. *The Power of the People: Active Nonviolence in the United States.* Culver City, Calif.: Peace Press, 1977.

Cortright, David. *Soldiers in Revolt: The American Military Today.* Garden City, N.Y.: Doubleday/Anchor, 1975.

Cummings, Richard. *The Pied Piper: Allard K. Lowenstein and the Liberal Dream.* New York: Farrar, Straus, and Giroux, 1973.

DeBenedetti, Charles. *The Peace Reform in American History*. Bloomington: Indiana University Press, 1980.

DeBenedetti, Charles, ed. *Peace Heroes in Twentieth-Century America*. Bloomington: Indiana University Press, 1986.

DeBenedetti, Charles, and Charles Chatfield. *An American Ordeal: The Antiwar Movement of the Vietnam Era*. Syracuse, N.Y.: Syracuse University Press, 1990.

Dellinger, David. *More Power Than We Know: The People's Movement Toward Democracy*. Garden City, N.Y.: Doubleday, 1975.

Ellsberg, Daniel. *Papers on the War*. New York: Simon and Schuster, 1972.

Evans, Sara. *Personal Politics: The Roots of Women's Liberation in the Civil Rights Movement and the New Left*. New York: Knopf, 1979.

Fairclough, Adam. "Martin Luther King, Jr., and the War in Vietnam." *Phylon* 45 (March 1984): 19–39.

Ferber, Michael, and Staughton Lynd. *The Resistance*. Boston: Beacon, 1971.

Finn, James. *Protest: Pacifism and Politics*. New York: Random House, 1968.

Fisher, Randall M. *Rhetoric and American Democracy: Black Protest Through Vietnam Dissent*. Lanham, Md.: University Press of America, 1985.

Foster, H. Schuyler. *Activism Replaces Isolationism: U.S. Public Attitudes, 1940–1975*. Washington, D.C.: Foxhall Press, 1983.

Fowler, Robert Booth. *Believing Skeptics: American Political Intellectuals, 1945–1964*. Westport, Conn.: Greenwood, 1976.

Fulbright, William J. *The Crippled Giant: American Foreign Policy and Its Domestic Consequences*. New York: Random House, 1972.

Gallup, George. *The Gallup Poll: Public Opinion, 1935–1971*. New York: Random House, 1972.

Gallup, George. *The Gallup Poll: Public Opinion, 1972–1977*. Wilmington, Del.: Scholarly Resources, 1978.

Gausman, William F. *Red Stains on Vietnam Doves*. Denver, Colo.: Veracity, 1989.

Gelb, Leslie H., and Richard K. Betts. *The Irony of Vietnam: The System Worked*. Washington, D.C.: Brookings Institution, 1979.

Gillon, Steven M. *Politics and Vision: The ADA and American Liberalism, 1947–1985*. New York: Oxford University Press, 1987.

Gitlin, Todd. *The Sixties: Years of Hope, Days of Rage*. New York: Bantam, 1987.

Gray, Francine du Plessix. *Divine Disobedience: Profiles in Catholic Radicalism*. New York: Vintage, 1971.

Halberstam, David. *The Making of a Quagmire*. New York: Knopf, 1965.

Halberstam, David. *Ho*. New York: McGraw-Hill, 1971.

Halberstam, David. *The Best and the Brightest*. New York: Random House, 1972.

Hall, Mitchell Kent. "Clergy and Laymen Concerned About Vietnam: A Study of Opposition to the Vietnam War." Ph.D. diss., University of Kentucky, 1987.

Hall, Mitchell K. *Because of Their Faith: CALCAV and Religious Opposition to the Vietnam War*. New York: Columbia University Press, 1990.

Hallin, Daniel C. *The Uncensored War: The Media & Vietnam*. New York: Oxford University Press, 1986.

Halstead, Fred. *Out Now! A Participant's Account of the American Movement Against the Vietnam War*. New York: Monad, 1978.

Hammond, William. *The Military and the Media*. Washington, D.C.: U.S. Army Center for Military History, 1991.

Harris, David. *Dreams Die Hard*. New York: St. Martin's Press, 1982.

Hayden, Tom. *Reunion: A Memoir*. New York: Random House, 1988.

Heath, G. Lewis, ed. *Mutiny Does Not Happen Lightly: The Literature of the American Resistance to the Vietnam War*. Metuchen, N.J.: Scarecrow, 1976.

Helmer, John. *Bringing the War Home: The American Soldier in Vietnam and After*. New York: Free Press, 1971.

Hensley, William E. "The Vietnam Anti-War Movement: History and Criticism." Ph.D. diss., University of Oregon, 1979.

Hertz, Martin F., and Leslie Rider. *The Prestige Press and the Christmas Bombing, 1972: Images and Reality in Vietnam*. Washington, D.C.: University Press of America, 1985.

Hoffman, Paul. *Moratorium: An American Protest*. New York: Tower, 1970.

Holsti, Ole, and James Rosenau. "Vietnam, Consensus, and the Belief Systems of American Leaders." *World Politics* 32 (October 1979): 1–56.

Horowitz, Irving. *The Struggle Is the Message: The Organization and Ideology of the Anti-War Movement*. Berkeley, Calif.: Glendessary Press, 1970.

Howell, Haney. *Roadrunners: Combat Journalists in Cambodia*. New York: Paladin Press, 1989.

Hurwitz, Ken. *Marching Nowhere*. New York: Norton, 1971.

Jacobs, Paul, and Saul Landau, eds. *The New Radicals: A Report with Documents*. New York: Vintage, 1966.

Karnow, Stanley. *Vietnam: A History*. New York: Viking, 1983.

Kasinsky, Renee G. *Refugees from Militarism: Draft-Age Americans in Canada*. New Brunswick, N.J.: Transaction Books, 1976.

Katz, Milton S. *Ban the Bomb: A History of SANE, the Committee for a Sane Nuclear Policy, 1957–1985*. New York: Greenwood, 1986.

Katz, Neil H. "Radical Pacifism and the Contemporary American Peace Movement: The Committee for Non-Violent Action, 1957–1967." Ph.D. diss., University of Maryland, 1974.

Kendrick, Alexander. *The Wound Within: America in the Vietnam Years, 1945–1974*. Boston: Little, Brown, 1974.

Keniston, Kenneth. *Young Radicals: Notes on Committed Youth*. New York: Harcourt, 1968.

Keniston, Kenneth. *Youth and Dissent: The Rise of a New Opposition*. New York: Harcourt, 1971.

Larner, Jeremy. *Nobody Knows. Reflections on the McCarthy Campaign of 1948*. New York: Macmillan, 1978.

Lens, Sidney. *Unrepentant Radical: An American Activist's Account of Five Turbulent Decades*. Boston: Beacon, 1980.

Levy, David W. *The Debate Over Vietnam*. Baltimore: Johns Hopkins University Press, 1991.

Lewy, Guenter. *Peace and Revolution: The Moral Crisis of American Pacifism*. Grand Rapids, Mich.: Erdmans, 1988.

Lunn, Hugh. *Vietnam: A Reporter's War*. New York: Scarborough House, 1987.

Lyttle, Bradford. *The Chicago Anti-Vietnam War Movement*. Chicago: Midwest Pacifist Center, 1988.

McGill, William J. *The Year of the Monkey: Revolt on the Campus, 1968–1969*. New York: McGraw-Hill, 1982.

Matusow, Allen J. *The Unraveling of America: A History of Liberalism in the 1960s*. New York: Harper and Row, 1984.

Meconis, Charles. *With Clumsy Grace: The American Catholic Left, 1961–1977*. New York: Seabury, 1979.

Mehnert, Klaus. *Twilight of the Young: The Radical Movements of the 1960s and Their Legacy*. New York: Holt, Rinehart, and Winston, 1976.

Menashe, Louis, and Ronald Rodosh, eds. *Teach-ins, U.S.A.: Reports, Opinions, Documents*. New York: Praeger, 1967.

Merton, Thomas. *The Nonviolent Alternative*. New York: Farrar, Strauss, and Giroux, 1971.

Miller, James. *"Democracy Is in the Streets": From Port Huron to the Siege of Chicago*. New York: Simon and Schuster, 1987.

Minnion, John. *The CND Story*. London: Allison and Busby, 1983.

Oates, Stephen B. *Let the Trumpet Sound: The Life of Martin Luther King, Jr*. New York: New American Library/Mentor, 1982.

Olson, James S., and Randy Roberts. *Where the Domino Fell: America and Vietnam, 1945–1990*. New York: St. Martin's Press, 1991.

O'Rourke, William. *The Harrisburg 7 and the New Catholic Left*. New York: Crowell, 1972.

Peterson, Richard E. *The Scope of Organized Student Protest in 1964–65*. Princeton, N.J.: Educational Testing Service, 1966.

Piehl, Mel. *Breaking Bread: The Catholic Worker and the Origin of Catholic Radicalism in America*. Philadelphia: Temple University Press, 1982.

Powers, Thomas. *Vietnam: The War at Home, Vietnam and the American People, 1964–1968*. Boston: Hall, 1984.

Quigley, E. *American Catholics and Vietnam*. Grand Rapids, Mich.: Erdmans, 1968.

Robinson, Jo Ann. *Abraham Went Out: A Biography of A. J. Muste*. Philadelphia: Temple University Press, 1970.

Rosenberg, Milton J. *Vietnam and the Silent Majority: The Dove's Guide*. New York: Harper and Row, 1970.

Rothman, Stanley, and S. Robert Lichter. *Roots of Radicalism: Jews, Christians, and the New Left*. New York: Oxford University Press, 1982.

Rubin, Jerry. *Growing (Up) at Thirty-Seven*. New York: Evans, 1976.

Sale, Kirkpatrick. *SDS*. New York: Vintage, 1974.

Salisbury, Harrison E. *Vietnam Reconsidered: Lessons from a War*. New York: Harper and Row, 1984.

Schalk, David L. *War and the Ivory Tower: Algeria and Vietnam*. New York: Oxford University Press, 1991.

Schlesinger, Arthur, Jr. *The Bitter Heritage: Vietnam and American Democracy, 1941–1966*. Boston: Houghton Mifflin, 1967.

Schuman, Howard. "Two Sources of Antiwar Sentiment in America." *American Journal of Sociology* 78 (November 1972): 513–36.

Sheehan, Neil. *A Bright and Shining Lie: John Paul Vann and America in Vietnam*. New York: Random House, 1988.

Skolnick, Jerome H. *The Politics of Protest*. New York: Ballantine, 1969.

Small, Melvin. *Johnson, Nixon, and the Doves.* New Brunswick, N.J.: Rutgers University Press, 1988.

Smith, Curt. *Long Time Gone: The Years of Turmoil Remembered.* South Bend, Ind.: Icarus Press, 1982.

Stavis, Ben. *We Were the Campaign: New Hampshire to Chicago for McCarthy.* Boston: Beacon, 1970.

Surrey, David S. *Choice of Conscience: Vietnam Era Military and Draft Resisters in Canada.* New York: Praeger, 1982.

Taylor, Clyde, ed. *Vietnam and Black America: An Anthology of Protest and Resistance.* Garden City, N.Y.: Doubleday/Anchor, 1973.

Turner, Kathleen J. *Lyndon Johnson's Dual War: Vietnam and the Press.* Chicago: University of Chicago Press, 1985.

Unger, Irwin. *The Movement: A History of the American New Left, 1959–1972.* New York: Dodd, Mead, 1974.

Useem, Michael. *Conscription, Protest, and Social Conflict: The Life and Death of a Draft Resistance Movement.* New York: Wiley, 1973.

Vietnam Veterans Against the War. *The Winter Soldier Investigation: An Inquiry into American War Crimes.* Boston: Beacon, 1972.

Viorst, Milton. *Fire in the Streets: America in the 1960s.* New York: Simon and Schuster, 1979.

Vogelgesang, Sandy. *The Long Dark Night of the Soul: The American Intellectual Left and the Vietnam War.* New York: Harper and Row, 1974.

Waterhouse, Larry, and Mariann Wizard. *Turning the Guns Around: Notes on the GI Movement.* New York: Praeger, 1971.

Wilson, E. Raymond. *Uphill for Peace: Quaker Impact on Congress.* Richmond, Ind.: Friends United Press, 1975.

Wittner, Lawrence S. *Rebels Against War: The American Peace Movement, 1933–1983.* Philadelphia: Temple University Press, 1984.

Woodstone, Norma Sue. *Up Against the War: A Personal Introduction to U.S. Soldiers and Civilians Fighting Against the War in Vietnam.* New York: Tower, 1970.

Zaroulis, Nancy, and Gerald Sullivan. *Who Spoke Up? American Protest Against the War in Vietnam, 1963–1975.* Garden City, N.Y.: Doubleday, 1984.

Zinn, Howard. *SNCC: The New Abolitionists.* Boston: Beacon, 1965.

17 Television and the Vietnam War

Sarah Farenick

The Vietnam War was like no other war in American history, and perhaps the most important reason for its uniqueness was the role played by television. More than a few commentators and scholars have discussed the fact that every day on the evening news the American public actually watched the war take place, with all of its carnage and absurdity, and they could not help but have their points of view shaped by the coverage. American policymakers found themselves in a unique political environment. They were unable to control the flow of information or shape the images of the war that the public consumed, and eventually that weakness undermined their political positions. After the war, television has also played a significant role in reflecting American public opinion about the Vietnam War.

After 1980 the popular image of the Vietnam veteran began to change on television. Like Michael in *The Deer Hunter* and Luke in *Coming Home*, the veteran was transformed into a figure of compassion and imbued with a sense of justice. Rather than threaten society, the new television veteran defends society, upholds justice, and restores order. In Vietnam he learned how to fight, use sophisticated weapons, and function in a tightly knit group, but the experience did not rob him of compassion. Indeed, it is suggested that the very traits that led him to Vietnam now compel him to battle evil and injustice in the United States. Television showcased this new veteran in such shows as "Magnum, P.I.," "The A-Team," and "Airwolf." Most of the heroes of these shows are unmarried, but their bachelorhood is not viewed as negative. The group functions as their family, and they display a healthy attraction to women that is amply reciprocated. Furthermore, they are not scarred emotionally or physically by their service in Vietnam. No guilt troubles their thoughts, no injuries plague their days.

Although these heroes were once in the military, they no longer act on behalf of the government. Crippled by red tape and bureaucratic lethargy, the modern state seems unable to act with speed and justice. The veteran heroes are part of the private sector—the United States of Ronald Reagan—and they function outside official channels. But they always get the job done; they ensure justice. As the viewer is told each week at the beginning of "The A-Team," "If you have a problem, if no one else can help, and if you can find them . . . you can hire the A-Team." But if the veteran heroes work outside the government, they are still willing to fight for their country. Often they combat external threats—drug smuggling, terrorism, and spying. Occasionally they travel outside the United States to solve problems. This they willingly do, for their cause is always just, and on television the ends justify the means. That the Vietnam War was a major historical and political event has always been obvious; less obvious, but certainly just as major, has been the cultural impact of the war on many aspects of American life. The Vietnam War has frequently been referred to as the "television war" because the American public could watch it every night on the six o'clock news, and it has been said that the network news programs greatly affected the public's perception of the war and possibly even the running of it (Winship). However, the war has had just as great an impact on television's entertainment programming, and that impact has continued into the 1990s. This impact can be examined by following certain patterns that show up through three basic chronological eras: the actual war years, arbitrarily set as 1965 to 1973, the immediate postwar years of 1973 to the early 1980s, and the later postwar years from the mid–1980s into the 1990s. Some of the patterns appear throughout all three eras. However, they follow an evolution that matched the public's perception of the war. Others would appear in only one era.

THE WAR YEARS

To a generation that has become used to made-for-television movies that mirror the major current events, often within months of their occurrence, it is difficult to realize that during the mid- to late 1960s very little was said about the Vietnam War. The first made-for-television movie to deal with the Vietnam War, *The Ballad of Andy Crocker*, was shown in 1969 and concerned a returning veteran and not the war itself (Marill). One of the few television shows to refer to the war was "Julia" starring Diahann Carroll. In it she played a widow whose husband had died in Vietnam (Castelman and Podrazik). Interestingly, "Gomer Pyle U.S.M.C." never mentioned the war even though the setting was a marine base and the audience followed the main character through boot camp and into his years of service. Of course, the point of the show was humor.

Prior to the Vietnam War the military was in most cases portrayed gallantly and heroically by television programming. In September 1965 the nighttime lineup included eleven shows with some sort of military background. Not all of these were new entries, because the military-oriented shows had been fairly popular for several years previously (Castelman). These shows included "12 O'Clock High," which told stories about an air force bomber group in England during World War II; "Wackiest Ship in the Army," another World War II show that took place in the South Pacific; "Combat!," which told the story of a World War II army combat unit; "Convoy," which portrayed the navy during the Battle of the Atlantic in World War II; "Mr. Roberts," a television version of the successful Broadway play and movie showing another side of World War II; "McHale's Navy," a slapstick comedy set in the South Pacific during World War II; and "Hogan's Heroes," which was a comedy set in a German prisoner-of-war camp. On a more modern note the public could see the military through the comedies of "Gomer Pyle," which gave us the ever-innocent country boy serving his country in the "peacetime marines" or watch the antics of an army sergeant married to a movie star on "Mona McCluskey." For the futurists, there was "Voyage to the Bottom of the Sea," where the sailors wearing some sort of military-like uniform battled aliens, undersea monsters, and enemies from some unnamed country (Brooks). All of these shows, even the comedies, were extremely promilitary. The screwups of "McHale's Navy" and "Hogan's Heroes" could still fight and outthink the enemy, even if in some highly unorthodox ways.

However, by the season of 1966–1967, the military-oriented show was losing its appeal to a nation that could watch a real war with increasing frequency on the six o'clock news. A prime example was the critically acclaimed series "Combat!" During the 1964–1965 season this show had ranked number 10, according to the Nielson ratings. Although its ratings had slipped some in the next two seasons, the viewing public was still tuning in to it in substantial numbers; but the show was still canceled at the end of the 1966 season. Several of the stars in the series, including Vic Morrow, would later attribute its cancellation to the growing criticism of the war in Vietnam. "Combat!" was not the only show to fade from television during the late 1960s. By 1966 the number of military shows was already down to eight. These included the returning shows: "Combat!," "Gomer Pyle," "F Troop," "Hogan's Heroes," "Twelve O'Clock High," and "Voyage to the Bottom of the Sea," as well as two new entries: "Rat Patrol" and "Jericho." One particular characteristic of these two shows was that they did not portray the "regular" military. "Rat Patrol" was the story of a unit of British and American soldiers fighting in the North Africa campaign of World War II. The men wore khaki shorts and raffish bush hats, and they drove a jeep that appeared to be the forerunner of the dune buggy. "Jericho" was the story of three "troubleshooters" operating undercover in Europe with the resistance groups of World War II—again not your ordinary soldiers.

The 1967 season saw only five shows with a military theme. By now "Combat!" and "Twelve O'Clock High" had been canceled, as had "F Troop" and "Jericho." One new show premiered with the military as its background—"Garrison's Gorillas," a "Dirty Dozen" clone that would last only one season. When the 1968 fall season began, the military was represented by only two shows: "Gomer Pyle" and "Hogan's Heroes." With the buildup of American troops in Vietnam and the disastrous Tet Offensive in January 1968, the viewing public was less and less in the mood to watch entertainment that appeared to glorify war (Castelman). From this point on, television increasingly portrayed the military either as bumblers or as bad guys.

The third pattern for the war years involved the ever-growing antiwar sentiment. In the earliest years of the war, some references to Johnson's policies were heard on a frequently controversial show called "That Was the Week That Was," which aired from January 1964 until May 1965. The show, which used satirical sketches and musical numbers, did not appeal to a broad audience (Castelman). Other shows offered up antiwar sentiments in more subtle forms, including one concerning a real-life frontier American. That show was "Daniel Boone," which ran from September 1964 through the 1969–1970 television season. Barry Rosenzweig supervised its writers, and he insisted that the Revolutionary War appear as England's Vietnam, with the colonials as the Vietcong and the English as the Americans (Gitlin). Another show, "Star Trek," consistently aired story lines that decried the evils and futilities of war (Fireman). Even "Mission: Impossible" stopped trying to overthrow governments in the early 1970s and switched to more domestic missions, such as dealing with organized crime. Interestingly, all the earlier missions focused on European or Central and South American governments. The writers wanted to steer clear of Southeast Asia.

Other shows were not so subtle in their antiwar sentiments. The list includes shows such as "Rowan and Martin's Laugh-In," where Goldie Hawn was frequently painted with peace symbols and other pointed comments were made about war (Harris). Two Norman Lear shows offered up antiwar comments. These were "All in the Family" and, for a short while, "Maude." On "All in the Family" Mike and Gloria constantly held forth on the wrongness of the war, much to the chagrin of Archie.

The Smothers Brothers were a singing-comedy act that had gained national fame during the folk music popularity explosion of the early sixties. In a midseason attempt to steal viewers from NBC's "Bonanza," CBS gave the brothers their own show on Sunday night. It quickly became very popular and extremely controversial. Among the more controversial shows was the one in September 1967 where the special guest was the folk singer Peter Seeger, making his first appearance on television after a sixteen-year blacklisting. He was scheduled to perform his violently antiwar song "Waist Deep in the Big Muddy," but the network cut the segment when Seeger, backed by the Smothers Brothers, refused to cut the most controversial verse. In February 1968, after a long battle with CBS, Tommy Smothers once again introduced Seeger on the show, and this time he was allowed to perform the song in its entirety. The Smothers Brothers continued to battle the network and its censors, but the show was finally canceled in 1969, while still extremely popular. The final straws were an interview with Joan Baez, who made a reference to her husband's prison term for draft evasion, and a segment featuring Dr. Benjamin Spock. Using a technical clause in the Smothers Brothers' contract relating to their furnishing the network affiliates with a broadcast tape prior to the showing, the network claimed breach of contract when the final tape of the April 14 show featuring Spock was several days late arriving at the affiliates. It was later shown that the network censors kept sending back parts of the tape for editing until it was too late for the show to furnish the final tape to the affiliates. The Smothers Brothers sued CBS and won their case (O'Connor).

In September 1972, with the war still going on, and the peace talks in Paris and the antiwar protests still continuing, a new show was aired on Sunday night. It was a spin-off of Robert Altman's popular movie *M*A*S*H* and was also called "M*A*S*H." Although all the major characters were carried over from the movie, only one of the original actors was. Instead, the television show starred Alan Alda, McClean Stevenson, Wayne Rodgers, Larry Linville, and Loretta Swit. From the beginning the producers, Larry Gelbart and Gene Reynolds, were committed to maintaining the antiwar stance of the show. The show attempted to show with humor as well as pathos the futility of war and especially the frustration that the doctors of a MASH unit felt in healing people only to have them shot at again. Since the show took place during the Korean conflict, the writers were able to express their views against the war without references to Vietnam itself, which might have led to network censoring (Winship).

In February 1973 the fighting in Vietnam was finally over, but the effect of the Vietnam War was not. CBS scheduled a hard-hitting drama about the less than positive experiences of returning war veterans entitled "Sticks and Bones." The show was to be broadcast in March 1973, just when the Vietnam prisoners of war were scheduled to begin coming home. The federal government worried that the show would be either inappropriate or too unsettling to viewing audiences, and they pressured CBS to remove the show from the schedule. The producer, Joseph Papp, was outraged that CBS would cave in and charged the network with censorship. He canceled his four-year agreement with CBS to produce movies and theatrical specials. The show was finally aired in August 1973 but without commercials. Sponsors were also worried about audience response. Only 94 of the 200 network affiliates carried the show. The incident was costly and disturbing for CBS (Montgomery). It was a lesson that all of the networks would remember in the coming years.

THE IMMEDIATE POSTWAR YEARS

With the end of the war, it appeared that most of the nation wanted to forget about Vietnam and war. Shows like "Happy Days," with its emphasis on the 1950s, became immensely popular in a nation that seemed to want to forget the tragedy and turbulence of the war years (Javna). "M*A*S*H" continued on the air, but it was one of the few programs with a military background from 1973 until 1983. Occasionally another military-oriented series premiered using the World War II motif, but seldom did it last more than one season. Although "M*A*S*H" began as an antiwar statement against Vietnam, it quickly evolved into more of a general antiwar program. As the show developed and the characters evolved themselves, the focus became more what war does to the individuals who find themselves in a foreign environment. The show remained extremely popular throughout its run, which ended in 1983. It still remains popular as a syndicated show.

"M*A*S*H" employed comedy as well as serious stories to portray the true horror of war. One show in particular, called "Sometimes You Hear the Bullet," brought these realities home when it introduced a correspondent who was Hawkeye's friend. The character was very sympathetic, and the audience was obviously supposed to like and care about him. Then, in the last scene, he is wounded, and Hawkeye is operating on him. Hawkeye is unable to save his friend, a fact he has difficulty accepting. Colonel Blake informs him that at officer training school he was taught that the facts of war guarantee that you cannot save them all and that war kills (Reiss). The show aired on January 28, 1973, the day after the Vietnam War ended (Javna).

Another of the powerful legacies of "M*A*S*H" was its decision to become the first television program to kill off a major character. Other shows had always written off characters who left the series by having them move away or marry or some such similar situation, even if the actor or actress playing the part had died. When McClean Stevenson decided to leave the series at the end of the 1974–1975 season, a special show was written to explain his leaving. Colonel Henry Blake receives his discharge and prepares to leave Korea and return home to his wife and kids. The show is spent saying farewell to Henry and presents the humorous escapades of Frank Burns, as he contemplates assuming command. Henry's chopper takes him to Seoul, where he is to catch a plane for Japan and then back home. In the final minutes of the show, with all the characters in their familiar places in the operating room, Radar enters holding a message that he reads to the working doctors, nurses, and orderlies. Henry's plane has been shot down over the Sea of Japan with no survivors. The final seconds of the show reveal the stunned and teary eyes above the operating room masks. Once again "M*A*S*H" broke new ground and broke the hearts of its viewers. Major characters were supposed to live happily ever after, even on a show about war. But one of the legacies of Vietnam was that the American public had learned that reality was something totally different by watching real soldiers and sometimes civilians dying on the evening news. Reality was invading their entertainment. Throughout the entire run of "M*A*S*H," the regular military was continually portrayed in a poor light. Front-line officers were either bumbling idiots or glory-hungry leaders with no concern for their men. The rear echelon officers fared no better, and even the regular enlisted man was frequently shown as corrupt at worst or at least more concerned with his own comforts and success. The draftees were usually the only ones shown to have true compassion. Colonel Potter was one of the few "regular army" officers who consistently came off sympathetically, although "Hot Lips" Hoolihan became a more sympathetic character toward the end of the series (Reiss).

During the war years another show that became as vocally antiwar was "All in the Family," and even after the ending of the active involvement, the show continued to broadcast its antiwar message on occasion. One such show was aired on December 15, 1976. The scene was the Bunker's dining room on Christmas Eve, 1976. Mike and Gloria had invited a friend, David, to have dinner with them. The problem was that he was a draft dodger living in Canada. At the same time Archie had invited his good friend, Pinky, whose son had been killed in Vietnam. The stage was set for a generational confrontation. Archie provides the opening shot. As Archie and Mike argue about the rightness or wrongness of David's prior actions and his presence at their dinner, David and Pinky sit there embarrassed. Archie ultimately brings up what he feels is the personal insult to Pinky, who had lost a son in the war that David had refused to fight. Then Pinky says his piece, which stuns the others. He accepts David and his actions and even shakes his hand. All of this is too much for Archie, who leaves the table, only to have Edith persuade him to return. The strong antiwar sentiment of the entire show was presented as the intelligent choice, with only bumbling Archie voicing support for the government's policies. The message was clear. Vietnam had showed the American viewing public that war, especially that war, was wrong.

Another show that attempted to show the horror of war was a made-for-TV movie that aired in April 1979. Its specific message was the personal tragedy of Vietnam for one middle-class American family. The movie was based on a true incident, and the actors were portraying real people. *Friendly Fire* was the account of an Iowa farm couple's efforts to discover how their son had been killed in Vietnam. When it aired in 1979, the nation was in the midst of trying to reinterpret the American involvement in Vietnam. The couple, the Mullens, were not protesters or powerful people at the beginning of the story. They were just an ordinary farm family that wanted to know why their son had died. Their actions after their son's death were not, however, typical of thousands of others who had lost sons. As the movie shows, they became frustrated with the evasions and insensitive treatment they received from the government and its agencies in their quest for answers, and this frustration led them to become anitwar activists. In the end, through the aid of a writer who had become interested in their story, the Mullens find that their son was accidentally killed by American artillery fire—so-called friendly fire. But the anger that began over their son's death eventually came to encompass the governmental policies that put him in Vietnam in the first place (Sklar).

The plight of the Vietnam vet and his compatriot, the prisoner of war (POW), was seldom portrayed in a favorable light during the years immediately following the war. In made-for-TV movies such as *The Desperate Miles*, *Green Eyes*, and *Just a Little Inconvenience*, the Vietnam vet was portrayed as either disgruntled, disillusioned, and/or out of place in the society to which he had returned. The vet almost always was handicapped in some way, either physically or emotionally (Marill). The picture of the Vietnam vet continued to be one of a misfit who had not adjusted to his return to the United States. Frequently, the maladjustment was complicated by drug abuse, which was always implied as having its origins in Vietnam. On the popular TV cop show "Kojak," after the crime of the week was committed, Lieutenant Kojak often requested that all Vietnam vets be brought in for questioning as just a matter of course. Gene Reynolds, who had helped to produce "M*A*S*H," was now producing "Lou Grant" for MTM. From the very beginning, the second show of the first season was the story of a Vietnam vet who holds the newsroom hostage until he gets the information he wants to the public. Throughout the series run, the theme of Vietnam, as seen through its effect on the vets, reappeared. During the second season, the series revealed that the scruffy-looking photographer "Animal" is a Vietnam vet, and his unresolved feelings about the war cause a constant questioning of life and the society around him. In the final season a story entitled "Immigrants" dealt with the growing problem of Vietnamese refugees (Feuer, Kerr, and Vahimagi). Interestingly enough, by 1981–

1982, the show's last season, Animal had apparently resolved his conflicts, dressed more appropriately, and was increasingly referred to by his real name—Dennis. By this time the specter of Vietnam was softening for the viewing public, and therefore the image of Vietnam and those who had been involved in it was changing.

In 1979–1980 all three networks decided that the viewing public might be ready to view the Vietnam War as entertainment. Three sitcoms were developed for the coming season. MTM had a series in development that was the idea of producer-writer Gary David Goldberg. It was about a Saigon-based news bureau similar to UPI or the AP. CBS liked the idea, and MTM went to work. The show, to be called "Bureau," was similar in format to the successful "Lou Grant." Unfortunately, the pilot was not all that funny, and it was far too anti-Establishment, antimilitary, and antiwar. The sample audience also felt that they were not quite ready for a comedy about Vietnam. CBS sent it back to the drawing board with instructions to make it lighter and to include an army press attaché who would be "more sympathetic." The second result was even worse, and neither the network nor MTM liked the product. The show was dead in the water. On NBC the Vietnam entry was a comedy called "Six O'Clock Follies." It was another show about the press corps in Vietnam, using as its title the term that the press corps in Saigon had used for the daily military press briefings that released the government's version about the day's action. Once again there was conflict between what the writers wanted—a hard-hitting black comedy—and what the network thought would sell—a lighthearted look at the war in Saigon. The result was a failure that lasted only six weeks, even as a summer fill-in. ABC's entry fared no better. According to its writers, "Bringing It Home" was to be a hard-hitting show about the men and women who covered the war. Conflicts began immediately between the writers and the network over every aspect of the show. ABC had in mind a show about a bunch of wild and crazy guys who just happened to be in Vietnam covering the war, while the writers wanted a vehicle to voice their sentiments about what had been wrong about the Vietnam War. The show was also doomed to failure. No one, it seemed, was quite ready for a show set in Vietnam (Gitlin).

By the end of the 1970s and into the early 1980s, more shows were referring to Vietnam in their programs. "Trapper John, M.D." premiered in 1979. Borrowing from "M*A*S*H," the series had a character called Alonzo Gates, who had been a surgeon at a Vietnam M*A*S*H unit. But while Trapper frequently referred to his experiences in Korea, after the first show Gonzo, as Gates was called, seldom referred to his war years. One exception was a show during the middle of the series that dealt with a nurse experiencing posttraumatic stress disorder. The character exhibited strange and even dangerous behavior that almost cost the life of a patient as well as her job until it was finally revealed that her "problem" was caused by her experiences in Vietnam. Another 1979 premiere was the comedy "WKRP in Cincinnati." One of the more powerful of its episodes dealt with one of the disc jockeys, Venus Flytrap, who never wanted to be photographed. In this episode it is revealed that he was absent without leave (AWOL) from the army and has changed his name to stay out of jail. Venus is urged to give himself up by the station owner, who cannot understand why he would have gone AWOL. In a moving scene, Venus explains to Mr. Carlson, the station owner, that after witnessing a prisoner in Vietnam being thrown from a flying helicopter and then experiencing the disjointing experience of flying back to a United States experiencing antiwar protests, he just kept walking and never looked back. He is now willing to face the consequences, but the viewer is left with the understanding that he, too, is one of the "walking wounded" of the war.

A third show that aired about this time was "Magnum, P.I.," which featured three buddies from Vietnam now living in Hawaii. The main character was Thomas Magnum, an Annapolis graduate and former naval intelligence officer who had resigned his commission, probably because of his Vietnam experiences. During the early years of the show the references to Vietnam were few and mostly negative. The continuing antimilitary theme was present in that Magnum was frequently in conflict with naval intelligence officer Buck Greene, a highly unsympathetic character. In order to get the help he needed to solve his cases, he had to con the information from his buddies still in naval intelligence. Colonel Green was always looming in the background as a quasi-villain.

The detective show "Simon and Simon" premiered in 1981. It was about two brothers running a detective agency in San Diego. The older brother, Rick, is a free spirit who shirks responsibility while the younger brother is a short-haired conservative. The kick was that Rick had been a marine serving in Vietnam, an experience he would like to forget. Once again, the concept that service in Vietnam left indelible scars on its veterans was carried out. Rick also had an oddball assortment of veteran friends who periodically showed up to assist in their cases. Frequently, these characters were just one-half step above the law. In the early 1980s the theme of the missing in action (MIAs) began to be reflected in several shows. Several shows such as "Magnum," "Simon and Simon," and others ran episodes dealing with the idea that there were still some of "our guys" left behind. It became something of a salve to the conscience to go back to rescue the "buddies" still wallowing in the jungles. These shows did not surface until almost ten years after the United States had withdrawn its troops from Vietnam, and it was also a signal that the public attitude toward Vietnam and its veterans was beginning to change.

THE LATER POSTWAR YEARS

During the late 1980s and early 1990s many of the earlier themes changed. In 1983 a new action-adventure show premiered called "The A-Team." The characters were all Vietnam vets. In fact, they were a crack counterinsurgency unit tried for a crime in Vietnam that they did not commit. After escaping from a U.S. military prison, they began to move underground across the United States, providing aid to the underdogs of America as they moved about. One of the characters, Howling Mad Murdock, was regularly broken out of a VA mental hospital. Supposedly his Vietnam experiences had left him a little out of touch with reality, but he was still one of the best pilots around. Along with the wrongs they righted each week, the A-Team had to stay one step ahead of the military police (the military was still the ultimate villain). But by the 1986 season, the A-team was working undercover for the government in order to "pay their debt."

Another show that showed the military and the government in a less than flattering light was "Airwolf," which featured a high-tech helicopter "appropriated" by the pilot who flew it for the supersecret governmental agency that had built it. He continued to fly missions, using the special helicopter, only as long as they continued to search for his MIA brother. Throughout the series run, various episodes referred to less than scrupulous Vietnam veterans, implying that they had been good men until military service in Vietnam ruined them.

But changing values were also appearing. Vietnam was no longer a taboo subject. On "Magnum, P.I." the viewing audience was finally allowed to know why the Vietnam experience so strongly affected Magnum. He had married a Eurasian woman who supposedly had perished in the fall of Saigon despite American military promises to get her out. In subsequent episodes, the wife was shown still to be living with her first husband, a North Vietnamese army officer secretly in the pay of the United States. Other shows continued to incorporate Vietnam and related issues into their story lines. Along with this trend was a major shift in the way that the Vietnam vet was perceived by the viewing public. A good example is "Hill Street Blues," which premiered in 1981. One of the major characters was Lt. Howard Hunter, the leader of the Special Weapons and Tactics police (SWAT) team. In the early years of the show, Hunter was a typical military-type buffoon. He made frequent references to his tour of duty in Vietnam, spouting the so-called government line. Over time on the series, Hunter began to exhibit psychological instabilities because of his war experience. As the nation's attitude toward the Vietnam veteran began to mellow, so, too, did the portrayal on this and other shows. Another character, Officer Joe Coffey, admitted that he, too, was a veteran, but he had dealt with his experience and put it behind him. At the same time, the character of Hunter was increasingly humanized, as were his references to Vietnam (Feuer).

In the mid–1980s the Vietnam War Memorial was dedicated in Washington, D.C., and the whole nation seemed to stop and take stock. HBO, the pay cable network, staged a huge telethon with big-name performers, many of whom had protested the war, to help defray some of the expenses of the memorial and the so-called traveling walls, which were to move around the country. It was called "Welcome Home, Vietnam Vets" and symbolized the change in attitude sweeping the country. Around the same time, more and more shows devoted episodes to the problems that vets were facing—especially posttraumatic stress disorder.

Finally, by the late 1980s, the war in Vietnam had become the in topic for entertainment. The huge success of movies like *Platoon* and *Full Metal Jacket* convinced the networks that the viewing audience was now ready for a weekly series set in Vietnam. However, with the change in the attitudes toward the Vietnam veteran, it was no longer necessary to focus on nonmilitary types as the main characters. In 1987, "Tour of Duty," TV's first regular drama about the Vietnam War, premiered. It focused on the men of Bravo Company, an infantry unit, in 1967. The show, which ran from the fall of 1987 until the spring of 1990, has been described as being the way the guys in Vietnam would have liked it to be (Henry). The show is very similar in style to all the television war shows and the war movies of the 1950s that portrayed World War II. Others have criticized the show for portraying the soldiers as "too nice" and too little affected by the war that they see around them (Anderson). The show did touch on some controversial topics, such as officer corruption, cowardice during battle, battle fatigue, and the dislocation that the men felt in flying out to Hawaii for rest and recreation/recuperation (R and R), only to fly back for the war. Much of the criticism about its somewhat unrealistic portrayal of the Vietnam War experience may have been due to the fact that in return for the free use of military equipment, including Huey helicopters, navy planes, and other military personnel, the show gave the Pentagon script review and often approval. According to the producer, Ron Schwary, this script review did not compromise the show's integrity (Koch). However, criticism from vets continued to be strong during most of the show's run. Regardless of the criticism about the realities on the show, it was a milestone in television's portrayal of the war. The relatively short run may have been more indicative of the lack of originality of the stories rather than the viewing audience's reaction to its setting.

Response to the show was strong enough for ABC to follow suit during the 1988 midseason premieres with its own show set in Vietnam. The show, called "China Beach," has a decidedly different perspective. Its main characters are a nurse, a Red Cross worker, two United Service

Organizations (USO) workers, and a woman who is sometimes a prostitute and always an "entrepreneur." The setting is the shores of the China Sea next to Da Nang, where a rest and relaxation facility was located next to an evacuation hospital. The remaining characters are the doctors and other men who work in the area, both soldiers and noncombatants. "China Beach" has received much critical acclaim for its writing and acting. Episodes have incorporated interviews with real nurses and Red Cross workers who served in Vietnam. Other episodes have tried to portray accurately the relationship with the Vietnamese population. During the fall 1990 season, the show shifted its perspective to the experiences that these characters had upon returning to the "real" world of the United States. Several shows during the 1990–1991 season moved throughout the decades, following the characters as their lives changed. "China Beach" was canceled in 1991.

Another recent program that has addressed the Vietnam experience, although from still another perspective, premiered at midseason in 1988. It was called "The Wonder Years," and the main character, Kevin Arnold, is just starting junior high school in 1969. Filled with images of the late 1960s and early 1970s, it gives a twelve-year-old's view of the world around him. Since that world included the Vietnam War, several episodes deal with the home front during the Vietnam War years. The very first episode had Kevin recognizing that the skinny tomboy across the street, Winnie, has turned into a lovely girl and his friendship has turned to puppy love. By the end of the episode, Kevin has had to comfort Winnie while dealing with his own confusion and sorrow over the death in Vietnam of Winnie's older brother. By the use of home movies, which became standard on the show, flashbacks were shown of the young man as he played around with the younger kids on the block. The show dealt poignantly with the reality of those left behind who were not sure why any of this had happened. Throughout the first season, Kevin's older sister participates in several antiwar protests, triggering conflict with her father, who had served in Korea. During the fall of 1988, the show aired an episode that dealt with the moratorium of 1969. The student council at Kevin's junior high, named ironically after Robert F. Kennedy, votes to stage a walkout in support of the moratorium. When the students find out that they could be suspended for carrying out the demonstration, some have second thoughts; in the end, unwittingly and accidentally, Kevin starts the walkout. In another episode, Winnie's parents split up due in part to their inability to share their individual grief over the death of their only son. Through episodes such as this, and in a seriocomic mode, "The Wonder Years" has given a different outlook to the Vietnam War years.

Another program with an interesting perspective on the war has been "Quantum Leap." The show is unique in its premise of time travel, as well as its concept that history might be changed by small differences in the way events happen. The main character, Sam, "leaps" in and out of other people's lives during the decades of his own life span. In the first season, during a show that dealt with the college protest movement, he reveals that his own brother had been killed in Vietnam. Another show featured Sam's holographic sidekick, who had been a POW in Vietnam. During the second season Sam was able to leap into the life of a soldier in his brother's platoon and save his own brother's life, thus changing history.

Today, in the early 1990s, it is not unusual to skim through the television guide on any given week and find references to a variety of shows using Vietnam and more specifically Vietnam veterans as their theme. Made-for-TV movies have addressed the MIA issue both pro and con, using the viewpoint of the family left behind, the buddies who survived, and even occasionally an MIA who has escaped to make it back. The fall of Saigon was the subject of one such movie. Others have been made showing American efforts, both official and private, to rescue Vietnamese orphans. The Vietnamese refugee theme, an outgrowth of the war, has turned up on several shows, including "21 Jump Street" and "Night Court." Once called the "television war" because of its coverage on the news, Vietnam has now become "television's war." Television reflects the fact that America itself was a victim of the war; the casualty was its innocence.

BIBLIOGRAPHY

Books

Allman, Kevin. *TV Turkeys*. New York: Putnam, 1987.

Asherman, Allan. *The Star Trek Compendium*. New York: Simon and Schuster, 1981.

Barnouw, Eric. *Tube of Plenty: The Evolution of American Television*. New York: Oxford University Press, 1975.

Brooks, Tim, and Earle Marsh. *The Complete Directory to Prime Time Network TV Shows 1946–Present*. New York: Ballantine Books, 1988.

Brown, Les. *Les Brown's Encyclopedia of TV*. New York: Zoetrope, 1982.

Capa, Cornell, and Buprenda Karia, eds. *Robert Capa 1913–1954*. New York: Grossman, 1974.

Castleman, Harry. *Watching TV: Four Decades of American TV*. New York: McGraw-Hill, 1982.

Castelman, Harry, and Walter J. Podrazik. *Harry and Wally's Favorite TV Shows*. Englewood Cliffs, N.J.: Prentice-Hall, 1989.

Clauss, J. T., ed. *The Star Trek Guide*. New York: Aeonion Press, 1976.

Collins, Max, and John Javna. *The Best of Crime and Detective Shows: Perry Mason to Hill Street Blues*. New York: Harmony Books, 1988.

Feuer, Jane, Paul Kerr, and Tise Vahimagi, eds. *MTM "Quality Television."* London: British Film Institute, 1984.

Fireman, Judy, ed. *TV Book, the Ultimate Television Book.* New York: Workman, 1985.

Gitlin, Todd. *Inside Prime Time.* New York: Pantheon, 1985.

Greene, Graham. *Ways of Escape.* New York: Simon and Schuster, 1980.

Harris, Jay, ed. *TV Guide, the First 25 Years.* New York: New American Library, 1980.

Javna, John. *Cult TV.* New York: St. Martin's Press, 1985.

Kalter, Suzy. *The Complete Book of M*A*S*H.* New York: Abrams, 1984.

Kelly, Katie. *My Prime Time: Confessions of a TV Watcher.* New York: Seaview Books, 1980.

Lowe, Carl, ed. *TV and American Culture.* New York: Wilson, 1981.

McDonald, J. Fred. *Television and the Cold War: The Video Road to Vietnam.* New York: Praeger, 1985.

McNeil, Alex. *Total Television, A Complete Guide to Programming from 1948 to the Present.* New York: Penguin Books, 1984.

Marill, Alvin H. *Movies Made for Television.* New York: Da Capo Press, 1980.

Montgomery, Kathryn C. *Target: Prime Time, Advocacy Groups and the Struggle over Entertainment Television.* New York: Oxford University Press, 1989.

O'Connor, John E., ed. *American History/American Television, Interpreting the Video Past.* New York: Unger, 1983.

Reiss, David S. *M*A*S*H.* New York: Bobbs-Merrill, 1980.

Rollins, Peter C., and David H. Cuthbert. *Television's Vietnam: The Impact of Visual Images.* Stillwater: Oklahoma State University Audiovisual Center, 1983.

Sklar, Robert. *Prime Time America, Life on and Behind the Television Screen.* Englewood Cliffs, N.J.: Prentice-Hall, 1988.

Steinberg, Corbett. *TV Facts.* New York: Facts on File, 1985.

Taylor, Ella. *Prime-Time Families, Television Culture in Postwar America.* Berkeley: University of California Press, 1989.

Terrace, Vincent. *Encyclopedia of Television Series, Pilots, and Specials 1974–1984, Vol. 2.* New York: Zoetrope, 1985.

Terrace, Vincent. *Television 1970–1980.* San Diego, Calif.: Barnes, 1981.

Winship, Michael. *Television.* New York: Random House, 1988.

Periodicals

Anderson, Kent. "Call It Neglect of Duty." *TV Guide* (March 12–18, 1988): 34–36.

Henry, William A. "Return of the Living Room War." *Channels* 7 (October 1987): 76.

Koch, Tom. "Pentagon Previews." *Common Cause Magazine* (January-February 1988): 8.

Morrison, Mark. "China Beach Salutes the Women of Vietnam." *Rolling Stone* (May 19, 1988): 75–76, 79.

Panitt, Merrill. "Review: *China Beach.*" *TV Guide* (February 18–24, 1989): 56.

Pekurney, Robert G., and Leonard D. Bart. "Sticks and Bones: A Survey of Network Affiliate Decision Making." *Journal of Broadcasting* 19 (Fall 1975): 427–38.

Reddicliffe, Steven. "The Brothers Come in from the Cold." *Rolling Stone* (February 11, 1988): 40.

Reddicliffe, Steven. "Suburban Serenade." *Rolling Stone* (June 16, 1988): 45–46.

Rollins, Peter C. "Television's Vietnam: The Visual Language of Television News." *American Journal of Culture* 4 (1981): 114–35.

Rollins, Peter C. "The Vietnam War: Perceptions Through Literature, Film, and Television." *American Quarterly* 36 (1984): 419–33.

TV Guide. September 1965 to present, various issues.

Zoglin, Richard. "War as Family Entertainment." *Time* (February 20, 1989): 84.

Television Programs

"Airwolf." CBS, 1980–1988.
"All in the Family." Tandem Productions for CBS, 1971–1983.
"The A-Team." NBC, 1983–1987.
"The Ballad of Andy Crocker." Thomas/Spelling Productions, 1969.
"China Beach." ABC, 1988–1991.
"Combat!" ABC, 1962–1967.
"Convoy." NBC, 1965.
"Daniel Boone." Twentieth-Century Fox for NBC, 1964–1970.
"The Desperate Miles." Universal, 1975.
"Friendly Fire." Marble Arch Productions, 1979.
"F Troop." ABC, 1965–1967.
"Garrison's Gorillas." ABC, 1967–1968.
"Gomer Pyle, U.S.M.C." CBS, 1964–1970.
"Green Eyes." Lorimar Production, 1977.
"Happy Days." ABC, 1974–1984.
"Hill Street Blues." MTM for NBC, 1981–1987.
"Hogan's Heroes." CBS, 1965–1971.
"Jericho." CBS, 1966–1967.
"Julia." NBC, 1968–1971.
"Just a Little Inconvenience." Universal, 1977.
"Kojak." CBS, 1973–1978.
"Lou Grant." MTM for CBS, 1977–1982.
"McHale's Navy." ABC, 1962–1966.
"Magnum, P.I." CBS, 1984–1987.
"M*A*S*H." Twentieth-Century Fox for CBS, 1972–1983.
"Maude." Tandem Productions for CBS, 1972–1978.
"Mission: Impossible." Desilu Studios for CBS, 1966–1973.
"Mr. Roberts." NBC, 1965–1966.
"Mona McCluskey." NBC, 1965–1966.
"Night Court." NBC, 1984–.
"Quantum Leap." CBS, 1989–.
"Rat Patrol." ABC, 1966–1968.
"Rowan and Martin's Laugh-In." NBC, 1968–1973.
"Simon and Simon." CBS, 1982–1989.

"Six O'Clock Follies." NBC, 1980.
"Star Trek." NBC, 1966–1969.
"Sticks and Bones." CBS, 1973.
"That Was the Week That Was." NBC, 1964–1965.
"Tour of Duty." CBS, 1987–1989.
"Trapper John, M.D." CBS, 1979–1986.
"Twelve O'Clock High." Quinn Martin Productions for ABC, 1964–1967.
"21 Jump Street." Fox, 1987–.
"Voyage to the Bottom of the Sea." ABC, 1964–1968.
"Wackiest Ship in the Army." NBC, 1965–1966.
"Welcome Home, Vietnam Vets." HBO, 1987.
"WKRP in Cincinnati." MTM for CBS, 1978, 1979–1982.
"The Wonder Years." ABC, 1988–.

18 American Literature and the Vietnam War

The April 30, 1990, issue of *Time* magazine said it all. The cover photograph showed a Vietnamese peasant walking through a rice field. The issue was devoted to "Vietnam: 15 Years Later." "In America, the pain endures." "In Cambodia, the killing continues." The lead story claimed that "guilt and recrimination still shroud America's perceptions of the only war it ever lost." Vietnam is still with us. In fact, it has become part of the popular culture as well as the political culture in the United States. Middle-aged Americans are still trying to sort out their feelings about the war, and a new generation of young adults has grown up wondering what all the fuss is about. They, too, are now ready for answers. It is fifteen years since the helicopters lifted off the roof of the U.S. embassy in Saigon (Ho Chi Minh City). That's still too soon for definitive judgments, but it is also enough time to have gained perspective about the war, to have learned whatever lessons there are to learn.

Because of its peculiar nature—so bloody yet undeclared, so efficient yet so unpopular—the Vietnam War has had an extraordinary impact on American culture, shaping the way Americans view themselves and their history. A whole generation of students are fascinated with a war they know little about, except that it has virtually dominated popular culture during their most formative years. But unfortunately, there still is not much perspective about the war, at least not in the public mind. Several years ago a student of mine vociferously argued that the United States lost the war intentionally by not really trying, by holding back on its might and power. When I asked him to elaborate on his argument, he cited the movie *Rambo II* to support his claims. I wondered how a reasonably intelligent American college student could have had his ideas about the war shaped by such a film. Tens of millions of other Americans have had their views of the war shaped by literature, television, and

*Lenna Allred collaborated in the preparation of this chapter.

films. Few experiences in American history have been more painful or confusing than the Vietnam War. W. D. Earhart, in his novel *Vietnam-Perkasie* (1983), captures the pain in describing the battle for the city of Hue in 1968:

I fought back passionately, in blind rage and pain, without remorse, conscience or deliberation. I fought back . . . at the Pentagon Generals and the Congress of the United States, and the *New York Times*; at the draft-card burners, and the Daughters of the American Revolution . . . at the teachers who taught me that America always had god on our side and always wore white hats and always won; at the Memorial Day parades and the daily Pledge of Allegiance . . . at the movies of John Wayne and Audie Murphy, and the solemn statements of Dean Rusk and Robert McNamara. (P. 214)

PREWAR LITERATURE

Oddly enough, the literature of the Vietnam War appeared before there really was much of a war in Indochina. As early as 1955, long before the Vietnam War captured the public imagination and became a political issue, novelist Graham Greene protested American policy there. His novel *The Quiet American* is full of good intentions, idealism, and a dangerous innocence. The quiet American is Alden Pyle, a character who closely resembles the real-life Edward Lansdale, who at the time was directing American counterinsurgency programs in South Vietnam. Pyle believes in coldly passionate abstractions—democracy, freedom, monolithic Communism, falling dominoes, and the love of God. *The Quiet American* is written from the perspective of character Thomas Fowler, a British journalist in South Vietnam who tries to convince Pyle that the American attempt to build democracy and destroy Communism is hopelessly naive. Firmly believing that truth is on his side, Pyle continues nonetheless, with the best intentions, to ruin lives and kill innocent people. When one of his schemes goes particularly bad and kills several Vietnamese civilians, Pyle simply observes: "They were only war casualties. . . . It was a pity, but you can't always hit your target. Anyway they died in the right cause. . . . In a way you could say they died for democracy" (237).

Of course, Greene's objective was to expose the fallacies of U.S. military policies in Vietnam. Stationed in Saigon as a war correspondent in the early 1950s, Greene watched France go and the United States arrive. The Americans had young, fresh faces and crew cuts; they were more and more Alden Pyles intent on doing good "not to any individual person but to a country, a continent, a world." That was just the problem. Americans defined good and evil in universal abstractions. Few Americans were ready for Greene's prophetic message; most found it cynical and anti-American. Fowler tells Pyle that "in five hundred years there may be no New York or London, but they'll be growing paddy in these fields.... Do you think the peasant sits and thinks of God and Democracy when he gets inside his mud hut at night?... Isms and ocracies. Give me facts" (219). In the end, Alden Pyle is murdered. Michael Herr, in his book *Dispatches* (1977, 49), said: "Maybe it was already over for us in Indochina when Alden Pyle's boy washed up under the bridge at Dakao, his lungs full of mud."

The most powerful late–1950s novel dealing with the war took Graham Greene to task, arguing that Americans should be criticized not for being too idealistic but for not being idealistic enough. William J. Lederer and Eugene Burdick's *The Ugly American* was published in 1958 and spent seventy-eight weeks on the best-seller list. The books sold 4 million copies and was made into a movie starring Marlon Brando. *The Ugly American* is set in the fictionalized Southeast Asian country of Sarkhan. The book focuses on the failures of American policy and the diplomats who were hopelessly ill-equipped to carry out that policy. The leading character is a Colonel Hillandale, who happens to be bright and able, moving through Sarkhan winning the trust of the indigenous people and weaning them away from Communism. Unfortunately, few of the other Americans in the novel are as capable.

The real enemy in *The Ugly American* is the U.S. foreign service. Although communication is its main function, the foreign service is unable to communicate in the language of the host country. Chosen too often for their "personal wealth, political loyalty, and the ability to stay out of trouble," America's ambassadors rarely have any language training. They hear only what their interpreters want them to hear, obtain from newspapers only what their readers want them to obtain, and are subject to costly leaks and security problems. Isolated in the cities, they spend their days entertaining visiting American VIPs, socializing with other Western diplomats, and occasionally meeting with members of the local elite. They ignore the vast percentage of the population who live in rural poverty and speak only their own language. They have no knowledge of their enemy. They have not read the works of Mao Zedong, Karl Marx, or Vladimir Lenin. Instead they believe that American dollars will lead to victory. The Communists in *The Ugly American*, on the other hand, speak the native language and work closely with rural peasants, building loyalties and political support. The United States was losing the fight for the Third World, but it could still win against Communism. In that sense, the novel is a jeremiad. The solution is to fill the Third World with more Colonel Hillandales—competent, confident, and linguistically gifted Americans who can show the virtues of democracy and capitalism.

During the next decade and ever since, the debate over Vietnam has not really transcended those initial contrasting worldviews of *The Quiet*

American and *The Ugly American*. Graham Greene's novel was about the naive assumption that money, power, and ideology could transform a Third World country, while William L. Lederer and Eugene Burdick called for just the opposite—more American money, expertise, and power, as if those alone would be enough to assure the future of the world. During and after the war, Americans would continue to debate the same question, whether American power should have been used in Vietnam at all or whether not enough power was used there.

When John Kennedy entered the White House, the Vietnam debate began to assume more urgency. The president faced difficult decisions about that debate. Some of his advisors, such as Maxwell Taylor and Walt Rostow, were calling for more direct military intervention, while others, like George Ball and Douglas MacArthur, were warning him to be careful about getting mired in a land war in Asia. Kennedy thought he found a middle ground in counterinsurgency strategies designed to strengthen the South Vietnamese military and political system while keeping the Vietcong at bay. His fascination with the Green Berets symbolized the president's faith in counterinsurgency. During the Kennedy years the Green Berets were perceived as missionaries with muscle. They seemed to be the perfect fulfillment of Colonel Hillandale in *The Ugly American*. They formed a tightly knit elite whose object was duty and whose family was the other people who wore the Green Beret. In addition to training in demolition, communications, scuba diving, unarmed combat, jungle survival, and field medicine, the Green Berets read the works of Mao Zedong and Vo Nguyen Giap, prepared their bodies for combat, and became fluent in the language of the people they were going to help.

The novel that reflected the new optimism was Robin Moore's *The Green Berets*, published in 1965, just as the American militarization of the war began. In the novel, the "ugly American" is transformed into a bright and shining knight, a warrior for democracy. The book rocketed to the top of the best-seller lists. Special Forces troops are portrayed as "good guys" out to rescue South Vietnam from its own incompetence and venality. South Vietnamese troops are cowardly and corrupt, quick to desert when real combat begins. The Vietcong and North Vietnamese are depicted as uniformly evil, bent on torture, murder, and atrocity. The book also celebrates the genius of American technology and the virtues of democracy and capitalism. There were other clones of Moore's novel. Gene D. Moore's *The Killing at Ngo Tho* (1967) focuses on Colonel Scott Leonard, a Special Forces officer whose mission is to locate and destroy a Vietcong base. *The Coasts of War* (1966), by Scott S. Stone is about Lieutenant Eriksen, a "black beret" naval advisor to South Vietnam. He commands a small flotilla of patrol boats in the Mekong Delta whose mission is to stop the shipment of supplies to the Vietcong. Peter Derrig's *The Pride of the Green Berets*

(1966) read like an enlistment brochure for the Special Forces. In *The Last Bridge* (1966), Brian Garfield writes of a combined force of American and South Vietnamese soldiers who operate behind enemy lines. Their mission, which is successful, is to rescue an American prisoner of war and destroy an important bridge in North Vietnam. Richard Newhafer's *No More Bugles in the Sky* (1966) revolves around a group of veteran CIA fliers who go to Indochina and bomb Chinese airfields along the North Vietnamese border, ostensibly to prevent Chinese air power from playing any role in the war. They, too, succeed in their mission.

The Green Berets still looked heroic in Robin Moore and Henry Rothblatt's 1971 novel *Court Martial*, but by then the enemy was the regular army, the Pentagon bureaucracy, and the CIA, all of whom saw to the court-martial of five Special Forces officers because of the alleged killing of a Vietnamese double agent. The image of the Vietnam War in 1971 was far different than it had been in 1965 when Moore's *The Green Berets* first appeared. By that time the novel, which had appeared so heroic in 1965, had become a caricature, almost laughable in its naïveté and innocence. Between 1967 and 1973, the bulk of American fiction about the Vietnam War could not have been more different from the early works of people like Robin Moore, Peter Derrig, Brian Garfield, and Scott Stone.

During the rest of the war years, most of the fiction portrayed Indochina as an alien place for Americans, a region of the world where they ought not be involved. In 1967 David Halberstam wrote *One Very Hot Day*. Early in the 1960s, Halberstam was a *New York Times* correspondent in South Vietnam who won a Pulitzer Prize for his reporting on the war. As early as 1963 Halberstam was arguing that U.S. policy in Vietnam was badly flawed, and he put those ideas to fiction in *One Very Hot Day*. The novel revolves around several American advisors who are trying to train the South Vietnamese army. The central character is a Captain Beaupre, who views the whole country as a worthless hellhole. A veteran of World War II and Korea, he has no illusions about the Vietnam War, and his only objective is to stay alive in the hot, sticky, despair-ridden environment. But Beaupre's second in command—the young, idealistic Lieutenant Anderson—has high hopes for successfully training the South Vietnamese soldiers and winning the war against Communism. In the end, the South Vietnamese troops fail to fight, Beaupre manages to survive, but Anderson dies in a firefight. Beaupre is unable to find any reason for his death, any meaning for an American to be dead in a nowhere place called Ap Than Thoi. As far as Beaupre is concerned, Anderson had died for nothing on a hot day in nowhere.

President Lyndon Johnson made the fateful decision early in 1965 to introduce regular American ground troops into the conflict, militarizing and Americanizing the conflict. By the end of the year, there were more than 184,000 U.S. troops in Vietnam, and a total of 636 soldiers had been killed since 1954. One year later, however, the number of troops had increased to more than 385,000, and the number of American deaths had risen tenfold—to 6,644 people. The antiwar movement was steadily gaining power, and the absurdities of the war became more and more manifest. Not surprisingly, the literature of the early years of the conflict reflected those changes.

John Sack's *M* (1967) was one of the first of the antiwar novels. The novel focuses on M Company, a training unit of American soldiers, and follows them from basic training at Fort Dix, New Jersey, through several months of combat in Vietnam. Sack juxtaposes Specialist 4 Demirgian, a gung ho American soldier committed to the philosophical rationale of the war, with the corruption of ARVN troops, the inability to distinguish between Vietcong and civilians, and the unbelievably poor morale among U.S. soldiers. The novel climaxes in a tragic killing of a Vietnamese girl by an American grenade lobbed into a shelter to kill Vietcong. Martin Russ's *Happy Hunting Ground* (1968) also exposes the irrationality of Vietnam violence and the way it affected the men who fought there, as does Charles Coe's *Young Man in Vietnam* (1968). In *The Prisoners of Quai Dong* (1967), Victor Kolpacoff's writes about a fictitious prisoner-of-war camp in North Vietnam inhabited by American POWs and their North Vietnamese captors. Through the lens of an interrogation room, where Americans are regularly tortured to extract confessions, Kolpacoff eventually describes everyone there—American POWs, Vietnamese officials, and innocent witnesses—as victims of the war.

James Crumley's novel *One Count to Cadence* (1969) centers on a ten-man communications detachment stationed first at Clark Air Base in the Philippines and then in Vietnam during the early stages of the war. Sergeant "Slag" Krummel is the narrator, and his foil is Joe Morning, a self-destructive loser. The novel exposes the gratuitous violence of military life—bars, brothels, fights, and profanity—as well as the futility of the war in Vietnam. The sergeant eventually betrays a best friend and buddy, and the team is decimated. The novel ends with the unit's returning to the Philippines, where Joe Morning joins the Communist-inspired Huk Rebellion there. William Turner Huggett's *Body Count* (1973) uses the battle at Khe Sanh in 1967 and 1968 to expose the futility of American policy in Vietnam. In the novel, Lieutenant Chris Hawkins takes over a marine platoon and evolves into an experienced leader. But the abandonment of their position soon after sacrificing so many lives to take it proves the futility of the war.

The problems of the "system" are portrayed in Josiah Bunting's *The Lionheads* (1972), which focuses on George Lemming, commander of the 12th Division in Vietnam. The time frame is March and April of 1968, in the wake of the Tet Offensive, when Lemming does anything he can, including the needless sacrifice of many of his own troops, to attack a North Vietnamese division and promote his own career. In *The Killing Zone* (1970), William Crawford Woods portrays the Vietnam War as an example of liberal extremism, a dangerous faith in technology and systems analysis. He writes of a training camp where an outdated professional soldier must train new recruits in the new age of high-tech warfare. But in the end there is a grisly training camp accident where several young soldiers are accidentally killed when a computer at the base incorrectly orders the use of live rounds in a training exercise. The novel exposes the intellectual arrogance of the programmers, systems analysts, accountants, statisticians, and experts who organized and conducted the war.

Some of the wartime novels used black comedy to characterize the folly of the war. *Incident at Muc Wa* was the title of Daniel Ford's 1967 novel about the Vietnam War. The book centers on Corporal Stephen Courcey, a demolitions expert who has just arrived in Vietnam. Along with several other American soldiers, he establishes an outpost at Muc Wa. The novel proceeds to expose the absurdities of the war through tragicomedy. Courcey's girlfriend from the States shows up at Muc Wa as a war correspondent, but she is unable to meet him because he is off in the jungles with a visiting general and army captain who are trying to earn their Combat Infantry Badges. The novel provides a caricature of stupid officers fighting a war for the wrong reasons. In the end, the troops at Muc Wa fight off a Vietcong attack, and the Vietcong, in Ford's words, "exfiltrate" the area. In the end, Courcey is killed in action. William Pelfry's *The Big V* (1972), in a similar vein, is one of the bleakest war novels ever written.

Two of the protest novels during the Vietnam War were surrealistic in their approaches to the conflict. Norman Mailer's *Why Are We in Vietnam?* (1967) is not actually set in Indochina. Placed in Texas, New York City, and the Brooks Range of Alaska, it is an antiwar story without ever being in Vietnam. A cast of characters—D. J. Jellicoe, Rusty Jellicoe, Alice Lee Jellicoe, Medium Asshole Pete, Medium Asshole Bill, and Tex Hude—end up in the Brooks Range of Alaska on a hunting trip. There, in a pristine and naturally savage environment, they use all the hunting technology they can muster and literally slaughter wolves, caribou, bighorn sheep, and bears. The carnage is extraordinary and, for Norman Mailer, symbolic of what American military technology was doing to the life and habitat of Southeast Asia.

Even more bizarre is William Eastlake's *The Bamboo Bed*, published in 1969. The novel begins with the suicide of a Madame Dieudonne after she hears of the death of her American Ranger lover Captain Clancy. Eastlake tries to describe the absurdity of the war with implausible fantasy images: peace-loving hippie flower children wandering aimlessly through the Indochinese jungles; helicopter pilots having sex with med-evac nurses while airborne; American Rangers topped with Roman hel-mets and accompanied by drummer boys airlifted into French-Vietnamese villas. The war in Vietnam makes no sense at all, just as the strange images of *The Bamboo Bed* cannot fit into any rationale world.

The American military presence in Vietnam came to an end in 1973, and in 1975 North Vietnamese troops overran South Vietnam, leaving the American public with the powerful and depressing images of U.S. personnel and desperate South Vietnamese evacuating the country via the roof of the American embassy in Saigon. The war was over. America lost. The war was not the only thing that was over. Most Americans wanted to forget about the conflict and its humiliation and absurdity. Neither the publishing world in New York nor the film industry in Hollywood wanted much to do with the war, and between 1973 and 1977 there was an extraordinary dearth of fiction about the conflict. There were a few novels—Robert Stone's *Dog Soldiers* (1973), Stephen Smith's *American Boys* (1975), and James Kirkwood's *Some Kind of Hero* (1975)—but they were exceptions rather than the rule, and their quality did not match what came before and what would come later. Americans were pretending that the war never happened.

The only major piece of literature to emerge during the lean years of 1973 to 1977 was Ron Kovic's *Born on the Fourth of July* (1977). Like a number of other pieces of Vietnam War literature, its theme revolves around the loss of innocence—how a naive, enthusiastic young American leaves a fine home, nurturing family, and wonderful country to fight for freedom, only to find himself in the Vietnamese quagmire. Ron Kovic grew up in a Roman Catholic family on Long Island, New York, and he joined the Marine Corps after high school to fight for his country. But the war was not what he expected. During combat he kills a friend accidentally, participates in the slaughter of Vietnamese children, and then takes a spinal wound, leaving him a paraplegic to suffer in VA hospitals when he returns home. Kovic eventually finds redemption only through his own opposition to the Vietnam War.

In 1977 the dam burst on Vietnam War literature, and for the next decade American publishers produced an array of excellent fiction and fine personal narratives. Philip Caputo's *A Rumor of War* (1977) picked up the loss of innocence theme and continued it. Hypnotized by John F. Kennedy's call on Americans to serve their country and the world, Caputo also joined the Marine Corps, was temporarily desensitized by the senseless brutality of the conflict, and ordered the murder of a Vietnamese civilian. Michael Herr's *Dispatches* (1977) portrays the black romanticism of Vietnam—how Americans found themselves desensi-tized, dehumanized, and engaged in an orgy of violence to fulfill their own mythological expectations. W. D. Ehrhart's *Vietnam-Perkasie* (1978) is a novel that shows how an innocent American boy is transformed by the Vietnam War into a killing machine, a crazed murderer for whom violence has become an end in itself. Gustav Hasford's *The Short-Timers* (1979) is an extraordinarily violent book that focuses on the fictional character William "Joker" Doolittle, a marine combat reporter in Vietnam who refuses promotion to sergeant and insists on wearing a peace button. With his time running "short"—only forty-nine days left on the tour of duty—Doolittle's insubordination rankles a superior officer, and he finds himself reassigned to a vulnerable combat unit. Supposedly fighting for freedom, the troops are actually prisoners of the war itself. James Webb's *Fields of Fire* (1978) follows a platoon of marines slogging through the rice paddies and jungles outside An Hoa, suffering violent death, horrible injuries, wretched living conditions, and poor morale because they see no rationale for the sacrifice, no reason to die. The central character is Will Goodrich, a Harvard student who enlists in the Marine Corps Band only to be assigned by mistake to Vietnam.

Novels about women in Vietnam followed the same themes. John Newman's 1988 edition of *Vietnam War Literature* lists over 700 works, poetry, drama, short stories, and novels. Of those 700 works, only about twenty deal with American women who served in Vietnam. Only one of the twenty treats the contributions of American women seriously. Most works of fiction about American servicewomen in Vietnam are either adolescent nurse novels, romance novels, or adult fiction bordering on or blatantly pornographic. Characterization of the women in these novels tends to be thinly drawn stereotypes. Newman's annotated bibliography lists five stories entitled either *Vietnam Nurse* or *Nurse in Vietnam*. The plot of these romance novels revolves around the relationship between a beautiful nurse and a handsome, very masculine officer. They fall in love and manage to have one or more dangerous adventures. In most of these stories the officer rescues the nurse, and they live happily ever after. Other works are blatantly pornographic. These include Parma Malik's *Viet Cong Defilers* (1976), in which a WAC corporal is captured and sexually tortured by the Viet Cong, *Vietcong Rape Raiders* (1983), a story about the brutal violation of an American nurse by her Vietcong captors, and several other anonymous works published by the War Horrors Press—*Nurse Prisoners of the Cong, Captive Nurses of the Viet Cong*, and *Victims of the Cong*. These works provide little insight into the real experiences of women who served in Vietnam.

One romance novel, *Bend with the Wind* (1980) by Elizabeth Simms Moore, is unique in its attempt to provide cultural background on Vietnam. The love story of nurse Marty Fountain and Dr. Peter Cain, set in a small civilian hospital in Quang Ngai province in 1962, is interspersed with thinly disguised lectures about the people, culture, and government of Vietnam. Moore brings some firsthand experience to the work. Her biographical information indicates that she worked as an X-ray technician in Vietnam but does not tell when she was there or in what part of the country. While this work presents information on such things as Vietnamese wedding customs, the Buddhist and Cao-Dai religions, the Montagnards, and efforts to help the Vietnamese people through international relief organizations, the stereotypical portrayals of the female characters provide little insight into the reality of their experiences in Vietnam.

Forever Sad the Hearts (1982) by Patricia L. Walsh is undoubtedly the best novel about women in the Vietnam War. In contrast to the other novels, characterization, language, and experiences presented in this work are completely consistent with Van Devanter's memoir and the oral histories. The story is told by Kate Shea, a nurse anesthetist, who volunteers for an eighteen-month tour of duty in Vietnam with the government-funded Better World Organization (BWO). Arriving in Saigon in early 1967, she is assigned to a civilian hospital in Da Nang. Walsh vividly describes the deplorable conditions in the hospital—the stench of rotted flesh and blood, garbage cans overflowing with putrid dressings, swarms of flies crawling over the operating tables, inadequate equipment, and lack of supplies. Kate quickly learns that most of the supplies that BWO sends the hospital are siphoned off to the black market. Because agency officials refuse to face the problem, nurses "crumshaw" most of their supplies from the navy and air force to keep the hospital going.

Like most Vietnam novels, *Forever Sad the Hearts* is a novel of initiation—of lost innocence. In this version, however, innocence is lost through treating the victims of combat rather than through participation in combat. Kate came to Vietnam believing the American myth. Americans were the good guys in the white hats who were in Vietnam to help fight Communism and preserve democracy. She was soon disillusioned. When the marines brought truckloads of wounded civilians to the hospital, Kate asked, "Why are American military called to pick up civilians?" "They don't have to be called," she was told. "They're the other half of the fire fight." A young lieutenant put it more bluntly when he exclaimed, "You mean we shoot 'em and you fix them up? . . . You're over here risking your life to save the people I'm risking my life to shoot." Here, the paradox of this war is brought clearly in focus. The patients that the American government was paying her to heal, were wounded by the soldiers the government paid to fight.

Unlike most of the other works presented, *Forever Sad the Hearts* seriously examines the politics of war and its consequences. Kate becomes increasingly concerned as she observes numerous discrepancies between what is being reported and what she can see firsthand. After an attack that leaves a large number of Americans dead, Kate wonders how the government would report this back home. She notes the difference between what the papers report and "the stacks of manila envelopes in the Air Force post office containing the records of Americans killed or missing in action." She also hears "men laugh about who'd be stupid enough to stay behind to count the enemy dead." There is another concern. What would happen to the young men Uncle Sam so casually offered up for slaughter who come home mutilated but still alive? "There seemed to be numbers and labels for everyone—K.I.A.s, M.I.A.s, wounded in action, enemy killed," Kate muses. "But this war needed a new category, a name for those who could be saved by rapid evacuation and modern technology, but could never return to a normal life.... They were the Viet Nam War's M.I.L.s. Missing in Life."

The finest novel of the Vietnam War appeared in 1978 with the publication of Tim O'Brien's *Going After Cacciato*. Unlike other works of fiction and nonfiction about the war, *Going After Cacciato* makes no attempt to re-create the Vietnamese environment. Instead, the book is surrealistic, highly symbolic, even though it retains the violence, capriciousness, and absurdity of the war. The novel begins when Cacciato, an American soldier, decides to desert. But he does not leave the service by way of Saigon or during a rest-and-recreation holiday in Honolulu or Hong Kong or Bangkok. Cacciato decides to head for Paris, France, by foot, through 8,600 miles of Southeast Asian jungles, South Asian mountains, Near East deserts, and European villages and cities. Since desertion is a crime, the third squad is assigned to go get Cacciato. The narrator is Paul Berlin, one of the soldiers in the squad. While the squad makes its way across Asia and Asia Minor, Paul Berlin survives the war physically by street smarts and emotionally by an active imagination.

John Del Vecchio's *13th Valley* (1982) is a more heavily intellectual piece, a novel of Alpha Company at the battle of Khe Ta Laou Valley. The main characters are college-educated, black 1st lieutenant Brooks; Jan, a highly articulate, politicized Afro-American; Silvers, a Jewish writer; El Paso, a college-educated, Hispanic radio operator; and Egan, who possesses an engineering degree. The book reads like a history of the battle, complete with a description of reality as well as official documents, which have no relationship at all to what happened. Such was the Vietnam War. U.S. military and political officials, through systems analysis and powerful technology, tried to create a reality, but in the end the only reality was defeat, depression, guilt, racial tension, and hostility toward officers. The characters articulate these themes throughout the novel's dialogue.

Stephen Wright's *Meditations in Green* (1983) pulls together most of the negative themes emerging from earlier novels. It revolves around a young soldier who goes off to Vietnam full of dreams of glory, but during his stay there he loses his naive innocence. He interprets aerial photographs and becomes appalled at the indiscriminate effects of carpet bombing—the mutilation and destruction of innocent civilians. To deal with his guilt, he turns to heroin and becomes a full-fledged addict, like tens of thousands of other American soldiers. Eventually, the young man slips into a lunacy that even he can recognize.

The attitudes of American soldiers toward the Vietnamese—South Vietnamese, Vietcong, and North Vietnamese—as well as the feelings of the Vietnamese toward the Americans is the central theme in Anthony Grey's *Saigon* (1982). It is a historical novel that follows Joseph Sherman from his youth, when his father takes him on a trip to Indochina, to the years of World War II, when he is an Office of Strategic Services (OSS) agent there, and finally to his years in Vietnam during the war. The central message is that the Vietnamese viewed Americans as an alien presence who would have preferred it if none of them had ever arrived. *Officers' Wives* (1981) by Thomas Fleming views most South Vietnamese as hopelessly corrupt and inept. Larry Heinemann's *Close Quarters* (1983) tells of Philip Dosier, who mans an armored personnel carrier during the war and randomly kills Vietnamese—enemies as well as civilians.

By the late 1980s and early 1990s, there were still fine literary works being produced about the Vietnam War, such as Tim O'Brien's *The Things They Carried* (1990), but there was also a new supply of "comic book" literature, a "Ramboization" of the conflict. Distrustful of their government in the 1970s and early 1980s, many Americans became mesmerized by the idea that there were still American POWs being held in Indochina. Films and novels reflected that fascination. In Franklin Allen Leib's *Valley of the Shadow* (1992), Lieutenant William Stuart discovers that one of his men, whom he thought was killed in action, is actually a prisoner of war in Laos. He tries to stage a heroic rescue of the friend. J. C. Pollock's *Mission M.I.A.* (1982) and Brian Freemantle's *The Vietnam Legacy* (1984) have similar themes. After the Gulf War of 1991, Americans became even more convinced that the war in Vietnam had been lost because politicians placed too many restrictions on the military. Joe Weber's novel *Rules of Engagement* (1992) exploits that conviction. It is the story of Brad Austin, a marine F–4 pilot who, after the death of his squadron leader, goes after North Vietnamese pilots and disregards the rules of engagement imposed by the White House. Stephen Coonts's *Flight of the Intruder* (1987) has a similar theme. Jake Grafton, a naval A–6 pilot, realizes toward the end of the war that the targets he is being sent to bomb have little strategic value and that the navy is primarily interested in boosting their sortie counts in competition with the air force. He decides to take the rules of engagement into his own hands and attacks on a rogue mission. Zalin Grant's *Over the Beach* (1986) is similar in its theme.

Other novels made the Vietnam War part of American popular culture through what scholars call mass market fiction. There have been literally hundreds of pulp novels dealing with the war, but several of the more recent ones reveal the primary themes. Franklin Leib's *The Fire Dream* deals in the male rituals of the World War II genre immortalized by such novels as *Battle Cry*, *From Here to Eternity*, and *The Young Lions*. It is pretty standard stuff, full of characters like Stuart, a gifted young white man who seeks glory in combat; Coles, a black man anxious to prove he is Stuart's equal; Hunter, a neurotic man driven by his own fears; Moser, the savant who can see into the future; and Beaurive, who leads the group and insists that there are glory and redemption in combat and victory. In the end, most of the men are killed, but they believe that they have nonetheless achieved "honor, duty, and glory." Danielle Steele's *Message from Nam* (1990) is even cornier. It is loaded with clichés. The characters are idealistic college students, black and white, who join the civil rights movement in the early 1960s, learn politics in the heady atmosphere of the University of California, Berkeley, fall in love, and complete law school, but the men are drafted and end up in the jungles of Vietnam. History continues. Some live and some die, but love survives.

The best of the recent mass market novels is Kurt Vonnegut's *Hocus Pocus* (1990). The central character is Eugene V. Debs Hartke, a West Point graduate who ends up against his will in Vietnam and becomes a professional killer. He ends up back in the United States years later married to a crazy alcoholic and teaching at a second-rate college. Hartke is a cynic who becomes a rummy womanizer. He takes a job at a local prison teaching illiterate African-American inmates and becomes involved in an uprising against the prison in particular and the Establishment in general. Arrested for his deeds, Hartke begins writing his memoirs from a jail cell. The novel is vintage Vonnegut, loaded with the American landscape and the theme that words—whether Lyndon Johnson's, Richard Nixon's, or Eugene V. Debs-Hartke's—are the hocus pocus that allowed America to explain away Vietnam.

BIBLIOGRAPHY

Books

Arco, Ronald. *Year of the Monkey*. New York: Simon and Schuster, 1982.

Baber, Asa. *Land of a Million Elephants*. London: Hutchinson, 1970.

Balaban, John. *After Our War*. Pittsburgh, Pa.: University of Pittsburgh Press, 1972.

Ballard, J. G. *Hello America*. London: Triad/Granada, 1981.

Berry, D. C. *Saigon Cemetery*. Athens: University of Georgia Press, 1972.

Bodey, Donald. *F.N.G.* New York: Viking, 1985.

Briley, John. *The Traitors*. New York: Putnam's, 1969.

Bunting, Josiah. *The Lionheads*. New York: George Braziller, 1972.

Butler, Robert Olen. *The Alleys of Eden.* New York: Horizon Press, 1981.

Caputo, Philip. *A Rumor of War.* New York: Ballantine, 1977.

Caputo, Philip. *DelCorso's Gallery.* New York: Holt, Rinehart, and Winston, 1983.

Coe, Charles. *Young Man in Vietnam.* New York: Four Winds, 1968.

Collingwood, Charles. *The Defector.* New York: Harper and Row, 1970.

Coonts, Stephen. *Flight of the Intruder.* New York: Simon and Schuster, 1987.

Corder, E. M. *The Deer Hunter.* New York: Exeter Books, 1978.

Crumley, James. *One Count to Cadence.* New York: Random House, 1969.

Dann, Jean Van Buren, and Jack Dunn, eds. *In the Field of Fire.* New York: TOR, 1987.

Del Vecchio, John. *The 13th Valley.* New York: Bantam, 1982.

Derrig, Peter. *The Pride of the Green Berets.* New York: Paperback Library, 1966.

Diehl, William. *Thai Horse.* New York: Villard Books, 1988.

Donovan, David. *Once a Warrior King.* London: Corgi, 1987.

Downs, Frederick. *The Killing Zone: My Life in the Vietnam War.* New York: Norton, 1978.

Duncan, Donald. *The New Legions.* New York: Random House, 1967.

Ehrhart, W. D. *Vietnam-Perkasie: A Combat Marine Memoir.* Jefferson, N.C.: McFarland, 1983.

Eastlake, William. *The Bamboo Bed.* New York: Simon and Schuster, 1969.

Fleming, Thomas. *Officers' Wives.* Garden City, N.Y.: Doubleday, 1981.

Ford, Daniel. *Incident at Muc Wa.* Garden City, N.Y.: Doubleday, 1967.

Frankland, Mark. *The Mother-of-Pearl Men.* London: John Murray, 1985.

Freemantle, Brian. *The Vietnam Legacy.* New York: Doherty Associates, 1984.

Fuller, Jack. *Fragments.* New York: Morrow, 1984.

Garfield, Brian. *The Last Bridge.* New York: David McKay, 1966.

Garson, Barbara. *MacBird.* New York: Grove Press, 1967.

Gellhorn, Martha. *The Face of War.* London: Virago, 1986.

Glasser, Ronald J. *365 Days.* New York: George Braziller, 1971.

Gold, Jerome. *The Negligence of Death.* Seattle, Wash.: Black Heron Press, 1990.

Grant, Zalin. *Over the Beach.* New York: Norton, 1986.

Greene, Graham. *The Quiet American.* Harmondsworth, England: Penguin Books, 1956.

Grey, Anthony. *Saigon.* Boston: Little, Brown, 1982.

Groom, Winston. *Better Times than These.* New York: Berkeley, 1978.

Halberstam, David. *One Very Hot Day.* Boston: Houghton Mifflin, 1967.

Haldeman, Joe. *The Forever War.* London: Futura, 1984.

Harrison, Marshall. *The Delta.* Novato, Calif.: Presidio Press, 1992.

Hasford, Gustav. *The Short-Timers.* New York: Harper and Row, 1979.

Heinemann, Larry. *Close Quarters.* New York: Farrar, Straus, and Giroux, 1974.

Heinemann, Larry. *Paco's Story.* Harmondsworth, England: Penguin, 1986.

Herr, Michael. *Dispatches.* London: Picador, 1977.

Huggett, William Turner. *Body Count.* New York: Putnam's, 1973.

Just, Ward. *Stringer.* Port Townsend, Wash.: Graywolf Press, 1974.

Just, Ward. *The American Blues.* New York: Viking, 1984.

Kalb, Bernard, and Marvin Kalb. *The Last Ambassador.* Boston: Little, Brown, 1981.

Karlin, Wayne. *Free Fire Zone.* Coventry, Conn.: First Casualty Press, 1973.

Kim, Samuel. *The American POWs*. Boston: Branden Press, 1979.

Kirkwood, James. *Some Kind of Hero*. New York: Crowell, 1975.

Kolpacoff, Victor. *The Prisoners of Quai Dong*. New York: New American Library, 1967.

Kolpit, Arthur. *Indians*. New York: Bantam, 1971.

Kovic, Ron. *Born on the Fourth of July*. New York: Pocket Books, 1977.

Lederer, William J., and Eugene Burdick. *The Ugly American*. New York: Norton, 1958.

Leib, Franklin Allen. *The Fire Dream*. Novato, Calif.: Presidio Press, 1984.

Leib, Franklin Allen. *Valley of the Shadow*. Novato, Calif.: Presidio Press, 1992.

Little, Loyd. *Parthian Shot*. New York: Viking Press, 1975.

Little, Loyd. *In the Village of the Man*. New York: Viking Press, 1978.

McCarthy, Mary. *Vietnam*. London: Weidenfeld and Nicolson, 1967.

McDonough, James R. *Platoon Leader*. Novato, Calif.: Presidio Press, 1985.

McKeown, Bonni. *Peaceful Patriot: The Story of Tom Bennett*. New York: Peaceful Patriot Press, 1987.

McQuinn, Donald. *Targets*. New York: Tom Doherty, 1980.

Mailer, Norman. *Why Are We in Vietnam?* New York: Putnam's, 1967.

Mason, Bobbie Ann. *In Country*. London: Flamingo, 1985.

Mason, Robert. *Chickenhawk*. London: Corgi, Transworld, 1983.

Mayer, Tom. *The Weary Falcon*. Boston: Houghton Mifflin, 1971.

Mecklin, John. *Mission in Torment: An Intimate Account of the U.S. Role in Vietnam*. New York: Doubleday, 1965.

Merritt, William E. *Where the Rivers Ran Backward*. Garden City, N.Y.: Doubleday, 1990.

Miller, Franklin D., and Elwood J. C. Kureth. *Reflections of a Warrior*. Novato, Calif.: Presidio Press, 1991.

Miller, Stephen P. *An Act of God: Memories of Vietnam*. Boston: Northeast View Press, 1987.

Moore, Elizabeth Simms. *Bend with the Wind*. Port Washington, N.Y.: Ashley Books, 1980.

Moore, Gene D. *The Killing at Ngo Tho*. New York: Norton, 1967.

Moore, Robin. *The Green Berets*. New York: Crown, 1965.

Moore, Robin, and Henry Rothblatt. *Court Martial*. Garden City, N.Y.: Doubleday, 1971.

Newhafer, Richard. *No More Bugles in the Sky*. New York: New American Library, 1966.

O'Brien, Tim. *If I Die in a Combat Zone: Box Me Up and Ship Me Home*. New York: Delacorte, 1973.

O'Brien, Tim. *Going After Cacciato*. New York: Delacorte, 1978.

O'Brien, Tim. *The Things They Carried*. Boston: Houghton Mifflin, 1990.

Pelfry, William. *The Big V*. New York: Liveright, 1972.

Phillips, Jayne Anne. *Machine Dreams*. New York: Dutton, 1984.

Pollock, J. C. *Mission M.I.A.* New York: Crown, 1982.

Rabe, David W. *The Basic Training of Pavlo Hummel/Sticks and Bones*. New York: Viking Press, 1973.

Rabe, David W. *Streamers*. New York: Knopf, 1982.

Ray, Michele. *Two Shores of Hell*. London: John Murray, 1967.

Ribman, Ronald. *The Final War of Ollie Winter*. New York: Dell, 1975.

Roth, Robert. *Sand in the Wind*. Boston: Little, Brown, 1973.

Russ, Martin. *Happy Hunting Ground*. New York: Atheneum Press, 1968.

Sack, John. *M*. New York: New American Library, 1967.

Sloan, James Park. *War Games*. Boston: Houghton Mifflin, 1971.

Smith, Stephen. *American Boys*. New York: Avon Books, 1975.

Steele, Danielle. *Message from Nam*. New York: Delacorte, 1990.

Stone, Robert. *Dog Soldiers*. Boston: Houghton Mifflin, 1973.

Stone, Robert. *A Flag for Sunrise*. London: Picador, 1981.

Stone, Scott C. S. *The Coasts of War*. New York: Pyramid, 1966.

Terry, Megan. *Viet Rock*. New York: Simon and Schuster, 1967.

Tiede, Tom. *Coward*. New York: Random House, 1968.

Van Lustbader, Eric. *French Kiss*. New York: Fawcett Colombine, 1989.

Vonnegut, Jurt. *Hocus Pocus*. New York: Putnam, 1990.

Walsh, Patricia L. *Forever Sad the Hearts*. New York: Avon Books, 1982.

Webb, James. *Fields of Fire*. Englewood Cliffs, N.J.: Prentice-Hall, 1978.

Webb, James. *A Sense of Honor*. New York: Bantam Books, 1981.

Webb, Kate. *On the Other Side*. New York: Quadrangle, 1972.

Weber, Joe. *Rules of Engagement*. Novato, Calif.: Presidio Press, 1992.

Weigl, Bruce. *The Monkey Wars*. Athens: University of Georgia Press, 1985.

West, Morris. *The Ambassador*. New York: Morrow, 1965.

Williams, Reese. *Unwinding the Vietnam War: From War into Peace*. Seattle, Wash.:
Real Comet Press, 1991.

Winn, David. *Gangland*. New York: Knopf, 1982.

Woods, William Crawford. *The Killing Zone*. New York: Random House, 1970.

Wright, Stephen. *Meditations in Green*. New York: Scribner's, 1983.

Scholarly Publications

Anisfield, Nancy, ed. *Vietnam Anthology: American War Literature*. Bowling Green,
Ohio: Bowling Green State University Press, 1985.

Baritz, Loren. *Backfire: A History of How American Culture Led Us into Vietnam and
Made Us Fight the Way We Did*. New York: Morrow, 1985.

Bartz, Michael Omar. "United States Cultural Movements as Reflected in the
Fiction, Journals, and Oral Histories of the Vietnam War." Ph.D. Diss.
Saint Louis University, 1987.

Beidler, Philip D. "Truth-Telling and Literary Values in the Vietnam Novel."
South Atlantic Quarterly 78 (Spring 1979): 141–56.

Beidler, Philip D. *American Literature and the Experience of Vietnam*. Athens: University of Georgia Press, 1982.

Beidler, Philip D. *Re-Writing America: Vietnam Authors in Their Generation*. Athens:
University of Georgia Press, 1991.

Beidler, Philip D. "Bad Business: Vietnam and Recent Mass-Market Fiction."
College English 54 (January 1992): 64–75.

Bellhouse, Mary L., and Lawrence Litchfield. "Vietnam and Loss of Innocence:
An Analysis of the Political Implications of the Popular Literature of the
Vietnam War." *Journal of Popular Culture* 16 (Winter 1982): 157–74.

Bergonzi, Bernard. "Vietnam Novels: First Draft." *Commonweal* 27 (October 1972): 84–88.

Brown, Harvey Ray Brown, Jr. "Modern American War Drama." M.A. Thesis. Lamar University, 1981.

Bryan, C.D.B. "Barely Suppressed Screams." *Harper's* 268 (June 1984): 67–72.

Calloway, Catherine. "The Vietnam War Novel: A Descent into Hell." Ph.D. Diss. University of South Florida, 1987.

Christie, Norton Bradley. "Another War and Postmodern Memory: Remembering Vietnam." Ph.D. Diss. Duke University, 1988.

Chung, Youn-Son. "War and Morality: The Search for Meaning in American Novels of World War I, World War II, and the Vietnam War." Ph.D. Diss. Emory University, 1985.

Colonnese, Tom Graydon. "The Vietnam War in American Literature." Ph.D. Diss. Arizona State University, 1981.

Creek, Mardena Bridges. "Myth, Wound, Accommodation: American Literary Response to the War in Vietnam." Ph.D. Diss. Ball State University, 1982.

Cronin, Cornelius A. "Historical Background to Larry Heinemann's *Close Quarters*." *Critique* 24 (Winter 1983): 119–30.

Ehrhart, W. D. "Soldier-Poets of the Vietnam War." *Virginia Quarterly Review* 63 (Spring 1987): 246–65.

Ehrhart, W. D., ed. *Carrying the Darkness: The Poetry of the Vietnam War*. Lubbock: Texas Tech University Press, 1989.

Felstiner, John. "American Poetry and the War in Vietnam." *Stand* 19 (No. 2, 1978): 4–11.

Furniss, David West. "Making Sense of the War: Vietnam and American Prose." Ph.D. Diss. University of Minnesota, 1988.

Gaspar, Charles Jamieson, Jr. "Reconnecting: Time and History in Narratives of the Vietnam War." Ph.D. Diss. University of Connecticut, 1983.

Gilman, Owen W., Jr., and Lorrie Smith, eds. *America Rediscovered: Critical Essays on Literature and Film of the Vietnam War*. New York: Garland, 1990.

Gitlin, Todd. "Notes in War Poetry." *Confrontation* 8 (Spring 1974): 145–47.

Hall, Henry Palmer, Jr. "The Enlisted Man's War: A Study of Vietnam War Novels." Ph.D. Diss. The University of Texas at Austin, 1984.

Harris, Norman. "Blacks in Vietnam: A Holistic Perspective Through Fiction and Journalism." *The Western Journal of Black Studies* 10 (No. 3, 1986): 121–31.

Heiss, Andrea Brandenburg. "On Foreign Grounds: Portrayal of Americans in Vietnam." Ph.D. Diss. The University of Iowa, 1983.

Hellmann, John. "The New Journalism and Vietnam: Memory as Structure in Michael Herr's *Dispatches*." *South Atlantic Quarterly* 79 (Spring 1980): 141–51.

Herzog, Tobey C. "Writing about Vietnam: A Heavy Heart-of-Darkness Trip." *College English* 41 (February 1980): 680–95.

Hidesaki, Yasuro. "Black Humor and Vietnam War Novels." *Kyushu American Literature* 27 (1986): 97–106.

Jason, Philip K., ed. *Fourteen Landing Zones. Approach to the Vietnam War Literature*. Iowa City: University of Iowa Press, 1991.

Kakutani, Michiko. "Novelists and Vietnam: The War Goes On." *New York Times Book Review* (April 15, 1984): 38–41.

Karaguezian, Maureen. "Irony in Robert Stone's *Dog Soldiers*." *Critique* 24 (Winter 1983): 65–73.

Keating, Kletus. "The Rhetoric of Extreme Experience: Michael Herr's Non-Fiction Vietnam Novel, *Dispatches*." Ph.D. Diss. University of Denver, 1987.

Lennox, William J., Jr. "American War Poetry." Ph.D. Diss. Princeton University, 1982.

Lewis, Lloyd B. *The Tainted War: Culture and Identity in Vietnam War Narratives.* Westport, Conn.: Greenwood Press, 1985.

Limon, John. "War and Play: A Theory of the Vietnam Sports Novel." *Arizona Quarterly* 46 (Autumn 1990): 65–90.

Lippard, Lucy. *A Different War: Vietnam in Art.* Seattle, Wash.: Real Comet Press, 1990.

Lister, Paul Antony. "War in Norman Mailer's Fiction." Ph.D. Diss. Kansas State University, 1987.

Lomperis, Timothy J., and John Clark Pratt, eds. *Reading the Wind: The Literature of the Vietnam War.* Durham, N.C.: Duke University Press, 1987.

Louvre, Alf, and Jeffrey Walsh, eds. *Tell Me Lies About Vietnam: Cultural Battles for the Meaning of the War.* New York: Open University Press, 1988.

Luce, Don, and John Sommer. *Viet Nam: The Unheard Voices.* Ithaca, N.Y.: Cornell University Press, 1969.

Malone, Anne. "Once Having Marched: American Narratives of the Vietnam War." Ph.D. Diss. Indiana University, 1983.

McInerney, Peter. " 'Straight' and 'Secret' History in Vietnam War Literature." *Contemporary Literature* 22 (Spring 1981): 187–204.

Melling, Philip H. *Vietnam in American Literature.* Boston: Twayne, 1990.

Mersmann, James F. "Out of the Vortex: A Study of Poets and Poetry Against the Vietnam War." Ph.D. Diss. University of Kansas, 1972.

Meyers, Kate Beaird. "Fragmentary Mosaics: Vietnam War 'Histories' and Post-modern Epistemology." *Genre* 21 (Winter 1988): 535–52.

Mitchell, Verner D. "I, Too, Sing America: Vietnam as Metaphor in *Coming Home*." *Vietnam Generation* 1 (Spring 1989): 188–24.

Myers, Thomas. "Dispatches from Ghost Country: The Vietnam Veteran in Recent American Fiction." *Genre* 21 (Winter 1988): 409–28.

Myers, Thomas. *Walking Point: American Narratives of Vietnam.* New York: Oxford University Press, 1988.

Newman, John. *Vietnam War Literature.* Metuchen, N.J.: Scarecrow Press, 1988.

Palm, Edward Frederick. "American Heart of Darkness: The Moral Vision of Five Novels of the Vietnam War." Ph.D. Diss. University of Pennsylvania, 1983.

Palm, Edward Frederick. "James Webb's *Fields of Fire*: The Melting Pot Platoon Revisited." *Critique* 24 (Winter 1983): 105–18.

Palm, Edward Frederick. "The Search for a Usable Past: Vietnam Literature and the Separate Peace Syndrome." *South Atlantic Quarterly* 82 (Spring 1983): 115–28.

Puhr, Katheline Marie. "Novelistic Responses to the Vietnam War." Ph.D. Diss. Saint Louis University, 1982.

Ringnalda, Donald. "Chlorophyll Overdose: Stephen Wright's *Meditations in Green.*" *Western Humanities Review* 40 (Summer 1986): 125–40.

Ringnalda, Donald. "Fighting and Writing: America's Vietnam War Literature." *Journal of American Studies* 22 (April 1988): 25–42.

Rollins, Peter. "The Vietnam War: Perceptions through Literature, Film, and Television." *American Quarterly* 36 (1984): 419–32.

Roundy, Peter Edward. "Images of Vietnam: *Catch-22*, New Journalism, and the Postmodern Imagination." Ph.D. Diss. The Florida State University, 1980.

Sanders, Joseph Elwood. "Modern American War Plays." Ph.D. Diss. University of California–Los Angeles, 1975.

Scheurer, Timothy E. "Myth to Madness: America, Vietnam and Popular Culture." *Journal of Popular Culture* 4 (Summer 1981): 149–65.

Schroeder, Eric James. "Truth-Telling and Narrative Form: The Literature of the Vietnam War." Ph.D. Diss. University of California–Los Angeles, 1984.

Schroeder, Eric James. "Two Interviews: Talks with Tim O'Brien and Robert Stone." *Modern Fiction Studies* 30 (1984): 135–64.

Searle, William J. "The Vietnam War Novel and the Reviewers." *Journal of Popular Culture* 4 (Summer 1981): 83–94.

Searle, William J. *Search and Clear: Critical Response to Selected Literature and Films of the Vietnam War.* Bowling Green, Ohio: Bowling Green State University Press, 1988.

Shelton, Frank W. "Robert Stone's *Dog Soldiers*: Vietnam Comes Home to America." *Critique* 24 (Winter 1983): 74–81.

Slocock, Caroline. "Winning Hearts and Minds: The 1st Casualty Press." *Journal of American Studies* 16 (April 1982): 107–17.

Smith, Julian. *Looking Away: Hollywood and Vietnam.* New York: Scribner's, 1975.

Smith, Lorrie. "A Sense-Making Perspective in Recent Poetry by Vietnam Veterans." *American Poetry Review* 15 (November-December 1986): 13–18.

Sossaman, Stephen. "American Poetry from the Indochina Experience." *Long Island Review* 2 (Winter 1973): 30–33.

Stewart, Margaret E. "Death and Growth: Vietnam-War Novels, Cultural Attitudes, and Literary Traditions." Ph.D. Diss. The University of Wisconsin–Madison, 1981.

Stewart, Matthew C. "Making Sense of Chaos: Prose Writing, Fictional Kind, and the Reality of Vietnam." Ph.D. Diss. Emory University, 1988.

Stringer, Kenneth Thompson, Jr. "A Substitute for Victory? Fictional Portraits of the American Soldier and Combat in Vietnam." Ph.D. Diss. The American University, 1984.

Stromberg, Peter Leonard. "A Long War's Writing: American Novels About the Fighting in Vietnam Written While Americans Fought." Ph.D. Diss. Cornell University, 1974.

Taylor, Gordon O. "Americans Personal Narrative of the War in Vietnam." *American Literature* 52 (May 1980): 294–308.

Van Deusen, Marshall. "The Unspeakable Language of Life and Death in Michael Herr's *Dispatches.*" *Critique* 24 (Winter 1983): 82–87.

Walsh, Jeffrey, and James Aulich, eds. *Vietnam Images: War and Representation.* New York: St. Martin's Press, 1989.

Willson, David A. *Wilson's Bibliography: War in Southeast Asia.* Auburn, Wash.: Green River Community College Press, 1991.

Wilson, James C. *Vietnam in Prose and Film.* Jefferson, N.C.: McFarland, 1982.

Winner, Carol Ann. "A Study of American Dramatic Productions Dealing With the War in Vietnam." Ph.D. Diss. University of Denver, 1975.

Wittman, Sandra. *Writing About Vietnam: A Bibliography of the Literature of the Vietnam Conflict.* Boston: Hall, 1989.

Yoshida, Sanroku. "Takeshi Kaiko's Paradox of Light and Darkness." *World Literature Today* 62 (Summer 1988): 391–96.

19   Film and the Vietnam War

Randy Roberts

During World War II the government and Hollywood cooperated. Blatant propaganda was accepted and applauded. Japanese were portrayed as weak-eyed, sadistic killers, and Russians were characterized as handsome, heroic soldiers of freedom. As early as 1942 a writer for *Variety* commented, "War has put Hollywood's traditional conception of the Muscovites through the wringer, and they have come out shaved, washed, sober, good to their families, Rotarians, brother Elks, and 33rd Degree Mason." Encouraged by Franklin D. Roosevelt (FDR), Hollywood turned out such films as the *Song of Russia, Three Russian Girls, Boys from Stalingrad, North Star, Counter-Attack,* and *Mission to Moscow,* which made the Soviet Union look like the United States with onion-shaped church domes. Evaluating *Mission to Moscow,* a censor for the Bureau of Motion Pictures of the Office of War Information wrote that it would "make a great contribution" to America's war effort.

In the years between the end of World War II and the Vietnam War, Hollywood changed dramatically. It became at once both more conservative and less political. The change began in 1947, when the House Un-American Activities Committee (HUAC) traveled to Hollywood to investigate Communist infiltration of the motion picture industry. Martin Dies, the conservative Texan who chaired HUAC, had watched with anger the cooperation between Hollywood and the FDR administration. He tended to see Communist influences everywhere—from the American Civil Liberties Union and the American League for Peace and Democracy to the Girl Scouts, Boy Scouts, and Shirley Temple. The investigation of Hollywood allowed Dies to extract revenge on the film industry and garner headlines for HUAC. Studio heads, fearful that his charges would hurt them at the box office, cooperated with HUAC. Actors, screenwriters, directors, and other members of the industry who did not cooperate with HUAC or who adhered too closely to their constitutional rights were blacklisted. HUAC returned to Hollywood in1951 and continued its hearings sporadically until 1954. During those years— years that saw the Korean War, the rise and fall of Joseph McCarthy, and the worst of the Red Scare—hundreds of witnesses were called to testify before HUAC. Again they either cooperated or found themselves unemployed and unemployable. For those who had joined the Communist party—which was no crime—cooperation entailed "naming names," the systematic and ritualistic naming of everyone the witness knew who was Communist or was suspected of being a Communist. This was a humiliating and emotionally draining experience. The first person in 1951 whom HUAC asked to name names, actor Larry Parks, made a desperate plea: "Don't present me with the choice of either being in contempt of this committee and going to jail or forcing me to really crawl through the mud to be an informer." HUAC insisted, and Parks eventually did crawl through the mud. So, too, did leading Hollywood composer David Raskin, who later admitted, "The only thing a decent person could do was not talk—I still believe that." People such as actor Zero Mostel who refused to name names—he told a producer that "as a Jew, if I inform, I can't be buried on sacred ground"—were blacklisted.

Structural changes in the film industry contributed to Hollywood's cooperation with HUAC. Simply stated, the industry was running scared. The late 1940s and the 1950s were bad years. Movie attendance was down, and the prospect of its rising again seemed remote. Returning GIs married; bought homes, automobiles, and electrical appliances; went to college; and had families—all of which meant less money and time for movies. Instead, they and their families listened to the radio and, after 1948, increasingly watched television. In Hollywood, television was the bogeyman, the specter of the future of American entertainment. In 1947 only 14,000 American families owned television sets. By the end of the 1950s over 90 percent of American homes had at least one TV set. To make matters worse, the major studios suffered a legal defeat in the Paramount case and were forced to sell their theater holdings. No longer could they depend upon their own theaters to show their films. Block booking, the fixing of admission prices, and discriminatory purchasing and pricing agreements with affiliated theaters ended. Responding to all these changes, the major studios trimmed their budgets by cutting back on production and taking actors, writers, producers, and directors off long-term contracts.

Faced by these structural problems, the industry's leaders were in no mood to court controversy. Employing a writer or actor who refused to name names might lead to a boycott by the Wage Earners Committee or the Catholic War Veterans or some other conservative group. The blacklist seemed a small price to pay for avoiding such problems. To demonstrate their public spirit, the major companies also began to make anti-Communist films. As a whole, they comprised a bad lot—badly written, badly acted, badly directed, and badly filmed. Even their titles were bad—*I Married a Communist, I Was a Communist for the FBI, The Red Menace, The Whip Hand, The Red Nightmare, Walk East on Beacon,* and *My Son John.* In all, the studios made over fifty such films. The films trafficked in crude stereotypes. Communists invariably had cruel faces, foreign accents, and compulsive mannerisms, and they could be detected by their quirky behavior. They hated animals, almost never had children, exhaled cigarette smoke slowly through their nostrils, seldom kept promises, and seemed to hate their own kind more than their democratic enemies. The theme of these anti-Communist films seemed to be that America's Red foes were singularly unattractive and inefficient.

By the mid–1950s the hysterical phase of the Red Scare had passed, and Hollywood stopped making overtly anti-Communist films. But the blacklist continued and the major studios avoided controversial social films. Gimmicks replaced content as a lure. Hollywood countered television by offering the viewer entertainment technology that could not be reproduced on a twelve-inch screen. Not only did Hollywood increasingly use color, but it also experimented with CinemaScope, 3-D, Cinerama, VistaVision, and even Smell-O-Vision and AromaRama, which pumped smells into the theaters to enhance the atmosphere of the story. The major studios also relied more heavily on the blockbuster epic. From *Samson and Delilah* (1949) and *The Robe* (1953) to *Ben Hur* (1959) and *Cleopatra* (1963), these "toga epics" provided an alternative to television. They did not, however, deal with controversial subjects, especially social and political themes. The "message film," which had been so important to the industry during the 1930s and 1940s, was one alternative to television that the leading producers chose not to try.

As the industry changed, however, a new force was gaining momentum. Independent producers became more important. In the wake of the Paramount decision, when the major studios were looking for ways to cut costs, independent producers saw an opportunity. Not only could independents find an outlet for their pictures, but they could also obtain financing and studio space from the underutilized majors. These same majors before the Paramount decision had actively discouraged independent productions. If at first the independent producers were as conservative as their counterparts in the major studios, by the late 1960s they were becoming bolder. The new political mood of the nation and court decisions that relaxed censorship signaled a change in the film industry.

The struggle of Americans to come to terms with the Vietnam War was contested largely outside the corridors of power. Politicians, diplomats, and military leaders lost their chance to influence popular opinion.

Many Americans no longer trusted their answers to fundamental questions. With the war lost and the peace concluded, politicians gave way to intellectuals and artists and media executives, a diverse collection of historians, writers, and film and television producers. It was now their turn to explain the war and its impact upon American society. The time to ask, What should we do? had passed. Now the questions What did we do? and Why did we do it? occupied center stage. Americans struggled with three central issues. Consider first the veterans of the war. How did Vietnam change them? Could they peacefully return to American society? How did their experiences scar them? Second was the war itself. What did it accomplish? What did it mean? How did it change America? Third was the loss of the war. Why did the United States lose? Who or what was to blame? How did that experience change America?

During the war itself, from the early 1960s through the early 1970s, a variety of films addressed the Vietnam War and the validity and morality of the American effort there. The cold war mentality prevailing in the United States during the early 1960s when American policymakers were deciding how to deal with Vietnam is clearly illustrated in the films of the era. First, Americans were clearly preoccupied with the nuclear threat posed by the superpowers. A series of films between 1959 and 1964 dealt with the possibility of nuclear holocaust. The first of them was *On the Beach* (1959), starring Gregory Peck, Ava Gardner, and Fred Astaire. The film is set in Australia after a global nuclear war. Deadly radiation is steadily drifting south, dooming all the people of Australia. It has already killed all human beings in more northern latitudes. Another film in that genre was *Fail Safe* (1963), starring Henry Fonda as the president of the United States who deals with an accidental American nuclear attack on Moscow by destroying New York City. Only that step prevented an all-out Russian retaliation. *The Bedford Incident* (1963) tells a similar story. It stars Richard Widmark as the commander of an antisubmarine U.S. naval vessel and Sidney Poitier as a journalist writing about him. Widmark locates a Soviet submarine and plays a game of cat-and-mouse that gets out of hand and leads to a nuclear confrontation. The best of these films was Stanley Kubrick's *Dr. Strangelove or: How I Learned to Stop Worrying and Love the Bomb* (1964). The film made fun of liberals' faith in technology and systems management and conservatives' paranoia over the Soviet threat. It also made the Russians look just as silly in their fears as the Americans.

The second mood of the early 1960s involved the Kennedyesque commitment on the part of the United States to defend freedom around the world. The James Bond spy movies, starring Sean Connery, pitted the freedom-loving West against diabolical fascists and Communists. In such films as *Dr. No* (1962) and *From Russia with Love* (1964), James Bond employed the latest technological innovations to foil the dictators. The spaghetti westerns of the era also portrayed larger than life superheroes. In films like *A Fistful of Dollars*, a superhero could be counted on to save the "poor downtrodden victim" from gangsters and criminals. America had the responsibility and the will to help the oppressed.

Vietnam was the place on the other side of the world where that commitment found its greatest expression. The very first of the Vietnam films was Joseph Mankiewicz's *The Quiet American* in 1975. The film was based on Graham Greene's 1956 novel of the same name (see Chapter 18).

Most Americans in the late 1950s interpreted Greene's novel as cynical and anti-American, and no filmmaker with any hope of commercial success was going to transfer its sarcasm to celluloid. The film that Joseph Mankiewicz eventually produced had none of the novel's sarcasm. Ironically, it cast Audie Murphy as a gentle American trying to aid the Vietnamese with food instead of bullets. It was quite a departure from Murphy's World War II films, where the only good Asian is a dead one. Murphy plays Alden Pyle, and the narrator in the film is Thomas Fowler, a British journalist. The film opens with Fowler commenting on the decline of European imperialism and the rise of American power. The message of the film is subtly, but definitely, anti-Communist.

In 1958, as a counter to Greene's novel, William J. Lederer and Eugene Burdick wrote *The Ugly American*, which became a runaway best-seller. The book attacks the American foreign service but praises American values. It accuses American ambassadors of being unable to speak the language of the country in which they are serving and of therefore being isolated by culture and geography from what is really happening. They do not understand the country, and they do not understand the Communist enemy. In contrast, the Communists speak the native languages and work closely with rural peasants, building loyalties and political support. If America is going to win the war with Communism, foreign service personnel must do a much better job of working with Third World peoples. In 1962 the film version of *The Ugly American* was released. Starring Marlon Brando, it was set in fictitious Sarkhan, where American diplomats are hopelessly ill-equipped to carry out American policy. The film also has a character, however, based on Edward Lansdale, who moves among the people of Sarkhan winning their trust and fighting Communism.

It was not until 1965, when President Lyndon B. Johnson committed regular ground forces to Vietnam, that Indochina became a divisive issue in American politics. Soon the controversy was reflected on the screen. In 1965 Robin Moore published his novel *The Green Berets*, and it became an immediate best-seller. The novel told the story of the Green Berets, the army's elite corps of counterinsurgency experts and nation builders. John Wayne loved the novel, hated the antiwar movement, and in 1968 produced his own film—*The Green Berets*. The filming enjoyed substantial support from the White House and the Pentagon.

The result was a controversial film that faithfully presented the administration position. The central focus of the film is the political awakening of a "liberal" journalist (David Janssen) to the real nature of the American involvement. At first he is skeptical; he doubts the domino theory, the threat of Communism, and the viability of the government in South Vietnam. But after following the activities of the Green Beret lieutenant colonel Michael Kirby (John Wayne), he reverses his opinions. Even then, he realizes that it will be difficult to tell the "truth" about Vietnam because of the liberal bias of the American press. In the end, the film suggests that the United States' biggest fight is not against North Vietnam but against the liberal Establishment that threatens the war effort by its opposition. *The Green Berets* was viciously attacked by critics but proved to be a commercial success.

The Green Berets was the only pro-Vietnam film released to general audiences. By the late 1960s and early 1970s, the film industry reflected the attitudes of much of the rest of the United States—that for a variety of reasons the effort in Vietnam was badly flawed. In 1970 four films make strong, if sometimes indirect, statements about the war: *Joe*, *M*A*S*H**, *Little Big Man*, and *Catch–22*. The films almost swept the Academy Award nominations that year. *Joe*, starring Peter Boyle as a "hard-hat" guy with right-wing views on Vietnam, centered on the war's effect on people at home. The main character goes through changes in attitude that reflect the shift in consciousness many Americans underwent during the 1960s. Joe has to deal with "the counter-culture" and antiwar activists, and he comes to face his own feelings about American involvement in the war. *Joe* was about as subtle as an M–16; he has to confront personal violence as well as the violence of the war.

Little Big Man, on one level, was a comedy and quasi-historical film about the Cheyenne and the "massacre" at Little Big Horn. It begins with 121-year-old Jack Crabbe (Dustin Hoffman) recounting his life to a researcher who is studying the life-style of Plains Indians. The film then follows the life of Jack Crabbe as he is captured by the Cheyenne, lives with them, is recaptured by the whites, returns to live with the Cheyenne, and is with the Cheyenne when Custer's troops are annihilated at Little Big Horn. There are obvious parallels with Vietnam throughout the film. Indian villages are destroyed as "pay back," often the wrong village and wrong tribe. Innocent women, children, and old men are brutally murdered, often because they are of a different color. Many critics saw reflections of the My Lai incident in Arthur Penn's movie, and some compared the near genocide of the Cheyenne with our treatment of "gooks" in Vietnam. The Cheyenne are shown to have a more ancient and more humane culture than the whites, who show little respect for ways they did not understand. The parallels need no explanation. The film is based on a 1964 novel by Thomas Berger and reflects the attitudes of director Arthur Penn more overtly than the antiwar *Alice's Restaurant*.

Neither one of the two ultimate antiwar movies of 1970 is set in Vietnam. Both films were highly critical of the military. For a while, the Pentagon would not let *M*A*S*H** be shown on military bases. Both of these films were set in different times and locales, but it was obvious that the war they were talking about was in Vietnam. *Catch–22*, based on the novel by Joseph Heller, is set in World War II, while *M*A*S*H** is set in Korea.

The message of *Catch–22* is woven into the black comedy of the novel and film. Yossarian, the protagonist, is just numbly trying to understand and maybe survive what has become an insane situation. He tries to escape the insanity by pretending to be insane. That then becomes the catch–22, because it is normal—sane—to want to escape from insane situations. Yossarian's squadron is asked to bomb towns so that they can produce nice, "tight" bombing patterns that look very efficient in aerial photographs. Movies like *Catch–22* demonstrated how far from victory the United States was and how contradictory were the goals of winning the "hearts and minds" of the Vietnamese people by destroying their country.

Black comedy is also central to *M*A*S*H** The initials stand for Mobile Army Surgical Hospital. This film stars Eliott Gould, Donald Sutherland, Tom Skerrit, Robert Duvall, and Sally Kellerman. Robert Altman directed it. The plot revolves around three army surgeons (draftees) during the Korean War. It is antimilitary in the extreme and perhaps matches America's mood in 1970. *M*A*S*H** is antiestablishment and antiauthority as well. *M*A*S*H** and *Catch–22* both reflect a growing feeling that the United States made a mistake in trying to be the global policeman. Whether one felt that the war was wrong on moral grounds or being waged badly by the administration, the mood of a large number of Americans reflected distrust.

Two powerful documentaries appeared in 1970 and 1972, and they were highly critical of the American war effort in Vietnam. Emile De Antonio's *In the Year of the Pig* received an Academy Award nomination for best documentary. It looked carefully at the Tet Offensive, the year 1968, and the war from a North Vietnamese perspective. It emphasized that American firepower, rather than winning the war, was actually losing the war politically. Two years later, the documentary *Hearts and Minds* employed a similar theme but also argued that the anti-Asian racism of so many American political and military officials was going to cause them to lose the war. *Hearts and Minds* also won the Academy Award for best documentary.

Two other trends in films in the late 1960s and early 1970s were connected to Vietnam. The first was a dramatic swing toward a more graphic depiction of violence. Because of the racial rebellions in American cities, the political assassinations of John F. Kennedy, Robert F. Kennedy, Malcolm X, and Martin Luther King, Jr., and the nightly television news shows presenting pictures of mayhem, slaughter, and atrocities, the perception of America as a violent society became much stronger. In April 1969 Nixon invaded Cambodia, and four students were killed at Kent State University and two more at Jackson State. The My Lai massacre was uncovered, and *The Wild Bunch*, directed by Sam Peckinpah, was released. There was violence at home and in Southeast Asia, and it was reflected on the screen. Peckinpah's violent images were very much like those Americans watched each night on television: violence dissected, in slow motion, with many of the same images repeated on all the networks. Villages, children, refugees, soldiers, blood, and bodies all danced together in slow motion as they were riddled with bullets. The plot unfolds as the outlaws, having outlived their time, flee into Mexico chased by people hired by the railroad. The group that represents law and order is just as bad or worse than "the Bunch," perhaps parodying the growing feeling by some Americans after My Lai and other similar incidents that U.S. soldiers were not always the "good guys."

The second major trend was the horror film genre. In the early 1970s with the American involvement in Vietnam winding down, the number of stylized horror movies increased. Americans began to discover what came to be called posttraumatic stress disorder or, in the words of the combat field, the "thousand-year stare." The victims were not unlike the "pod people" of *Invasion of the Body Snatchers* from the 1950s. In 1968 George Romero had made a "horror" film called *Night of the Living Dead*, which some critics saw as a satire that indirectly portrayed American warriors as mindless, soulless creatures who required living flesh to survive. Americans did not like to view themselves as monsters, but atrocities like My Lai made them wonder.

At first the Vietnam veteran loomed large in American popular culture. He came to symbolize the war that the nation wished to forget, and far from being portrayed as a hero, he was transformed into a villain. Somehow his participation in the "immoral" war, even if it had not been voluntary, set him apart from the civilians at home and made him a misfit. Often he was seen as a person not to pity or hate or love but to fear, for he was a ticking time bomb waiting to explode, waiting to carry the war home. The American public was not without a sense of sympathy for what had happened to the veterans. Wars leave terrible physical scars. In 1971 one movie dealt with that theme—Dalton Trumbo's *Johnny Got His Gun*. The film, about a World War I veteran who returns from the war a quadruple amputee, made a strong antiwar statement and raised sympathy for the people who were damaged by it.

But the most enduring image of the Vietnam War was not the physically handicapped veteran. Americans were far more preoccupied with psychologically scarred men and women. Such a presentation of the returning veteran was not unique to the Vietnam War. In Edward Dymtryk's film *Crossfire* (1947), Robert Ryan plays a psychotic returning veteran consumed by his hatred for Jews. Palpable violence pervades the film. A civilian correctly notes, "You can feel the tension in the air. A whole lot of fight and hate that doesn't know where to go." Ryan clearly does have deadly potential, and he can and does kill. But he is not portrayed as the typical returning GI. His hate is deeper; it is the fruit of a lifetime of psychological troubles, not the product of war. Other veterans might have some difficulty adjusting to civilian life—as they do in *The Best Years of Our Lives* (1946)—but if they threaten anyone, it is only themselves. By the end of that film, the returning veterans do adjust; they are successfully reintegrated into civilian society.

Few people doubted the moral fiber of the World War II veteran. After all, he had fought in the "good war," and his cause was just. Korean War veterans faced greater difficulties. The war was more ambiguous; the peace, less satisfying. In fact, was it a war at all? Or was it a "police action" or simply a "conflict"? The veterans knew the answer, but civilians had called into question their very performance. Reports that the Communists had successfully brainwashed POWs frightened civilians and led to speculation that some of the returning soldiers might be spies. The novel (1959) and later the film (1962) *The Manchurian Candidate* centered on the idea that Communists had programmed some returning POWs to kill. But even in the case of the brainwashed killer—the Manchurian candidate—psychological problems are rooted more in his relationship with his mother than in his wartime experiences. On this point the novel and the film are clear: the war did not create misfits and psychotics; only a lifetime of maladjustment—and perhaps a dash of Communist brainwashing—could produce an unbalanced person.

The psychotic or maladjusted Vietnam War veteran, however, was portrayed as a product of the war. In most cases he is a man without a background, a man without a home or parents or life before his service in Vietnam. It is almost as if he were bred in the country's steamy jungles and fertile rice fields. All he knows is war, and when he returns to the United States he continues to ply his trade. Sometimes he joins an outlaw motorcycle gang in which violence is a way of life and a reason for being. Such B-movies as *Angels from Hell* (1968), *Satan's Sadists* (1969), *Chrome and Hot Leather* (1971), and *The Losers* (1970) transport the veteran from a helicopter to a Harley. Other times the veteran remains a loner. But once again the potential for violence seethes beneath the surface. In *Taxi*

Driver (1976) Travis Bickle (Robert De Niro) ticks quietly in New York City. He has no past and no future; he seems to invent both out of thin air. Although he writes his parents, he fills his letters with lies, and one suspects that his parents are part of his fantasy life. The only reality in his life is the war that he cannot articulate but that drives him toward violence as surely as he drives his taxi. He waits to explode. That in the end he kills a pimp is irrelevant. He might just as easily have killed a politician or anyone else, including himself. His violence knows no reason. It is not directed toward society or politicians or any particular person. It just is.

Violence is given greater direction and logic in *Tracks* (1976), a low-budget film directed by Henry Jaglom. In the film an army sergeant, played by Dennis Hopper, escorts the body of a friend killed in Vietnam back to the soldier's home for burial. On the cross-country train trip he tries to tell his fellow passengers about the dead soldier, a black hero who saved his life. He asks the civilians about the war and wonders why the United States was in Vietnam. Most of the other passengers are not interested in the sergeant, his dead comrade, or his questions; some are hostile, a few embarrassed. His war is not their war; his sufferings are not their sufferings. The film ends with the burial. Alone, the sergeant watches the coffin being lowered into the ground. Then he jumps in after it. When he emerges from the hole, he is dressed for battle and fully armed. "You want to go to Nam?" he cries out. "I'll take you there." A sympathetic character has once again been transformed into violence incarnate. Avenging angel or not, violence is implicit in his being, the answer to an uncaring nation.

Even when the veteran wishes to avoid violence, it follows him like an albatross. In Karel Reisz's *Who'll Stop the Rain?* (1978), based on Robert Stone's novel *Dog Soldiers* (1974), the action centers on a veteran who is involved in smuggling a shipment of heroin into the United States. Not only does he bring the corruption of Saigon back home with him—for the heroin will ruin civilians just as it did soldiers—but violence and death follow in his wake. As in the other films, the ultimate threat of the veterans is the Vietnamization of the United States.

Starting in the late 1970s the image of the Vietnam veteran began to change. Hollywood signaled the shift with two successful movies—*Coming Home* (1978) and *The Deer Hunter* (1978). In *Coming Home*, director Hal Asby continued his interest in Vietnam. Three years earlier he had directed *Shampoo*, a film about wealthy southern Californians set during the 1968 presidential election. As the characters in *Shampoo* get ready for a Nixon victory party, news of the horrors of Vietnam assaults them from radio and television. But they pay no mind; it is not their war, not their concern. *Coming Home* brings the war to southern California. Its central characters are Luke Martin (John Voight), a bitter paraplegic, and Sally Hyde (Jane Fonda), the wife of a marine captain (Bruce Dern) serving a tour in Vietnam. Viewed from the perspective of the early 1990s, *Coming Home* is sentimental stuff. It is too pat. During the course of the film the conservative, sexually repressed Sally flowers into a liberal, liberated woman. She puts on Levis, allows her hair to follow its natural frizzy disposition, and experiences an orgasm—with Luke—for the first time in her life. Luke is also transformed. Bitter and angry at the start of the film, he becomes introspective and gentle. *Coming Home* suggests that love can cure the trauma of Vietnam, that understanding can erase the pain of bad memories.

In 1978, however, *Coming Home* was an original film. Frank Rich of *Time Magazine* called it "one long, low howl of pain," and others agreed that it was an important statement. It also showed Hollywood that a film about the Vietnam War could be political and profitable. At the same time it contributed to the rehabilitation of the popular image of the Vietnam veteran. Influenced by paraplegic Ron Kovic in *Born on the Fourth of July* (1976), *Coming Home* portrays the veteran not only as someone who needs to be healed but also as a healer. Luke is not a loner; he is not a ticking bomb; he is not a threat to society. His anger flows from the unwillingness of America to recognize his plight. "When people look, they don't see me," Luke tells Sally. He wants America to take notice and to remember, for his crippled body is an important legacy of Vietnam. Toward the end of the film, he tells a group of high school students: "There was a lot of shit over there I find fucking hard to live with. But I don't feel sorry for myself. I'm just saying that there's a choice to be made." That choice is as present in the United States as it was in Vietnam. Luke has to decide whether he will live consumed by bitterness or use his pain to help others. He chooses the latter course and is reintegrated into society.

The Deer Hunter contains the same message. Directed by Michael Cimino, the film shows how the war changed the lives of three men from a western Pennsylvania steel town. Of the three, the most important is Michael (Robert De Niro). He begins the film as a loner, and violence seems an integral part of his character. He kills a deer with one shot and is intolerant of his friends' shortcomings. In Vietnam, it seems, surrounded by death and terror, he finds compassion. He saves the lives of two friends, and when one becomes addicted to heroin and Russian roulette, Michael even risks his own life in an attempt to reach him. "I love you," he says just before Nicky's (Christopher Walken) luck runs out and he loses his final game of Russian roulette.

Vietnam changes Michael for the better. It purges him of aggression and anger. He no longer wants to kill deer or any other animals. He is at peace with himself and his surroundings. He can even love now and is able to relate to women. The film ends on a note of affirmation. After

Nicky's funeral, Michael joins his other friends—women as well as men—in singing "God Bless America." He is finally a whole person, reconciled with himself, his community, and his country. That same message comes through in Oliver Stone's 1989 film *Born on the Fourth of July*, in which Tom Cruise portrays Ron Kovic, a crippled Vietnam veteran who finally comes to terms with the war. His way of coming to terms, however, is a bit different from Luke's in *Coming Home*. Kovic finds a political outlet for his frustrations, and in campaigning for a "never again" philosophy about Vietnam, he finds redemption.

The transformation of the Vietnam veteran in movies and on television is part of the more general rehabilitation of the popular image of the U.S. military, an image that Operation Desert Storm in 1991 raised to World War II levels of reverence. During the 1970s films and television shows portrayed the military as a corrupt, bloodthirsty institution. Although enlisted men were occasionally presented as decent people, officers were invariably pictured as incompetent, self-serving, and destructive. "The bullshit piled up so fast in Vietnam you needed wings to stay above it," Captain Willard remarks in *Apocalypse Now* (1979). In the same movie, Lieutenant Colonel Kilgore orders his men into battle to secure a strip of beach that has "good surf." In such films as *An Officer and a Gentleman* (1982), *Taps* (1981), *Lords of Discipline* (1983), *Private Benjamin* (1980), and *Stripes* (1981), Hollywood revitalized the military. Instead of being an institution that kills boys it is viewed as a place where boys become men, or in the case of *Private Benjamin*, spoiled girls become independent women.

At the start of *An Officer and a Gentleman*, Zack Mayo (Richard Gere) is a self-centered punk. He wants to be an officer but cares nothing for discipline or traditions and exploits his fellow officer candidates. During the course of the film he learns to respect and love the navy. "I will never forget you," he tells his ruthless drill instructor (DI) upon completing officer candidate school. For him the navy has become the home he never had. His spit-and-polish black DI becomes his true father, replacing his drunken, prostitute-chasing biological father. Mayo and his classmates are ideal types—clean, honorable, and disciplined. By contrast, civilians in the film are portrayed as beer-swilling, pool-shooting troublemakers. They provoke fights—which they promptly lose—and generally exist to envy the officer candidates. As for the candidates who do not have the "right stuff," life appears bleak. Mayo's friend who quits just before graduation informs his fiancée that he can return to Oklahoma and get his old job back at J. C. Penney. Faced with that prospect, she dumps him, and he commits suicide.

In part, the promilitary films reflect the economy of the late 1970s and early 1980s. High-paying jobs in heavy industry were becoming scarce, and there was little glamour or money in flipping hamburgers at McDonald's. For many young Americans the military became "a great place to start." Enlistments in the armed forces jumped in the 1980s, and enrollment in Reserve Officers' Training Corps (ROTC) programs doubled. The mood of Reagan's era—with its overt patriotism and promise of restored greatness—contributed to the popularity of the films. It contrasted especially with the malaise and perceived impotency of the Carter years. Americans yearned for a return to greatness. They wanted a military with teeth, equipped to act and fortified by a commitment to a higher code.

As Americans reappraised the Vietnam veteran and the military, they also attempted to understand the war itself. Historians sifted through the "facts" of the war. Aided by the illegally released Pentagon Papers, they searched for its causes. During the 1960s and most of the 1970s, two schools of thought emerged. The first believed that the war, in Arthur Schlesinger, Jr.'s, words, was a "tragedy without villains." It resulted from unfortunate decisions made by well-meaning officials. The second school rejected this benign view and asserted that the war was the result of an imperialistic American foreign policy. Such historians as William Appleman Williams, Walter LaFeber, and Gabriel Kolko claimed that the United States had a history of expansion and domination and that at least since the turn of the century it had been establishing its hegemony over the Pacific. The Vietnam War marked a setback in this policy of expansion, but the decision to fight in Vietnam was very much a part of the policy.

During the 1980s a third school of historical thought gained ascendancy. It maintained that the war was a "noble crusade" against Communism, a shining expression of American commitment to democracy and liberty. Not only did these historians believe that the United States should have fought in Vietnam, but they argued that the military could have won the war. These historians absolve the military of all guilt. As Guenter Lewy writes in *America in Vietnam* (1978, vii), "The sense of guilt created by the Vietnam War in the minds of many Americans is not warranted and the charges of officially condoned illegal and grossly immoral conduct are without substance." Instead of being the villains, the soldiers who fought the war were the heroes; they did their duty under taxing circumstances. That the war was ultimately lost was not their fault. Rather, civilians back home—both inside and outside the government—failed to understand what the war was about and refused to live up to their country's honorable commitment to South Vietnam. Of course, this perception reflected the changing political face of the United States. By 1980 politicians were once again talking about dominoes and the obligations the United States had to countries struggling to stay free. In 1980 Ronald Reagan said that the United States had "an inescapable duty to act as the tutor and protector of the free world."

This profound sense of confusion about the meaning of, and the reasons for, the war also found its way into films about the war. Francis Ford Coppola's *Apocalypse Now* attempted to translate that confusion into a narrative film. "The most important thing I wanted to do in the making of *Apocalypse Now*," Coppola wrote in the program notes for the film, "was to create a film experience that would give the audience a sense of the horror, the madness, the senselessness, and the moral dilemma of the Vietnam War." Captain Willard's voyage up the river into the "heart of darkness" is as much a quest for answers as it is a mission of death. In trying to understand the sanity behind Colonel Kurtz's insanity, Willard is attempting to fathom the logic of the illogical conflict. Everywhere there is madness. The coldly unemotional military and civilian officials who tell Willard that Kurtz's command must be "terminated with extreme prejudice" are mad. They speak the language of madness; the meanings of their words cannot be found in a dictionary. Kilgore is mad. He attacks the enemy not to win the war but to secure a good surfing beach. Even Willard remarks, "After seeing the way Kilgore fought the war, I began to wonder what they had against Kurtz." Kurtz is quite mad. He is like a computer thrown into an Alice-in-Wonderland world and fed bits of illogical data. His response to his environment is to become insane, for as the film demonstrates, only the insane survive.

Apocalypse Now may be the best film about the war, and its theme of madness may be accurate on a psychological level, but it does not help the viewer understand how or why the United States became involved in the war. It does not deal with what the war accomplished or how it changed the country. Its major political criticism is aimed not at the war itself but at the management of the war. Willard describes his superior officers as "a bunch of four-star clowns who are giving the whole circus away." He openly sympathizes with the outlaw Kurtz: "Charging someone with murder in a place like this is like handing out speeding tickets at the Indianapolis 500."

Sidney J. Furie's *The Boys in Company C* (1978) similarly exposes the absurdities of the war. The film deals with a group of recruits bound for Vietnam in 1967. It follows them through boot camp and into combat, describing a group of young marines dealing with drugs, fragging, kill-ratios, and body counts. The film ends with a symbolic soccer match between the marines in Company C and a Vietnamese team. The marines are ordered to play but not to win, a parody on the U.S. conduct of the war. In spite of clichés such as throwing themselves on grenades to save the platoon, the film was one of the first to project the idea the war was "thrown" and the "fix was in."

Two films in 1987 continue to emphasize the themes of waste, carnage, and absurdity: *Gardens of Stone* and *Full Metal Jacket*. The "garden of stone" is Arlington Cemetery in Washington, D.C. The film stars James Earl Jones, James Caan, Michael Levy, and Anjelica Huston. Jones and Caan play battle-hardened career soldiers whose current duty assignment is the funeral detail at the national cemetery. Caan's character is torn between trying to dissuade a zealous soldier who wants to follow in his father's path and test himself in Vietnam and his girlfriend, who is passionately against the war. Caan tries to take the middle road, but the increasingly disillusioned letters from the young soldier, as well as his eventual death in combat, leave Caan with a feeling of ultimate futility.

Full Metal Jacket is producer-director Stanley Kubrick's Vietnam film. It follows the same formula as films such as *The Boys in Company C* and *Rumor of War*. The plot follows a group of marines through basic training and on to Vietnam. The film is based on the novel *The Short-Timers*, by Gustav Hasford. It stars Matthew Modine as another "everyman." He wears "born to kill" on his helmet and a peace sign on his shirt. He explains to an officer that this represents the "duality of man." We cannot be sure if this is symbolism or sarcasm, but Kubrick does not veer from the formula war movie very far. He has the "sensitive guy" versus the "tough DI" but with a twist. He has a psycho return the violence by killing the drill instructor.

Kubrick is sensitive to the racial tone of the war on one level: as a black soldier is put on "point" during a search and destroy patrol, the black says, "That's right, put the nigger on the trigger." On the other hand, Kubrick points out the anti-Vietnamese racism of American soldiers when one of the men says, "Inside of every gook there is an American trying to get out." A gunner on a Huey helicopter remarks: "Anyone who runs is a V.C. Anyone who stands still is a well-disciplined V.C." There are no subtleties here and few metaphors. The last third of the film, except for graphic violence, could have come straight from a John Wayne war movie. The time is Tet, the Year of the Monkey. The North Vietnamese are launching an all-out offensive against the Americans. The city of Hue is in flames, but one of the grunts says, "This is how I thought war was supposed to be." Kubrick seems to be saying that if the war had been a conventional one, then we would have won. *Full Metal Jacket* has muddled themes, as if Kubrick is saying that there were no easy answers or choices in Vietnam. The film ends with the GIs marching through a burning Hue singing the theme song of "The Mickey Mouse Club."

The Boys in Company C and *Full Metal Jacket* contrast sharply with the post–World War II films. Two cases in point are *To Hell and Back* and *The Sands of Iwo Jima*, films starring Audie Murphy and John Wayne, respectively. Both films reflected postwar feelings of patriotism and nationalism. John Wayne and the marines taking on the Japanese at Iwo

Jima and Murphy winning the war against Germany almost single-hand-edly have become clichés, but they mirror the jubilant and fiercely pa-triotic attitudes of many Americans after the war.

The world of John Wayne and Audie Murphy is far removed from such films as *Platoon* (1986) or its companion *Casualties of War* (1989). They do not address questions of causation or results but revolve instead around a conflict of good and evil. The plot in *Platoon* follows Chris Taylor (Charlie Sheen) as he arrives "in country" and loses his innocence to the brutality of the war. Oliver Stone wrote and directed *Platoon* and has refused to comment about the film's symbolism. Certainly Chris Taylor's odyssey parallels his country's. In *Platoon*, the Vietnam War is fought much of the time by young, black, and poor men. Taylor's platoon has two sergeants, one the gung-ho killing machine Sergeant Barnes, and the other the laid-back, pot-smoking Sergeant Elias, both seasoned veterans who know how to kill and how to survive. Both seem to be aware of the politics of the war but cope with the brutality differently. The film is set late in the war. Drugs are widely used, and morale is low. Taylor, as the innocent, is torn between Elias (Willem Dafoe) and Barnes (Tom Berringer). He finally sides with Elias but is fascinated by Barnes. Taylor asks Elias if he believes in the war, and Elias answers that he did in 1965 "but now . . . no. . . . We're going to lose this war." In the end, Barnes murders Elias, and Taylor kills Barnes. The war becomes a stage, and although there is an attempt to relate something of the combat experience, the meaning of the war is irrelevant. In one voice-over in *Platoon*, Chris Taylor remarks: "I think now, we did not fight the enemy, we fought ourselves. And the enemy was in us." In both films, the good guys and the bad guys are the Americans, represented by a caring ser-geant and a mindless, killing-machine sergeant. They could have been set in any war. They just happen to be set in Vietnam. Like *Apocalypse Now*, *Coming Home*, and *The Deer Hunter*, *Platoon*, and *Casualties of War* are about self-discovery, not war.

Films that have taken a political stand have not been particularly suc-cessful at the box office. Burt Lancaster starred in two of those early political films—*Twilight's Last Gleaming* (1977) and *Go Tell the Spartans* (1978). *Twilight's Last Gleaming* was a Robert Aldrich film. Lancaster again plays a renegade general, a role he had played in the 1964 film *Seven Days in May*. But this time he is a liberal who wants to tell the American public about American involvement in Vietnam. He takes control of a Strategic Air Command missile base and threatens to launch nuclear warheads unless the president makes public a memo that shows the Vietnam War was fought only to show the Russians that the United States would fight a limited war to prevent nuclear war. In this film, unlike early war movies, the good guys do not win. *Go Tell the Spartans* deals with the early years of the American combat presence in Vietnam.

In theory these were years of youthful innocence, a time when the struggle for "hearts and minds" was taken seriously by Americans in Vietnam and in the United States. But as the film illustrates, the war was already over, and Lancaster plays an American officer who understood the futility of the struggle. The United States had lost but did not know it. The film's final scene—a long shot of a cemetery of war dead—suggests that the only act remaining in the war was death—futile, meaningless death.

If filmmakers dealt poorly with the origins and meaning of the war, they were even worse at coming to terms with defeat. To be sure, most of the films depict a thoroughly corrupt or stupid officer corps. But beyond this limited explanation of failure, few producers were willing to go. Part of the reason was financial; industry leaders maintained that Americans would not pay to watch a film about their country losing a war. During the 1970s, when there was a mood of self-criticism in the country, few films about the war were made. When producers turned to the subject of war, the age of self-criticism had passed. The Reagan years affirmed patriotic values. Heroes dominated popular culture. Rock star Bruce Springsteen, at his 1986 concert in Dallas, expressed frustration that his anti-Vietnam megahit "Born in the U.S.A." had actually become a patriotic anthem in the popular mind.

The best expression of this new mood was Sylvester Stallone's films *First Blood* (1982) and *Rambo: First Blood Part II* (1985). In the first film John Rambo is an ex-Green Beret who is mistaken for a hippie. By nature a loner and even a peaceful man, he is forced by a series of inept government officials to defend his freedom in the wilds of the Pacific Northwest. The movie suggests that men like John Rambo did not lose the war; politicians back home did. In the climactic scene Rambo tells his former Special Forces commanding officer: "Nothing is over, nothing! You just don't turn it off. It wasn't my war—you asked me, I didn't ask you . . . and I did what I had to do to win—but somebody wouldn't let us win." Yet there is no examination of just what "winning" means in the context of the war in Vietnam. It is enough for Rambo and his audience that the war could have been won.

In the second film Rambo returns to Vietnam to find and rescue Americans missing in action (MIAs) from Vietnam—a popular scenario in the mid–1980s that was central to such films as *Uncommon Valor* (1983), *Missing in Action* (1984), *Missing in Action II: The Beginning* (1985), *P.O.W.: The Escape* (1986), and *The Hanoi Hilton* (1987). But Rambo was really returning to Vietnam to win the war. When Colonel Trautman (Richard Crenna), his former commander, tells him, "The old war's dead, John," Rambo replies: "I'm alive. It's still alive." Later Rambo asks, "Do we get to win this time?" Trautman answers, "This time it's up to you." Since winning is again never defined, Rambo rewrites history. He "wins."

During the 1980s, there was a powerful resurgence of patriotism in the United States, beginning with the Reagan administration and steadily escalating to the euphoria of Desert Storm in 1991. In the process, Americans once again began to look at Communism as an evil force in the world. George Lucas's *Star Wars* trilogy—*Star Wars* (1979), *The Empire Strikes Back* (1981), and *Return of the Jedi* (1983) revived the idea of a world caught in a great struggle between an "evil empire" (as Ronald Reagan dubbed the Soviet Union in 1981) and "the Force." There were other, far more explicitly anti-Communist films in the 1980s, the most blatant of which was *Red Dawn* (1984), a silly movie built around the ludicrous premise that Soviet and Cuban troops could be airlifted into the interior of the United States and conquer Colorado. Far more effective was the monumental *The Killing Fields* (1984), the true story of *New York Times* reporter Sidney Schanberg (Sam Waterston) and his Cambodian photographer Dith Pran (Haing Ngor). When the Khmer Rouge Communists take control of Cambodia in 1975, Pran is left behind while Schanberg and the Americans evacuate Phnom Penh. Pran spends several years in Khmer Rouge "reeducation" camps, and the film explores the genocidal mania of the Khmer Rouge and the process by which they systematically slaughtered 2 million Cambodians in the late 1970s. There is no doubt about the reality of Communist evil in *The Killing Fields*.

By the late 1980s the American view of the Vietnam War, at least as it was portrayed in films, was more complex than ever before. The old debates of the 1960s and 1970s—when American liberals viewed the Vietcong as peace-loving nationalists and the American government as a war-mongering machine or when conservatives saw the Vietcong as Commie terrorists and the American government as the defender of liberty in Vietnam—had evolved to a new level. Both sides in the war were capable of incredible violence and genuine sincerity at the same time. In *Good Morning Vietnam*, Robin Williams plays Adrian Cronauer, an American disc jockey for armed forces radio in South Vietnam. Although the film viciously satirizes American policy in Vietnam and makes a strong case for the extraordinary commitment of the Vietcong, it nevertheless views both sides as real people caught in a very confusing situation. Eric Weston's *The Iron Triangle* (1989) follows a similar theme. It stars Beau Bridges and Haing S. Ngor. Bridges is captured by the North Vietnamese and saved by a young Vietcong. The film revolves around the growing respect that develops between the American and the Vietnamese.

Some of the Vietnam War films also took on the aura of the older generation of American war films, not so much in viewing the enemy as bloodthirsty savages but in viewing the GIs as normal young men fighting the war for a variety of reasons. The war films reflected the revived reputation of the American military during the 1980s. In the 1990 film *Memphis Belle*, which looks at American bombing crews flying over Germany during World War II, the American boys are innocent, committed, courageous, frightened—in short, very human. Vietnam films like *Hamburger Hill* (1987) and *The Hanoi Hilton* (1987) have a similar appeal. The 1988 HBO documentary *Dear America* consists of actors like Michael J. Fox and Sean Penn reading actual letters written by GIs in Vietnam. The film uses combat footages as a backdrop to the letters and brilliantly demonstrates how painful and confusing the war was for the men sent there to fight it.

Of course, Americans remained concerned about the impact of the Vietnam War on the United States, and those fears continued to be reflected in films. The film *Distant Thunder* (1988) stars John Lithgow as an emotionally scarred Vietnam War veteran who abandons civilization for a life in the national forests of rural Washington. Louis Malle's *Alamo Bay* (1985) was concerned with the violent dispute in the early 1980s between shrimpers along the coast of south Texas and the recently arrived Vietnamese immigrant fishermen who began, with great financial success, to fish those waters in the late 1970s. The confusing war and its ambiguous results, it seems, will continue to occupy moviemakers for the next generation.

BIBLIOGRAPHY

Adair, Gilbert. *Hollywood's Vietnam: From the Green Berets to Apocalypse Now*. New York: Proteus, 1981.

Aldgate, Anthony, and Jeffrey Richards. *Britain Can Take It: The British Cinema in the Second World War*. New York: Blackwell, 1986.

Alloway, Lawrence. *Violent America: The Movies 1946–1964*. New York: Museum of Modern Art, 1971.

Anderegg, Michael, ed. *Inventing Vietnam: Film and Television Constructions of the U.S.-Vietnam War*. Ann Arbor, Mich.: University Microfilms, 1990.

Auster, Albert, and Leonard Quart. "Hollywood and Vietnam: The Triumph of the Will." *Cineaste* 9 (Spring 1979): 4–9.

Auster, Albert, and Leonard Quart. *How the War Was Remembered: Hollywood and Vietnam*. Westport, Conn.: Praeger, 1988.

Baitaille, Gretchen M., and Charles L. P. Silet. *Images of American Indians on Film*. New York: Garland, 1985.

Baker, M. Joyce. *Images of Women in Film: The War Years, 1941–45*. Ann Arbor, Mich.: University Microfilms, 1980.

Basinger, Jeanine. *The World War Two Combat Film: Anatomy of a Genre*. New York: Columbia University Press, 1988.

Belmans, Jacques. "Cinema and Man at War." *Film Society Review* 7 (February 1972): 22–37.

Berg, Rick. "Losing Vietnam: Covering the War in an Age of Technology." *Cultural Critique* 3 (Spring 1986): 111.

Bogue, Ronald L. "The Heartless Darkness of *Apocalypse Now.*" *Georgia Review* 35 (Fall 1981): 611–26.

Bohn, Thomas William. *An Historical and Descriptive Analysis of the "Why We Fight" Series.* New York: Arno, 1977.

Bonoir, David E., Steven M. Champlin, and Timothy S. Kelly. *The Vietnam Veteran: A History of Neglect.* New York: Praeger, 1984.

Boyd, David. "*The Deer Hunter*: The Hero and the Tradition." *Australian Journal of American Studies* 1 (No. 1, 1980): 41–51.

Broderick, Mick. *Nuclear Movies: A Filmography.* Northcote, Australia: Post-Modem, 1988.

Brownlow, Kevin. *The War, the West and the Wilderness.* New York: Knopf, 1979.

Buckley, Tom. "Hollywood's War." *Harper's* 258 (April 1979): 84–86.

Burke, Frank. "In Defense of *The Deer Hunter* or: The Knee Jerk Is Quicker Than the Eye." *Literature-Film Quarterly* 11 (No. 1, 1983): 22–27.

Butler, Ivan. *The War Film.* New York: Barnes, 1974.

Calder, Jenni. *There Must Be a Lone Ranger: The American West in Film and Reality.* New York: McGraw-Hill, 1977.

Campbell, Craig W. *Reel America and World War I: A Comprehensive Filmography and History of Motion Pictures in the United States, 1914–1920.* Jefferson, N.C.: McFarland, 1985.

Chabal, P. R., and P. S. Chabal. "Copping Out with Coppola." *Cambridge Quarterly* 13 (No. 3, 1984): 187–203.

Christensen, Terry. *Reel Politics.* New York: Blackwell, 1987.

Cieutat, M. T. "Hollywood Films Dealing with the Vietnam War and Related Themes." *Positif* (No. 320, 1987): 50–57.

CineBooks. *War Movies.* Evanston, Ill.: CineBooks, 1989.

The Civil War in Motion Pictures: A Bibliography of Films Produced in the United States Since 1897. Compiled by Paul C. Spehr and the Staff of the Motion Picture Section. Washington, D.C.: Library of Congress, 1961.

Condon, Richard. *The Manchurian Candidate.* New York: McGraw-Hill, 1959.

Culbert, David, ed. *Film and Propaganda in America: A Documentary History.* 5 vols. New York: Greenwood, 1990–1992.

Curley, Stephen J., and Frank J. Wetta. "War Film Bibliography." *Journal of Popular Film and Television,* 18 (Summer 1990), 72–79.

Del Vecchio, John. *The 13th Valley.* New York: Bantam Books, 1982.

Deming, Barbara. *Running Away from Myself: A Dream Portrait of America Drawn from the Films of the Forties.* New York: Grossman, 1969.

Dempsey, Michael. "*Apocalypse Now.*" *Sight and Sound,* 49 (Winter 1979–1980), 5–9.

Dempsey, Michael. "Four Shots at *The Deer Hunter.*" *Film Quarterly* 32 (Summer 1979): 10–22.

Denby, David. *Film 70/Film 71.* New York: Simon and Schuster, 1971.

Dick, Bernard. *The Star-Spangled Screen: The American World War II Film.* Lexington: University Press of Kentucky, 1985.

Dittmar, Linda, and Gene Michaud, eds. *From Hanoi to Hollywood: The Vietnam War in American Film.* New Brunswick, N.J.: Rutgers University Press, 1990.

Dolan, Edward F., Jr. *Hollywood Goes to War.* New York: Smith, 1985.

Dowling, John. "Nuclear War and Disarmament." *Sightlines* 15 (1982): 19–21.

Dworkin, Martin S. "Clean Germans and Dirty Politics." *Film Comment* 3 (Winter 1965): 36–41.

Eiserman, Frederick A. *War on Film: Military History Education.* Historical Bibliography No. 6. Fort Leavenworth, Kans.: U.S. Army Command and General Staff College, 1987.

Evans, Gary. *John Grierson and the National Film Board: The Politics of Wartime Propaganda.* Toronto: University of Toronto Press, 1984.

Farmer, James H. *Celluloid Wings: The Impact of the Movies on Aviation.* Blue Ridge Summit, Pa.: Tab, 1984.

Francis, Don. "The Regeneration of America: Uses of Landscape in *The Deer Hunter.*" *Literature-Film Quarterly* 11 (No. 1, 1983): 16–21.

Furhammar, Leif, and Foke Isaksson. *Politics and Film.* New York: Praeger, 1971.

Furia, R. D. "*Apocalypse Now*: The Ritual Murder of Art." *Western Humanities Review* 34 (Winter 1980): 85–89.

Fyne, Robert. "The Unsung Heroes of World War II." *Literature/Film Quarterly* 7 (1979): 1489–54.

Garland, Brock. *War Movies: The Complete Viewer's Guide.* New York: Facts on File, 1987.

Gehring, Wes D., ed. *Handbook of American Film Genres.* Westport, Conn.: Greenwood, 1985.

Gillet, John. "Westfront 1957." *Sight and Sound* 27 (Winter 1957–1958): 122–27.

Gilman, Owen W., Jr., and Lorrie Smith, eds. *America Rediscovered: Critical Essays on Literatures and Film of the Vietnam War.* New York: Garland, 1990.

Grant, Barry Keith, ed. *Film Genre Reader.* Austin: University of Texas Press, 1986.

Greene, Graham. *The Quiet American.* Harmondsworth, England: Penguin, 1956.

Hasford, Gustav. *The Short-Timers.* New York: Harper and Row, 1979.

Heilbrom, Lisa M. "Coming Home a Hero: The Changing Image of the Vietnam Vet as Prime-Time Television." *Journal of Popular Film and Television* 13 (Spring 1985): 25–30.

Hellmann, John. "Vietnam and the Hollywood Genre Film: Inversions of American Mythology in *The Deer Hunter* and *Apocalypse Now.*" *American Quarterly* 34 (Fall 1982): 418–39.

Hilger, Michael. *The American Indian in Film.* Metuchen, N.J.: Scarecrow, 1986.

Hughes, Robert, ed. *Film, Book 2: Films of Peace and War.* New York: Grove, 1962.

Hutton, Paul Andrew. " 'Correct in Every Detail': General Custer and Hollywood." *Montana: The Magazine of Western History* 41 (Winter 1991): 29–57.

Isaacs, Hermine Rich. "Shadows of War on the Silver Screen." *Theatre Arts* 26 (November 1942): 689–96.

Isenberg, Michael T. "An Ambiguous Pacifism: A Retrospective on World War I Films, 1930–38." *Journal of Popular Film* 4 (1975): 98–115.

Jackson, Kathy Merlock. *Images of Children in American Film.* Metuchen, N.J.: Scarecrow, 1986.

Jacobs, Lewis. "World War II and the American Film." *Cinema Journal* 7 (Winter 1967–1968): 1–21.

Jacobson, Herbert L. "Cowboy, Pioneer and American Soldier." *Sight and Sound* 22 (1953): 189–90.

Jacoby, Monica E., and Frederick C. Fulfer. *Reel Wars: A Facts Quiz Book About War Films*. Middletown, Conn.: Southfarm, 1986.

Jeavons, Clyde. *A Pictorial History of War Films*. Secaucus, N.J.: Citadel, 1974.

Jeffords, Susan. "The New Vietnam Films: Is the Movie Over?" *Journal of Popular Film and Television* 13 (Winter 1986): 186–94.

Johnston, Winifred. *Memo on the Movies: War Propaganda, 1914–1939*. Norman: University of Oklahoma Press, 1939.

Jones, Ken D., and Arthur F. McClure. *Hollywood at War: The American Motion Picture and World War II*. New York: Barnes, 1973.

Jowett, Garth. *Film: The Democratic Art*. Boston: Little, Brown, 1976.

Kagan, Norman. *The War Film: A Pyramid Illustrated History of the Movies*. New York: Pyramid, 1974.

Kane, Kathryn. *Visions of War: Hollywood Combat Films of World War II*. Ann Arbor: University of Michigan Press, 1982.

Kanfer, Stefan. *Film 69/Film 70*. New York: Simon and Schuster, 1970.

Kauffman, Stanley. *Before My Eyes*. New York: Harper and Row, 1980.

Kinney, Judy Lee. "The Mythical Method: Fictionalizing the Vietnam War." *Wide Angle* 75 (No. 4, 1985): 35–40.

Koppes, Clayton R., and Gregory D. Black. *Hollywood Goes to War: How Politics, Profits and Propaganda Shaped World War II Movies*. New York: Free Press, 1987.

Kovic, Ron. *Born on the Fourth of July*. New York: McGraw-Hill, 1976.

Kozloff, Max, William Johnson, and Richard Corliss. "Shooting at Wars: Three Views." *Film Quarterly* 21 (Winter 1967–1968): 27–36.

Kracauer, Siegfried. *From Caligari to Hitler: A Psychological History of the German Film*. Princeton, N.J.: Princeton University Press, 1947.

Kuiper, John B. "Civil War Films: A Quantitative Description of a Genre." *Journal of the Society of Cinematologists* 5 (1965): 81–89.

Kunz, Don. "Oliver Stone's Film Adaptation of *Born on the Fourth of July*: Redefining Masculine Heroism." *War, Literature and the Arts* 2 (Fall 1990): 1–25.

Landrum, Larry M., and Christine Eynon. "World War II in the Movies: A Selected Bibliography of Sources." *Journal of Popular Film* 1 (Spring 1972): 147–53.

Langman, Larry, and Ed Borg. *Encyclopedia of American War Films*. New York: Garland, 1989.

Lewis, Leon, and William David Sherman. *In the Landscape of Contemporary Cinema*. Buffalo, N.Y.: Buffalo Spectrum, 1967.

Lewy, Gunter. *America in Vietnam*. New York: Oxford University Press, 1978.

Lingeman, Richard R. *Don't You Know There's a War On? The American Home Front, 1941–1945*. New York: Putnam, 1970.

Look Magazine, ed. *Movie Lot to Beachhead: The Motion Picture Goes to War and Prepares for the Future*. Salem, N.H.: Ayer, 1980.

McClure, Arthur F. "Hollywood at War: The American Motion Picture and World War II, 1939–1945." *Journal of Popular Film* 1 (Spring 1972): 123–35.

McInerney, Peter. "Apocalypse Then: Hollywood Looks Back at Vietnam." *Film Quarterly* 33 (Winter 1979–1980): 21–32.

McKinney, Devin. *"Born on the Fourth of July."* *Film Quarterly* 44 (Fall 1990): 44–47.

Madsen, Alex. "Vietnam and the Movies." *Cinema* 4 (Spring 1968): 10–13.

Manchel, Frank. *Film Study: A Resource Guide*. Rutherford, N.J.: Fairleigh Dickinson University Press, 1973.

Manvell, Roger. *Films and the Second World War*. New York: Barnes, 1974.

Mariani, John. "Let's Not Be Beastly to the Nazis." *Film Comment* 15 (January-February 1979); 49–53.

Martin, Andrew Victor. "Critical Approaches to American Cultural Studies: The Vietnam War in History, Literature, and Film." Ph.D. diss. University of Iowa, 1987.

Mast, Gerald. *The Movies in Our Midst: Documents in the Cultural History of Film in America*. Chicago: University of Chicago Press, 1982.

Mellen, Joan. *Big Bad Wolves*. New York: Pantheon, 1977.

Moore, Robin. *The Green Berets*. New York: Crown, 1965.

Morella, Joe, Edward Z. Epstein, and John Griggs. *The Films of World War II*. Secaucus, N.J.: Citadel, 1973.

Mould, David H. *American Newsfilm, 1914–1919: The Underexposed War*. New York: Garland, 1983.

Norden, Martin F. "The Disabled Vietnam Veteran in Hollywood Film." *Journal of Popular Film and Television* 13 (Spring 1985): 16–23.

O'Connor, John E., and Martin A. Jackson, eds. *American History/American Film: Interpreting the Hollywood Image*. New York: Ungar, 1988.

Palmer, William J. "The Vietnam War Films." *Film Library Quarterly* 13 (No. 4, 1980): 4–14.

Paris, Michael. "The American Film Industry and Vietnam." *History Today* 37 (April 1987): 19–26.

Parish, James Robert. *The Great Combat Pictures: Twentieth-Century Warfare on the Screen*. Metuchen, N.J.: Scarecrow, 1990.

Pendo, Stephen. *Aviation in the Cinema*. Metuchen, N.J.: Scarecrow, 1985.

Perlmutter, Tom. *War Movies*. Secaucus, N.J.: Castle, 1974.

Pickard, Roy. *A Companion to the Movies: From 1903 to the Present Day*. London: Lutterworth, 1972.

Pitts, Michael R. *Hollywood and American History: A Filmography of Over 250 Motion Pictures Depicting U.S. History*. Jefferson, N.C.: McFarland, 1984.

Polan, Dana. *Power and Paranoia: History, Narrative, and the American Cinema, 1940–1950*. New York: Columbia University Press, 1986.

Pursell, Michael. *"Full Metal Jacket*: The Unravelling of Patriarchy." *Literature-Film Quarterly* 16 (No. 4, 1988): 216–22.

Ray, Robert B. *A Certain Tendency of the Hollywood Cinema, 1930–1980*. Princeton, N.J.: Princeton University Press, 1985.

Reaves, Michael. "From Hasford's *The Short-Timers* to Kubrick's *Full Metal Jacket*: The Fracturing of Identification." *Literature-Film Quarterly* 16 (No. 4, 1988): 232–37.

Renov, Michael. *Hollywood's Wartime Woman: Representation and Ideology*. Ann Arbor, Mich.: University Microfilms, 1988.

Rollins, Peter C., ed. *Hollywood as Historian: American Film in a Cultural Context.* Lexington: University Press of Kentucky, 1983.

Rollins, Peter C. "The Vietnam War: Perceptions Through Literature, Film, and Television." *American Quarterly* 36 (1984): 419–32.

Rubin, Steven Jay. *Combat Films: American Realism, 1945–1970.* Jefferson, N.C.: McFarland, 1981.

Sarria, Andrew. *On the Cinema, 1955/1969.* New York: Simon and Schuster, 1970.

Sayre, Nora. *Running Time: Films of the Cold War.* New York: Dial Press, 1982.

Searle, William J., ed. *Search and Clear: Critical Response to Selected Literature and Films of the Vietnam War.* Bowling Green, Ohio: Bowling Green State University Press, 1988.

Shaheen, Jack G. *Nuclear War Films.* Carbondale: Southern Illinois University Press, 1978.

Shain, Russell Earl. *An Analysis of Motion Pictures About War Released by the American Film Industry, 1930–1970.* New York: Arno Press, 1976.

Shindler, Colin. *Hollywood Goes to War: Films and American Society, 1939–1952.* New York: Routledge, 1979.

Short, K.R.M., ed. *Film and Radio Propaganda in World War II.* Knoxville: University of Tennessee Press, 1983.

Sklar, Robert. *Movie-Made America: A Cultural History of American Movies.* New York: Random House, 1975.

Skogsberg, Bertil. *Wings on the Screen: A Pictorial History of Air Movies.* San Diego, Calif.: Barnes, 1981.

Smith, Claude J., Jr. "The Rehabilitation of the U.S. Military in Films Since 1978." *Journal of Popular Film and Television* 11 (Winter 1984): 145–51.

Smith, Julian. *Looking Away, Hollywood and Vietnam.* New York: Scribners, 1975.

Smith, Myron J. *Air War, Southeast Asia, 1961–1973: An Annotated Bibliography and 16mm Film Guide.* Metuchen, N.J.: Scarecrow Press, 1979.

Smith, Ralph. "The Vietnam War." *History Today* 34 (October 1984): 45–48.

Soderbergh, Peter A. "Aux Armes! The Rise of the Hollywood War Film, 1916–1930." *South Atlantic Quarterly* 65 (Autumn 1966): 509–22.

Solomon, Stanley J. *Beyond Formula: American Film Genres.* New York: Harcourt, Brace, Jovanovich, 1976.

Stevenson, James A. "Beyond Stephen Crane: *Full Metal Jacket.*" *Literature-Film Quarterly* 16 (No. 4, 1988): 238–43.

Stone, Robert. *Dog Soldiers.* Boston: Houghton-Mifflin, 1974.

Studlar, Gaylyn, and David Desser. "Never Having to Say You're Sorry: *Rambo's* Rewriting of the Vietnam War." *Film Quarterly* 42 (Fall 1988): 9–16.

Sturken, Marita. "The Camera as Witness: Documentaries on the Vietnam War." *Film Library Quarterly* 13 (No. 4, 1980): 15–20.

Suid, Lawrence H. *Guts & Glory: Great American War Movies.* Reading, Mass.: Addison Wesley, 1978.

Suid, Lawrence H. "Hollywood and Vietnam." *Film Comment* 15 (September-October 1979): 20–25.

Syers, William. *Flashbacks.* New York: Ungar Press, 1987.

Thomas, Tony. *The Cinema of the Sea: A Critical Survey and Filmography, 1925–1986.* Jefferson, N.C.: McFarland, 1988.

Thompson, Lawrence, Richard Welch, and Philip Stephens. "A Vietnam Filmography." *Journal of Popular Film and Television* 9 (Spring 1981): 61–67.

Tyler, Parker. *Magic and Myth in the Movies.* New York: Simon and Schuster, 1947.

Virilio, Paul. *War and Cinema: The Logics of Perception.* New York: Routledge, 1988.

Wilson, James C. *Vietnam in Prose and Film.* Jefferson, N.C.: McFarland, 1982.

Wood, Robin. *Hollywood from Vietnam to Reagan.* New York: Columbia University Press, 1986.

Zinsser, William. *Seen Any Good Movies?* New York: Doubleday, 1958.

20 The Vietnam War and Comic Books

Bradford Wright

The Vietnam War looms as the central subject in contemporary American politics, society and culture. Much has been written about the Vietnam War in the mass media and popular culture. One popular mass entertainment medium, however, has so far received little scholarly attention. In many respects the Vietnam War period was a watershed for the American comic book industry, which recovered from the doldrums of the late 1950s to reestablish itself as a major purveyor of entertainment for the young and for adults. This study will explore how the Vietnam War and American society were reflected in the contemporary comic books of the industry's major publishers. It is an analysis of the relationship among war, society, and popular culture during a critical period of American history.

The comic book industry thrived during the early 1950s, largely due to the popularity of crime and horror comic books that featured graphic violence, sexual overtones, and other adult themes. Parents, psychologists, government officials, and other concerned groups suspected that comic books contributed to a rise in juvenile delinquency. The public crusade against comic books resulted in a U.S. Senate investigation into the industry in 1954, after which the publishers established the self-censoring Comics Code Authority. In order to ensure the national distribution of their comic books, the code required publishers to adhere to the standards, which have been described by one of the code's proponents as "the most stringent for any media" (Goldwater, 8). The code was intended to uphold the principles of "good taste" in comic books and to preserve the medium as a "wholesome form of entertainment." Among the code's standards was the provision that "policemen, judges, government officials and respected institutions shall never be presented in such a way as to create disrespect for established authority" (*Code of the Comics Magazine Association of America*, 1). The code, therefore, dictated that comic book stories after 1954 would be not only sanitized and juvenile, but devoid of social and political criticism as well.

The establishment of the Comics Code Authority had an immediate and depressing effect on the comic book industry as a whole. Many publishers who had relied upon themes forbidden by the code were unable to distribute their comic books and went out of business within a few years. The industry was further hurt by the rise of television, which had more to offer discerning teenagers and young adults than the code-approved comic books (Witek, 49–50). The *New York Times* reported that by 1962 annual comic book sales had dropped from 800,000,000 in 1952 to 350,000,000 in 1962. The comic book industry, which had once consisted of over fifty publishers, began the 1960s with fewer than a dozen publishing houses (*New York Times*, 1962, 12).

The code did not affect all publishers equally, however, and some were not hurt by it at all. DC Comics survived the 1950s in good shape, and by 1962 it had acquired 30 percent of the market (*New York Times*, 1962, 12). DC had never participated heavily in the controversial crime or horror trends, and the content of its comic books was restrained even before the code, featuring such widely recognizable characters as Superman, Batman, and Wonder Woman (Benton, 104). Throughout the 1950s these titles remained targeted at an unsophisticated juvenile readership and were, therefore, unchanged by the editorial standards of the code (*Superman*, 210–328; *Batman*, 90–215). DC was also probably hurt less by television than other publishers because the popularity of the televised "Adventures of Superman" may have actually boosted the sales of Superman comic books. In 1956 DC initiated what comic book historians have termed the "silver age" of superhero comic books by reviving some of its stock superheroes from the 1940s and giving them revised origins with more contemporary settings (Jacobs and Jones, 9). The popularity of titles like *The Flash*, *Green Lantern*, and *The Justice League of America* helped reestablish the superhero comic book as the industry's most popular genre of the 1960s.

The Dell Publishing Company was one comic book publisher that may have actually benefited from the establishment of the code. Dell's top-selling comic books were its "funny animal" titles that featured characters from the cartoons of Walt Disney and Warner Brothers. The company was proud of its reputation for producing clean, wholesome comic books that were held up as positive examples by those who criticized the rest of the industry. The president of Dell was one of the few publishers who refused to submit their comic books to the Code Authority, because Dell already maintained its own code for decency and good taste (*New York Times*, 1954, 29). The company thrived during the late 1950s, selling more comic books worldwide than any other publisher, but circulation dropped dramatically in the early 1960s. Dell's attempt to diversify its publishing operation by producing titles in genres such as war and science fiction failed to capture a large audience, and the company remained a second-rate publisher until it left the comic book field in 1973 (Benton, 110).

Marvel Comics had been among the most prolific of comic book publishers since its entry into the field in 1939. During its first two decades, Marvel followed changing industry trends, publishing titles in every comic book genre. Marvel's war and horror comic books were its most visible titles prior to the code. The former were inspired by the Korean War and have been described by one writer as perhaps the most anticommunist of all 1950s war comics (Benton, 133). The latter were among those specifically condemned by the U.S. Senate investigation into the industry (U. S. Senate Committee on the Judiciary). Marvel entered the 1960s as a much smaller publishing operation, whose most notable comic books were fantasy stories inspired by Saturday matinee monster films. That the *New York Times* failed even to mention Marvel in its report on the status of the industry in 1962 attests to the publisher's small share of the market (*New York Times*, 1962, 12).

The publisher of Marvel Comics noticed the success of DC's superhero titles and asked his staff to put out a comic book featuring a team of superheroes modeled after DC's *The Justice League of America*. Stan Lee, who served as Marvel's comic book editor, art director, and head writer, conceived a comic book that actually bore little resemblance to any DC comic (Lee, *Origins of Marvel Comics*, 16). Lee, working with writer Jack Kirby, created an experimental group of superheroes who displayed a depth of characterization beyond anything that had yet been attempted in the genre. The "Fantastic Four" were portrayed as human beings with diverse personalities and human failings who had accidentally acquired superpowers. One member of the group, Ben Grimm, gained his superstrength at the expense of his humanity, when "comic rays" transformed him into a hulking, orange, rock-skinned monster. Grimm, calling himself simply "the Thing," was overtly envious of, and hostile toward, his friends and teammates who retained their human appearance. The Thing was a new kind of superhero for the 1960s—one who was deeply alienated from and resentful of, the society that he was sworn to protect ("The Fantastic Four").

The success of *The Fantastic Four* prompted Marvel to produce another innovative superhero comic book. *The Incredible Hulk* featured Dr. Bruce Banner, a mild-mannered physicist reminiscent of Dr. Jekyll, who periodically transforms into a tremendously strong, green-skinned brute. The Hulk's bestial nature and his hatred of the human race, which constantly hounds him, make him an outsider far removed from the traditional ideal of a superhero ("The Incredible Hulk").

Spider-Man was destined to become Marvel's most popular character. Peter Parker is a shy, socially inept high school science student whose only family and friends are his elderly aunt and uncle. He accidentally gains the proportionate powers of a spider when he is bitten by a radioactive spider at a science demonstration. Upon discovering his powers, however, he is not inspired to use them to help mankind, but instead seeks personal fame and wealth. After his debut performance on television, Spider-Man witnesses a fugitive escape from a pursuing police officer. When the angry policeman asks him why he did not help stop the criminal, Spider-Man replies that he is looking out only for himself. Soon thereafter, Parker discovers that his beloved Uncle Ben has been killed by a burglar. He tracks the murderer down only to discover that the killer is the very fugitive whom he had allowed to escape earlier. Only then does he realize that "with great power comes great responsibility," and he pledges himself to a life of crime fighting ("Spider-Man"). Here was a young superhero whose service to society was motivated not by a noble heroic ideal, but rather by an intense sense of personal obligation born of guilt. This set the tone for the *Spider-Man* comic book series, in which the hero had to contend with society's problems, phobias, and his own self-pity as often as he had to battle supervillains.

These and other comic books injected a renewed vitality into the industry, which had stagnated since the establishment of the code. Working within the constraints of the code, Stan Lee brought a sense of contemporary realism to superhero comic books despite the obviously fantastic premise of the genre. In this sense, the Marvel comic books were very different from DC's. While DC stories were set in such mythical locations as "Metropolis," "Gotham City," and "Star City," Marvel superheroes operated in and around New York City. DC editorial policy dictated that its comic books would appeal almost exclusively to a juvenile audience, but Stan Lee searched for an older readership (*New York Times*, 1962, 12). Lee maintained that it was possible to capture a postadolescent audience without alienating the younger readers by presenting comic book stories on two levels: "color, costumes, and exaggerated action for the kids, [and] science-fiction, satire, and sophisticated philosophy for the adults and near-adults" (Lee, 15).

This creative strategy brought success to Stan Lee and Marvel Comics. Although Marvel remained well behind DC in overall sales, the gap between the two publishers narrowed considerably throughout the 1960s (Benton, 136). Marvel also won a devoted following among older readers. The popularity of Marvel Comics on college campuses was noted by *Esquire* magazine, which reported in 1966 that Stan Lee had become a popular visiting lecturer ("Okay You Passed the 2-S Test," 115). Another issue noted that Spider-Man and the Hulk ranked alongside Bob Dylan, Che Guevara, and Malcolm X as the most popular revolutionary figures among the collegiate New Left (*Esquire*, 97).

Marvel Comics employed a realism in both characterization and setting in its superhero titles that was unequaled in the comic book industry. Marvel Comics were the most popular among college students—a socially aware audience that Marvel strove to retain. For these reasons, the Marvel comic books, more than any other, serve as a barometer of the changing political and social mood during the Vietnam War. They will be dealt with in greater detail later in this chapter.

The Dell Publishing Company was the first to portray the Vietnam War in comic books. *Jungle War Stories* featured tales set in South Vietnam as early as July 1962, marking one of the war's earliest appearances in American popular culture. Unlike most Dell titles, which were targeted at young children, this war comic book aimed at a slightly older readership. Each issue of *Jungle War Stories* consisted of three or four short war stories that usually featured soldiers of the U.S. Special Forces. The emphasis of these stories was not on characterization—of which there was virtually none—or even on action. Above all, they sought to educate the audience about America's increasing involvement in the Vietnam conflict. Because the series ran during the earliest stage of American military involvement, it is likely that many of the teenagers who read the comic book gleaned from it their initial knowledge of the Vietnam situation. *Jungle War Stories* merits a careful analysis because it was the closest that the comic book industry came to a careful and deliberate propaganda effort for American policy in Vietnam.

The early issues of *Jungle War Stories* were devoted primarily to an explanation and justification of the U.S. presence in South Vietnam. One such story, entitled "Day of Reckoning," was unusual in that it was told from the viewpoint of a Russian military advisor to the Vietcong. The protagonist, who is referred to only as "Comrade," recounts the history of his life to some of his Vietcong troops. His life has been endless frustration. As a boy he was chosen by the "Party" for special training in guerrilla warfare. It was a promising start for a career, because "this was the first step of the communist ladder." He was given his first great opportunity to prove himself when "the movement swept over China." He leads an attack against some of Chiang Kai-shek's supply junks, but his ambush is defeated when the supposedly "helpless" ships return fire with American-supplied machine guns. "Curse the Yankee. . . . Curse him!" exclaims the Comrade. Later he seeks to redeem himself in the eyes of his superiors by aiding the Communist guerrillas in Greece, but again he is frustrated by "American weapons speaking from the hands of Greek Government troops." Likewise, his efforts in the Malayan insurrection fail due to "Yankee arms." The Comrade angrily concludes, "It was the Yankee weapons that ended all hopes!" The Soviet's ravings are cut short by a Green Beret, airborne assault on his position. The Vietcong are defeated, and the Comrade meets a fitting end when he himself is killed by American soldiers ("Day of Reckoning"). The message in this story is that American military aid to South Vietnam is needed to confront the Communist Menace, which must be contained. The story supports the Truman Doctrine and suggests that Communism is a monolithic threat. It even hints that defeat in Vietnam might compel the Soviet "comrades," who are apparently directing the insurrection, finally to realize the futility of their efforts.

South Vietnam, however, needed more than just American weapons to stop the Vietcong. American military advisors were needed to instruct and lead the Army of the Republic of Vietnam (ARVN), which could not do anything right on its own. *Jungle War Stories* made this point clear as early as issue number one. In the first story, American Green Berets parachute into Phu-Yen province in order to lead some ARVN troops and soon conclude that "these people got no belly for fighting the Viet Cong guerrillas." Under American leadership, however, the South Vietnamese score their first success against the Communists ("Requiem for a Red").

The South Vietnamese civilian population similarly needed American guidance to put them on the path to victory and peace. In "A Walk in the Sun," some Green Berets come to a village with orders to move the inhabitants to a nearby strategic hamlet. Upon arriving in the village, one American soldier comments to another that "it's a crazy mixed-up war." His friend agrees, adding, "Half the peasants want no part of it ...either side." He concludes that "there'll always be folks who figure the world owes them a living." Later, the Americans are confronted by the village leader, who tells them, "The sides of this cursed war are like grains of rice...no difference!" As the villagers are led through the jungle by the Americans, they witness some scenes that make a strong impression upon them: entire villages burned and destroyed by the Communists, contrasted by scenes of Green Berets giving medical attention and food to injured peasants. When the group finally arrives at the strategic hamlet, the Vietnamese peasants have undergone a profound change of attitude. The village leader acknowledges: "We were fools. You [Americans] showed us today that as you fed our hungry, buried our dead and saved our children from [the Vietcong's] horrors." He pledges the villagers' allegiance to the South and the American leadership, promising to "do our part to fight the Red dogs" ("A Walk in the Sun"). The Green Berets had won the hearts and minds of the Vietnamese people.

Not all Vietnamese were so quick to come to this conclusion, however. The South Vietnamese population remained deeply divided, and this was reflected in the comic book as well. "The Year of the Cat" is set in a village that is about to be turned into a strategic hamlet. It features two villagers—a female Songtoi and her lover, Van Xuan. Songtoi is angered by the Americans' presence in her village. Moreover, she is unhappy with the Saigon regime. She tells her lover: "Those with intelligence realize how evil the [South] Vietnamese are! And unworthy of our allegiance." Van Xuan remains committed to the South, arguing that "the government helps arm us so that we can defend ourselves against the raids of the Viet Cong!" Songtoi defends the ruthless tactics of the Communists by claiming that "people must be forced to accept what is just for them!" She eventually leaves her lover, joins the Vietcong, and is killed when they launch an unsuccessful attack on the village. Van Xuan mourns her death, but he is pleased with the battle's outcome: "It is good that the [South] Vietnamese armed us for such a time!" ("The Year of the Cat").

It is interesting to note that both the loyalist Vietnamese and the Vietcong refer to those loyal to the Saigon regime as simply "the Vietnamese." South Vietnam is simply "Vietnam." In this sense the Vietcong are portrayed not as Vietnamese but as an exterior threat to the legitimate government and people of the South—the only true Vietnam.

In addition to the regular war stories, *Jungle War Stories* often contained pages of straightforward information on the Vietnam conflict. One such page, entitled "The Enemy in Vietnam," described the Vietcong guerrilla as a "scrawny, unkempt 100-pounder who barely comes up to the average G.I.'s shoulders." Despite his diminutive size, though, the enemy is "cruel, cunning and tough" and capable of traveling "up to forty miles a day on fabric rubber-soled shoes." This "fact page" went on to describe some of the tactics employed by the Vietcong. According to the comic book, the Communists would have children play "for days on end" near a fort that is targeted for an attack so that "the coming and going of its personnel can be carefully noted." Supposedly innocent Vietnamese children, therefore, may actually work for the enemy—an ambiguous foe indeed ("The Enemy in Vietnam"). Information pages like this one usually contained a combination of established facts and unsupported assertions. One, entitled "Viet Cong: The Face of the Enemy," introduces the reader to Vo Nguyen Giap, "the little-known author of the master plan for conquest by subversion." Vietcong tactics, as directed by Giap, include "a brutal succession of village burnings, road minings and bridge burnings... together with the capture of vital rice barges and incessant extortion of money and food from Vietnamese peasants." According to the comic book, "Viet Cong soldiers are frequently hard to distinguish from the rest of the Vietnamese population because of the typical black pajamas which they wear." While this information could have been read in the *New York Times*, the next panel states: "Reminiscent of the brutal war in North Korea is the 'Human Wave' technique practiced by the Viet Cong. Accompanied by the wild blowing of bugles, the North Vietnamese Communists attack in overwhelming numbers" ("Viet Cong: The Face of the Enemy"). This claim bore less resemblance to the true military situation in Vietnam than to the racist notion that Asians, whether they be Japanese, Chinese, North Korean, or North Vietnamese, must employ their "overwhelming numbers" on the battlefield in order to compensate for their inferiority as individual soldiers and human beings. In any case, this juxtaposition of fact and assertion in *Jungle War Stories* would have made it difficult for the otherwise uninformed reader to distinguish what is true and what is false about the situation in Vietnam.

The Vietcong in *Jungle War Stories* are portrayed as a dangerous and treacherous foe, more likely to cut their adversary's throat from behind than assault him frontally. In one story, the Vietcong take over a village and masquerade as the inhabitants in order to fool the U.S. Special Forces and the ARVN ("Deadly Masquerade"). In the next issue the Communists again disguise themselves, this time as ARVN soldiers, in order to deceive an American pilot ("Surprise Party"). The next issue's story, entitled "The Enemy Has Many Faces," tells how the Vietcong, disguised as Buddhist monks, try to infiltrate a strategic hamlet. This absurd premise is taken even further in another story when the Vietcong kidnap some Vietnamese children and masquerade as their teachers in order to sneak into a school on the outskirts of Saigon ("The Big Blow-Up"). The point, which is overstated in these stories, is that the enemy in Vietnam can appear in any number of forms. What appears to be a harmless villager, teacher, or other Vietnamese civilian may well be a Communist waiting to stab a trusting American in the back. The series suggested that it was difficult to tell friend from foe in the Vietnam War.

The American soldier in *Jungle War Stories* exhibited superior qualities of military prowess, humanitarianism, and leadership. The troops of the U.S. Special Forces were usually featured as the protagonists in the stories. Several Green Berets, in particular, appeared as recurring characters, but their individual personalities are so shallow and indistinguishable from one another that the reader is not able to identify with any of them. Their deeds are not portrayed as individual accomplishments, but rather are representative of the entire American military effort in Vietnam. A page entitled "Vietnam Battle Facts," which appeared in a 1963 issue, stated simply that "our job in Vietnam is to supply and instruct [the South Vietnamese] in ways of halting the Red guerrillas' terror." The Green Berets pursue this directive successfully, whether they are organizing militarily incompetent ARVN troops or winning the hearts and minds of the population with the Strategic Hamlets program.

"The Attack Begins," proclaimed the cover of the January-March, 1965, issue of *Jungle War Stories*. The inside cover of the comic book displayed a picture of the USS *Maddox*, flanked by North Vietnamese gunboats. It briefly described the Tonkin Gulf incident as "the first major naval engagement of the Vietnam conflict" (*Jungle War Stories*).

The nature of the war had clearly changed, and the increasing American involvement in Vietnam was reflected in *Jungle War Stories*. The Green Berets were no longer as concerned with training and leading the South Vietnamese as they were with winning the war. American GIs were now fighting alongside the Special Forces. As early as 1965, the comic book drew attention to difficulties that would continue to frustrate the American military effort for the duration of the war. In one story an American pilot is forced to abandon his pursuit of retreating Vietcong soldiers when they cross the border into Laos. The Vietcong laugh at the American's predicament, noting "a little thing like a border . . . saps their strength and turns them into cowards." When the pilot returns to headquarters, he complains that "if that crazy [border is] gonna stop us every time we chase . . . well that's a dang fool way to fight a war!" ("Pinch the Devil"). As early as 1965, the series hinted that the war might be lost because government policy tied the hands of our troops.

The South Vietnamese themselves were portrayed as a significant obstacle to victory. The ARVN had always appeared as confused and inept in the series, but by 1965 the South Vietnamese leadership was seen to be dangerously corrupt, incompetent, and jealous of their American allies. In "Frontal Assault," the South Vietnamese military commanders devise a plan that they keep secret from the Americans because they want to "show our American colleagues that we Vietnamese can work out a battle scheme just as clever as [the Americans] might suggest." The plan, of course, fails miserably. Later, the American commanders discover that this and other ARVN military fiascos have come about because the plans were leaked to the enemy by a spy among the ARVN planning staff in Saigon ("Frontal Assault"). If the United States was going to win the war in Vietnam, according to this comic book, it would have to do so not with the help of its South Vietnam allies, but in spite of them.

A curious item appeared in the April-June 1965 issue of *Jungle War Stories*. "A Letter from Vietnam" was a one-page letter from "Jim," an American serviceman in South Vietnam, to his teenage brother, "Billy." There were no accompanying pictures or explanation for the letter, and it is not clear whether it was fictional or an actual, reprinted letter. In it the soldier writes of his close friend Johnny, who, while stationed in Vietnam, spent his free time studying in order to earn his high school diploma. The soldier then describes an incident in which Johnny was killed in action before he had received his diploma. Jim urges his young brother to stay in high school until he earns his diploma and then to go to college. The last line of the letter reads, "I just don't want my kid brother to waste his life when it isn't necessary" ("A Letter from Vietnam").

This downbeat letter was highly uncharacteristic of the usual content of *Jungle War Stories*. In one page, Dell offered a pessimistic account of a war that was crueler than anything that had been depicted in its comic books. The first comic book publisher to come out in support of the American effort in Vietnam was also the first to discourage enlistment, however obliquely. With the rapidly escalating U.S. presence in Vietnam in 1965, it is possible that the staff at Dell feared the possible success of their own propaganda.

Because Dell did not give public credit to its comic book writers, it is not known whether there was a change of view in one writer's mind or a change in the creative staff behind *Jungle War Stories*. Whichever the case, the tone of the comic book shifted slightly after 1965. "Face of the Enemy," appearing in the same issue as "A Letter from Vietnam," tells of an American pilot who is forced to bail out over North Vietnam. He encounters a Communist soldier, who does not capture or kill the American but instead leads him safely back to the South Vietnamese border. The Communist returns to the North, where he maintains that he is doing his best to end the war, "for the benefit of all Vietnam" ("Face of the Enemy"). Never before in the comic book had the enemy been depicted with such humane characteristics.

Another story, "Big Surprise," features no Americans. It is about a South Vietnamese member of the Civilian Irregular Defense group, who is portrayed as a hero—albeit a reluctant one—who defeats a company of Vietcong single-handedly. His success is a result of accidental circumstances—he deceives the enemy because his appearance is identical to that of their commander—but, nevertheless, for the first time the South Vietnamese have demonstrated that, with a little luck, they can defeat the enemy without American help ("Big Surprise").

With the July-September 1965 issue, Dell changed the title of *Jungle War Stories* to *Guerrilla War*, a more appropriate title for a Vietnam War comic book, but the series was canceled by the beginning of 1966. The contribution of *Jungle War Stories* and *Guerrilla War* to the comic book field was marginal. The series lasted only fourteen issues and was greatly overshadowed and outsold by the more popular superhero titles of Marvel and DC. Still, the series was significant for several reasons. It represented the first attempt by a publisher to portray the Vietnam conflict in comic books, and it did so several years before the Gulf of Tonkin Resolution truly made Vietnam an American war. The comic book was also the closest that the industry came to a propaganda effort in support of American policy in Vietnam. It should be noted that *Jungle War Stories*, like all privately published comic books, was in no way licensed by the U.S. government for propaganda purposes. Indeed, the comic book contained some themes and ideas, such as the unfavorable portrayal of our South Vietnamese allies, that would not have been encouraged by the Johnson administration. Still, by incorporating an impressive amount of information into the comic books—whether it was true or not—the creators of *Jungle War Stories* gave even their fictional features an air of authority that could lead the reader to believe that these stories, which usually followed the official government line, were an accurate reflection of the situation in Vietnam. It is impossible to determine what influence this series had upon its adolescent audience, but it is likely that many readers who came of age during the height of the Vietnam War initially learned of the conflict in the pages of this comic book.

The last significant point to make about *Jungle War Stories* is that it was the first Vietnam War comic book to fail commercially. Although the series lasted for over three years, a run of only fourteen issues is a fair to poor one by industry standards. That the title was canceled at the same time that the American military presence in Vietnam was nearly 200,000 strong and growing is probably not a coincidence. The more that people were bombarded by images and information about the war in the mass media, the less they wanted to be exposed to it in escapist popular entertainment. Whether its cancellation was a result of a conscious editorial decision or falling sales or a combination of both, the demise of *Jungle War Stories* was an early indication that the Vietnam War would be difficult to sell to the American people.

Subsequent efforts to portray the Vietnam War in comic form were also short-lived. The Green Beret continued to be the popular protagonist for Vietnam War comic books. Robin Moore's well-received novel *The Green Berets* (Olson and Roberts, 204) and Sgt. Barry Sadler's hit song "Ballad of the Green Berets" seemed to demonstrate the marketability of the U.S. Special Forces. According to Robin Moore, he was approached in 1966 by General Yarborough, the commander of the J.F.K. Special Warfare Center at Fort Bragg, to start a comic strip "extolling the heroism of the Green Berets" (Moore and Kubert, 1). Moore, working with artist Joe Kubert, an illustrator who had done work for DC's line of war comic books, produced a syndicated newspaper strip entitled "Tales of the Green Beret," which was based upon Moore's novel. Although Kubert maintained that he and Moore were not "taking any side, either hawk or dove" ("Pop Goes the War," 66), the strip read like propaganda for the Johnson administration's Vietnam policy (Moore and Kubert).

The "Tales" strip was not well received. Newspapers that carried it began to drop the strip when they received complaints from readers. Some deplored the strip's "paramilitary bloodthirstiness," while others complained that it played "propaganda on the comic page." Newspaper editors also feared reader indifference. As the managing editor of the *Charlotte Observer* put it: "People were reading about the war on the front page and throughout the newspaper. By the time they got to the comic page they wanted relief." Joe Kubert admitted that portraying the Vietnam War in comics created problems of reader empathy, because the United States in Vietnam was "the big guy fighting the little guy and the American has always been for the underdog" ("Pop Goes the War," 66).

"Tales of the Green Beret" was terminated by the end of 1967. Robin Moore blamed the cancellation of his strip on "the left-leaning portion of the academic community [who] ... waged a vituperative campaign against the newspapers carrying [it]" (Moore and Kubert, 1). Efforts by the comic book industry to portray the Vietnam War in its publications, however, met with a similar lack of success. Dell tried once again to sell the war to readers with its own comic book adaptation of Moore's "Tales" strip. Dell's *Tales of the Green Beret* depicted the bitter fighting in Vietnam in a more grim and realistic manner than *Jungle War Stories*. In one story a Green Beret is even prepared to kill innocent Vietnamese civilians in order to get at the Vietcong, claiming that there was "no such thing as a non-combatant in this war!" ("My Enemy—My Brother"). The comic book, which proclaimed on the cover of its first issue that "if we must fight ... we will win!" (*Tales of the Green Beret*) was a loser with readers. Dell published only five issues of *Tales* over a period of two and a half years before it canceled the title.

The Milson Publishing Company was a short-lived operation that tried in 1967 to capitalize on the public fascination with the Green Berets and the popularity of superhero comic books. Milson's *Super Green Beret* featured a teenager who turns into a full-grown superpowered Green Beret soldier when he dons a magical green beret. This, the most absurd of all Vietnam War comic books, failed miserably. It lasted only two issues, and Milson folded shortly thereafter.

DC and Marvel, the two leading publishers by 1968, avoided the Vietnam War for the most part. DC published five war comic books, but only one of them ever featured stories set in Vietnam. From the start of 1966 to the middle of 1967, *Our Fighting Forces* starred Captain Hunter, a retired Green Beret who has been captured by the Vietcong. Although Captain Hunter frequently encounters the Vietcong, the search for his brother, not the war itself, motivates him and serves as the dramatic focus of the series. The published reader response to the "Captain Hunter" feature was generally favorable, but some maintained that the Vietnam War belonged in the newspapers and not in comic books (Letters page, *Our Fighting Forces*, no. 102). Others criticized the writers for portraying Captain Hunter as being too preoccupied with finding his brother at the expense of helping America win the war (Letters page, *Our Fighting Forces*, no. 106). Hunter, ultimately unable to appeal to either hawks or doves, found his brother and was banished from *Our Fighting Forces*. Such a theme was consistent with the other DC war comic books featuring stories set during World War II, a more popular war with a clearly defined purpose.

Marvel's only 1960s war comic book was also set in World War II. *Sgt. Fury and His Howling Commandos* featured a cast a diverse characters who starred in action-packed adventures that, as one writer has noted, "read like an unintentional parody of bad war movies" (Jacobs and Jones, 111). The 1967 *Sgt. Fury King-Size Special*, however, was set during contemporary times and featured Fury and his commandos in Vietnam. Fury, now the head of SHIELD—a high-tech espionage agency modeled after television's "UNCLE"—is approached by President Johnson to undertake a secret mission into North Vietnam in order to prevent what Washington believes is an attempt by Hanoi to build a hydrogen bomb. Fury then recruits the old members of his World War II commando unit from their civilian lives. Johnson insists that the mission must be performed by civilians, because "we cannot afford to risk escalation of the war by having our troops invade North Vietnam" ("Vietnam: The Valor and the Victory").

The reunited "Howling Commandos," now middle-aged but apparently still capable of taking on the Vietnamese, parachute into Haiphong in order to sabotage the suspected nuclear weapons plant. Outside the factory, two North Vietnamese sentries are having a conversation; one asks the other if he thinks that the Americans might invade the North. The soldier laughs and replies: "But of course not.... I hear that many of them would rather invade Washington!" While the comic book implied that the American war effort might be threatened by domestic dissent, it was certainly not in danger of being defeated militarily by the enemy. The North Vietnamese soldiers in the story are hopelessly inept. An entire North Vietnamese battalion is unable to prevent the escape of any one of the seven Americans who successfully complete their mission ("Vietnam: The Valor and the Victory"). Indeed, the Vietnamese enemy is remarkably similar to the bungling Germans who were the prototypical antagonists in the regular *Sgt. Fury* series. While the idea of American civilians conducting covert missions in Vietnam was revived with popular success in the 1980s with movies like *Rambo* and *Missing in Action*, the comic book audience was not ready for it in 1967. Marvel, highly conscious of its sales figures and reader response, was not impressed enough with the reaction to the story to publish a similar comic book. Sergeant Fury returned permanently to the more familiar and more marketable Second World War.

The failure of Vietnam War comic books to command the interest and support of readers was similar to the trouble that the Johnson administration had rallying popular support for its Vietnam policy. The Vietnam conflict was a grim struggle for unclear objectives against an enemy that was not well defined. The American Green Beret was marketed in comics as the ideal heroic figure in an otherwise inglorious war. Readers, however, identified more with the superpowered comic book heroes who at times seemed more believable than their counterparts in the war comic books. While Vietnam War comic books represented only a very marginal portion of the industry's output during the 1960s, the war itself had a tremendous impact on American society that was, in turn, reflected in the more popular and prolific superhero comic books.

Marvel comic books are the most useful for the purpose of this chapter, because they differed from those of DC and other publishers in some key respects. Marvel was the first to publish code-approved comic books that appealed to an audience that was more sophisticated than the code presumed. Feedback from this older readership, which included an avid following among college students, was an important factor determining the content of the comic books. Unlike the DC superheroes who remained entrenched within the realm of fantasy for much of the 1960s, the Marvel superheroes were placed in identifiable contemporary settings like New York City, the New Mexican desert, or even Vietnam. Marvel was also the first publisher to give any of its superhero comic books a political focus during the Vietnam War period. An analysis of these Marvel comic books and the reader response to them will illustrate the degree to which they reflected the contemporary American political and social mood between 1963 and 1975.

Stan Lee wrote in 1975 that "Marvel Comics has never been very much into politics. . . . We have no official party line—I issue no editorial edicts as to what the political tone of our stories should be" (Lee, *Son of Origins of Marvel Comics*, 45). Marvel comic books of the early 1960s, however, frequently had a political focus that followed the line of the Johnson administration. The early superhero plots, which were written almost exclusively by Lee, regularly featured the hero as the defender of American interests against evil Communist forces.

The Hulk in his first appearance prevents a spy named Igor from stealing the formula for America's secret "Gamma-ray bomb" ("The Coming of the Hulk"). In subsequent issues the Hulk battles both Soviet troops that seek to capture him ("The Gladiator from Outer Space") and Red Chinese forces under "General Fang" that try to overrun a peaceful Himalayan nation ("The Hordes of General Fang"). Comic book historians have pointed out that these stories were inappropriate for this comic book because "the [Hulk] was cast as an antihero with no concern for human society [but] Lee insisted upon pitting him against evil communists" (Jacob and Jones, 54). Thor was another Marvel superhero who was made to endure a series of implausible adventures laden with the clichés of cold war propaganda. In one issue, the Norse God of Thunder helps the inhabitants of a fictional Latin American nation over-throw a ruthless Communist dictator. ("The Mighty Thor vs the Exe-cutioner"). Later he thwarts a Soviet plot to capture some top American scientists ("Prisoner of the Reds"). In another story, Thor even defends an Indian outpost against an attack by the Red Chinese ("The Mysterious Radioactive Man").

On one occasion, in 1965, Thor's adventures took him to the jungles of Vietnam. After being knocked unconscious by a Vietcong mortar shell, the Thunder God wakes up to find himself in the hut of a Vietnamese family. The villagers think that Thor is a "messenger of Buddha" who was been sent in answer to their prayers to "destroy the guerrillas" who have been terrorizing them. Looking about the village, Thor observes that "there is little food.... The Red guerrillas have brought famine to the land." He sees some American helicopters on patrol but notes that "they are so few, and the communist foe is so many ... and so cunning" ("Into the Blaze of Battle").

The villain in the story is a ruthless Vietcong commander whose troops routinely round up hostages from captured Vietnamese villages. Among those captured is the family that had aided Thor. It is revealed that the Vietcong officer is actually the family's eldest son, who had abandoned them years earlier in order to join the Communist cause. The younger brother, who remains loyal to the Saigon regime, accuses the elder of betraying his family by "serving the Red terrorists." The Communist shoots and kills his brother in a fit of rage, shouting: "You do not matter! Nobody matters! Only the communist cause is important! People mean nothing! Human lives mean nothing!" Thor eventually rescues the family and defeats the Vietcong. The commander, overcome with grief as a result of his own actions, comes to his senses, renounces Communism, and commits suicide. His last words are: "It was communism that made me what I am ... that shaped me into a brutal, unthinking instrument of destruction.... may it vanish from the face of the earth and the mem-ory of mankind!"

At the end of the story Thor vows, "I shall return, and when I do, the hammer of Thor shall be heard in every village ... in every home ... in every heart throughout this tortured land!" Despite his dramatic pledge, however, the Thunder God never did return to Vietnam. It is possible that even at this early stage of the conflict, comic book readers understood that the situation was far more complex than this cliché-ridden plot suggested. Perhaps the 1960s readership was too sophisti-cated to accept the kind of simplistic scenarios that had been popular in the comic books of World War II. In any case, the Thor comic book with its trappings of Norse mythology was a highly inappropriate vehicle for conveying political messages.

Another Marvel superhero was much better suited for this. Stan Lee created "Iron Man" in 1973 and gave the character and the series a political focus that it would retain, in one way or another, throughout the Vietnam War years. A brief analysis of the "Iron Man" series during this period will illustrate how the political tone of the comic book changed according to the evolving political and social mood of America.

The origin of Iron Man was set in South Vietnam. Anthony Stark is introduced as a millionaire industrialist and scientist who invents and manufactures weapons for the U.S. government. He travels to South Vietnam in order to demonstrate his latest invention to some high-ranking American military advisors. While accompanying a group of ARVN soldiers into the jungle to observe his weapons in action, Stark accidentally sets off a Vietcong land mine, which leaves him critically wounded. When he awakens, Stark discovers that he has been captured by Vietcong forces led by a ruthless tyrant named Wong Chu. The Communists know that a piece of shrapnel lodged near Stark's heart gives him only days to live, but they convince him to construct a weapon for them in return for an operation that will save his life. Stark agrees to build a weapon, but he secretly plans not to turn it over to the Communists, but to use it for himself. The "weapon" that Stark constructs is actually a suit of armor that keeps his heart beating and gives him augmented strength, among other powers. Taking the name "Iron Man," Stark escapes, defeats the Vietcong, kills Wong Chu, and destroys the Communist base. Like other Marvel superheroes, however, Iron Man pays a price for his new powers—he must forever wear the metal chest plate under his clothes in order to keep his heart beating ("Iron Man Is Born").

The elements in this story set the tone for future Iron Man comic books. The Communist villain Wong Chu is the epitome of evil: ugly, rotund, and smoking cigarettes, he has no concern whatsoever for human life. The Red guerrilla cares nothing about the Vietnamese people. Even the advancement of Communism is important only as a means to achieving personal power. Tony Stark, meanwhile, is the very symbol of America, a noble hero helping the South Vietnamese with his superior wealth and technology. Marvel's portrayal of the Vietnam conflict is not only childishly simplistic, but ethnocentric as well. The war is not so much a Vietnamese phenomenon as it is a battleground in the greater global struggle between the democratic West and the Communist East. Vietnam is a domino that America must not allow to fall.

Tony Stark devoted both of his lives to keeping the United States ahead in the cold war. As Stark the industrialist and inventor, he builds new weapons like his "atomic naval cannon" for the Defense Department. In his Iron Man identity, he battles "America's enemies from within and without" ("The Stronghold of Dr. Strange"). His efforts as both Stark and Iron Man were appreciated by the government officials with whom he often worked. In one story, Iron Man is thanked by an FBI agent for thwarting a "commie spy ring." Later, a general at the Pentagon compliments Stark on his latest invention: "The Reds would probably give up half of Asia if they could steal the plans of what you've invented so far" ("Trapped by the Red Barbarian"). No other superhero was so closely associated with the U.S. government.

Iron Man fought a series of Communist villains in battles symbolic of the struggle between the West and the East. Among these adversaries were the Red Barbarian—a Soviet general who works directly for Comrade K ("Trapped"); the Crimson Dynamo—Iron Man's armor-clad Soviet counterpart ("Iron Man Faces the Crimson Dynamo"); the Black Widow—a Soviet spy and seductress ("The Crimson Dynamo Strikes Again"); and the Titanium Man—another armored Soviet supersoldier ("If I Must Die, Let It Be with Honor"). Even Nikita Khrushchev made an occasional appearance; he once worked out a plan to sabotage Stark industries so that "the U.S. would lag behind . . . in the arms race" ("Iron Man Faces"). In each of these stories, Iron Man triumphs on behalf of the U.S. government. Even when things went badly, the armored hero maintained his patriotic zeal. Once, when he was captured, he defiantly exclaimed: "If this is to be my finish, I'll show how an American faces death! I'll show that nothing can shatter the faith of a man who fights for freedom!" ("The Mandarin's Revenge").

From time to time Iron Man would return to the war-torn country where his heroic career was born. In a 1967 story he thwarts a plot by the Titanium Man and a Red Chinese villain called Half-Face to score a Communist propaganda victory by destroying a peaceful Vietnamese village at night and making it appear that American bombers were responsible for the carnage. Iron Man saves the village, preserves America's good international reputation, and takes the opportunity to smash some Vietcong in the process ("The Golden Gladiator and the Giant").

For the most part, though, Iron Man left the fighting in Vietnam to the American military, while he engaged Communist enemies in a more symbolic show of support for U.S. policy. When the Titanium Man issued a public challenge to Iron Man, Stark felt compelled to accept, because it was a "matter of national pride and prestige" ("If I Must Die"). He defeats his much larger Soviet foe and exclaims: "You thought you'd just have to flex your muscles and show your strength, and your enemies would fall by the wayside! . . . You made the worst mistake any Red can make . . . you challenged a foe who isn't afraid of you!" ("What Price Victory?"). Iron Man's stand underscored the need to preserve American prestige by containing the Communist menace however and wherever it threatens American interests.

Two things happened in 1968 that forever changed the political tone
of the *Iron Man* series. One was the Tet Offensive. The other was the
expansion of the Marvel Comics publishing operation. The magnitude
of the National Liberation Front offensive stunned the American people
and called into serious question the administration's entire Vietnam policy, which had been so doggedly defended by Iron Man. Disillusioned
Americans, especially among the young generation, felt that they had
been misled and misinformed by the government. It would have been
commercially unwise to present the same government line in a comic
book. At the same time, Marvel's financial success allowed the publisher
to expand and hire new writers and artists. *Iron Man* was one of the
titles that was handed over to these new young comic book writers, who
tended to be politically liberal. (Lee, *Son of Origins*, 45). The content of
Iron Man comic books was thereafter affected by change in both the
Marvel staff and the mood of comic book readers.

After 1968 all cold war themes were abandoned in the *Iron Man* series.
Even when Soviet foes like the Crimson Dynamo returned, they acted
more like other apolitical supervillains than the Communist stereotypes
that they had once been ("From the Conflict . . . Death"). Iron Man himself spent less time working the U.S. government and turned his attention
inward toward such domestic issues as race relations and pollution control ("This Doomed Land, This Doomed Sea"). The new writers played
upon the Tony Stark/Iron Man character as a well-meaning but misdi-
rected defender of the establishment. He is pitted against a new enemy
called the Firebrand, who claims to have been "an all-American boy who
started out to make this nation a better place . . . sat in for civil rights,
marched for peace, and demonstrated on campus, and got spat on by
bigots, [and] beat on by 'patriots' ". Firebrand whips up riots and hysteria
among young demonstrators because he has concluded that America
"doesn't want to be changed. The only way to build anything decent is
to tear down what's here and start over" ("The Fury of the Firebrand").

Although Firebrand was portrayed as a dangerous villain, his message
elicited some reader empathy. One letter pointed out that "while Firebrand was marching, trying to bring about a more peaceful world, Stark
Industries was probably building weapons for Vietnam where we 'destroyed a city in order to save it' " (Letters page, *Iron Man*, no. 31).
Before 1968, most of the printed response to the series did not comment
on the hero's politics, although an occasional letter praised his patriotism:
"Not since George M. Cohen has anyone so waved their country's flag—
and it wouldn't hurt if there were more of this sort of thing" (Letters
page, *Tales of Suspense*, no. 59). By the early 1970s, however, *Iron Man*'s
readers became increasingly concerned with the character's political
stance. One wrote that "Tony Stark is going to have to do some pretty
big restructuring of his life to avoid being classified as an enemy of the

people" (Letters page, *Iron Man*, no. 33). Another insisted that "the time is right for Tony Stark to quit being a weapons manufacturer" (Letters page, *Iron Man*, no. 35). Although some conservative readers did not object to Iron Man's role as a defender of authority, most of the printed mail demanded a change.

Anthony Stark was, according to one reader, "a profiteering, capitalistic, war-mongering defense contractor.... [who] produces devices to kill people" (Letters page, *Iron Man*, no. 38). Recognizing that the political mood of their readership had shifted, *Iron Man*'s writers tried to improve the hero's image. In one issue, Iron Man argues with a right-wing U.S. senator who claims that "there's a new breed of people in this country today.... who want to destroy the government that made America great." Iron Man counters that the American people, not the government, makes the country great. The senator then calls him an anarchist ("When Demons Wail"). This was change, indeed, from the superhero who once claimed that "no one has the right to defy the wishes of his government" ("The Return of the Titanium Man").

Iron Man's political about-face is confirmed after a student demonstration outside of Stark Industries turns into a riot, and the crowd is fired on by Stark's own security force. The demonstrators cry out, "It's another Kent State!" and stone Iron Man when he arrives on the scene. He criticizes the students for "preaching peace while resorting to violence," but one of them justifies their action as "the only way we can make your generation hear us" ("Menace at Large"). These events leave the hero deeply disturbed. He later reevaluates his image as a defender of government policy and a weapons manufacturer: "I designed... weapons that can be used to kill one people... to save another.... I find myself pondering every action I ever made" ("Why Must There Be an Iron Man?"). Finally, Stark resolves to end his corporation's association with weapons research and development and to diversify into areas such as pollution control and consumer goods ("Deathplay").

A powerful story entitled "Long Time Gone" serves as a fitting epilogue for the political metamorphosis of Iron Man. Published in 1975 simultaneously with the fall of Saigon, the story opens with Tony Stark sitting alone in his office, pondering his own experiences in Vietnam. Looking into a mirror, he questions himself and searches his soul for the answers: "As Iron Man you beat the commies for democracy without ever questioning just whose democracy you were serving... or just what those you served intended to do with the world once you'd saved it for them. Vietnam raised all those questions.... like: what right had we to be there in the first place?"

Stark relives through a flashback sequence a time when, as Iron Man, he observed the horrors of the Vietnam War firsthand. He sees confused and weary American troops fight and die. He sees a high-tech artillery piece of his own design lay waste to a village, killing enemy and innocent alike. He comes across a blind Vietnamese boy who has been orphaned by the day's fighting. Moved to tears by the death and carnage that have resulted in part from his own action, Iron Man buries the dead in a mass grave and marks it with the epitaph "WHY?" Returning to the present, Tony Stark dons his Iron Man armor, strikes a dramatic pose, and pledges "to avenge those whose lives have been lost through the ignorance of men like the man I once was . . . or I will die trying!" ("Long Time Gone"). The end of the Vietnam War brings with it Iron Man's final repudiation of the government actions that he had once so zealously defended.

It would seem that a comic book featuring a star-spangled hero named Captain America should have been an appropriate series for a political focus. In 1964, Marvel revived this World War II comic book hero, who was a living symbol of patriotism and the American ideal. Stan Lee, though, seemed unsure of what to do with the Captain America character. Captain America confronts apolitical villains in New York for a few issues. Then he travels to Vietnam—not to fight alongside American troops as he did in the Second World War, but to rescue a friend who has been captured by the Vietcong. While American objectives in the war remained ambiguous, a rescue mission presented the hero with a clear and attainable goal. While he's there, of course, he battles some Communists, who are portrayed much like the other evil Red caricatures of early Marvel Comic books. Beyond this, however, there is no mention of the need to defend South Vietnam from the Communist threat, a message that was overstated in the *Iron Man* comic book ("The Strength of the Sumo").

After his brief adventure in Vietnam, Captain America is sent back to World War II, where he once again battles Hitler's hordes for nine issues, before returning to contemporary times. In an effort to find the proper tone and setting for Captain America, Stan Lee had unintentionally portrayed the patriotic hero as an appropriate symbol of a confused America that preferred to relive past glories, rather than recognize and adapt to the new world situation.

Captain America, more than any other comic book, generated a political controversy among its readers. As early as 1965, a letter from an American serviceman suggested that "the war in Vietnam would make an endless amount of adventures for . . . Cap." Lee responded, though, that other readers wanted Captain America to stay out of Vietnam (Letters page, *Tales of Suspense*, no. 71). After 1968 the difference in opinion over the hero's role became more pronounced. Some readers argued that Cap should stop being a defender of the Establishment. One letter asserted, "It would fit the standards of today . . . if [Captain America was] more liberal" (Letters page, *Captain America*, no. 110). Another, more sophisticated response pointed out that Cap "is a very strange mixture of individualism and statism, in that when he lectures on freedom, he seems to be talking about the nation rather the people who make it up" (Letters page, *Captain America*, no. 113).

Marvel also printed letters from those who continued to urge Captain America to go to Vietnam. One of these stressed that "Captain America should be devoted to uniting our nation against foes who are killing our soldiers in Vietnam. Regardless if . . . our foreign policy is right or wrong, we should stand behind the men who are dying to preserve our liberty." Stan Lee maintained, however, that informal polls taken by Marvel over the years indicated that the great majority of readers wanted Cap to stay out of the fighting in Vietnam (Letters page, *Captain America*, no. 116).

Stan Lee wrote most of the *Captain America* comic books until 1972. By then the tone of the character had changed in a way similar to that of Iron Man's. Lee wrote in 1971 that Captain America "simply doesn't lend himself to the John Wayne-type character he once was. . . . We just cannot see any of our characters taking on a role of super-patriotism in the world as it is today" (Letters page, *Captain America*, no. 142). Consequently, Captain America went through a period of soul-searching and self-doubt about his role in the Vietnam era:

Throughout the world, the image of Captain America has become a symbol . . . a living embodiment of all that democracy stands for. But now . . . there are those who scorn love of our flag . . . love of country . . . those to whom patriotism is just a square, out-moded word. Those who think of me . . . as a useless relic . . . of a meaningless past. . . . This is the day of the antihero . . . the age of the rebel and the dissenter. It isn't hip to defend the establishment . . . only to tear it down. And in a world rife with injustice, greed, and endless war . . . who's to say the rebels are wrong? . . . I've spent a lifetime defending the flag . . . and the law. Perhaps . . . I should have battled less . . . and questioned more. ("The Sting of the Scorpion")

Stan Lee maintained that because Americans could not agree on a common enemy in Vietnam and because the administration's objectives were unclear, "Captain America would not be serving America by taking sides. For the sake of unity, Cap [remained] on the home front" (Letters page, *Captain America*, no. 128). Therefore, when Captain America does go to Vietnam in one story, he avoids conflict with either side and tries only to facilitate the peace negotiations ("Captured in Vietnam"). Captain America, instead, turned his attention toward America's domestic concerns. Together with his black, superhero sidekick the Falcon, who leads a civilian life as a social worker in Harlem, Captain America tackled such problems as inner-city crime, poverty, and social dislocation. The Captain America of the 1970s symbolized a nation, weary of confusing and painful overseas adventures, that had turned inward to confront serious domestic ills, brought on, in part, by a decade of war.

Captain America's disassociation from the U.S. government was completed after the revelations of the Watergate scandal. The hero discovers that an organization called CRAP—the Committee to Regain America's Principles—led by a man named Quentin Harderman, is actually a front for the "Secret Empire," a fascist organization that seeks to overthrow the U.S. government. Tracking down the mysterious leader of the Secret Empire leads Captain America to the White House and the Oval Office. Although the face of the villain is obscured in shadow, the reader is left with little doubt as to the true identity of the man who sought to overthrow the U.S. Constitution ("Before the Dawn"). Captain America is so stunned and disillusioned that he temporarily changes his name to "Nomad—the man without a country." He later readopts the name Captain America, however, and pledges to help restore legitimacy to the perennial American ideals of freedom and democracy that have been corrupted by a self-serving government ("Nomad, No More").

The radical shift in the political tone and character of *Iron Man* and *Captain America* was a result of changes in popular American values and changes in the comic book industry itself. After 1968 it became fashionable among the younger generation to oppose the Establishment, which had brought America the Vietnam War. The culture of dissent, which was reflected in popular music and film, was also mirrored in comic books. Cognizant of the views held by the majority of their readers, Stan Lee and the new generation of comic book creators abandoned the cold war clichés of early Marvel stories. Evil communist caricatures were replaced by villainous right-wing authority figures. Before this could happen, however, Marvel had to confront an authority figure of its own—the Comics Code Authority.

By the beginning of the 1970s it had become clear that the comic book audience had outgrown the naive presumptions of the code. The code's insistence that "in every instance good shall triumph over evil" and that "policemen, judges, government officials and respected institutions shall never be presented in such a way as to create disrespect for established authority" (*Code*) could not be taken seriously by a generation that had watched the Chicago police riot of 1968, read about the Pentagon Papers, and followed a war that defied such simplistic concepts as "good" and "evil."

Adapting to growing reader sophistication led Marvel to brush against certain code restrictions. A character called Tribune, who appeared in the *Daredevil* comic book, was typical of the new right-wing comic book villains. The Tribune is a self-styled judge, jury, and executioner who "convicts" and sentences to death antiwar demonstrators, draft dodgers, and anyone else whom he judges to be a "commie pinko" ("The Tribune"). In the *Spider-Man* comic book, a character named Sam Bullitt is introduced as a retired police officer who runs for New York City district attorney. His platform is one of "law and order" that promises to stamp out "left-wing anarchists who are trying to destroy this great proud nation of ours." It is revealed that Bullitt is not only a crypto-fascist, but also a crook with ties to organized crime ("To Smash the Spider"). Although these story lines were not technically in violation of the code, because the Tribune is not really a judge and Bullitt is not an acting policeman or an elected official, they clearly presented the authority figure as an antagonistic element and thus ran contrary to the spirit of the code.

In 1971 Stan Lee wrote several issues of *The Amazing Spider-Man* that dealt with the problem of drug abuse ("And Now the Goblin"). The code implicitly forbade any mention of drugs in comic books, and the stories were rejected by the Code Authority. Lee published the comic books without the authority's seal of approval, and they sold well in spite of it. Marvel's successful defiance compelled the Code Authority to revise its outdated standards. Among the provisions that were dropped was one that forbade the unfavorable portrayal of authority figures (*New York Times*, 1971, 37). Comic book writers at both Marvel and DC, which together accounted for about two-thirds of all comic books sold at that time, took advantage of the liberalized guidelines to produce stories that were more reflective of the concerns of American society ("Comic Realities").

The Comics Code Authority was established in 1954, when it was unpopular and unwise to criticize traditional American values and institutions. By 1971 the cold war consensus had broken down, and it had become popular to question authority and to challenge the Establishment. The young generation's disillusionment and alienation during the Vietnam War years gave rise to the culture of dissent, which was reflected in the superhero comic books of Marvel and, by this time, of DC as well. The contemporary media took notice of the comic book industry's trend toward relevance but pointed out that its new social awareness was self-conscious and self-serving as well. Slumping sales by the end of the 1960s led the major publishers to do market surveys of their collegiate readership ("Comic Realities"). Whatever their motivations, the comic book creators' attempts to reflect contemporary values and concerns forced a revision of the code, which ultimately broadened the potential of comic books as a medium and an art form.

Comic books since the end of the Vietnam War have tended to deal with the conflict in a manner similar to that of other popular entertainment media (Olson and Roberts, 269–74). The Vietnam veteran in comic books has generally been portrayed as a figure who is left alienated from society by his Vietnam experience. The first veteran to return from the war was Flash Thompson, a supporting character in the *Spider-Man* comic book. Flash, a friend of Peter Parker (Spider-Man), is an all-

American-boy—a high school football star, voted most likely to succeed, popular with his classmates and with women in particular. He forsakes a college football scholarship to serve his country in the Vietnam War ("In the Hands of the Hunter"). When he returns, Flash is a very different character. He has trouble adjusting to civilian life. He keeps to himself and snaps at his friends when they offer to help him. Later, it is revealed that Flash is deeply disturbed by his participation in a war that had victimized the peaceful Vietnamese people ("Vengeance from Vietnam"). Flash never really could readjust to American society after the war. By 1986 he had bounced "from one dead-end job to the next," suffered a failed relationship with a Vietnamese American woman, and felt betrayed by his friends who had stayed at home during the war and enjoyed more happiness and success than himself. ("The Choice and the Challenge").

While Flash Thompson's war experience left him embittered and depressed, another comic book veteran has suffered an even deeper alienation. Frank Castle was a captain in the U.S. Marine Corps who served in Vietnam for five years. Soon after the end of the war, his wife and children are murdered by the mob after they accidentally witness a gangland killing. The traumatized marine hunts down and kills the murderers himself, and thereafter, armed with a Vietnam-era M–16, assorted pistols, knives, and grenades and calling himself "the Punisher," he wages a one-man war against crime. The Punisher's ruthless and sometimes psychotic vigilantism frequently brought him into conflict with superheroes as well as criminals during the 1970s, when he was first introduced. In the 1980s the Punisher was revised slightly into a more heroic and sympathetic figure, and he had become one of Marvel's most popular characters. Mirroring popular films like *Rambo* and *Missing in Action*, the Punisher acts outside of the law, because his experience in Vietnam has taught him that the government cannot or will not get the job done. The streets of New York become a war zone, criminals are the elusive enemy, and the Punisher is the soldier who is forever fighting his own personal war against crime ("The Punisher").

This chapter has attempted to explore the comic book industry's response to the Vietnam War and American society. Although much analysis has been devoted to relevant comic books, it must be emphasized that the industry as a whole, like much of America, had trouble coming to grips with the war. Compared with World War II and Korea, the Vietnam War itself elicited a marginal response from the publishers. Few Vietnam War comic books were published, and none succeeded commercially. To avoid alienating any segment of their politically divided readership, Marvel and DC rarely mentioned the Vietnam War in their contemporary comic books. The impact that the war had on American society, however, was reflected in the content of these comic books and was ultimately recognized by the revised Comics Code Authority. The national consensus that had united America during World War II and cold war dissolved during the Vietnam War. The diversity of views on the war was mirrored in the comic books, ranging from the propaganda of *Jungle War Stories* to the antiwar and anti-Establishment Marvel comic books of the early 1970s. Considering the preponderance of the Vietnam War in the American media overall, though, the comic book industry's treatment of the conflict was quite restrained. In the final analysis, comic books, indeed, reflected America's subconscious wishes: some endorsed the war, and others criticized it, but many simply offered readers an escape from the tragedy of Vietnam.

BIBLIOGRAPHY

"And Now the Goblin." *The Amazing Spider-Man*, no. 95 (April 1971), Marvel Comics Group.

Batman from the Thirties to the Seventies. New York: Crown, 1971.

"Before the Dawn," *Captain America*, no. 175 (July 1974), Marvel Comics Group.

Benton, Mike. *The Comic Book in America*. Dallas: Taylor, 1989.

"The Big Blow-Up." *Jungle War Stories*, no. 11 (April-June 1965), Dell.

"Big Surprise." *Guerrilla War*, no. 12 (July-September 1965), Dell.

"Captured in Vietnam," *Captain America*, no. 125 (May 1970), Marvel Comics Group.

"The Choice and the Challenge." *The Amazing Spider-Man*, no. 275 (April 1986), Marvel Comics Group.

Code of the Comics Magazine Association of America. General Standards, Part A, 1954.

"Comic Realities." *Newsweek* (November 23, 1970): 98.

"The Coming of the Hulk." *The Incredible Hulk*, no. 1 (May 1972), Marvel Comics Group.

"The Crimson Dynamo Strikes Again." *Tales of Suspense*, no. 52 (April 1964), Marvel Comics Group.

"Day of Reckoning." *Jungle War Stories*, no. 2 (January-March 1963), Dell.

"Deadly Masquerade." *Jungle War Stories*, no. 7 (April-June 1964), Dell.

"Deathplay." *Iron Man*, no. 50 (September 1972), Marvel Comics Group.

"The Enemy Has Many Faces." *Jungle War Stories*, no. 9 (October-December 1964), Dell.

"The Enemy in Vietnam." *Jungle War Stories*, no. 2 (January-March 1963), Dell.

Esquire (September 1965): 97.

"Face of the Enemy." *Jungle War Stories*, no. 11 (April-June 1965), Dell.

"The Fantastic Four." *The Fantastic Four*, no. 1 (November 1961), Marvel Comics Group.

"From the Conflict . . . Death." *Iron Man*, no. 22 (February 1970), Marvel Comics Group.

"Frontal Assault." *Guerrilla War*, no. 12 (July-September 1965), Dell.

"The Fury of the Firebrand." *Iron Man*, no. 25 (May 1970), Marvel Comics Group.

"The Gladiator from Outer Space." *The Incredible Hulk*, no. 4 (November 1962), Marvel Comics Group.

"The Golden Gladiator and the Giant." *Tales of Suspense*, no. 93 (September 1967), Marvel Comics Group.

Goldwater, John L. *Americana in Four Colors*. New York: Comics Magazine Association of America, 1964.

"The Hordes of General Fang." *The Incredible Hulk*, no. 5 (January 1963), Marvel Comics Group.

"If I Must Die, Let It Be with Honor." *Tales of Suspense*, no. 69 (September 1965), Marvel Comics Group.

"The Incredible Hulk." *The Incredible Hulk*, no. 1 (May 1962), Marvel Comics Group.

"In the Hands of the Hunter." *The Amazing Spider-Man*, no. 48 (May 1967), Marvel Comics Group.

"Into the Blaze of Battle." *Journey into Mystery*, no. 117 (June 1965), Marvel Comics Group.

"Iron Man Faces the Crimson Dynamo." *Tales of Suspense*, no. 46 (October 1963), Marvel Comics Group.

"Iron Man Is Born." *Tales of Suspense*, no. 39 (March 1963), Marvel Comics Group.

Jacobs, Will, and Gerard Jones. *The Comic Book Heroes*. New York: Crown, 1985.

Jungle War Stories, no. 10 (January-March 1965), Dell.

Lee, Stan. *Origins of Marvel Comics*. New York: Simon and Schuster, 1974.

Lee, Stan. *Son of Origins of Marvel Comics*. New York: Simon and Schuster, 1975.

"A Letter from Vietnam." *Jungle War Stories*, no. 11 (April-June 1965), Dell.

Letters page. *Captain America*, no. 110 (February 1969), Marvel Comics Group.

Letters page. *Captain America*, no. 113 (May 1969), Marvel Comics Group.

Letters page. *Captain America*, no. 116 (August 1969), Marvel Comics Group.

Letters page. *Captain America*, no. 128 (August 1970), Marvel Comics Group.

Letters page. *Captain America*, no. 142 (October 1971), Marvel Comics Group.

Letters page. *Iron Man*, no. 31 (November 1970), Marvel Comics Group.

Letters page. *Iron Man*, no. 33 (January 1971), Marvel Comics Group.

Letters page. *Iron Man*, no. 35 (March 1971), Marvel Comics Group.

Letters page. *Iron Man*, no. 38 (June 1971), Marvel Comics Group.

Letters page. *Our Fighting Forces*, no. 102 (August 1966), National Periodical.

Letters page. *Our Fighting Forces*, no. 106 (April 1967), National Periodical.

Letters page. *Tales of Suspense*, no. 59 (November 1964), Marvel Comics Group.

Letters page. *Tales of Suspense*, no. 71 (November 1965), Marvel Comics Group.

"Long Time Gone." *Iron Man*, no. 78 (September 1975), Marvel Comics Group.

"The Mandarin's Revenge." *Tales of Suspense*, no. 54 (June 1964), Marvel Comics Group.

"Menace at Large." *Iron Man*, no. 46 (May 1972), Marvel Comics Group.

"The Mighty Thor vs the Executioner." *Journey into Mystery*, no. 84 (September 1962), Marvel Comics Group.

Moore, Robin, and Joe Kubert. *Tales of the Green Beret, vol. 1*. El Cajon, Calif.: Blackthorne, 1985.

"My Enemy—My Brother." *Tales of the Green Beret*, no. 2 (June 1967), Dell.

"The Mysterious Radioactive Man." *Journey into Mystery*, no. 93 (June 1963), Marvel Comics Group.

The *New York Times*, September 27, 1954, 29.

The *New York Times*, September 23, 1962, Section 3, 12.

The *New York Times*, February 4, 1971, 37.

"Nomad, No More," *Captain America*, no. 183 (March 1975), Marvel Comics Group.

"Okay You Passed the 2-S Test; Now You're Smart Enough for Comic Books." *Esquire* (September 1966): 115.

Olson, James, and Randy Roberts. *Where the Domino Fell*. New York: St. Martin's Press, 1991.

"Pinch the Devil." *Jungle War Stories*, no. 8 (April-June 1965), Dell.

"Pop Goes the War." *Newsweek* (September 12, 1966): 66.

"Prisoner of the Reds." *Journey into Mystery*, no. 87 (December 1962), Marvel Comics Group.

"The Punisher." *Handbook of the Marvel Universe*, no. 10 (September 1986), Marvel Comics Group.

"Requiem for a Red." *Jungle War Stories*, no. 1 (July-September 1962), Dell.

"The Return of the Titanium Man." *Iron Man*, no. 81 (September 1966), Marvel Comics Group.

"Spider-Man." *Amazing Fantasy*, no. 15 (August 1962), Marvel Comics Group.

"The Sting of the Scorpion." *Captain America*, no. 122 (February 1970), Marvel Comics Group.

"The Strength of the Sumo." *Tales of Suspense*, no. 61 (January 1965), Marvel Comics Group.

"The Stronghold of Dr. Strange." *Tales of Suspense*, no. 41 (May 1963), Marvel Comics Group.

Super Green Beret, no. 1 (April 1967), Milson.

Superman from the Thirties to the Seventies. New York: Crown, 1971.

"Surprise Party." *Jungle War Stories*, no. 8 (July-September 1964), Dell.

Tales of the Green Beret, no. 1 (January 1967), Dell.

"This Doomed Land, This Doomed Sea." *Iron Man*, no. 23 (March 1970), Marvel Comics Group.

"To Smash the Spider." *The Amazing Spider-Man*, no. 91 (December 1970), Marvel Comics Group.

"Trapped by the Red Barbarian." *Tales of Suspense*, no. 42 (June 1963), Marvel Comics Group.

"The Tribune." *Daredevil*, no. 70 (November 1970), Marvel Comics Group.

U.S. Senate Committee on the Judiciary. *Hearings Before the Subcommittee to Investigate Juvenile Delinquency, 83d Congress, 2nd Session*. Washington, D.C.: U.S. Government Printing Office, 1955.

"Vengeance from Vietnam." *The Amazing Spider-Man*, no. 108 (May 1972), Marvel Comics Group.

"Viet Cong: The Face of the Enemy." *Jungle War Stories*, no. 4 (July-September 1963), Dell.

"Vietnam Battle Facts." *Jungle War Stories*, no. 2 (January-March 1963), Dell.

"Vietnam: The Valor and the Victory." *Sgt. Fury King-Size Special*, no. 3 (August 1967), Marvel Comics Group.

"A Walk in the Sun." *Jungle War Stories*, no. 2 (January-March 1963), Dell.

"What Price Victory?" *Tales of Suspense*, no. 71 (November 1965), Marvel Comics Group.

"When Demons Wail." *Iron Man*, no. 42 (October 1971), Marvel Comics Group.

"Why Must There Be an Iron Man?" *Iron Man*, no. 47 (June 1972), Marvel Comics Group.

Witek, Joseph. *Comic Books as History*. Jackson: University Press of Mississippi, 1989.

"The Year of the Cat." *Jungle War Stories*, no. 4 (July-September 1963), Dell.

PART VII

Aftermath of the War

21   The Indochinese Refugees

Ever since the seventeenth century, America has been viewed by much of the rest of the world as the land of opportunity where oppressed and poverty-stricken people can start a new life. During the 1600s and 1700s, most immigrants to the United States were Protestants coming from the British Isles and Germany. That migration broadened somewhat to include the French, Scandinavians, and Chinese in the first half of the nineteenth century, and during the late 1800s and early 1900s, the immigrants came increasingly from Southern and Eastern Europe. After World War II, the immigrants came primarily from the Western Hemisphere and from Asia. The migration of the Indochinese—Vietnamese, Cambodians, and Laotians—in the 1970s, 1980s, and 1990s was part of that most recent migration.

One of the most dramatic outcomes of the Vietnam War was the series of demographic changes that occurred throughout Indochina. Social scientists around the world have long realized that immigration does not begin in a vacuum; long before people begin moving across continents, they begin moving within their own countries because of major social and economic changes occurring around them. The great migration of people from Indochina to the United States in the late 1970s and 1980s fits that demographic pattern. During the 1950s and 1960s, the American presence in Indochina stimulated monumental demographic changes. In 1954, nearly 1 million Roman Catholics from North Vietnam relocated to South Vietnam under protocols established by the Geneva Accords. As more and more American money poured into South Vietnam beginning in the early 1960s, and especially after 1964, the country's economy changed. South Vietnamese gravitated toward Saigon, looking for jobs spawned by the American war machine. Between 1960 and 1970, the population of Saigon increased from just over 1 million people to nearly 4 million people. Most of them were peasants who had lived their lives in rural villages. The sheer destructiveness of the war, by blowing up thousands of villages throughout South Vietnam, also set in motion a vast migration within South Vietnam, as did U.S. policies to resettle peasants into militarily secure areas.

Similar demographic changes came to Laos and Cambodia. The American invasion of Cambodia in 1970 drove large numbers of Vietcong and North Vietnamese soldiers deeper into Cambodia, and it had the same effect on Cambodian peasants. The population of Phnom Penh grew dramatically in the 1960s and 1970s; peasants headed for the city, where they thought they might be free of military action at the hands of American soldiers and bombers and various factions of Cambodian guerrillas. In Laos, the Central Intelligence Agency recruited an army among the Hmong tribe to fight the Vietcong and North Vietnamese along the Ho Chi Minh Trail. The combined American-South Vietnamese invasion of Laos in 1971 also destabilized hundreds of communities throughout the country. For a look at these events in Cambodia and Laos, see William Shawcross's *Sideshow: Kissinger, Nixon, and the Destruction of Cambodia* (1979) and John Prados, *President's Secret Wars: CIA and Pentagon Covert Operations Since World War II* (1986).

The story of the Indochinese migration to the United States is still incomplete, although historians now identify three basic stages of the immigration process. The best general survey is Paul Rutledge's *The Vietnamese Experience in America* (1992). Until the early 1960s, there was only a handful of Vietnamese, Cambodians, and Laotians in the United States. Most of them were students enrolled in scientific and engineering programs at American universities. Those numbers increased along with the American escalation of the war in the 1960s, but even then the number of permanent Indochinese immigrants living in the United States numbered only a few thousand people. Many of them were the wives of American soldiers who had completed a tour of duty in South Vietnam. By 1975 a total of only 20,038 Indochinese immigrants had settled in the United States during the previous decade. The vast majority of them were Vietnamese. The Immigration and Naturalization Service did not even keep track of the number of Laotians and Cambodians because there were so few of them.

The second wave of Indochinese immigrants began in 1975 when North Vietnam completed its conquest of South Vietnam, the Khmer Rouge overran Phnom Penh, and the Pathet Lao assumed power in Laos. Indochina had fallen to the Communists, and those Indochinese who came to the United States consisted of the people most closely associated, politically and economically, with the anti-Communist regimes of Nguyen Van Thieu in South Vietnam, Lon Nol in Cambodia, and Souvanna Phouma in Laos. Le-Thi-Que, A. Terry Rambo, and Gary

D. Murfin make that clear in their article "Why They Fled: Refugee Movement During the Spring 1976 Communist Offensive in South Vietnam" (1976), as does Gail P. Kelly in *From Vietnam to America: A Chronicle of the Vietnamese Immigration to the United States* (1977). The initial wave of Indochinese immigrants after the Communist takeover totaled approximately 170,000 people, of whom 155,000 were Vietnamese, 7,500 were Cambodians, and 7,500 were Laotians. The vast majority of them were former employees of the United States or the previous regimes in power. More than 40 percent of the Vietnamese were Roman Catholics who had been born in North Vietnam, migrated south in 1954, and then worked for South Vietnam during the intervening twenty years. Most of the Laotian immigrants were Hmong tribesmen who had cooperated with the CIA in attacking the North Vietnamese during the war. By the end of 1975, the United States had received 130,000 Indochinese refugees at receiving centers in Guam and the Philippines, while another 60,000 were waiting in refugee camps in Hong Kong and Thailand.

As John H. Leba, Ba Kong Le, and Anthony T. Leba *(The Vietnamese Entrepreneurs in the U.S.A.: The First Decade*, 1985) and Darrel Montero *(Vietnamese Americans: Patterns of Settlement and Socioeconomic Adaptation in the United States*, 1977) point out in their studies, this second wave of Vietnamese immigrants tended to be well educated and blessed with good job and professional skills. Back in South Vietnam they had been large-landowners, physicians, dentists, attorneys, civil servants, small-businessmen, and employees of large U.S. corporations doing business in South Vietnam, and when they settled in the United States they brought their educations and entrepreneurial skills with them. Many of them were Roman Catholics and already spoke English or at least understood English. They were accustomed to the economic and social rhythms of modern industrial society, and they had enjoyed substantial contact with Americans during the previous ten years. Their culture shock upon arrival, though considerable, was less than what subsequent waves of Vietnamese immigrants would undergo.

Life in those initial refugee camps and reception centers is described in William T. Liu and Alice K. Murata's *Vietnamese Refugees in America* (1978). The refugees centers in 1975 left much to be desired, but they were infinitely better than the camps the later waves of Indochinese immigrants would encounter. They received bed linens, clothing, toiletries, cots, and tents to live in, and they were given basic medical care, food, and occupational evaluations before being sent on to the United States. Schools were established for Vietnamese children and English as a Second Language programs were implemented for all of the refugees. The U.S. government took a systematic approach to the settlement of the Indochinese refugees, making sure that they were not concentrated in any single geographic location. Thousands of small and large communities throughout the United States were asked to sponsor immigrant families, and the government often employed the services of local charitable organizations and churches in settling the immigrants into apartments, jobs, and schools. Darrel Montero's *Vietnamese Americans: Patterns of Settlement and Socioeconomic Adaptation in the United States* (1977) looks at how those first large numbers of Indochinese immigrants adjusted to the United States.

The third wave of Indochinese immigrants began arriving in the United States in the late 1970s and throughout the 1980s. They were political and economic refugees from the brutal and ineffective policies imposed by the Communist regimes after 1975 in Vietnam, Laos, and Cambodia. North Vietnam reunited the country under the name Socialist Republic of Vietnam, and political authorities in Hanoi implemented sweeping collectivization schemes all over the economy of the former South Vietnam. As Joel Charney and John Spragens, Jr., point out in *Obstacles to Recovery in Vietnam and Kampuchea* (1984), the economies of Vietnam and Cambodia (Kampuchea) went into tailspins. The gross national product fell dramatically, as did labor productivity. Income levels fell precipitously as capital and the countries' most talented people fled. William J. Duiker's *Vietnam Since the Fall of Saigon* (1980) describes the economic chaos in southern Vietnam, as does Nguyen Long's *After Saigon Fell: Daily Life Under the Vietnamese Communists* (1981), Nguyen Tien Hung's *Economic Development of Socialist Vietnam, 1955–1980* (1977), Nguyen Van Canh's *Vietnam Under Communism: 1975–1982* (1983), and Robert E. Long's *Vietnam Ten Years After* (1985). For a look at the Cambodian economy, see François Ponchaud's *Cambodia: Year Zero* (1977). In addition to the Communists' policies, the economies of Indochina were suffering from rapid drop in American spending, which had fueled income and employment for the previous decade. Large numbers of Vietnamese and Cambodians suddenly found themselves living in cities but out of work.

The Communist takeover also led to a variety of ethnic discriminations throughout Indochina. In Laos, the Hmong and Mien tribesmen who had cooperated with the Americans found themselves the objects of discrimination. In Cambodia, the Vietnamese and Cham Muslims became the objects of scorn by the ruling Khmer majority. The ethnic Chinese in Saigon, as well as the ethnic Khmers in the Mekong Delta, were targeted for discrimination by the Vietnamese government. Also, the rural mountain peoples of Laos and Vietnam, particularly those who were living in the cities, were treated as second-class citizens by the more urbane groups in Cambodia and Vietnam. Because of the ethnic discrimination, there were strong pockets of discontented people anxious to leave their respective countries.

In addition to severe economic and social problems imposed by Communist economic dictates and the end of U.S. military spending there, the people of Indochina were also suffering from severe political problems. The government of the Socialist Republic of Vietnam began relocating large numbers of southern Vietnamese out of Saigon back out into the countryside, and many former employees of the United States and South Vietnam who had not been able to escape in 1975 found themselves subject to political "reeducation." Ginetta Sagan and Stephen Downey, in *Violations of Human Rights in the Socialist Republic of Vietnam, April 30, 1975–April 30, 1983* (1983), describe that reeducation process. Politically suspect individuals were forced out into reeducation camps in rural areas where they engaged in hard manual labor, received political indoctrination, and participated in mortification programs where they confessed their sins. Once political authorities decided they were "rehabilitated," they were reassigned to new jobs, usually where their skills could be employed effectively. International human rights authorities protested the entire business, but to little avail.

But the violation of civil rights in Vietnam was nothing compared with the genocidal rage that swept through Cambodia in the late 1970s. Pol Pot and the Khmer Rouge came to power and launched a liquidation campaign aimed at eliminating everyone who had ever held political power in Cambodia, who had worked as a professional or intellectual, who had owned a small business, or who had worked for a foreign entity—in short, everyone except peasants. Declaring "Year Zero," Pol Pot and the Khmer Rouge virtually depopulated the cities and major towns of Cambodia and went on a killing rampage. Some scholars and American intelligence experts estimate that between 1975 and 1979, when Vietnam invaded Cambodia in order to stop the slaughter, the Khmer Rouge assassinated more than 1 million people, including the elite and middle class of the entire country. The best works describing the holocaust in Cambodia are William Shawcross's *The Quality of Mercy: Cambodia, Holocaust, and Modern Conscience* (1984), Martin Stuart-Fox's *The Murderous Revolution: Death in Pol Pot's Kampuchea* (1986), and Ben Kiernan's *Cambodia: The Eastern Zone Massacres* (1986).

These economic, social, and political disasters in the late 1970s and 1980s produced the third wave of Indochinese immigration to the United States. They tended to be less educated than the original wave of immigrants, and they were more ethnically diverse, often consisting of Vietnamese, Cambodians, Cham, Hmong, Mien, Chinese, and a variety of other tribal people from the highlands. Comparatively few of them were Roman Catholics. They were desperate to escape the political oppression and economic blight of Indochina. Many of them also had family members who had already escaped to the United States with the earlier immigrants. They came out of Vietnam, Cambodia, and Laos illegally, either crossing overland through the mountains and jungles into Thailand, where they ended up in refugee camps, or escaping by sea in boats.

The so-called boat people are described in Nathan Caplan, John K. Whitmore, and Marcella Choy, *The Boat People and Achievement in America: A Study of Family Life, Hard Work, and Cultural Values* (1989); Bruce Grant, *The Boat People* (1979); and John C. Knudsen, *Boat People in Transition* (1985). By far most of the Indochinese getting away after 1976 left by sea in small boats, hoping to make it to Indonesia, Thailand, Malaysia, or the Philippines. Demographers now estimate that as many as 1.3 million people fled Indochina by boat, earning the title "boat people." Their voyages were beset with danger. Pirates in the South China Sea regularly victimized them, and Indonesia and Malaysia and, later, Hong Kong frequently rejected them even when they did make landfall. Barry Wain's *The Refused: The Agony of the Indochinese Refugees* (1981) looks at the plight of those Indochinese who were refused and had to be repatriated to Vietnam, Laos, and Cambodia. Most historians suspect that only half of those who left Indochina in boats survived the journey. For a look at the pirates who plagued and exploited the refugees, see Nhat Tien, Duong Phuc, and Vu Thanh Thuy, *Pirates on the Gulf of Siam* (1981). Although most of the refugees ended up in the United States, a small number of them had different destinations, as made clear in Rewi Alley, *Refugees from Viet Nam in China* (1980), John K. Knudsen, *Vietnamese Survivors: Processes Involved in Refugee Coping and Adaptation* (1988), and Nancy Viviani, *The Long Journey: Vietnamese Migration and Settlement in Australia* (1984).

There are a number of moving, highly informative, first-person accounts of the Indochinese migration. The best of them is James M. Freeman, *Hearts of Sorrow: Vietnamese American Lives* (1989), which takes an anthropological approach to what is essentially oral history. Also see Muriel Stanek, *We Came from Vietnam* (1985). Several individual autobiographies portray the danger of the escape from Indochina as well as the pain of adjusting to a new life in the United States. For especially poignant works, see Huynh Quang Nhuong, *The Land I Lost* (1982) and Nguyen Ngoc Ngan and E. E. Richey, *The Will of Heaven: A Story of One Vietnamese and the End of His World* (1982). The autobiographical portrayals of the holocaust in Cambodia during the late 1970s are even more dramatic. Sydney H. Schanberg's *The Death and Life of Dith Pran* (1980) is a moving account of Dith Pran, a Cambodian photographer working for the *New York Times* who was captured by, but eventually escaped from, the Khmer Rouge. The book became the basis of the Academy Award-winning film *The Killing Fields* in 1984. Haing Ngor, *Haing Ngor: A Cambodian Odyssey* (1987) and Molyda Szymusiak, *The Stones Cry Out: A Cambodian Childhood, 1975–80* (1986), provide highly personal views of the Cambodian tragedy.

At first the United States welcomed the new immigrants. Congress passed the Indochinese Migration and Refugee Assistance Act of 1975, renewed in 1977, which provided unprecedented economic assistance to the immigrants. Most Americans, even those who opposed the war, felt a certain responsibility toward its victims. The government paid for their airfare to the United States, extended loans for those who wanted to start businesses of their own, and provided scholarship assistance for Vietnamese children wishing to attend college. The federal government also provided funds to local school districts to assist them in teaching the Vietnamese immigrants.

But that assistance was not permanent, as Gil Loescher and John A. Scanlon make clear in *Calculated Kindness: Refugees and America's Half-Open Door, 1945–Present* (1986). The third-wave immigrants who came to the United States in the late 1970s and 1980s were not as well educated or as well-off as the first immigrants. They came from rural backgrounds and did not adjust as well to economic life in America. Because they came in such large numbers, they raised nativist concerns in the United States. The country was full of American veterans who did not like the Vietnamese anyway, and economic problems in the United States created fears that the immigrants would take jobs from natives and lower prevailing wage levels. Another problem involved the definition of a refugee. The term *refugee* in U.S. immigration refers to an individual who is fleeing his or her homeland to escape political repression and persecution. The United States does not recognize poverty or economic suffering, at least in terms of conferring refugee status, and the Immigration and Naturalization Service began denying entry to many Vietnamese in the 1980s on the grounds that they were not true political refugees.

A number of excellent works by historians and sociologists have focused on the process of settlement and adaptation among Indochinese immigrants. For some of the immigrants, especially uneducated, rural peasants and mountain people from the Central Highlands of South Vietnam and Laos, the adjustment was particularly difficult. The classic work on the people of the Central Highlands is Gerald C. Hickey's *Free in the Forest: Ethnohistory of the Vietnamese Central Highlands, 1954–1976* (1982). Bruce T. Downey and Douglas P. Olney, in *The Hmong in the West: Observations and Reports* (1982), describe the Hmong communities in places like Sacramento and Oakland, California. Because the Hmong were essentially a premodern people practicing an animistic religion before the Vietnam War, their arrival in California in the late 1970s was an especially wrenching experience. The experience of many Cambodian refugees living in San Diego, California, was quite similar. Many of the mountain people went into clinical depressions after their arrival in the United States, and an astonishingly large number of them died of a type of sudden death syndrome. Books like Tom Choken Owan's *Southeast Asian Mental Health: Treatment, Prevention, Services, Training, and Research* (1985) were designed to acquaint mental health professionals with the problem.

A number of studies have looked at particular Vietnamese communities in the United States. Interested readers should look at Jacqueline Desbarats and Linda Holland's article "Indochinese Settlement Patterns in Orange County" (1983); Elizabeth A. Hagerty's *Vietnamese in Southern California* (1986); Darrel Montero, *Vietnamese Americans: Patterns of Settlement and Socioeconomic Adaptation in the United States* (1977); and Charles C. Muzny, *The Vietnamese in Oklahoma City: A Study of Ethnic Change* (1989). By far the best works to date on the settlement and adjustment of the Vietnamese are Paul James Rutledge's *The Vietnamese Experience in America* (1992) and Nathan Caplan, John K. Whitmore, and Marcella Choy, *The Boat People and Achievement in America: A Study of Family Life, Hard Work, and Cultural Values* (1989).

Like other immigrants who came before them, the Indochinese have created a vibrant community life in the United States. During the 1980s, most of them gravitated to urban centers, especially in the West and Southwest, where the presence of tens of thousands of other Indochinese gave them a sense of community and security. They formed Buddhist churches or groups within Roman Catholic parishes, and they established a variety of community groups, such as the Cambodian Association of San Diego, California, and the Association for the Positive Promotion of Lao Ethics. Vietnamese newspapers like *Dat Lanh* and *Thong Bao* and *Chan Troi Moi* appeared. Rutledge argues in *The Vietnamese Experience in America* that the Vietnamese are unique among Asian immigrants—not nearly as clannish as the Chinese, but not as assimilationist-oriented as the Japanese.

The Boat People and Achievement in America is a highly analytical, quantitative study of 1,300 Vietnamese and Laotian households. Caplan, Whitmore, and Choy found that the unemployment rate was extremely high among the immigrants, with more than 60 percent of the families living below the poverty level and 75 percent receiving public assistance of some kind. When improvement in that status occurs over time, it is usually attributable to the entry of additional household members into the work force. Those Indochinese with the most years in the United States, the smallest families, and the best English skills enjoyed increasingly higher living standards over time. In most cases, Laotian immigrants were more likely than the Vietnamese to fare poorly. They also found, however, that Vietnamese immigrant children were relatively successful in school, particularly in mathematics and science—more successful than native American students.

In 1992, only seventeen years had passed since the end of the Vietnam

War and the beginning of the large-scale Indochinese migration to the United States. A total of more than 1 million people from Indochina had settled here. Like other immigrant groups, they stirred up resentment as well as admiration among native Americans, and they had also established ethnic institutions needed to maintain their personal identity and begin the assimilation process in the United States. At the present time there are tens of thousands of Vietnamese languishing in refugee camps in Thailand, Malaysia, Indonesia, and Hong Kong waiting for the chance to come to the United States, and hundreds of thousands more in Vietnam hoping for the same opportunity.

BIBLIOGRAPHY

Alley, Rewi. *Refugees from Viet Nam in China.* New York: New World Press, 1980.

Archdeacon, Thomas J. *Becoming American: An Ethnic History.* New York: Free Press, 1983.

Baer, Florence S. "Give Me ... Your Huddled Masses: Anti-Vietnamese Refugee Lore and the 'Image of Limited Good.' " *Western Folklore* 41 (1982): 275–91.

Bosquet, Gisele. "Living in a State of Limbo: A Case Study of Vietnamese Refugees in Hong Kong Camps." In *People in Upheaval*, ed. Scott M. Morgan and Elizabeth Morgan. New York: Center for Migration Studies, 1987.

Butler, David. *The Fall of Saigon.* New York: Simon and Schuster, 1985.

Caplan, Nathan, John K. Whitmore, and Marcella Choy. *The Boat People and Achievement in America: A Study of Family Life, Hard Work, and Cultural Values.* Ann Arbor: University of Michigan Press, 1989.

Charney, Joel, and John Spragens, Jr. *Obstacles to Recovery in Vietnam and Kampuchea.* New York: Oxfam America, 1984.

Desbarats, Jacqueline, and Linda Holland. "Indochinese Settlement Patterns in Orange County." *Amerasia Journal* 10 (1983): 23–46.

Doan Van Toai and David Chanoff. *The Vietnamese Gulag.* New York: Simon and Schuster, 1986.

Downey, Bruce T., and Douglas P. Olney, eds. *The Hmong in the West: Observations and Reports.* Minneapolis: University of Minnesota Center for Urban and Regional Affairs, 1982.

Duiker, William J. *Vietnam Since the Fall of Saigon.* New York: Center for International Studies, 1980.

Finan, Christine. "A Community Affair: Occupational Assimilation of Vietnamese Refugees." *Journal of Refugee Resettlement* 1 (1980): 1–21.

Freeman, James M. "Vietnamese War Widow." *San Jose Studies* 14 (Spring 1988): 59–70.

Freeman, James M. *Hearts of Sorrow: Vietnamese American Lives.* Stanford, Calif.: Stanford University Press, 1989.

Freeman, James M., Huu Nguyen, and Peggy Haretsell. "The Tribal Lao Training Project." *Cultural Survival Quarterly* 9 (1985): 10–12.

Gough, Kathleen. *Ten Times More Beautiful: The Rebuilding of Vietnam.* New York: Monthly Review Press, 1978.

Grant, Bruce. *The Boat People.* New York: Penguin, 1979.

Hagerty, Elizabeth A. *Vietnamese in Southern California.* New York: AMS Press, 1986.

Haing Ngor. *Haing Ngor: A Cambodian Odyssey.* New York: Macmillan, 1987.

Henkin, Alan B., and Liem Thanh Nguyen. *Between Two Cultures: The Vietnamese in America.* San Francisco: R and E, 1981.

Hickey, Gerald C. *Free in the Forest: Ethnohistory of the Vietnamese Central Highlands, 1954–1976.* New Haven, Conn.: Yale University Press, 1982.

Huynh Quang Nhuong. *The Land I Lost.* New York: Harper and Row, 1982.

"Indochinese Refugees." *Editorial Research Report* 2 (1977): 639–60.

Kelly, Gail P. *From Vietnam to America: A Chronicle of the Vietnamese Immigration to the United States.* Boulder, Colo.: Westview Press, 1977.

Kelly, Gail P. "Schooling, Gender and the Reshaping of Occupational and Social Expectations: The Case of Vietnamese Immigrants in the United States." *International Journal of Women's Studies* 1 (1978): 323–35.

Kiernan, Ben. *Cambodia: The Eastern Zone Massacres.* New York: Columbia University, Center for the Study of Human Rights, 1986.

Kiernan, Ben. "Conflict in the Kampuchean Communist Movement." *Journal of Contemporary Asia* 10 (1980): 7–74.

Kiernan, Ben. "Origins of Khmer Communism." *Southeast Asian Affairs* 6 (1981): 161–80.

Kiernan, Ben. *How Pol Pot Came to Power.* London: Verso, 1984.

Kiernan, Ben. "Kampuchea's Ethnic Chinese Under Pol Pot: A Case of Systematic Social Discrimination." *Journal of Contemporary Asia* 16 (1986): 18–29.

Kiernan, Ben. "Orphans of Genocide: The Cham Muslims of Kampuchea Under Pol Pot." *Bulletin of Concerned Asian Scholars* 20 (1988): 2–23.

Kiernan, Ben, and Chandthou Boua, eds. *Peasants and Politics in Kampuchea, 1942–1981.* London: Zed Press, 1982.

Kinzie, J. David, et al. "An Indochinese Refugee Psychiatric Clinic: Culturally Accepted Treatment Approaches." *American Journal of Pyschiatry* 137 (1980): 1429–32.

Kirayama, Kasumi K. "Evaluating Effects of the Employment of Vietnamese Refugee Wives on Their Family Roles and Mental Health." *California Sociologist* 5 (1982): 96–110.

Knudsen, John C. *Boat People in Transition.* New York: Barber Press, 1985.

Knudsen, John K. "Health Problems in the Refugee Career: Refugees from Vietnam via Transit Camps to Norway." In *Health and International Life-Courses,* ed. K. T. Ask. Bergen, Norway: Bergen University Press, 1986.

Knudsen, John K. *Vietnamese Survivors: Processes Involved in Refugee Coping and Adaptation.* Bergen, Norway: Bergen University, 1988.

Leba, John H., Le, Ba Kong, and Anthony T. Leba. *The Vietnamese Entrepreneurs in the U.S.A.: The First Decade.* New York: Zieleks, 1985.

Le-Thi-Que, A. Terry Rambo, and Gary D. Murfin. "Why They Fled: Refugee Movement During the Spring 1976 Communist Offensive in South Vietnam." *Asian Survey* 16 (September 1976): 855–63.

Liu, William T., and Alice K. Murata. *Vietnamese Refugees in America.* Nashville, Tenn.: Charter House, 1979.

Loescher, Gil, and John A. Scanlon. *Calculated Kindness: Refugees and America's Half-Open Door, 1945–Present*. New York: Free Press, 1986.

Long, Robert E., ed. *Vietnam Ten Years After*. New York: Wilson, 1985.

Marx, Rani. "The In Mien." *Migration Today* 9 (1981): 22–26.

Matthews, Ellen. *Culture Clash*. Chicago: International Press, 1982.

Montero, Darrel. *Vietnamese Americans: Patterns of Settlement and Socioeconomic Adaptation in the United States*. Boulder, Colo.: Westview Press, 1977.

Montero, Darrel, and Ismael Dieppa. "Resettling Vietnamese Refugees: The Service Agency's Role." *Social Work* 27 (1982): 74–81.

Muzny, Charles C. *The Vietnamese in Oklahoma City: A Study of Ethnic Change*. New York: AMS Press, 1989.

Nguyen Long. *After Saigon Fell: Daily Life Under the Vietnamese Communists*. Berkeley: University of California Press, 1981.

Nguyen Manh Hung. "Vietnamese." In *Refugees in the United States: A Reference Handbook*, ed. David W. Haines. Westport, Conn.: Greenwood Press, 1985.

Nguyen Ngoc Ngan, and E. E. Richey. *The Will of Heaven: A Story of One Vietnamese and the End of His World*. New York: Dutton, 1982.

Nguyen Tien Hung. *Economic Development of Socialist Vietnam, 1955–80*. New York: Praeger, 1977.

Nguyen Van Canh. *Vietnam Under Communism: 1975–1982*. Stanford, Calif.: Hoover Institution Press, 1983.

Nhat Tien, Duong Phuc, and Vu Thanh Thuy. *Pirates on the Gulf of Siam*. San Diego, Calif.: Boat People S.O.S. Committee, 1981.

O'Ballance, Edgar. *The Wars in Vietnam, 1954–1980*. New York: Hippocrene Books, 1981.

Olson, James S. *The Ethnic Dimension in American History*. New York: St. Martin's Press, 1979.

Owan, Tom Choken, ed. *Southeast Asian Mental Health: Treatment, Prevention, Services, Training, and Research*. Washington, D.C.: U.S. Government Printing Office, 1985.

Pickwell, Sheila M. "Nursing Experiences with Indochinese Refugee Families." *Journal of School Health* 53 (1983): 86–91.

Ponchaud, François. *Cambodia: Year Zero*. New York: Holt, Rinehart, and Winston, 1977.

Prados, John. *President's Secret Wars: CIA and Pentagon Covert Operations Since World War II*. New York: Morrow, 1986.

Redick, Liang Tien, and Beverly Wood. "Cross-Cultural Problems for Southeast Asian Refugee Minors." *Child Welfare* 61 (1982): 365–73.

Rutledge, Paul. *The Role of Religion in Ethnic Self-Identity: A Vietnamese Community*. Lanham, Md.: University Press of America, 1985.

Rutledge, Paul. *The Vietnamese in America*. New York: Lerner, 1987.

Rutledge, Paul. *The Vietnamese Experience in America*. Bloomington: Indiana University Press, 1992.

Sagan, Ginetta, and Stephen Downey. *Violations of Human Rights in the Socialist Republic of Vietnam, April 30, 1975–April 30, 1983*. Atherton, Calif.: Atherton Foundation, 1983.

Salzburg, Joseph S. *Vietnam: Beyond the War*. New York: Sovereign Books, 1975.

Schanberg, Sydney H. *The Death and Life of Dith Pran*. New York: Penguin, 1980.

Schultz, Sandra. "How Southeast Asian Refugees in California Adapt to Unfamiliar Health Care Practices." *Health and Social Work* 7 (1983): 148–56.

Shawcross, William. *Sideshow: Kissinger, Nixon, and the Destruction of Cambodia.* New York: Simon and Schuster, 1979.

Shawcross, William. *The Quality of Mercy: Cambodia, Holocaust, and Modern Conscience.* New York: Simon and Schuster, 1984.

Silverman, Edwin B. "Indochina Legacy: The Refugee Act of 1980." *Publius* 10 (1980): 29–41.

Skinner, Kenneth A. "Vietnamese in America: Diversity in Adaptation." *California Sociologist* 3 (1980): 103–24.

Stanek, Muriel. *We Came from Vietnam.* New York: Whitman, 1985.

Starr, Paul D., and Alden E. Roberts. "Attitudes Toward Indochinese Refugees: An Empirical Study." *Journal of Refugee Resettlement* 1 (1981): 51–66.

Starr, Paul D., and Alden E. Roberts. "Attitudes Toward New Americans: Perceptions of Indo-Chinese in Nine Cities." *Research in Race and Ethnic Relations* 3 (1982a): 165–86.

Starr, Paul D., and Alden E. Roberts. "Community Structure and Vietnamese Refugee Adaptation: The Significance of Context." *International Migration Review* 16 (1982b): 595–618.

Stein, Barry N. "Occupational Adjustment of Refugees: The Vietnamese in the United States." *International Migration Review* 13 (1970): 25–45.

Stern, Lewis M. "Response to Vietnamese Refugees: Surveys of Public Opinion." *Social Work* 26 (1981): 306–11.

Stuart-Fox, Martin, ed. *Contemporary Laos: Studies in the Politics and Society of the Lao People's Republic.* New York: St. Martin's Press, 1982.

Stuart-Fox, Martin. *The Murderous Revolution: Death in Pol Pot's Kampuchea.* Chippendale, N.S.W., Australia: Alternative, 1986.

Szymusiak, Molyda. *The Stones Cry Out: A Cambodian Childhood, 1975–80.* New York: Hill and Wang, 1986.

Takaki, Ronald. *Strangers from a Different Shore: A History of Asian Americans.* Boston: Little, Brown, 1989.

Tobin, Joseph Jay, and Joan Friedman. "Spirits, Shamans, and Nightmare Death: Survivor Stress in a Hmong Refugee." *American Journal of Orthopsychiatry* 53 (1983): 439–49.

Vats, Bhagat. *The Kampuchea Holocaust and Its Aftermath.* Helsinki, Finland: World Peace Council, 1981.

Viviani, Nancy. *The Long Journey: Vietnamese Migration and Settlement in Australia.* Melbourne, Australia: Melbourne University Press, 1984.

Wain, Barry. *The Refused: The Agony of the Indochinese Refugees.* New York: Simon and Schuster, 1981.

Westmeyer, Joseph, et al. "Migration and Mental Health Among Hmong Refugees: Association of Pre- and Postmigration Factors with Self-Rating Scales." *Journal of Nervous and Mental Disease* 171 (1982): 92–96.

Zasloff, Joseph, and Leonard Unger. *Laos: Beyond the Revolution.* New York: St. Martin's Press, 1991.

22 Prisoners of War, Missing in Action

Frances Arlene Leonard

As a result of the stipulations of the Paris Peace Accords of 1972, a total of 587 American prisoners-of-war—564 military personnel and 23 civilians—were released by the North Vietnamese and Vietcong in February and March of 1973. Several other people had already escaped after being POWs for a period of time. There were also more than 2,500 others who were classified as MIAs—Missing in Action. Most of the American prisoners-of-war were Air Force or Navy pilots shot down by North Vietnamese antiaircraft fire during bombing raids over North Vietnam and South Vietnam. Most of them spent their time in captivity in North Vietnamese prisons, although a few ended up in Vietcong or Laotion camps. Many former POWs wrote books about their ordeal, and most of the books had similar themes, dealing with their capture, interrogation, torture, boredom, resistance, release, homecoming, and adjustment.

A central issue for the POWs, and for the military in general, was the relevancy of the Code of Conduct. The Code of Conduct for Members of the Armed Forces of the United States was developed by the Pentagon and enacted following the Korean War. Forty-three percent of men captured had collaborated with the enemy in some way. Code of Conduct posters were printed and hung outside the company commander's offices in boot camps. Nathan Hale, the Revolutionary War hero who said he regretted having only one life to give for his country, was the symbol chosen to illustrate the poster. Until 1977 it read as follows:

1. I am an American fighting man. I serve in forces which guard my country and our way of life. I am prepared to give my life in their defense.
2. I will never surrender of my own free will. If in command I will never surrender my men while they still have the means to resist.

3. If I am captured I will continue to resist by all means available. I will make every effort to escape and aid others to escape. I will accept neither parole nor special favors from the enemy.

4. If I become a prisoner of war, I will keep faith with my fellow prisoners. I will give no information or take part in any action which might be harmful to my comrades. If I am senior, I will take command. If not, I will obey the lawful orders of those appointed over me and will back them up in every way.

5. When questioned, should I become a prisoner, I am bound to give only name, rank, service number, and date of birth. I will evade answering further questions to the utmost of my ability. I will make no oral or written statements disloyal to my country and its allies or harmful to their cause.

6. I will never forget that I am an American fighting man, responsible for my actions, and dedicated to the principles which made my country free. I will trust in my God and in the United States of America. (Hackworth and Sherman, p. 360)

President Jimmy Carter approved one change in the code. In paragraph five, the word *bound* was changed to *required*. This allowed POWs who were being tortured and brutalized to give more than name, rank, service number, and birth date without losing their honor. But the message was still clear that POWs were to resist their captors and withstand as much torture as they could before submitting to enemy demands.

Colonel David H. Hackworth and Julie Sherman, in Hackworth's autobiography *About Face*, say he was surprised to find that many mornings at reveille, the troops had to recite the Code of Conduct. To him, it "was a silly and degrading exercise. If the soldiers who had fought in Korea had been well trained and well led, there would not have been so many POWs to begin with." Perhaps so, but for many American POWs in Vietnam, it was the terra firma from which they based their daily activities. However, most POWs realized that it was not physically possible to refrain from giving their captors information. Their only other option was death by torture or beatings.

The single major underlying issue for American prisoners of war during the Vietnam conflict was to return home with honor. POWs occupied themselves with how to handle interrogations by the North Vietnamese, with how to escape, and with establishing and maintaining communications with other prisoners. The following quote is from *P.O.W.: A Definitive History of the American Prisoner-of-War Experience in Vietnam, 1964–1973* by John G. Hubbell. Major Larry Guarino, an air force pilot captured in June 1965 and imprisoned in Hanoi, reveals the major objective of the North Vietnamese captors. During an interrogation by a North Vietnamese Army senior officer the POWs called "Dog," he told Guarino:

You must understand that your position here is and will always be that of a criminal. You are not now or ever going to be treated in accordance with the Geneva agreements, because this is an undeclared war. You have criminally attacked our people, and it has been decided that you are always to be treated as a criminal. You must cooperate and show repentance for your crimes to earn good treatment. Sooner or later, you are going to show repentance. You are going to admit you are a criminal. You are going to denounce your government. You are going to beg our people for forgiveness. (P. 54)

The POWs were treated as war criminals until late 1969. Solitary confinements for extended periods, some exceeding a year or more, were not unusual. Medical attention was withheld, and the food was considered vile at best. For a prisoner to receive "good treatment," he had to cooperate with the North Vietnamese in their quest to gain propaganda yardage. Noncompliance with their demands meant beatings and torture. Meanwhile, the North Vietnamese claimed "lenient and humane treatment" as their policy. Although North Vietnam signed the 1949 Geneva Convention regarding treatment of prisoners of war, there was an ambiguity: those who committed "crimes against humanity" were not protected. The North Vietnamese considered air bombings as genocide, and therefore pilots were "war criminals" as well as useful propaganda tools and as hostages in negotiations with the United States. Their treatment was cruel and harsh. Senior POWs, particularly those who refused to cooperate in any way with the interrogators, were routinely tortured to get information or to force them to cooperate by making antiwar statements. Not until April 1967 would national attention be given to the conditions of POWs. Photographs taken at a press conference of Commander Richard Stratton mechanically bowing like a robot and with a void look in his eyes were printed in *Life* magazine. Some consciousness was finally raised of the treatment that American POWs might be receiving. But the Vietnamese resisted pressure from the United States for another two years before conditions would improve for POWs.

In the foreword of *A Code to Keep* by Ernest C. Brace, Senator John McCain opens with a quote from *Man's Search for Meaning* by Victor Frankel. He writes that under conditions of captivity, "everything can be taken from a man but one thing: the last of human freedoms—to choose one's attitude in any given set of circumstances, to choose one's own way." McCain acknowledges that Ernest Brace certainly chose his own way. Brace was an ex-marine pilot who flew secret supply missions to Laos as part of a CIA operation during the Vietnam War. He was captured May 21, 1965, at a small airstrip in Laos, marched to Dien Bien Phu, and locked in a bamboo cage for over three years before being transported to Hanoi. His bamboo cage was three feet wide, four feet tall, and seven feet long. He attempted three escapes. Although a civilian and not bound by the Military Code of Conduct for Prisoners of War, Brace was determined to give as little accurate information as he could to his captors and to attempt to escape whenever possible.

Brace was a civilian captured in Laos, a country that forbade foreign troops under an international agreement that North Vietnam had signed. He did not appear on any POW lists released by the Communists to the outside world. Terry Burke, a coordinator assigned to the CIA secret army in Laos, escaped during the attack on the airstrip only minutes before Brace's plane landed and he was taken prisoner. Burke searched for Brace for several weeks. The information he received on Brace's locations was accurate but always too late. His assignment up, Burke was sent back to the United States. The State Department informed Brace's family that he had been captured by enemy military forces and that it would try to establish contact with his captors in order to negotiate his release. It would be four years before they had any further news of him.

Brace was seldom allowed to bathe and never allowed to exercise during his first year of captivity. His two trips a day to the latrine were the only opportunities he had to stand upright. Brace endured rats, snakes, malaria-carrying mosquitoes, scorpions, large red ants, and other insects that paid nightly visits to his cage or lived with him. He was bitten repeatedly on his bare feet and ankles by the large rats that came out at night in search of food. On more than one occasion he was sprayed with urine from a rat. "I had to lie in disgust, unable to wipe my face" (Brace, 96). Snakes were attracted to the cage by the increasing rat population.

The beating he received after his first escape attempt did not discourage him from trying again. Eleven months after his capture he found the opportunity he had been waiting for, only to be recaptured five days later, starving and exhausted. His cage was wrapped with barbed wire, and a piece of structural steel formed into a U was pinned snugly around his neck and secured to his bed board. Before being put back in his cage, he was held against the barbed wire surrounding it and beaten again. A couple of weeks later he was moved to a new place of confinement. Four months later he attempted another escape.

The morning after being recaptured, he was placed standing in a hole in the ground and buried up to his lower jaw. On the third day a bowl of rice soup was poured into his mouth, the only meal he would receive during his seven-day ordeal. When he was removed from the hole, Brace had lost all motor functions, including his ability to stand. It was weeks before he regained any bodily functions. His legs remained paralyzed.

Brace made bamboo picks to untie his hand and neck ropes so he could sleep more comfortably until a guard discovered the loose ropes and he was beaten again. This time a severe kick to his head caused another loss of the few motor skills he had regained. By November, he had no control of his bowels and kidneys. He sat or lay in his filth until March, when he took his first bath in six months and his cage was cleaned. He spoke for the first time in over a year. Early in October he was taken to Hoa Lo Prison, referred to as the Hanoi Hilton by American POWs. He was questioned briefly, then taken to Plantation Gardens, also referred to as the Country Club, one of four camps in Hanoi.

The first American voice he had heard in three and a half years belonged to John McCain, a resident of the Plantation for one year. McCain explained the tap code they used for communication. "Shave and a haircut" was tapped as the signal to come to the wall, and "two bits" was the "go ahead" reply. The alphabet was divided into a five-by-five grid. The letter *K* was omitted to make it come out even. The letter *A* was tap, pause, tap. *B* was tap, pause, tap, tap. *F* was the first letter of the second line, tap, tap, pause, tap, and so on. Communication was important. Contact with other prisoners was necessary to reinforce the Code of Conduct and maintain a chain of command.

Lieutenant Colonel Ted Guy was the Senior Ranking Officer (SRO) at the Plantation. Lieutenant Commander Richard Stratton was also a resident. Stratton's story is told in *Prisoner at War: The Survival of Commander Richard A. Stratton* by Scott Blakey. Peter Heinegen, in his review of *Prisoner at War*, states

Blakey first made a television documentary about Stratton called "2,551 Days" and now he's expanded his material into a book. He writes, for the most part, an acceptable brand of journalese in the staccato, masculine manner of Jimmy Breslin.... he's got a good story and he doesn't let it get away from him.... Blakey turns what might have been just another wartime saga into a pointed moral tale.... Today's reader will find it a vivid and unsteeling reminder of our all-too-recent past. (Blakey, 248)

Survivors by Zalin Grant contains the stories of nine American pilots and soldiers who were held prisoners for five years. All nine were captured between January and March 1968. Ted Guy assumed command of the Plantation in July 1968. The previous SRO, Harvey Stockman, beaten by the North Vietnamese in an attempt to extract a confession from him, was isolated in a section of the camp that cut him off from any communication with other prisoners. The Plantation had originally been the home of the Vietnamese mayor during French occupation. Guy said it was thought that the North Vietnamese wanted a showplace, a camp where foreign dignitaries and international reporters could be shown carefully screened POWs in relatively pleasant surroundings for maximum propaganda advantage. In the center of the walled compound was a two-story, colonial-style villa that served as the camp staff's offices and quarters. The POWs called it the Big House. They were familiar with the interrogation room inside.

There were forty-four POWs at the Plantation when Stratton arrived; one was Doug Hegdahl, the rest were air force and navy pilots. Hegdahl had fallen off his ship and was rescued by North Vietnamese fishermen. He was nineteen years old. Hegdahl was ordered to accept early release in July 1969. He had memorized the names of 260 prisoners held in Hanoi prisons. It was for this reason only that Commander Stratton convinced Colonel Guy to order Hegdahl to accept release. The Vietnamese had thought the navy kid simple-minded and of no value except as a bargaining tool. Many of the POWs' names were unknown outside the walls of the Hanoi Hilton, and Hegdahl was their only means to let families know that their husbands, fathers, and sons were still alive. Prior to late 1969, only a few prisoners had received any mail or been allowed to write to their families. Some had not received any mail since their captivity. The only way to receive any privileges was through cooperating with the North Vietnamese by making antiwar and propaganda tapes and writing or signing antiwar appeals and letters. Most men resisted these demands only to be tortured, broken, and forced to sign confessions and make antiwar propaganda tapes anyway.

SRO policies were about the same in all the camps. POWs were not to write anything, tape anything, or give out classified information. They were to withstand torture as long as possible. Those who willingly cooperated with the Vietnamese were kept separate from other POWs and given special treatment. They were a small group known as the Peace Committee (PC). PCs were allowed out of their cells from morning until late night. Not only were they free to talk with one another, exercise, and bathe when they wanted to, but they also took trips outside the prison walls to museums, the circus, and to other special events. They were given coffee, sugar, condensed milk, eggs, meat, cigarettes, fruit, candy, and, occasionally, beer. PCs voluntarily made antiwar propaganda tapes to be aired over Hanoi's "Voice of Vietnam" and the Vietcong's "Liberation Radio." John Young, a Green Beret, claimed to have made thirty-three tapes. Near the end of the war, the PCs requested asylum in other countries. According to Young, the Vietnamese encouraged them to return to the United States to prove that they believed in their antiwar protests and to promote Communism in America. Colonel Guy pressed charges of misconduct against the PCs after repatriation. All charges were dismissed.

Hanoi sustained four air strikes in December 1966. Public outrage in the United States over the bombings afforded the Vietnamese an opportunity to make the attacks a major issue in their antiwar propaganda. American public sentiment regarding the Vietnam conflict was a tinderbox. There were 389,000 American troops in Vietnam at the time, and the media brought the war into the homes of millions of Americans. Our soldiers were "smoking marijuana and killing innocent women and children." The Vietnamese needed a malefactor to exploit. Lieutenant Commander Richard A. Stratton, a navy pilot, was captured January 5. The NVA had their "mad bomber of Hanoi." Stratton was viciously tortured and interrogated for two weeks. He had never been to Hanoi before his capture, but he signed the "confession" saying he had led the air strikes. Stratton believed his selection as archfiend in the subsequent melodrama was simply luck of the draw.

POWs in Hanoi were assured that they had not been forgotten. In 1970 Colonel Arthur Simon led a raid on Son Tay prison camp, twenty miles north of Hanoi. However, the prisoners held at Son Tay had been removed four months before Simon and his seventy Green Berets made their move. The Vietnamese began moving all prisoners to Hanoi and eventually to the Hilton. More than 300 men were imprisoned between the walls of Hoa Lo. The number of POWs and the information they brought with them stirred communications within the compounds. By 1972, the men were receiving more mail, although not all that was sent to them. Pictures of children that had not been born yet when their fathers had been sent to Nam were seen for the first time. The POWs heard rumors of peace talks. On January 27, 1973, the Paris Peace Agreement was signed. Robert Molyneaux of Virginia Polytechnic in his review of *Survivors* says: "The Vietnam POW stories continue to filter out, revealing quiet accounts of desperate men determined to survive imprisonment by a ruthless enemy. . . . The writing is choppy at times, as we switch from one story to another, but Grant lets the men speak for themselves—even when they dislike each other. This is a straightforward but powerful book" (Molyneaux, 792).

Everett Alvarez, Jr., was the first U.S. Navy pilot shot down over North Vietnam. He was taken to the later-named Hanoi Hilton, where he was tortured until he confessed to committing "war crimes" against the Vietnamese people. He was kept in solitary confinement for fifteen months before he was allowed contact with other POWs. Alvarez was in the first group to be released following the Paris Peace Agreement. He had been a POW for eight and a half years. He was awarded the Silver Star, two Legions of Merit, two Purple Hearts, and several other medals. Alvarez remained in the navy until he retired in 1980. He then attended George Washington University, earning a law degree and serving as deputy administrator of the Veterans Administration. His and Anthony S. Pitch's book *Chained Eagle* is an excellent account of the physical and mental abuses endured by POWs and also of a truly optimistic spirit.

During February and March 1973, 591 military and civilian POWs returned home. The army, air force, and navy began a study on the long-term effects of captivity. The army and air force discontinued their studies in the early 1980s, but the navy has continued to monitor 168 former POWs. The overall health of the group has been surprising, according to Captain Robert E. Mitchell, the navy physician who now runs the study at the Pensacola Naval Air Station, where most navy pilots are trained. In an article appearing in the *Journal of the American Medical Association*, Timothy Kern reported his interview with Mitchell. Mitchell said that whipworm was "the most common parasitic infestation. . . . skin problems were not remarkable and there was no serious problem with malnutrition. . . . there has been no tuberculosis" (2777). Coronary artery disease and cancer rates are the same as in the general population. Mitchell says "the POWs appear to be experiencing little of the post-Vietnam stress syndromes or psychological trauma reported so commonly in other Vietnam veterans. Their divorce rate and the rate of psychiatric care has been about the same, or better, than those of the general public. . . . Only about six Navy POWs have not done as well as expected" (2779). Mitchell suggests the reason navy POWs have done so well is that they were pilots. "Almost all were officers, and—as officers—they had college degrees. These POWs tended to be older, more mature, better educated, and probably more motivated than the average soldier" (2780). Mitchell adds that the POWs did not return unharmed. Kern reports about 40 percent have shoulder problems. "Next in order of prevalence and severity are elbow problems, hand injuries, and hip bursitis or hip degenerative joint disease. Neck problems are also common (27%)" (2781). As the former POWs go into retirement, Mitchell says they have characteristics that weigh in their favor; the former POWs have demonstrated that they tend to be not defensive, can admit problems, and can deal with them readily.

Following the repatriation of American POWs, only 2,546 personnel (2,505 servicemen and 41 civilians) were unaccounted for, 4 percent of the 58,152 killed. In contrast, 78,750 are still unaccounted for from World War II (19.4 percent), and 8,300 (15 percent) of the dead are still unaccounted for from the Korean War. There are currently 2,273 Americans still missing from the Vietnam War, of whom 1,101 were killed in action but whose remains have not been recovered. However, special teams of Americans and Vietnamese are investigating known crash sites to recover bones for forensic study and identification. Locating these sites is easier since Hanoi opened its classified war files in a step toward normalization with the United States. The likelihood of finding the remains of missing pilots is slight for several reasons. H. Bruce Franklin states in "The POW/MIA Myth" the following:

A U.S. Navy study of all fatal noncombat accidents from 1969 to 1975 involving the type of combat aircraft flown in Vietnam showed that in 40 percent of the cases remains were insufficient for positive identification through autopsy, even though naval investigators arrived on the scene within hours of a crash and identities of the airmen were already known. Bodies in Indochina would additionally suffer the ravages of the tropical climate, with its monsoon rains, engulfing mud, and vegetative overgrowth, and would likely be torn apart and scattered by animals. (P. 47)

Franklin adds that the MIA issue remains a quagmire that has "attained a prominence and importance out of all proportion to the minuscule chance that any of the men so listed are alive" (49).

The MIA status is a somewhat ambiguous category. Servicemen whose deaths or captures are uncertain are designated as missing in action until their true status is determined by evidence. A study by Captain Douglas L. Clarke on MIAs argues: "Missing in action is an accounting limbo. It reflects a lack of knowledge concerning an individual rather than being truly descriptive of his condition. In only the most isolated and bizarre cases. . . . are men able to evade capture in enemy territory for any length of time. Virtually all MIAs are either dead or in enemy hands from the day they disappear—except this information is not available to their country" (1).

Vietnamese officials are also frustrated. An effort to provide the fullest possible accounting for all Americans missing in action has gone beyond the issue of accountability. Franklin cites an example from the House Select Committee that discovered hundreds of cases for which the United States was demanding an accounting, although there was virtually no possibility whatsoever that the Indochinese governments could have any information. His example is that of a UH–1H helicopter with five U.S. Army men on board that crashed into a mountain and exploded into flames. An army investigation team could find only a small amount of bone fragments, determined useless for identification. The five men had been classified as missing in action, and the Vietnamese were to account for each one.

The debate over live POWs still remaining in Vietnam, Laos, and Cambodia is as inconclusive as trying to identify charred bone fragments. As yet, there is no concrete evidence that they exist. Captain Clarke's thesis in his very readable and well-documented study *The Missing Man* is that the government has gone beyond its responsibilities to MIAs at the expense of "the legitimate interests of the United States government, the missing men, and their next of kin" (4).

The other side of the debate has been fueled by politicians, the CIA, and Hollywood. A number of films were made in the 1980s depicting the heroic American POWs still being tortured in jungle prison camps and rescued by maverick Vietnam veterans. *The Deer Hunter* (4 Academy Awards, 1978), *Uncommon Valor* (1983), *Missing in Action* (1984), *Missing in Action II* (1985), *Rambo: First Blood II* (1985), *POW: The Escape* (1986), and *The Hanoi Hilton* (1987) raised public awareness to new heights. A recent *Wall Street Journal*/NBC News poll shows "69 percent of the American people believe that U.S. prisoners of war are still being held in Southeast Asia," nearly twenty years after the United States called its troops home. They hold this belief because of the cynical way the Nixon and subsequent administrations exploited the POW/MIA issue. Where Washington left off, Hollywood picked up, until fact and fantasy got hopelessly mingled in people's minds.

James S. Olson and Randy Roberts, in their book *Where the Domino Fell*, state that the POW-MIA issue that Reagan emphasized during efforts by the Vietnamese to normalize relations between the two countries "was largely imaginary": "Fueled by a series of POW-MIA movies and the incendiary rhetoric of the Reagan administration, a large portion of the American public became convinced that there were thousands of prisoners of war and other American soldiers listed as missing in action still alive in Vietnam. . . . Although several government investigations of the issue reached that conclusion that there were no live POWs or MIAs in Vietnam, still the suspicion lingers" (274).

The Bush administration and the League of Families agree there is no evidence to support the case for live prisoners of war, yet both operate under the assumption that at least some Americans may still be captive. Military intelligence agencies have received nearly 1,500 eyewitness reports of prisoners still in Indochina, but most of the sightings have been investigated and resolved. The Department of Defense has also investigated thousands of reports of dog tags used by Vietnamese refugees to barter their way into the United States. Most of the dog tags belong to servicemen who returned during the troop removal in 1973. In August 1991, the Senate adopted a resolution (S Res 82) creating a Select Committee on POW/MIA Affairs. The twelve-member committee, chaired by Senator John Kerry, a decorated veteran of the Vietnam War, will investigate the fate of American prisoners of war and those missing in action. The Senate also adopted an amendment requiring that a POW/MIA flag designed by the National League of Families of American Prisoners and Missing in Southeast Asia be displayed at all federal buildings designated by the General Services Administration and at the Vietnam Veterans Memorial in Washington, D.C., until such time as the fullest possible accounting has been made of POW/MIAs in Southeast Asia. Officially, Colonel Charles Shelton is the only man listed as MIA or POW, and he is known to have died about twenty-five years ago, according to Bruce Franklin. Shelton was shot down over Laos in April 1965. He is "listed as POW as a symbolic gesture of the Administration's commitment to this issue," according to the Defense Department statement in Franklin's "The POW/MIA Myth." All other known or presumed prisoners of war have been either returned or determined to have died in captivity.

American POW/MIAs are still used as bargaining chips. Article 8(b) of the Paris Peace Agreement signed in 1973 deals specifically with MIA information and provides that the parties to the agreement would assist each other in locating all missing-in-action personnel. Article 8(b) has become a justification by the United States for not complying with Article 21, in which the United States agrees to contribute to postwar reconstruction in Indochina in the amount of $3.5 billion. The MIA issue has become a barrier between American and Indochina relations. The U.S. government has stated that normalization will not take place until "the fullest possible accounting for the missing, the return of all Americans who may still be held in captivity, and the repatriation of all recoverable remains" are resolved (D. Clarke, 52–53).

Early in the 1990s, especially because of the presidential candidacy of H. Ross Perot in 1992, the issue of American MIAs once again surfaced into the American political consciousness. Perot had long believed that there had been a conspiracy in the Pentagon to cover-up information about surviving prisoners-of-war, and he articulated the issue repeatedly to a number of American audiences. Also, early in 1992, President Boris Yelstin of Russia confessed that he believed it was possible that some American POWs ended up in Soviet prison camps. Subsequent investigations revealed that some American MIAs from World War II had ended up in the Soviet camps, but there were no discoveries of Vietnam POWs there. In September 1992, in testimony before a Senate investigating committee, several high-ranking officials in the Nixon administration, including former Secretary of Defense James Schlesinger and General Alexander Haig, admitted the possibility that some American POWs in Laos were listed as MIAs and left behind after the 1973 Paris Peace Accords. The last chapter on the question of Americans still listed as missing-in-action in Indochina has yet to be written.

BIBLIOGRAPHY

Alvarez, Everett Jr., and Anthony S. Pitch. *Chained Eagle*. Garden City, N.Y.: Doubleday, 1991.

Anderson, William C. *BAT–21*. Englewood Cliffs, N.J.: Prentice-Hall, 1980.

Ashmore, Harry S., and William C. Baggs, with Ellen H. Burnell. *Mission to Hanoi: A Chronicle of Double-dealing in High Places*. New York: Putnam's, 1968.

Barnes, Scott, and Melva Libb. *Bohica*. Canton, Ohio: Daring Books, 1987.

Berrigan, Daniel. *Night Flight to Hanoi: War Diary with 11 Poems*. New York: Perennial Library/Harper and Row, 1968.

Blakey, Scott. *Prisoner at War: The Survival of Commander Richard A. Stratton.* New York: Anchor Press, 1978.

Brace, Ernest C. *A Code to Keep.* New York: St. Martin's Press, 1988.

Camp, Norman M., ed. *Stress, Strain and Vietnam: An Annotated Bibliography of Two Decades of Psychological and Social Science Literature Reflecting the Effect of the War on the American Soldier.* Westport, Conn.: Greenwood Press, 1989.

Chesley, Larry. *Seven Years in Hanoi: A POW Tells His Story.* Salt Lake City, Utah: Bookcraft, 1973.

Clarke, Douglas L. *The Missing Man.* Washington, D.C.: U.S. Government Printing Office, 1981.

Clarke, Jeffrey J. *Advice and Support.* Washington, D.C.: Center of Military History, U.S. Army, 1988.

Daly, James A., and Lee Bergman. *A Hero's Welcome: The Conscience of Sergeant James Daly Versus the United States Army.* Indianapolis: Bobbs-Merrill, 1975.

David, Heather. *Operation Rescue.* New York: Pinnacle Books, 1971.

Dengler, Dieter. *Escape from Laos.* San Rafael, Calif.: Presidio, 1979.

Denton, Jeremiah A. *When Hell Was in Session.* New York: Reader's Digest Press, 1976.

Des Pres, Terrence. *The Survivor: An Anatomy of Life in the Death Camps.* New York: Oxford University Press, 1976.

Doyle, Edward, and Terrence Maitland. *The Vietnam Experience: The Aftermath.* Boston: Boston, 1985.

Dramesi, John A. *Code of Honor.* New York: Norton, 1975.

Dudman, Richard. *Forty Days with the Enemy.* New York: Livewright, 1971.

Dunn, Joe P. "The Vietnam War POW/MIAs" An Annotated Bibliography." *Bulletin of Bibliography* 45 (June 1988): 152–57.

Effros, William G. *Quotations Vietnam: 1945–1970.* New York: Random House, 1970.

Ellsberg, Daniel. *Papers on the War.* New York: Simon and Schuster, 1972.

Fall, Bernard B. *Viet-Nam Witness: 1953–1966.* New York: Praeger, 1966.

Fall, Bernard B., and Marcus G. Raskin. *The Viet-Nam Reader: Articles and Documents on American Foreign Policy and the Viet-Nam Crisis.* New York: Vintage, 1965.

Fifield, Russell H. *The Diplomacy of Southeast Asia, 1945–1958.* New York: Harper, 1958.

Fitzgerald, Frances. *Fire in the Lake: The Vietnamese and the Americans in Vietnam.* New York: Vintage, 1973.

Franklin, H. Bruce. "The POW/MIA Myth." *Atlantic Monthly* (December 1991): 45–51.

Gaither, Ralph, and Steve Henry. *With God in a P.O.W. Camp.* Nashville, Tenn.: Broadman, 1973.

Gettleman, Marvin E., ed. *Vietnam.* Greenwich, Conn.: Fawcett, 1966.

Grant, Zalin. *Survivors.* New York: Norton, 1975.

Groom, Winston, and Duncan Spencer. *Conversations with the Enemy: The Story of PFC Robert Garwood.* New York: Putnam, 1983.

Hackworth, David H., and Julie Sherman. *About Face.* New York: Simon and Schuster, 1989.

Halberstam, David. *The Best and the Brightest*. New York: Random House, 1972.

Heineger, Peter. "Prisoner at War." *America* (October 14, 1978): 248.

Heslop, J. M. *From the Shadow of Death, Stories of POWs*. Salt Lake City, Utah: Desert Book, 1973.

Hickey, Gerald C. *Village in Vietnam*. New Haven, Conn.: Yale University Press, 1967.

Homolka, William. *Americans in Southeast Asia: The POW/MIA Issue*. New York: New World Books, 1986.

Hubbell, John G. *P.O.W.: A Definitive History of the American Prisoner-of-War Experience in Vietnam, 1964–1973*. New York: Reader's Digest Press, 1976.

Jensen, Jay Roger. *Six Years in Hell*. Salt Lake City, Utah: Horizon, 1974.

Kern, Timothy. "Follow-Up: 15 Years After Captivity in SE Asia." *Journal of the American Medical Association* (May 19, 1989): 2776–84.

Kilbourne, Jimmy. *Escape and Evasion: 17 True Stories of Downed Pilots Who Made It Back*. New York: Macmillan, 1973.

Kimball, William K. *The Other Side of Glory—Vietnam: The Untold Story*. Canton, Ohio: Daring Books, 1987.

Knightly, Phillip. *The First Casualty*. New York: Harvest/Harcourt Brace Jovanovich, 1975.

Lowery, Timothy S. *And Brave Men, Too*. New York: Crown, 1985.

McConnell, Malcolm. *Into the Mouth of the Cat: The Story of Lance Sijan, Hero of Vietnam*. New York: Norton, 1985.

McCubbin, Hamilton I., ed. *Family Separation and Reunion, Families of Prisoners of War and Servicemen Missing in Action*. San Diego, Calif.: Naval Health Research Center, 1974.

McDaniel, Eugene, and James Johnson. *Scars and Stripes: The True Story of One Man's Courage in Facing Death As a Vietnam POW*. Irving, Calif.: Harvest House, 1980.

McDaniel, Norman A. *Yet Another Voice*. New York: Hawthorne Books, 1975.

McGrath, John. *Prisoner of War*. Annapolis, Md.: U.S. Naval Institute, 1975.

Mauer, Harry. *Strange Ground: Americans in Vietnam, 1945–1975, An Oral History*. New York: Holt, 1989.

Miller, Carolyn P. *Captured!* Chappaqua, N.Y.: Christian Herald, 1977.

Molyneaux, Robert. Review of *Survivors*. *Library Journal* (March 15, 1974): 792.

Mulligan, James A. *The Hanoi Commitment*. Virginia Beach, Va.: RIF Marketing, 1981.

Norman, Geoffrey. *Bouncing Back*. Boston: Houghton Mifflin, 1981.

O'Daniel, Larry J. *Missing in Action: Trail of Deceit*. Arlington, Va.: Arlington House, 1979.

O'Daniel, Larry J. *Help Me, I'm Still Alive: Story of a P.O.W. Cover-Up*. St. Petersburg, Fla.: Forget Me Not Association, 1986.

Olson, James S., and Randy Roberts. *Where the Domino Fell*. New York: St. Martin's Press, 1991.

Patterson, Charles J., and G. Lee Tippin. *The Story of Heroes Who Fell from Grace: The True Story of Operation Lazarus, the Attempt to Free American POWs from Laos in 1982*. Canton, Ohio: Daring Books, 1985.

Plumb, Charlie, and Glen H. DeWerff. *I'm No Hero: A POW Story*. Independence, Mo.: Independence Press, 1973.

Plumb, Charlie. *The Last Domino? A POW Looks Ahead.* Independence, Mo.: Independence Press, 1975.

"Prisoners of War: Slow-Fading Hope." *Economist* 317 (November 24, 1990): 24–25.

Ray, Michele. *The Two Shores of Hell.* New York: McKay, 1968.

Risner, Robinson. *The Passing of the Night: My Seven Years as a Prisoner of the North Vietnamese.* New York: Random House, 1973.

Roberts, James C. *Missing in Action.* Washington, D.C.: Fund for Objective News Reporting, 1980.

Rowan, Stephen A. *They Wouldn't Let Us Die: The Prisoners of War Tell Their Story.* New York: Jonathan David, 1973.

Rowe, James N. *Five Years to Freedom.* Waltham, Mass.: Little, Brown, 1971.

Rutledge, Howard, and Phyllis (with Mel and L. White). *In the Presence of Mine Enemies: A Prisoner of War, 1965–1973.* Old Tappan, N.J.: Fleming H. Revell Company, 1973.

Salisbury, Harrison E. *Behind the Lines—Hanoi: December 23, 1966–January 7, 1967.* New York: Harper and Row, 1967.

Santoli, Al. *Everything We Had: An Oral History of the Vietnam War by Thirty-three American Soldiers Who Fought It.* New York: Random House, 1981.

Santoli, Al. *To Bear any Burden: The Vietnam War and Its Aftermath in the Words of Americans and Southeast Asians.* New York: Dutton, 1985.

Schemmer, Benjamin F. *The Raid.* New York: Harper and Row, 1976.

Schlesinger, Arthur M. *The Imperial Presidency.* Boston: Houghton Mifflin, 1973.

Schwinn, Monika, and Bernhard Dichl. *We Came to Help.* New York: Harcourt, Brace, Jovanovich, 1976.

"Senate Approves POW/MIA Panel." *Congressional Quarterly Weekly Report* 49 (August 10, 1991): 2261.

Sheehan, Neil. *A Bright and Shining Lie.* New York: Random House, 1988.

Shemmer, Benjamin F. *The Raid.* New York: Harper and Row, 1976.

Smith, George Edward, and Donald Duncan. *POW, Two Years with the Viet Cong.* Berkeley, Calif.: Ramparts, 1971.

Stockdale, James B. *A Vietnam Experience: Ten Years of Reflection.* Stanford, Calif.: Hoover Institution Press, 1984.

Stockdale, James B., and Sybil Stockdale. *In Love and War: The Story of a Family's Ordeal and Sacrifice During the Vietnam Years.* New York: Harper and Row, 1984.

Wallace, Terry. *Bloods: An Oral History of the Vietnam War by Black Americans.* New York: Random House, 1984.

Webb, Kate. *On the Other Side: Twenty-three Days with the Viet Cong.* New York: Time Books, 1972.

Willenson, Kim. *The Bad War: An Oral History of the Vietnam Conflict.* New York: New American Library, 1987.

Wyatt, Barbara Powers, and Frederic A. Wyatt. *We Came Home.* Toluca Lake, Calif.: P.O.W. Publications, 1977.

23 What Should We Teach About the Vietnam War?: The Evolution of the Debate

Joe P. Dunn

Courses on Vietnam appearing in the 1960s were usually offered by opponents of the war. Many of them reflected the values of an emergent new generation of academics dedicated to teaching and scholarship for political purposes, often to promote radical activity. A lively debate over what should be taught had surfaced by the time most of the first generation of Vietnam courses disappeared with the end of the conflict. Although Vietnam was less evident in the classroom in the late 1970s, the search for the lessons of the experience continued with conservatives, liberals, and radicals advancing very different propositions.[1] As Vietnam courses reemerged and proliferated in the curriculum in the 1980s, the question of what should be taught revived. The first three articles to address this subject in the new environment were published in November 1981.

H. Bruce Franklin's op-ed piece, "Teaching the Vietnam War Today: Who Won and Why?" in *The Chronicle of Higher Education* attracted the most attention. Franklin, a professor of American literature, proclaimed that teaching the war "now may be more subversive" than in the 1960s. Wishing to resuscitate the activism of the earlier decade, he espoused a radical agenda and bragged that many of his students went off to Washington to join demonstrations against America's intervention in El Salvador. Asserting that defense of the war depended upon ignorance and that some of his students' ideas "had to be dispelled right away," he offered his own "factual" correctives. The article stimulated numerous hostile responses. Critics charged that many of Franklin's "facts" were simply wrong. His readings all reflected the same ideological slant; some were very dubious sources. Others challenged Franklin's pedagogy, simplistic analyses, and political agenda. Several commentators questioned his competency for the course.[2]

Diplomatic historian Sandra C. Taylor's "Teaching the Vietnam War" in *The History Teacher* was a more thorough and less passionate exposition. Taylor's earlier article with Rex Casillas—"Dealing with Defeat: Teaching the Vietnam War"—gave the results of a survey of professors who dealt with the conflict. In *The History Teacher* article, Taylor discussed possible sources for a course. Although tending toward antiwar sources, her appraisals were balanced and judicious. She briefly noted the two prevalent positions at the time—the conventional wisdom that the war was a mistake and the "new revisionists" who argued that victory had been possible. Explaining that many of the questions that Vietnam raised remained unresolved and that "Most students have the uneasy sense, as do their teachers, that Vietnam was not the last time that we will call upon arms to impose our version of world order on others," she challenged historians to teach the subject to a generation who already did not know the experience.

Joe P. Dunn's "Teaching the Vietnam War as History" made a strong argument for teaching the war by emphasizing how Vietnam served as a microcosm of the forces of the twentieth century—nationalism, imperialism, colonialism, revolution, communism, liberalism, Third World developmental problems, nation building, and the Cold War—as well as a case study in American decisionmaking and the changing nature of American society in the 1960s. Although he makes the point clearer and more emphatically in later writings, Dunn also implies that significant attention should be given to Vietnamese history, culture, society, and politics. Finally, the article served as one of the earliest annotated bibliographies on teaching sources.

In the same issue, Dunn responded to an earlier book review of *Teaching the Vietnam War* by William L. Griffen and John Marciano, a self-styled expose of high school textbook treatment of Vietnam and a radical alternative interpretation. Franklin had proclaimed the text invaluable, the most useful tool for his course, and Taylor also cited the book. Dunn, however, called the work a "superficial, ideological tract." He charged that the revisionist narrative, which ignored the best recent scholarship in favor of emotional rhetoric, such as comparing the United States in Vietnam to the Nazi invasions of Europe, was little more than a polemic. The authors' rejoinder echoed Franklin's agenda as they articulated a rather limited dichotomy of interpreting the war as either American imperialism or apologists for the war.[3]

In the next years, a small literature began to develop on teaching and sources. Dan B. Fleming and Ronald J. Nurse's "Vietnam Revised: Are Our Textbooks Changing" (1982) and Joe P. Dunn's "Teaching the Vietnam War in High School" (1983) looked at sources for the secondary level. Fleming and Nurse found textbooks less pernicious than Griffen and Marciano, and Dunn restated his views on teaching Vietnam while noting appropriate sources for the high school level. Karen J. Winkler's 1982 article "Scholars of the Vietnam War Consider How the Crucial Decisions Were Made" in *The Chronicle of Higher Education* interviewed leading scholars who called for serious attention to studying the decision process and related questions.

Fox Butterfield's 1983 article "The New Vietnam Scholarship" in the *New York Times Magazine*, which spoke about some of the early courses on the war, played a major role in the growing interest in teaching Vietnam. The article "Vietnam as the Past" (1983) by Richard K. Betts, Douglas Pike, and Harry G. Summers, Jr. was also a signal contribution in the evolving literature including one of the best early bibliographies. Both the Woodrow Wilson International Center for Scholars and the University of Southern California held high-profile conferences on the "lessons of Vietnam" in 1983. The latter conference especially played a key role in the revival of attention to the war.[4]

However, the most important event of 1983 was the Public Broadcasting System's thirteen-part, "The Vietnam Experience," the single greatest spur to the teaching of the war. Over 150 colleges and universities offered credit courses on the war based on the series. The $3 million series, supported by a $1.2 million grant from the National Endowment for the Humanities, received glowing reviews from the *New York Times*, *Time*, *TV Guide*, and many academics. Critics responded equally emphatically.

R. C. Raack, professor of history and a film expert, concentrated upon technique. His 1984 "Caveat Spectator" explained how purposeful techniques were employed to distort and propagandize. He cited such manipulative and deceptive practices as carefully edited interviews, intercut edits (intersplicing shots of other events overshadowing or counterpointing the words of a speaker), juxtaposition of irrelevant emotive scenes to evoke sympathy with the narrator's conclusions, ambient sound and music, an omniscient narrator, and one-sided archival sources. Raack concluded that the flawed product should be withdrawn from distribution. The "omniscient narrator's lecture with pictures" only served to prove that "History is too important to be left to television producers."

While Raack condemned the technical flaws, Stephen J. Morris's "Vietnam, A Dual-Vision History" in *The Wall Street Journal* (December 20, 1983) dissected content. More generous to producers Richard Ellison and Stanley Karnow than Raack, Morris explained that the two members of the liberal antiwar movement were fair-minded individuals who did seek a balanced product. However, finances forced them to allocate nearly half of the episodes to French and British producers, individuals with strong, radical commitments. Morris believed that the American-produced episodes had flaws, but the British and French episodes were largely ideological tracts, a purposeful whitewash of the Communists.

Calling the series a failure, Morris explained that while there was truth to the charge that few American policymakers understood Vietnamese history, "There was even more truth in the charge that few Western antiwar movement supporters even understood modern totalitarianism. That is one indubitable lesson of Vietnam." The PBS series is further tragic evidence of it.

The greatest enemy of the PBS series was Reed Irvine, founder of Accuracy in Media, Inc. (AIM). His 1984 "The Flawed History of Vietnam" is an emotional, even polemical, assessment branded "The Vietnam Experience," an insidious "waste of public funds." It distorted the truth in favor of the Communists and perpetuated the myths that the liberal media actually created during the war. Specifically, Irvine excoriated the "leftist" producers and experts, the "straight Vietnamese Communist Party-line history" of the nationalist movement and false depiction of Ho Chi Minh as a nationalist hero, the exculpation of the media's role in getting the United States involved in South Vietnam and later in abandonment of the country, the transformation of the U.S. victory during Tet 1968 into a perception of defeat, the unwarranted emphasis upon atrocities, and the failure to depict the Vietnamese gulag after 1975. Irvine feared that the series would have a powerful and pernicious impact on how the war was portrayed to the next generation and called on the National Endowment for the Humanities to fund a full-scale critique. NEH did provide some funds, and in July 1984, AIM conducted a two-day conference on the PBS program. Two later AIM videos, "Vietnam: The Real Story" (1984) and "Vietnam: The Impact of Media" (1985) provided more detailed critiques. The latter especially is quite useful as a classroom source particularly in counterpoint to the PBS series segment on the 1968 Tet Offensive.

Vietnam courses proliferated in the mid–1980s largely as a result of "The Vietnam Experience." A 1986 national poll by the Center for the Study of the Vietnam Generation found over 400 courses concentrating on the war. A poll underway by the Indochina Institute most likely will demonstrate a significant increase since that date.

Most of the new Vietnam courses drew large enrollments.[5] Probably the two largest were Theodore R. Kennedy's "Vietnam Involvements Symposium," taught under an anthropology label at the State University of New York–Stony Brook, which enrolled 800, and Walter H. Capp's religion course at the University of California–Santa Barbara, which accepted over 900 and turned away hundreds others. Kennedy, a Korean War veteran, started the course as a tribute to his brother who died from the deterioration of his lungs after returning from Vietnam (assumed to be from agent orange exposure). Kennedy spent several thousand dollars of his own money to bring in an array of speakers which the course featured. Financial and psychological costs caused Kennedy to drop the course after two years in 1986 and 1987.

While Kennedy's symposium was a local phenomenon, Walter Capps's course remains the highest-profile Vietnam offering in the nation. It was featured on "Sixty Minutes," discussed in *The Chronicle of Higher Education*, and mentioned in almost every article on teaching the war. However, Capps's 1985 article "On Teaching Today's Students About the Vietnam War" is disappointing. A justification for a course of such partisan political division as a proper expression of the humanities, it did not address pedagogy or materials. Capps's concern is values: "The course offers an illustration of how values are transmitted within contexts of highly volatile social and political change." He continued that the fundamental questions addressed are "about the nature of virtue, the claims that vested national interests make upon justice, the properties of the good society, how far patriotism and the dictates of warfare are trustworthy guides for achieving one's *telos* as a human being."[6]

Political scientist Douglas Pike's "Teaching the Vietnam Experience as a Whole Course" (1985) also began with the issue of values and the problem of perspectives. His purpose was quite different from Capps. Pike bemoaned that so little expertise about Vietnam existed. Even at the height of the war, America produced few Indochina experts, and the situation worsened with the end of the conflict. Scholarship on Vietnam focused on a few topics with essential areas of research untouched. But worse yet, he asserted, was the appalling paucity of good teaching materials. The available curriculum materials were avowedly left wing and no decent textbooks existed. Pike contended that at this early stage when "we have not yet reached the starting gate of truth determined, but are still wandering in a maze of competing perceptions," when teaching about the event was still dictated by "an inordinately high level of interpretative passion," focus should be upon students understanding the various perceptions of the war and the implications of each. His article outlined the various perceptions to which students should be exposed on the major questions of the war. Both Capps and Pike wished to expose students to the myriad range of arguments. It was clear that they each began from very different perspectives and stood at opposite ends of the scale of interpretations.

Historian Ronald H. Spector's 1986 article "What Did You Do in the War Professor?" in *American Heritage* more pointedly addressed the same themes as Pike. Spector suggested that faculty for most of the new Vietnam courses were ill prepared by either experience or formal study and continued that "the problem with the present-day crop of history courses about Vietnam is not so much attitudes or experiences as lack of knowledge." He asserted that "since the 1960s, academic historians have contributed little if anything to our knowledge of the Vietnam War," and the books that have shaped the debates on the subject were by journalists and former participants rather than by academics. He concluded that "if the present trend continues, we can be reasonably confident that despite the vogue of Vietnam history courses, American historians will have little influence on how we remember the Vietnam War."

Former foreign service Indochina specialist Frederick Z. Brown echoed Spector's concerns. His "Myths and Misperception Abound in Our Courses on the War in Vietnam" (1988) reiterated that "There are precious few Vietnam scholars with genuine knowledge—as opposed to a ditty bag of war stories—and the amount of first-rate scholarship falls far short of the need and the untapped potential." While Spector lamented the scanty scholarly contributions by historians, Brown charged political scientists with default. He maintained that ample documentation was released under the Freedom of Information Act for significant investigations. Most particularly, he contended, the decision process in the post–1968 years needed scholarly attention. Brown also criticized the overly American orientation on Vietnam. Most courses, texts, and scholarship focused upon the experience of Americans at war and at home. This displayed intellectual chauvinism: the message was that what America did was important; what the Vietnamese did or thought did not matter. He branded "such a narcissistic approach not only misleading, but grossly unfair to the South Vietnamese, who were fighting for their survival." In sum, "The war and its consequences must be understood in terms of the historical, political, and social realities in Vietnam itself."

Brown continued that ignorance about the Vietnamese perspective, both Communist and non-Communist, and the abysmal misunderstanding of Vietnamese nationalism, led to the myths and misperceptions in courses on the war. He explained that the standard cliché that Ho Chi Minh represented the true expression of Vietnamese nationalism is subject to serious question, and that other nationalist perspectives, such as that expressed in Bui Diem's *In the Jaws of History*, deserve greater consideration than ordinarily is accorded. For Brown, these are more important questions than some of the superficialities which dominate many Vietnam courses.

As controversy swirled over what should be taught in college courses, the subject surfaced in high school curricula (as anticipated by Dunn and others in the articles noted above). Dunn conducted a grant-funded, two-week summer institute in June 1986, which trained nineteen high school teachers from the Southeast to teach the war. A number of the participants introduced Vietnam War units and even whole courses in their school. The most ambitious effort was by Carol Transou of Science Hill High School, Johnson City, Tennessee, the 1987 Tennessee Teacher of the Year. Transou's course on the war attracted national attention, and as a recipient of a *Readers' Digest*–National Endowment for the Humanities Sabbatical Leave Year in 1989–90, she undertook a year-long personal study of the war and traveled to Vietnam herself.[7] Union High School in South Carolina initiated a year-long, schoolwide program on the war featuring Vietnam units in many parts of the curriculum, a series of nationally prominent speakers, a play, a project newspaper, and community activities such as bringing "The Traveling Wall," the replica of the Vietnam Memorial, to the town.

In a different type of approach, an Oklahoma junior high school teacher wrote to policymakers and other key figures in the Vietnam War to ask what should be taught to the next generation. Bill McCloud's 1988 article "What Should We Tell Our Children About Vietnam" and a book with the same title relates the wide diversity of responses he received.

More importantly, sociology professor Jerold M. Starr issued *The Lessons of the Vietnam War* (1988), a compilation of individual units on various aspects of the war written primarily for secondary teachers and students. Starr served as guest editor of the January 1988 issue of *Social Education*, journal of the National Council for the Social Studies, which was devoted to teaching the war. The sixteen articles on the topic, many by participants in the forthcoming volume, publicized the curriculum collection. Appearing at an opportune time and supported by a strong publicity effort, *The Lessons of the Vietnam War* attracted considerable attention and a number of adoptions by high school and college level courses. Starr also organized speakers' bureaus, a teacher-training institute, and other activities to support adoptions of the curriculum.

Despite its apparent success, the curriculum had severe problems. It had a difficult history before it even appeared. The original funding and the first group of authors came from peace and leftist groups. Reviewers' criticism of the original unit manuscripts caused several authors and the project editor to leave. Starr recruited a more prominent group of contributors including George Herring and William Duiker, but many of the conceptional inadequacies of the project remained. The attempt to reduce complex issues into brief treatment and basic vocabulary led to simplistic narrative and interpretations. Apparent haste to get the manuscript into print resulted in embarrassing factual inaccuracies. As author or coauthor of more than half of the units and pervasive editor of all of them, Starr's lack of expertise and his political perspectives dominate the entire curriculum. The final product is disappointing, which is unfortunate since good curriculum material for the secondary level is badly needed.

Allan Goodman, associate dean of the Georgetown University School of Foreign Service and respected authority on the negotiating process during the Vietnam War, concurs that materials to deal with the war at the secondary and college level are needed. After speaking to his daughter's high school American history class, Goodman wrote "Scholars Must Give More Serious Thought to How They Teach and Write About the War in Vietnam" (1990). He complained that despite the attention of recent years, the war is still ignored by many history and foreign-policy professors and by high school teachers. Furthermore, most who do teach it are locked into "the old debates and questions that exercised them during the conflict itself." Goodman particularly criticized the penchant for "anecdotal accounts of what the fighting and decision making were like (at home and abroad), as well as the longer-standing approach of teaching about Vietnam as an episode in the cold war." He asserted the need for a deeper, more sophisticated approach that viewed the war in larger political and societal context as "a fundamental clash between cultures and ways of thinking about power and history."

In his article, which appeared one week prior to Iraq's invasion of Kuwait, Goodman offered prophetic advice as he stated that the study of Vietnam should raise questions about when to use force and when to use diplomacy. He challenged teachers and scholars to address how to avoid Vietnams in the future at a point in history when the decline of superpower confrontation might make the employment of military power a more appealing option. Students need to learn that wars affect not just those who participated but shape the cultural and political alignments of an entire generation. He ended by asking historians to help students consider whether wars, even for justified means, are worth the social and economic costs. Teachers should help students to question their generation's ability to control and limit the negative effects of war.

Joe P. Dunn's "The Vietnam Experience: A Syllabus for an Interdisciplinary History/Political Science Course" in *Teaching the Vietnam War: Resources and Assessments* and his contributions in Marc Jason Gilbert's *The Vietnam War: Teaching Approaches and Resources* offer other course models. Besides being the most complete collections on resources and teaching strategies available, both books speak to how the war should be taught. Dunn's perspectives are evident in his bibliographic essays. Gilbert's volume is a larger work that offers fourteen essays by experienced teachers in the field. To quote from reviewer Douglas Pike, "There is gold amid the dross." Actually, there is much gold. Several of the essays are excellent sources of practical information, and the book is an outstanding contribution.[8]

Beyond the published sources, an even larger dialogue about teaching the war exists at scholarly conferences. Sessions on teaching the war are commonplace at history, political science, international studies, Asian studies, and increasingly at literature, sociology, media, and other conferences. Often teaching sessions are more prevalent at regional rather than national conferences. For instance, the Southeast Conference of the Association of Asian Studies usually has at least one session annually on teaching Vietnam, and two books, including Gilbert's above, have emerged primarily from these sessions. In recent years a growing number of specific conferences, symposia, or workshops on Vietnam have been held across the country.

The largest forum on the war, one which emphasizes teaching the subject, is the Popular Culture Association (PCA) annual conference. Peter Rollins, president of the association in the early 1980s, introduced Vietnam as a specialty area, and it has grown to one of the association's largest interest areas. By the end of the decade, more than eighty papers, many on teaching the subject, were presented annually. The participants in the Vietnam sessions tend to be younger academics with specialties in literature, movies, film, media, or other such areas. Frustrated with their lack of specific expertise on Vietnam, one critic responded that "most of the individuals could not find Vietnam on a map and that the war was too important to leave this collection of Vietnam groupies." A new journal, *Vietnam Generation*, arose from participants in PCA sessions.

Another important venue on the teaching of the war is the Indochina Institute at George Mason University. The Institute hosted a National Conference on Teaching the Vietnam War in April 1988, and in 1990, conducted a six-week National Endowment for the Humanities Summer Institute on the teaching of the war. It also publishes a newsletter that serves as the national clearinghouse of information on the study and teaching of Vietnam.

CONCLUSION

Just as some were beginning to question if the teaching of Vietnam had reached a saturation point, the Gulf War provided a new relevance. Iraq and Vietnam obviously were quite different, but many of the old political questions about presidential power in making war, the role of Congress, the impact of an antiwar movement, the short and long-term costs of war, and the understanding and appreciation of different cultures were renewed; and military debates such as the efficacy of military means to send political messages, the ability of airpower and bombing to win wars, the length of tours of duty, and the question of a possible draft resurfaced. Invoked subtly or overtly, Vietnam hung over every thought and action of Desert Shield and Desert Storm. The media poured forth lessons from Vietnam and comparisons between the two situations. Several scholarly comparative studies are in progress, and some of the old Vietnam debates have reemerged with new vigor. Undoubtedly, the next round of essays will provide us new insight on what we should teach about Vietnam in the wake of the Gulf War.

To paraphrase Mark Twain, the rumors of the death of Vietnam are greatly exaggerated. As once more we confront the old adage that each generation writes its own history, we can look forward to the continuing quest for meanings and lessons from the Vietnam experience.

NOTES

1. See Joe P. Dunn, "In Search of Lessons: The Development of a Vietnam Historiography," in *Parameters: The Journal of the U.S. Army War College*, which used the lessons motif in an interpretive bibliograpic essay of sources at the time. Over the years, the author has published a number of specialized bibliographic essays. For the most comprehensive bibliographic essays on teaching sources including a list of all published Vietnam bibliographies, see Joe P. Dunn, *Teaching the Vietnam War: Resources and Assessments*, and Joe P. Dunn, "Texts and Auxiliary Resources," *The Vietnam War: Teaching Approaches and Resources*, edited by Marc Jason Gilbert.

2. See the many letters to the editor in the December 9 and 16 issues, especially one by Earl H. Tilford, Jr.

3. Griffen and Marciano, *Teaching the Vietnam War*; "On Teaching Recent History: An Exchange," in *Teaching History*, 94–95; also see Margaret E. Stewart, "Vietnam-War Novels in the Classroom," in *Teaching History*, 60–66.

4. Excerpts from the papers presented at the conference are collected in Harrison E. Salisbury, ed., *Vietnam Reconsidered: Lessons from a War*. However, it does not capture the controversy, violent emotion, and turmoil that characterized the conference.

5. Journalist articles on the new Vietnam courses include Fox Butterfield, "Disparity in College Courses on Vietnam," *New York Times* (April 27, 1988), B–11; Stephen Goode, "Taking a Trip Back to the Sixties," *Insight on the News* 4 (April 15, 1988): 50–52; David Moniz, "Learning the Lessons of Vietnam," Columbia, S.C., *The State* (October 2, 1988), 1E, 3E (syndicated nationally); and Pam Kelley, "When Vietnam Is Lesson, Teachers Don't Agree," *The Charlotte Observer* (April 24, 1989), 1A, 3A (syndicated nationally).

6. Also see Capps's book, *The Unfinished War: Vietnam and the American Conscience*.

7. See the article on the summer institute by Joe P. Dunn, "Teaching Teachers to Teach the Vietnam War," *Social Education* 52 (January 1988): 37–38. On Transou's activities, see Alvin P. Sanoff, "Vietnam Comes of Age," *U.S. News and World Report* 102 (February 2, 1987): 58–59; Karen Franklin, "Making Peace with Vietnam," *Teacher Magazine* (March 1990), 33–34; and Karen Franklin, "Everything I Need to Know I Learned in Vietnam," *Veteran* 10 (May 1990): 15–17.

8. Pike's comments on the Dunn book are found in *Indochina Chronology*, April–June 1991 issue, 18; and on the Gilbert book in October-December 1991 issue, 20.

BIBLIOGRAPHY

Berman, David M. "Vietnam Through Vietnamese Eyes: A Review of the Literature." *Asia Pacific Community* 28 (Spring 1985): 88–104.

Berman, David M. "Perspectives on the Teaching of Vietnam." *The Social Studies* 77 (July-August 1986): 165–68.

Berman, David M. "Every Vietnamese Was a Gook: My Lai, Vietnam, and American Education." *Theory and Research in Social Education* 16 (Spring 1988): 141–59.

Berman, David M. "In Cold Blood: Vietnam in Textbooks." *Vietnam Generation* 1 (1989): 1–17.

Berman, David M. "Rethinking Vietnam." *The New England Journal of History* 47 (Winter 1990): 31–41.

Betts, Richard K., Douglas Pike, and Harry G. Summers, Jr. "Vietnam as the Past." *The Wilson Quarterly* 6 (Summer 1983): 95–139.

Brown, Frederick Z. "Myths and Misperception Abound in Our Courses on the War in Vietnam." *The Chronicle of Higher Education* 34 (May 25, 1988): A 48.

Butterfield, Fox. "The New Vietnam Scholarship." *New York Times Magazine* (February 13, 1983): 26–35, 45–61.

Capps, Walter. *The Unfinished War: Vietnam and the American Conscience*. Boston: Beacon Press, 1982.

Capps, Walter. "On Teaching Today's Students About the Vietnam War." *Federation Review* 8 (May-June 1985): 10–13.

Daniels, R. Steven, and Carolyn L. Clarke-Daniels. "Teaching the Vietnam War: An Examination of History, Policy, and Impact." *The Political Science Teacher* 3 (Fall 1990): 13–16.

Dunn, Joe P. "In Search of Lessons: The Development of a Vietnam Historiography." *Parameters: The Journal of the U.S. Army War College* (December 1979): 28–40.

Dunn, Joe P. "On Teaching Recent History: An Exchange." *Teaching History: A Journal of Methods* 6 (Fall 1981): 94–95.

Dunn, Joe P. "Teaching the Vietnam War as History." *Teaching History: A Journal of Methods* 6 (Fall 1981): 50–59.

Dunn, Joe P. "Teaching the Vietnam War in High School." *The Social Studies* 74 (September-October 1983): 198–200.

Dunn, Joe P. "The Vietnam Experience: A Syllabus for an Interdisciplinary History/Political Science Course." *Teaching the Vietnam War: Resources and Assessments* (Los Angeles: Center for the Study of Armament and Disarmament, 1990): 84–90.

Fleming, Dan B., and Ronald J. Nurse. "Vietnam Revised: Are Our Textbooks Changing." *Social Education* 46 (May 1982): 338–43.

Franklin, H. Bruce. "Teaching the Vietnam War Today: Who Won and Why?" *The Chronicle of Higher Education* 23 (November 4, 1981): 64.

Gilbert, Marc Jason, ed. *The Vietnam War: Teaching Approaches and Resources*. Westport, Conn.: Greenwood Press, 1991.

Goldstein, Jonathan. "Teaching the American-Indochina War: An Interdisciplinary Experiment." *Teaching History* 12 (Spring 1987): 3–9. (An earlier version appeared in *Contemporary Southeast Asia* 7 [March 1986]: 320–27.)

Goldstein, Jonathan. "Using Literature in a Course on the Vietnam War." Appeared simultaneously in *College Teaching* 37 (Summer 1989): 91–95, and *Teaching History* 14 (Fall 1989): 59–69.

Goodman, Allan. "Scholars Must Give More Serious Thought to How They Teach and Write About the War in Vietnam." *The Chronicle of Higher Education* 36 (July 25, 1990).

Griffen, William L., and John Marciano. *Teaching the Vietnam War*. Montclair, N.J.: Allenheld, Osman, 1979.

Irvine, Reed. "The Flawed History of Vietnam." *AIM Report* (January 1984).

McCloud, Bill. "What Should We Tell Our Children About Vietnam." *American Heritage* 38 (May-June 1988): 55–77.

McCloud, Bill. *What Should We Tell Our Children About Vietnam*. Norman: University of Oklahoma Press, 1989.

Morris, Stephen J. "Vietnam, A Dual-Vision History." *The Wall Street Journal* (December 20, 1983), 30.

Pike, Douglas. "Teaching the Vietnam Experience as a Whole Course." *Teaching Political Science: Politics in Perspectives* 12 (Summer 1985): 144–51.

Raack, R. C. "Caveat Spectator." *OAH Newsletter* 12 (February 1984): 25–28.

Salisbury, Harrison E., ed. *Vietnam Reconsidered: Lessons from a War*. New York: Harper and Row, 1984.

Spector, Ronald H. "What Did You Do in the War Professor?": Reflections on Teaching About Vietnam." *American Heritage* 38 (December 1986): 98–102.

Starr, Jerold M. *The Lessons of the Vietnam War*. Pittsburgh, Pa. Center for Social Studies Education, 1988.

Stewart, Margaret E. "Vietnam-War Novels in the Classroom." *Teaching History: A Journal of Methods* 6 (Fall 1981): 60–66.

Taylor, Sandra C. "Teaching the Vietnam War." *The History Teacher* 15 (November 1981): 57–66.

Taylor, Sandra, and Rex Casillas. "Dealing with Defeat: Teaching the Vietnam War." *Newsletter of the Society for Historians of American Foreign Relations* 11 (December 1980): 10–18, and 12 (March 1981): 1–10.

Winkler, Karen J. "Scholars of the Vietnam War Consider How the Crucial Decisions Were Made." *The Chronicle of Higher Education* (July 14, 1982): 19–20.

Appendix: Filmography

Air America	1990	Roger Spottiswoode
Alamo Bay	1985	Louis Malle
Alice's Restaurant	1969	Arthur Penn
All Quiet on the Western Front	1930	Lewis Milestone
An Officer and a Gentleman	1982	Taylor Hackford
Angkor: Cambodia Express	1986	Lek Kitiparaporn
The Annihilators	1985	Charles E. Sellier
Apocalypse Now	1979	Francis F. Coppola
Bat 21	1988	Peter Markle
The Bedford Incident	1965	James Harris
Best Years of Our Lives	1946	Frank Capra
Big Jim McClain	1952	James E. Grant
Big Wednesday	1978	John Milus
Bonnie and Clyde	1967	Arthur Penn
Born on the Fourth of July	1989	Oliver Stone
The Boys in Company C.	1978	Sidney J. Furie
Braddock: Missing in Action III	1988	Aaron Norris
The Candidate	1972	Jeremy Larner
Casualties of War	1989	Brian De Palma
Catch–22	1970	Mike Nichols
Che!	1969	Richard Fleishner
Chinatown	1974	Roman Polanski
Coming Home	1978	Hal Ashby
The Crazy World of Julius Vrooder	1974	Arthur Hiller

Crossfire	1947	Edward Dmytryk
Dear America	1988	George S. Brown
The Deer Hunter	1978	Michael Cimino
Distant Thunder	1988	Rick Rosenthal
Dr. Strangelove	1964	Stanley Kubrick
Don't Cry It's Only Thunder	1982	Peter Werner
84 Charlie Mopic	1989	Patrick Duncan
The Empire Strikes Back	1981	George Lucas
Fail Safe	1964	Sidney Lumet
First Blood	1982	Ted Kotcheff
A Fistful of Dollars	1964	Sergio Leone
Flight of the Intruder	1991	John Milius
The Fountainhead	1949	King Vidor
Friendly Fire	1985	David Greene
Full Metal Jacket	1987	Stanley Kubrick
Gardens of Stone	1987	Francis F. Coppola
Good Morning Vietnam	1988	Barry Levinson
Go Tell the Spartans	1978	Ted Post
The Green Berets	1968	John Wayne
Hail Hero	1969	David Miller
Hamburger Hill	1987	John Irwin
The Hanoi Hilton	1987	Lionel Chetwynd
Hearts and Minds	1970	Documentary
Heroes	1977	Jeremy Kagan
In Country	1989	Norman Jewison
In the Year of the Pig	1970	Emile De Antonio
Invasion of the Body Snatchers	1956	Don Siegel
The Iron Triangle	1989	Eric Weston
Jacknife	1989	David Jones
Joe	1970	John G. Alvidson
Johnny Got His Gun	1971	Dalton Trumbo
The Killing Fields	1984	Roland Joffe
The Last Hunter	1984	Anthony Dawson
Limbo	1972	Mark Robson
The Line	1982	Robert J. Siegel
Little Big Man	1970	Arthur Penn
The Lords of Discipline	1983	Franc Roddam
The Losers	1970	Jack Starrett

Lost Command	1966	Mark Robson
The Manchurian Candidate	1962	John Frankenheimer
M*A*S*H*	1970	Robert Altman
Memphis Belle	1990	Michael Caton-Jones
Missing in Action	1984	Joseph Zito
Missing in Action II: The Beginning	1985	Lance Hool
Night of the Living Dead	1968	George Romero
Off Limits	1988	Christopher Crowe
On the Beach	1959	Stanley Kramer
Operation CIA	1965	Christian Nyby
Outside In	1972	Allen Baron
Parades	1972	Robert J. Siegel
Patton	1969	Franklin Schaffner
Platoon	1986	Oliver Stone
P.O.W.: The Escape	1986	Gideon Amir
Private Benjamin	1980	Howard Zieff
P.T. 109	1963	Leslie Martinson
Purple Hearts	1984	Sidney Furie
The Quiet American	1957	Joseph Mankiewicz
Rambo	1982	George Cosmatos
Rambo: First Blood Part II	1985	George Cosmatos
Red Dawn	1984	John Milus
Return of the Jedi	1983	George Lucas
Rolling Thunder	1977	John Flynn
Rumor of War	1980	Charles Fris
Salvador	1986	Oliver Stone
The Sand Pebbles	1966	Richard Attenborough
Sands of Iwo Jima	1949	Allan Dwan
Search and Destroy	1981	William Fruet
Seven Days in May	1964	J. Frankenheimer
Shampoo	1975	Hal Ashby
Soldier Blue	1974	Joseph E. Levine
Some Kind of Hero	1982	Michael Pressman
Southern Comfort	1981	Walter Hill
Star Wars	1979	George Lucas
Stripes	1981	Ivan Reitman
Taps	1981	Harold Becker
Taxi Driver	1976	Martin Scorcese

There Is No. 13	1977	William Sachs
To Hell and Back	1955	Jesse Hibbs
To the Shores of Hell	1966	Will Zens
Tracks	1976	Henry Jaglom
Twilight's Last Gleaming	1977	Robert Aldrich
The Ugly American	1962	George Englund
Uncommon Valor	1983	Ted Kotcheff
War Is Hell	1964	Burt Topper
Welcome Home Soldier Boys	1972	Richard Compton
Who'll Stop the Rain?	1978	Karel Reisz
The Wild Bunch	1970	Sam Peckinpah
A Yank in Viet-Nam	1964	Marshall Thompson

Author Index

Subject Index

Contributors

LENNA ALLRED is a graduate student in the Department of History at Texas A&M University in College Station, Texas.

GARY M. BELL is professor of history at Sam Houston State University in Huntsville, Texas.

MARILYN CLARK teaches at Tomball College in Tomball, Texas.

JOAN L. COFFEY is assistant professor of history at Sam Houston State University in Huntsville, Texas.

JOE P. DUNN is Charles A. Dana Professor of History at Converse College in Spartanburg, South Carolina.

SARAH FARENICK is a graduate student in the Department of History at Sam Houston State University in Huntsville, Texas.

STEVEN HEAD, a former graduate student in history at Sam Houston State University, is a professional accountant in Houston, Texas.

MARK LAMBERT is a graduate student at University of Texas at Austin.

FRANCES ARLENE LEONARD is a graduate student at Sam Houston State University in Huntsville, Texas.

IRIS LOVE teaches at Tomball College in Tomball, Texas.

ERNEST M. B. OBADELE-STARKS is a graduate student in the Department of History at the University of Houston in Houston, Texas.

RANDY ROBERTS is professor of history at Purdue University in West Lafayette, Indiana.

AMILCAR SHABAZZ is a graduate student in the Department of History at the University of Houston in Houston, Texas.

KAREN SLEEZER is a graduate student in the Department of History at Sam Houston State University in Huntsville, Texas.

WILLIAM J. TOPICH is a graduate student in the Department of Political Science at Arkansas State University in Jonesboro, Arkansas.

BRADFORD WRIGHT is a graduate student in the Department of History at Purdue University in West Lafayette, Indiana.